advantage interactive cd-rom

Place
Postage
Here

Irwin/McGraw-Hill
Attn: Jim Rogers, Marketing Manager
1333 Burr Ridge Parkway
Burr Ridge, IL 60521

Microsoft® Office 97 Professional

No
Short
answer

Session 1
P. 43-46 hands on
stop @ case prob.

Session 2
P. 91-96
stop@ case prob.

Session 3
Hands on
& case prob

Session 4
Work on

Microsoft® Office 97 Professional

Sarah E. Hutchinson

Glen J. Coulthard

THE IRWIN/McGRAW-HILL ADVANTAGE SERIES FOR COMPUTER EDUCATION

**Irwin
McGraw-Hill**

Boston, Massachusetts Burr Ridge, Illinois Dubuque, Iowa
Madison, Wisconsin New York, New York San Francisco, California St. Louis, Missouri

Irwin/McGraw-Hill

A Division of The McGraw-Hill Companies

MICROSOFT® Office 97 Professional

This book is printed on acid-free paper.

3 4 5 6 7 8 9 0 WC/WC 1 0 9 8 7

ISBN 0-256-26004-4

Publisher: *Tom Casson*
Sponsoring editor: *Garrett Glanz*
Developmental editor: *Kristin Hepburn*
GTS production coordinator: *Cathy Stotts*
Marketing manager: *James Rogers*
Senior project supervisor: *Denise Santor-Mitzit*
Production supervisor: *Pat Frederickson*
Art director: *Keith McPherson*
Prepress buyer: *Heather D. Burbridge*
Compositor: *GTS Graphics, Inc.*
Typeface: *11/13 Bodoni Book*
Printer: *Webcrafters, Inc.*

http://www.mhcollege.com

Microsoft® Word 97 for Windows®

Contents

SESSION 1
Fundamentals

SESSION 2
Character and Paragraph Formatting

SESSION 3
Editing and Proofing Tools

SESSION 4
Printing and Document Management

SESSION 5
Increasing Your Productivity

APPENDIX
Microsoft Word 97 for Windows Toolbar Summary 207

Microsoft® Excel 97 for Windows®
Contents

SESSION 1
Fundamentals

SESSION 2
Working with Spreadsheets

SESSION 3
Increasing Your Productivity

SESSION 4
Managing a Workbook

SESSION 5
Creating Charts

APPENDIX
Toolbar Summary 208

INDEX 219

Microsoft® PowerPoint® 97 for Windows®
Contents

SESSION 1
Fundamentals 97

SESSION 2
Creating a Presentation

SESSION 3
Designing a Presentation

SESSION 4
Adding Visual Effects

SESSION 5
Notes, Handouts, and Printing

APPENDIX
Toolbar Summary 169

INDEX   173

Microsoft® Access 97 for Windows®

Contents

SESSION 1
Fundamentals

SESSION 2
Working with Tables

SESSION 3
Retrieving Information

SESSION 4
Presenting Your Data

SESSION 5
Working with Forms

Integrating Microsoft® Office 97 Professional for Windows®
Contents

SESSION 1
Fundamentals

SESSION 2
Sharing Information

SESSION 3
Working with Objects

SESSION 4
Managing Your Desktop

SESSION 5
Step-by-Step with OLE

SESSION 6
Comprehensive Case Study

Microsoft® Word 97 for Windows®

Sarah E. Hutchinson

Glen J. Coulthard

THE IRWIN/MCGRAW-HILL ADVANTAGE SERIES FOR COMPUTER EDUCATION

Boston, Massachusetts Burr Ridge, Illinois Dubuque, Iowa
Madison, Wisconsin New York, New York San Francisco, California St. Louis, Missouri

Irwin/McGraw-Hill

A Division of The **McGraw·Hill** *Companies*

MICROSOFT® WORD 97 for WINDOWS®

This book is printed on acid-free paper.

3 4 5 6 7 8 9 0 WC/WC 9 0 9 8 7

ISBN 0-256-25996-8

Publisher: *Tom Casson*
Sponsoring editor: *Garrett Glanz*
Developmental editor: *Kristin Hepburn*
GTS production coordinator: *Cathy Stotts*
Marketing manager: *James Rogers*
Senior project supervisor: *Denise Santor-Mitzit*
Production supervisor: *Pat Frederickson*
Art director: *Keith McPherson*
Prepress buyer: *Heather D. Burbridge*
Compositor: *GTS Graphics, Inc.*
Typeface: *11/13 Bodoni Book*
Printer: *Webcrafters, Inc.*

http://www.mhcollege.com

WELCOME TO THE IRWIN ADVANTAGE SERIES

The Irwin Advantage Series has evolved over the years to become one of the most respected resources for software training in the world—to date, over 200,000 students have used one or more of our learning guides. Our instructional methodologies are proven to optimize the student's ability to learn, yet we continually seek ways to improve on our products and approach. To this end, all of our learning guides are classroom tested and critically reviewed by dozens of learners, teachers, and software training experts. We're glad you have chosen the Irwin Advantage Series!

KEY FEATURES

The following features are incorporated into the new Microsoft Office 97 student learning guides to ensure that your learning experience is as productive and enjoyable as possible:

CASE STUDIES

Each session begins with a real-world **case study** that introduces you to a fictitious person or company and describes their immediate problem or opportunity. Throughout the session, you obtain the knowledge and skills necessary to meet these challenges. At the end of the session, you are given an opportunity to solve **case problems** directly related to the case scenario.

CONCEPTS, SKILLS AND PROCEDURES

Each learning guide organizes and presents its content in logically structured session topics. Commands and procedures are introduced using **hands-on examples in a step-by-step format,** and students are encouraged to perform the steps along with the guide. These examples are clearly identified by the text design.

PERFORM THE FOLLOWING STEPS

Using this new design feature, the step progression for all hands-on examples and exercises are clearly identified. Students will find it surprisingly easy to follow the logical sequence of keystrokes and mouse clicks. No longer do you have to worry about missing a step!

END OF SESSION EXERCISES

Each session concludes with **short answer questions** and **hands-on exercises.** These comprehensive and meaningful exercises are integrated with the session's objectives; they were not added as an afterthought. They serve to provide students with opportunities to practice the session material. For maximum benefit, students should complete all the exercises at the end of each session.

IN ADDITION BOXES

These content boxes are placed strategically throughout the guide and provide information on related topics that are beyond the scope of the current discussion. For example, there are three typical categories that are visually identified by the following icons:

Integration
The key to productive and efficient use of Office 97 is in the integration features for sharing data among the applications. With a few mouse clicks, for example, you can create a PowerPoint presentation from a Word document, copy an Access database into an Excel workbook, and incorporate professional Office Art into your annual report. Under this heading, you will find methods for sharing information among the Microsoft Office 97 applications.

Advanced
In a 200+-page learning guide, there are bound to be features that are important but beyond the scope of the text. Therefore, we call attention to these features and offer suggestions on how to apply techniques or to search for more information.

Internet
The Internet is fast becoming a standard tool for gathering and exchanging information. Office 97 provides a high level of Internet connectivity, allowing the user to draw upon its vast resources and even publish documents directly on the World Wide Web. Although not every student will have a persistent Internet connection, you can review the content under this heading to learn about Office's Internet features.

Real life situations introduce the topics

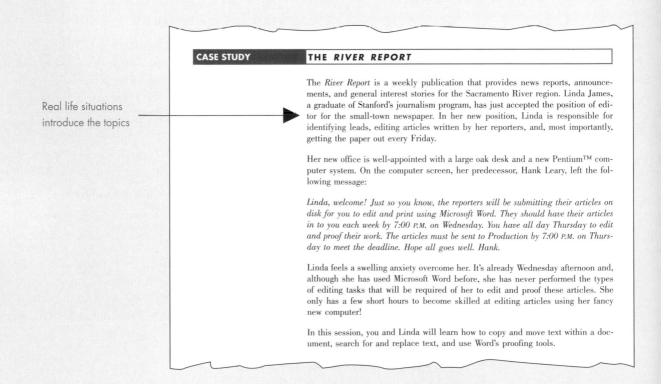

CASE STUDY   **THE *RIVER REPORT***

The *River Report* is a weekly publication that provides news reports, announcements, and general interest stories for the Sacramento River region. Linda James, a graduate of Stanford's journalism program, has just accepted the position of editor for the small-town newspaper. In her new position, Linda is responsible for identifying leads, editing articles written by her reporters, and, most importantly, getting the paper out every Friday.

Her new office is well-appointed with a large oak desk and a new Pentium™ computer system. On the computer screen, her predecessor, Hank Leary, left the following message:

Linda, welcome! Just so you know, the reporters will be submitting their articles on disk for you to edit and print using Microsoft Word. They should have their articles in to you each week by 7:00 P.M. on Wednesday. You have all day Thursday to edit and proof their work. The articles must be sent to Production by 7:00 P.M. on Thursday to meet the deadline. Hope all goes well. Hank.

Linda feels a swelling anxiety overcome her. It's already Wednesday afternoon and, although she has used Microsoft Word before, she has never performed the types of editing tasks that will be required of her to edit and proof these articles. She only has a few short hours to become skilled at editing articles using her fancy new computer!

In this session, you and Linda will learn how to copy and move text within a document, search for and replace text, and use Word's proofing tools.

Large figures guide
learning

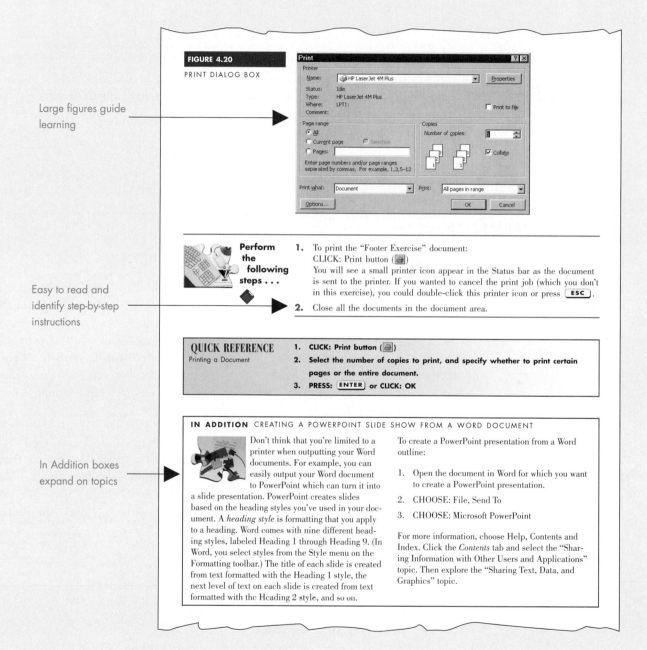

FIGURE 4.20

PRINT DIALOG BOX

Perform the following steps . . .

1. To print the "Footer Exercise" document:
   CLICK: Print button (🖨)
   You will see a small printer icon appear in the Status bar as the document is sent to the printer. If you wanted to cancel the print job (which you don't in this exercise), you could double-click this printer icon or press ESC.

Easy to read and
identify step-by-step
instructions

2. Close all the documents in the document area.

QUICK REFERENCE
Printing a Document

1. **CLICK: Print button (🖨)**
2. **Select the number of copies to print, and specify whether to print certain pages or the entire document.**
3. **PRESS: ENTER or CLICK: OK**

IN ADDITION CREATING A POWERPOINT SLIDE SHOW FROM A WORD DOCUMENT

In Addition boxes
expand on topics

Don't think that you're limited to a printer when outputting your Word documents. For example, you can easily output your Word document to PowerPoint which can turn it into a slide presentation. PowerPoint creates slides based on the heading styles you've used in your document. A *heading style* is formatting that you apply to a heading. Word comes with nine different heading styles, labeled Heading 1 through Heading 9. (In Word, you select styles from the Style menu on the Formatting toolbar.) The title of each slide is created from text formatted with the Heading 1 style, the next level of text on each slide is created from text formatted with the Heading 2 style, and so on.

To create a PowerPoint presentation from a Word outline:

1. Open the document in Word for which you want to create a PowerPoint presentation.

2. CHOOSE: File, Send To

3. CHOOSE: Microsoft PowerPoint

For more information, choose Help, Contents and Index. Click the *Contents* tab and select the "Sharing Information with Other Users and Applications" topic. Then explore the "Sharing Text, Data, and Graphics" topic.

Students practice with
real life projects

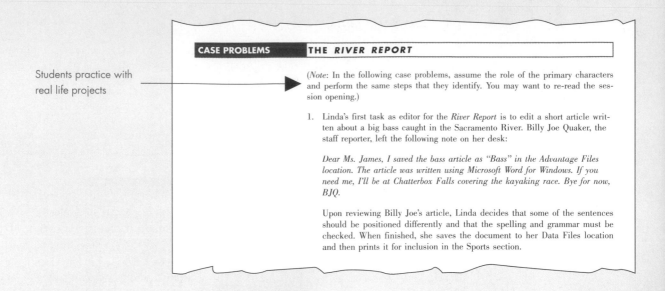

CASE PROBLEMS **THE *RIVER REPORT***

(*Note*: In the following case problems, assume the role of the primary characters and perform the same steps that they identify. You may want to re-read the session opening.)

1. Linda's first task as editor for the *River Report* is to edit a short article written about a big bass caught in the Sacramento River. Billy Joe Quaker, the staff reporter, left the following note on her desk:

    Dear Ms. James, I saved the bass article as "Bass" in the Advantage Files location. The article was written using Microsoft Word for Windows. If you need me, I'll be at Chatterbox Falls covering the kayaking race. Bye for now, BJQ.

    Upon reviewing Billy Joe's article, Linda decides that some of the sentences should be positioned differently and that the spelling and grammar must be checked. When finished, she saves the document to her Data Files location and then prints it for inclusion in the Sports section.

TEXT SUPPLEMENTS

ADVANTAGE FILES

Certain hands-on examples and exercises are marked with a disk ◆ icon, indicating the need to retrieve a document file from the **Advantage Files location.** These document files may be provided to you in a number of ways: packaged on a diskette accompanying this text, or on the computer network at your school. You may also download the files from the ***Advantage Online*** Web site (http://www.irwin.com/cit/adv). *These documents files are extremely important to your success.* Check with your instructor or lab advisor for details on how to acquire the Advantage Files.

In addition to identifying the Advantage Files location, you will also need to specify a **Data Files location.** This location is used to save the documents that you create and may either be a blank diskette or a folder on the network server. Again, your instructor or lab advisor will specify the proper locations. More information on the file locations and the proper techniques for retrieving and saving information is provided inside the back cover of this book.

CD-ROM INTERACTIVE TUTORIALS

In addition to using this book, you may have access to our *Advantage Interactive* software. These interactive multimedia tutorials are fully integrated with the material from each session and make effective use of video clips, screen demonstrations, hands-on exercises, and quizzes. You will enjoy the opportunity to explore these tutorials and learn the software at your own pace. For ordering information, please refer to the coupon inside the front cover.

INSTRUCTOR'S RESOURCE KIT

For instructors and software trainers, each learning guide is accompanied by an **Instructor's Resource Kit (IRK).** This kit provides suggested answers to the short-answer questions, hands-on exercises, and case problems appearing at the end of each session. Furthermore, the IRK includes a comprehensive test bank of additional short-answer, multiple-choice, and fill-in-the-blank questions, plus hands-on exercises. You will also find a diskette copy of the Advantage Files which may be duplicated or placed on your network for student use.

SUPPORT THROUGH THE WWW

The Internet, and more specifically the World Wide Web, is an important component in our approach to software instruction for the Office 97 application series. The *Advantage Online* site at http://www.irwin.com/cit/adv is a tremendous resource for all users, providing information on the latest software and learning guide releases, download options for the Advantage Files, and supplemental files for the Instructor Resource Kits. We also introduce new methods for you to communicate with the authors, publisher, and other users of the series. As a dynamic venture, *Advantage Online* will evolve and improve over time. Please visit us to see the latest developments and contribute your valuable feedback.

NETWORK TESTING

Evaluation and assessment are important components of any instructional series. We are committed to providing quality alternatives to traditional testing instruments. With our Irwin Network Test Interactive software, instructors can select questions, create and administer tests, and then calculate grades—all on-line! Visit the *Advantage Online* site for more information on how we are progressing in this exciting area.

Before you begin

As with any software instruction guide, there are standard conventions that we use to indicate menu options, keystroke combinations, and command instructions.

MENU INSTRUCTIONS

In Office 97, all Menu bar options and pull-down menu commands have an underlined or highlighted letter in each option. When you need to execute a command from the Menu bar—the row of menu choices across the top of the screen—the tutorial's instruction line separates the Menu bar option from the command with a comma. Notice also that the word "CHOOSE" is always used for menu commands. For example, the command for quitting Windows is shown as:

CHOOSE: File, Exit

This instruction tells you to choose the File option on the Menu bar and then to choose the Exit command from the File pull-down menu. The actual steps for choosing a menu command are discussed later in this guide.

KEYSTROKES AND KEYSTROKE COMBINATIONS

When two keys must be pressed together, the tutorial's instruction line shows the keys joined with a plus (+) sign. For example, you can execute a Copy command in Windows by holding down CTRL and then pressing the letter c.

The instruction for this type of keystroke combination follows:

PRESS: CTRL +c

COMMAND INSTRUCTIONS

This guide indicates with a special typeface and color the data that you are required to type in yourself. For example:

TYPE: Income Statement

When you are required to enter unique information, such as the current date or your name, the instruction appears in italic. The following instruction directs you to type your name in place of the actual words: "your name."

TYPE: *your name*

Acknowledgments

This series of learning guides is the direct result of the teamwork and heart of many people. We sincerely thank the reviewers, instructors, and students who have shared their comments and suggestions with us over the past few years. We do read them! With this valuable feedback, our guides have evolved into the product you see before you. We also appreciate the efforts of the instructors and students at Okanagan University College who classroom tested our guides to ensure accuracy, relevancy, and completeness.

We also give many thanks to Garrett Glanz, Kristin Hepburn and Tom Casson from Irwin for their skillful management of this text. In fact, special recognition goes to all of the individuals mentioned in the credits at the beginning of this guide. And finally, to the many others who weren't directly involved in this project but who have stood by us the whole way, we appreciate your encouragement and support.

Write to us

We welcome your response to this book, for we are trying to make it as useful a learning tool as possible. Write to us in care of Garrett Glanz, Richard D. Irwin, 1333 Burr Ridge Parkway, Burr Ridge, IL 60521. Thank you.

Sarah E. Hutchinson
sclifford@mindspring.com

Glen J. Coulthard
current@junction.net

Contents

SESSION 1
Fundamentals

SESSION 2
Character and Paragraph Formatting

SESSION 3
Editing and Proofing Tools

SESSION 4
Printing and Document Management

SESSION 5
Increasing Your Productivity

APPENDIX
Microsoft Word 97 for Windows Toolbar Summary 207

INDEX   210

Microsoft Word 97 for Windows

Fundamentals

SESSION OUTLINE

INTRODUCTION

Word processing is the most popular application for microcomputers. Whether you write term papers or business letters, a word processing software package lets you easily create, edit, format, and permanently store documents. Nowadays you are expected to use a computer and word processor to create your work—handwritten correspondence just isn't acceptable in formal business and educational environments. In this session, you explore the features and benefits of word processing using Microsoft Word 97 for Windows.

THE EXPERT HANDYMAN, INC.

George Perrera has lived in Irvine, California, for over 25 years. Sometimes he feels as if he knows everyone in town. His phone rarely stops ringing because he is *the* person to call when you need a household handyman. Although George has been working as a handyman for over ten years, he just recently gave his business a name: The Expert HandyMan.

George operates his business from his basement at 1990 Jillson Street. To get new clients, he relies on word-of-mouth advertising and the occasional newsletter. He currently performs an average of eight house calls per day and always seems to have more business than he can comfortably handle himself. Hoping to spend less time performing administrative tasks like creating invoices, George has purchased a new computer for his business.

Now let's focus on the problem. Invoices, invoices, invoices! With all this business, George generates eight invoices a day, nearly 40 per week. To create invoices, George uses a ball-point pen to fill out a page in a carbon-copy invoice book. He gives one copy to the customer and keeps the other for his records. George believes that it would be much more efficient to create the invoice with a word processing program, save it on the computer's hard disk, and then print a copy of the invoice for his customer. Although George has used Microsoft Windows, he doesn't know the first thing about using a word processing program.

In this session, you and George learn how to create simple documents, access Word's Help facility, edit documents, use the Undo command, and save and print your work.

INTRODUCING MICROSOFT OFFICE 97

Microsoft Office for Windows combines the most popular and exciting software programs available into a single suite of applications. In the Standard edition, Office 97 includes Microsoft Word, Microsoft Excel, Microsoft PowerPoint, and the all-new Microsoft Outlook, a desktop information tool that manages your e-mail, calendar, contacts, to-do lists, journal, and Office documents. In the Professional edition, you also get Microsoft Access, a relational database management system that fully integrates with the other Office applications. Office 97 also provides shared applications (sometimes called "servers") that let you create and insert clip art, word art, charts, and mathematical equations into your word processing documents, electronic spreadsheets, and presentations.

All software products are born with specific design goals. For Office 97, Microsoft concentrated on optimizing Office for use in Windows' 32-bit environments, including Windows 95 and Windows NT. In addition to enjoying performance improvements, Office 97 offers integration with the Internet and World Wide Web (WWW) and benefits from many usability enhancements. For example, you can name your documents using up to 250 characters, place shortcuts to documents directly on the desktop, save documents in HTML format, post documents to your corporate intranet or to the Web, use the Windows Briefcase program to compare and synchronize files, and multitask your applications with single-click functionality from the taskbar.

All of Office's primary applications use Intellisense technology, helping users to focus on their work and not on their software. Examples of Intellisense are automatic spell and grammar checking, wizards that lead you through performing basic and complex tasks, and the *Auto Web Link*, which automatically converts a World Wide Web address into a hyperlink. (*Note*: We define *hyperlinks* shortly, in the Internet Features section.) Office 97 offers additional help system features, including an animated and customizable character called the Office Assistant who provides helpful information as you work.

INTEGRATION FEATURES

Many would say that the essence of Office 97 is its ability to integrate data between applications. For example, you can include an Excel chart in a Word document, a Word document in a PowerPoint presentation, an Access database in an Excel worksheet, and so on. You can also create an object using a shared application—such as Microsoft Art Gallery, Microsoft Map, Microsoft Equation Editor, or Microsoft Organization Chart—and insert it in your document without ever leaving the current Office application.

Further blurring the line between applications, Microsoft Binder allows you to assemble, print, and distribute collections of varied documents. Like working with a real three-ring binder, you can insert documents that you create in Word, Excel, and PowerPoint into a single binder document and withdraw them. Then, you can print the contents of the binder complete with consistent headers and footers and with consecutive page numbering. A binder document also provides an easy way to transfer information from one computer to another, since all the documents are stored in a single file.

INTERNET FEATURES

One of the most exciting innovations in Office 97 is its ability to take advantage of the World Wide Web and the Internet. For those of you new to the online world, the **Internet** is a vast collection of computer networks that spans the entire planet, made up of many smaller networks connected by standard telephone lines, fiber optics, and satellites. More than just an electronic repository for information, the Internet is a *virtual community* with its own culture and tradition. The term **Intranet** refers to a private and usually secure local or wide area network that uses Internet technologies to share information. To access the Internet, you need a network or modem connection that links your computer to your account on the university's network or an independent Internet Service Provider (ISP).

Once you are connected to the Internet, you can use web browser software, such as Microsoft Internet Explorer or Netscape Navigator, to access the **World Wide Web** (WWW). The WWW provides a visual interface for the Internet and lets you search for information by simply clicking on highlighted words and images, known as **hyperlinks**. When you click a link, you are telling your computer's web browser to retrieve a page from a web site and display it on your screen. Each web page on the Internet has a unique location or address specified by its *Uniform Resource Locator* or **URL**. One example of a URL is: http://www.microsoft.com. For more information on the Internet and World Wide Web, visit your local bookstore, campus computing center, or computer users group.

Microsoft Office 97 provides a consistent set of tools for publishing documents, spreadsheets, presentations, and databases to the web and for accessing help information directly from Microsoft's corporate web site. Specifically, each Office application includes a Web toolbar that lets you quickly open, search, and browse through any document on your local computer, corporate or university Intranet, and the Internet. Furthermore, you can create your own hyperlinks and share your documents with the entire world after publishing them to a web server. As you proceed through this manual, look for the Internet integration features found in the In Addition boxes.

WORD PROCESSING WITH WORD

Word processing is the most commonly used application for microcomputers and is often cited as the primary reason for purchasing a computer. **Word processing** is the method by which documents (for example, letters, reports, and other correspondence) are created, edited, formatted, and printed using a computer. Microsoft Word is one of the most popular word processing software programs available today. Let's explore some of its features in further detail.

- *Entering text.* You create a document in Word by typing information onto the screen. As you type on the computer keyboard, text appears at the **insertion point** or cursor. When entering text, you should be aware of a feature called **word wrap**. Word wrap automatically moves the insertion point to the beginning of the next line when the end of the current line is reached.

- *Editing text.* Microsoft Word has numerous editing features to help you make corrections and modify existing documents. Two of the most important features let you insert and rearrange text. Insert mode enables you to insert text anywhere in a document. This feature works well for inserting a sentence or phrase in the middle of an existing paragraph. Also, copy and move commands allow you to change the order of paragraphs or sections in a document and limit the need to retype similar information.

- *Formatting text.* Formatting refers to changing the appearance of text in a document. There are four different levels of formatting: (a) *Character formatting* selects typefaces, font sizes, and styles for text. (b) *Paragraph formatting* specifies text alignment, line spacing, indentations, tab settings, and borders. (c) *Section formatting* lets you specify page numbers, *headers*, and *footers* for different sections or chapters of a document. (*Note:* Do not be concerned if these terms are unfamiliar; each is described in this guide.) (d) *Document formatting* specifies the overall page layout for printing.

- *Proofing tools.* Word 97 offers an integrated spell- and grammar-checking capability. When you request a Spelling and Grammar check, Word compares each word in your document to the words stored in a standard dictionary. If no match is found, the **spelling checker** typically marks the word and suggests alternative spellings or other words. Word also analyzes your document's punctuation, sentence structure, and word usage. Another writing tool in Word is the electronic thesaurus. A **thesaurus** provides a list of synonyms (and antonyms) for a given word or phrase.

- *Printing.* After creating, editing, formatting, and proofing a document, you'll want to send it to the printer. Before performing this step, make sure your computer is connected to a printer and that the printer is turned on. Your print options include printing multiple copies and limiting the print selection to specific pages. Word also allows you to preview a document on-screen before printing. Besides saving trees, this feature allows you to see the effects of formatting changes immediately without having to print the document.

- *Merging.* One of the most powerful features of Word is the ability to insert a list of names and addresses into a standard document for printing. This process, called **mail merge**, allows you to create a single document and then print personalized copies for numerous recipients. Mail merge activities are not limited, however, to producing form letters. Merging can be used to print a batch of invoices, promotional letters, or legal contracts

- *Wizards.* As you will see in this learning guide, Word employs many wizards to help you get your work done. These software features make short order of tasks that might otherwise be repetitive, time-consuming, or difficult. For example, the tasks involved in setting up a standard letter or fax cover sheet can be handled entirely by a wizard. You simply follow on-screen directions to define the document's layout.

- *"Auto" features.* Word performs a number of procedures for you automatically as you type. For example, Word's AutoCorrect feature will automatically replace "teh" with "the" and "ast he" with "as the" and ensure that your sentences begin with an uppercase letter. Other "auto" features include *AutoFormat As You Type*, *AutoComplete*, and *AutoSummarize*.

- *The Office Assistant.* Think of the Office Assistant, a component of Word's Help system, as your own personal computer guru. When you have a question about how to accomplish a task in Word, you can "talk" to the Office Assistant using typed English phrases. The Office Assistant analyzes your request and provides a resource list of potential help topics. The Assistant can also provide step-by-step instructions on how to complete a task and even perform certain tasks for you.

- *Sound.* If you have a set of speakers connected to your computer, don't be surprised if you hear sounds when you perform such common tasks as opening, closing, and saving files, deleting text, and choosing menu commands. Office 97 has added the dimension of sound to all of your Office 97 applications. You can change the sounds in the Sounds Properties dialog box of the Windows Control Panel.

Now, let's begin our journey through Microsoft Word 97.

STARTING WORD

This session assumes that you are working on a computer with Windows and Microsoft Word 97 loaded on the hard disk drive. Before you load Windows and Word, let's look at how to use the mouse and keyboard.

USING THE MOUSE AND KEYBOARD

Microsoft Word 97 for Windows is a complex yet easy-to-learn program. As you proceed through this guide, you will find that there are often three methods for performing the same command or procedure in Word:

- Menu   Select a command or procedure from the Menu bar.
- Mouse   Point to and click a toolbar button or use the Ruler.
- Keyboard   Press a keyboard shortcut (usually CTRL + *letter*).

Although this guide concentrates on the quickest and easiest methods, we recommend that you try the others and decide which you prefer. *Don't memorize all of the methods and information in this guide! Be selective and find your favorite methods.*

Although you may use Word with only a keyboard, much of the program's basic design and operation relies on using a mouse. Regardless of whether your mouse has two or three buttons, you use the left or primary mouse button for selecting text and menu commands and the right or secondary mouse button for displaying shortcut menus. The most common mouse actions used in Word are:

- Point   Slide the mouse on your desk to position the tip of the mouse pointer over the desired object on the screen.
- Click   Press down and release the left mouse button quickly. Clicking is used to position the insertion point in the document, select menu commands, and choose options in a dialog box.
- Right-Click Press down and release the right mouse button. Right-clicking the mouse on text or an object displays a context-sensitive shortcut menu.
- Double-Click Press down and release the mouse button twice in rapid succession. Double-clicking is used in Word to select text.
- Drag   Press down and hold the mouse button as you move the mouse pointer across the screen. When the mouse pointer reaches the desired location, release the mouse button. Dragging is used to select a block of text or to move objects or windows.

You may notice that the mouse pointer changes shape as you move it over different parts of the screen or during processing. Each mouse pointer shape has its own purpose and may provide you with important information. There are five primary mouse shapes you should be aware of:

⬉	left arrow	Used to choose menu commands, access the toolbars, and make selections in dialog boxes.
⬈	right arrow	Used to select text in the document window's Selection area.
⧖	Hourglass	Informs you that Word is occupied with another task and requests that you wait.
I	I-beam	Used to modify and edit text and to position the insertion point.
☞	Hand	In a Help window, the hand is used to select shortcuts and definitions.

As you proceed through this guide, other mouse shapes will be explained in the appropriate sections.

Aside from being the primary input device for creating a document, the keyboard offers shortcut methods for performing commands and procedures. For example, several menu commands have shortcut key combinations listed to the right of the command in the pull-down menu. Therefore, you can perform a command by simply pressing the shortcut keys rather than accessing the Menu bar. Many of these shortcut key combinations are available throughout Windows applications.

LOADING WINDOWS

Because Windows is an operating system, it is loaded automatically into the computer's memory when you turn on the computer.

Perform the following steps . . .

1. Turn on the power switches to the computer and monitor. After a few seconds, the Windows desktop will appear (Figure 1.1). (*Note*: The desktop interface on your computer may look different from Figure 1.1.)

2. If a Welcome to Windows dialog box appears, do the following:
   CLICK: Close button (☒) in the top right-hand corner of the window

FIGURE 1.1

THE WINDOWS DESKTOP

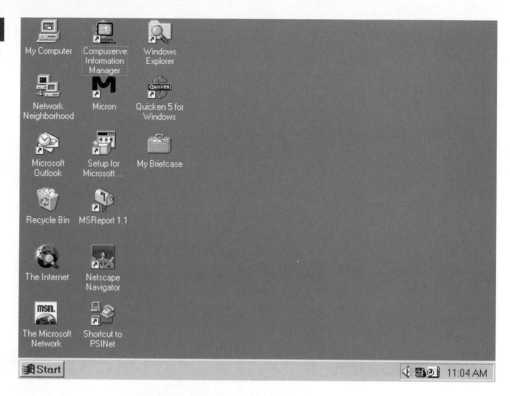

QUICK REFERENCE
Loading Windows

Turn on your computer to load Microsoft Windows (or Microsoft Windows NT 3.51 or later).

LOADING MICROSOFT WORD 97

In this section, you load Microsoft Word.

Perform the following steps . . .

1. Point to the Start button () on the taskbar and then click the left mouse button once. The Start menu appears as a pop-up menu.

2. Point to the Programs command using the mouse. Notice that you do not need to click the left mouse button to display the list of programs in the fly-out or cascading menu.

3. Move the mouse pointer horizontally to the right until it highlights an option in the Programs menu. You can now move the mouse pointer up and down the Programs menu. Notice that you still haven't clicked the left mouse button.

4. Point to the Microsoft Word menu item and then click the left mouse button once to execute the command. After a few seconds, the Microsoft Word screen appears.

5. If the Office Assistant (shown at the right) appears:
   CLICK: Close button (☒) in its top right-hand corner

| **QUICK REFERENCE** | 1. | **CLICK: Start button** () |
| Loading Microsoft Word 97 | 2. | **CHOOSE: Programs, Microsoft Word** |

THE GUIDED TOUR

Software programs designed for Microsoft Windows, such as Word, have many similarities in screen design and layout. Each program operates in its own application window, while the letters, spreadsheets, and brochures you create appear in separate document windows. This section explores the various parts of Word, including the tools for manipulating application and document windows.

APPLICATION WINDOW

The Word screen consists of the **application window** and the **document window**. The application window (Figure 1.2) contains the Title bar, Menu bar, Standard toolbar, Formatting toolbar, Status bar, and document area. Document windows contain the actual documents that you create and store on the disk.

FIGURE 1.2

MICROSOFT WORD'S
APPLICATION WINDOW

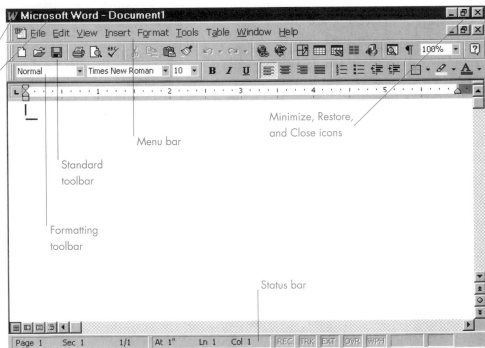

The primary components of the application window are:

Control icon (W)   Used to size and position the application window using
                                   the keyboard. (*Note*: It is easier to use the mouse to
                                   choose the same options available in the Control menu.)

Minimize (⬕) and Maximize (⬜), Restore (⬕), and Close (✕) icons	Located in the top right-hand corner of the application window, these icons are used to control the display of the application window using the mouse. (*Note*: The Maximize button doesn't appear in Figure 1.2.)
Title bar	The Title bar contains the name of the program or document file. Using a mouse, you can move a window by dragging its Title bar. (*Note*: The Office Shortcut bar may also appear in the Title bar area.)
Menu bar	Contains the Word menu commands.
Standard toolbar	The Standard toolbar displays buttons for opening and saving documents, editing text, and accessing special features using the mouse.
Formatting toolbar	The Formatting toolbar displays buttons for accessing character and paragraph formatting commands using the mouse.
Status bar	Located at the bottom of the application window and above the taskbar, the Status bar displays status or mode information and tracks your current position in a document.

Although the application window is typically maximized, you can size, move, and manipulate the Word application window on the Windows desktop to customize your work environment.

DOCUMENT WINDOW

The document window provides the viewing and editing area for a document. When Word is first loaded, this window is maximized to fill the entire document area. Figure 1.3 shows an example of a document window that is not maximized, as it would appear in the document area of Word's application window.

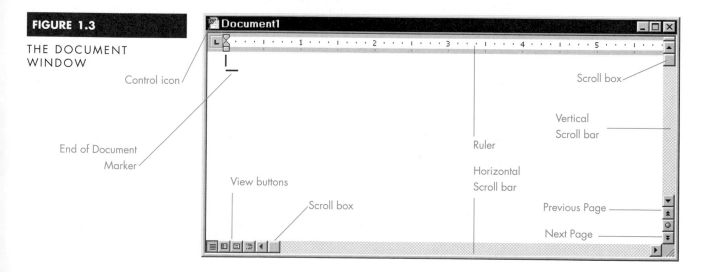

FIGURE 1.3

THE DOCUMENT WINDOW

Control icon

End of Document Marker

View buttons

Scroll box

Scroll box

Ruler

Horizontal Scroll bar

Vertical Scroll bar

Previous Page

Next Page

The parts of a document window are listed below:

Control icon (⊞)	Used to size and position the application window using the keyboard. (*Note*: It is easier to use the mouse to choose the same options available in the Control menu.)
Ruler	Located beneath the Formatting toolbar in a maximized window, each document window has its own Ruler that provides information about tab settings, paragraph indentations, and margins.
Scroll bars	Placed at the right and bottom borders of the document window, scroll bars facilitate moving around a document using the mouse. By dragging the scroll box along the scroll bar, you can skim quickly through a document.
View buttons	Located at the bottom left-hand corner of the document window, the View buttons let you easily switch between Normal View, Online Layout View, Page Layout View, and Outline View. The Normal View is used for the majority of your work. The Online Layout View is the best view to use if you want to read a document online. The Page Layout and Outline views provide additional features for finalizing and managing documents.
End of Document Marker and Paragraph symbol	The End of Document Marker informs you that you can not move the insertion point beyond this point in the document. Although not always displayed, the Paragraph symbol (¶) shows where you have pressed the ENTER key to start a new line.
Office Assistant	When you load Word, the Office Assistant appears if it was displaying when you last exited the program. The Office Assistant helps you complete tasks by providing helpful tips and answering your questions.

You should recognize some familiar components in the document window that appear in all windows. For example, the Minimize and Maximize buttons appear in the top right-hand corner of the document window. To restore a maximized document to a window, you click the Restore button (⊟). To maximize the document window, you click the Maximize button (□). Before proceeding, make sure that your document window is maximized, resembling Figure 1.2.

MENU BAR

Word commands are grouped together on the Menu bar, as shown below.

⊞ File Edit View Insert Format Tools Table Window Help   _ ⊟ ✕

Commands in this guide are written in the following form: Edit, Copy, where Edit is the Menu bar option and Copy is the command to be selected from the pull-down menu. To execute a command, click once on the Menu bar option and then click once on the pull-down menu command. Commands that are not available for selection appear dimmed. Commands that are followed by an ellipsis (. . .) require further information to be collected in a dialog box. If you choose a command that is followed by a sideways triangle (▶), an additional pull-down menu will appear.

In this section, you practice accessing the Menu bar.

Perform the following steps . . .

1. To choose the Help command, position the tip of the mouse pointer on the word Help in the Menu bar and click the left mouse button once. A pull-down menu appears below the Help option. (*Note*: If your computer is set up to output sound, you will hear an audible click when you make a menu selection.)

2. To see the pull-down menus associated with other menu options, drag the mouse slowly to the left over the additional options on the Menu bar.

3. To leave the Menu bar without making a command selection, use one of the following methods: (a) click in the Title bar, (b) click on the current Menu bar option, (c) click in the document area, or (d) press ⌐ESC⌐ twice.

4. To display the pull-down menu for the File option:
   CHOOSE: File
   This instruction tells you to click the left mouse button once with the pointer on the File option in the Menu bar. (*Note*: All menu commands that you execute in this guide begin with the word "CHOOSE.")

5. To leave the Menu bar without making a selection:
   CHOOSE: File

SHORTCUT MENUS

Word uses context-sensitive shortcut menus for quick access to menu commands. Rather than searching for commands in the Menu bar, you position the mouse pointer on text or an object, such as a table or a graphic, and click the right mouse button. A pop-up menu appears with the most commonly selected commands for the text or object.

Now you practice accessing a shortcut menu.

Perform the following steps . . .

1. To display a shortcut or pop-up menu, position the mouse pointer over any button on the Standard toolbar and click the right mouse button. The shortcut menu at the right should appear.

2. To remove the shortcut menu from the screen, move the mouse pointer into the document area and click the left mouse button. The shortcut menu disappears.

QUICK REFERENCE
Using Shortcut Menus

1. **Position the mouse pointer over an item, such as a toolbar button.**

2. **CLICK: the right mouse button to display a shortcut or pop-up menu**

3. **CHOOSE: a command from the menu, or**

    CLICK: the left mouse button in the document area to remove it

TOOLBARS

Assuming that you haven't yet customized your Word screen, you will see the Standard and Formatting toolbars appear below the Menu bar. Word provides thirteen toolbars and hundreds of buttons[1] for quick and easy mouse access to its more popular features. Don't worry about memorizing the button names appearing in the following graphics—the majority of these buttons are explained elsewhere. You can also point at any toolbar button and pause until a yellow ToolTip appears with the button name.

The Standard toolbar provides access to file management and editing commands in addition to special features like Insert Hyperlink, Insert Table, and Columns:

The Formatting toolbar lets you access character and paragraph formatting commands:

To select additional toolbars, you point to an existing toolbar and click the right mouse button. From the shortcut menu that appears, you can display and hide toolbars by choosing their names in the pop-up menu. If a toolbar is currently being displayed, a check mark appears beside its name.

In this section, you practice displaying and hiding toolbars.

---

[1]Sometimes called *icons*.

Perform the following steps . . .

1. Position the mouse pointer over any button on the Standard toolbar.

2. CLICK: right mouse button to display the shortcut menu

3. To display the Picture toolbar:
   CHOOSE: Picture
   The new toolbar appears somewhere in the document window.

4. To remove the Picture toolbar:
   RIGHT-CLICK: Picture toolbar
   This instruction tells you to position the mouse pointer over the Picture toolbar and click the right mouse button.

5. CHOOSE: Picture
   The Picture toolbar disappears from the application window.

RULER

The Ruler (shown below) displays the tab, paragraph, and margin settings for the current line. Rather than accessing menu commands to adjust paragraph and document formatting options, you can move the symbols provided on the Ruler using the mouse.

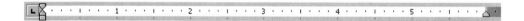

STATUS BAR

The Status bar (shown below) provides editing and status information for a document, including the current page number, section number, and total number of pages. The insertion point's current depth from the top of the page is displayed in inches, along with the line and column numbers.

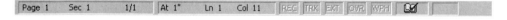

The Status bar also provides some helpful information. For example, when "OVR," which stands for Overtype mode, appears dimmed in the Status bar, Word is in Insert mode. You can toggle between Overtype and Insert modes by double-clicking the "OVR" indicator on the Status bar. The book icon, which we describe later in this session, is used to correct spelling and grammar errors.

DIALOG BOX

A dialog box is a common mechanism in Windows applications for collecting information before processing a command or instruction (Figure 1.4). In a dialog box, you indicate the options you want to use and then click the OK button when you're finished. Dialog boxes are also used to display messages or to ask for the confirmation of commands.

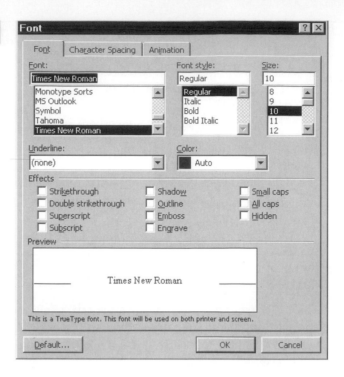

A dialog box uses several methods for collecting information. We describe each method in Table 1.1.

Most dialog boxes provide a question mark button (☐?☐) near the right side of the Title bar. If you have a question about an item in the dialog box, click the question mark and then click the item to display some helpful information. You should also know that dialog boxes have a memory. For example, the tab that appears when you exit the dialog box will be selected the next time you open the dialog box.

THE WINDOWS TASKBAR

The Windows taskbar is usually located on the bottom of your screen below the Status bar. (*Note*: We say "usually" because you can move the taskbar around on your desktop.) Each application that you are currently working with is represented by a button on the taskbar. To switch between applications, click the appropriate application button on the taskbar. At this point, you should see a button for Microsoft Word on the taskbar.

Getting Help

Word provides several **context-sensitive help** features and a comprehensive library of online documentation. Like many developers trying to minimize the retail price of software and maximize profits, Microsoft has stopped shipping volumes of print-based documentation in favor of disk-based Help systems. However, a Help system is only as good as the search tools that it provides. Fortunately for us, Windows gives developers the tools and capability to create consistent and easy-to-use

TABLE 1.1	Name	Example	Action
Parts of a Dialog Box	Check box	☑ Always ☐ Never	Click an option to turn it on or off. The option is turned on when a "☑" appears in the box.
	Command button	OK / Cancel	Click a command button to execute an action. You accept or cancel the selections in a dialog box by clicking the OK or Cancel command buttons, respectively.
	Drop-Down list box	Screen Saver / None	Make a choice from the list that appears when you click the down arrow next to the box; only the selected choice is visible.
	List box	Wallpaper / [None] / Arcade / Argyle	Make a choice from the scrollable list; several choices, if not all, are always visible.
	Option button	Display: ⦿ Tile ○ Center	Select an option from a group of related options.
	Slide box	Desktop area / Less — More / 640 by 480 pixels	Drag the slider bar to make a selection, like using a radio's volume control.
	Spin box	Wait: 6 ↕ minutes	Click the up and down arrows to the right of the box until the number you want appears.
	Tab	General | Letters & Faxes	Click a named tab at the top of the window to access other pages of options in the dialog box.
	Text box	File name: untitled	Click inside the text box and then type the desired information.

Help systems. This section describes the context-sensitive help features found in Word and then describes where to find more detailed information using the Help Topics window.

CONTEXT-SENSITIVE HELP

Context-sensitive help refers to a software program's ability to retrieve and present helpful information reflecting your current position in the program. In Word, you can access context-sensitive help for menu options, toolbar buttons, and dialog box items. The help information is presented concisely in a small pop-up window that you can remove with the click of the mouse. This type of help lets you access information quickly and then continue working without interruption. Table 1.2 describes some methods for accessing context-sensitive help while working in Word.

TABLE 1.2	*To display . . .*	*Do this . . .*
Displaying context-sensitive Help information	A description of a dialog box item	Click the question mark button ([**?**]) in a dialog box's Title bar and then click an item in the dialog box. A helpful description of the item appears in a pop-up window. Additionally, you can often right-click a dialog box item to display its description.
	A description of a menu command	Choose Help, What's This? from the Menu bar and then choose the desired command using the question mark mouse pointer. Rather than executing the command, a helpful description of the command appears in a pop-up window.
	A description of a toolbar button	Point to a toolbar button to display its ToolTip label; a full description of the toolbar button also appears in the Status bar. You can also choose Help, What's This? from the Menu bar and then click a toolbar button to display more detailed help information in a pop-up window.

Now you will access context-sensitive help.

Perform the following steps . . .

1. In the next few steps, you practice choosing Help, What's This? to access Help for the File, New command and one of the toolbar buttons. Let's start with the File, New command.
   CHOOSE: Help

2. To activate the question mark mouse pointer:
   CHOOSE: What's This?

3. CHOOSE: File, New
   Rather than executing the command, Word provides a description of the command.

4. After reading the description, close the window by clicking on it once.

5. To display information about a toolbar button:
   CHOOSE: Help, What's This?
   CLICK: Save button ([⊟]) on the Standard toolbar
   The following pop-up window appears:

   > **Save (File menu)**
   >
   > Saves the active file with its current file name, location, and file format.

6. CLICK: the pop-up window once to remove it

7. Word also provides a special Help tool called the Office Assistant. The Office Assistant watches your keystrokes as you work and offers suggestions and shortcuts. The Office Assistant may appear as a paperclip (by default) or as another character. To display the Office Assistant:
CLICK: Office Assistant button ([?])
The Office Assistant and its associated tip window appear. Your screen should appear similar to Figure 1.5.

FIGURE 1.5

OFFICE ASSISTANT AND TIP WINDOW

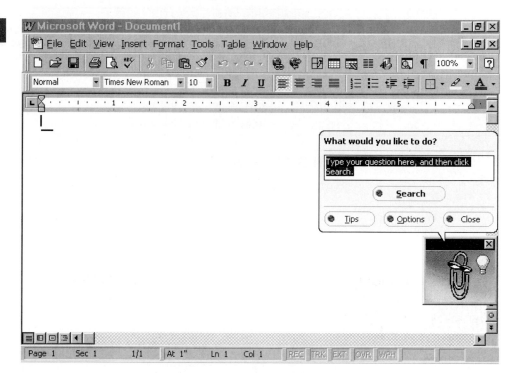

8. To type in a question about page numbers, perform the following steps:
TYPE: insert page numbers in a document

9. To display information about your topic, you click the Search button.
CLICK: Search button in the tip window
A list of related topics appears.

10. To close the tip window:
CLICK: Close button

11. The Office Assistant box, without the tip window, appears in the document window. By simply clicking the animated character, the Office Assistant will display information about the procedure you are performing. To illustrate, do the following:
CHOOSE: Format, Columns

12. To obtain additional information about creating columns:
CLICK: Office Assistant character
A list of topics related to columns appears in the tip window.

13. To remove the Office Assistant box and tip window:
CLICK: Close icon ([x]) in the Office Assistant dialog box

14. To close the Columns dialog box:
   CLICK: Cancel command button

Occasionally an illuminated light bulb will appear in the Office Assistant box. This is the Office Assistant's way of telling you it has a new tip or suggestion. You tell the Office Assistant that you want to view the tip by clicking the light bulb.

QUICK REFERENCE
Displaying Context-Sensitive
Help

1. **CHOOSE: Help, What's This?**

2. **Using the question mark mouse pointer, select the desired item for which you want to display a help pop-up window:**
    *   **CHOOSE: a menu command, or**
    *   **CLICK: a toolbar button, or**
    *   **CLICK: a dialog box item**

HELP TOPICS WINDOW

The primary way that you access Word's Help system is by choosing the Help, Contents and Index command from the menu. This command displays the Help Topics window, as shown in Figure 1.6. You can think of the Help Topics window as the front door to Word's vast help resources.

FIGURE 1.6

HELP TOPICS WINDOW:
CONTENTS TAB

The Help Topics window provides three different tools, each on its own tab, to help you find the information you need quickly and easily. You point to and click a tab using the mouse to make the tab active in the window. Refer to the following tab descriptions to determine which tool you should use when requiring assistance:

- *Contents* tab   Displays a list of help topics organized as a hierarchy of books and pages. Think of this tab as the Table of Contents for the entire Help system. You navigate through categories by double-clicking book icons (📖) until reaching the desired help topic (❓). Notice in Figure 1.6 that there are three different types of icons displayed:

    📖   represents a help category; double-click a book icon to view the books and topics it contains

    📖   represents an open category that is currently displaying its contents; double-click an open book icon to close (or collapse) the book

    ❓   represents a help topic; double-click a topic icon to display a help window

- *Index* tab   Displays an alphabetical list of keywords and phrases, similar to a traditional book index. To search for a topic using this tab, you type a word (or even a few letters) into the text box, which, in turn, makes the list box scroll to the first matching entry in the index. When the desired entry appears in the list box, double-click it to display the help topic. If a keyword has more than one associated topic, a Topics Found window appears and you can select a further topic to narrow your search.

- *Find* tab   Provides the ability to conduct a full-text search of the Help system for finding a particular word or phrase. Although similar to the *Index* tab, this tab differs in its ability to look past indexed keywords and search the help text itself.

When you double-click a help topic, it is displayed in a *secondary* window. You may find that secondary windows include some unfamiliar buttons, like ⏩ and ⬆, embedded in the help text. The ⏩ symbol, which we'll call the Chiclet button, represents a "See Also" link that you can click to move to a related help topic. The ⬆ symbol, called the Show Me button, initiates the command you're interested in. You may also notice that some words or phrases in the help window have a dotted underline. If you click such a word or phrase, a definition pop-up window appears.

Now you will access the Help Topics window.

Perform the following steps . . .

1. To access the Help Topics window:
   CHOOSE: Help, Contents and Index

2. CLICK: *Contents* tab
   Your screen should now appear similar to Figure 1.6, except that your book categories will appear collapsed. (*Note*: The Help Topics window remembers the tab that was selected when it was last closed. It will automatically

return to this tab the next time you access the Help system. For example, if you close the Help Topics window with the *Index* tab active, it will again appear active the next time you display the window.)

3. To display the contents of a book:
DOUBLE-CLICK: "📕 Editing and Sorting" book
(*Note*: You can double-click the book icon (📘) or the book's title. If you find it difficult to double-click using the mouse, you can also select or highlight the book by clicking it once and then click the Display command button.) This particular book contains six topic pages and five additional book categories.

4. To further clarify the search:
DOUBLE-CLICK: "📕 Correcting and Deleting" book
Notice that this book contains multiple topics.

5. To display a help topic:
DOUBLE-CLICK: "❓ Automatically correct text" topic
The Help Topics window is removed from view and a secondary window appears with the topic information.

6. To print the help topic:
RIGHT-CLICK: anywhere in the help text of the secondary window
CHOOSE: Print Topic (as shown in Figure 1.7)
(*Note*: You can also print help information directly from the *Contents* tab. If you select a book by clicking on it once and then click the Print command button, the entire book (including the additional book categories that may be contained within the book) is sent to the printer. If you select an individual topic and click Print in the Help Topics window, only the highlighted topic is sent to the printer.)

FIGURE 1.7

DISPLAYING A HELP TOPIC AND A SHORTCUT MENU

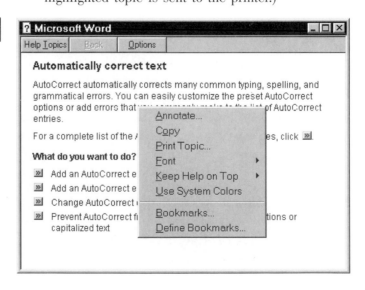

7. In the Print dialog box that appears:
- CLICK: OK command button to print the topic, or
- CLICK: Cancel command button if you do not have a printer

Whatever your selection, you are returned to the secondary window. (*Note*: If you selected to print the topic and your computer does not have a printer connected, you may be returned to Word with an error message. In this case, choose Help, Contents and Index to redisplay the Help Topics window and then proceed to Step 10.)

8. To close the secondary window and return to the Help Topics window:
CLICK: Help Topics button (immediately under the Title bar)

9. To close the current book:
CLICK: ▲ on the vertical scroll bar repeatedly
DOUBLE-CLICK: "📖 Editing and Sorting" book
Notice that the list of books and topics is collapsed under the book icon.

10. Let's search for some information using the keyword index:
CLICK: *Index* tab

11. To find the topics related to Word's AutoFormat feature:
TYPE: **autoformat**
The list automatically scrolls to highlight "AutoFormat."

12. In the topic list:
DOUBLE-CLICK: AutoFormat
A secondary window appears with additional topics.

13. In the Topics Found window:
DOUBLE-CLICK: "Turn automatic changes on or off"

14. You may have noticed that a term in this secondary window appears with a dotted underline. To view this definition term, do the following:
CLICK: "AutoText" with the hand mouse pointer (🖑)
A pop-up window appears with a definition.

15. After reading the help text, remove the definition pop-up window:
CLICK: the pop-up window once

16. To return to the Help Topics window:
CLICK: Help Topics button

17. Let's close the Microsoft Word Help system. To do so:
CLICK: Cancel command button (in the lower right-hand corner)
The Help Topics window is removed. (*Remember*: The next time you open the Help Topics window, the *Index* tab will be selected.)

QUICK REFERENCE
Searching for Help Using the Help Topics Window

1. **To display the Help Topics window:**

CHOOSE: Help, Contents and Index

2. CLICK: *Contents* tab to navigate a hierarchical Help system

CLICK: *Index* tab to search for a word or phrase in a keyword index

CLICK: *Find* tab to conduct a full-text search of the Help system

IN ADDITION CUSTOMIZING THE OFFICE ASSISTANT

To customize the Office Assistant, you do the following:

1. Ensure that the Office Assistant box appears.

2. RIGHT-CLICK: the Office Assistant character in the box

3. CHOOSE: Choose Assistant from the menu

4. Use the *Gallery* tab to select your favorite Office Assistant.

5. Select or remove features in the *Options* tab.

6. When finished, press (**ENTER**) or CLICK: OK

CREATING A DOCUMENT

Creating a document in Word is easy. You type information onto the screen, save the document to the disk, and, if desired, send it to the printer. Before you begin typing, make sure that you have a blinking insertion point in the upper left-hand corner of the document window. This marks the location where text is inserted. Below the insertion point, you should see a horizontal black bar called the **End of Document Marker**. As you enter information, this marker automatically moves downward.

In the next few sections, you will create the paragraph appearing in Figure 1.8.

FIGURE 1.8

PRACTICE PARAGRAPH

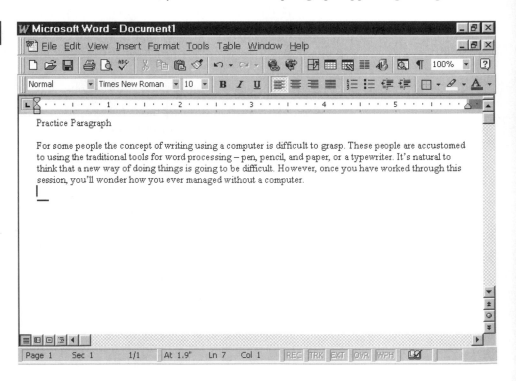

BEFORE YOU BEGIN: CHECKING YOUR "AUTO" SETTINGS

Before you create the document in Figure 1.8, let's look at the AutoCorrect, Auto-Format, and spelling and grammar settings on your computer. If necessary, we recommend that you change the settings to match those shown in Figures 1.9, 1.10, and 1.11. (*Note*: These settings correspond to Word's default settings; that is, these settings are in effect after Word is first installed.) Then, the Figures in this learning guide will match what you view on your screen.

Perform the following steps . . .

1. To check the AutoCorrect settings:
CHOOSE: Tools, AutoCorrect from the Menu bar
CLICK: *AutoCorrect* tab
Your screen should now appear similar to Figure 1.9.

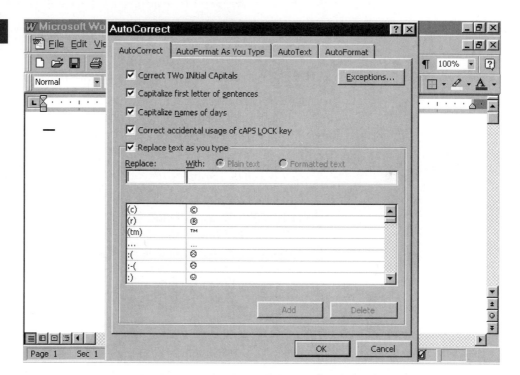

2. If necessary, change the settings in the AutoCorrect tab to match those in Figure 1.9. To select or deselect a check box, point to the box and click the left mouse button.

3. To check the "AutoFormat As You Type" settings:
CLICK: *AutoFormat As You Type* tab
Your screen should now appear similar to Figure 1.10.

FIGURE 1.10

THE AUTOCORRECT
DIALOG BOX:
AUTOFORMAT AS YOU
TYPE TAB

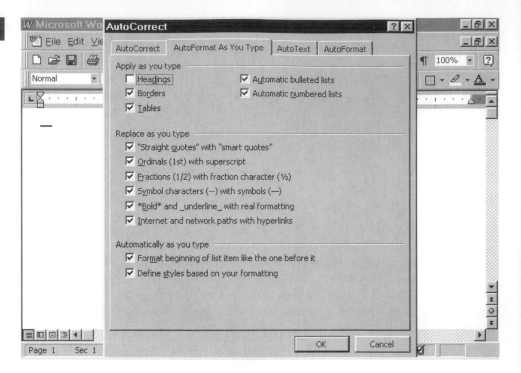

4. If necessary, change the settings in the *AutoFormat As You Type* tab to match those in Figure 1.10. (*Note*: We describe the options available in the *AutoFormat As You Type* tab later in this guide.)

5. To close the AutoCorrect dialog box:
CLICK: OK button

6. To check the spelling and grammar settings:
CHOOSE: Tools, Options
CLICK: *Spelling & Grammar* tab
Your screen should now appear similar to Figure 1.11.

FIGURE 1.11

THE OPTIONS DIALOG
BOX: SPELLING &
GRAMMAR TAB

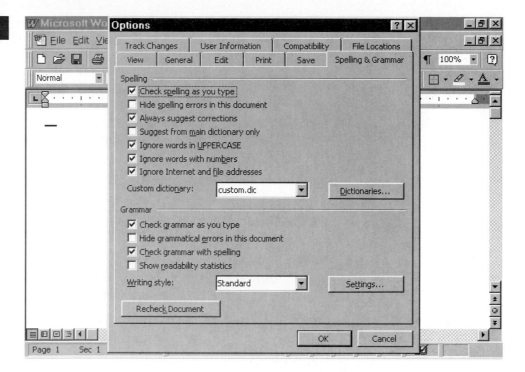

7. If necessary, change the settings in the *Spelling & Grammar* tab to match those in Figure 1.11. (*Note*: We describe the options available in the *Spelling & Grammar* tab later in this guide.)

8. To close the Options dialog box:
CLICK: OK button

INSERTING TEXT

To illustrate the fundamentals of inserting text, this section leads you through an exercise for editing the words "Practice Paragraph." You will also learn about Word's AutoCorrect feature which automatically corrects simple typographical errors in spelling and capitalization. For example, you can type "teh" and Word replaces the text with "the" as soon as you press the Space Bar. For typographical errors that aren't so straightforward, don't be surprised if Word displays a wavy red underline beneath the offending word. Because Word checks your spelling and grammar as you type, some words in your document may appear with a red (spelling error) or green (grammar error) wavy underline. For now, ignore any underlines that you may encounter.

Perform the following steps . . .

1. TYPE: **Paragraph**
The insertion point appears one character to the right of the word "Paragraph."

2. To move the insertion point back to the beginning of the line:
PRESS: HOME
The insertion point should now appear to the left of the "P" in "Paragraph."

3. Make sure that the letters OVR in the Status bar appear dimmed. This tells you that Word's current mode is Insert mode and not Overtype mode. If the letters OVR are not dim, double-click the letters in the Status bar before continuing. Type the following, exactly as it appears:
TYPE: **PRactice**
PRESS: Space Bar
Notice that Word's AutoCorrect feature automatically corrected your capitalization error at the beginning of the word. Also, the Insert mode let you insert text and spaces at the current position by simply typing the characters and pressing the Space Bar. The existing information was pushed to the right.

4. To illustrate the difference between Insert mode and Overtype mode, position the insertion point to the left of the letter "P" in the word "Practice."

5. Locate OVR, the abbreviation for Overtype mode, on the Status bar.
DOUBLE-CLICK: OVR
The letters OVR appear highlighted (not dimmed) in the Status bar.

6. TYPE: **My**
The word "My" overwrites the first two characters of "Practice."

7. To toggle back to Insert mode:
DOUBLE-CLICK: OVR in the Status bar
The letters OVR should now appear dimmed.

8. Let's complete the phrase:
PRESS: Space Bar to insert a space
TYPE: **Pr**
The line should now read "My Practice Paragraph."

9. The (**ENTER**) key inserts blank lines into a document and signifies the end of a paragraph. To illustrate, position the insertion point to the left of the letter "P" in the word "Paragraph."

10. PRESS: (**ENTER**) four times
The word "Paragraph" moves down with the insertion point and blank lines are inserted into the document.

In the next section, you learn how to delete blank lines from a document.

QUICK REFERENCE
Inserting Text

- **Insert text into a document by typing.**
- **Insert spaces between words by pressing the Space Bar in Insert mode.**
- **Insert blank lines in a document by pressing the (ENTER) key.**
- **To toggle between Insert and Overtype modes:**
  PRESS: (INSERT) or DOUBLE-CLICK: OVR in the Status bar

DELETING TEXT

The **BACKSPACE** and **DELETE** keys are the most common keystrokes for removing information from a document one character at a time. Let's now practice using these keystrokes.

Perform the following steps . . .

1. To quickly move to the top of the document:
   PRESS: **CTRL** + **HOME**
   This instruction tells you to press and hold down the **CTRL** key and tap **HOME** once. You then release both keys. The insertion point jumps to the first column of the first line in the document. (*Note:* If your keyboard does not have separate arrow keys, ensure that the Num Lock status is off before performing this keystroke combination.)

2. To move to the end of the line:
   PRESS: **END**

3. In order to get the word "Paragraph" back to its original location, you must delete the blank lines.
   PRESS: **DELETE** four times

4. To illustrate the use of the **BACKSPACE** key, position the insertion point to the left of the word "Practice" using the mouse or keyboard.

5. PRESS: **BACKSPACE** three times
   The word "My" and the space are deleted. The text now reads "Practice Paragraph" once again.

6. To move the insertion point down two lines without moving the text:
   PRESS: **END** to move to the end of the line
   PRESS: **ENTER** twice
   The insertion point is now in the correct position for you to begin typing the practice paragraph.

QUICK REFERENCE
Deleting Text

- **PRESS: DELETE** to delete text to the right of the insertion point
- **PRESS: BACKSPACE** to delete insertion point

WORD WRAP

The word wrap feature of Word allows you to continuously type without having to press the **ENTER** key at the end of each line. If you have worked on a typewriter, resist the temptation to hit a carriage return (**ENTER**)) when the right margin approaches. Word will take you to the next line automatically. In this section, you complete the practice paragraph.

Perform the following steps . . .

1. TYPE: For some people the concept of writing using a computer is difficult to grasp. These people are accustomed to using the traditional tools for word processing -- pen, pencil, and paper, or a typewriter. It's natural to think that a new way of doing things is going to be difficult. However, once you have worked through this session, you'll wonder how you ever managed without a computer.

2. PRESS: (ENTER)
   Your screen should now appear similar to Figure 1.8. Notice that Word automatically formatted your double-dash into a continuous dash, called an *em dash*.

QUICK REFERENCE

Word Wrap

When typing a paragraph, do not press the (ENTER) key at the end of each line. The (ENTER) key is used only to end a paragraph or to insert a blank line in a document.

IN ADDITION HYPHENATING WORDS

Words sometimes wrap to the next line in such a way that your paragraphs have a very ragged right margin. You can hyphenate words yourself or direct Word to hyphenate long words where needed.

To access the hyphenation feature, choose Tools, Language, Hyphenation from the Menu bar. For more information, choose Help, Contents and Index. Click the *Index* tab, and then type **hyphenation.**

AUTOMATIC SPELL AND GRAMMAR CHECKING

If Word's "Check spelling as you type" and "Check grammar as you type" features have been selected (see the "Before You Begin" section), one or two words in your document may already be marked with a wavy underline.

Red underline indicates that the Spelling Checker can't find a match for a word in its main dictionary. It may be that the typed word isn't misspelled at all; perhaps it's a proper name like "Carlos Rodriguez." To correct a misspelled word, point to the word using the mouse and then right-click. A shortcut menu will appear with a list of suggested correct spellings and a few additional options. You can either select the correct word from the list, choose the Ignore All command if the word is spelled correctly, or edit the word yourself. Use a similar procedure to correct grammar errors.

To correct all of your spelling and grammar errors at once, use the book icon on the Status bar. If your document is free of spelling and grammar errors, a check mark will appear on the book icon. Otherwise, an "☒" will appear. To jump through the spelling and grammar errors in a document, double-click the book icon.

In this section, you practice correcting a spelling error and a grammar error.

Perform the following steps . . .

1. In this step, you will force a spelling error in the first line of the practice paragraph. Edit the word "**concept**" so that it becomes "**concpt.**"

2. Click once with the mouse in another part of the paragraph. Notice that a red wavy underline appears beneath the misspelled word.

3. To correct the word, point to the word and then right-click using the mouse. Your screen should now look similar to Figure 1.12.

FIGURE 1.12

THE SPELLING
SHORTCUT MENU

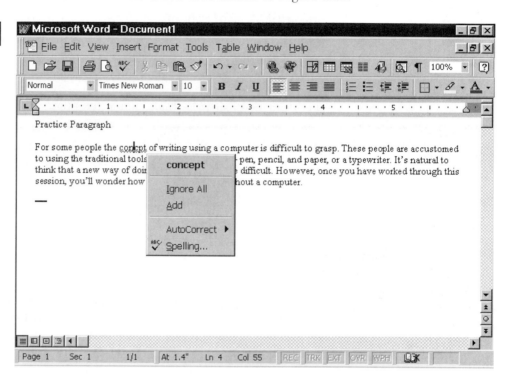

4. Using the mouse, choose the word "concept" in the menu. The word "concept" should have replaced "concpt" in the document.

5. To create a grammar error, delete the apostrophe (') in the word "It's" located at the beginning of the third sentence.

6. Click the mouse pointer in another part of the paragraph. A green wavy underline should appear.

7. To correct the error, point to the word and then right-click using the mouse.

8. Using the mouse, choose the word "It's" from the menu. The word "It's" should have replaced "It's" in the document.

9. On your own, correct any spelling and grammar errors that may still exist in your document by double-clicking the book icon on the Status bar.

1. **Point to a word with a wavy red or green underline and then right-click
   with the mouse.**

2. **Choose Word's suggestion from the shortcut menu, choose the Ignore All or
   Ignore Sentence command if no error has been made, or edit the error
   yourself.**

USING THE UNDO COMMAND

The **Undo command** allows you to cancel the last several commands you per-
formed in a document. There are three methods for executing the Undo command.
You can choose Edit, Undo from the menu, press the keyboard shortcut of
CTRL +z, or click the Undo button (⤺▾) on the Standard toolbar.

Let's practice using the Undo button (⤺▾):

**Perform
the
following
steps . . .**

1. Make sure that you are in Insert mode (the letters OVR should appear
   dimmed in the Status bar) and then insert another blank line at the end of
   the document:
   PRESS: CTRL + END to move the cursor to the end of the document
   PRESS: ENTER

2. TYPE: This is a test of the Undo command.

3. To undo the typing you just performed:
   CLICK: Undo button (⤺▾) on the Standard toolbar
   (*CAUTION*: You place the tip of the mouse pointer over the curved arrow
   on the left side of the button, as opposed to the downward pointing arrow,
   before clicking the left mouse button.)

4. TYPE: This is a test of the Menu bar method.

5. To undo the typing again:
   CHOOSE: Edit, Undo Typing

6. To view all the actions that you can undo:
   CLICK: down arrow beside the Undo button (⤺▾)
   To see additional Undo actions, drag the scroll box downward.

7. To remove the drop-down list without selecting an item:
   CLICK: down arrow beside the Undo button (⤺▾) again

CLICK: Undo button (⤺▾) on the Standard toolbar, or

CHOOSE: Edit, Undo, or

PRESS: CTRL +z

SAVING AND CLOSING A DOCUMENT

When you are creating a document, it exists only in the computer's RAM (random access memory), which is highly volatile.[2] To permanently store your work, you must save the document to the hard disk or to a floppy diskette. Saving your work to a disk is similar to placing it into a filing cabinet. For important documents (ones that you cannot risk losing), you should save your work every 15 minutes, or whenever you're interrupted, to protect against an unexpected power outage or other catastrophe.

To save a document to a disk, you click the Save button (🖫) on the Standard toolbar or you select the File, Save command from the menu. If you haven't saved the document before, a dialog box appears with a suggested filename. You can either accept the suggested filename or type in a new name. When naming a file for use with Windows, you can use up to 255 characters, including spaces. You can't use the following characters in filenames:

$$\backslash \quad / \quad : \quad * \quad ? \quad " \quad < \quad > \quad |$$

When you are finished typing the filename, press ENTER or click the Save command button. As the document is being written to the disk, a series of boxes appears in the Status bar indicating its progress.

In the next few steps, you will save the document to one of the following locations:

- *Advantage Files location*—This location may be on a diskette, in a folder on your local hard drive, or in a folder on a network server. The Advantage Files are the document files that have been created for you and that you will retrieve in the remaining exercises in this guide.

- *Data Files location*—This location may also be on a diskette, in a hard drive folder, or in a network folder. It may even be the same disk or folder where you keep the Advantage Files. You will save the documents that you create or modify to the Data Files location.

> **IMPORTANT:** *Before continuing, ensure that you know the location of your Advantage Files and where to store your Data Files. If necessary, ask your instructor or lab assistant for additional information.*

Now let's save the current document.

Perform the following steps . . .

1. Make sure that you have identified the location for storing your data files. If you require a diskette, place it into the diskette drive now.

---

[2]RAM is wiped clean when you turn off your computer or experience a power failure.

2. CLICK: Save button (▣)
    The Save As dialog box should appear (Figure 1.13); the filenames and directories may differ from your dialog box.

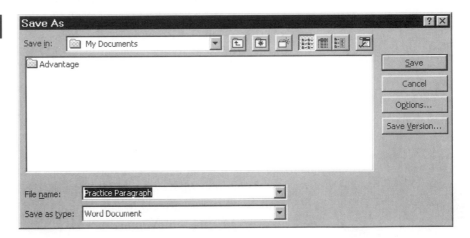

3. To specify a filename for the document, you would type it into the *File name* text box. Since the name "Practice Paragraph" already appears in the *File name* text box, let's move to the next step.

4. To specify where the document will be saved, do the following:
    CLICK: down arrow beside the *Save in* drop-down list box
    SELECT: *your Data Files location*
    PRESS: (ENTER) or CLICK: Save command button
    Note: In this guide, we save documents to the "My Documents" folder on the hard disk and retrieve documents from the "Word97" sub-folder, which is located at the following path:
    \My Documents\Advantage\Word97

5. When you are finished working with a document, you close the file to free up valuable RAM. To close the "Practice Paragraph" file:
    CHOOSE: File, Close

There are times when you'll want to save an existing document under a different filename. For example, you may want to keep different versions of the same document on your disk. Or, you may want to use one document as a template for future documents that are similar in style and format. Rather than retyping an entirely new document, you can retrieve an old document file, edit the information, and then save it under a different name using the File, Save As command. If you want to replace the old file instead, choose File, Save or click the Save button (▣).

IN ADDITION SAVING A DOCUMENT AS A PROTECTED FILE

If you're sharing your computer with other people, but don't want anyone else to be able to look at or modify your files, consider assigning a password to your individual files. Before opening or modifying a protected file, you must type in the correct password.

To assign a password to a document, choose File, Save As and then click the Options command button. The *Save* tab should already be selected with the file sharing options appearing at the bottom.

For more information, choose Help, Contents and Index. Click the Index tab and then type in **password-protected documents.**

IN ADDITION SAVE A DOCUMENT TO AN FTP SITE

If you want your document to be accessible to others on the Internet, consider saving it to an FTP site. *FTP (File Transfer Protocol)* makes it possible for users to transfer documents over the Internet. You can save to an FTP site if your computer has an Internet connection that supports saving files. To save to an FTP site:

1. CHOOSE: File, Save As

2. SELECT: Internet Connections (FTP) from the Save in drop-down list

3. DOUBLE-CLICK: the site you want to save to (*Note:* You can add FTP sites to the list by selecting Add/Modify FTP Locations in the file area.)

4. TYPE: a name for your document

5. PRESS: (ENTER) or CLICK: Save command button

IN ADDITION SAVE AS HTML

To publish your Word document on the Web, you must save it in an HTML format first. *HTML (Hypertext Markup Language)* is a system for marking up documents so they can be viewed on the World Wide Web. To save a document as an HTML document:

CHOOSE: File, Save as HTML

(*Note:* It is a good idea to choose File, Save to save your Word document in a Word format before saving it in an HTML file format. Then, you can make changes to your Word document later.)

When you are finished working with a document, you should close the file to free up valuable RAM. To close a document window, simply click the Close button (☒) in the upper right-hand corner of the document window. When the document window is maximized, its Close button appears on the right side of the Menu bar. Let's close the "Practice Paragraph" document file.

Perform the following steps . . .

1. CLICK: Close button (☒) of the document window
(*CAUTION*: If you click the Close button for the application window, Word will close.)

2. If other documents appear in the document area, repeat step 1 to clear them from memory.

BEGINNING A NEW DOCUMENT

When Word is first loaded, a blank document automatically appears on the screen. If you have already typed information into this document and would now like to work with a new document, you must choose the File, New command or click the New button ([🗋]) on the Standard toolbar.

Now let's display a new blank document.

Perform the following steps . . .

1. Ensure that there are no open documents in the document area.

2. CLICK: New button ([🗋]) on the Standard toolbar
   A new document appears.

OPENING AN EXISTING DOCUMENT

Now that your document is stored in this electronic filing cabinet called a disk, how do you retrieve the document for editing? To modify or print an existing document, click the Open button ([📂]) on the Standard toolbar or choose File, Open from the Menu bar. Once the Open dialog box appears, you select the file's location by clicking in the *Look in* drop-down list box. You then double-click the document name appearing in the file list.

In this section, you open the "Practice Paragraph" document from the Data Files location.

Perform the following steps . . .

1. Make sure you have identified the location for retrieving your Data Files. If you require a diskette, place it into the diskette drive now.

2. To practice using the Open dialog box:
   CLICK: Open button ([📂]) on the Standard toolbar

3. To view your Data Files:
CLICK: down arrow beside the *Look in* drop-down list box
SELECT: *your Data Files location*
Your screen should now appear similar to Figure 1.14. (*Note*: If your Advantage Files are stored along with your Data Files, additional files will appear in the file list on your computer. Figure 1.14 shows the contents of a hard disk folder named *My Documents*.)

FIGURE 1.14

THE OPEN DIALOG BOX

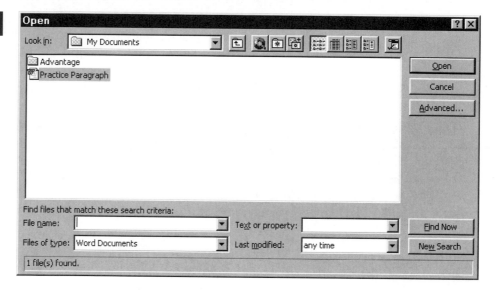

4. To change the display in the Open dialog box, try the following:
CLICK: Detail button ( ) to see each document's file size and date
CLICK: Properties button ( ) to see summary information
CLICK: Preview button ( ) to see a document preview
CLICK: List button ( ) to see a multiple-column format

5. To open the "Practice Paragraph" document:
DOUBLE-CLICK: Practice Paragraph
The document is loaded into Word's document window.

QUICK REFERENCE
Opening a Document

1. **CLICK: Open button ( ), or**
   CHOOSE: File, Open from the Menu bar
2. **CLICK: down arrow beside the *Look in* drop-down list box**
3. **SELECT: a file location**
4. **DOUBLE-CLICK: the desired document**

IN ADDITION OPENING A DOCUMENT FROM THE WINDOWS DESKTOP

From the Windows desktop, you can open a document that you've worked with recently. Click the Start button on the taskbar and then choose the Documents command. Then, choose

the document's name. The application you used to create the document loads automatically.

IN ADDITION OPEN AN INTERNET DOCUMENT

If your computer has an Internet connection, you can open documents on the World Wide Web or at an FTP site directly from the Open dialog box. In the Open dialog box, you click the Search the Web button (🔍) to launch your Web browser program. Using the procedure specific to your browser, you type in a *URL* (*Uniform Re-*

source Locator), an address that points to a specific location on the Internet. All Web URLs begin with "http://". All FTP URLs begin with "ftp://". For more information about opening Internet documents, choose Help, Contents and Index from the Menu bar. Then select the Index tab and type **opening documents on the Internet.**

Printing a Document

Now that you've learned how to create a document, you will learn how to send it to the printer. This section provides only a brief glimpse at the tools available. A more detailed discussion on printing appears in Session 4.

The quickest method for sending the active document to the printer is to click the Print button (🖨) on the Standard toolbar. When you click this button, no dialog boxes appear asking you to confirm your choice, so ensure that the printer is online and has sufficient paper. You may want to save a few trees by previewing the document on-screen first using the Print Preview button (🔍). You can always click the Print button (🖨) from the Print Preview screen if you want to send the document to the printer.

Now you will print a document.

Perform the following steps . . .

1. Ensure that the "Practice Paragraph" document appears in the document window.

2. To display a preview of how the "Practice Paragraph" document will appear when printed:
   CLICK: Print Preview button (🔍)
   Your screen should now appear similar to Figure 1.15. This view provides an overall picture of the document's layout.

3. At this point it's hard to decipher any of the text. To zoom in a bit further:
   CLICK: down arrow in the Zoom box (29% ▾)
   SELECT: 50% from the drop-down menu

FIGURE 1.15

PRINT PREVIEW

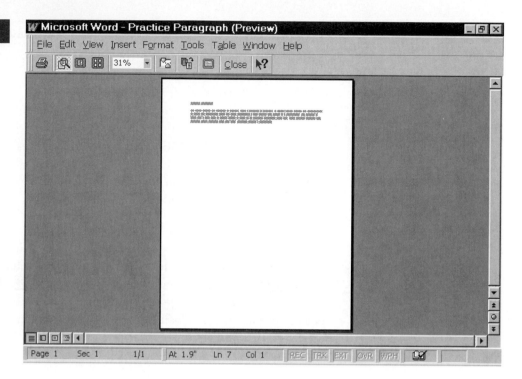

4. Assuming that you are pleased with the Print Preview results:
CLICK: Print button (🖨)
The "Practice Paragraph" document will print to your default printer.

5. Close the "Practice Paragraph" document.

QUICK REFERENCE
Quick Printing

1. **CLICK: Print Preview button (🔍) to see a preview of your document**
2. **CLICK: Print button (🖨) to send your document to the printer**

LEAVING WORD

When you are finished using Word, save your work and exit the program by click-ing the Close button (☒) or by choosing the File, Exit command. If you have made modifications to the active document and have not saved the changes, Word asks whether the document should be saved or abandoned before exiting the program.

Perform the following steps . . .

1. To exit Word:
CLICK: Close button (☒) of the application window
Assuming that no changes were made to the document, the application is closed and you are returned to the Windows desktop.

2. To exit Windows:
CHOOSE: Start, Shut Down
SELECT: *Shutdown the computer?* option button
CLICK: Yes command button

Summary

We began by introducing Microsoft Office 97 and describing the most notable features of Microsoft Word 97. After loading Microsoft Windows and Word, you were led on a guided tour of the program's major components. We also used the Help facility to retrieve information on menu commands, toolbar buttons, and general procedures.

In the latter half of the session, you created a practice document using the Insert and Overtype modes. You learned how to remove characters using **DELETE** and **BACKSPACE** and how to enter blank lines using **ENTER**. In addition, you learned about Word's automatic spelling and grammar feature. The session finished with discussions on saving, closing, opening, and printing document files. Many of the commands and procedures appearing in this session are provided in the command summary in Table 1.3.

TABLE 1.3

Command Summary

Task Description	Menu Command	Toolbar Button	Keyboard Shortcut
Create a new document file	File, New	🗋	**CTRL**+n
Open an existing document file	File, Open	📂	**CTRL**+o
Close a document file	File, Close		
Save a document to the disk	File, Save	💾	**CTRL**+s
Preview a document for printing	File, Print Preview	🔍	
Print a document	File, Print	🖨	**CTRL**+p
Save a document to the disk, specifying the filename	File, Save As		
Leave Word	File, Exit	☒	
Reverse the last command(s) executed	Edit, Undo	↺▾	**CTRL**+z
Access the Word Help facility	Help, Contents and Index		
Access the Office Assistant	Help, Microsoft Word Help	❓	**F1**

KEY TERMS

application window

In Microsoft Windows, each running application program appears in its own application window. These windows can be sized and moved anywhere on the Windows desktop.

document window

In Microsoft Windows, each open document appears in its own document window. These windows can be sized and moved anywhere within the document area.

End of Document Marker

The black, horizontal bar that appears at the end of a Word document. You cannot move the insertion point beyond this marker.

grammar checker

In word processing programs, a program that checks the grammar and word usage in a document.

hyperlinks

These are highlighted words or phrases that appear when viewing information on the World Wide Web. You click the hyperlink to view a different document.

insertion point

The vertical flashing bar in Word that indicates your current position in the document. The insertion point shows where the next typed characters will appear.

Internet

A collection of computer networks that spans the globe.

Intranet

A local or wide area network that uses Internet technologies to share information.

mail merge

A procedure that typically involves combining data that is stored in a data file with a form letter created in a word processing software program.

spelling checker

In word processing programs, a program that checks the spelling of words in a document.

thesaurus

In word processing programs, a program that provides a list of synonyms and antonyms for a selected word.

Undo command

In a software application, a command that reverses the last command executed.

URL

Standing for *Uniform Resource Locator*, a name given to an address or location on the Internet.

word processing

Preparation of a document using a microcomputer.

word wrap

When the insertion point reaches the right-hand margin of a line, it automatically wraps to the left margin of the next line; the user does not have to press **ENTER** at the end of each line.

World Wide Web

A visual interface for the Internet.

EXERCISES

SHORT ANSWER

1. What is the purpose of the Office Assistant?

2. What Internet features are included in Office 97?

3. What are the four levels of formatting in a document?

4. What are some examples of mail merge activities?

5. Why is it significant to know that the default mode in Word is the Insert mode?

6. Why is it important to close a document before retrieving another file?

7. What happens if you press **ENTER** when the insertion point is in the middle of a paragraph?

8. How do you delete a single character to the left of the insertion point?

9. What can you do to remove the red wavy underlines from a document?

10. What is the difference between the File, Save and File, Save As commands?

 ### HANDS-ON

(*Note*: Ensure that you know the location of your Advantage Files and where to store your Data Files. If necessary, ask your instructor or lab assistant for additional information.)

1. Create the document pictured in Figure 1.16.

WE'RE MOVING TO SPAIN on May 15, 1997!

Our new address and phone are:

    Calle Blanca de Rivera, 19
    28010 Madrid, Spain
    Local Phone: 311-0001

ADIOS!

a. Save the document as "Moving Announcement" to your Data Files location.

b. Close the "Moving Announcement" document.

c. Retrieve the "Moving Announcement" document from the Data Files location and insert the following text after the first sentence: **Please come visit us!**

d. Save the "Moving Announcement" document to your Data Files location once again.

e. Print and then close the document.

2. Pretend you're having a garage sale. Open the "Garage" document from the Advantage Files location and edit it to include the date March 16, 1997; the time 10 A.M. to 12 P.M.; and your address. When finished, save it to the Data Files location as "Garage Sale." (*Hint*: If your Data Files location is different from your Advantage Files location, you will need to choose File, Save As from the Menu bar to choose a different disk location.) Close the "Garage Sale" document.

3. Create the document appearing in Figure 1.17. Make sure you include your name and job title (real or imaginary) in the closing of the letter. Save this document to the Data Files location as "Al Martino."

FIGURE 1.17

"AL MARTINO"
DOCUMENT

September 24, 1997

Mr. Al Martino
210 Spruce Way
Stanford, CA 94305

Dear Mr. Martino:

Thank you for your letter regarding the upcoming
event. I am in complete agreement with you that the
number of persons attending must be limited to 200.
Your idea of having this event catered sounds
fantastic!

Moving to a different subject, I noticed that the
letter you wrote me was typed using a typewriter.
(You certainly make use of correction fluid!) With
the number of letters you write, you really should
consider purchasing a microcomputer and word
processing software program.

If you are interested, come over to my office and
I'll show you some word processing fundamentals. We
could even use my computer to design and print the
invitations for the event.

Best regards,

Your name

a. Insert the following text between the second and third paragraphs:

Specifically, word processing software makes it
easier to change a document by allowing you to do the
following:

    1. Insert text
    2. Delete text
    3. Move text
    4. Copy text

b. In the first line of the last paragraph, delete the words "If you are inter-ested," and start the sentence with "You should."

c. In the second paragraph, replace the phrase "correction fluid" with "white-out" using Overtype mode and the **DELETE** key.

d. Save the document back to the Data Files location as "Al Martino," replacing the original version.

e. Print the "Al Martino" document.

f. Close the "Al Martino" document.

g. Open a new document.

4. Create the document appearing in Figure 1.18. Make sure you include your name in the closing of the letter. Save this document to the Data Files location as "ABC Realty."

FIGURE 1.18

"ABC REALTY"
DOCUMENT

June 28, 1997

Mr. S. Luis Obispo
Manager, Sales
ABC Realty Inc.
1388 Primrose Lane
Albany, GA 31705

Dear Luis:

Per our conversation yesterday, please accept this letter as confirmation for your order of computer equipment, deliverable next week.

As discussed, five computers will be installed: one at reception, two for sales, one for accounting, and the last one for yourself. We will also be installing DOS 3.3 and WordPerfect 5.1 at that time.

Training on these software programs will begin the week after installation, per the schedule arranged in our conversation. By the way, I've included the cost for training in the total cost of the equipment.

If I can be of further assistance or if you have any questions, please do not hesitate to contact me.

Yours sincerely,
Tech Talk Technology

Your name
Accounts Representative

a.   In the second paragraph, perform the following editing changes:

Text Before Editing	Text After Editing
`DOS 3.3`	`Windows`
`WordPerfect 5.1`	`Microsoft Word 97`
`at that time`	`the next morning`

b.   Remove the entire third paragraph, starting with "Training on."

c.   Enter the phone number (800) 581-8799 below the last line.

d.   Using the Save button (🖫), save the document as "ABC Realty" to the Data Files location.

e.   Close the document.

f.   Retrieve the "ABC Realty" document from the Data Files location.

g.   Edit the phone number to read (800) 588-1799.

h.   Save the document once again to the Data Files location.

i.   Print and then close the document.

5.   On your own, write a letter to a friend. This document should begin with the current date, include at least two paragraphs, and end with your name in the closing. Make sure to correct any spelling or grammar errors. Save the document as "On Your Own-1" to the Data Files location and then print the document. *Extra Credit*: If you don't want anyone besides yourself to be able to open or edit this letter in the future, protect the letter with a password.

6.   On your own, explore a Microsoft Word Help topic. Pick a Microsoft Word Help topic that interests you and write about it in a few paragraphs. Make sure to explain why you chose the topic and how to perform the procedures described. (For example, you may be interested in creating indexes.) Insert your name and the current date at the beginning of the document. Save the document as "On Your Own-2" to the Data Files location and then print the document.

CASE PROBLEMS   **THE EXPERT HANDYMAN, INC.**

(*Note*: In the following case problems, assume the role of the primary characters and perform the same steps that they identify. You may want to re-read the session opening.)

1.   George is determined to use Microsoft Word to create invoices. He has outlined the information by hand (as shown below) that he wants to include on every invoice.

The Expert HandyMan, Inc.
1990 Jillson Street
Irvine, California 92718

Invoice Number:
Date:
Customer Name:
Address:
City, State, Zip:

[Insert a sentence describing the job performed and result.]

[Number of hours] hours at $30 per hour = [Insert total amount due]

We appreciate your business.

Sincerely,

George Perrera
President, The Expert HandyMan, Inc.

Referring to the handwritten notes, create a generic invoice document that George can edit each time he needs to generate a new invoice. When finished, save the document as "Invoice" to the Data Files location. Print "Invoice."

2. Yesterday, George completed a job for Kenneth Richards at 436 Wetlands Way, Irvine, California, 92718. Kenneth's dryer wasn't working properly, and George had to clean the fan unit and replace the main airflow tube. George must now generate an invoice for the two hours spent at Mr. Richards' house. Retrieve the blank invoice stored in the Data Files location, edit the invoice to reflect Mr. Richards' information, add the Invoice Number GP-946, and then save the document as "Invoice - Kenneth Richards" to the Data Files location.

3. George feels so confident with his new word processing skills that he decides to tackle a proposal using Word. In a conversation with a friend, George heard that Isabel Perez at the Holiday Retreat Hotel is looking for someone to spend five days performing odd jobs around the hotel. The problems include doors that won't close properly, locks that stick, faucets that leak, and tables that wobble.

    George wants the business at the Holiday Retreat Hotel. He decides to prepare a written proposal stating his hourly wage and describing some of his accomplishments, including the job he just completed for Kenneth Richards. The Holiday Retreat Hotel is located at 2987 W. Howard Street, Irvine, California, 92718. Prepare a proposal document for George and save it as "Proposal - Holiday Retreat Hotel" to the Data Files location. Print the document.

4. George has decided to put an advertisement in the local paper for The Expert HandyMan, complete with his address, phone number, and his new slogan: "We can fix anything that needs fixing!" He wants the ad to run for the next month in the Business Classifieds section of the weekend edition. Two hours after calling the local paper for information on submitting an ad, George receives a message on his answering machine. The message is from Rachel Yenkel, the advertising manager.

Hi, Mr. Perrera. Please send me the text for your advertisement. Insert the words "BEGIN TEXT" one line above the text of your advertisement and "END TEXT" one line below. Send the ad text in a letter to my attention at 4910 S. Commerce Street, Irvine, California, 92718. Also, you will have to let me know what section you want the ad to appear in and how many days you want the ad to run. Bye.

When you have created the advertisement, save the document to the Data Files location as "Local Advertisement." Print the advertisement.

Microsoft Word 97 for Windows

Character and Paragraph Formatting

SESSION

2

IRWIN

COMPUTER & INFORMATION TECHNOLOGY

SESSION OUTLINE

Word's Default Settings
Moving Through a Document
Selecting Text
Character Formatting Commands
Paragraph Formatting Commands
AutoCorrect Features
Summary
Key Terms
Exercises

INTRODUCTION

Word processing programs make assumptions about how a document should appear when printed. For most business documents, these assumptions or default settings work well. However, you may also want to tailor a document to meet a specific need. This session teaches you how to use Word's formatting commands to enhance your work.

CASE STUDY	ADVANCED SOFTWARE DESIGN, INC.

Advanced Software Design, Inc. (ASD) is a software development company that specializes in writing Windows-based software applications. Upon request, ASD submits a proposal to a company or individual who expresses a need for a custom-written application. For example, Harry Zidell of Business Assistance Services, an employment agency, recently contracted with ASD to build a performance evaluation program for testing his candidates. A few days after talking to Alethia Montera, a consultant at ASD, Harry received a proposal in the mail. The proposal looked fair, and the project is now underway.

While speaking to a client on the phone or in person, Alethia takes handwritten notes outlining the client's needs. After the conversation or meeting, she estimates the number of hours required to complete the project and calculates the cost of the job. She then sends her notes to Mary, who types them up using Microsoft Word and returns them to Alethia for final review. Mary likes working for Alethia and hopes that one day she can work side-by-side with her in assessing clients' needs. To show her initiative and desire for advancement, Mary decides to improve the look of ASD's proposals using Word's formatting commands. But where to begin? Mary has never tried to format a document using Word.

In this session, you and Mary learn more about Word's default settings and how they affect your documents, how to select text, and how to format characters and paragraphs.

WORD'S DEFAULT SETTINGS

While the words in a document contain the message, a formatted document can better communicate that message. Not only does formatting let you add your own personality to your work, it also improves a document's readability. With proper formatting, you can direct readers' attention to important concepts, improve overall comprehension of the material, and better the reader's chance of recalling the material. And last, it can look really nice!

You begin this session by learning how to change Word's formatting assumptions or default settings. These settings affect how your documents appear on the screen and how they look when printed. This session teaches you Word's most commonly used character and paragraph formatting commands. With these commands, you can produce professional-looking resumes, letters, and reports with minimal effort.

When you first load Word or click the New button ([D]) on the Standard toolbar, a new document appears based upon Word's Normal template. This template provides a set of basic formatting assumptions about your new document, including paper size, margin widths, and default font. You can modify these initial assumptions directly in the template or you can start with a new document based on the template and customize the settings later. The **default settings** for a new document based on the Normal template are listed in Table 2.1.

TABLE 2.1	*Option*	*Setting*
Settings for the Normal template	Paper Size	8.5 inches wide by 11 inches tall
	Top and Bottom Margins	1 inch
	Left and Right Margins	1.25 inches
	Page Numbering	None
	Line Spacing	Single space
	Font (Typeface)	Times New Roman
	Font Size	10 point
	Tabs	Every 0.5 inch
	Justification	Left-justified with a ragged right margin

In this section you practice modifying the default page layout options.

Perform the following steps . . .

1. Make sure that you have identified the location for retrieving your Advantage Files and for saving your Data Files. If you require a diskette, place it in the diskette drive now.

2. A new document should appear in the Word application window. [*Hint*: If a document currently appears on your screen, close it by clicking its Close button ([X]) and then click the New button ([D]) on the Standard toolbar.]

3. To view the default page layout settings for this new document:
   CHOOSE: File, Page Setup
   CLICK: *Margins* tab
   Your screen should now appear similar to Figure 2.1. Notice that there are four tabs along the top of this dialog box: Margins, Paper Size, Paper Source, and Layout.

PAGE SETUP
DIALOG BOX:
MARGINS TAB

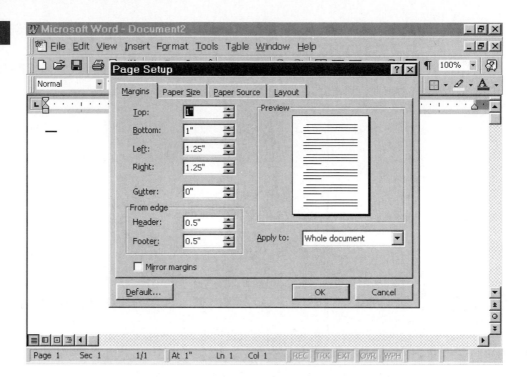

4. To increase and decrease the values for the margin settings, you click the up and down triangular-shaped increment buttons, sometimes called *Spin box controls*, positioned to the right of each text box. Let's increase the top margin to 1.5 inches:
CLICK: up increment button until 1.5 appears in the *Top* text box
The *Preview* area immediately shows the increase in the top margin. (*Note*: The margin settings increase in increments of .1 of an inch on each click. You can also type a number into the text box to enter a more detailed measurement.)

5. To ensure that you are using letter-size paper:
CLICK: *Paper Size* tab
Your screen should now appear similar to Figure 2.2. As you can see in this figure, the default paper size is Letter with a Portrait orientation.

FIGURE 2.2

PAGE SETUP
DIALOG BOX:
PAPER SIZE TAB

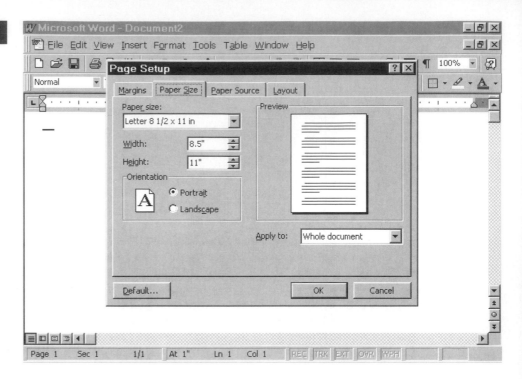

6.   To return to the document:
       PRESS: **ENTER** or CLICK: OK
       The document now has a 1.5-inch top margin.

For now, we're finished looking at the default page layout options. In the next few sections, you learn how to move efficiently through a document and to block text using the mouse and keyboard. These skills are important in learning how to select text and issue character and paragraph formatting commands.

Moving through a document

Before inserting or editing text in a document, you must position the insertion point using the mouse or keyboard. Like many procedures in Word, the mouse provides the easiest method for navigating through a document. To position the insertion point, you scroll the document window until the desired text appears and then click the I-beam mouse pointer in the text. Contrary to what you might think, scrolling the document window does not automatically move the insertion point! If you forget to click the mouse and start typing or press an arrow key, Word takes you back to the original location of the insertion point before you started scrolling.

Common methods for scrolling the document window are provided below:

To scroll the window . . .	Do this . . .
One line at a time	Click the up (▲) and down (▼) arrowheads on the vertical scroll bar.
One screen at a time	Click the vertical scroll bar itself, above and below the scroll box (▢).
One page at a time	Click on these scroll bar symbols to move to the previous page (▲) or to the next page (▼) in a document.
Pages at a time	Drag the scroll box (▢) along the vertical scroll bar.

In addition to the above methods, you can select to browse through a specific type of object using the Select Browse Object button (⊙) on the vertical scroll bar. When used in conjunction with the Next Page and Previous Page buttons you can browse through specific types of objects such as endnotes, footnotes, headings, sections, graphics, or tables.

Although not as intuitive as using the mouse, there are several keyboard shortcuts for moving the insertion point through a document. If you are a touch-typist, you may prefer these methods over using a mouse. Table 2.2 provides a summary of the more popular keystrokes.

TABLE 2.2

Using the keyboard to move the Insertion Point

Key	Description
↑ or ↓	Moves up or down one line
CTRL + ↑	Moves to the previous paragraph
CTRL + ↓	Moves to the next paragraph
← or →	Moves to the previous or next character
CTRL + ←	Moves to the beginning of the previous word
CTRL + →	Moves to the beginning of the next word
PgUp or PgDn	Moves up or down one screen
HOME or END	Moves to the beginning or end of the current line
CTRL + HOME	Moves to the beginning of the document
CTRL + END	Moves to the end of the document
F5 (GoTo)	Moves to a specific line, section, or page number
SHIFT + F5 (GoBack)	Moves to the last three areas, in order, that you have edited in a document

In this section you practice moving through a document.

Perform the following steps . . .

1. To display your Advantage Files:
   CLICK: Open button (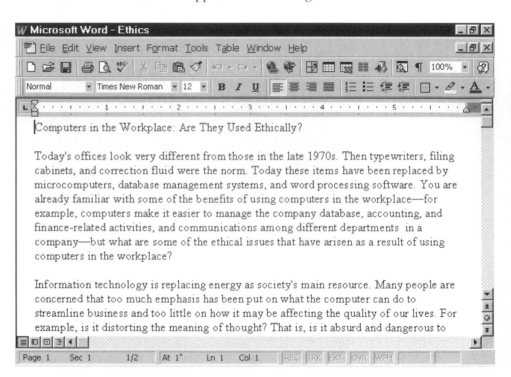) on the Standard toolbar
   CLICK: down arrow beside the *Look in* drop-down list box
   SELECT: *your Advantage Files location*

2. To retrieve the "Ethics" document:
   DOUBLE-CLICK: "Ethics" in the file area
   Your screen should now appear similar to Figure 2.3.

FIGURE 2.3

THE "ETHICS"
DOCUMENT

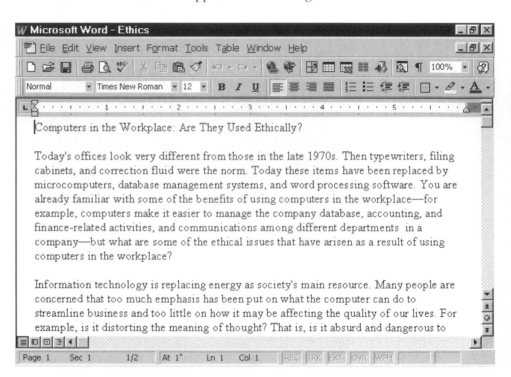

3. To move down through the document one screen at a time:
   CLICK: below the scroll box on the vertical scroll bar repeatedly

4. To move to the top of the document:
   DRAG: the scroll box to the top of the vertical scroll bar
   Notice that as you drag the scroll box along the scroll bar, Word displays the current page number.

5. To move to the bottom of the document using the keyboard:
   PRESS: CTRL + END

6. To move back to the top of the document using the keyboard:
   PRESS: CTRL + HOME

7. To move to the end of the current line:
   PRESS: END

8. To move to the beginning of the current line:
   PRESS: HOME

9. To move to the top of the second page in the document:
CLICK: Next Page button (▼) on the vertical scroll bar
The insertion point automatically moves to the first line of page 2.

10. To practice using the Go To dialog box:
DOUBLE-CLICK: on the page area ("Page 2") in the Status bar
Your screen should now appear similar to Figure 2.4.

FIGURE 2.4

THE GO TO DIALOG BOX

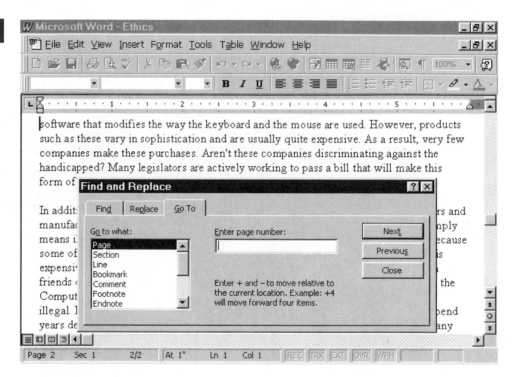

11. TYPE: **P1L8**
CLICK: Go To button or PRESS: ENTER
CLICK: Close command button
The "P" tells Word that the following number is a page number, and the "L" tells Word that the next number is a line number. The letters can be typed in either uppercase or lowercase characters. In this step, the insertion point is moved to line 8 on page 1.

12. To move to the top of the document:
PRESS: CTRL + HOME

QUICK REFERENCE
Accessing the
Go To Dialog Box

- **DOUBLE-CLICK: on the page area in the Status bar, or**
- **PRESS:** F5 **(Go To), or**
- **PRESS:** CTRL **+g, or**
- **CHOOSE: Edit, Go To**

IN ADDITION MARKING LOCATIONS WITH BOOKMARKS

You can also name locations, called *bookmarks,* in your document and then use the Go To dialog box when you want to move to them quickly.

To create a bookmark, position the cursor at the location you want to name and then choose Insert,

Bookmark from the Menu bar. Type a name for th-bookmark (up to 40 characters) and then click the Add button.

To move to a bookmark, display the Go To dialog box, select Bookmark from the *Go to what* list box, and then select the bookmark's name from the *Enter bookmark name* drop-down list box.

SELECTING TEXT

Once text has been typed into a document, you make formatting changes by first selecting the text and then issuing the appropriate command. Selected text always appears highlighted in reverse video (white text on a black background). A selection may include letters, words, lines, paragraphs, or even the entire document. When you finish formatting a selection, press an arrow key or click anywhere in the document to remove the highlighting from the text.

BLOCKING TEXT

Word provides an invisible column in the extreme left margin of the document window called the **Selection bar.** When the mouse is moved into this area, the pointer changes from an I-beam to a right-pointing diagonal arrow ( ). The Selection bar provides shortcut methods for selecting text using the mouse, as summarized in Table 2.3 along with other selection methods.

TABLE 2.3	To select this . . .	Do this . . .
Selecting text using the Mouse	Single Letter	Position the I-beam pointer to the left of the letter you want to select. Press down and hold the left mouse button as you drag the mouse pointer to the right.
	Single Word	Position the I-beam pointer on the word and double-click the left mouse button.
	Single Sentence	Hold down **CTRL** and click once with the I-beam pointer positioned on any word in the sentence.
	Block of Text	Move the insertion point to the beginning of the block of text and then position the I-beam pointer at the end of the block. Hold down **SHIFT** and click once.
	Single Line	Move the mouse pointer into the Selection bar, beside the line to be selected. Wait until the pointer changes to a right-pointing arrow and then click once.
	Single Paragraph	Move the mouse pointer into the Selection bar, beside the paragraph to be selected. Wait until the pointer changes to a right-pointing arrow and then double-click. You can also triple-click with the I-beam mouse pointer positioned inside a paragraph.
	Entire Document	Move the mouse pointer into the Selection bar. Wait until the pointer changes to a right-pointing arrow and then hold down **CTRL** and click once. You can also triple-click with the I-beam mouse pointer positioned in the Selection bar.

Next you practice selecting text using the "Ethics" document.

Perform the following steps . . .

1. To select the word "Computers" in the title, first position the I-beam mouse pointer on the word.

2. DOUBLE-CLICK: Computers
   The word and its trailing space should be highlighted in reverse video.

3. To select the letters "Work" in the word "Workplace," you must first position the I-beam pointer to the left of the "W" in "Workplace."

4. PRESS: left mouse button and hold it down
   DRAG: I-beam to the right until Work is highlighted

5. To select the first sentence in the first paragraph below the title, first position the I-beam pointer on the word "offices." (*Note:* The mouse pointer can be placed over any word in the sentence.)

6. PRESS: **CTRL** and hold it down
   CLICK: left mouse button once
   The first sentence, including the period and spaces, are highlighted.

7. To select only the third line in the first paragraph, position the mouse pointer to the left of the line in the Selection bar. The mouse pointer should change from an I-beam to a right-pointing diagonal arrow.

8. CLICK: the Selection bar beside the third line

9. To select the entire first paragraph:
    DOUBLE-CLICK: the Selection bar beside the first paragraph
    (*Note*: You can also position the I-beam pointer on any word in the paragraph and triple-click the left mouse button to select the entire paragraph.)

10. To select the entire document:
    PRESS: (CTRL) and hold it down
    CLICK: once anywhere in the Selection bar
    (*Note*: You can also position the mouse pointer in the Selection bar and triple-click the left mouse button to select the entire document.)

11. To remove highlighting from the text:
    CLICK: once anywhere in the text area

12. To return to the top of the document:
    PRESS: (CTRL) + (HOME)

To select text using the keyboard, you can use any combination of the keyboard shortcuts for moving the insertion point around the document while holding down the (SHIFT) key. Most people, however, find that the mouse methods provide all the flexibility they need for selecting blocks of text.

DELETING BLOCKS OF TEXT

Previously, you were told to delete text one character at a time using the (BACKSPACE) and (DELETE) keys. However, the ability to select characters, paragraphs, and documents allows you to delete larger blocks of text easily. Now you will practice deleting and replacing text in a document.

Perform the following steps . . .

1. To select the phrase in the title that reads "Are They Used Ethically?" first position the I-beam pointer to the left of the word "Are."

2. PRESS: left mouse button and hold it down
    DRAG: I-beam to the right until the question mark is highlighted
    (*Note*: If you select the space following the question mark, the next line will be deleted too.)

3. To remove this phrase from the title:
    PRESS: (DELETE)

4. Move the I-beam pointer on the word "Computers" in the title:
    DOUBLE-CLICK: Computers
    The word is selected.

5. TYPE: **Technology**
    Rather than using the Overtype mode, you can select the text to be replaced and then type in the new information. The typing automatically replaces the text selection.

6. To Undo this last editing change:
CLICK: Undo button (⟲▾) in the Standard toolbar
The word "Computers" reappears.

7. To demonstrate a basic formatting command, let's change the capitalization of the selected word "Computers":
CHOOSE: Format, Change Case
SELECT: UPPERCASE
PRESS: ENTER or CLICK: OK
The word changes from "Computers" to "COMPUTERS." (*Note*: You can also use SHIFT + F3 to toggle the selected text between uppercase, lowercase, and initial caps.)

8. Close the document window without saving the changes:
CLICK: Close button (✖) of the document window
CLICK: No command button

Now that you know how to move through documents and select text, formatting your documents will be much easier. The next section begins with an introduction to the character formatting commands.

CHARACTER FORMATTING COMMANDS

In word processing software, enhancing the appearance of text is referred to as character formatting. Specifically, character formatting involves selecting typefaces, font sizes, and attributes for text. Some of the attributes available in Word include bold, italic, underline, highlight, font color, strikethrough, shadow, outline, superscript, and subscript. You can even add animated effects, such as a blinking background or a shimmer, to text. Although these enhancement features are effective in drawing the reader's attention, they can also detract from the message you are trying to communicate. Most publishing professionals advocate using no more than four typefaces or fonts in a document. Still, there is no better gauge than common sense and good taste.

Word's character formatting commands are accessed through the Font dialog box (Figure 2.5), the Formatting toolbar, or by using shortcut keyboard combinations. Since many of the features are accessible from the Formatting toolbar and shortcut keys, you may never need to use the Format, Font menu command except to see a preview of a desired font or other attribute in the dialog box. Table 2.4 summarizes the mouse and keyboard methods for choosing character formatting commands.

FIGURE 2.5

FONT DIALOG BOX

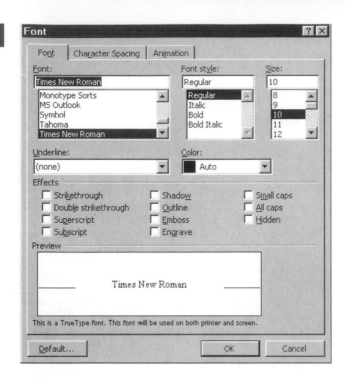

TABLE 2.4	*Toolbar Button*	*Keyboard Shortcut*	*Description*
Character Formatting Summary	**B**	CTRL + b	Makes the selected text **bold**
	I	CTRL + i	*Italicizes* the selected text
	U	CTRL + u	Applies a single underline
		CTRL + SHIFT + d	Applies a double underline
		CTRL + SHIFT + w	Applies underlining to words only
	(highlight)		Applies color highlighting to text
	A		Changes the font color
	Times New Roman	CTRL + SHIFT + f	Specifies a font or typeface
		CTRL + [	Decrease the point size by 1 point
		CTRL +]	Increase the point size by 1 point
	10	CTRL + SHIFT + p	Specifies a point size for the font
		CTRL + SHIFT + a	CAPITALIZES the selection
		CTRL + SHIFT + k	Applies SMALL CAPS

TABLE 2.4 *Continued*	*Toolbar Button*	*Keyboard Shortcut*	*Description*
		CTRL + F3	Changes the case of the selection
		CTRL + =	Applies a $_{sub}$script style
		CTRL + SHIFT + =	Applies a ^{super}script style
		CTRL + Space Bar	Removes all character formatting

BOLDFACE, ITALIC, AND UNDERLINES

In Word, you can apply character formatting commands as you type or after you have selected text. In this section you apply boldface, italic, and underlines to the "Ethics" document.

Perform the following steps . . .

1. Retrieve the "Ethics" document from the Advantage Files location. (*Note*: The last four documents that you opened are listed at the bottom of the File pull-down menu. Choose "Ethics" from this list.)

2. To insert a new line between the title and the first paragraph:
   PRESS: END
   PRESS: ENTER

3. To add an italicized subtitle for this document:
   CLICK: Italic button (*I*) on the Formatting toolbar
   TYPE: **The Information Age and the Age of Humanity**

4. To stop typing in italic:
   CLICK: Italic button (*I*)

5. To select this subtitle, position the mouse pointer in the Selection bar to the left of the line and click the left mouse button once.

6. Make the subtitle bold and underlined using the buttons on the Formatting toolbar:
   CLICK: Bold button (**B**)
   CLICK: Underline button (U)

7. To better see the changes you've made:
   CLICK: anywhere in the text area

8. Make the following formatting changes in the first paragraph using either the Formatting toolbar buttons or the keyboard shortcuts.

Text to be formatted	*Formatting to apply*
microcomputers	italic and bold
database management system	italic
word processing software	italic
ethical issues	word underline only

QUICK REFERENCE
Boldface, Italic, and
Underlines

- To make text bold, click the Bold button (**B**) or press CTRL +b
- To italicize text, click the Italic button (*I*) or press CTRL +i
- To underline text, click the Underline button (U) or press CTRL +u

---

TYPEFACES, FONTS, AND POINT SIZES

One of the more interesting character formatting options is the ability to select from a variety of typefaces. A **typeface** is a style of print. A **font** is defined as all the symbols and characters of a particular typeface for a given point size. Many DOS word processing programs do not utilize a variety of fonts, unless they are available through an individual software vendor or resident in the printer's memory. Microsoft Windows, on the other hand, provides easy access to several popular typefaces.

The font and point size can be changed before typing new text or after selecting text. Although you can use the Font dialog box to set the font and point size, it is easier to use the drop-down lists on the Formatting toolbar. In this section you change some of the fonts and point sizes in the "Ethics" document.

Perform the following steps . . .

1. SELECT: the main title on the first line

2. To display a list of the available fonts:
    CLICK: down arrow beside the *Font* drop-down list (Times New Roman ▼)

3. Scroll through the font choices by clicking the up and down arrows on the drop-down list's scroll bar or by dragging the scroll box.

4. SELECT: Arial (or a font that is available on your computer)
    (*Hint*: You select a font from the drop-down list by clicking on it.)

5. To display the range of available font sizes:
    CLICK: down arrow beside the *Font Size* drop-down list (10 ▼)

6. SELECT: 16-point font size
    CLICK: Bold button (**B**)
    PRESS: HOME to remove the highlighting
    Your screen should now appear similar to Figure 2.6.

FIGURE 2.6

THE "ETHICS" DOCUMENT
AFTER CHARACTER
FORMATTING

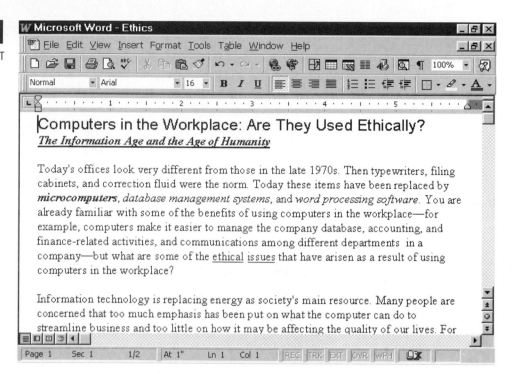

QUICK REFERENCE
Typefaces, Fonts,
and Point Sizes

- To select a typeface, click the *Fonts* drop-down list (Times Roman) in the Formatting toolbar and then click on the desired font.
- To change the font size, click the *Font Size* drop-down list (10) in the Formatting toolbar and then click on the desired point size.

HIGHLIGHT, COLOR, AND ANIMATION

A number of features exist for enhancing how a document appears on the screen. These features are especially useful when others will be reviewing your document online and you want to draw attention to certain elements. In this section, we describe how to highlight text and add color and animation to a document. You highlight and add color to text using the Highlight ( ) and Font Color ( ) buttons on the Formatting toolbar. You add animation using the Font dialog box.

In this section you practice highlighting text and adding color and animation to a document.

Perform the following steps . . .

1. To highlight the first sentence:
   SELECT: the first sentence

2. CLICK: Highlight button ( )
   (*Note*: Make sure that you click the left side of the button and not the down arrow.) The sentence should be highlighted in yellow, or in the currently selected color. Your screen should now appear similar to Figure 2.7.

FIGURE 2.7

HIGHLIGHTING TEXT

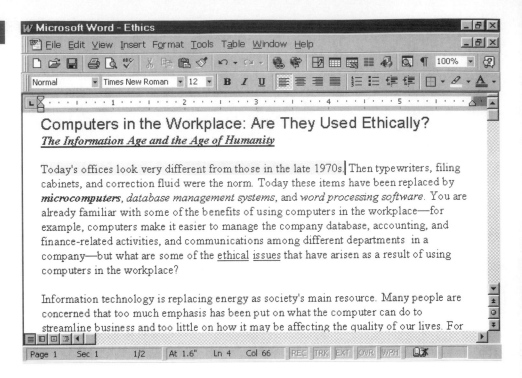

3. To remove the text highlight:
   SELECT: the first sentence
   CLICK: down arrow in the Highlight button (⟦🖉▾⟧)
   SELECT: None
   The text is no longer highlighted. (*Note*: Before you can highlight text in the future, you will have to re-select a color option using the Highlight button.)

4. Let's try adding color to the first paragraph.
   SELECT: the first paragraph
   CLICK: Font Color button (⟦🅰▾⟧)
   (*Note*: Make sure that you click the left side of the button and not the down arrow.)
   CLICK: in the document window to remove the highlighting
   The paragraph text should now appear red, or in the currently selected color. Your screen should now appear similar to Figure 2.8.

FIGURE 2.8

COLORING TEXT

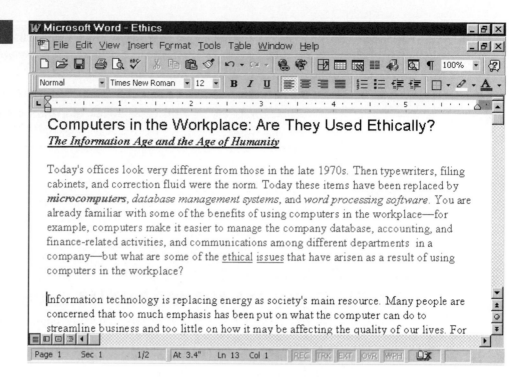

5. To select a new color, you click the down arrow in the Font Color button ([A▾]). On your own, color the first paragraph blue.

6. Now let's try animating the subtitle of the document. To do this, you will use the *Animation* tab in the Font dialog box.
SELECT: the main title (1st line) at the top of the document

7. CHOOSE: Format, Font
CLICK: *Animation* tab

8. Experiment with the different effects by clicking them in the Animations list box. Before continuing:
CLICK: Sparkle Text
PRESS: (ENTER) or CLICK: OK

9. To save the file to your Data Files location:
CHOOSE: File, Save As

10. To specify a filename for the document:
TYPE: **Ethics-Version 2**

11. To specify where the document will be saved, do the following:
CLICK: down arrow beside the *Save in* drop-down list box
SELECT: *your Data Files location*
PRESS: (ENTER) or CLICK: Save command button

12. Print the "Ethics-Version 2" document. (*Note:* Your highlighting and coloring will appear as shades of gray when printing on a black and white printer, and your animated effects only appear on the screen.)

USING THE FORMAT PAINTER

Word's Format Painter feature lets you copy character and paragraph formatting
from one area in your document to another area. To copy character formatting, you
select the text with the desired formatting and click the Format Painter button (◁)
on the Standard toolbar. When you move the mouse pointer into the document area,
it becomes an I-beam attached to a paintbrush. To apply the formatting, you drag
the mouse pointer over the text that you want to format. When you release the
mouse button, the formatting characteristics are copied from the original selection
to your new selection.

To copy formatting to multiple areas in a document, you double-click the Format
Painter button (◁) after selecting the originally formatted text. As described in the
previous paragraph, you paint the first selection by dragging the mouse pointer over
the desired text. However, this time the paintbrush mouse pointer doesn't disappear
when you finish applying the first coat. You continue applying formatting to additional
text selections and then click the Format Painter button (◁) when you are done.

In this section you practice using the Format Painter.

Perform the following steps . . .

1. Retrieve a document called "Paint" from the Advantage Files location.

2. SELECT: Features

3. To format the heading:
   CLICK: Bold button ([**B**])
   CLICK: Italic button ([*I*])
   SELECT: Arial font from the *Font* drop-down list ([Times New Roman ▾])
   SELECT: 14-point size from the *Font Size* drop-down list ([10 ▾])
   (*Note*: If you don't have the Arial font on your computer, select an alternate
   font.)

4. To copy the formatting characteristics that you just selected:
   DOUBLE-CLICK: Features
   (*Note*: "Features" may already be selected.)

5. CLICK: Format Painter button ()

6. Move the mouse pointer into the document area. Notice that it becomes an I-beam attached to a paintbrush.

7. To copy the formatting to the second heading:
   DRAG: mouse pointer over the subheading "Future Expectations"
   When you release the mouse button, the second heading is formatted with the same characteristics as the first heading.

8. To format "Windows 95" in the first sentence:
   SELECT: Windows 95

9. CLICK: Bold button (**B**)
   CLICK: Italic button (*I*)

10. To copy this formatting to several areas in the document:
    DOUBLE-CLICK: Format Painter button ()

11. Using the I-beam paintbrush mouse pointer, select all occurrences of "Windows 95" and "Windows NT" in the document. (*Tip*: You can double-click words as you would with the regular I-beam mouse pointer to apply the formatting.)

12. To finish using the paintbrush mouse pointer:
    CLICK: Format Painter button ()

13. Save the document as "Painted" to your Data Files location. (*Remember*: You must use the Save As command if your Data Files are stored in a different location from your Advantage Files.)

14. Close the document.

QUICK REFERENCE
Using the Format Painter Button ()

1. **SELECT: the text with the desired formatting characteristics**
2. **CLICK: Format Painter button ()**
3. **SELECT: the text that you want to format**

IN ADDITION FORMATTING CHARACTERS WITH STYLES

A *character style* is a set of formats that can contain any specification found in the Font dialog box (Figure 2.5), such as font type, type style, and point size. When you apply a style to a selection of text, all the formatting instructions in the style are executed at once. When you edit a style, any text that conforms to the style is updated immediately.

If you work with documents that contain lots of formatting, styles will (1) save you time, (2) promote consistent formatting throughout your documents, and (3) make it easier for you to edit a document's format.

To find out more about styles, choose Help, Contents and Index. Select the Index tab and then type **styles** to display a list of topics.

IN ADDITION FORMATTING CHARACTERS WITH WORDART

 To add special effects to your document text, consider entering or formatting your text using WordArt. WordArt provides a collection of commands for adding special effects, such as a wavy look, to your text.

1. Position the insertion point where you want to insert text formatted by WordArt, or select existing text that you want to format with WordArt.

2. CHOOSE: Insert, Picture, WordArt
    (*Note:* You can also click the WordArt button on the WordArt toolbar.)

3. Select a style in the WordArt Gallery dialog box and then press (**ENTER**) or click OK.

4. TYPE: the desired text into the Edit WordArt Text dialog box

5. Format the text using buttons in the Edit WordArt Text dialog box.

6. When you're finished:
    CLICK: OK

7. Enhance the selected WordArt object using the WordArt toolbar, if necessary.

8. To resize the object, point to it and click. Selection handles appear around the object. Drag a selection handle in the desired direction. (*Note:* To delete an object, point to it and click. Then press (**DELETE**).)

PARAGRAPH FORMATTING COMMANDS

Paragraph formatting involves changing indentation, alignment, line spacing, and tab settings for a paragraph. As with character formatting, many paragraph formatting commands are accessible using the mouse or keyboard shortcut combinations. Using a mouse, you can change alignments and indent paragraphs by clicking buttons on the Formatting toolbar or create hanging indents and set tab stops by dragging symbols on the Ruler. For entering specific measurements and accessing the full gamut of paragraph formatting options, choose the Format, Paragraph command to display the dialog box shown in Figure 2.9.

FIGURE 2.9

PARAGRAPH DIALOG BOX

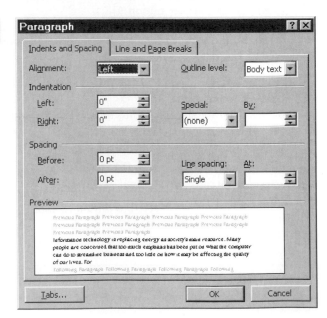

Word stores formatting information in the **Paragraph Symbol** (¶). To apply paragraph formatting commands to a paragraph, position the insertion point anywhere in the paragraph—you do not need to select any text—and then issue the desired command. To remove paragraph formatting, you can press ENTER +q to return to the Normal style. You can also delete the paragraph mark to make the current paragraph assume the formatting characteristics of the subsequent paragraph.

When you first install Word onto your computer, the paragraph marks are hidden from view. To display the paragraph marks and all other hidden symbols, click the Show/Hide button (¶) on the Formatting toolbar. Along with the paragraph marks, Word reveals spaces (as dots), tabs (as right-pointing arrows →), and other formatting codes and symbols. It's very important to note that these are *nonprinting symbols*—they will not show up on the printed page.

A favorite feature in Word is the ability to display a help bubble showing you the formatting characteristics of your text. To display the bubble, choose Help, What's This? from the Menu bar and then click the question mark mouse pointer on the desired text area. A bubble will appear with character and paragraph formatting information. To remove the Help bubble, you press ESC or choose Help, What's This? again.

In this section you display the hidden symbols and formatting information for the "Ethics-Version 2" document.

Perform the following steps . . .

1. Ensure that the "Ethics-Version 2" document appears on your screen.

2. If not already displayed, show all of the hidden symbols in the document by doing the following:
    CLICK: Show/Hide button (¶)
    Paragraph marks (¶) appear in the document wherever the ENTER key was pressed. This view is useful for checking codes and spaces but you may find it distracting.

3. To show the formatting characteristics for the main title:
    CHOOSE: Help, What's This?

4. Position the question mark mouse pointer over any letter in the main title:
    CLICK: left mouse button once
    Your screen should now appear similar to Figure 2.10.

FIGURE 2.10

HELP BUBBLE FOR
SHOWING FORMATTING
CHARACTERISTICS

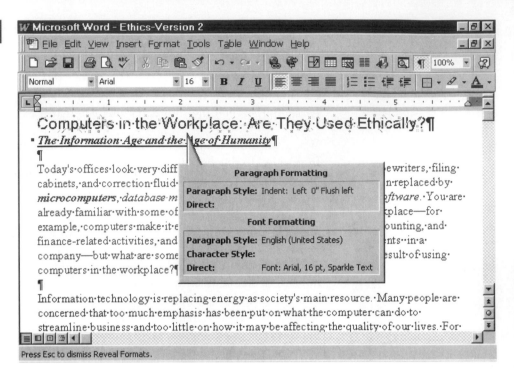

5. To remove the Help bubble:
PRESS: ESC

6. Before proceeding, let's hide the symbols:
CLICK: Show/Hide button (¶)

INDENTING PARAGRAPHS

Indenting a paragraph means to move a body of text in from the normal page margins. When you indent a paragraph, you temporarily change the text's positioning relative to the left and right margins. You can indent a paragraph on the left side only, right side only, or on both sides (known as a *nested paragraph*).

If you use the Increase Indent (⬛) and Decrease Indent (⬛) buttons on the Formatting toolbar, indentation is determined by the tab settings in the Ruler. If the tab positions have not been modified, Word assumes you want to use the default 0.5 inch settings. Each time you indent a paragraph, the text moves to the next tab stop. Therefore, to create larger indentations you can set larger gaps between tabs or select the indent command multiple times. You can also customize your indents by dragging the indent markers on the Ruler (shown below).

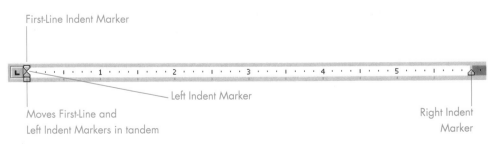

- *First-Line Indent Marker*
  This indent marker moves only the first line of a paragraph in from the left margin. This paragraph format is often used in letters to avoid having to press the (**TAB**) key at the start of each new paragraph.

- *Left Indent Marker*
  The left indent marker moves the body of the entire paragraph in from the left margin.

- *Right Indent Marker*
  The right indent marker moves the body of the entire paragraph in from the right margin. Left and right indents are often used together to set quotations apart from normal body text in a document.

By default, Word positions the first-line and left indent markers on the left margin, and the right indent marker on the right margin. You will now practice changing the paragraph indents using the mouse.

Perform the following steps . . .

1. Ensure that the "Ethics-Version 2" document appears on your screen.

2. Move the insertion point to the second paragraph, starting with the words "Information technology." Position the insertion point to the left of the letter "I" in the word "Information."

3. To add a left indent to this paragraph:
   CLICK: Increase Indent button (⬛)
   The paragraph moves 0.5 inch to the next tab stop. Notice the new location of the indent markers on the Ruler.

4. To view the new settings as they appear in the Paragraph dialog box, position the mouse pointer on the paragraph and click the right mouse button to bring up the shortcut menu.

5. CHOOSE: Paragraph
   The Paragraph dialog box appears. Notice the new value in the *Left Indentation* text box and the sample paragraph in the *Preview* area.

6. To return to the document:
   CLICK: Cancel button

7. To indent the paragraph 1 inch from the right margin:
   DRAG: right indent marker to the left by 1 inch (to 5 inches on the Ruler)

8. To remove the left indent:
   CLICK: Decrease Indent button (⬛)
   Notice that this button has no effect on the right indent marker.

9. To remove the right indent:
   DRAG: right indent marker back to the right margin (at 6 inches on the Ruler)

10. Move the cursor to anywhere in the last paragraph of the "Ethics-Version 2" document.

11. To indent the last paragraph by 1 inch:
CLICK: Increase Indent button (⬚) twice

12. A handy keystroke to remember is `CTRL` +**q**; it removes all paragraph formatting characteristics from the current paragraph. To demonstrate:
PRESS: `CTRL` +**q**
The paragraph indentations return to their normal settings against the left and right margins.

13. Move to the end of the document and insert a new blank line.

14. In this next step, you insert a hanging indent where the first line of the paragraph lines up with the left margin and the remainder of the paragraph is indented. To begin:
DRAG: left indent marker to 1 inch on the Ruler
(*Caution:* Make sure that the tip of your mouse pointer points to the triangle and not to the bottom rectangle when dragging. If performed correctly, the first-line indent marker should remain at the margin.)

15. TYPE: **Summary**
PRESS: `TAB`

16. TYPE: **Information systems technology provides a clear opportunity for the disabled to perform in the workplace.**
Your screen should now appear similar to Figure 2.11.

FIGURE 2.11

INDENTING
PARAGRAPHS IN THE
"ETHICS-VERSION 2"
DOCUMENT

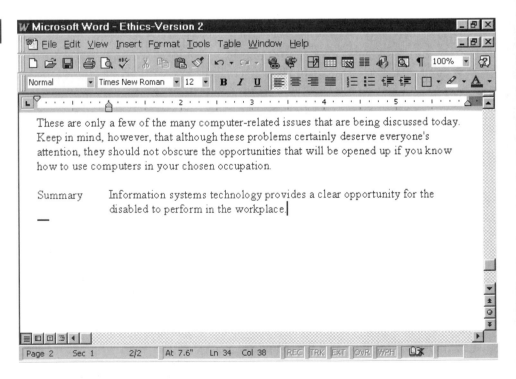

17. Save the "Ethics-Version 2" document to your Data Files location.

18. Close the document.

CREATING BULLETED AND NUMBERED LISTS

Word provides a utility for automatically creating lists with leading **bullets** or numbers. Although round circles are the standard shape for bullets, you can select shapes from a variety of symbols. Numbered lists can use numerals, letters, or numbers. If you want to modify the bullet symbols or numbering scheme, choose the Format, Bullets and Numbering command to display the dialog box appearing in Figure 2.12. This screen graphic also shows the resulting dialog box when you click the Customize button.

FIGURE 2.12

BULLETS AND
NUMBERING
DIALOG BOX

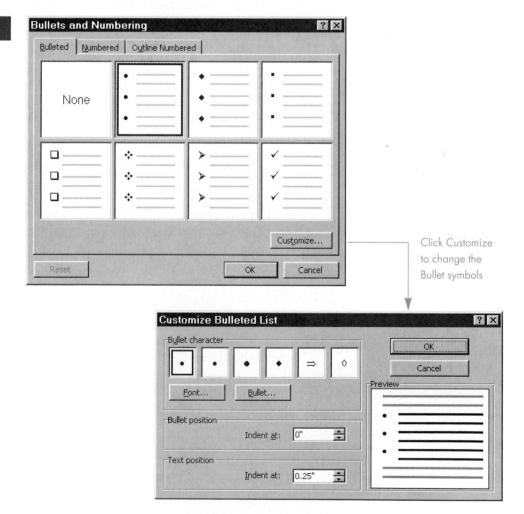

Click Customize
to change the
Bullet symbols

In this section you create bulleted and numbered lists.

 **Perform the following steps . . .**

1. If you do not have an empty document on the screen, open a new document using the New button ([🗋]).

2. TYPE: **To Do List**
   PRESS: [ENTER] twice

3. To create a bulleted list:
   CLICK: Bullets button ([≣])
   A bullet appears and the left indent marker is moved on the Ruler.

4. Enter the following text, pressing [ENTER] at the end of each line:
   Pick up dry cleaning
   Meet Jesse at the gym
   Go grocery shopping
   Mail letter to Mom

5. You will notice that Word automatically starts each new line with a bullet when you press [ENTER]. To turn off the bullets, ensure that your insertion point is on the line below "Mail letter to Mom" and then:
   CLICK: Bullets button ([≣])

6. PRESS: [ENTER]

7. In this next example, you create a numbered list after you've already entered information into your document. To begin:
   TYPE: **Travel Itinerary**
   PRESS: [ENTER] twice

8. Enter the following lines of text, as before:
   Aug 12: Flight 455 to Sydney.
   Aug 28: Flight 87 to Auckland.
   Aug 29: Flight A101 to Christchurch.
   Sep 11: Flight 110 to Vancouver.

9. Using the mouse pointer in the Selection bar, select the text that you just entered in step 8.

10. CLICK: Numbering button ([≣])
    The selected text is automatically numbered.

11. To use letters rather than numbers for the list, position the mouse pointer over the highlighted text and click the right mouse button. From the shortcut menu that appears:
    CHOOSE: Bullets and Numbering

12. Ensure that the *Numbered* tab is selected in the dialog box.

13. SELECT: the option that shows a), b), and c)

14. PRESS: [ENTER] or CLICK: OK
    CLICK: anywhere in the document to remove the highlighting
    Your document should now appear similar to Figure 2.13.

FIGURE 2.13

NUMBERED AND
BULLETED LISTS

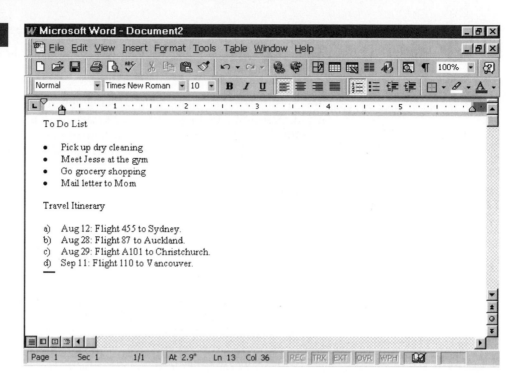

15. To add an item to your travel itinerary between Christchurch and Vancouver, position the I-beam pointer at the end of the Christchurch line or item c) and press **ENTER**.

16. TYPE: **Sep 10: Flight 904 to Seattle.**
Notice that Word automatically renumbers, or in this case re-letters, the list for you when you insert new entries.

17. Save the document as "To Do List" to the Data Files location.

18. Close the document.

QUICK REFERENCE
Bulleted and
Numbered Lists

- To create a bulleted list, click the Bullets button (🔲)
- To create a numbered list, click the Numbering button (🔲)
- To modify the bullet symbols or numbering scheme:
  CHOOSE: Format, Bullets and Numbering

CHANGING PARAGRAPH ALIGNMENT

Justification refers to how text aligns with the margins of a document. You can align or apply justification to a paragraph either before or after text is typed. Word provides four different types of justification or alignment:

- *Left justification* aligns text at the left margin but leaves jagged right edges as a typewriter does.

- *Center justification* centers the line or paragraph between the margins.

- *Right justification* positions text flush against the right margin.

- *Full justification* provides even text columns at the left and right margins by automatically spacing words on the line.

You specify the justification for a paragraph using the Format, Paragraph command, Formatting toolbar buttons, or keyboard shortcut combinations (summarized in Table 2.5). Remember, paragraph formatting requires the insertion point to be placed in the paragraph to be formatted, but you need not select any text.

TABLE 2.5	*Toolbar Button*	*Keyboard Shortcut*	*Description*
Alignment options	▤	CTRL +l	Left-aligns the selected paragraph
	▤	CTRL +e	Centers the selected paragraph
	▤	CTRL +r	Right-aligns the selected paragraph
	▤	CTRL +j	Fully justifies the selected paragraph

In this section you practice changing justification.

Perform the following steps . . .

1. Retrieve the "Ethics" document from the Advantage Files location.

2. To change the justification for the title, first position the insertion point at the beginning of the title.

3. CLICK: Center button (▤)
   The line is immediately centered between the two margins.

4. CLICK: Align Right button (▤)
   The line is positioned flush against the right margin.

5. To move the line back to its original position:
   CLICK: Align Left button (▤)

6. Practice changing the first paragraph's justification using the buttons on the Formatting toolbar.

IN ADDITION ALIGNING TEXT VERTICALLY

On a page, text is usually aligned with the top margin. That is, the first line of text that you type prints on the first line after the top margin. In some cases, such as when including a cover page or a table of data in your document, you may want the text to be centered or justified between the top and bottom margins.

To align text vertically, choose File, Page Setup from the Menu bar. Select the *Layout* tab. In the *Vertical alignment* list, select Center to center the text on the page or *Justified* to spread the paragraphs evenly between the top and bottom margins.

CHANGING LINE SPACING

Another common paragraph formatting procedure lets you change the line spacing in a document. The standard options for line spacing are single- and double-spaced, but your choices aren't limited to these. You can specify various line spacing options using the Format, Paragraph dialog box. However, the shortcut keys in Table 2.6 provide the quickest methods for selecting line spacing in a paragraph.

TABLE 2.6	*Keyboard Shortcut*	*Description*
Changing Line Spacing	CTRL +1	Single-spaces the selected paragraph
	CTRL +2	Double-spaces the selected paragraph
	CTRL +5	Applies 1.5-line spaces to the selected paragraph

Now you practice changing line spacing.

Perform the following steps . . .

1. Move the insertion point into the first paragraph of the "Ethics" document.

2. To double-space this paragraph:
   PRESS: CTRL +2
   Notice that only the first paragraph is double-spaced.

3. To apply 1.5-line-spacing:
   PRESS: CTRL +5

4. To return the paragraph to single spacing:
   PRESS: CTRL +1

5. To double-space the document, you need to first select the entire document. Move the mouse pointer into the Selection bar and triple-click the left mouse button. The entire document should be highlighted in reverse video before proceeding.

6. PRESS: CTRL +2
   The "Ethics" document should be double-spaced.

7. CLICK: anywhere in the document to remove the highlighting

8. Close the document and do not save the changes.

CHANGING TAB SETTINGS

Tabs enable you to neatly enter text and numbers into columns. If your past experience includes using a typewriter, you are likely familiar with using the Space Bar to line up columns of text on a page. This works fine when you are using a monospaced font in which all letters are an equal width. However, most word processing fonts are not monospaced and, therefore, you cannot line up columns by simply pressing the Space Bar a fixed number of times. To accomplish the same objective in Word, you place tabs on the Ruler and use the TAB key to move the insertion point between tab stops. The four basic types of tabs are described in Table 2.7 below.

TABLE 2.7	Tab Name	Ruler Symbol	Description
Types of Tabs	Left-Aligned	⌊L⌋	Starting at the tab, text extends to the right as you type
	Center-Aligned	⌊⊥⌋	Starting at the tab, text is centered on the tab stop.
	Right-Aligned	⌊⌐⌋	Starting at the tab, text extends to the left as you type.
	Decimal-Aligned	⌊⊥⌋	At the tab, the integer portion of a number extends to the left and the decimal fraction extends to the right.

Before you start adding your own tabs to the Ruler, you should be aware that Word supplies left-aligned tabs every 0.5 inch by default. If you require greater flexibility, you begin by selecting a tab type using the Tab Alignment button (⌊L⌋) located at the far left of the Ruler. On each mouse click, Word switches to the next tab symbol. Once the desired tab type appears, you position the tip of the mouse pointer on the Ruler and click once to place the tab. If you need to fine-tune a tab's position on the Ruler, you simply drag it back and forth. To remove a tab, you drag it downwards and off the Ruler. Be forewarned that all the default tabs to the left of the new tab are automatically cleared.

You can also set tabs using the Format, Tabs command (its dialog box appears in Figure 2.14.) An added benefit to using the Tabs dialog box to set tabs is that you can also set leaders. A tab **leader** is a dotted, dashed, or solid line that fills the space between text and tab stops. Leaders are commonly used in tables of contents to visually join the section headings with the page numbers. Some examples of leaders are provided below:

Dot leader ....A Right-Aligned tab
Dashed leader ----------------------------Another Right-Aligned tab
Solid leader _____And yet a third Right-Aligned tab

FIGURE 2.14

TABS DIALOG BOX

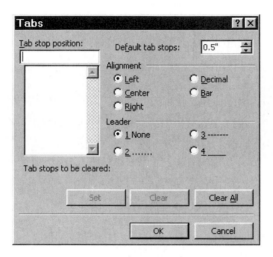

Next you create a document that uses customized tabs.

Perform the following steps . . .

1. If you do not have an empty document on the screen, open a new document using the New button (🗋).

2. To center the title and specify double spacing:
   CLICK: Center button (▤)
   PRESS: CTRL +2

3. TYPE: **Marketing Memo**
   PRESS: ENTER

4. To change the paragraph alignment to fully justified:
   CLICK: Justify button (▤)

5. TYPE: **It is my pleasure to announce to Sporting Life's marketing and sales staff that sales have increased steadily for the past six months. As you well know, Sporting Life is known for carrying quality sporting items at reasonable prices. But without you, Sporting Life would be "just another sports store." Keep up the good work!**

6. To add a blank line and change to single spacing:
PRESS: `ENTER`
PRESS: `CTRL`+1

In the remainder of the document, you will create an income and expense report for January through June. The first step is to label the columns that will contain the figures. The first column heading will be centered at 3 inches and the second column heading at 4.5 inches on the Ruler.

Now you set tab stops for the table heading and the data.

Perform the following steps . . .

1. CLICK: Tab Alignment button at the far left of the Ruler until the center-aligned tab symbol (⊥) appears

2. Position the tip of the mouse pointer on the 3-inch mark of the Ruler and click the left mouse button once. If done properly, you will see a center-aligned tab mark appear on the Ruler. If the tab stop is not placed correctly, drag the tab mark into position using the mouse. If you need to, you can delete the tab and start over by dragging the tab downward and off the Ruler.

3. To position the second tab stop, position the mouse pointer on the 4.5-inch mark and click the left mouse button once.

4. PRESS: `TAB`
The insertion point moves to the first tab stop. Notice that Word deletes the default tab stops to the left of the customized tabs.

5. TYPE: **REVENUE**
PRESS: `TAB`

6. TYPE: **EXPENSES**
PRESS: `ENTER` twice
The headings are centered on their respective tab marks.

7. The next step is to set the decimal tabs for aligning the numbers correctly. Before proceeding, remove the two center-aligned tab stops by dragging them down and off the Ruler.

8. To specify a tab position for the row headings:
SELECT: Left-aligned tab (L) using the Tab Alignment button
CLICK: 1 inch on the Ruler

9. To specify a tab position for the REVENUE figures:
SELECT: Decimal-aligned tab (⊥) using the Tab Alignment button
CLICK: 3.25 inches on the Ruler
(*Tip*: To display a measurement helper, try holding down the `ALT` key as you drag the tab symbol on the Ruler.)

10. To specify a tab position for the EXPENSES figures:
CLICK: 4.75 inches on the Ruler

11. For fun, let's turn on the Show/Hide symbols feature:
CLICK: Show/Hide button (¶)

12. Now, let's enter January's REVENUE and EXPENSES:
PRESS: **TAB**
TYPE: **January**
PRESS: **TAB**
TYPE: **18,900.75**
PRESS: **TAB**
TYPE: **13,534.67**
PRESS: **ENTER**
Notice that each press of the **TAB** key results in the tab symbol (→).

13. Enter the following information in the Month, Revenue, and Expense columns to finish the Marketing Memo:

February	22,050.00	15,356.48
March	17,354.45	11,225.32
April	18,239.00	15,006.95
May	26,884.69	19,322.55
June	28,677.41	21,632.10

14. Save the document as "Marketing Memo" to the Data Files location. Your screen should now appear similar to Figure 2.15.

15. Print the "Marketing Memo" document.

FIGURE 2.15

SPORTING LIFE
MARKETING MEMO

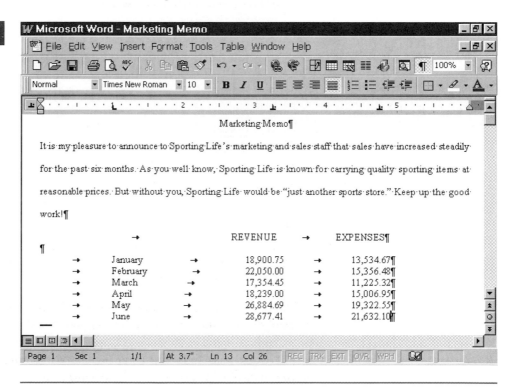

FORCING A PAGE BREAK

Word automatically repaginates a document as you insert and delete text. In Word's Normal view, a dotted line appears wherever Word inserts a floating page break, sometimes splitting an important paragraph or a table of figures. Rather than leaving the text on separate pages, you can instruct Word to start a new page at the insertion point by inserting a hard page break. The quickest way to force a hard page break is to press CTRL + ENTER. You can also choose the Insert, Break command from the Menu bar.

In this section, you force a page break so that the table created in the "Marketing Memo" document appears on a separate page.

Perform the following steps . . .

1. Position the insertion point at the beginning of the line containing the headings REVENUE and EXPENSES. Make sure that the insertion point is in the first column, next to the left margin.

2. PRESS: CTRL + ENTER
   A solid line with the words "Page Break" appears above the headings. The Status bar should now contain "Page 2" and "2/2."

3. To delete the hard page break, position the insertion point directly on the page break line and press DELETE.

4. Close the "Marketing Memo" document without saving.

QUICK REFERENCE
Inserting a Forced Page Break

1. Position the insertion point at the beginning of the line that you want moved to the top of a new page.

2. PRESS: CTRL + ENTER

AUTOCORRECT FEATURES

Word is pretty eager to please. In fact, Word can perform a number of formatting tasks for you automatically. Depending on your preference, Word will format your documents as you type or once you're finished. You specify what you want Word to do for you by choosing Tools, AutoCorrect from the Menu bar.

By default, Word formats your documents automatically as you type. Word can format your documents with borders, numbered and bulleted lists, quotations, em dashes, ordinal numbers such as 1st, fractions such as ¼, and symbols such as © and ™. It can even help you complete certain words, such as the months of the year, the names of Fortune 1000 companies, and cities with a population greater than 30,000. In this section, you create a small document that illustrates some of these features.

Perform the following steps . . .

1. To begin a new document:
   CLICK: New button ( ) on the Standard toolbar

2. While you work through this section, we assume the *AutoCorrect* and *Auto-Format As You Type* tabs on your computer look the same as those in Figure 2.16. To check these settings:
   CHOOSE: Tools, AutoCorrect from the Menu bar
   CLICK: *AutoCorrect* tab
   Ensure that the settings match those in Figure 2.16.
   CLICK: *AutoFormat As You Type* tab
   Again, ensure that the settings match those in Figure 2.16.

FIGURE 2.16

AUTOCORRECT DIALOG
BOX: CHECKING YOUR
SETTINGS

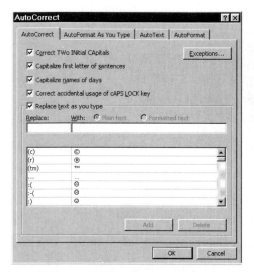
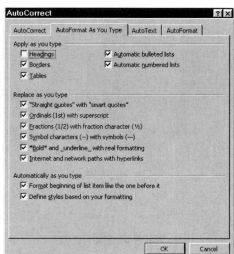

3. When you are finished:
   PRESS: (ENTER) or CLICK: OK button

4. Let's begin by typing a heading for our document.
   TYPE: **AutoFormat As You Type**
   PRESS: (ENTER)
   Word thinks "As" should be "as" and has thus underlined "As" with a wavy green underline. Ignore this suggestion.

5. To apply a border using the AutoFormat feature:
   TYPE: ---
   PRESS: (ENTER)
   A border now appears beneath the title.

6. To insert a blank line after the border:
   PRESS: (ENTER)

7. To automatically create a numbered list, you type the first number, press (TAB), type some text, and then press (ENTER). To illustrate:
TYPE: **1.**
PRESS: (TAB) once
TYPE: **Apples**
PRESS: (ENTER)
TYPE: **Oranges**
PRESS: (ENTER)
TYPE: **Bananas**

8. To stop the automatic numbering:
PRESS: (ENTER) twice

9. To automatically create a bulleted list, you type an asterisk (*), press (TAB), type some text, and then press (ENTER). To illustrate:
TYPE: *****
PRESS: (TAB) once
TYPE: **Cookies**
PRESS: (ENTER)
TYPE: **Ice Cream**
PRESS: (ENTER)
TYPE: **Cake**

10. To stop the automatic bullets:
PRESS: (ENTER) twice

11. In this step, you'll see how Word automatically formats ordinal numbers, fractions, and other symbols. Just type the characters you see; Word will do the formatting for you.
To type an ordinal number:
TYPE: **1**
TYPE: **s**
TYPE: **t**
TYPE: **,** (comma)
PRESS: Space Bar

On the same line, type the following literals to display the associated symbols. Type a comma and then press the Space Bar after each symbol appears.

You Type:	To display:
1/4	¼
(c)	©
(r)	®
(tm)	™
-->	→
==>	➔
:)	☺
:|	☺
:(	☹

12. To insert a blank line:
PRESS: [ENTER]

13. Using the mouse pointer in the Selection bar, select the row of symbols you entered in step 11. Then:
SELECT: 14-point size from the *Font Size* drop-down list ([10 ▼])
CLICK: anywhere in the document to remove the highlight
Your screen should now appear similar to Figure 2.17.

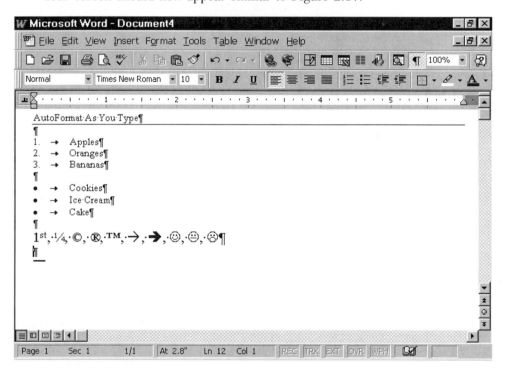

14. Word 97 includes a feature called AutoText, which automatically finishes commonly used words such as "January," "Respectfully," and "CONFIDEN-TIAL." You simply type a few characters and Word will help you type the rest. Before illustrating the use of this feature, move the cursor to the end of the document.
PRESS: [CTRL]+[END]
PRESS: [ENTER] twice

15. TYPE: `I leave for vacation in Janu`
Your screen should now appear similar to Figure 2.18.

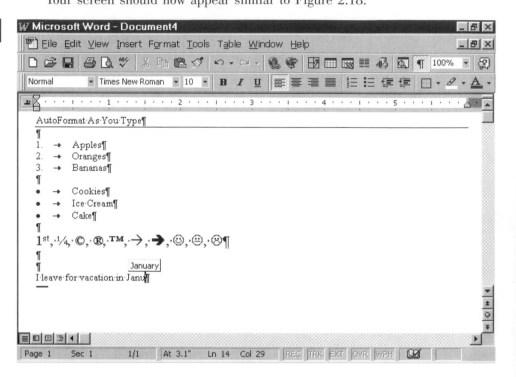

16. To let Word complete the Word for you, you press ENTER.
PRESS: ENTER
"January" should now appear. Type a period (.) to end the sentence.

17. To see the complete list of words that Word will help you type:
CHOOSE: Tools, AutoCorrect
CLICK: *AutoText* tab

18. Scroll through the list of words and phrases in the *Enter AutoText entries here* list box. In a later session, we show you how to create your own Auto-Text entries.

19. To return to your document:
CLICK: Cancel button

20. Save the document as "AutoFormat" to your Data Files location.

21. Close the document.

IN ADDITION AUTOMATIC HYPERLINK FORMATTING

By default, Word will format any In-ternet, network, and e-mail addresses that you include in your documents as hyperlinks. You then simply click the hyperlink to go to the specified location. Word automatically underlines and applies a blue attribute to your hyperlinks. For example, the following shows a hyperlink to Microsoft Word on the web: http://www.microsoft.com/word/

SUMMARY

This session introduced several methods for moving around a document and selecting text. As with most Windows programs, Word is based upon a Select and then Do approach to formatting and editing. Therefore, the proper selection of text is extremely important for executing commands and working effectively with Word.

This session concentrated on character and paragraph formatting commands. Besides applying boldface, italic, and underline character styles to text, character formatting involves changing the typeface, font, and point size. Paragraph formatting commands enable you to customize paragraphs in your text without affecting the entire document. This section explored indenting paragraphs, creating bulleted and numbered lists, aligning text, setting tabs, and forcing page breaks. You then practiced using some of Word's AutoFormat features.

Table 2.8 provides a summary of the commands introduced in this session.

TABLE 2.8

Command Summary

Task Description	Menu Command	Toolbar Button	Keyboard Shortcut
Move to a specific location in your document	Edit, Go To		CTRL +g, or F5
Make text bold	Format, Font	B	CTRL +b
Italicize text		I	CTRL +i
Underline text		U	CTRL +u
Highlight text			
Color text			
Animate text	Format, Font, Animation tab		
Select a typeface	Format, Font	Times New Roman	
Change the font size		10	
Increase Indent	Format,		
Decrease Indent	Paragraph		
Create a bulleted list	Format, Bullets		
Create a numbered list	and Numbering		
Specify bullet symbols or numbering schemes	Format, Bullets and Numbering		
Provide options for setting up your page layout	File, Page Setup		

TABLE 2.8
Continued

Task Description	Menu Command	Toolbar Button	Keyboard Shortcut
Left-align a paragraph	Format,	▤	`CTRL` +1
Center-align a paragraph	Paragraph	▤	`CTRL` +e
Right-align a paragraph		▤	`CTRL` +r
Justify a paragraph		▤	`CTRL` +j
Single-space a paragraph	Format,		`CTRL` +1
Space a paragraph by 1.5 lines	Paragraph		`CTRL` +5
Double-space a paragraph			`CTRL` +2
Specifies tab positions and leaders	Format, Tabs		
Copy formatting options		⬦	
Force a page break	Insert, Break		`CTRL` + `ENTER`

KEY TERMS

bullets

The symbols used to set apart points in a document. Bullets are typically round dots and appear in paragraphs with a hanging indent.

default settings

Assumptions made by Word, if no other specific selections are made.

font

All of the symbols and characters of a particular typeface for a given point size.

leader

The symbols, lines, dots, or dashes that fill the gap between text and tab stops.

Paragraph Symbol

The symbol (¶) at the end of a paragraph that stores all of Word's paragraph formatting information.

Selection bar

The leftmost column of the document window. The Selection bar provides shortcut methods for selecting text in a document using the mouse.

typeface

A style of print.

EXERCISES

SHORT ANSWER

1. How do you select an entire document using the mouse?

2. What are Word's default settings?

3. What procedure would you use to move efficiently to page 2, line 16?

4. How would you go about selecting a single sentence?

5. Describe the four types of tabs you can include in a document.

6. Describe some methods for moving the cursor around a document.

7. Provide an example of when you would use a dot leader.

8. How would you set line spacing to 1.5 lines?

9. Describe the most efficient procedure for selecting and then adding animation to a paragraph.

10. What is the difference between a hard page break and a floating page break? How can you tell the difference between the two in a Word document?

HANDS-ON

(*Note:* Ensure that you know the location of your Advantage Files and where to store your Data Files. If necessary, ask your instructor or lab assistant for additional information.)

1. Create the memo appearing in Figure 2.19. Make sure to include the current date in the DATE: area and your name in the FROM: area of the memo.

FIGURE 2.19

"KATHY JORDAN"
DOCUMENT

MEMORANDUM

DATE: *current date*

  TO: Kathy Jordan
           Administrative Support Manager

FROM: *your name*
           V.P., Marketing

 SUBJECT: Appearance of Documents

It has come to my attention that our two clients
are finding our proposals difficult to read. When
queried further, they both mentioned (as personal
preference dictates) that the sentences seemed to
have gaps between the words. (Similar to this
paragraph.)

After speaking with several people in our Word
Processing department, I understand that we have
been using full justification for paragraphs. As
these two clients are our lifeblood, please prepare
a letter to the staff stating that the use of full
justification in documents is no longer acceptable.
All documents are to be typed using left
justification only.

Please send me a draft of the letter by Monday.

                              Enjoy your weekend!

---

a. Make sure that your memo has the following formatting features:

- Center the title "MEMORANDUM."
- Use tabs to right-align the memo headings for DATE:, TO:, FROM:, and SUBJECT:.
- Fully justify the first paragraph.
- Left-align (or left-justify) the second and third paragraphs.
- Right-align (or right-justify) the last line.

b. Make the title and the memo headings (DATE:, TO:, FROM:, and SUBJECT:) bold.

c. Italicize the word "justification" throughout the memo.

    d.   Underline "Monday" in the third paragraph.

    e.   Save the document as "Kathy Jordan" to your Data Files location.

    f.   Print the document.

    g.   Close the document.

2.   This exercise uses tabs to align a table of numbers.

    a.   Open a new document.

    b.   Specify decimal tab settings on the Ruler at 2 inches, 3.5 inches, and 5 inches.

    c.   Enter the following information into the document.

	January	February	March
East	50,000	65,000	75,000
West	125,000	105,000	100,500
Central	55,000	50,000	75,000

    d.   PRESS: `ENTER` three times.

    e.   TYPE: **These are the forecasted commissions for the first part of 1997. Please add a discussion of these figures to the Sales Planning agenda next week.**

    f.   Save the document as "Forecast" to your Data Files location.

    g.   Print the document.

    h.   Close the document.

3.   The objective of this exercise is to practice using tabs, leaders, and character formatting commands.

    a.   Open a new document.

    b.   Create the document appearing in Figure 2.20.

FIGURE 2.20

"SALES PLANNING
AGENDA" DOCUMENT

SALES PLANNING AGENDA

DATE: October 4th, 1997   TIME: 9 A.M. to 4 P.M.

Who Is Our Customer?
     Demographic Analysis . . . . . . 9:00-9:45 A.M.
     Psychographic Analysis . . . . . 9:50-10:30 A.M.
     Lifestyles and AIO Study . . 10:45 A.M.-12 P.M.

What Are We Selling?
     Research and Development . . . . 1:00-2:00 P.M.
     Product Packaging . . . . 2:05-2:45 P.M.
     Pricing Structures . . . . 3:00-3:30 P.M.

Incentives and Commissions . . . . . 3:35-4:00 P.M.

Please be prepared to give a ten-minute impromptu
presentation on the status of your department.
Specifically, mention the following issues:

- Employee Productivity
- Employee Satisfaction
- Resource Management
- Future Requirements

                         Your faithful V.P. of Marketing,

                                          your name

c. Make the first two lines of the agenda, including the title, date, and time, bold.

d. Increase the font size for the title to 18 points.

e. Select the Arial font for the main agenda items. (*Note:* If Arial isn't present on your computer, select a different font.)

f. Make the three main agenda items bold and 14 points in size.

g. Underline the word "faithful" in the closing of the document.

h. Save the document as "Sales Planning Agenda" to your Data Files location.

i. Print the agenda.

j. Close the document.

4. The objective of this exercise is to practice including a page break in a document, changing the font of an entire document, indenting, and changing line spacing.

a. Create the document pictured in Figure 2.21 (make sure to perform the steps described in brackets):

THE POPULAR POINTING DEVICES
USED WITH MICROCOMPUTERS

DATE: *current date*
BY: *your name*

[*insert a page break here*]

The following is a summary of the types of pointing
    devices that are commonly used with
    microcomputers:

The mouse: A small, hand-held device connected to
    the computer by a cable and rolled around the
    desktop to move the cursor around the screen.

The trackball: Essentially an upside down mouse.
    The ball is rolled around in a socket to move
    the cursor. Trackballs are used where space is
    limited.

The light pen: A pen-shaped input device that uses
    a photoelectric (light-sensitive) cell to
    signal screen position to the computer. The
    pen, which is connected to the computer by a
    cable, is placed on the display screen at the
    desired location.

The touch screen: A special display screen that is
    sensitive to touch. The user touches the screen
    at desired locations, marked by labeled boxes,
    to "point out" choices to the computer.

The digitizer: A tablet covered by a grid of wires
    that are connected to the computer by a cable.
    Drawings placed on the tablet can be traced
    with a special pen or mouse-like device to
    translate the image into computer-usable code.

Pen-based computing: Uses special software and
    hardware to interpret handwriting done directly
    on the screen.

b. Before you continue, save the document to your Data Files location as "Pointing Devices."

c. Double-space the entire document.

d. Change the font of the entire document to Arial.

e. Increase the point size of the title on the first page to 16 point.

f. Center all the text positioned on the first page.

g. Boldface the name of each pointing device on page 2.

h. Save the document as "Pointing Devices" to your Data Files location.

i. Print the document.

j. Close the document.

5. On your own, create a resume that includes your name and address centered at the top of the page. (*Note*: Except for your name, it is acceptable to use fictitious information in the resume.) Include character and paragraph formatting to emphasize important events. Make sure to review the page setup settings (margins, etc.) and edit them if you think your resume will look better. Save the resume as "On Your Own-3" to your Data Files location and then print the resume. *Extra Credit*: Align the resume so that it is centered vertically on the page.

6. On your own, create an itinerary. Your destination is a city you have never been to but would like to visit. For each day in this weeklong vacation, detail the types of activities, such as taking a tour or visiting a monument, that you will be doing. Be sure to use character, paragraph, and page formatting commands when creating the itinerary in order to describe your vacation in an organized fashion. Save the itinerary as "On Your Own-4" to your Data Files location and then print the itinerary.

CASE PROBLEMS	ADVANCED SOFTWARE DESIGN, INC.

(*Note:* In the following case problems, assume the role of the primary characters and perform the same steps that they identify. You may want to re-read the session opening.)

1. For the past year, Mary's proposals have all looked similar to the one appearing in Figure 2.22. She wants to create a new document that contains the same information but with formatting enhancements. For example, she would like to make the company's name and address look more like a letterhead on printed stationery, perhaps centered and with a different font at the top of the page. She would also like to add emphasis to the different titles on the proposal (Date, Client Name, Project Description, and so on).

Create the document appearing in Figure 2.22 and then perform the steps that Mary has identified. Print it and then save the document as "ASD Proposal" to your Data Files location. Lastly, close the document before proceeding.

FIGURE 2.22

A STANDARD ASD
PROPOSAL DOCUMENT

ADVANCED SOFTWARE DESIGN, INC.
221 FOREST DRIVE
Lakewood, NJ 08701
Tel: 333-333-3333
Fax: 333-333-3331

DATE: [enter current date]

CLIENT NAME: [enter client name]

PROJECT DESCRIPTION: [enter project description]

HOUR ESTIMATE: [enter hours]

COST ESTIMATE: [multiply the hours by $50]

Signature _____
            Alethia Montera, Vice President

2. Having just completed a telephone conversation with Mountain Wear, Inc., Alethia hands Mary her proposal notes for typing. The project description reads as follows:

   Mountain Wear, Inc., a manufacturer of rugged footwear, needs a better program for keeping track of its inventory. It has one warehouse, with several truckloads of shoes coming and going each day. The company would like to generate hourly reports and gather demographic data on the people who buy Mountain Wear shoes. I estimate this job will take 122 programming hours.

   Mary retrieves the "ASD Proposal" document from the Data Files location and edits it to include the information from Alethia's notes. When finished, she prints it and then saves the proposal as "MWI Proposal" to the Data Files location. Lastly, Mary closes the document.

3. Now that Alethia has seen what Mary can do with Microsoft Word, she asks Mary to format the company's client list for the upcoming board meeting. She gives Mary the following instructions:

   Mary, you will find the document file, called "Clients," at the Advantage Files location. Please format the contents to make it look more professional. Thanks, Alethia.

Upon retrieving the "Clients" document, Mary decides to print it so that she can get a complete picture of the document before she applies any formatting commands. With the printed document in hand, Mary sees clearly that she needs to center and apply a larger point size to the title. Also, she decides to indent and number the names, format all text using the Times New Roman font, and add emphasis to the company names by making them italic. After incorporating her changes, she saves the file to the Data Files location as "Clients-Formatted."

Mary now decides to preview the "Clients-Formatted" document on the screen to see if she likes the overall look of the document. Although pleased with the list, she decides to insert some extra blank lines at the top of the document and a few just below the main heading to balance the page. Mary saves the document again, prints it, and puts a copy in the message box outside Alethia's office.

4.   Upon returning to her cubicle, Mary finds a note tacked to her computer monitor from Alethia.

Mary, I need someone to create a splashy advertising piece for an upcoming customer mailing, and I think you're the one to do it! Use one side of an 8x10 piece of paper. I want you to make the following points: (1) Advanced Software Design can satisfy any programming requirement because of its staff of highly talented programmers. (2) ASD always supplies accurate cost estimates. (3) Your satisfaction is guaranteed—should you be dissatisfied with a product, we'll either modify it at our own cost or give you a full refund. (4) ASD provides a 24-hour support hotline should questions arise once an application is delivered. And lastly, after the name, address, and phone number of our company (positioned at the top of the page), try to draw the reader's attention to the following sentence: The Small Business Association, in conjunction with the Hapstead Publishing Group, did an assessment of software development companies and gave Advanced Software Design the "Best Pick" award for 1996. By the way, I need this by tomorrow. Let me know if you have any questions. Thanks, Alethia.

Although she's flattered, it's already late in the day and Mary is concerned about completing the advertising piece on time. She realizes that without Microsoft Word she won't stand a chance at finishing this ad. When you finish the project, print the document and then save it as "ASD Advertisement" to the Data Files location. Lastly, close the document and Exit Word.

Editing and Proofing Tools

SESSION

3

IRWIN

COMPUTER & INFORMATION TECHNOLOGY

INTRODUCTION

By the completion of this session, you will know the editing commands required to develop error-free documents. Also, you'll learn how to use Word's proofing tools including the Spelling and Grammar Checker and the Thesaurus. Whether you require assistance with spelling, sentence structure, or just finding the right word, these tools are invaluable.

CASE STUDY	THE *RIVER REPORT*

The *River Report* is a weekly publication that provides news reports, announcements, and general interest stories for the Sacramento River region. Linda James, a graduate of Stanford's journalism program, has just accepted the position of editor for the small-town newspaper. In her new position, Linda is responsible for identifying leads, editing articles written by her reporters, and, most importantly, getting the paper out every Friday.

Her new office is well-appointed with a large oak desk and a new Pentium™ computer system. On the computer screen, her predecessor, Hank Leary, left the following message:

Linda, welcome! Just so you know, the reporters will be submitting their articles on disk for you to edit and print using Microsoft Word. They should have their articles in to you each week by 7:00 P.M. on Wednesday. You have all day Thursday to edit and proof their work. The articles must be sent to Production by 7:00 P.M. on Thursday to meet the deadline. Hope all goes well. Hank.

Linda feels a swelling anxiety overcome her. It's already Wednesday afternoon and, although she has used Microsoft Word before, she has never performed the types of editing tasks that will be required of her to edit and proof these articles. She only has a few short hours to become skilled at editing articles using her fancy new computer!

In this session, you and Linda will learn how to copy and move text within a document, search for and replace text, and use Word's proofing tools.

WORKING WITH MULTIPLE DOCUMENTS

Word allows you to simultaneously display and work with as many documents as your computer's memory will allow. This feature enables you to open multiple documents at the same time and share information among them. You can also use the Window, New Window command to open multiple windows or views of the same document. For example, you might want to view page 10 of a document while working on page 30. Each document or window view appears in its own document window. These windows can be sized, moved, and arranged anywhere in the document area.

In this section you display multiple documents.

Perform the following steps . . .

1. Make sure that you've loaded Microsoft Word and that you've identified the location for retrieving your Advantage Files and the location for storing your Data Files. If you require a diskette, place it into the diskette drive now.

2. To close all open documents that may appear in the document area:
PRESS: (SHIFT) and hold it down
CHOOSE: File, Close All
(*Note*: By holding down the (SHIFT) key, Word changes the command in the pull-down menu from Close to Close All.)

3. Retrieve the "Spelling" document from the Advantage Files location.

4. Retrieve the "Sailboat" document from the Advantage Files location.

5. When the "Sailboat" document is opened, the "Spelling" document disappears. Actually, the "Sailboat" document is just temporarily covering the "Spelling" document. To display the "Spelling" document:
CHOOSE: Window, 2 Spelling

6. Notice that the names of the open documents appear at the bottom of the Window pull-down menu. To move between open documents, you simply select the document name. To move back to "Sailboat":
CHOOSE: Window, 1 Sailboat

7. Although this method allows you to work on several documents at the same time, sometimes it's desirable to compare documents side-by-side. To simultaneously display both documents:
CHOOSE: Window, Arrange All
Your screen should now appear similar to Figure 3.1.

FIGURE 3.1

USING THE WINDOW, ARRANGE ALL COMMAND TO VIEW TWO DOCUMENTS

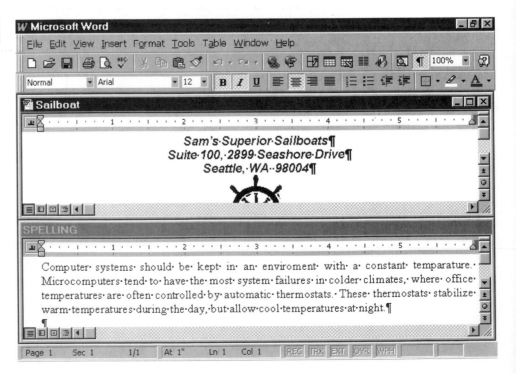

8. The document window with the 🚩 icon (Sailboat) is the active window. Any editing and formatting commands that you execute will affect the active window only. To move between documents, you click the mouse pointer on a window to make it active:
CLICK: anywhere in the "Spelling" document window
The "Spelling" Title bar should change color to reflect that it is active and the 🚩 icon will appear at the left side of the Title bar.

9. CLICK: anywhere in the "Sailboat" document window
The "Sailboat" Title bar changes to reflect that it is now active.

10. Notice that the active window has its own Minimize (⬚), Maximize (⬚), and Close buttons (☒). To maximize the "Sailboat" window:
CLICK: Maximize icon (⬚) on the "Sailboat" document window

11. CHOOSE: Window, Arrange All to view both windows again

12. PRESS: (SHIFT) and hold it down
CHOOSE: File, Close All
Both documents are closed and removed from the document area.

QUICK REFERENCE
Viewing Multiple Documents

- **CHOOSE: Window, filename to display an open document**
- **CHOOSE: Window, Arrange All to show multiple windows on-screen**
- **CHOOSE: Window, New Window to open a new document window**

IN ADDITION LINKING YOUR DOCUMENT TO THE INTERNET
AND OTHER MICROSOFT OFFICE DOCUMENTS

You can create links in your document to Internet addresses or to other Microsoft Office documents on your hard drive or network drive. When you click the link, you move to the desired location. These links are called *hyperlinks*. To include hyperlinks in your document, you click the Insert Hyperlink button (🔗) on the Standard

toolbar and then answer the questions in the Insert Hyperlink dialog box.

For more information, choose Help, Contents and Index. Click the *Contents* tab and select the "Working with Online and Internet Documents" topic. Then explore the "Working with Hyperlinks" topic.

COPYING AND MOVING INFORMATION

There are several different methods for copying and moving text in a document. Similar to most Windows applications, Word provides the **Clipboard** for sharing information within a document, among documents, and among applications. For quick "from-here-to-there" copy and move operations, Word provides the **drag and drop** method where you use the mouse to drag text and graphics in a document. This section provides examples using both methods for copying and moving information.

USING THE CLIPBOARD

If the drag and drop method is quicker and easier, why use the Clipboard to copy and move information? The Clipboard provides greater flexibility, allows you to copy information to multiple locations in a document, and allows you to copy and move information to and from other applications. The general process for copying and moving information using the Clipboard is summarized in the following steps:

a. Select the text that you want to copy or move.

b. Cut or copy the selection to the Clipboard.

c. Move the insertion point to where you want to place the information.

d. Paste the information from the Clipboard into the document.

e. Repeat steps c. and d., as desired.

The Clipboard tools for cutting, copying, and pasting text and graphics appear in Table 3.1.

TABLE 3.1 Copying and Moving Information Using the Clipboard	*Task Description*	*Menu Command*	*Toolbar Button*	*Keyboard Shortcut*
	Moves the selected text from the document to the Clipboard	Edit, Cut	✂	**CTRL** +X
	Copies the selected text to the Clipboard	Edit, Copy	📋	**CTRL** +C
	Inserts the contents of the Clipboard at the insertion point	Edit, Paste	📋	**CTRL** +V

In this section you practice using the Clipboard.

Perform the following steps . . .

1. Retrieve the "Hardware" document from the Advantage Files location.

2. If the document window isn't maximized, click its Maximize button (☐).

3. Insert two lines at the top of the document using the **ENTER** key.

4. To copy the phrase "Computer systems" from the first sentence to the top of the document, first you must select the text:
    SELECT: Computer systems

5. To copy the selection to the Clipboard:
    CLICK: Copy button (📋)

6. PRESS: ⬆ twice

7. To paste the contents of the Clipboard into the document:
    CLICK: Paste button (📋)

8. To center the title:
    CLICK: Center button (≡)

9. To change the case of the letters in the title:
SELECT: Computer systems
PRESS: [SHIFT] + [F3] once
The title should now read "COMPUTER SYSTEMS." (*Note*: You can also choose the Format, Change Case command.)

10. Let's move the entire second paragraph to the end of the document:
DOUBLE-CLICK: beside the second paragraph in the Selection bar

11. To move the selected paragraph to the Clipboard:
CLICK: Cut button (✂)
Notice that the paragraph is removed from the document.

12. Move to the bottom of the document and add a blank line:
PRESS: [CTRL] + [END]
PRESS: [ENTER]

13. CLICK: Paste button (📋)
The paragraph is inserted at the bottom of the document.

14. Insert another blank line at the end of the document:
PRESS: [ENTER]

15. When information is placed on the Clipboard, it can be pasted multiple times. To illustrate, you will insert another copy of the paragraph:
CLICK: Paste button (📋)
A second copy of the paragraph appears.

QUICK REFERENCE
Copying and Moving Information Using the Clipboard

- To move information using the Clipboard:
  CLICK: Cut button (✂)

- To copy information using the Clipboard:
  CLICK: Copy button (📋)

- To paste information using the Clipboard:
  CLICK: Paste button (📋)

IN ADDITION COPYING AND MOVING BETWEEN MICROSOFT OFFICE APPLICATIONS

1. Select the text, data, or other object that you want to move or copy. Then click the Cut button (✂) or the Copy button (📋).

2. Switch to the application you want to move or copy into and then position the cursor.

3. Click the Paste button (📋) to insert the contents of the Clipboard at the cursor location. (*Note*: If you choose Edit, Paste Special from the Menu bar and then choose the Paste Link option, the pasted information will be linked to its source application. Any changes you make to the data in the source application will show up in the linked application.)

IN ADDITION INSERTING AN EXCEL WORKSHEET IN A WORD DOCUMENT

1. Open both the Word document and the Excel workbook.

2. In the Excel workbook:

   a. Select the worksheet or range of cells that you want to copy to Word.

   b. CLICK: Copy button ()

3. In the Word document:

   a. Position the cursor where you want to insert the worksheet.

   b. CHOOSE: Edit, Paste Special

   c. Choose Paste (to embed) or Paste link (to link).

IN ADDITION INSERTING AN ENTIRE POWERPOINT PRESENTATION IN A WORD DOCUMENT

1. Open the presentation in PowerPoint for which you want to create a Word document.

2. CHOOSE: File, Send To

3. CHOOSE: Microsoft Word

4. In the Write-Up dialog box, choose how the slides should appear in Word.

5. Choose Paste (to embed) or Paste link (to link).

USING DRAG AND DROP

The drag and drop method is the easiest way to copy and move information short distances. The Clipboard is not used during a drag and drop operation; therefore, you can only copy or move text from one location to another. In other words, you are not able to perform multiple "pastes" of the selected text. This method is extremely quick for simple copy and move operations.

Next you practice using drag and drop.

Perform the following steps . . .

1. In the "Hardware" document, select the first sentence of the first paragraph by positioning the I-beam mouse pointer over any word in the sentence, holding down the CTRL key, and clicking once.

2. Position the mouse pointer over the selected text. Notice that the pointer shape is a left-pointing diagonal arrow and not an I-beam. To move this sentence using drag and drop:
   CLICK: left mouse button and hold it down

3. The mouse pointer changes shape to include a phantom insertion point at the end of the diagonal arrow. Drag the new mouse pointer into the second paragraph, immediately *after* the first sentence.

4. Position the mouse pointer and phantom insertion point to the left of the letter "T" in the word "The."

5. Release the left mouse button. Notice that the sentence is inserted at the mouse pointer, causing the existing text to wrap to the next line.

6. To remove the highlighting from the text:
   CLICK: anywhere in the unselected area of the document

7. The drag and drop method can also be used to copy text. Select the word "failures" in the first paragraph:
DOUBLE-CLICK: failures
The word should be highlighted.

8. To copy this word into the title area:
PRESS: CTRL and hold it down

9. Position the mouse pointer over the highlighted word and then drag the selection to the right of the word "SYSTEMS" in the title.

10. Release the left mouse button and then the CTRL key. Notice that Word automatically places a space between the word "SYSTEMS" and the word "failures."

11. To change the copied text to uppercase:
PRESS: SHIFT + F3 twice
The title should now read "COMPUTER SYSTEMS FAILURES."

12. Close the document and do not save the changes.

QUICK REFERENCE
Using Drag and Drop

- **To move information, select the text to move and then drag the selected text to the desired location.**

- **To copy information, select the text to copy, press** CTRL **and hold it down, and then drag the selected text to the desired location.**

IN ADDITION USING DRAG AND DROP BETWEEN OFFICE APPLICATIONS

The procedure for dragging and dropping between applications is identical to performing the procedure within the same document. Be-

fore initiating the drag and drop procedure, ensure that both applications (for example, Word and Excel) appear on the screen at once.

FINDING AND REPLACING TEXT

Imagine that you have just completed a 200-page proposal supporting the importation of llamas as household pets in North America. As you are printing the final pages, a colleague points out that you spelled *llama* with one *l* throughout the document. The Spell Checker didn't catch the error since both *llama*, the animal, and *lama*, the Tibetan monk, appear in Word's dictionary. Therefore, you must use another of Word's editing features—the Find and Replace utility—to correct your mistake.

The Find and Replace commands under the Edit menu allow you to search for and replace text, nonprinting characters like the Paragraph Symbol (¶), and formatting characteristics. Next you demonstrate the power of these two commands.

Perform the following steps . . .

1. Retrieve the "Hardware" document from the Advantage Files location.

2. To begin a search for a word or phrase in the document:
   CHOOSE: Edit, Find
   Your screen should now appear similar to Figure 3.2. (*Note*: The dialog box may look similar to Figure 3.3.)

FIGURE 3.2

FIND AND REPLACE
DIALOG BOX

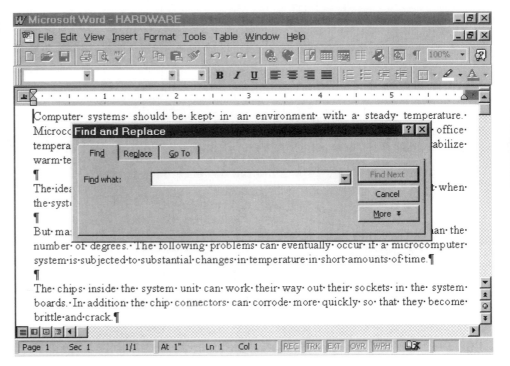

3. With the insertion point in the *Find what* text box:
   TYPE: **can**

4. In this step, you instruct Word to only retrieve whole words. That is, you don't want Word to retrieve all words containing the letters "can" (for example, you don't want to retrieve words like *can*non or s*can*). To do this you must click the More button.
   CLICK: More button
   Your screen should appear similar to Figure 3.3. (*Note*: If your dialog box now looks like Figure 3.2, click the More button again.)
   CLICK: *Find whole words only* check box

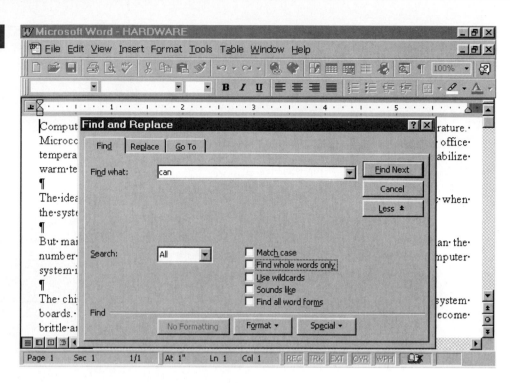

5. To tell Word to begin the search:
PRESS: (ENTER) or CLICK: Find Next

6. Word stops at the first occurrence of "can." (*Note*: You will probably need to drag the dialog box downward to see that "can" is now selected in your document.) To continue the search:
PRESS: (ENTER) or CLICK: Find Next

7. To cancel the search at this point:
CLICK: Cancel button

8. Return to the top of the document to begin a new search operation:
PRESS: (CTRL) + (HOME)

9. Let's replace the word "can" with "will" throughout the document:
CHOOSE: Edit, Replace
Notice that the word "can" already appears in the *Find what* text box from the last time we performed the Edit, Find command.

10. To enter the replacement text, you must first click the I-beam mouse pointer in the *Replace with* text box to position the insertion point.

11. TYPE: will
Your screen should now appear similar to Figure 3.4.

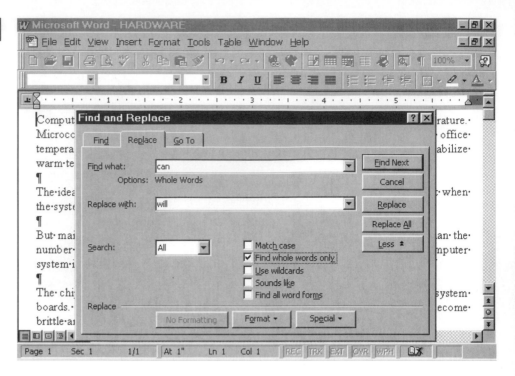

12. To execute the replacement throughout the document:
CLICK: Replace All command button
A dialog box appears informing you that four replacements were made in the document.

13. To close the dialog boxes:
PRESS: **(ENTER)** or CLICK: OK
CLICK: Close command button

14. Now let's make all occurrences of the word "will" bold:
CHOOSE: Edit, Replace

15. In the *Find what* text box:
TYPE: **will**

16. Position the insertion point in the *Replace With* text box by clicking the I-beam mouse pointer in the text box.

17. Since the word "will" already appears in this text box, you need only specify the bold formatting option. For this exercise:
CLICK: Bold button (**B**) on the Formatting toolbar
Notice that the formatting characteristics appear below the text box.

18. To perform the replacement:
CLICK: Replace All command button
Similar to last time, four replacements are made in the document.

19. To close the dialog boxes:
PRESS: **ENTER** or CLICK: OK
CLICK: Close button (**X**)
If you browse through the document, you will notice that all occurrences of the word "will" have been made bold.

20. Save the document as "Replaced" to the Data Files location.

21. Close the document.

QUICK REFERENCE	**1.** **CHOOSE: Edit, Find, or Edit, Replace**
Finding and Replacing Text	**2.** **TYPE: text to find and, if necessary, the replacement text**
	3. **To refine your search, click the More button.**
	4. **SELECT: Find Next, Replace, Replace All, or Cancel**

USING AUTOTEXT

In Session 2 you saw that by simply typing a few characters, Word will complete certain words for you, such as the months of the year. In this section, you learn more about this feature, called AutoText. With AutoText, you can store frequently used words, phrases, and even graphics, such as a company logo, for easy access. Once defined, you retrieve an **AutoText entry** by typing an abbreviated code and then pressing **F3**. Word replaces the code with the full text or graphic it represents.

Perform the following steps . . .

1. Retrieve the "Sailboat" document from the Advantage Files location.

2. The company name, used quite frequently in this sample letter, is quite long and difficult to type. Therefore, it provides a perfect candidate for an AutoText entry. To define it as an AutoText entry, you begin by selecting the full text in the first sentence:
SELECT: Sam's Superior Sailboats
(*Caution*: Do not select the formatted company name that appears in the heading area.)

3. To define the selected text as an AutoText entry:
CHOOSE: Insert, AutoText
CHOOSE: New
Your screen should now appear similar to Figure 3.5.

FIGURE 3.5

AUTOTEXT DIALOG BOX

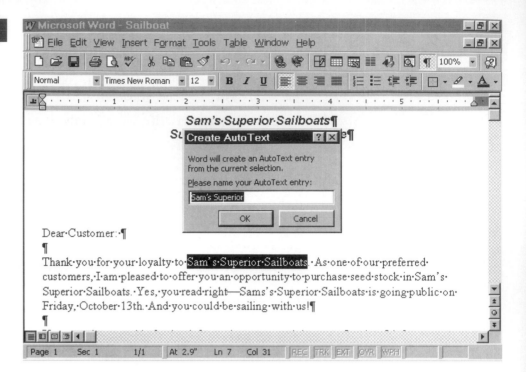

4. Although Word provides an optional name for this entry, you should enter your own abbreviation to use in retrieving the company name.
   TYPE: **sss**
   PRESS: (ENTER) or CLICK: OK

5. Move to the bottom of the document and try out the AutoText entry:
   PRESS: (CTRL) + (END)
   PRESS: Space Bar
   TYPE: **of sss**

6. To replace the abbreviated code with the full text:
   PRESS: (F3)

Before	*After*
Sincerely,	Sincerely,
Sam Silverton	Sam Silverton
Founder of sss	Founder of Sam's Superior Sailboats

7. You are now going to add a graphic to the AutoText library. To select the graphic at the top of the page, position the mouse pointer on the wheel and click the left mouse button once. When properly selected, the graphic appears within a framed box. The Picture toolbar automatically appears.

8. To add the graphic as an AutoText entry:
   CHOOSE: Insert, AutoText
   CHOOSE: New

9. Enter the following code:
TYPE: **logo**
PRESS: (ENTER) or CLICK: OK

10. Move to the bottom of the document:
PRESS: (CTRL) + (END)

PRESS: (ENTER) to add a new line

11. To insert the logo:
TYPE: **logo**
PRESS: (F3)
The logo appears below the text.

12. Save the document as "AutoText" to the Data Files location and then close the document.

QUICK REFERENCE		
Creating an AutoText Entry	**1.**	**SELECT: the desired text for an AutoText entry**
	2.	**CHOOSE: Insert, AutoText, New**
	3.	**TYPE: the abbreviated code for accessing the entry**
	4.	**PRESS: (ENTER) or CLICK: OK**

IN ADDITION INSERTING AUTOSHAPES

Word 97 provides AutoShapes, such as circles, stars, and banners, that you can insert and resize in your document. To insert an AutoShape:

1. CHOOSE: Insert, Picture, AutoShapes

2. SELECT: a category from the AutoShapes toolbar

3. Select a shape from the pull-down menu.

4. In your document, drag with the mouse to position and size the shape.

5. To add formatting to the object, point to it and double-click. Make selections in the Format AutoShape dialog box and then press (ENTER) or click OK.

6. To resize the object, point to it and click. Selection handles appear around the object. Drag a selection handle in the desired direction. (*Note*: To delete an object, point to it and click. Then press (DELETE).)

USING THE SPELLING AND GRAMMAR CHECKER

Word provides the following major proofing tools: the Spelling and Grammar Checker and the Thesaurus. In this section, you use the Spelling and Grammar Checker to review a single word, a selection of text, or an entire document. In addition, you learn how to add items to the AutoCorrect feature. Below, we describe some of the spelling and grammar features that you will encounter.

Using AutoCorrect

AutoCorrect is duly named for its ability to automatically correct your typographical and capitalization errors as you type. You will find this feature extremely handy if you habitually misspell or mistype particular words. For example, people commonly type "thier" instead of "their"—knowing perfectly well how to spell the word but making a simple typing mistake. By adding this word to the AutoCorrect list, you can have Word correct this error automatically.

Correcting Spelling Errors

Word can perform a spelling check automatically as you type (Word's default setting) or all at once if you click the Spelling and Grammar button (ABC) on the Standard toolbar. When Word performs a spelling check, it begins by comparing each word to entries in Word's main dictionary, which contains well over 100,000 words. If a word cannot be found, the Spelling Checker attempts to find a match in a custom dictionary that you may have created. Custom dictionaries usually contain proper names, abbreviations, and technical terms.

When you use the Spelling and Grammar button (ABC) to correct a document's spelling, a dialog box appears when the Spelling Checker cannot identify a word and believes it to be misspelled. The Spelling Checker also flags errors relating to repeated words (for example, "the ball was was red") and mixed case (for example, "the baLL was rEd"). The Spelling and Grammar dialog box provides options for correcting or ignoring the entry and for adding words to the custom dictionary or to the AutoCorrect feature.

Correcting Grammar Errors

Word contains grammatical rules and style considerations for every occasion. Word offers the following styles of grammar checking: Casual, Standard (the default setting), Formal, Technical, and Custom. You can also customize Word to check only for specific rules and wording styles. The procedure for correcting grammar errors is almost identical to the one for correcting spelling errors.

Another feature of the Grammar Checker is the **readability statistics** dialog box (Figure 3.6) that can appear at the completion of the spelling and grammar check. By default, it doesn't appear. You can select to display it by choosing Tools, Options and then selecting *Show readability statistics* in the *Spelling & Grammar* tab. Besides counting the number of words, the Readability Statistics dialog box measures the readability of a document, basing its scores on the number of words per sentence and the average number of syllables per word.

FIGURE 3.6

READABILITY STATISTICS
DIALOG BOX: "SPELLING"
DOCUMENT

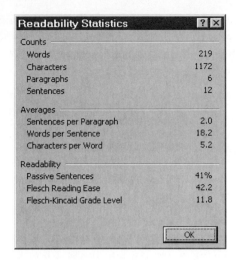

In this section you practice using the Spelling and Grammar button (⌨) on the Standard toolbar.

Perform the following steps . . .

1. Retrieve the "Spelling" document from the Advantage Files location. This document is a copy of the "Hardware" document with several intentional typographical errors and misspellings.

2. To start a spelling check:
   CLICK: Spelling and Grammar button (⌨)
   (*Note:* You can also start a spelling check by choosing the Tools, Spelling and Grammar command.) When Word finds the first misspelled word, it displays a dialog box (Figure 3.7) and waits for further instructions.

FIGURE 3.7

SPELLING AND GRAMMAR
DIALOG BOX

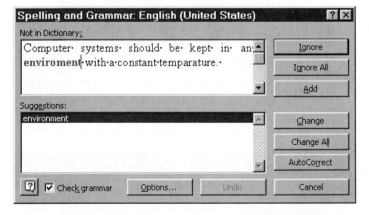

3. You have several options when the Spelling and Grammar Checker cannot find a word in its dictionary or detects a grammar error:
   - If a word is misspelled and the proper version appears in the *Suggestions* list box, highlight the word in the list box and click the Change or Change All buttons. You should consider adding the word to the Auto-Correct feature as well.

- If the word is misspelled and none of the suggestions is correct, type the proper version into the *Not in Dictionary* text box and then click the Change or Change All buttons. You should consider adding the word to the AutoCorrect feature as well.

- If the word is spelled correctly and not frequently used, click the Ignore or Ignore All buttons to proceed to the next word.

- If the word is spelled correctly and frequently used, click the Add button to add it to the custom dictionary.

- If a grammar error is detected and the proper grammar appears in the *Suggestions* list box, highlight the word in the list box and click the Change button.

- If a grammar error is detected and none of the suggestions is correct, type the proper version into the text box, located on the top of the dialog box, and then click the Change button.

- If a grammar error detected by Word is actually correct grammar, click the Next Sentence button to continue.

To correct the misspelled word "enviroment," ensure that the correct spelling of the word appears in the *Suggestions* text box and then:
CLICK: Change command button

4. The next word that the Spelling Checker finds is "temparature." Let's add this word to the AutoCorrect feature. Make sure the correct spelling of the word appears in the *Suggestions* text box and then do the following:
CLICK: AutoCorrect command button

5. The next word that the Spelling Checker finds is "Farenheit." Make sure the correct spelling of the word (Fahrenheit) appears in the *Suggestions* text box and then do the following:
CLICK: Change command button

6. Word has now detected a grammar error. Your screen should appear similar to Figure 3.8. The dialog box shows the offending phrase and suggests why it was flagged. Word thinks you should delete the comma (,) after "Operating." To accept this suggestion:
CLICK: Change command button

FIGURE 3.8

SPELLING AND GRAMMAR
DIALOG BOX: CHECKING
THE GRAMMAR

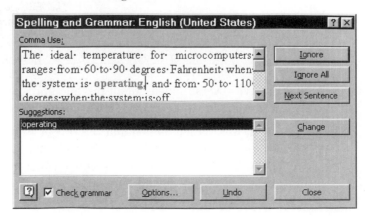

7. On your own, continue the spelling and grammar check for the rest of the document. A message dialog box will appear when it is finished. To clear this dialog box:
PRESS: (ENTER) or CLICK: OK
(*Note*: If the Readability Statistics dialog box appears, press (ENTER) or click OK again.)

8. The Word Count command is another useful tool that provides some basic document statistics. To display the Word Count dialog box:
CHOOSE: Tools, Word Count

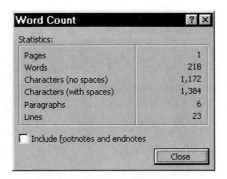

9. To close the Word Count dialog box:
PRESS: (ENTER) or CLICK: Close

10. Save the document as "Spelling-Done" to the Data Files location.

11. Close the document.

<table>
<tr><td>

QUICK REFERENCE
Using the Spell and
Grammar Checker

</td><td>

1. **CLICK: Spelling and Grammar button (⬚), or**

2. **CHOOSE: Tools, Spelling and Grammar**

3. **When a misspelled word is found, you can accept Word's suggestion, change the entry, ignore the word and the suggested alternatives provided by Word, or add the term to the AutoCorrect feature or custom dictionary. When a grammar error is detected you can accept Word's suggestion, change the entry, or ignore the sentence.**

</td></tr>
</table>

USING THE THESAURUS

Have you ever found yourself with the "perfect" word at the tip of your tongue—only to have it stay there? This situation is not limited to authors and professional writers. In fact, most people experience this sensation whenever they sit down to set their thoughts on paper. Fortunately, Word provides a helping hand with its built-in **Thesaurus.** A thesaurus provides quick access to synonyms (words with similar meanings) and antonyms (words with opposite meanings) for a given word or phrase. You invoke Word's Thesaurus utility by choosing Tools, Language, Thesaurus from the menu or by pressing (SHIFT) + (F7).

In this section, you choose a synonym.

Perform the following steps . . .

1. Retrieve the "Hardware" document from the Advantage Files location.

2. Using the mouse, select the word "steady" at the end of the first sentence in the first paragraph.

3. CHOOSE: Tools, Language, Thesaurus
   Your screen should now appear similar to Figure 3.9.

FIGURE 3.9

THESAURUS DIALOG BOX

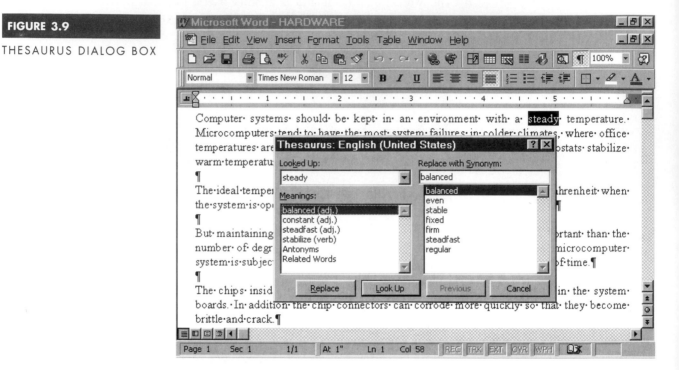

4. Since a word may have several interpretations, you can select the appropriate meaning from the *Meanings* list box. The *Replace with Synonym* list box displays the synonyms for the highlighted meaning. You have three options available after selecting a word from the *Replace with Synonym* list box:

   - Select the Replace command button to replace the word in the document with the highlighted word.

   - Select the Look Up command button to display additional synonyms for the highlighted word.

   - Type a word into the *Replace with Synonym* text box and then select the Look Up or Replace command buttons.

   To change the word "steady," select the word "stable" in the *Replace with Synonym* list box and then do the following:
   SELECT: Replace command button

5. Let's find a synonym for the word "ideal," appearing near the beginning of the first sentence in the first paragraph. To begin, select the word "ideal."

6. PRESS: (SHIFT) + (F7)

7. In the *Replace with Synonym* list box:
SELECT: perfect

8. To look up synonyms for "perfect":
CLICK: Look Up command button

9. To display the previous list of synonyms:
CLICK: Previous command button

10. To replace the word "ideal," select the word "perfect" in the *Replace with Synonym* list box and then do the following:
CLICK: Replace command button

11. Close "Hardware" without saving.

QUICK REFERENCE
Using the Thesaurus

1. **Select a word to look up in the Thesaurus.**
2. **CHOOSE: Tools, Language, Thesaurus or PRESS:** `SHIFT` + `F7`
3. **Select the desired word in the *Replace with Synonym* list box.**
4. **SELECT: Replace command button**

IN ADDITION INSERTING COMMENTS

When a document is produced as part of a collaborative effort, it is important that you are able to insert comments directly into the document. To do this in Word:

1. Display the Reviewing toolbar.

2. In the Word document, select the text that you want to comment on.

3. CLICK: Insert Comment button () on the Reviewing toolbar

4. TYPE: a comment into the bottom half of the document window

5. CLICK: Close command button

Word highlights words that have an associated comment and, as you move the I-beam pointer over the highlighted text, the comment appears above.

SUMMARY

This session focused on Word's editing and proofing tools. After a discussion on working with multiple document windows, the session described two methods for copying and moving information: using the Clipboard and using drag and drop. You also used the Find and Replace commands to search for and replace text and formatting in a document. The section on AutoText demonstrated how easy it is to insert frequently used text and graphics into a document by typing abbreviated codes. The last half of this session concentrated on proofing documents using the Spelling and Grammar Checker and the Thesaurus.

Table 3.2 provides a list of the commands covered in this session.

TABLE 3.2

Command Summary

Task Description	Menu Command	Toolbar Button	Keyboard Shortcut
Select a window to make active	Window, *document name*		
Size and display all open document windows	Window, Arrange All		
Create a new window view for the active document	Window, New Window		
Copy the selected text to the Clipboard	Edit, Copy	🗐	CTRL + C
Move the selected text to the Clipboard	Edit, Cut	✂	CTRL + X
Insert or paste the Clipboard's contents	Edit, Paste	📋	CTRL + V
Find text in a document	Edit, Find		CTRL + F
Find and replace text in a document	Edit, Replace		CTRL + H
Create an AutoText entry	Insert, AutoText		
Retrieve an AutoText entry			F3
Perform a spelling and grammar check of a document	Tools, Spelling and Grammar	ABC	F7
Display a list of synonyms for the selected word	Tools, Language, Thesaurus		SHIFT + F7
Count the number of words in a document	Tools, Word Count		

KEY TERMS

AutoText entry
A frequently used text or graphic that is inserted into a document by typing an abbreviated code and then pressing F3.

Clipboard
In Windows, the Clipboard is a program that allows you to copy and move information within an application or among applications.

drag and drop
A feature of Windows that allows you to copy and move information by dragging objects or text from one location to another using the mouse.

readability statistics

A statistics page appears after the Grammar Checker has completed its check; provides a grade-level reading equivalency for a document.

Thesaurus

In Microsoft Word, a proofing tool that provides synonyms and antonyms for the selected word or phrase. A synonym is a word that has the same meaning as another word. An antonym has the opposite meaning.

EXERCISES

SHORT ANSWER

1. How many windows can be open in the document area at one time?

2. How do you move between open documents using the mouse?

3. What are the two methods for copying and moving information? How do they differ?

4. Name three types of information that can be searched for using the Find command.

5. How do you create an AutoText entry?

6. How do you insert an AutoText entry?

7. Explain what you would do if the Spell Checker came across a frequently used word that is correctly spelled but Word cannot find it in its main dictionary.

8. How is the Thesaurus tool used?

9. Besides counting words, what other statistics appear in the Word Count dialog box?

10. How are grade levels awarded for the readability statistics?

 ## HANDS-ON

(*Note*: Ensure that you know the location of your Advantage Files and where to store your Data Files. If necessary, ask your instructor or lab assistant for additional information.)

1. The objective of this exercise is to practice performing copy and move operations using the Clipboard and drag and drop methods.

   a. Create the document appearing in Figure 3.10.

FIGURE 3.10

"ORDERS" LETTER

Alpha Beta Computer Rentals
5900 Algonquin Road
Suite 775
Ashton, NC 28804

September 3, 1997

Ms. Lolita Balfour
2910 Freemont Road
Raleigh, NC 27610

Dear Ms. Balfour:

Thank you for your order! I am writing to confirm
that the following items will be delivered to your
premises on September 25th.

Items Shipped

MONITOR: TLC SVGA Color Monitor
OPTIONS: 28.8K Baud Internal Fax/Modem
HARD DISK: MaxStore 1.6 GB Hard Drive
CPU: Compact Pentium 100 with 32MB RAM
VIDEO CARD: ABC Ultrasonic Graphics Card

Yours truly,

your name
Accounts Representative

P.S. If I can be of any assistance, please call me
at 704-250-9987.

b. Save the document as "Orders" to your Data Files location.

c. Using the Clipboard, move the text after "P.S." (starting at the word "If") above the line "Yours truly." Leave the "P.S." at the bottom of the letter.

d. Using the Clipboard, move the first sentence in the first paragraph ("Thank you for your order!") after the "P.S." on the last line.

e. Using the drag and drop method, change the order of the Items Shipped to the following: CPU, HARD DISK, MONITOR, VIDEO CARD, OPTIONS.

f. Using the drag and drop method, copy the company name "Alpha Beta Computer Rentals" from the top of the page to below the title "Accounts Representative" in the closing.

g. Save the document again, replacing the original version.

h. Print the document.

i. Close the document.

2. This exercise gives you practice using AutoText entries and the Find and Replace commands.

a. Open a new document.

b. Enter the following information at the top of the page, substituting your name and address for the italicized text shown below:

your name
your address
your city, state   zip code

c. Define one AutoText entry for all of the text, using your initials as the abbreviated code.

d. PRESS: **ENTER** twice

e. TYPE: **Management Information Systems Department**

f. Define an AutoText entry called MIS for this term. (*CAUTION*: Do not select the paragraph mark, just the text.)

g. PRESS: **ENTER** twice

h. TYPE: **OS/2 Version 2.2 Batch Release 2.299**

i. Define an AutoText entry called OS for this term. (*CAUTION*: Do not select the paragraph mark, just the text.)

j. Open a new document.

k. Create the document appearing in Figure 3.11, using the AutoText entries wherever possible.

FIGURE 3.11

"MIS DEPARTMENT"
MEMO

DATE: February 14, 1997

TO: Mr. Tyler French
           Director of Operations
           Management Information Systems Department

FROM: *your name*
           your address
           your city, state   zip code

SUBJECT: OS/2 Version 2.2 Batch Release 2.299

Please be forewarned that the OS/2 Version 2.2
Batch Release 2.299 operating system will not be
available for the Management Information Systems
Department on March 1, 1997, as previously promised.

Although we understand the requirement for OS/2
Version 2.2 Batch Release 2.299, Research and
Development must fully test the product before
allowing any department access to the code–and that
includes the Management Information Systems
Department.

If you require further clarification, please have
Alan Johansen, V.P., Management Information Systems
Department, contact me at the following address:

    your name
    your address
    your city, state   zip code

Thanks for your patience.

---

l. Save the document as "MIS Department" to the Data Files location.

m. Using the Replace command, change the name of the department from "Management Information Systems Department" to "Office Automation Division."

n. Using the Replace command, make every occurrence of "OS/2 Version 2.2 Batch Release 2.299" boldface in the document.

o. Save the document again, replacing the original version.

     p.   Print the document.

     q.   Close all the open documents in the document area. Do not save the original document that you used to define the AutoText entries.

3.   The following exercise uses the proofing tools to correct a poorly written and misspelled document.

     a.   Retrieve the "Badmemo" document from the Advantage Files location.

     b.   Correct the misspelled words and grammar errors with the help of the Spelling and Grammar Checker.

     c.   Save the document as "Goodmemo" to the Data Files location. (*Note*: You will need to choose File, Save As if you are saving to a different disk.)

     d.   Print the document.

     e.   Close the document.

4.   The objective of this exercise is to practice move operations using the Clipboard, Find and Replace commands, the Thesaurus tool, and the Spelling and Grammar Checker.

     a.   Open "Input" from the Advantage Files location.

     b.   Using the Clipboard, change the order of the hardware components to match the following: pen-based computing, touch screen, digitizer, mouse, trackball, light pen.

     c.   Using the Replace command, change every occurrence of "computer" to "PC." (*Note*: Make sure that you select the *Find whole words only* check box.)

     d.   Use the Thesaurus to find a different word for "Essentially" in the first sentence of the Trackball description.

     e.   Correct the misspelled words with the help of the Spelling and Grammar Checker.

     f.   Save the document as "Input Hardware" to the Data Files location. (*Note*: You will need to choose File, Save As if you are saving to a different disk.)

     g.   Print the document.

     h.   Close the document.

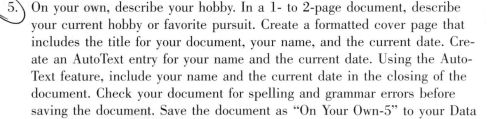

5.   On your own, describe your hobby. In a 1- to 2-page document, describe your current hobby or favorite pursuit. Create a formatted cover page that includes the title for your document, your name, and the current date. Create an AutoText entry for your name and the current date. Using the Auto-Text feature, include your name and the current date in the closing of the document. Check your document for spelling and grammar errors before saving the document. Save the document as "On Your Own-5" to your Data Files location and then print the document.

6. On your own, design a flyer that describes an upcoming event, such as an auto show or school picnic. The objective of the flyer is to get the word out about the event and to motivate people to attend. Include your name at the end of the flyer as the contact person for the event. Check your document for spelling and grammar errors before saving the document. Save the flyer as "On Your Own-6" to your Data Files location and then print the flyer. *Extra Credit*: Add special text effects to the flyer using WordArt.

CASE PROBLEMS	**THE *RIVER REPORT***

(*Note*: In the following case problems, assume the role of the primary characters and perform the same steps that they identify. You may want to re-read the session opening.)

1. Linda's first task as editor for the *River Report* is to edit a short article written about a big bass caught in the Sacramento River. Billy Joe Quaker, the staff reporter, left the following note on her desk:

   Dear Ms. James, I saved the bass article as "Bass" in the Advantage Files location. The article was written using Microsoft Word for Windows. If you need me, I'll be at Chatterbox Falls covering the kayaking race. Bye for now, BJQ.

   Upon reviewing Billy Joe's article, Linda decides that some of the sentences should be positioned differently and that the spelling and grammar must be checked. When finished, she saves the document to her Data Files location and then prints it for inclusion in the Sports section.

2. At 5:00 P.M. on Wednesday, reporter Tola McPherson submitted her article about Saturday's baseball game. The article is named "Baseball" and is stored in the Advantage Files location. As it is one of the first articles that Linda has had to review, she doesn't know what to expect when she opens the document. She is pleasantly surprised, however, because the article seems relatively error-free. To be on the safe side, however, Linda runs the document through Word's Spelling and Grammar Checker and implements its suggestions where appropriate.

   Sounding embarrassed, Tola calls Linda at 5:45 P.M. to tell her to change the name "Collin Lamas" to "Victor Lamas." Linda swiftly makes the change using Word's Replace command. Now that she has put her stamp of approval on the article, she saves it to her Data Files location and sets it aside until Thursday evening, when she will give it to Production.

3. As Linda is organizing the articles to give to Production, Tola rushes in with a last-minute change. "Linda, I have some very interesting information about Victor Lamas and I think we need to include it in our 'Baseball' article. The information is stored in a file named 'Lamas' in the Advantage Files location. I've gotta run to follow up on a lead." With 6:00 P.M. appearing on

her desk clock, Linda knows that she doesn't have much time to make the changes! She opens the "Baseball" document from the Data Files location into one window and the "Lamas" document from the Advantage Files location into another. After reading both documents, she decides to move the first paragraph from the "Lamas" document and position it immediately after the second paragraph in the "Baseball" document. She then moves the second paragraph from the "Lamas" document and positions it after the last paragraph in the "Baseball" document.

Satisfied with the revised "Baseball" document, Linda saves "Baseball" to her Data Files location and prints her work at 6:30 P.M. She just makes the 7:00 P.M. deadline!

4. As tradition would have it, a complimentary ad is published each year in the *River Report* announcing the upcoming Pear Fair on June 15th. Linda is responsible for creating the advertisement. To begin, she reviews some of the previous document files left by Hank Leary. Fortunately, she finds a file named "Pearfair" stored in the Advantage Files location. After opening the file, she is even more comfortable with the task at hand. Hank had included bracketed notes throughout the document to help him create the advertisement for this year's fair.

Linda reviews the document and incorporates all of Hank's suggestions. She then deletes each of his bracketed notes from the document. After saving the document as "Pearfair-Final" to her Data Files location, she prints it for inclusion in the Special Events section.

5. Linda must write a short article describing the 4th of July parade. She attended the parade and jotted down some notes that are now stored in "Parade" in the Advantage Files location. But the notes are rough and were not placed in a particular order. Therefore, she must edit and move around the text to form a legible paragraph. Also, she has since learned that Bruce Towne drove the fire engine, not Bill Darsie. She can fix that mistake using the Replace utility. As a final step, she corrects the spelling and grammar. She saves the document to her Data Files location as "Parade-Final" and prints it for inclusion in the Special Events section.

Microsoft Word 97 for Windows

Printing and Document Management

SESSION

4

HTTP:// WWW.

IRWIN

COMPUTER & INFORMATION TECHNOLOGY

SESSION OUTLINE

INTRODUCTION

After the final editing and proofing of a document, there remain only a few optional steps for finalizing its appearance. Some of these steps include specifying the page layout, preventing widows and orphans, inserting page numbers, and creating headers and footers; each helps to keep your audience on track when reading your document. This session also introduces several printing and file management commands. To work efficiently with a word processing software program, it is important that you know how to find, copy, and print a document without having to open each file stored on your hard disk. This session provides you with the knowledge and experience to perform these functions confidently.

CASE STUDY	GINO'S PIZZA KITCHEN

Gino Lerma is the owner of four pizza restaurants in the Boston metropolitan area. He started with one restaurant 15 years ago and, through hard work and careful planning, Gino was able to open a new restaurant every few years. Gino now considers himself semi-retired, even though he works around the clock and requires a full-time assistant, Larry Ingla. Although he is no longer part of the daily activities, Gino fondly remembers his many years working until midnight, six days per week, in the restaurants.

Each month, Gino's managers use Microsoft Word to create a summary report of their restaurant's activities. Each manager then sends his or her report to Larry Ingla. Larry uses the Windows Clipboard to create a single document from the four reports and then prints the consolidated report for Gino to review. With feedback from his bank manager on the consolidated reports, Gino has asked Larry to format the reports with headers, footers, and page numbers. He also wants Larry to improve the general page layout of the reports and has given him specific suggestions for improvement. Larry immediately agreed to Gino's request, but in truth, he doesn't know where to begin.

In this session, you and Larry will learn how to take control of the way your document appears on the screen and when printed, how to use document formatting commands, and how to manage the files you create using several file management commands.

CUSTOMIZING YOUR WORK AREA

Microsoft Word has many advantages over character-based word processing programs like WordPerfect 5.1. Not only can you see the effects of character and paragraph formatting commands immediately on-screen, you can also edit text using features such as drag and drop. One of the disadvantages of working in this WYSIWYG environment is that it may take longer to page through a document on-screen. For example, Word must continuously update the screen with all of the special fonts and graphics that you have selected, unlike a character-based program which simply displays basic characters. Since most people haven't learned how to type faster than the computer can think, this last point may be a little academic.

As a compromise, Word provides four primary views for working with documents: Normal, Online Layout, Page Layout, and Outline. While each view has its own advantages, it is their combination that gives you the best overall working environment. For faster data entry, you can also select a Draft Font for the Normal and Outline views. Since the Draft Font presents text without WYSIWYG formatting, the screen is updated and redrawn as fast as most character-based word processing programs. This section describes and demonstrates the Normal, Online Layout, and Page Layout views.

SELECTING A VIEW

You select a view for your document using the View command on the Menu bar or by clicking the desired View button on the horizontal scroll bar. On the pull-down menu, a bullet appears next to the active or currently selected view. Table 4.1 summarizes the view options.

TABLE 4.1

View Options

Task Description	Menu Command	View Button
Change to Normal view	View, Normal	
Change to Online Layout view	View, Online Layout	
Change to Outline view	View, Outline	
Change to Page Layout view	View, Page Layout	

Your selection of a view depends upon the type of work that you are performing, as described in the following guidelines:

- *Perform most of your work using the Normal view.*
  The Normal view displays text with character and paragraph formatting, but does not show headers, footers, or newspaper-style text columns. The Normal view separates pages in a document with a dotted line, dividing the last line of one page from the first line of the next. Figure 4.1 shows a sample document in the Normal view.

FIGURE 4.1

A DOCUMENT DISPLAYED IN NORMAL VIEW

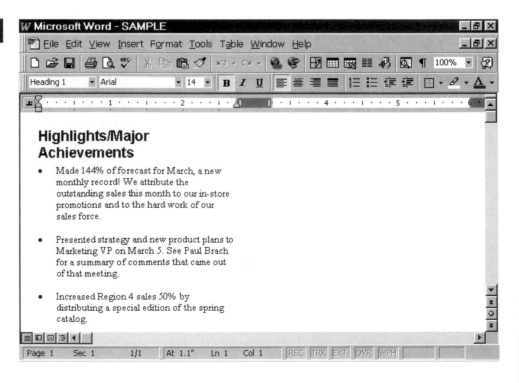

• *Read a document on the computer screen in Online Layout view.*
The Online Layout view is optimized for reading on screen. The document
appears in a larger font and with more space in between lines. The page
layout is determined based on the computer screen rather than by the paper.
Also, by default Word displays a separate pane called the *document map* in
Online Layout view. You use the document map to navigate your document.
Figure 4.2 shows a document in Online Layout view.

FIGURE 4.2

A DOCUMENT DISPLAYED
IN ONLINE LAYOUT VIEW

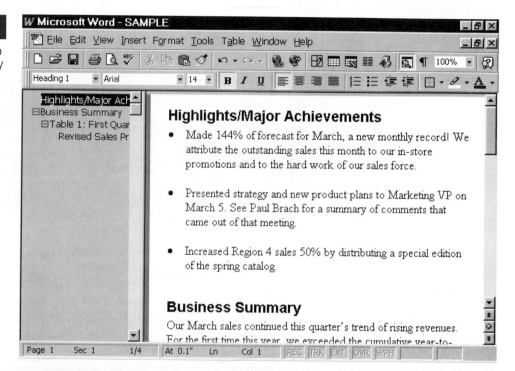

• *Edit the final document before printing in the Page Layout view.*
The Page Layout view displays a document in almost full WYSIWYG pre-
view mode. All character, paragraph, and document formatting options are
displayed, along with headers, footers, and newspaper-style text columns.
The document is separated on-screen into what appear to be real pages.
Figure 4.3 shows a document in the Page Layout view.

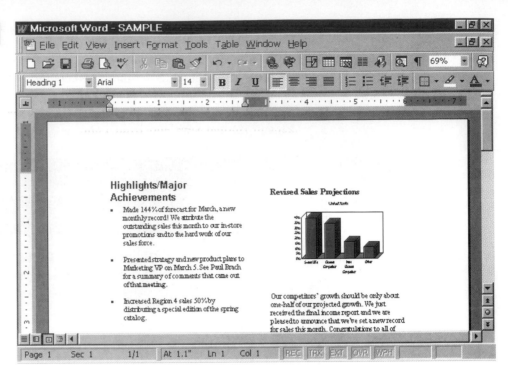

- *Organize and plan your document using the Outline view.*
  The Outline view displays a document as an outline with expandable and collapsible heading levels. This view is used for rearranging entire sections of a document or for moving to a specific section in a long document quickly. Figure 4.4 shows a document in the Outline view, collapsed to show only the major headings.

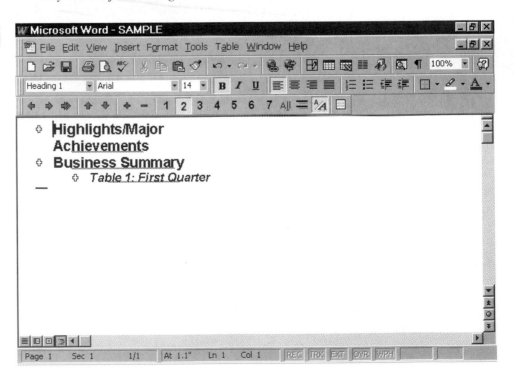

- *Enter large amounts of text quickly using the Draft Font.*
  The Draft Font mode speeds up the display of a document by not showing WYSIWYG character formatting. Although you continue to select the desired formatting, the formatted text only appears underlined in the document. You select the *Draft Font* check box by choosing Tools, Options from the Menu bar and then clicking the *View* tab. Figure 4.5 displays a document in Normal view and Draft Font.

FIGURE 4.5

A DOCUMENT DISPLAYED IN NORMAL VIEW AND DRAFT FONT

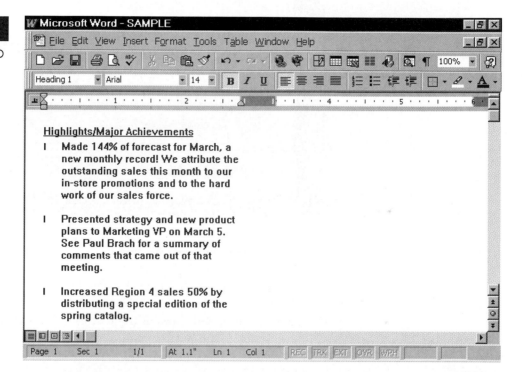

- *Work with the largest text area possible using Full Screen mode.*
  The Full Screen mode lets you work on a document without the clutter of Word's Menu bar, toolbars, or Ruler. Indeed, the only indication that you are still using Word is the Full Screen button (shown at right) that appears in the document area. To change to Full Screen mode, choose View, Full Screen from the menu. To return to the regular Word workspace once you are in Full Screen mode, choose Close Full Screen from the Full Screen button or press ESC .

In this section you practice selecting different views.

Perform the following steps . . .

1. Retrieve the "Newsltr" document from the Advantage Files location.

2. To change to a Page Layout view:
   CHOOSE: View, Page Layout
   Your screen should now appear similar to Figure 4.6.

FIGURE 4.6

THE "NEWSLTR"
DOCUMENT IN PAGE
LAYOUT VIEW

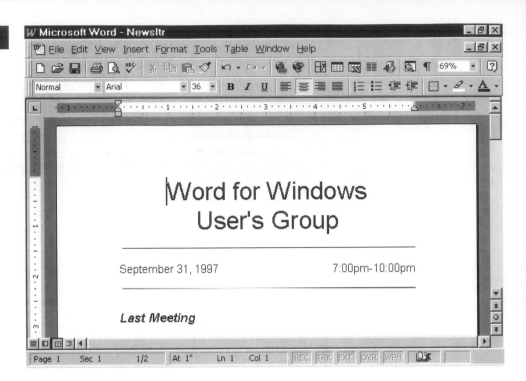

3. To change to Full Screen mode:
   CHOOSE: View, Full Screen
   You may be asking, "How do I choose commands if Word removes the Menu bar and toolbars?" In Full Screen mode, you must use the keyboard shortcut keys and shortcut (right-click) menus. (*Tip*: You can sometimes access the Menu bar by pointing to the very top of the screen and clicking the left mouse button.)

4. To return to the regular Word workspace:
   PRESS: (**ESC**) or SELECT: Close Full Screen in the Full Screen box

5. Now let's change to Online Layout view:
   CHOOSE: View, Online Layout
   Your screen should appear similar to Figure 4.7.

FIGURE 4.7

THE "NEWSLTR"
DOCUMENT IN
ONLINE LAYOUT VIEW

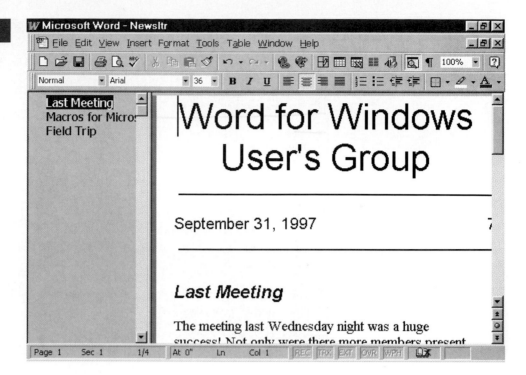

6. You can move to other parts of the document by clicking in the document map, the pane located on the left. To illustrate:
CLICK: "Macros for Micros" in the left pane
As you can see, the cursor moved to the new location.

7. If you work with documents that contain many headings and subheadings, you should know that you can expand and collapse the headings in the document map. For example:
RIGHT-CLICK: a document heading in the document pane
With the menu that appears you can select which headings appear in the document map. This document contains only main headings (Heading 1).

8. To return to the document without making a selection:
CLICK: in the document area

9. You can also change the background color to enhance your online viewing. Any color you choose appears only in Online Layout view. To illustrate:
CHOOSE: Format, Background
CLICK: the color of your choice

10. To change back to the Normal view:
CHOOSE: View, Normal
Notice that the background color you chose in the previous step doesn't appear in Normal view.

11. Now let's change to the Draft Font:
CHOOSE: Tools, Options
CLICK: *View* tab
SELECT: *Draft Font* check box in the *Show* area
Your screen should now appear similar to Figure 4.8.

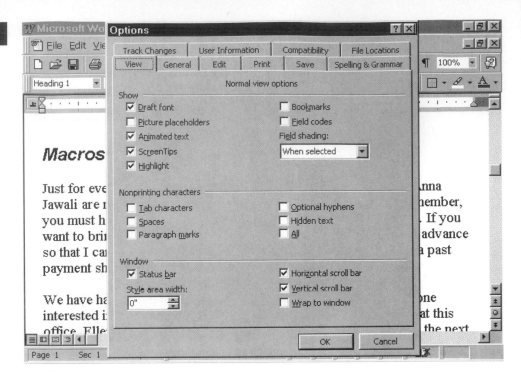

FIGURE 4.8

OPTIONS DIALOG BOX
WITH DRAFT FONT
SELECTED

12. To return to the document:
PRESS: (**ENTER**) or CLICK: OK
You should notice that the document changes to an almost character-based display.

13. To remove the Draft display mode:
CHOOSE: Tools, Options
SELECT: *Draft Font* until no "✔" appears in the check box
PRESS: (**ENTER**) or CLICK: OK

14. To move to the top of your document:
PRESS: (**CTRL**) + (**HOME**)

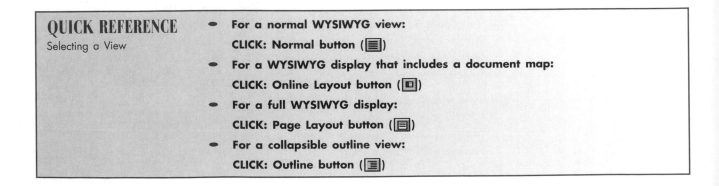

QUICK REFERENCE
Selecting a View

- **For a normal WYSIWYG view:**
  CLICK: Normal button (▤)
- **For a WYSIWYG display that includes a document map:**
  CLICK: Online Layout button (▣)
- **For a full WYSIWYG display:**
  CLICK: Page Layout button (▤)
- **For a collapsible outline view:**
  CLICK: Outline button (▤)

ZOOMING THE DISPLAY

Regardless of the view you select, Word lets you zoom in and out on a document, increasing and decreasing its display size. For example, you may want to enlarge Word's normal view to 200% of its original size when working with detailed graphics. To modify Word's zoom setting, you choose the View, Zoom command or select the Zoom Control box (100%) on the Standard toolbar.

Let's demonstrate how to zoom the display.

Perform the following steps . . .

1. To zoom the "Newsltr" document to 200% its original size:
   CLICK: down arrow beside the Zoom Control box (100%)

2. From the resulting drop-down list:
   SELECT: 200%
   The document is immediately magnified twice its original size.

3. To find the best-fit magnification:
   CLICK: down arrow beside the Zoom Control box (100%)
   Your screen should now appear similar to Figure 4.9.

FIGURE 4.9

ZOOMING THE DISPLAY
USING THE ZOOM
CONTROL BOX

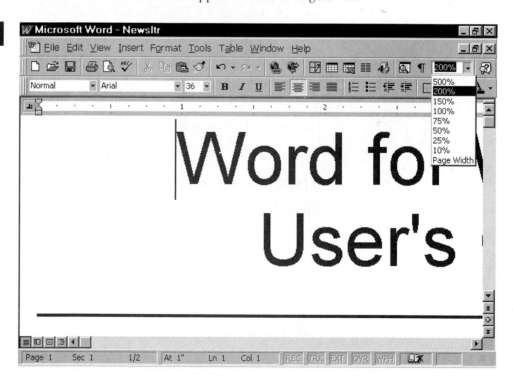

4. SELECT: Page Width from the drop-down list
   The view is zoomed to the best fit for your screen's resolution.

5. In addition to using the Zoom Control box (100%) to select a magnification factor, you can use the Zoom dialog box:
   CHOOSE: View, Zoom
   Your screen should now appear similar to Figure 4.10.

FIGURE 4.10

ZOOM DIALOG BOX

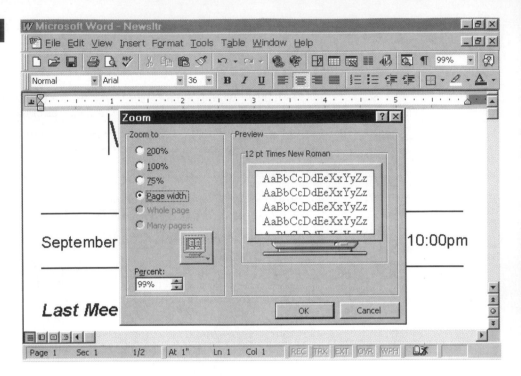

6. SELECT: the various magnification options in the *Zoom to* area
Notice that the text displayed on the monitor in the *Preview* area is updated after each selection.

7. Before you proceed to the next section:
SELECT: Page Width
PRESS: **ENTER** or CLICK: OK

DISPLAYING AND HIDING TOOLBARS

Another method for customizing the work area involves manipulating the toolbars in Word. Most people work with only the Standard and Formatting toolbars displayed. However, you can open the additional eleven toolbars (AutoText, Control Toolbox, Database, Drawing, Forms, Picture, Reviewing, Tables and Borders, Visual Basic, Web, and WordArt) and move them anywhere within the application window. Don't get carried away and display all of the toolbars on the screen at all times. You should attempt to keep your screen as clear as possible to maximize your document's work area.

Let's demonstrate some of the features that are available for manipulating toolbars.

Perform the following steps . . .

1. To display the shortcut or pop-up menu for accessing toolbars, position the mouse pointer on any button in the Standard toolbar and click the right mouse button once. The shortcut menu on page 141 should appear.

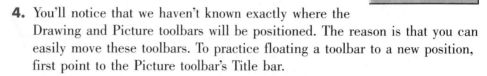

2. To display the Drawing toolbar:
CHOOSE: Drawing
Remember to click the command using the left mouse button. You should see the Drawing toolbar appear, usually positioned at the bottom of the screen. (*Note*: You can also display the Drawing toolbar by clicking the Drawing button () on the Standard toolbar.)

3. To display the Picture toolbar using the Menu bar:
CHOOSE: View, Toolbars
SELECT: Picture
The Picture toolbar will appear somewhere in the document area.

4. You'll notice that we haven't known exactly where the Drawing and Picture toolbars will be positioned. The reason is that you can easily move these toolbars. To practice floating a toolbar to a new position, first point to the Picture toolbar's Title bar.

5. CLICK: left mouse button and hold it down
DRAG: the toolbar to the right side of the document window
You should notice that the shadowed frame changes from a horizontal bar to a vertical bar.

6. Now drag the Picture toolbar back to the center of the screen. Do this by pointing to the line that separates two buttons and then dragging the toolbar to the center.

7. To make the Picture toolbar appear more compact, drag the bottom border of the Picture toolbar downward. The toolbar on your screen may appear similar to the example at right.

8. Using the shortcut menu, remove the Drawing and Picture toolbars from the screen.

9. One last item for customizing your work area—you can hide the Ruler to create more screen real estate using the following command:
CHOOSE: View, Ruler

10. To re-display the Ruler:
CHOOSE: View, Ruler

QUICK REFERENCE
Customizing Your Work Area

- **To zoom in or out on your document:**
  CHOOSE: View, Zoom, or click the Zoom Control box (100% ▼)
- **To display or hide toolbars:**
  CHOOSE: View, Toolbars, or right-click a toolbar to display a menu
- **To display or hide the Ruler:**
  CHOOSE: View, Ruler

DOCUMENT FORMATTING COMMANDS

Simply stated, document formatting involves preparing a document for the printer. This section provides lessons on setting margins, specifying paper sizes and orientation, preventing widows and orphans, inserting page numbers, and lastly, creating headers and footers in a document.

SPECIFYING YOUR PAGE LAYOUT

Your document's page layout is affected by many factors, including the margins or white space desired around the edges of the page, the size of paper you are using, and the print orientation. Fortunately for us, Word provides a single dialog box for controlling all of these factors. Accessed by choosing File, Page Setup from the menu, the Page Setup dialog box provides four tabs: Margins, Paper Size, Paper Source, and Layout. Figure 4.11 shows the Page Setup dialog box with the *Margins* tab selected. The entry areas for the other three tabs are provided below the dialog box.

FIGURE 4.11

PAGE SETUP DIALOG
BOX: MARGINS TAB

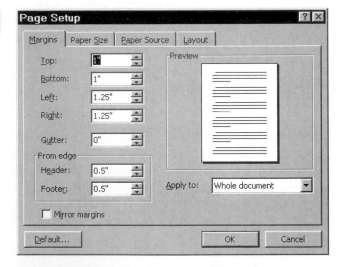

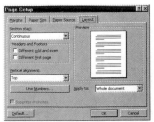

Not surprisingly, Word allows you to set the top, bottom, left, and right margins for a page. In addition, you can set a gutter margin to reserve space for binding a document. The **gutter** is where pages are joined in the center of the binding or hole-punched for a ring binder. Word provides default settings of 1.25 inches for the left and right margins and 1 inch for the top and bottom margins. The gutter margin is initially set at 0 inch, as most documents are not bound. With respect to paper size, typical options include using letter- or legal-sized paper with a **por-trait orientation** (8.5 inches wide by 11 inches tall) or a **landscape orienta-tion** (11 inches wide by 8.5 inches tall). For the purposes of this section, you will not modify the paper source or section layout options.

Let's now practice changing the page layout settings.

Perform the following steps . . .

1. Close all the open documents in the document area without saving.

2. Retrieve the "Proposal" document from the Advantage Files location.

3. To change the margins from the default settings to an even 1 inch around the entire page:
CHOOSE: File, Page Setup

4. Ensure that you are viewing the margin settings:
CLICK: *Margins* tab

5. To change the left and right margins to 1 inch:
CLICK: down triangle beside the *Left margin* text box repeatedly, until the value decreases to 1 inch
CLICK: down triangle beside the *Right margin* text box repeatedly, until the value decreases to 1 inch
(*Note*: As you click the symbols, the *Preview* area at the right-hand side shows the effect of the change on your document.)

6. To illustrate the use of a gutter, you will increase the counter in the *Gutter* text box to 0.5 inch:
CLICK: up triangle beside the *Gutter* text box repeatedly, until the value increases to 0.5 inch
(*Note*: The shaded area in the *Preview* area represents the binding.)

7. Reset the Gutter margin to 0 inch.

8. To select legal-size paper with a landscape orientation for this document, first display the paper size and orientation information:
CLICK: *Paper Size* tab

9. SELECT: Legal 8½ × 14-in from the *Paper Size* drop-down list

10. SELECT: *Landscape* option button from the *Orientation* area
Notice that the *Preview* area changes with each selection.

11. PRESS: (ENTER) or CLICK: OK

12. When you return to the document, the page may be too wide to fit in the current view. To remedy this problem:
CLICK: Page Layout button (▣)
CLICK: Zoom Control box (100% ▾)
CHOOSE: Page Width
Your screen should now appear similar to Figure 4.12.

FIGURE 4.12

PAGE LAYOUT VIEW
WITH A LANDSCAPE
ORIENTATION

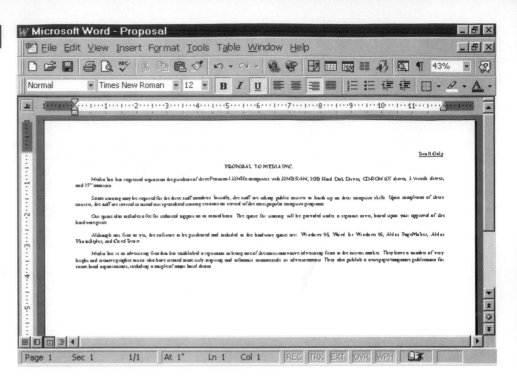

13. To return the document to letter-size paper with a portrait orientation, you will call up the Page Setup dialog box using a shortcut method:
DOUBLE-CLICK: gray area in the Ruler (see diagram below)

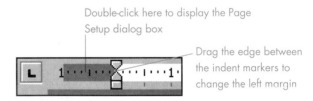

Double-click here to display the Page
Setup dialog box

Drag the edge between
the indent markers to
change the left margin

14. When the Page Setup dialog box appears:
CLICK: *Paper Size* tab
SELECT: Letter 8½ × 11-in from the *Paper Size* drop-down list
SELECT: *Portrait* option button from the *Orientation* area
PRESS: **ENTER** or CLICK: OK
The document is immediately redrawn in the Page Layout view.

15. To change a document's margins using the mouse, you position the mouse pointer over the margin boundary (the line between the gray area and the white area on the Ruler) and then drag the boundary to increase and decrease the margin setting. (See the diagram in step 13.) If you've positioned your mouse pointer correctly, it changes from a white arrow to a black, two-headed arrow. To have Word display the margin measurements in the Ruler as you drag the margin boundary, you hold down the **ALT** key.

Let's proceed—do the following:
PRESS: [**ALT**] and hold it down
DRAG: left margin boundary to the right until 1.3 appears as the measurement on the horizontal Ruler
(*Note*: In Normal view, the double-headed arrow doesn't appear.) Your screen should now appear similar to Figure 4.13.

FIGURE 4.13

CHANGING MARGINS IN PAGE LAYOUT VIEW USING THE MOUSE AND [**ALT**] KEY

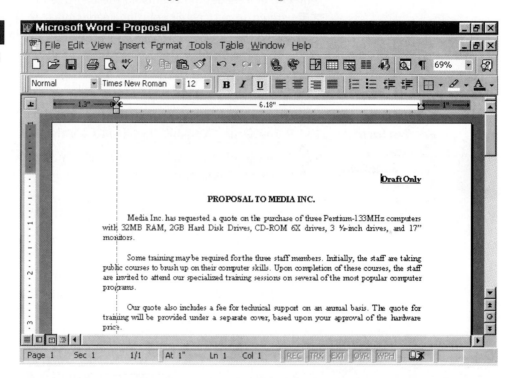

16. Release the mouse button and the [**ALT**] key.

17. Using the same method as outlined in step 16, change the right margin to 1.3 inches. (*Note*: You can use this same method to change left, right, top, and bottom margins in a document.)

18. Save the document as "Proposal-Revised" to the Data Files location. (*Note*: If you are saving to a different disk you will need to use the File, Save As command.)

19. Close the document.

QUICK REFERENCE
Using the Page Setup
Dialog Box

1. **CHOOSE: File, Page Setup**
2. **CLICK:** *Margins* **tab to display the settings page for margins**
3. **Specify a gutter margin if binding the document, as well as the top, bottom, left, and right margins.**
4. **CLICK:** *Paper Size* **tab**
5. **Specify the paper size and either portrait or landscape orientation.**

PREVENTING WIDOWS AND ORPHANS

Although the heading implies a plan for abolishing family suffering, this section deals with a much less serious topic—straggling sentences that are separated from their paragraphs by a page break. A **widow** is created when the last sentence in a paragraph flows to the top of the next page. An **orphan** is created when the first sentence of a paragraph begins on the last line of a page. When a single sentence is separated from a paragraph, the reader must work harder to keep up with the flow of the text. Fortunately, Word has a widow and orphan protection feature that automatically prevents these breaks from occurring.

In this section, you check the widow/orphan settings on your computer.

 Perform the following steps . . .

1. Retrieve the "Newsltr" document from the Advantage Files location.

2. To ensure that the Widow and Orphan protection feature is turned on:
   CHOOSE: Format, Paragraph
   The Paragraph dialog box appears.

3. CLICK: *Line and Page Breaks* tab

4. Under the Pagination group, ensure that the *Widow/Orphan Control* check box is selected:
   SELECT: *Widow/Orphan Control* check box
   Remember, a "✓" in the check box means that the option is selected.

5. PRESS: (ENTER) or CLICK: OK

QUICK REFERENCE
Protecting Against Widows and Orphans

1. **CHOOSE: Format, Paragraph**
2. **CLICK: *Line and Page Breaks* tab**
3. **SELECT: *Widow/Orphan Control* check box in the *Pagination* area**
4. **PRESS: (ENTER) or CLICK: OK**

INSERTING PAGE NUMBERS

Page numbers assist a reader in finding and referencing sections within a document. In Word, you can position page numbers at the top or bottom of a document and align the page number with the left, center, or right margins. Furthermore, you can select the format and starting page for the numbering scheme based on personal preference. For example, you can use standard numbers (1, 2, 3 . . .), letters (a, b, c . . . or A, B, C . . .), or Roman numerals (i, ii, iii . . .) for the numbering format and change the format for different sections in a document.

To add page numbers to a document, you choose the Insert, Page Numbers command. When the Page Numbers dialog box appears, you specify the position and alignment desired for the page numbers. Depending on your selections, Word creates a header or footer using the default numbering format (1, 2, 3 . . .), starting at page 1.

Let's now demonstrate how to insert page numbers.

Perform the following steps . . .

1. CHOOSE: Insert, Page Numbers
   The dialog box in Figure 4.14 should appear on your screen. (*Note:* Figure 4.14 also shows the dialog box for changing the numbering format from standard numbers to letters or Roman numerals.)

FIGURE 4.14

PAGE NUMBERS DIALOG BOX

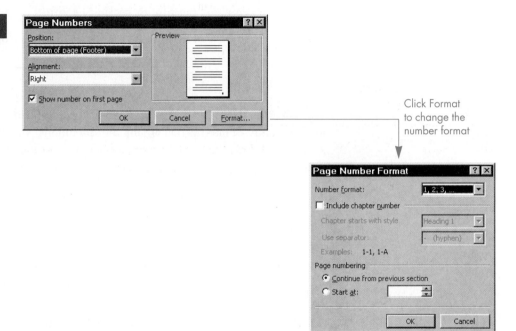

Click Format to change the number format

2. To position the page number in the bottom right-hand corner of the page:
   SELECT: Bottom of Page (Footer) in the *Position* drop-down list box
   SELECT: Right in the *Alignment* drop-down list box

3. PRESS: (ENTER) or CLICK: OK
   Word automatically changed the view to Page Layout view.

4. To see the page number on the bottom of Page 1, you're going to first position the cursor on the top of Page 2 and then press the (↑) key.
   DRAG: the horizontal scroll box to the top of Page 2
   CLICK: in the heading (Field Trip) of page 2
   PRESS: (↑)
   In the bottom right-hand corner, a "1" appears as the page number.

5. To change back to the Normal view:
   CLICK: Normal button (▤)

Because Word places the page numbering scheme into the header or footer of a document, you can further customize the page numbers by selecting a font and style for them.

QUICK REFERENCE

Inserting Page Numbers

1. **CHOOSE: Insert, Page Numbers**
2. **SELECT: an option from the *Position* drop-down list box**
3. **SELECT: an option from the *Alignment* drop-down list box**
4. **PRESS: ⟨ENTER⟩ or CLICK: OK**

CREATING HEADERS AND FOOTERS

A document **header** and **footer** appear at the top and bottom of each page. The header often contains the title or section headings for a document while the footer might show the page numbers or copyright information. Adding a header or footer produces a more professional-looking document and makes longer documents easier to read.

In the last section, you inserted page numbers in the "Newsltr" document. When you specified that the numbering should appear at the bottom of the page, Word automatically created a header for the document. To view the page numbers, you switched to Page Layout view since headers and footers are not visible in Normal view. In the next exercise, you learn how to edit and format the header in Page Layout view.

In this section, you create a footer.

Perform the following steps . . .

1. Make sure that the "Newsltr" document is open in the document area.

2. To edit the header and footer for the "Newsltr" document:
    CHOOSE: View, Header and Footer
    Upon choosing this command, Word switches you to Page Layout view, displays the Header and Footer toolbar, creates a framed editable text area for the header and footer, and dims the document's body text. Your screen should now appear similar to Figure 4.15. Figure 4.16 identifies the buttons in the Header and Footer toolbar.

FIGURE 4.15

VIEWING A DOCUMENT'S
HEADER AND FOOTER IN
PAGE LAYOUT VIEW

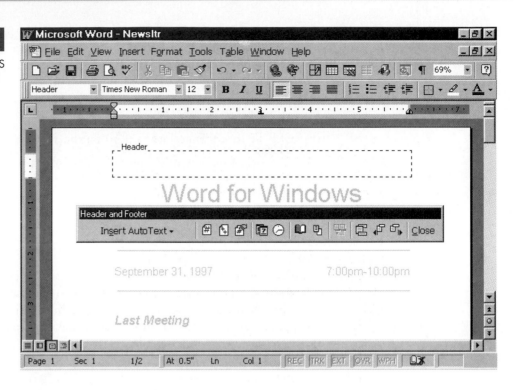

FIGURE 4.16

HEADER AND FOOTER
TOOLBAR

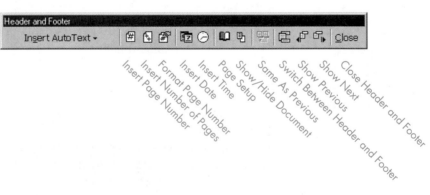

3. Let's leave the header area unchanged. To view the footer:
CLICK: Switch Between Header and Footer button (⊞) on the Header and
Footer toolbar

4. The page number, inserted last section, appears at the far right-hand side of
the first line in the footer area. Your insertion point should appear flashing
at the left edge. Let's now enter information about when the document was
last printed.
TYPE: **Printed on**
PRESS: Space Bar

5. To place the date and time in the footer and have them automatically updated when you print the document:
CLICK: Insert Date button (⊞) on the Header and Footer toolbar
PRESS: Space Bar
TYPE: **at**
PRESS: Space Bar
CLICK: Insert Time button (🕐) on the Header and Footer toolbar

6. To format this new title, you must first select the text:
SELECT: Printed on (current date) at (time)
SELECT: Arial from the *Font* drop-down list (│Times New Roman ▼│)
SELECT: 10 point from the *Font Size* drop-down list (│10 ▼│)
CLICK: Bold button (│**B**│)
(*Note*: If the Arial font isn't available on your computer, choose a different font.)

7. As in the previous step, you format the page number by first selecting the text. However, Word places the page number in a special box called a frame. To select text inside a frame, you must position the I-beam pointer carefully and drag across the text. Do not drag the mouse pointer when it appears as a pointer with a cross-shaped, four-headed arrow—this moves the entire frame.

Now, do the following:
DRAG: I-beam mouse pointer across the page number
The page number should appear highlighted and surrounded by a shaded box (see below).

(*Note*: An anchor may also appear to the left of the framed text box indicating that the page number is anchored to the right border of the footer. Anchors are used when framing text and graphics, a topic beyond the scope of this guide.)

8. To format the page number with the same options as the title:
SELECT: Arial from the *Font* drop-down list (│Times New Roman ▼│)
SELECT: 10 point from the *Font Size* drop-down list (│10 ▼│)
CLICK: Bold button (│**B**│)
Congratulations, you've finished creating and formatting the footer! Your screen should now appear similar to Figure 4.17 (with a different date and time in the footer, of course).

FIGURE 4.17

COMPLETED FOOTER FOR
THE "NEWSLTR"
DOCUMENT

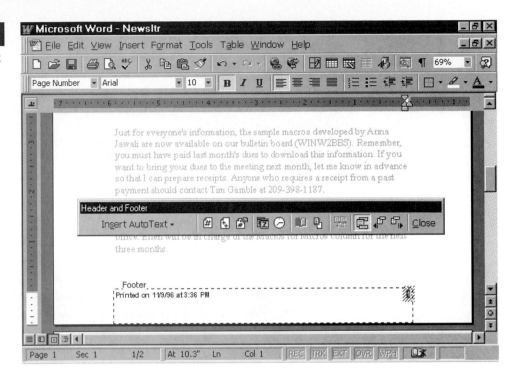

9. To finish editing the footer and return to your document:
CLICK: Close button (Close) on the Header and Footer toolbar
You are returned to the view you were using prior to choosing the View,
Header and Footer command.
(*Tip*: You can double-click the dimmed body text in the Page Layout view
to return to editing the document. To switch back to the header and footer
in Page Layout view, you double-click its dimmed text.)

10. Ensure that you are viewing the document in Normal view:
CLICK: Normal button (▤)

11. Save the document as "Footer Exercise" to the Data Files location. (*Note*: If
you are saving to a different disk, you will need to use the File, Save As
command.)

QUICK REFERENCE
Creating a Header or Footer

1. CHOOSE: View, Header and Footer

**2. Edit and format the header and footer using the regular formatting
commands and the buttons on the Header and Footer toolbar.**

3. CLICK: Close button (Close)

IN ADDITION WORKING WITH TEMPLATES

If your proposals, for example, all use the same margin settings, headers and footers, character formatting commands, and perhaps display the company logo on the top of the page, consider creating a template that stores all the elements that you typically include in a document proposal.

A *template* is a file that contains all the parts and features of a particular type of document. A template can contain text, headers, footers, graphics, page and paper layouts, and more.

For more information, choose Help, Contents and Index. Click the *Index* tab, and then type **templates** to display a list of topics.

PRINTING A DOCUMENT

This section introduces the printing commands for Word, including setting print options and previewing the output. The Windows Printers folder provides a centralized location for tasks relating to printing, including installing a new printer, changing printer settings, and checking or changing the status of scheduled print jobs. You access the Printers folder from the taskbar by clicking the Start button and then choosing Settings, Printers.

To coordinate the printing of multiple documents, Windows places documents temporarily in a print spooler or **queue** on the hard disk. When the printer has completed one print job, Windows takes the next print job from the queue and feeds it to the printer. Because this spooling process occurs in the background, you can continue working in an application immediately after you send a document to the printer. The Windows print spooler is a full 32-bit application, which means you realize little or no slow-down when you send a document to the printer.[1] In other words, there is no waiting for the printer to complete its work before you can continue your own work.

PREVIEWING THE DOCUMENT

A primary benefit of working with today's sophisticated word processing programs, including Word, is the ability to preview documents in a full-page display before sending them to the printer. To access Word's Print Preview mode, you choose File, Print Preview from the menu or click the Print Preview button (🔍) on the Standard toolbar. Some of the features of Print Preview include the following:

- View one page (▣) or multiple pages (▦) at the same time.
- Select Zoom mode to view your document or Edit mode to modify and format your document without leaving Print Preview.
- Make last minute changes to margin settings by dragging the margin boundaries on the Ruler, similar to Page Layout view.

---

[1]In Windows 3.1, print spooling was handled by the Print Manager program.

Let's demonstrate how to preview a document.

Perform the following steps . . .

1. Make sure that the "Footer Exercise" document is open in the document area.

2. CLICK: Print Preview button (🔍)
Upon selecting this command, Word switches you to Print Preview mode. Your screen should now appear similar to Figure 4.18. Figure 4.19 identifies the buttons on the Print Preview toolbar.

FIGURE 4.18

PREVIEWING THE "FOOTER EXERCISE" DOCUMENT

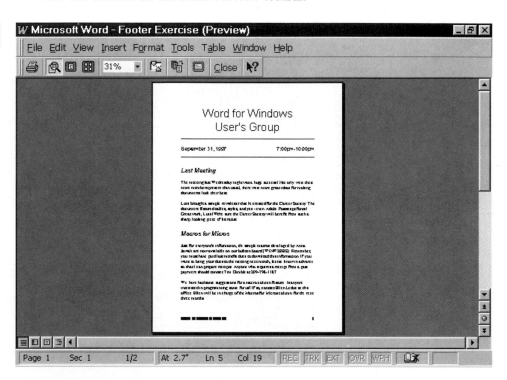

FIGURE 4.19

PRINT PREVIEW TOOLBAR

3. To zoom in on the document, move the mouse pointer over the first paragraph until it changes to a magnifying glass with a plus sign.

4. CLICK: left mouse button once to zoom the view to 100%
Notice that the plus sign in the magnifying glass mouse pointer changes to a minus sign.

5. To switch Print Preview from Zoom mode to Edit mode:
CLICK: Magnifier button (🔍)

6. Move the mouse pointer over the document. Notice that the mouse pointer becomes an I-beam, as opposed to a magnifying glass.

7. To format the title text:
   SELECT: Word for Windows

8. To display the shortcut menu for formatting text:
   RIGHT-CLICK: the selected text
   CHOOSE: Font

9. In the Font dialog box:
   SELECT: 48 point from the *Size* list box
   SELECT: Bold from the *Font Style* list box
   PRESS: **ENTER** or CLICK: OK

10. To change back to Zoom mode:
    CLICK: Magnifier button (🔍)

11. To zoom out, position the magnifying glass mouse pointer over the document and click the left mouse button once.

12. To exit Print Preview:
    CLICK: Close button (Close)

13. Save the "Footer Exercise" document to the Data Files location, replacing the original version.

QUICK REFERENCE
Previewing a Document

1. **CLICK: Print Preview button (🔍)**
2. **Use Zoom mode to view the document and Edit mode to change margin settings, edit text, and format your document.**
3. **CLICK: Close button (Close) to return to the document**

IN ADDITION KEEPING LINES TOGETHER

After previewing a document, you may decide that you don't want a page break to appear in the middle of a paragraph:

1. CHOOSE: Format, Paragraph
2. CLICK: *Line and Page Breaks* tab
3. SELECT: *Keep Lines Together* check box

PRINTING THE DOCUMENT

If you are satisfied with your document after viewing it in Page Layout view and Print Preview, it's time to send it to the printer. The quickest and easiest method for printing a single copy of every page in a document is to click the Print button (🖨) on the Standard toolbar. If you want to print specific pages only, or if you want multiple copies of a document, you must choose the File, Print command and make your selections in the Print dialog box (shown in Figure 4.20).

FIGURE 4.20

PRINT DIALOG BOX

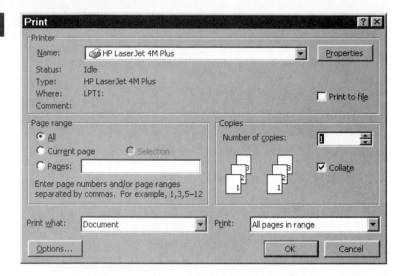

Perform the following steps . . .

1. To print the "Footer Exercise" document:
CLICK: Print button ()
You will see a small printer icon appear in the Status bar as the document is sent to the printer. If you wanted to cancel the print job (which you don't in this exercise), you could double-click this printer icon or press **ESC**.

2. Close all the documents in the document area.

QUICK REFERENCE
Printing a Document

1. **CLICK: Print button ()**
2. **Select the number of copies to print, and specify whether to print certain pages or the entire document.**
3. **PRESS: ENTER or CLICK: OK**

IN ADDITION CREATING A POWERPOINT SLIDE SHOW FROM A WORD DOCUMENT

Don't think that you're limited to a printer when outputting your Word documents. For example, you can easily output your Word document to PowerPoint which can turn it into a slide presentation. PowerPoint creates slides based on the heading styles you've used in your document. A *heading style* is formatting that you apply to a heading. Word comes with nine different heading styles, labeled Heading 1 through Heading 9. (In Word, you select styles from the Style menu on the Formatting toolbar.) The title of each slide is created from text formatted with the Heading 1 style, the next level of text on each slide is created from text formatted with the Heading 2 style, and so on.

To create a PowerPoint presentation from a Word outline:

1. Open the document in Word for which you want to create a PowerPoint presentation.

2. CHOOSE: File, Send To

3. CHOOSE: Microsoft PowerPoint

For more information, choose Help, Contents and Index. Click the *Contents* tab and select the "Sharing Information with Other Users and Applications" topic. Then explore the "Sharing Text, Data, and Graphics" topic.

FILE MANAGEMENT COMMANDS

While creating, formatting, and printing documents are definitely major topics in this guide, the importance of file management should not be understated. Without file management commands, you could not back up your work, free up disk space for more files, or organize your documents into a logical filing system. Specifically, file management refers to copying, moving, deleting, renaming, and sorting documents that reside on your hard disk and floppy diskettes.

CREATING A DOCUMENT INVENTORY

Most of Word's file management utilities can be accessed through the Open dialog box. While primarily a document retrieval tool, you can also print, preview, copy, delete, rename, sort, and search for files. In addition, you can create a shortcut to a document on the Windows desktop and send a file to an e-mail or fax recipient. This section provides an example of how you can use the Open dialog box to search for documents and change how files are viewed.

In this section, you locate files and change the document view.

Perform the following steps . . .

1. Ensure that there are no open documents in the document area.

2. CLICK: Open button (📁)

3. To display the types of files that you can search for:
CLICK: down arrow beside the *Files of type* text box (near the bottom of the dialog box)

From this drop-down list, you can limit your search to Word Documents, Document Templates, Rich Text Format files, Text files, or many other types of files. Or, you can perform a broad search for All Files. You can also type in your own file specification if you want to search for specific files not included in the drop-down list.

4. SELECT: Word Documents from the *Files of type* drop-down list

5. To have Word search the Advantage Files location for Word Documents:
CLICK: down arrow beside the *Look in* text box
SELECT: *your Advantage Files location*
All of the Word Document files in the Advantage Files location will appear in the file list area. (*Note*: This same procedure can be used to search an entire hard disk.)

6. To narrow the search to files that begin with the characters "Gino":
CLICK: *File name* text box
TYPE: **Gino**
CLICK: Find Now button
Five files should appear in the file list area.

7. To refresh the search criteria:
CLICK: New Search button
All of the Word Document files in the Advantage Files location again appear in the file list area.

8. There are four views available in the Open dialog box. Each can be accessed using the Open dialog box toolbar.

- List (⊞)   Displays folder and filenames with small icons.

- Details (▤)   Displays standard file information, including the document's name, size, type, and the date it was last modified.

- Properties (▦)   Displays a summary screen for the highlighted file, containing document statistics, comments, and other useful information.

- Preview (▦)   Displays a preview of the highlighted file in the list.

To display a preview of a document file:
SELECT: "Software" document in the file list area
CLICK: Preview button (▦)
Your screen should now appear similar to Figure 4.21.

FIGURE 4.21

PREVIEWING A
DOCUMENT

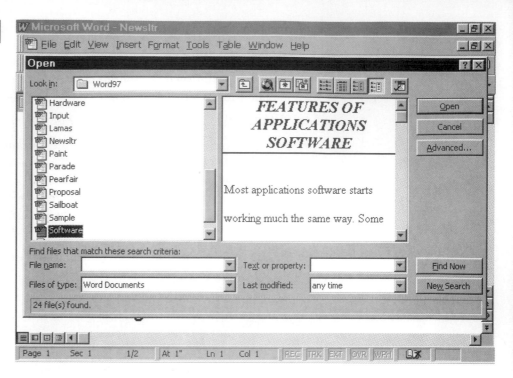

9. To display all the files in the Advantage Files location in the Details view:
   CLICK: Details button ( )

10. To display the files in a list view:
    CLICK: List button ( )

11. To sort the list by file size, you use the Commands and Settings button in the Open dialog box toolbar. Do the following:
    CLICK: Commands and Settings button ( )
    CHOOSE: Sorting

12. CLICK: down arrow beside the *Sort files by* text box
    SELECT: Size from the drop-down list
    PRESS: (ENTER) or CLICK: OK button
    The list is sorted in ascending order by file size. (*Hint:* You can also click the column headings in the Details view to sort documents in the file list area. Click the heading twice to switch between ascending and descending order.)

13. On your own, sort the files in ascending order by the filename.

14. To close the Open dialog box:
    CLICK: Cancel button

QUICK REFERENCE

Changing the View
and Sorting Files

1. **CLICK: Open button (** 🖼️ **)**

2. **To change the view, click the List (▦), Detail (📊), Properties (📋), or Preview button (📄).**

3. **To change the sort order, click the Commands and Settings button (🔽) and then choose the Sorting command.**

MANAGING INDIVIDUAL FILES

Besides displaying and opening files, the Open dialog box provides commands for copying, moving, renaming, and deleting files. These file management tasks are among the most common performed in word processing. The Copy and Cut commands enable you to copy or move a file to a new drive or directory. The Rename command renames the selected file, and the Delete command removes the file from the current drive or directory.

Another useful feature is the ability to select more than one file at a time for copying, moving, deleting, and printing documents. There are two methods for selecting a group of documents.

First, to select a group of contiguous files (all files are next to each other in the list box), you select the first file, hold down the (**SHIFT**) key, and then click the last file. All the documents between the first and last files are automatically highlighted. Second, to select a group of noncontiguous files, you select the first file and then hold down the (**CTRL**) key while clicking on each additional file. Once the files are highlighted, you right-click with the mouse to issue a file management command from the shortcut menu.

In this section, you copy a file to the hard disk, delete the copied file, and then rename a file.

Perform the following steps . . .

1. CLICK: Open button (🖼️)

2. To place a copy of the "Newsltr" document on the hard disk, point to the file and then right-click with the mouse.

3. CHOOSE: Copy

4. You will copy the "Newsltr" file to the root directory of the hard disk (drive C:) and then delete it later. Do the following:
   CLICK: down arrow beside the *Look in* drop-down list box
   SELECT: the icon that represents drive C:

5. To paste the document into the root directory of drive C:
   RIGHT-CLICK: an empty area in the file list area
   CHOOSE: Paste
   A dialog box appears briefly informing you that the file is being copied. Although this example teaches you how to copy files from drive A: to drive C:, you are more likely to copy files from your hard disk to a diskette in order to back up your documents.

6. To delete the "Newsltr" file from drive C:, point to the file and then right-click with the mouse.

7. CHOOSE: Delete
SELECT: Yes when asked to confirm the deletion (see below)

Confirm File Delete

Are you sure you want to send 'Newsltr' to the Recycle Bin?

Yes   No

(*Note*: Word provides another method for deleting a file. After you select a file, you can delete it by pressing the (DELETE) key.)

8. Before renaming a file in the next step, change the search path back to the Advantage Files location:
CLICK: down arrow beside the *Look in* drop-down list box
SELECT: *your Advantage Files location*

9. To change the name of the "Gino1996" document to "1996Gino," point to the "Gino1996" document and then right-click with the mouse.

10. CHOOSE: Rename
TYPE: **1996Gino**
A text editor box still appears around the new name.

11. To remove the text editor box:
PRESS: (ENTER)

12. On your own, rename the "1996Gino" document back to its original name (Gino1996).

13. To close the Open dialog box:
CLICK: Cancel button

QUICK REFERENCE
Copying and Deleting Files

1. **CLICK: Open button ( )**
2. **Copy, cut (move), delete, or rename a file by pointing to the file and right-clicking with the mouse. You then choose the appropriate command from the shortcut menu that appears.**

PRINTING FILES

Word allows you to print one document or multiple documents directly from the Open dialog box. As in the process for copying and deleting files, you highlight the desired file or files, right-click with the mouse, and then choose the Print command. When the Print dialog box appears, you specify the number of copies you want printed and then press (ENTER) or click OK.

Perform the following steps . . .

1. CLICK: Open button ()
   The files in the Advantage Files location should appear.

2. To print both the "Newsltr" and "Proposal" documents, first select the files from the file area:
   SELECT: "Newsltr" in the file area

3. Position the mouse pointer over the "Proposal" document.

4. PRESS: CTRL and hold it down
   CLICK: left mouse button once
   Both files should now be highlighted.

5. Release the CTRL key.

6. Point to one of the selected files and then right-click with the mouse.

7. CHOOSE: Print
   Both documents are sent to the printer and the document screen reappears.

QUICK REFERENCE
Printing Documents

1. **CLICK: Open button ()**

2. **Print a file by pointing to it, right-clicking with the mouse, and then choosing the Print command.**

CREATING A DOCUMENT SHORTCUT

If you frequently use a particular document file, you might consider placing a shortcut to the file on the Windows desktop. Shortcuts are used to open a file or program quickly. After you load Windows, you simply double-click the shortcut on the Windows desktop to open Word and then the document. You can create a shortcut using the shortcut menu in the Open dialog box.

Perform the following steps . . .

1. CLICK: Open button ()
   CLICK: down arrow beside the *Look in* drop-down list box
   SELECT: *your Advantage Files location*
   The files in the Advantage Files location should appear.

2. Let's say that you use the "Newsltr" file often. To create a shortcut for this file, first point to the file with the mouse and then do the following:
   RIGHT-CLICK: "Newsltr" file
   CHOOSE: Create Shortcut
   A shortcut icon named "Shortcut to Newsltr" is created.

3. To copy the shortcut to the desktop, point to the shortcut file and then right-click with the mouse.

4. CHOOSE: Copy
   CLICK: Cancel button to exit the Open dialog box

5. Before you paste the shortcut onto the desktop, minimize Word so that you can see the desktop. The Windows desktop appears.

6. To paste the shortcut onto the desktop:
RIGHT-CLICK: an empty area on the desktop
CHOOSE: Paste
CLICK: an empty area of the desktop to remove the highlighting
Your screen should now appear similar to Figure 4.22.

7. To test the shortcut:
DOUBLE-CLICK: "Shortcut to Newsltr" icon on the desktop
After a few moments, Word will load and the "Newsltr" document should appear in the document window.

8. Exit Word.

9. The Windows desktop appears. To delete the shortcut from the desktop, point to the shortcut and then right-click with the mouse.

10. CHOOSE: Delete
CLICK: Yes command button

SUMMARY

This session introduced the document formatting commands for preparing a document to send to the printer. The majority of page layout options are selected from the Page Setup dialog box, including margins, paper size, print orientation, and paper source. Other formatting topics covered this session included preventing widows and orphans, inserting page numbers, and creating headers and footers. Because the WYSIWYG capabilities of Word can sometimes slow the text entry process, Word provides several alternative views for a document. Whereas the Normal view is used for the majority of your work, you'll find that the Online Layout, Page Layout and Outline views provide additional features for finalizing and managing documents.

The second half of the session examined printing options and file management commands. Topics included using the Zoom and Edit modes in Word's Print Preview and using the Open dialog box to find, copy, delete, rename, and print documents. You also learned how to create a document shortcut and then move the shortcut to the Windows desktop. Table 4.2 provides a list of the commands and procedures covered in this session.

TABLE 4.2	Task Description	Menu Command	Toolbar Button	Keyboard Shortcut
Command Summary	Display text with character and paragraph formatting only	View, Normal	▤	
	Display text with the document map pane	View, Online Layout	▣	
	Display text with all formatting (headers, footers, and columns)	View, Page Layout	▣	

TABLE 4.2 Continued	Task Description	Menu Command	Toolbar Button	Keyboard Shortcut
	Display a document as a collapsible outline	View, Outline	▤	
	Access the Zoom dialog box	View, Zoom	100% ▾	
	Display or hide Word's toolbars	View, Toolbars		
	Display or hide the Ruler line	View, Ruler		
	Set page layout options	File, Page Setup		
	Set paragraph pagination options (widows and orphans)	Format, Paragraph, Line and Page Breaks tab		
	Insert page numbers in the header or footer of a document	Insert, Page Numbers		
	Change to Page Layout view for editing the header and footer	View, Header and Footer		
	Display a document in Print Preview mode	File, Print Preview	🔍	
	Send a document to the printer	File, Print	🖨	CTRL +p
	Perform file management functions	File, Open	📂	

KEY TERMS

footer
Descriptive text that appears at the bottom of each page in a document. The footer usually contains page numbers or copyright information.

gutter
The gutter is where pages are joined together in a bound document.

header
Descriptive text that appears at the top of each page in a document. The header usually contains titles or section headings.

landscape orientation
Describes how a page is printed. Letter-size paper with a landscape orientation measures 11 inches wide by 8.5 inches high. Legal-size paper with a landscape orientation measures 14 inches wide by 8.5 inches high.

orphan
In printing, a single sentence that appears at the bottom of a page, separated from the rest of its paragraph on the next page.

165

portrait orientation

Describes how a page is printed. Letter-size paper with a portrait orientation measures 8.5 inches wide by 11 inches high. Legal-size paper with a portrait orientation measures 8.5 inches wide by 14 inches high.

queue

In printing, a program that uses memory and the disk to line up and prioritize documents waiting for printer time.

widow

In printing, a single sentence that appears at the top of a page, separated from the rest of its paragraph on the previous page.

EXERCISES

SHORT ANSWER

1. When might you want to create a document shortcut?

2. When would you use the Draft Font?

3. How do you return to Word's application window when you are in Full Screen mode?

4. Name the four tabs in the Page Setup dialog box.

5. How do you prevent widows and orphans in a document?

6. What are two methods for inserting page numbers?

7. What are two methods for changing the margins in a document?

8. How do you preview a document before sending it to the printer?

9. What are the two modes available in Print Preview?

10. Name two methods for selecting multiple files in the Open dialog box.

HANDS-ON

(*Note*: Ensure that you know the location of your Advantage Files and where to store your Data Files. If necessary, ask your instructor or lab assistant for additional information.)

1. This exercise uses some character and paragraph formatting commands, as well as document formatting commands. Open "Software" from the Advantage Files location and then perform the following steps:

   a. Include a header that displays the current date in the flush right position.

   b. Ensure that the document is protected against widows and orphans.

   c. Left-justify the entire document.

   d. Include your name and the current page number in a footer.

   e. Check the spelling and grammar in the document.

f. Save the file as "Software" to the Data Files location. (*Remember*: If you are saving to a different disk, you will need to choose File, Save As.)

g. Print the document.

h. Close the document.

2. The following exercise retrieves an existing file from the Advantage Files location and modifies its page layout settings.

a. Retrieve "Bedford" from the Advantage Files location.

b. Change to a Page Layout view.

c. Using the Zoom Control box, shrink the display until you can see the entire page on the screen.

d. Access the Page Setup dialog box by double-clicking the Ruler.

e. Change the top, bottom, left, and right margins to 1.5 inches.

f. Using the mouse, change all the margins to 1.2 inches by dragging the margin boundaries.

g. Add a footer to the letter that centers the following phrase: "From the Desk of *your name*." Substitute your own name for the italicized words.

h. Format the footer with an Arial typeface (or another typeface on your computer) and a 10-point font size.

i. Close the footer area and return to the Normal view.

j. View the document using Print Preview.

k. Using the mouse in Print Preview, change the top and bottom margins to 1 inch.

l. Send the document to the printer from the Print Preview screen.

m. Save the document as "Bedford - Reference" to the Data Files location. (*Remember*: If you are saving to a different disk, you will need to choose File, Save As.)

n. Print the document.

o. Close the document.

3. This exercise creates a document with headers and footers.

a. Open a new document.

b. Center the title "Budget Forecast - 1997" at the top of the page.

c. Center the subtitle "ABC Realty Inc." on the next line immediately below the title.

d. Enhance the title with an Arial, 18-point font and make it bold. (*Note*: Use another font if Arial doesn't exist on your computer.)

e. Enhance the subtitle with an Arial, 14-point font and make it bold and italic.

f. Enter four blank lines and left-justify the new paragraph.

g. Make sure that the font is Times New Roman, 12 point, before proceeding.

h. Type the text appearing in Figure 4.23.

FIGURE 4.23

"BUDGET 1997" DOCUMENT

Introduction

Now that we are in the first quarter of 1997, it is time we stopped to review our direction for the remainder of the year. We had a tough year in 1996, but it seems that the economy is well on its way to recovery. We are anticipating a good year for all the staff.

This report is confidential and should not be circulated outside of this office. It is intended to be a planning document for the Sales Team in 1997. Any questions or suggestions can be directed to your immediate supervisor.

---

i. Return to the top of the document.

j. Create a header and footer for the document. Center-align the text "ABC Realty Inc." in the header. Left-align the text "Prepared by *your name*" in the footer, along with a right-aligned page number. Substitute your name for the italicized text in the footer.

k. View the document using Print Preview.

l. Print the document.

m. Save the document as "Budget 1997" to the Data Files location. Keep the document open for use in the next exercise.

4. In this exercise you practice using some commands from previous sessions as well as document formatting commands.

a. Ensure that "Budget 1997" appears in the document area.

b. Change to a Normal view.

c. Set the following page dimensions:

Paper Size:	Letter
Paper Orientation:	Portrait
Top Margin:	1 inch
Bottom Margin:	1 inch
Left Margin:	1 inch
Right Margin:	1 inch

ABC REALTY INC.

1997

Revenue
    Commercial Properties $125,500,000
    Residential Properties   35,000,000
    Leased Properties   875,000

Total Revenue $161,375,000

Expenses
    Insurance $50,000
    Salaries   750,000
    Commissions   15,500,000
    Office Supplies   25,000
    Office Equipment   20,000
    Utilities   15,000
    Leased Automobiles   50,000
    Travel   250,000
    Advertising & Promotion   25,000,000

Total Expenses   41,660,000

Net Income $119,715,000

d. Enter the information in Figure 4.24. (*Hint*: Use tabs.)

e. Preview the document.

f. Print the document.

g. Save the document to the Data Files location, replacing the original version.

h. Close the document.

5. On your own, create an outline describing a course you would like to take, either one that is currently offered at your school or an entirely new course. The description should consist of a cover page and two additional pages. Ensure that the correct page number and other pertinent information prints on pages two and three. Describe the topics/tasks/activities that should take place each week in a 15-week semester. Save the outline as "On Your Own-7" to your Data Files location and then print it. *Extra Credit*: Create the outline in Outline view and then output it to a PowerPoint presentation. Print the PowerPoint presentation.

CASE PROBLEMS   **GINO'S PIZZA KITCHEN**

(*Note*: In the following case problems, assume the role of the primary characters and perform the same steps that they identify. You may want to re-read the session opening.)

1. After a relaxing Christmas holiday, Larry arrives at the office to find the following note on his desk:

   Larry, I trust you had a wonderful time on Nantucket Island. Sorry to be a pain, but I'd like to see the monthly restaurant report ASAP. This time, please include the current page number and date at the bottom of each page. Also, could you leave some room on the left side of each page so that I have a place to make notes? Thanks. Gino.

   With his favorite mug in tow, Larry heads directly for the coffee machine, planning his strategy along the way. When he returns to his desk, Larry turns on the computer, launches Word, and locates the four manager's reports stored in the Advantage Files location. These files are named "GinoNo," "GinoSo," "GinoEast," and "GinoWest." He loads the four documents into separate windows. He then moves the cursor to the end of the "GinoNo" document. After switching to the "GinoSo" document, Larry copies all the text in this document to the Clipboard. Next, he switches back to the "GinoNo" document, pastes the text into the document, and then performs this same procedure for the "GinoEast" and "GinoWest" documents. When finished, the "GinoNo" window contains the four summary reports. He saves this document as "Gino's-December" to the Data Files location.

   Now that he has a single document to work with, Larry begins by inserting a formatted title on the first page of the report that reads:

   Gino's Pizza Kitchen
   Monthly Summary: December

   Using character formatting commands, Larry makes the text in the long document easier to read. He selects a 1.5-inch gutter so that Gino has a place to make notes and then creates a footer displaying the current date and page number. To ensure that the document's text flows nicely, Larry uses a command to make sure that widows and orphans are suppressed. He then saves the document back to the Data Files location, prints the document, and places a copy on Gino's desk.

2. Larry wants additional practice working with headers, footers, and other document formatting commands. He decides to make a copy of the "Gino's-December" document, stored in the Data Files location. He names the copy "Larry," which he will easily recognize as a practice file.

3. Before giving Gino the yearly summary report, Larry decides to format the document to improve its readability. It currently uses only a single font and doesn't incorporate headers, footers, or page numbers. The report is stored in the Advantage Files location as "Gino1996." Larry also decides to include a title page for the report. When finished, he saves the document as "Gino1996-Revised" to the Data Files location and then prints it for Gino's review.

Microsoft Word 97 for Windows

Increasing Your Productivity

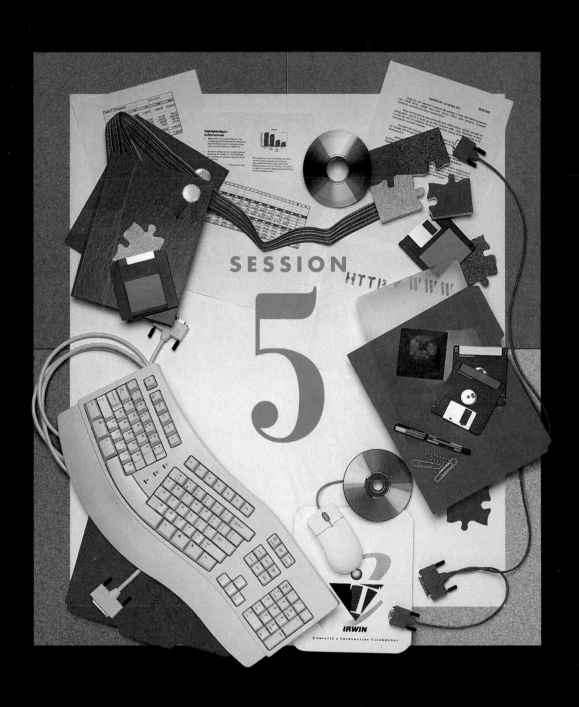

SESSION

5

SESSION OUTLINE

Using Wizards to Create Documents
Table Fundamentals
Merging Fundamentals
Customizing Word
Summary
Key Terms
Exercises

INTRODUCTION

Computers are getting really smart! With the right tools, they balance our checkbooks, budget how much we're allowed to spend dining out per month, answer our phones when we're not home, and send faxes in the middle of the night to get the best long-distance rates. But what can a software company do to make a word processor smarter? Microsoft's answer: add Wizards to lead you step-by-step through creating professional-looking letters, resumes, and other documents. In this session, you'll meet some of Word's most popular Wizards.

You will also learn how to create tables for organizing columns and rows of information and how to merge address information from a list of respondents into a standard form letter. The session concludes with a discussion on how to customize Word to best fit your working environment.

CASE STUDY   **THE UNION TENNIS CLUB**

Jerry Garcia is the manager of the beautiful Union Tennis Club in Fort Lauderdale, Florida. He has worked at the club for three years and runs a very tight operation. The club's Board of Directors is pleased with his performance and he has a good relationship with most of his employees. Also, the ones who pay the bills, the members, find him approachable, capable, responsive, and friendly.

Jerry uses a computer to keep track of the club's finances and membership list. Although primarily self-taught on the computer, Jerry has received some help from a few computer-literate members. Jerry is now preparing to put the name of each member with an overdue account into a Microsoft Word document. He remembers his frustrations when performing this task the last time. First, he had trouble aligning the data for each member. And second, he didn't know how to use Word to send a reminder letter to each person in the list. Instead, he grudgingly used the standard "Overdue Account" form on which he wrote the name of the offending member. Jerry knows there's a better way—he just doesn't know where to begin.

In this session, you and Jerry will learn how to create tables for lining up information, how to merge data with a standard form letter, and customize Word to meet your particular needs.

USING WIZARDS TO CREATE DOCUMENTS

Wizards help you to do your work quicker and more efficiently. Whether you need to write a term paper or create an agenda for tomorrow's meeting, a **wizard** gets you started and headed in the right direction. It's not necessary to understand how a wizard works; but it is important to know that wizards are available and easily accessible. You can select from a variety of wizards to create specialized documents, as summarized in Table 5.1.

TABLE 5.1	*Name*	*Description*
Some of Word's Wizards	Envelope	Creates a single envelope or multiple envelopes for a mailing list
	Fax	Creates a fax cover sheet; formatting options include Professional, Contemporary, and Elegant
	Letter	Creates the structure for a normal, contemporary, or professional letter format or a newsletter.
	Mailing Label	Creates a single page of labels or multiple pages
	Memo	Creates a standard memo with an optional distribution list
	Resume	Creates an entry-level, chronological, functional, or professional resume

Because the documents created by wizards are based on standard document templates, you can easily edit and format them once they've been created. A **template** is a predesigned and preformatted document into which you put your own information. Word comes with many document templates that you can fill in directly including: Contemporary Resume, Elegant Resume, Contemporary Letter, Professional Letter, Elegant Memo, and Contemporary Report, to name a few. With a little more education and experience, you can also learn how to customize your own templates.

IN ADDITION DOWNLOADING ADDITIONAL TEMPLATES AND WIZARDS FROM THE WEB

If you have access to the World Wide Web, you can download additional templates and wizards from Microsoft's Web site. To do this:

1. CHOOSE: Help, Microsoft on the Web

2. CHOOSE: Free Stuff

Then follow the instructions on the Web page to download the files you want.

To access a wizard or template, you choose the File, New command, select the appropriate tab from the New dialog box, and then double-click the wizard or template that you want to use. When you invoke a wizard, the selected wizard will display a series of questions and options on the screen regarding how you want the document formatted. On the last page, you click the Finish button and watch as the wizard creates the document right before your eyes.

Although we cannot show you every wizard's creation, we will lead you through one example. In this section, you use a wizard to create a fax cover sheet.

Perform the following steps . . .

1. Open "Software" from the Advantage Files location.

2. To create a new document using a wizard:
   CHOOSE: File, New
   CLICK: *Letters & Faxes* tab
   Your screen should now appear similar to Figure 5.1.

FIGURE 5.1

NEW DIALOG BOX:
LETTERS & FAXES TAB

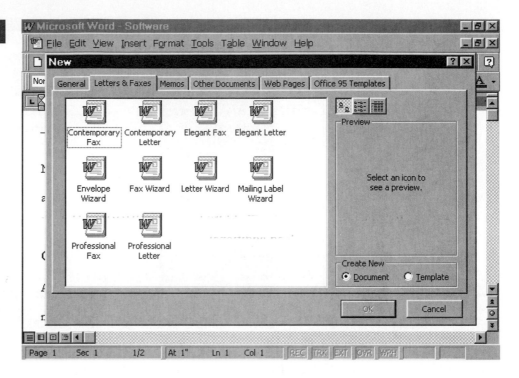

3. Let's start with a relatively simple wizard that is used quite frequently by business people:
DOUBLE-CLICK: Fax Wizard in the *Template* area
The Fax Wizard is launched and presents the initial Fax Wizard screen. Your screen should now appear similar to Figure 5.2. On the left side of the dialog box, you see the steps the Fax Wizard will go through in order to format the final document. To skip to a particular step, you click its name or associated box. Otherwise, if you click Next, the next step will occur.

FIGURE 5.2

FAX WIZARD:INITIAL
SCREEN

4. To proceed to the next screen (Document to Fax):
CLICK: Next button

5. On this screen, ensure that "Software.doc" appears in the *The following document* text box and the *With a cover sheet* option is selected. (*Note:* As you proceed, if you change your mind, you can always review your selections by clicking the Back button or a step in the chart.)

6. Now we're going to skip to the Recipients screen. Since you aren't going to actually fax the document in this exercise, it doesn't matter what you select on the Fax Software screen.
CLICK: Recipients on the left side of the dialog box

7. In the first row, type the name of a friend in the *Name* text box and the corresponding fax number in the *Fax Number* text box. If you prefer fictitious information, refer to Figure 5.3.

FAX WIZARD: ENTERING
THE RECIPIENT'S
INFORMATION

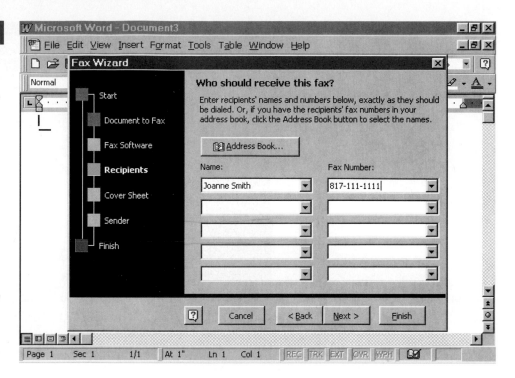

8. To go to the next step (Cover Sheet):
CLICK: Next button

9. Now the Fax Wizard wants to know whether you prefer a Professional, Contemporary, or Elegant fax cover:
SELECT: *Elegant* option button (it's not really that elegant!)

10. To go to the next step (Sender):
CLICK: Next button

11. Now type your information into the Sender screen. If you prefer a fictitious entry, refer to Figure 5.4. You begin by typing in the first text box.

FAX WIZARD: ENTERING
THE SENDER'S
INFORMATION

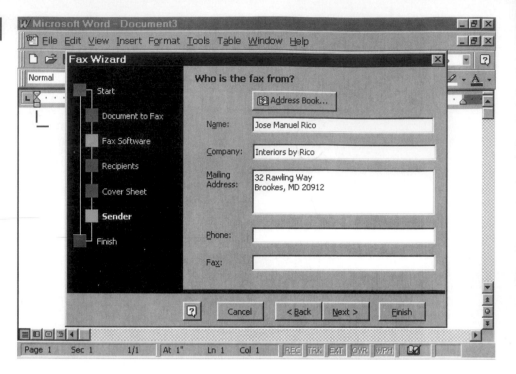

12. To go to the next step (Finish):
CLICK: Next button

13. To create the cover sheet:
CLICK: Finish

14. After several seconds (perhaps a minute on slower machines), the fax cover document appears in Page Layout view. You are looking at the bottom of the document and the Office Assistant appears offering guidance.

15. To remove the Office Assistant from the screen, click the Close icon (⊠) in the Office Assistant box.

16. To see the top of the fax cover sheet, drag the scroll box to the top of the vertical scroll bar. Your screen should now appear similar to Figure 5.5. (*Note:* An anchor may appear on your screen. Anchors are used when framing text and graphics, a topic beyond the scope of this guide.)

FIGURE 5.5

PARTIAL VIEW OF THE
COMPLETED FAX COVER
SHEET

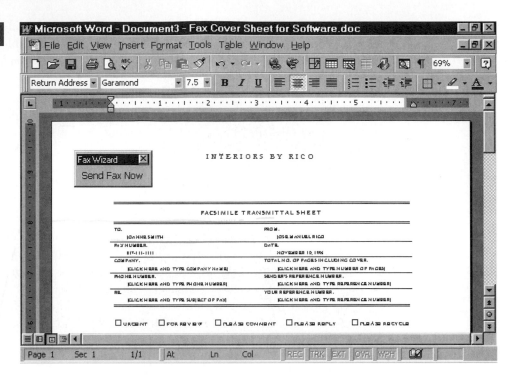

17. Your next step is to complete the fax cover and add any additional comments. Click on any bracketed instructions and either type in the requested information or press the **DELETE** key to remove the comment from the cover sheet.

18. Save the document as "My Fax" to the Data Files location.

19. To print the fax cover:
CLICK: Print button (🖨)

20. Close all documents.

QUICK REFERENCE
Using Wizards

1. CHOOSE: File, New

2. SELECT: a tab in the New dialog box

3. SELECT: a wizard from the *Template* area

4. Make selections in the Wizard's dialog box and then:
   CLICK: Next button to proceed

5. When you are satisfied with the options that you've chosen:
   CLICK: Finish button

TABLE FUNDAMENTALS

Word provides two methods, tabs and tables, for organizing information using a grid format. This session focuses on Word's table feature. You use a table to line up information into columns and rows. For example, a table works well for creating forms, phone lists, inventory lists, and even financial statements. Although Word provides a Table Wizard, you'll find that creating tables using the toolbar buttons and Word's AutoFormat feature is just as easy and more flexible.

CREATING A TABLE

Put your artist's cap on because Word 97 lets you draw tables. To draw a table, you click the Tables and Borders button () on the Standard toolbar, activating the Tables and Borders toolbar and the Draw Table tool. You simply drag the Draw Table tool on the screen to create the horizontal and vertical lines that make up a table. Using this method, you create each **cell,** the intersection of a row and column, one by one.

If you anticipate that your table will contain many cells, you may consider building the bulk of the table using the Table, Insert command or by clicking the Insert Table button (▦) on the Standard toolbar. With either of these methods you can create a table containing many cells in a few seconds. You place the insertion point where you want the table to appear and then choose the Table, Insert Table command or click the Insert Table button (▦) on the Standard toolbar. You must then specify the desired number of columns and rows.

As a final step, you can use the Tables and Borders toolbar or Word's AutoFormat feature to customize the table to your unique requirements. By the way, don't be concerned if you initially misjudge your requirements, adding and deleting columns and rows is quite straightforward. In this section, you create the cost estimate pictured in Figure 5.6 using the Insert Table button (▦) and the Tables and Borders button (▣).

FIGURE 5.6

"COST ESTIMATE"
DOCUMENT

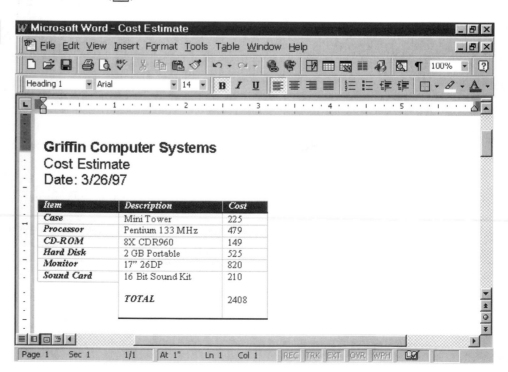

Perform the following steps . . .

1. Open a new document using the New button (⬜). Ensure that you are viewing the document in Normal view.

2. TYPE: `Griffin Computer Systems`
   PRESS: [ENTER]
   TYPE: `Cost Estimate`
   PRESS: [ENTER]
   TYPE: `Date: 3/26/97`
   PRESS: [ENTER] twice

3. To create a table that has 5 rows and 3 columns:
   CLICK: Insert Table button (▦) and hold it down
   DRAG: the mouse pointer downwards until a grid appears
   SELECT: 5 × 3 Table from the pop-up grid menu
   Your screen should now appear similar to Figure 5.7.

FIGURE 5.7

CREATING A TABLE
USING THE MOUSE

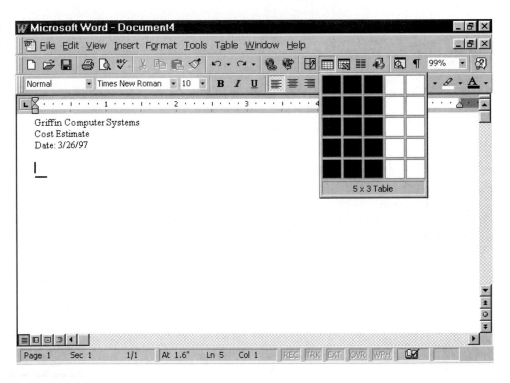

4. Release the mouse button. Word places a table with 5 rows and 3 columns at the insertion point.

QUICK REFERENCE
Creating a Table
Using the Mouse

1. **Position the insertion point where you want to insert the table.**
2. **CLICK: Insert Table button (▦) and hold it down**
3. **DRAG: the grid pattern to the desired number of rows and columns**
4. **Release the mouse button.**

IN ADDITION CREATING AN EXCEL WORKSHEET IN A WORD DOCUMENT

 If you know how to use Excel, you can easily create an Excel worksheet in a Word document using the Insert Microsoft Excel Worksheet (⊞) button on the Standard toolbar. You perform the following steps:

1. In the Word document, position the cursor where you want to position the Excel worksheet.

2. CLICK: Insert Microsoft Excel Worksheet (⊞)

3. By dragging with the mouse, select the size of the table from the pop-up grid menu.

4. Excel's Standard and Formatting toolbars will replace Word's toolbars. Type your data into the worksheet and use Excel's commands to complete the worksheet.

5. CLICK: in the document to return to Word

6. To edit the Excel worksheet, you point to the worksheet and double-click.

ENTERING DATA INTO A TABLE

A table consists of rows and columns. You type information into a cell, which is the intersection of a row and column. To position the insertion point in a cell, you can use the I-beam mouse pointer, press the arrow keys (⬆, ⬇, ⬅, and ➡), or press ⌨TAB. If the insertion point is positioned in the rightmost cell of the last row, pressing ⌨TAB will automatically add another row to the bottom of the table. You format text within a cell like any other text in the document.

Perform the following steps to enter data.

  Perform the following steps . . .

1. With the insertion point in the first cell, let's enter some information into the table, starting with the headings:
   TYPE: **Item**
   PRESS: ⌨TAB
   TYPE: **Description**
   PRESS: ⌨TAB
   TYPE: **Cost**
   PRESS: ⌨TAB
   Notice that the last ⌨TAB takes you to the next row in the table.

2. In the same manner as above, enter the following four items under the appropriate headings. You can press ⌨TAB to advance to the next cell, or you can try using the arrow keys and mouse pointer:

Item	*Description*	*Cost*
Case	**Mini Tower**	**225**
Processor	**Pentium 133 MHz**	**479**
Hard Disk	**2 GB Portable**	**525**
Monitor	**17" 26DP**	**820**

3. With the insertion point in the last cell (820), press the ⌨TAB⌨ key to add another row to the table. (*Note:* If you already pressed ⌨TAB⌨ in the previous step and a new row appeared, move to step 4.)

4. Enter one more item into the table:
TYPE: **Sound Card**
PRESS: ⌨TAB⌨
TYPE: **16 Bit Sound Kit**
PRESS: ⌨TAB⌨
TYPE: **210**
PRESS: ⬇
Notice that the insertion point leaves the table with this last keystroke.

5. To add a blank line:
PRESS: ⌨ENTER⌨

6. When you click inside a table, the Insert Table button (⊞) changes to the Insert Rows button (⊞⊏). To illustrate:
CLICK: in the fourth row of the table (Hard Disk)
Notice that the Insert Table button (⊞) changed to the Insert Rows button (⊞⊏).

7. To insert a row:
CLICK: Insert Rows button (⊞⊏)
A row was inserted above the fourth row.

8. Click in the first cell of the newly inserted row.

9. Type the following information:
TYPE: **CD-ROM**
PRESS: ⌨TAB⌨
TYPE: **8X CDR960**
PRESS: ⌨TAB⌨
TYPE: **149**
Your screen should now appear similar to Figure 5.8.

FIGURE 5.8

THE DATA HAS BEEN
ENTERED

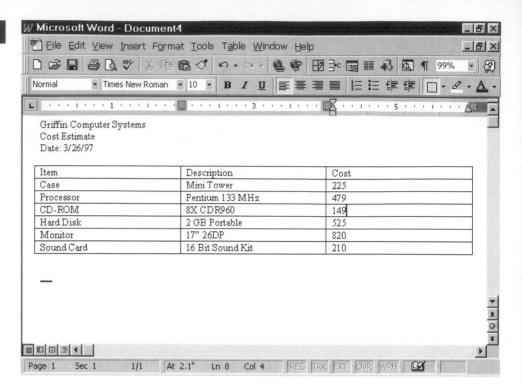

10. In the next few steps, you narrow the columns to better fit the data. Point with the mouse to the vertical border separating the first and second columns. The mouse pointer should change to a double-headed arrow.

11. By referring to Figure 5.6, hold down the mouse button and drag the border to the left. Repeat the procedure for the vertical border between the second and third columns and for the far-right vertical border.

DRAWING A TABLE

In this section, you complete the cost estimate by drawing the total cells at the bottom of the table. Before you can use the Draw Table tool, your document must appear in Page Layout view. If you don't switch to Page Layout view prior to activating the drawing pencil, Word will display a message indicating that you should switch. In this section, you practice drawing a few cells in a table.

Perform the following steps . . .

1. To switch to Page Layout view:
CLICK: Page Layout button (▣)

2. CLICK: Tables and Borders button
Your screen should appear similar to Figure 5.9. The Draw Table tool is activated and the Tables and Borders toolbar appears. Also, the Office Assistant may appear with a helpful tip. (*Note:* The Office Assistant doesn't appear in Figure 5.9.)

FIGURE 5.9

ACTIVATING THE
DRAW TABLE TOOL

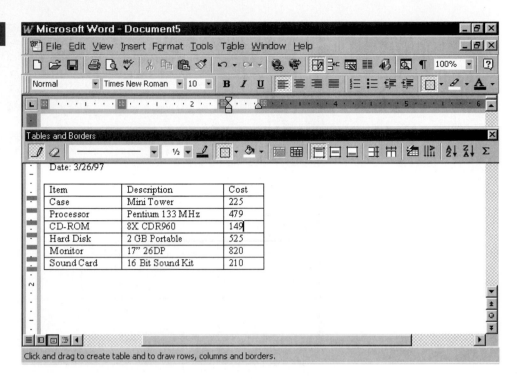

3. If necessary, drag the Tables and Borders toolbar to another area of the screen or reshape it so that you can see more of your document. Also, if the Office Assistant appears:
CLICK: Close icon (☒) in the Office Assistant box

4. To create the outside border of the two cells at the bottom of the table (see Figure 5.6), point to the bottom-left corner of the last cell in the Description column.

5. Hold the mouse button down and, by referring to Figure 5.6, drag downwards and to the right to create the two cells. Your screen should appear similar to Figure 5.10.

FIGURE 5.10

DRAWING A CELL

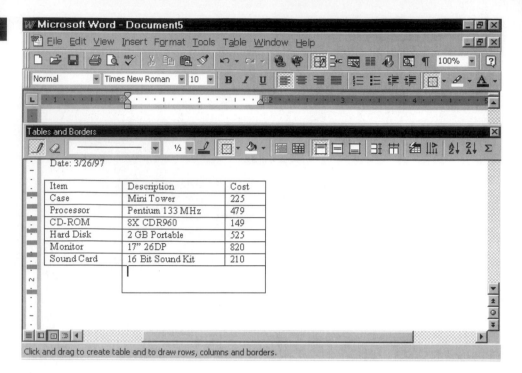

6. The Draw Table tool is still activated. On your own, create the vertical line that will divide the newly inserted cell into two cells.

7. To deactivate the Draw Table tool:
CLICK: Draw Table button ( ) in the Tables and Borders toolbar
The Tables and Borders toolbar no longer appears.

8. CLICK: in the leftmost cell
TYPE: **TOTAL**
PRESS: TAB

9. To total the amounts above, use the AutoSum button (Σ) on the Tables and Borders toolbar.
RIGHT-CLICK: a toolbar button
CHOOSE: Tables and Borders
CLICK: AutoSum button (Σ)
A total of the amounts above automatically appears in the cell.

10. In this step, you center vertically the data in the newly inserted cells.
SELECT: the two cells at the bottom of the table
CLICK: Center Vertically button ( ) on the Tables and Borders toolbar

11. Close the Tables and Borders toolbar.

12. Save the document as "Cost Estimate" to the Data Files location.

FORMATTING A TABLE

With Word's Table AutoFormat command, you can format your tables in just a few keystrokes or mouse clicks. Using the menu, you first place the insertion point in any cell of the table and then choose the Table, Table AutoFormat command. An easier method is to right-click the desired table and choose the Table AutoFormat command from its shortcut menu. Either way, the dialog box in Figure 5.11 appears, from which you can select one of over 30 professionally designed formats.

FIGURE 5.11

TABLE AUTOFORMAT
DIALOG BOX

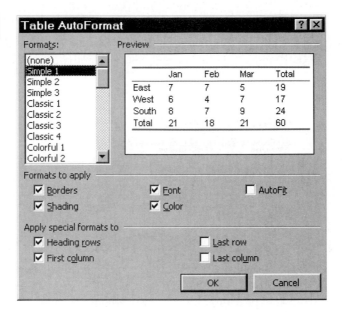

Let's demonstrate how to format a table.

Perform the following steps . . .

1. Ensure that the insertion point appears in the table. If not, move the insertion point into the table using the mouse or arrow keys.

2. To format the table:
   CHOOSE: Table, Table AutoFormat
   The dialog box in Figure 5.11 appears. (*Note:* Remember that you can also right-click the table to display the shortcut menu and then choose Table Autoformat from the menu.)

3. To view the formatting options:
   PRESS: ⬇ repeatedly, pausing between each press to view the formatting characteristics shown in the *Preview* area

4. SELECT: Colorful 2 in the *Formats* list box
   PRESS: (ENTER) or CLICK: OK
   The table is immediately formatted using the Colorful 2 options.

5. Let's format the titles at the top of the page before proceeding:
   SELECT: Griffin Computer Systems
   SELECT: Arial (or another font) from the *Font* drop-down list (Times New Roman ▾)
   SELECT: 14 point from the *Font Size* drop-down list (10 ▾)
   CLICK: Bold button (**B**)

6. Format the "Cost Estimate" and "Date: 3/26/97" information using the same commands as in step 5, but don't apply the bold attribute.

7. CLICK: near the end of the document to remove the highlighting
Your screen should now appear similar to Figure 5.6. (*Note:* The screen in Figure 5.6 is zoomed to 100%.)

8. Save the "Cost Estimate" document to the Data Files location, replacing the original version.

9. Close all the open documents in the document area.

10. Remove the Tables and Borders toolbar.

QUICK REFERENCE
Using Table AutoFormat

1. **Position the insertion point in the table you want to format.**

2. **CHOOSE: Table, Table AutoFormat**

3. **SELECT: formatting options from the *Formats* list box**

4. **PRESS: (ENTER) or CLICK: OK**

IN ADDITION CREATING COLUMNS

Tables are best used for keeping text, numbers, or dates aligned in a grid format. Word also provides you with the capability to create *newspaper columns,* also called *snaking columns,* whereby text wraps automatically to the top of the next column when it reaches the bottom of the current column.

To create columns, choose Format, Columns from the Menu bar or click the Columns button (▦) on the Standard toolbar. For more information, choose Help, Contents and Index from the Menu bar. Click the *Index* tab and then type **columns.** A list of topics will appear.

IN ADDITION INSERTING AN ACCESS TABLE IN WORD

Perform the following steps in Word:

1. In your Word document, position the cursor where you want the Access table to appear.

2. Display the Database toolbar.

3. CLICK: Insert Database (▫▫) on the Database toolbar

4. CLICK: Get Data command button

5. CLICK: MS Access Databases in the *Files of type* box

6. Select a database in the *filename* box and then click the Open command button.

7. Click the *Tables or Queries* tab and then select a table or query.

8. If you want Word to format the table for you: CLICK: Table AutoFormat command button

9. Choose how you want the table formatted and then click OK.

10. To copy the Access data into Word: CLICK: Insert Data command button

11. Select the records to include in the Insert Data dialog box.

12. If you want the inserted Access data to be linked to Access so that the data is updated automatically as it changes in Access: SELECT: Insert data as field check box

MERGING FUNDAMENTALS

Have you ever received a letter from a company or organization that you knew absolutely nothing about? Was your name typed in the salutation and perhaps mentioned in the body of the letter? This kind of document is called a *form letter*. Your name, along with thousands of others, is stored in a mailing list and placed into specific locations in a letter through a process called **merging**. Merging requires two files: the **data source** and the **main document**. The data source contains variable data, such as names and addresses, to be merged with the main document or form letter.

PREPARING A MERGE OPERATION

Word provides a utility called the Mail Merge Helper that leads you through performing a mail merge from scratch. In addition to creating form letters, the Mail Merge Helper can assist you with printing mailing labels, envelopes, and catalogs. You start the Mail Merge Helper by choosing the Tools, Mail Merge command from the menu. In this section, you will perform a simple merge of an employee mailing list with an interoffice memo.

Next, you merge a list of names with a memo.

Perform the following steps . . .

1. Open a new document using the New button (⬜). Ensure that you are viewing the document in Normal view.

2. To launch the Mail Merge Helper:
   CHOOSE: Tools, Mail Merge
   Your screen should now appear similar to Figure 5.12.

FIGURE 5.12

MAIL MERGE HELPER

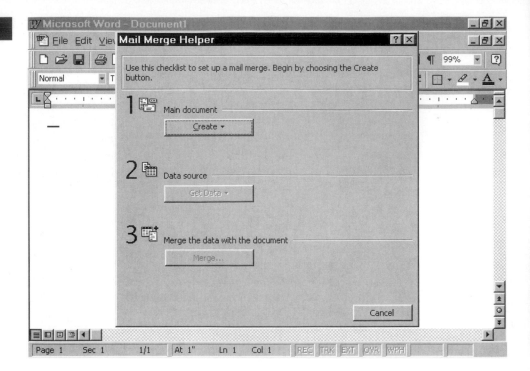

3. The Mail Merge Helper provides three steps as a checklist for performing a mail merge. The first step, according to the dialog box, is to create a main document file. To proceed:
SELECT: Create command button
A pop-up menu appears with four possible options: Form Letters, Mailing Labels, Envelopes, and Catalog.

4. To perform a merge for a letter or other such document (i.e., memo):
CHOOSE: Form Letters from the pop-up menu

5. To use the active document for creating the main document file:
SELECT: Active Window command button
Notice that the information you selected appears below the *Main document* area in the Mail Merge Helper dialog box.

6. Because you are starting this mail merge operation from scratch, you must create a new data source file. To proceed:
SELECT: Get Data command button
CHOOSE: Create Data Source from the pop-up menu
Your screen should now appear similar to Figure 5.13.

FIGURE 5.13

CREATE DATA SOURCE
DIALOG BOX

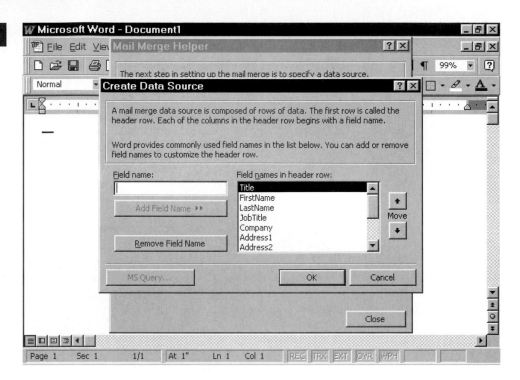

7. You use the Create Data Source dialog box to define the information you
will be merging with the main document file. For the employee mailing list,
you require entry blanks (also called **fields**) for their first name, last name,
city, state, postal or zip code, and phone number. Fortunately, these fields
are among the defaults provided in the *Field names in header row* list box.
To remove the other field names in the list box, you highlight a field name
and then select the Remove Field Name command button. Do the following:
SELECT: Title in the *Field names in header row* list box
SELECT: Remove Field Name command button

8. Using the procedure outlined in the previous step, remove all the field
names in the *Field names in header row* list box, except for FirstName,
LastName, City, State, PostalCode, and WorkPhone.

9. To proceed to the next step:
PRESS: (**ENTER**) or CLICK: OK
The Save As dialog box should appear.

10. Save the data source file as "Mail List" to the Data Files location.
After Word finishes saving the file, it displays a dialog box giving you the
choice of adding information to the data source or working in the main
document.

11. To add the employee information to the "Mail List" data source file:
SELECT: Edit Data Source command button
Your screen should now appear similar to Figure 5.14.

FIGURE 5.14

DATA FORM DIALOG BOX

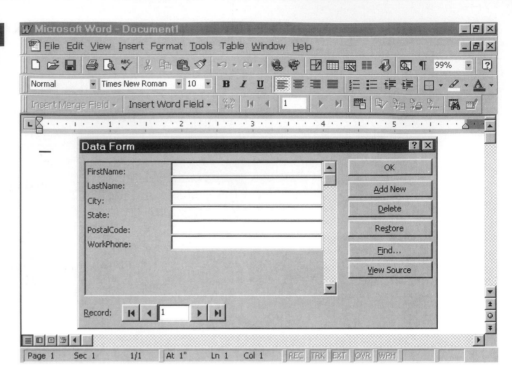

12. Enter the following information using the Data Form dialog box. To advance to the next field, you press **TAB** or use the mouse. When you reach the WorkPhone field, you press **ENTER** or click the Add New command button to add a new employee to the data file.

FirstName	LastName	City	State	PostalCode	WorkPhone
Janos	Sagi	Boston	MA	02116	617-552-4224
Becky	McFee	Chicago	IL	60637	312-654-9871
Sima	Veiner	Toronto	ON	M5B 2H1	416-599-1080
Jack	Yee	Seattle	WA	98004	206-787-3554

13. To finish adding information to the data source file:
    SELECT: OK command button
    You are placed in the main document file, where you will begin editing the form letter. Notice the Merge toolbar that appears below the Formatting toolbar.

14. Let's create a memo to the four employees in the data source file:
    TYPE: **DATE:**
    PRESS: **TAB** twice
    TYPE: *current date*
    PRESS: **ENTER** twice
    TYPE: **TO:**
    PRESS: **TAB** twice

15. To have Word automatically substitute the names of the employees into this memo, you need to specify the merge fields that contain the information:
CLICK: Insert Merge Field button in the Merge toolbar
CHOOSE: FirstName from the drop-down menu
PRESS: Space Bar
CLICK: Insert Merge Field button
CHOOSE: LastName from the drop-down menu

16. Now let's add the merge field codes for address information:
PRESS: **ENTER** to advance one line
PRESS: **TAB** twice
CLICK: Insert Merge Field button
CHOOSE: City from the drop-down menu
TYPE: **,** (a comma)
PRESS: Space Bar
CLICK: Insert Merge Field button
CHOOSE: State from the drop-down menu
PRESS: **ENTER** twice

17. TYPE: **FROM:**
PRESS: **TAB** twice
TYPE: *your name*
PRESS: **ENTER** four times

18. Enter the body text of the memo:
TYPE: **Please be advised that the meeting has been postponed until the 4th of January.**

19. Save the document as "Mail Merge Memo" to the Data Files location. Your screen should now appear similar to Figure 5.15.

FIGURE 5.15

"MAIL MERGE MEMO"
DOCUMENT

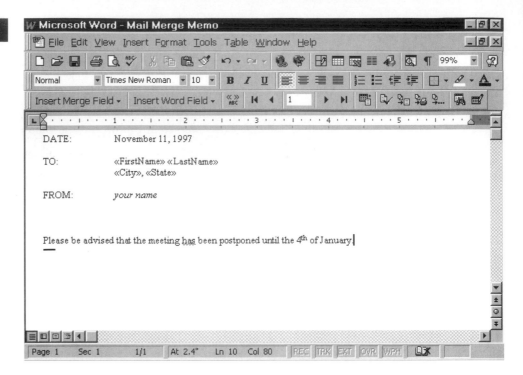

20. To return to the Mail Merge Helper dialog box:
CHOOSE: Tools, Mail Merge
(*Note:* You can also click the Mail Merge Helper button (▦) on the Merge toolbar.) The filenames of the main document and the data source file should appear below their respective steps in the dialog box.

21. Proceed to the next section.

QUICK REFERENCE Preparing a Mail Merge Operation	**1.** **CHOOSE: Tools, Mail Merge**
	2. **Specify a main document file.**
	3. **Specify an existing data source file or create a new data source file.**
	4. **If necessary, add information to the data source file.**
	5. **Edit the main document, inserting merge fields as desired.**

IN ADDITION USING AN EXCEL OR ACCESS DATA SOURCE WHEN PERFORMING A MERGE
OPERATION

1. CHOOSE: Tools, Mail Merge

2. Specify a main document file.

3. Specify an Excel worksheet file or an Access database file as the data source.

4. Specify the desired worksheet range, or Access table or query, containing the data for merging.

5. Edit the main document, inserting merge fields as desired.

6. On the merge toolbar, select either the Merge to New Document button or the Merge to Printer button.

PERFORMING THE MERGE

Once the data source file and the main document file have been created, you are ready to perform the merge. The output of the merge is typically sent to a new document or to the printer. If there are only a few records in the data source file, you may prefer to merge to a new document, save the document for review, and then print the document at a later time. If there are 2,500 records in the data source file and the main document file consists of ten pages, then merging the two files would result in a 25,000-page document—an unacceptable length by most standards. In this case, merging directly to the printer is your best option.

Let's now demonstrate how to perform a merge.

Perform the following steps . . .

1. With the Mail Merge Helper dialog box displayed:
    SELECT: Merge command button
    Your screen should now appear similar to Figure 5.16.

FIGURE 5.16

MERGE DIALOG BOX

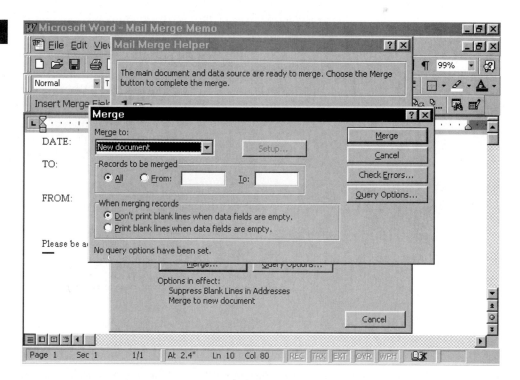

2. In the *Merge to* drop-down list box:
    SELECT: New Document

3. To perform the merge:
    CLICK: Merge command button
    The data source file is merged with the main document file and the result appears in a separate document.

4. Save the new document as "Merged Documents" to the Data Files location.

5. Close all the open documents in the document area. When asked to save changes to your documents, respond yes to all dialog boxes.

QUICK REFERENCE
Performing the Merge

1. **In the Mail Merge Helper dialog box:**
    SELECT: Merge command button

2. **In the Merge dialog box:**
    SELECT: Merge command button

CUSTOMIZING WORD

This section introduces you to some of the basic customization options available in Word 97. This section is not intended to be an all-inclusive discussion.

CHANGING WORD'S DEFAULT SETTINGS

You modify Word's default settings in the Options dialog box, accessed by choosing the Tools, Options command. There are a variety of customization topics contained in this dialog box. For example, you can remove the Status bar and scroll bars from the application window, display the Paragraph symbol on-screen at all times, change Word's default mode to Overtype, and tell the Spell Checker to ignore words in uppercase. This section is a guided tour of only some of these topics, providing you with enough information to explore them on your own.

Let's now demonstrate how to change default settings.

Perform the following steps . . .

1. Open a new document.

2. To access the Options dialog box:
CHOOSE: Tools, Options
Notice the topical tabs that appear in this dialog box.

3. Let's review the View settings first:
CLICK: *View* tab
There are three primary groups on this page: *Show, Nonprinting Characters,* and *Window.* The *Show* group provides an option for viewing your document using a draft font. One of our favorite features is the ability to display just the Paragraph symbol on-screen without having to show all the other hidden characters and codes. You select this option from the *Nonprinting Characters* group. The *Window* group lets you remove the Status bar and scroll bars from the application window to increase your document viewing area.

4. CLICK: *Save* tab
    The most popular save options (shown in Figure 5.17) include:
    - *Always create backup copy* check box
    - *Allow fast saves* check box
    - *Save AutoRecover info every* check box

    Although relatively self-explanatory, you can find more information about each option by clicking the question mark icon (⟦?⟧) in the Title bar and then clicking an element.

FIGURE 5.17

OPTIONS DIALOG BOX:
SAVE TAB

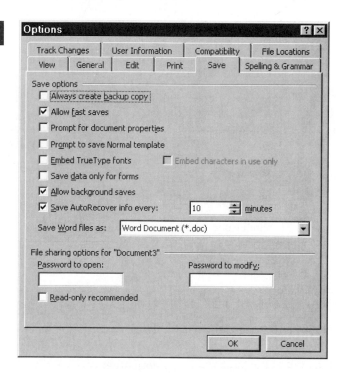

5. CLICK: *File Locations* tab
    To specify where on your disk you would like Word to look for documents, highlight the Documents option and then select the Modify command button. Word uses this information in the Open dialog box.

6. CLICK: *Spelling & Grammar* tab
    If you work with technical terms, abbreviations, figures, or Internet addresses, you will appreciate the three check boxes on this page for ignoring information during a spelling check. For example, when the *Ignore words in UPPERCASE* and *Ignore words with numbers* check boxes are selected, the Spell Checker progresses through a document without stopping on text like RAM, CPU, or 486. Figure 5.18 provides an example of the Spelling and Grammar options.

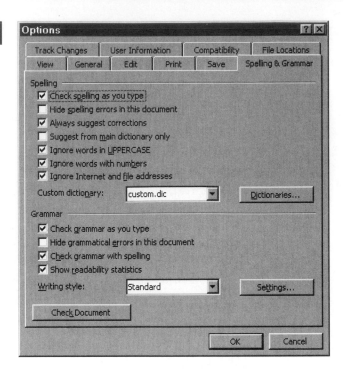

FIGURE 5.18

OPTIONS DIALOG BOX:
SPELLING TAB

7. To cancel our whirlwind tour through the Options dialog box:
PRESS: (ESC) or CLICK: Cancel

IN ADDITION OPTIONS DIALOG BOX: FOR MORE INFORMATION

To find out more information about any setting in the Options dialog box, select the tab of the page you want to learn more about and then

click the question mark icon ([?]). You can click any element in the dialog box to display helpful information.

UNDERSTANDING MACROS

A **macro** is a collection of keystrokes that has been recorded in order to automate a particular sequence of tasks. Once recorded, the procedure or task may be executed again and again by simply selecting the macro from a list or by pressing a shortcut key combination. You can also assign macros to buttons on the toolbar or create new pull-down menu commands. Macros are usually created to cut down on the amount of time and effort required to perform repetitive tasks specific to your work.

IN ADDITION MACROS: FOR MORE INFORMATION

Creating macros is beyond the scope of this session, but definitely not beyond your grasp to learn and use in your documents. To find out more about macros, choose Help, Con-

tents and Index from the Menu bar. Click the *Index* tab and then type **macros**. A list of topics will appear.

Summary

This session introduced you to creating complex documents using wizards. Word 97 provides wizards for creating many types of common documents including fax covers, resumes, letters, envelopes, and memos. Using the Fax Wizard in this session, you produced an attractive fax cover sheet within minutes. You also created and formatted tables in this session for organizing information into rows and columns.

With Word's Mail Merge Helper, you can easily produce form letters. A form letter is a standard document where only the addressee or other variable information changes. With the variable information entered into a data source file, only a single form letter needs to be created. The process of merging takes the information from the data source file and inserts it into the correct locations in the form letter. In this session, you merged names and addresses into a standard memo.

The session concluded with a brief discussion on customizing Word's default settings. Table 5.2 provides a list of the commands and procedures covered in this session.

TABLE 5.2	*Task Description*	*Menu Command*	*Toolbar Button*
Command Summary	Access wizards for creating new documents	File, New	
	Create or insert a table	Table, Insert Table	▦
	Draw a table	Table, Draw Table	▦
	Format a table based on predefined formatting guidelines	Table, Table AutoFormat	
	Start the Mail Merge Helper to lead you through a mail merge	Tools, Mail Merge	
	Access Word's default settings	Tools, Options	

KEY TERMS

cell
The intersection of a column and row in a table.

data source
A document file that uses a table to capture and store variable information for the merge process.

fields
In a data source file, the entry blanks or individual pieces of information. In a table, rows are complete records for items or people and columns are fields or pieces of information in each record.

macro
A collection of keystrokes that is recorded for playback at a later date. A macro enables you to perform a series of operations by pressing a shortcut key combination or clicking a toolbar button.

main document
A type of form letter document used by Word in the merge process. The main document file contains codes to insert information from the data source file.

merging
The process of taking information from a data source file and inserting it into a form letter or main document file, one record at a time. The results from merging these two files can be sent to a file or the printer.

template
A predesigned form into which you can enter your own information.

wizard
A Word feature that provides step-by-step assistance through the document creation process.

EXERCISES

SHORT ANSWER

1. List nine wizards that are available in Word 97.
2. How would you create a resume using a wizard?
3. When would you use a table in a document?
4. Name three methods for creating a table.
5. What is the quickest method for formatting a table?
6. Explain the merge process.
7. What is a data source file?

8. List two options for where the results of a print merge can be sent.

9. How do you tell Word to display the Paragraph symbol on-screen without displaying the other nonprinting characters and codes?

10. How do you create a macro?

HANDS-ON

(*Note*: Ensure that you know the location of your Advantage Files and where to store your Data Files. If necessary, ask your instructor or lab assistant for additional information.)

1. In the following exercise, you create and format a table.

   a. Open a new document.

   b. Create the document appearing in Figure 5.19.

FIGURE 5.19

"ROLAND GARROS"
DOCUMENT

current date

Mr. Roland Garros
Clay Supplies Inc.
1091 Panorama Ridge
Houston, TX 76798

Dear Mr. Garros:

Per your request, I am providing a list of the items that you ordered for your office last Wednesday.

Please confirm the order by placing your initials beside each item in the column provided, and then fax this letter back to me at 817-747-1234.

Yours sincerely,
Grand Slam Computer Sales

your name
Account Representative

c. Insert the following table between the first and second paragraph.

Client Initial	Qty	Description	Total Price
	5	Laser Printers	$10,250.00
	5	Printer Cables	76.00
	20	3.5" Diskettes	30.00
	5	Windows 95	450.00

d. Make the headings in the table bold.

e. Add a new row at the bottom of the table and enter the following:

TOTAL COST	$10,806.00

f. Apply a predefined format of your choice to the table using the Table, Table AutoFormat command.

g. Save the document as "Roland Garros" to the Data Files location.

h. Print the document.

i. Close the document.

2. In this exercise, you create a main document file and a data source file, and then perform a merge of the two documents to create a third file.

a. Open a new document.

b. CHOOSE: Tools, Mail Merge

c. Use the active window as the main document file.

d. Create a new file for the data source.

e. Use the following fields for the data file: FirstName, LastName, Address1, City, State, ZipCode.

f. Save the data source as "Customer Data" to the Data Files location.

g. Enter the following information into the data source file.

FirstName	LastName	Address1	City	State	ZipCode
Elliot	Lepinski	898 Burrard Ave.	Louisville	KY	40205
Red	Robinson	235 Johnson St.	Washington	DC	20052
Elaine	Maynard	1005 West 9th St.	Baton Rouge	LA	70803
Ranjitt	Singh	122 Cordova Ave.	Tacoma	WA	98416
William	Delaney	36 Primore Road	Wichita	KS	67208
Francisco	Ortez	875 Broadway	Albuquerque	NM	87131
Alice	Chan	29 Redmond Road	San Francisco	CA	92182
Jessica	Thomas	909 West 18th St.	Brooklyn	NY	11225
Jimmy	Kazo	888 East 8th Ave.	Billings	MT	59101

h. Create the document appearing in Figure 5.20. Do not type the merge codes. Use the Insert Merge Field button to add each merge code, such as <<FirstName>>, to the document.

FIGURE 5.20

"CUSTOMER FORM" DOCUMENT

---

current date

<<FirstName>> <<LastName>>
<<Address1>>
<<City>>, <<State>>   <<ZipCode>>

Dear <<FirstName>>:

                    We're Moving!

Please be informed that as of August 31st we are moving to new premises located at 8030 United Boulevard in Boston.

We are looking forward to this move with great anticipation. Because of your continued support, we are expanding our training facilities to accommodate two training rooms and a boardroom.

As a result of this move, we will be closed from the third week in August to the end of September. An invitation to the Open House will be forwarded to you, <<FirstName>>, as soon as we are settled.

Let us know if we can do anything for you!

Sincerely,

your name
President

---

i. Save the main file as "Customer Form" to the Data Files location.

j. Perform the merge to a new document, using the Mail Merge Helper. Print out the first page of the new document

k. Save the new file as "Customer - Merged Documents" to the Data Files location.

l. Close the document.

3. Guess what? You have been asked to distribute a memo to your entire class describing an upcoming field trip to Microsoft Corporation in Redmond, Washington. Perform the following steps.

    a. Use the Memo Wizard to create the memo.

    b. When requested, include your name and initials in the memo.

    c. Save the memo to your Data Files location as "Class Memo."

    d. Print the "Class Memo" document.

    e. Close the document.

4. On your own, create a form letter that describes what you've been up to lately. As you proceed, keep the following in mind:

    a. Choose Tools, Mail Merge to begin.

    b. Create a data source that contains the names and addresses of five or more family members and/or friends.

    c. Save the data source as "Friends" to the Data Files location.

    d. Create the form letter document. Insert the merge codes you defined in step a using the Insert Merge Field button.

    e. Save the main file as "My News" to the Data Files location.

    f. Perform the merge to a new document, using the Mail Merge Helper.

    g. Print the documents, but don't save them.

    h. Close all the documents.

5. On your own, create a table of names and addresses, recipes, expenses, To Do tasks, or whatever you would find useful. Without obscuring your data, incorporate as many formatting features into the table as you can. Save the table as "On Your Own-9" to your Data Files location.

CASE PROBLEMS   **THE UNION TENNIS CLUB**

(*Note*: In the following case problems, assume the role of the primary characters and perform the same steps that they identify. You may want to re-read the session opening.)

1. Now that he knows how to create tables, Jerry isn't dreading the task at hand. Nine members of the Union Tennis Club have overdue accounts and he must put their names and addresses (see below) into a table. When finished, he saves the file as "Overdue Accounts" to the Data Files location. (*Note*: Include the table headings in the first row of the table.)

FirstName	LastName	Address1	City	State	PostalCode
Muriel	Britzky	3710 Bush Street	San Francisco	CA	94111
Myron	Drexler	1485 Sonoma Hwy	Sonoma	CA	96555
Julie	Davis	100 Bosley Lane	New York	NY	90000
Mitch	Kaplanoff	20 Cactus Lane	Palm Desert	CA	98888
Michael	Reynolds	17 Windy Way	Lincoln	MA	09111
Jacob	Raggio	P.O. Box 145	Evergreen	CO	89777
Mary	Timberlake	151 Greer Road	Evanston	IL	60201
Todd	Bowman	200 Union Street	San Francisco	CA	14441
Valli	Terris	1871 Orrinton Ave	Chicago	IL	87555

2. Since he has already created the table of overdue members, Jerry decides to create a reminder letter complete with merge codes. During the process, Jerry selects "Open Data Source" to tell Microsoft Word where to "get" the data and specifies his "Overdue Accounts" document in the Data Files location. After creating the form letter, Jerry saves it to the Data Files location as "UTC - Form Letter." He then performs the merge and prints out the form letters. Because he's concerned about disk space on his computer, he doesn't save the merged form letters as a document to the Data Files location.

3. Jerry wants to include a table in the upcoming newsletter that lists the sale items available in the club's tennis shop. These items include:

Item	Description	Cost
Tennis Racket	Wilson Hammer	$139.00
Tennis Shirts	UTC logo	$14.95
Tennis Shorts	Navy-Mens	$21.99
Visors	White	$7.50
Tennis Balls	Wilson	$2.00
Tennis Bag	Penn	$24.99

After creating the table, Jerry formats and then prints it for the newsletter. He saves it to the Data Files location as "UTC - Sale" and closes the document. With his desk clear, Jerry pokes his head out of his office and asks politely: "Tennis, anyone?"

Appendix

Microsoft Word 97 for Windows Toolbar Summary

STANDARD

FORMATTING

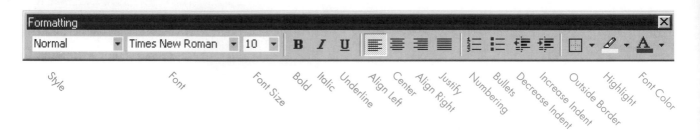

DRAWING

PICTURE

TABLES

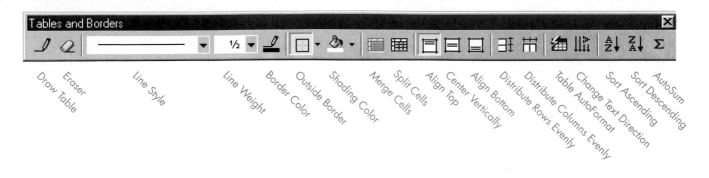

WORDART

Index

The page numbers in boldface indicate Quick Reference procedures.

Microsoft® Excel 97 for Windows®

Sarah E. Hutchinson

Glen J. Coulthard

Irwin/McGraw-Hill

A Division of The McGraw·Hill Companies

MICROSOFT® EXCEL 97 for WINDOWS®

This book is printed on acid-free paper.

3 4 5 6 7 8 9 0 WC/WC 9 0 9 8 7

ISBN 0-256-25997-6

Publisher: *Tom Casson*
Sponsoring editor: *Garrett Glanz*
Developmental editor: *Kristin Hepburn*
GTS production coordinator: *Cathy Stotts*
Marketing manager: *James Rogers*
Senior project supervisor: *Denise Santor-Mitzit*
Production supervisor: *Pat Frederickson*
Art director: *Keith McPherson*
Prepress buyer: *Heather D. Burbridge*
Compositor: *GTS Graphics, Inc.*
Typeface: *11/13 Bodoni Book*
Printer: *Webcrafters, Inc.*

http://www.mhcollege.com

WELCOME TO THE IRWIN ADVANTAGE SERIES

The Irwin Advantage Series has evolved over the years to become one of the most respected resources for software training in the world—to date, over 200,000 students have used one or more of our learning guides. Our instructional methodologies are proven to optimize the student's ability to learn, yet we continually seek ways to improve on our products and approach. To this end, all of our learning guides are classroom tested and critically reviewed by dozens of learners, teachers, and software training experts. We're glad you have chosen the Irwin Advantage Series!

KEY FEATURES

The following features are incorporated into the new Microsoft Office 97 student learning guides to ensure that your learning experience is as productive and enjoyable as possible:

CASE STUDIES

Each session begins with a real-world **case study** that introduces you to a fictitious person or company and describes their immediate problem or opportunity. Throughout the session, you obtain the knowledge and skills necessary to meet these challenges. At the end of the session, you are given an opportunity to solve **case problems** directly related to the case scenario.

CONCEPTS, SKILLS AND PROCEDURES

Each learning guide organizes and presents its content in logically structured session topics. Commands and procedures are introduced using **hands-on examples in a step-by-step format,** and students are encouraged to perform the steps along with the guide. These examples are clearly identified by the text design.

PERFORM THE FOLLOWING STEPS

Using this new design feature, the step progression for all hands-on examples and exercises are clearly identified. Students will find it surprisingly easy to follow the logical sequence of keystrokes and mouse clicks. No longer do you have to worry about missing a step!

END OF SESSION EXERCISES

Each session concludes with **short answer questions** and **hands-on exercises.** These comprehensive and meaningful exercises are integrated with the session's objectives; they were not added as an afterthought. They serve to provide students with opportunities to practice the session material. For maximum benefit, students should complete all the exercises at the end of each session.

IN ADDITION BOXES

These content boxes are placed strategically throughout the guide and provide information on related topics that are beyond the scope of the current discussion. For example, there are three typical categories that are visually identified by the following icons:

Integration

The key to productive and efficient use of Office 97 is in the integration features for sharing data among the applications. With a few mouse clicks, for example, you can create a PowerPoint presentation from a Word document, copy an Access database into an Excel workbook, and incorporate professional Office Art into your annual report. Under this heading, you will find methods for sharing information among the Microsoft Office 97 applications.

Advanced

In a 200+-page learning guide, there are bound to be features that are important but beyond the scope of the text. Therefore, we call attention to these features and offer suggestions on how to apply techniques or to search for more information.

Internet

The Internet is fast becoming a standard tool for gathering and exchanging information. Office 97 provides a high level of Internet connectivity, allowing the user to draw upon its vast resources and even publish documents directly on the World Wide Web. Although not every student will have a persistent Internet connection, you can review the content under this heading to learn about Office's Internet features.

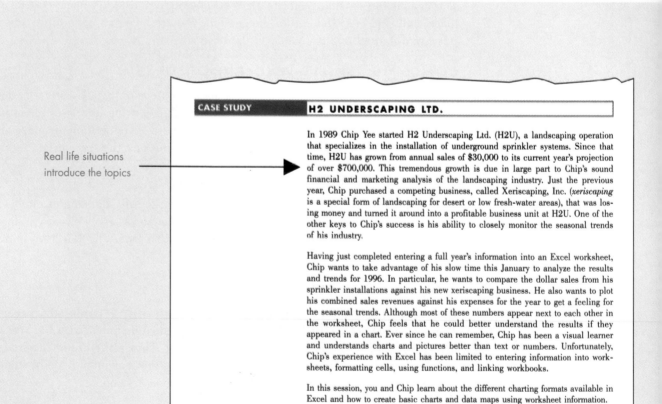

Real life situations introduce the topics

CASE STUDY   **H2 UNDERSCAPING LTD.**

In 1989 Chip Yee started H2 Underscaping Ltd. (H2U), a landscaping operation that specializes in the installation of underground sprinkler systems. Since that time, H2U has grown from annual sales of $30,000 to its current year's projection of over $700,000. This tremendous growth is due in large part to Chip's sound financial and marketing analysis of the landscaping industry. Just the previous year, Chip purchased a competing business, called Xeriscaping, Inc. (*xeriscaping* is a special form of landscaping for desert or low fresh-water areas), that was losing money and turned it around into a profitable business unit at H2U. One of the other keys to Chip's success is his ability to closely monitor the seasonal trends of his industry.

Having just completed entering a full year's information into an Excel worksheet, Chip wants to take advantage of his slow time this January to analyze the results and trends for 1996. In particular, he wants to compare the dollar sales from his sprinkler installations against his new xeriscaping business. He also wants to plot his combined sales revenues against his expenses for the year to get a feeling for the seasonal trends. Although most of these numbers appear next to each other in the worksheet, Chip feels that he could better understand the results if they appeared in a chart. Ever since he can remember, Chip has been a visual learner and understands charts and pictures better than text or numbers. Unfortunately, Chip's experience with Excel has been limited to entering information into worksheets, formatting cells, using functions, and linking workbooks.

In this session, you and Chip learn about the different charting formats available in Excel and how to create basic charts and data maps using worksheet information.

Large figures guide learning

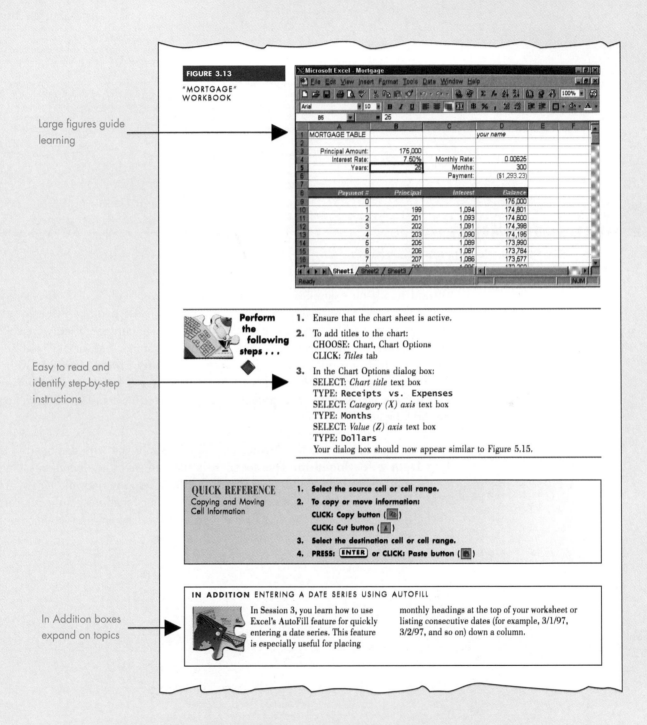

FIGURE 3.13

"MORTGAGE"
WORKBOOK

Easy to read and identify step-by-step instructions

Perform the following steps . . .

1. Ensure that the chart sheet is active.

2. To add titles to the chart:
   CHOOSE: Chart, Chart Options
   CLICK: *Titles* tab

3. In the Chart Options dialog box:
   SELECT: *Chart title* text box
   TYPE: Receipts vs. Expenses
   SELECT: *Category (X) axis* text box
   TYPE: Months
   SELECT: *Value (Z) axis* text box
   TYPE: Dollars
   Your dialog box should now appear similar to Figure 5.15.

QUICK REFERENCE
Copying and Moving
Cell Information

1. Select the source cell or cell range.

2. To copy or move information:
   CLICK: Copy button ( )
   CLICK: Cut button ( )

3. Select the destination cell or cell range.

4. PRESS: ENTER or CLICK: Paste button ( )

In Addition boxes expand on topics

IN ADDITION ENTERING A DATE SERIES USING AUTOFILL

In Session 3, you learn how to use Excel's AutoFill feature for quickly entering a date series. This feature is especially useful for placing monthly headings at the top of your worksheet or listing consecutive dates (for example, 3/1/97, 3/2/97, and so on) down a column.

Students practice with
real life projects

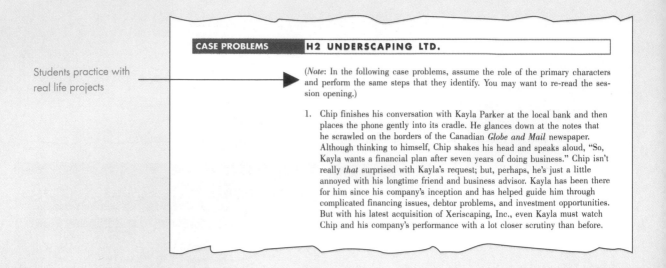

CASE PROBLEMS | **H2 UNDERSCAPING LTD.**

(*Note*: In the following case problems, assume the role of the primary characters and perform the same steps that they identify. You may want to re-read the session opening.)

1. Chip finishes his conversation with Kayla Parker at the local bank and then places the phone gently into its cradle. He glances down at the notes that he scrawled on the borders of the Canadian *Globe and Mail* newspaper. Although thinking to himself, Chip shakes his head and speaks aloud, "So, Kayla wants a financial plan after seven years of doing business." Chip isn't really *that* surprised with Kayla's request; but, perhaps, he's just a little annoyed with his longtime friend and business advisor. Kayla has been there for him since his company's inception and has helped guide him through complicated financing issues, debtor problems, and investment opportunities. But with his latest acquisition of Xeriscaping, Inc., even Kayla must watch Chip and his company's performance with a lot closer scrutiny than before.

TEXT SUPPLEMENTS

ADVANTAGE FILES

Certain hands-on examples and exercises are marked with a disk ◆ icon, indicating the need to retrieve a document file from the **Advantage Files location.** These document files may be provided to you in a number of ways: packaged on a diskette accompanying this text, or on the computer network at your school. You may also download the files from the ***Advantage Online*** Web site (http://www.irwin.com/cit/adv). *These documents files are extremely important to your success.* Check with your instructor or lab advisor for details on how to acquire the Advantage Files.

In addition to identifying the Advantage Files location, you will also need to specify a **Data Files location.** This location is used to save the documents that you create and may either be a blank diskette or a folder on the network server. Again, your instructor or lab advisor will specify the proper locations. More information on the file locations and the proper techniques for retrieving and saving information is provided inside the back cover of this book.

CD-ROM INTERACTIVE TUTORIALS

In addition to using this book, you may have access to our *Advantage Interactive* software. These interactive multimedia tutorials are fully integrated with the material from each session and make effective use of video clips, screen demonstrations, hands-on exercises, and quizzes. You will enjoy the opportunity to explore these tutorials and learn the software at your own pace. For ordering information, please refer to the coupon inside the front cover.

INSTRUCTOR'S RESOURCE KIT

For instructors and software trainers, each learning guide is accompanied by an **Instructor's Resource Kit (IRK).** This kit provides suggested answers to the short-answer questions, hands-on exercises, and case problems appearing at the end of each session. Furthermore, the IRK includes a comprehensive test bank of additional short-answer, multiple-choice, and fill-in-the-blank questions, plus hands-on exercises. You will also find a diskette copy of the Advantage Files which may be duplicated or placed on your network for student use.

SUPPORT THROUGH THE WWW

The Internet, and more specifically the World Wide Web, is an important component in our approach to software instruction for the Office 97 application series. The *Advantage Online* site at http://www.irwin.com/cit/adv is a tremendous resource for all users, providing information on the latest software and learning guide releases, download options for the Advantage Files, and supplemental files for the Instructor Resource Kits. We also introduce new methods for you to communicate with the authors, publisher, and other users of the series. As a dynamic venture, *Advantage Online* will evolve and improve over time. Please visit us to see the latest developments and contribute your valuable feedback.

NETWORK TESTING

Evaluation and assessment are important components of any instructional series. We are committed to providing quality alternatives to traditional testing instruments. With our Irwin Network Test Interactive software, instructors can select questions, create and administer tests, and then calculate grades—all on-line! Visit the *Advantage Online* site for more information on how we are progressing in this exciting area.

Before you begin

As with any software instruction guide, there are standard conventions that we use to indicate menu options, keystroke combinations, and command instructions.

MENU INSTRUCTIONS

In Office 97, all Menu bar options and pull-down menu commands have an underlined or highlighted letter in each option. When you need to execute a command from the Menu bar—the row of menu choices across the top of the screen—the tutorial's instruction line separates the Menu bar option from the command with a comma. Notice also that the word "CHOOSE" is always used for menu commands. For example, the command for quitting Windows is shown as:

CHOOSE: File, Exit

This instruction tells you to choose the File option on the Menu bar and then to choose the Exit command from the File pull-down menu. The actual steps for choosing a menu command are discussed later in this guide.

KEYSTROKES AND KEYSTROKE COMBINATIONS

When two keys must be pressed together, the tutorial's instruction line shows the keys joined with a plus (+) sign. For example, you can execute a Copy command in Windows by holding down CTRL and then pressing the letter C.

The instruction for this type of keystroke combination follows:

PRESS: CTRL +C

COMMAND INSTRUCTIONS

This guide indicates with a special typeface and color the data that you are required to type in yourself. For example:

TYPE: Income Statement

When you are required to enter unique information, such as the current date or your name, the instruction appears in italic. The following instruction directs you to type your name in place of the actual words: "your name."

TYPE: *your name*

ACKNOWLEDGMENTS

This series of learning guides is the direct result of the teamwork and heart of many people. We sincerely thank the reviewers, instructors, and students who have shared their comments and suggestions with us over the past few years. We do read them! With this valuable feedback, our guides have evolved into the product you see before you. We also appreciate the efforts of the instructors and students at Okanagan University College who classroom tested our guides to ensure accuracy, relevancy, and completeness.

We also give many thanks to Garrett Glanz, Kristin Hepburn and Tom Casson from Irwin for their skillful management of this text. In fact, special recognition goes to all of the individuals mentioned in the credits at the beginning of this guide. And finally, to the many others who weren't directly involved in this project but who have stood by us the whole way, we appreciate your encouragement and support.

WRITE TO US

We welcome your response to this book, for we are trying to make it as useful a learning tool as possible. Write to us in care of Garrett Glanz, Richard D. Irwin, 1333 Burr Ridge Parkway, Burr Ridge, IL 60521. Thank you.

Sarah E. Hutchinson
sclifford@mindspring.com

Glen J. Coulthard
current@junction.net

Contents

SESSION 1
Fundamentals

SESSION 2
Working with Spreadsheets

SESSION 3
Increasing Your Productivity

SESSION 4
Managing a Workbook

SESSION 5
Creating Charts

APPENDIX
Toolbar Summary 208

INDEX   219

Microsoft Excel 97 for Windows

Fundamentals

SESSION OUTLINE

INTRODUCTION

Be thankful for the electronic spreadsheet, one of the most commonly used business software tools! Just a few years ago, a spreadsheet existed only in paper form and its 7,500 or so tiny spaces had to be filled in by hand. Many a manager, accountant, and business planner wore down several pencils (and erasers) revising this paper instrument. Today, electronic spreadsheets such as Microsoft Excel enable you to insert and change numbers with ease. This session shows you how to begin using this valuable tool.

THE BONDABLE GROUP

Started in the spring of 1996, The Bondable Group is composed of three friends who formed a partnership after graduating together with degrees in business administration. The group offers investment advice to individuals wanting to expand their portfolios into the bond and stock markets. Jennifer Spalding is the undisputed leader of the group, having graduated with a Finance major. Although they don't possess the same financial skills as their associate, Pancho Valdez and Mackenzie Sherwood are definitely the sales backbone. Both Pancho and Mackenzie are marketing majors with excellent communication and presentation skills.

The group agreed recently to purchase notebook computers for Pancho and Mackenzie, since most of their work entails visiting clients' homes in the evening. To prepare for the arrival of their new computers, Jennifer suggested that the two men develop a simple financial planning tool using Microsoft Excel 97 for Windows. With an electronic spreadsheet, Pancho and Mackenzie could demonstrate the outcomes of different investment strategies to their clients. Unfortunately, neither of the two has ever used Microsoft Excel and they don't know the first thing about creating an electronic spreadsheet.

In this session, you and our two friends are led step-by-step through one of the most popular spreadsheet programs available, Microsoft Excel. You will initially concentrate on spreadsheet fundamentals like entering text, numbers, dates, and formulas. By the end of the session, you will know how to effectively design, create, and save a spreadsheet. You will also know how to retrieve advice from Excel's Help system and how to use the Undo command for reversing data entry and editing mistakes.

INTRODUCING MICROSOFT OFFICE 97

Microsoft Office for Windows combines the most popular and exciting software programs available into a single suite of applications. In the Standard edition, Office 97 includes Microsoft Word, Microsoft Excel, Microsoft PowerPoint, and the all-new Microsoft Outlook, an integrated desktop information tool that manages your e-mail, calendar, contacts, to do lists, journal, and Office documents. In the Professional edition, you also get Microsoft Access, a relational database management system that works directly with the other Office applications. Office 97 also provides shared applications (sometimes called "server applications") that let you create and insert clip art, organizational charts, and mathematical equations into your word processing documents, electronic spreadsheets, and presentations.

All software products are born with specific design goals. For Office 97, Microsoft concentrated on optimizing Office for use in Windows' 32-bit environments, including Windows 95 and Windows NT. In addition to enjoying performance improvements, Office 97 offers integration with the Internet and World Wide Web (WWW) and benefits from many usability enhancements. For example, Office 97 lets you do the following:

- name your documents using up to 250 characters,
- place shortcuts to documents directly on the Windows desktop,
- use the Windows Briefcase program to compare and synchronize files,
- multitask applications with single-click functionality from the taskbar,
- save documents in the web's Hypertext Markup Language (HTML) format, and
- post documents to your internal intranet or to the Web.

All of Office's primary applications use Intellisense technology, helping users to focus on their work and not on their software. Examples of Intellisense are automatic spelling and grammar checking and wizards that lead you through performing basic and complex tasks. Office 97 offers additional Help features, including an animated character called the Office Assistant who provides helpful tips and suggestions as you work.

INTEGRATION FEATURES

Many would say that the essence of Office 97 is its ability to share data among the suite of applications. For example, you can place an Excel chart in a report that you write using Word, a Word document in a presentation created in Power-Point, an Access database in an Excel worksheet, and so on. You can also create objects using shared applications—such as Microsoft Chart, Microsoft Equation Editor, or Microsoft Organization Chart—and insert them in your documents without ever leaving the current Office application.

Further blurring the line between applications, Microsoft Binder allows you to assemble, print, and distribute collections of varied documents. Like working with a real three-ring binder, you can insert documents that you create in Word, Excel, and PowerPoint into a single binder document and withdraw them. Then, you can print the contents of the binder complete with consistent headers and footers and with consecutive page numbering. A binder document also provides an easy way to transfer information from one computer to another, since all the documents are stored in a single file.

INTERNET FEATURES

One of the most exciting innovations in Office 97 is its ability to take advantage of the World Wide Web and the Internet. For those of you new to the online world, the **Internet** is a vast collection of computer networks that spans the entire planet, made up of many smaller networks connected by standard telephone lines, fiber optics, and satellites. More than just an electronic repository for information, the Internet is a *virtual community* with its own culture and tradition. The term **Intranet** refers to a private and usually secure local or wide area network that uses Internet technologies to share information within an organization. To access the Internet, you need a network or modem connection that links your computer to an account on the university's network or to an independent Internet Service Provider (ISP).

Once you are connected to the Internet, you can use web browser software, such as Microsoft Internet Explorer or Netscape Navigator, to access the **World Wide Web (WWW).** The WWW provides a visual interface for the Internet and lets you search for information by simply clicking on highlighted words and images, know as **hyperlinks.** When you click a link, you are telling your computer's web browser to retrieve a page from a web site and display it on your screen. Each web page on the Internet has a unique location or address specified by its *Uniform Resource Locator* or URL. One example of a URL is: http://www.microsoft.com. For more information on the Internet and World Wide Web, visit your local bookstore, campus computing center, or computer users group.

Microsoft Office 97 provides a consistent set of tools for publishing documents, spreadsheets, presentations, and databases to the web and for accessing help information directly from Microsoft's corporate web site. Specifically, each Office application includes a Web toolbar that lets you quickly open, search, and browse through any document on your local computer, corporate or university Intranet, and the Internet. Furthermore, you can create your own hyperlinks and share your documents with the entire world after publishing it to a web server. As you proceed through this manual, look for the Internet integration features found in the In Addition boxes.

WORKING WITH MICROSOFT EXCEL

For years, people used calculators and rolls of paper to perform numerical calculations. With the advancements in computers over the past decade, these manual tools are somewhat obsolete. Accountants, statisticians, and business people now use electronic spreadsheets to analyze their financial and statistical data more accurately and more quickly. However, spreadsheets are much more than glorified calculators; often they are the primary financial tool for a small business.

An electronic spreadsheet is similar to a manual worksheet or an accountant's ledger (Figure 1.1.) With a manual worksheet, you write descriptive labels down the first column or along the top row. Using Microsoft Excel 97, you create a worksheet in much the same way as before, by entering information into cells, or intersections of columns and rows. You can also create formulas, apply formatting options, and save the worksheet to a disk file. An Excel spreadsheet is called a *workbook* and may contain several independent or integrated worksheets. The number of worksheets you can create and store in a workbook is limited only by the memory within your computer.

FIGURE 1.1			

PARTIAL VIEW OF AN
ACCOUNTANT'S MANUAL
WORKSHEET

Date	Item	Debit	Credit
19-Jun-96	Sold photocopy machine		
	Dr. Cash in Bank	750.00	
	Cr. Equipment		750.00
25-Jun-96	Sold 20 units of inventory		
	Dr. Accounts Receivable	1000.00	

Some advantages of using Excel over manual worksheets are these:

- *An Excel worksheet is much larger than a manual worksheet.* While a manual worksheet is limited by paper size, each Excel worksheet contains 256 columns and 65,536 rows. Furthermore, you can enter up to 32,000 characters in a single cell!

- *Perform mathematical, statistical, and financial calculations quickly and accurately.* In addition to entering text and numbers into worksheet cells, you can calculate **formulas,** such as 200+350. A formula may consist solely of numbers or it may refer to the contents of other cells.

- *Perform what-if scenarios for planning and budgeting.* Changing a single number in a manual worksheet can mean hours of extra work in recalculating figures. Changing a number in an Excel worksheet, however, instantaneously produces a ripple effect of recalculations for all formulas dependent upon that cell's value. For example, you can quickly test scenarios like "What if my annual sales were only 5,000 units? How would that affect my net income?"

- *Build worksheets quickly using Excel's wizards and templates.* Wizards simplify the process of entering functions, analyzing your data, and working with databases, while templates provide prebuilt workbook solutions.

- *Create charts that visually represent worksheet data.* In addition to the usual line, bar, and pie charts, you can create geographical maps and pinpoint demographics (such as age, income, and education statistics) or analyze regional trends from worksheet information.

PLANNING YOUR WORKSHEET

Would you start building a house or an office building before receiving an architect's plans? Hopefully not! Even experienced builders rely heavily on the planning phase before breaking new ground. Likewise, you wouldn't want to create a spreadsheet without first having a clear objective. This section provides some basic guidelines to help you plan and develop your electronic spreadsheets.

Use the following steps to create a workbook using Excel:

1. Establish your objectives for creating a worksheet.
2. Design the worksheet based on your output or reporting requirements.
3. Construct the worksheet by entering data and creating formulas.
4. Manually test and evaluate the worksheet.
5. Modify, if necessary, and enhance the worksheet.
6. Document the worksheet for other users.

If you are new to electronic spreadsheets, you may not understand the full importance of the above discussion. Don't despair—you'll definitely understand the utility of these steps by the end of this guide. Now, let's begin our journey through Microsoft Excel.

STARTING EXCEL

This session assumes that you are working on a computer with Windows 95 (or Microsoft Windows NT 4.0) and Microsoft Excel 97 loaded on the hard disk drive. Before you load Windows and Excel, let's look at how to use the mouse and keyboard.

USING THE MOUSE AND KEYBOARD

Microsoft Excel 97 for Windows is a complex yet easy-to-learn program. As you proceed through this guide, you will find that there are often three methods for performing the same command or procedure in Excel:

- Menu   Select a command or procedure from the Menu bar.
- Mouse   Point to and click a toolbar button.
- Keyboard   Press a keyboard shortcut (usually CTRL + *letter*).

Although this guide concentrates on the quickest methods, we recommend that you try the others and decide which you prefer. *Don't memorize all of the information in this guide! Be selective and find your favorite methods.*

Although you may use Excel with only a keyboard, much of the program's basic design relies on using a mouse. Regardless of whether your mouse has two or three buttons, you will use the left or primary mouse button for selecting workbook items and menu commands and the right or secondary mouse button for displaying shortcut menus.

The most common mouse actions used in Excel are these:

- Point

  Slide the mouse on your desk to position the tip of the mouse pointer over the desired object on the screen.

- Click

  Press down and release the left mouse button quickly. Clicking is used to select a cell or an object in the worksheet and to choose menu commands.

- Right-Click

  Press down and release the right mouse button. Right-clicking the mouse pointer on a cell or an object displays a context-sensitive shortcut menu.

- Double-Click

  Press down and release the mouse button twice in rapid succession. Double-clicking is used to perform in-cell editing and to modify the worksheet tab names in a workbook.

- Drag

  Press down and hold the mouse button as you move the mouse pointer across the screen. When the mouse pointer reaches the desired location, release the mouse button. Dragging is used to select a group of cells and to copy or move data.

You may notice that the mouse pointer changes shape as you move it over different parts of the screen. Each mouse pointer shape has its own purpose and may provide you with important information. There are five primary mouse shapes that appear in Excel:

(arrow icon)	arrow	Used to choose menu commands and toolbars buttons.
(cross icon)	cross	Used to select cells in a worksheet.
(hourglass icon)	hourglass	Informs you that Excel is occupied and requests that you wait.
(I-beam icon)	I-beam	Used to modify and edit text.
(hand icon)	hand	Used to select hyperlinks in the worksheet and in the Help system.

Aside from being the primary input device for creating a worksheet, the keyboard offers shortcut methods for performing commands and procedures. For example, several menu commands have shortcut key combinations listed to the right of the command in the pull-down menu. Therefore, you can perform a command by simply pressing the shortcut keys rather than accessing the Menu bar. Many of these shortcut key combinations are available throughout Windows applications.

LOADING WINDOWS

Because Windows is an operating system, it is loaded automatically into the computer's memory when you turn on the computer. If you haven't already turned your computer on, perform the following steps.

Perform the following steps . . .

1. Turn on the power switches to the computer and monitor. After a few seconds, the Windows desktop will appear (Figure 1.2). (*Note:* The desktop interface on y computer may look different from Figure 1.2.)

2. If a Welcome to Windows dialog box appears, do the following:
   CLICK: Close button (☒) in the top corner of the dialog box window

FIGURE 1.2

THE WINDOWS DESKTOP

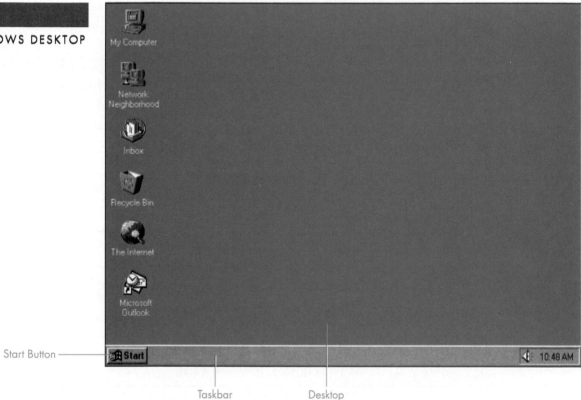

Start Button

Taskbar   Desktop

QUICK REFERENCE	Turn on your computer to automatically load Microsoft Windows 95 (or
Loading Windows	Microsoft Windows NT 4.0).

LOADING MICROSOFT EXCEL 97

Using the Start button ([Start]), you can readily access your favorite programs, documents, and system management tools. In this section, you load Microsoft Excel 97 and display a new workbook.

Perform the following steps . . .

1. Position the mouse pointer over top of the Start button ([Start]) and then click the left mouse button once. The Start pop-up menu appears.

2. Point to the Programs command using the mouse. Notice that you do not need to click the left mouse button to display the list of programs in the fly-out or cascading menu.

3. Move the mouse pointer horizontally to the right until it highlights an option in the Programs menu. You can now move the mouse pointer up and down the Programs menu. Notice that you still haven't clicked the left mouse button.

4. Point to the Microsoft Excel menu item and then click the left mouse button once to execute the command. After a few seconds, the Microsoft Excel screen appears.

5. If the Office Assistant window (shown at the right) appears:
   CLICK: Close button ([X]) in its top right-hand corner

The Windows taskbar is usually located on the bottom of your screen below the Status bar. Each application that you are currently working with is represented by a button on the taskbar. Switching between open applications on your desktop is as easy as clicking the appropriate taskbar button, like switching channels on a television set. At this point, you should see a button for Microsoft Excel on the taskbar.

QUICK REFERENCE Loading Microsoft Excel 97	1. **CLICK: Start button ([Start])** 2. **CHOOSE: Programs, Microsoft Excel**

THE GUIDED TOUR

Software programs designed for Microsoft Windows have many similarities in screen design and layout. Each program operates in its own application window, while the spreadsheets, letters, and presentations you create appear in separate document windows. This section describes the components found in the Excel application and document windows.

APPLICATION WINDOW

When you first load Excel, the screen displays the **application window** and a maximized **document window.** The application window (Figure 1.3) contains the Title bar, Menu bar, Standard toolbar, Formatting toolbar, Formula bar and Name box, and Status bar. You create new worksheets or open existing workbooks in the document area. In Figure 1.3, the document area is covered entirely by a maximized document window.

FIGURE 1.3

MICROSOFT EXCEL'S APPLICATION WINDOW

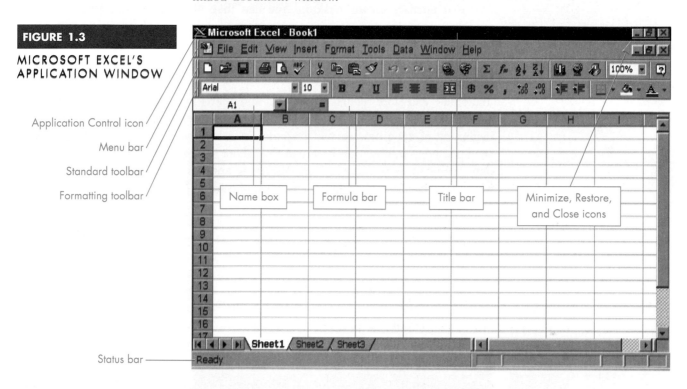

The primary components of the application window are:

Application Control icon (⊠)	Used to identify the application. You can double-click the Control icon to close Microsoft Excel.
Minimize (▭) and Maximize (❑), Restore (⬒), and Close (⊠) icons	Located in the top right-hand corner, these icons control the display of the application window using the mouse. (*Note:* Since the window is already maximized, the Maximize icon does not appear in Figure 1.3.)
Title bar	The Title bar contains the name of the program and/or workbook file. You can also move a window that is not maximized by dragging its Title bar.
Menu bar	Contains the Excel menu commands.
Standard toolbar	Displays buttons for accessing file management and editing commands using a mouse.
Formatting toolbar	Displays buttons for accessing character and cell formatting commands using the mouse.

Formula bar	Appears below the toolbars and includes the Name box and Edit Formula button ().
Status bar	Located at the bottom of the application window, the Status bar displays the current status or mode and other helpful information.

Although the application window is usually maximized, you can reduce it to a window that appears on the desktop. You can then size, move, and manipulate the application window to customize your work environment in Windows. In this guide, we assume that the Excel application window is always maximized.

DOCUMENT WINDOW

You create and store related worksheets and charts in a special file called a **workbook.** You can think of an Excel workbook as a three-ring binder with tabs at the beginning of each new section or topic. In a workbook, you can add and delete sections, copy information from one worksheet section to another, and summarize data in the entire workbook. Each workbook appears in its own document window which can be minimized to an icon, maximized to fill the entire document area, or displayed as a window.

Each new workbook contains three blank worksheets labeled Sheet1, Sheet2, and Sheet3. Similar to a large piece of ledger paper, a worksheet (Figure 1.4) is divided into vertical columns and horizontal rows. The rows are numbered and the columns are labeled from A to Z, then AA to AZ, and so on to column IV. The intersection of a column and a row is called a **cell.** Each cell is given a **cell address,** like a post office box number, consisting of its column letter followed by its row number (for example, B4 or FX400).

FIGURE 1.4

A DOCUMENT WINDOW

Document Control Icon

Cell

Scroll box

Active
Sheet tab

Vertical
Scroll bar

Tab Scrolling
Arrows

Inactive Sheet tab

Tab Split box

Scroll box

Horizontal
Scroll bar

A document window consists of the following parts:

Document Control icon (▣)	Used to size and position the window using the keyboard. You can double-click the Control icon to close the document window.
Scroll bars	Placed at the right and bottom borders of the document window, scroll bars facilitate moving around a worksheet using the mouse.
Sheet tabs	Sheet tabs identify the various pages or sections in a workbook. You click a tab to move to that worksheet or double-click a tab to change its name.
Tab Split box	Drag the tab split box to increase or decrease the space shared by the sheet tabs and the horizontal scroll bar.
Tab Scrolling arrows	Click the tab scrolling arrows to move quickly to the first sheet, previous sheet, next sheet, or last sheet in a workbook.

You should recognize some familiar components in the document window that appear in all windows. For example, the Minimize, Maximize, and Close buttons also appear in the top right-hand corner of the document window. To restore a maximized document to a window, you click the Restore button (▣). To maximize a document window, you click the Maximize button (▣). Before proceeding, make sure that the document window is maximized and that you can identify the window icons for both the application and the document window (as shown below):

Application window icons ──────

Document window icons ──────

You can display several workbooks concurrently within the application window. For example, you may want to view data from several departments on the screen at the same time. Assuming that the data is divided into separate workbooks, you can open each file in its own document window. Another method for accomplishing this type of summary perspective is to create and store multiple worksheets in a single workbook file. Similar to peeling off pages from a notepad, you enter each department's data on its own worksheet and then consolidate the data in a separate summary worksheet. In Session 4, you learn how to work with multiple workbook files and multiple-sheet workbooks.

MENU BAR

Excel commands are grouped together on the Menu bar, as shown in the example provided below.

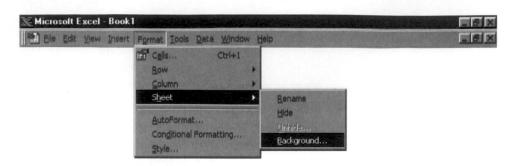

Commands in this guide are written in the following form:

CHOOSE: Format, Sheet, Background

where Format is the Menu bar option, Sheet is the command on the pull-down menu, and Background is the command on the fly-out menu. To execute a command, click once on the Menu bar option and then click once on the desired menu commands. Commands that are not available for selection appear dimmed. Commands that are followed by an ellipsis (Background..., for example) require further information to be collected in a dialog box.

In the following exercise, you practice accessing the Menu bar.

Perform the following steps . . .

1. To choose the Help command, position the tip of the mouse pointer on the word Help in the Menu bar and click the left mouse button once. A pull-down menu appears below the Help option.

2. To see the pull-down menus associated with other menu options, drag the mouse pointer slowly to the left over the additional options on the Menu bar. (*Note:* You need not hold down the left mouse button as you move the mouse pointer.)

3. To leave the Menu bar without making a command selection, position the pointer in a blank area of the Title bar and click once. On your own, try clicking the Help menu item repeatedly and notice how the pull-down menu appears and disappears.

4. To display the pull-down menu for the File option:
   CHOOSE: File
   This instruction tells you to click the left mouse button once with the pointer on the File option in the Menu bar. (*Note:* All menu commands that you execute in this guide begin with the word "CHOOSE.")

5. To leave the Menu bar without making a selection:
   CLICK: an empty area on the Excel Title bar

SHORTCUT MENUS

Excel provides context-sensitive shortcut menus for quick access to menu commands. Rather than searching for commands in the Menu bar, you position the mouse pointer on an object, such as a cell or toolbar, and click the right mouse button. A pop-up menu appears with the most commonly selected commands for the object.

Let's now practice accessing a shortcut menu.

Perform the following steps . . .

1. To display a shortcut menu, position the mouse pointer over any cell in the worksheet and click the right mouse button. The shortcut menu at the right should appear.

2. To remove the shortcut menu from the screen:
PRESS: ESC
The shortcut menu disappears.

QUICK REFERENCE
Using Shortcut Menus

1. **Position the mouse pointer over an object.**

2. **CLICK: shortcut or right mouse button to display a pop-up menu**

3. **CHOOSE: a command from the menu, or**
PRESS: ESC **to remove the menu**

TOOLBARS

In the application window, you will see the Standard and Formatting toolbars appear below the Menu bar. Excel provides several toolbars and hundreds of buttons for quick and easy mouse access to its more popular features. Don't worry about memorizing the button names appearing in the following figures, you can simply point to any toolbar button using the mouse and pause until a ToolTip label appears with the button's name.

The Standard toolbar (Figure 1.5) provides access to file management and editing commands, in addition to special features like the Office Assistant and the ChartWizard:

FIGURE 1.5

STANDARD TOOLBAR

The Formatting toolbar (Figure 1.6) lets you access character and cell formatting commands:

FORMATTING TOOLBAR

To display additional toolbars, you point to a visible toolbar and click the right mouse button to display a shortcut menu. You can show and hide toolbars by choosing their names in the resulting pop-up menu. If a toolbar is currently being displayed, a check mark appears beside its name.

You will now practice displaying and hiding toolbars.

Perform the following steps . . .

1. Position the mouse pointer over any button on the Standard toolbar.

2. To display the Drawing toolbar:
   CLICK: right mouse button to display the shortcut menu
   CHOOSE: Drawing

3. To remove the toolbar:
   RIGHT-CLICK: Drawing toolbar
   This instruction tells you to position the mouse pointer over the Drawing toolbar and click the right mouse button.

4. CHOOSE: Drawing
   The Drawing toolbar disappears from the application window.

IN ADDITION MOVING TOOLBARS

- To undock a toolbar, position the mouse pointer over the Move bar (▐) appearing at the left of the docked toolbar. Click the left mouse button and drag the toolbar into the application window. The toolbar turns into a floating window, complete with a Title bar and Close box.

- To redock a floating toolbar, position the mouse pointer over its Title bar and drag it toward one of the borders. Release the mouse button when the toolbar snaps into place.

DIALOG BOX

A dialog box is a common mechanism in Windows applications for collecting information before processing a command (Figure 1.7). In a dialog box, you indicate the options you want to use and then click the OK command button when you're finished. Dialog boxes are also used to display messages or to ask for confirmation of commands.

FIGURE 1.7

A DIALOG BOX

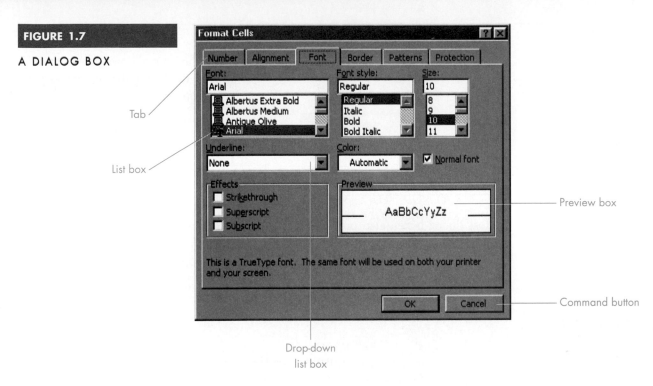

A dialog box uses several types of controls or components for collecting information. We describe the most common components in Table 1.1.

TABLE 1.1

Dialog Box Components

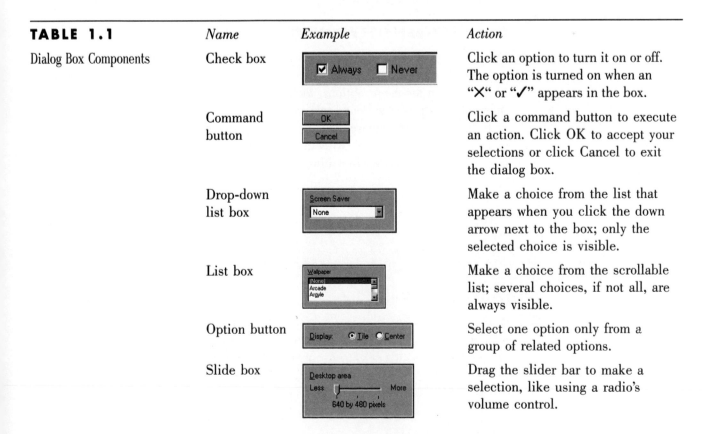

Name	Example	Action
Check box	☑ Always ☐ Never	Click an option to turn it on or off. The option is turned on when an "✗" or "✓" appears in the box.
Command button	OK / Cancel	Click a command button to execute an action. Click OK to accept your selections or click Cancel to exit the dialog box.
Drop-down list box	Screen Saver / None	Make a choice from the list that appears when you click the down arrow next to the box; only the selected choice is visible.
List box	Wallpaper / [None] / Arcade / Argyle	Make a choice from the scrollable list; several choices, if not all, are always visible.
Option button	Display: ⦿ Tile ◯ Center	Select one option only from a group of related options.
Slide box	Desktop area / Less — More / 640 by 480 pixels	Drag the slider bar to make a selection, like using a radio's volume control.

TABLE 1.1	*Name*	*Example*	*Action*
Continued	Spin box	Wait: 6 minutes	Click the up and down arrows to the right of the box until the number you want appears.
	Tab	Contents | Index | Find	Click a named tab to access other pages in the dialog box.
	Text box	File name: untitled	Click inside the text box and then type the desired information.

Most dialog boxes also provide a question mark icon (?) near the right side of the Title bar. If you have a question about an item in the dialog box, click the question mark and then click the item to display a pop-up help window. To remove the help window, click on it once.

GETTING HELP

Excel provides several **context-sensitive help** features and a comprehensive library of online documentation. Like many developers trying to minimize the retail price of software and maximize profits, Microsoft has stopped shipping volumes of print-based documentation in favor of on-line and web-based Help options. This section describes Excel's help features and how to find more detailed information.

CONTEXT-SENSITIVE HELP

Context-sensitive help refers to a program's ability to present helpful information reflecting your current position in the program. In Excel, you can access context-sensitive help for menu options, toolbar buttons, and dialog box items. The help information is presented concisely in a small pop-up window that you can remove with the click of the mouse. This type of help lets you access information quickly and then continue working without interruption. Table 1.2 describes some methods for accessing context-sensitive help while working in Excel.

TABLE 1.2	*To display . . .*	*Do this . . .*
Displaying Context-Sensitive Help Information	A description of a dialog box item	Click the question mark button (?) in a dialog box's Title bar and then click an item in the dialog box. A helpful description of the item appears in a pop-up window. Alternatively, you can often right-click a dialog box item and then chose the What's This? command from the shortcut menu.
	A description of a menu command	Choose Help, What's This? command and then choose a command using the question mark mouse pointer. Rather than executing the command, a helpful description of the command appears in a pop-up window.
	A description of a toolbar button	Point to a toolbar button to display its ToolTip label. You can also choose the Help, What's This? command and then click a toolbar button to display more detailed help information.

In the following exercise, you will access context-sensitive help.

Perform the following steps . . .

1. To display help for the File, New command, you must first activate the question mark mouse pointer. Do the following:
   CHOOSE: Help, What's This?
   Your mouse pointer should now appear with an attached question mark. (*Note:* You can also press **SHIFT** + **F1** to activate this pointer.)

2. Using the question mark mouse pointer (and not the keyboard):
   CHOOSE: File, New
   Rather than executing the command, Excel provides a description of the command in a pop-up window.

3. After reading the description, close the window by clicking on it once.

4. To display a ToolTip for a toolbar button, position the mouse pointer over the AutoSum button (**Σ**) on the Standard toolbar. After a second or two, a ToolTip will appear showing the button's name.

5. To display additional information for the AutoSum button:
   PRESS: **SHIFT** + **F1**
   This command tells you to hold down the **SHIFT** key and then tap the **F1** key. Then, release the **SHIFT** key.

6. CLICK: AutoSum button (Σ)
The following pop-up window appears:

> **AutoSum**
>
> In Microsoft Excel, adds numbers automatically with the SUM function. Microsoft Excel suggests the range of cells to be added. If the suggested range is incorrect, drag through the range you want, and then press ENTER.
>
> In Word, inserts an = (Formula) field that calculates and displays the sum of the values in table cells above or to the left of the cell containing the insertion point.

7. CLICK: the pop-up window once to remove it

QUICK REFERENCE	
QUICK REFERENCE Displaying Context-Sensitive Help	**1.** **CHOOSE: Help, What's This?** **2.** **Using the question mark mouse pointer, select the desired item for which you want to display a help pop-up window.**

OFFICE ASSISTANT

The Office Assistant is your personal and customizable computer guru. When you need to accomplish a particular task, you call up the Assistant by clicking the Office Assistant button (⊡) on the Standard toolbar. To conduct a search of the entire Help system, you simply type an English phrase in the form of a question. The Assistant analyzes your request and provides a resource list of suggested topics. Furthermore, the Assistant watches your keystrokes and mouse clicks as you work and can offer suggestions and shortcuts to make you more productive and efficient.

Let's put your Assistant to work.

Perform the following steps . . .

1. To display the Office Assistant:
CLICK: Office Assistant button (⊡)
The Office Assistant and its associated tip window appear as shown in Figure 1.8. Notice that the text in the tip window is selected, ready for you to begin typing your question.

FIGURE 1.8

OFFICE ASSISTANT AND
TIP WINDOW

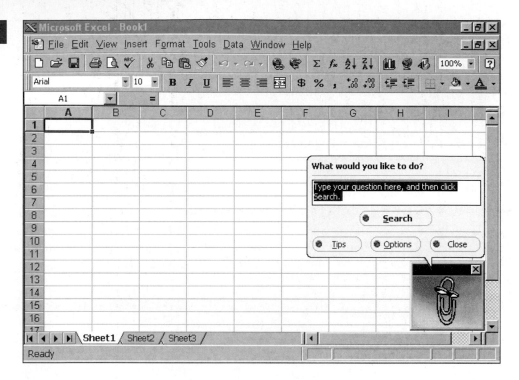

2. Type your request just as you would ask the question out loud. For this example, let's find out what a "function" is in an Excel worksheet.
   TYPE: **What is a function?**
   CLICK: Search button
   (*Note*: You need not be concerned about typing your questions using perfect grammar or punctuation. However, spelling does count!)

3. A tip window appears with several topics displayed. You must now refine your search by selecting one of these topics. Do the following:
   CLICK: About using functions to calculate values
   A Help Topics window appears with the requested information. You will learn more about working with this window in the next section.

4. CLICK: Close button ([**X**]) on the Help Topics window
   CLICK: Close button ([**X**]) on the Office Assistant window

Occasionally an illuminated light bulb will appear in the Office Assistant window. This light bulb informs you that the Assistant wants to share a new tip or suggestion with you. To view the tip, click the light bulb in the Office Assistant window. To close the window, click its Close button.

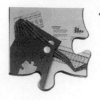

IN ADDITION CUSTOMIZING THE OFFICE ASSISTANT

- To customize your Assistant's appearance:
RIGHT-CLICK: Office Assistant window
CHOOSE: Choose Assistant from the pop-up menu

- To customize your Assistant's behavior:
RIGHT-CLICK: Office Assistant window
CHOOSE: Options from the pop-up menu

HELP TOPICS WINDOW

For a complete topical listing of Excel's Help system, choose the Contents and Index command from the Help menu. This command displays the Help Topics window, as shown in Figure 1.9. You can think of the Help Topics window as the front door to Excel's vast help resources.

FIGURE 1.9

HELP TOPICS WINDOW: *CONTENTS* TAB

The Help Topics window provides three different tools, each on its own tab, to help you find the information you need quickly and easily. You point to and click a tab using the mouse to make the tab active in the window. Refer to the following tab descriptions to determine which tool you should use when requiring assistance:

- *Contents* tab — Displays a list of help topics organized as a hierarchy of books and pages. This tab is your Table of Contents for the entire Help system. Notice in Figure 1.9 that there are three different types of icons displayed:

  represents a help category; double-click a book icon to view the books and topics it contains represents an open category that is currently displaying its contents; double-click an open book icon to close (or collapse) the book

? represents a help topic; double-click a topic icon to display a help window

- *Index* tab

Displays an alphabetical list of keywords and phrases, similar to a traditional book index. To search for a topic using this tab, type a word (or even a few letters) into the text box which, in turn, makes the list box scroll to the first matching entry in the index. Then, double-click the desired entry to display the help topic. If a keyword has more than one associated topic, a Topics Found window appears and you can select a further topic to narrow your search.

- *Find* tab

Provides the ability to conduct a full-text search of the Help system for finding a particular word or phrase. Although similar to the *Index* tab, this tab differs in its ability to look past indexed keywords and search the help text itself.

When you double-click a help topic, it is displayed in a *secondary* window. You may find that secondary windows include some unfamiliar buttons, like ≫ and ↰, embedded in the help text. The ≫ symbol, which we'll called the Chiclet button, represents a "See Also" link that you can click to move to a related topic. The Show Me symbol (↰) actually initiates the command you're interested in. You may also notice that some words or phrases in the help window have a dotted underline. If you click such a word or phrase, a definition pop-up window appears.

You will now access the Help Topics window.

Perform the following steps . . .

1. To display the Help Topics window:
   CHOOSE: Help, Contents and Index

2. CLICK: *Contents* tab
   Your screen should now appear similar to Figure 1.9, except that your book categories will appear collapsed. (*Note*: The Help Topics window remembers the tab that was selected when it was last closed. It will automatically return to this tab the next time you access Help.)

3. To display the contents of a book:
   DOUBLE-CLICK: "◆ Entering Data and Selecting Cells" book
   (*Note*: You can double-click the book icon (◆) or the book's title. If you find it difficult to double-click using the mouse, you can also select or highlight the book by clicking it once and then click the Open command button.) This particular book contains two additional categories.

4. To further clarify the search:
   DOUBLE-CLICK: "📕 Entering Data" book
   Notice that this book contains multiple topics.

5. To display a help topic:
   DOUBLE-CLICK: "❓ Entering data in worksheet cells" topic
   The Help Topics window is removed from view and a secondary window
   appears with the topic information.

6. To further refine your search:
   CLICK: "⟫ Enter numbers, text, a date, or a time"
   Notice that the mouse pointer changed to a hand.

7. To print the help topic that appears:
   CLICK: Options command button at the top of the window
   CHOOSE: Print Topic
   (*Note*: You can also print help information directly from the *Contents* tab. If
   you select a book and then click the Print command button, the entire
   book, including the additional book categories that may be contained within
   the book, is sent to the printer.)

8. In the Print dialog box that appears:

   • CLICK: OK command button to print the topic, or

   • CLICK: Cancel command button if you do not have a printer

   Whatever your selection, you are returned to the secondary window. (*Note:*
   If you selected to print the topic and your computer does not have a printer
   connected, you may be returned to Excel with an error message. In this
   case, you can skip the next step.)

9. To close the help window and return to Excel:
   CLICK: Close button (❎)

QUICK REFERENCE	1. **To display the Help Topics window:**
Searching for Help Using the Help Topics Window	**CHOOSE: Help, Contents and Index**
	2. **CLICK: *Contents* tab to navigate a hierarchical Help system**
	CLICK: *Index* tab to search for a word or phrase in a keyword index
	CLICK: *Find* tab to conduct a full-text search of the Help system

If you are connected to the Internet, you can keep current on product and company news by visiting Microsoft's web site. You'll also find helpful productivity tips and online support for all the Office 97 products.

Free Stuff
Product News
Frequently Asked Questions
Online Support
Microsoft Office Home Page
Send Feedback...
Best of the Web
Search the Web...
Web Tutorial
Microsoft Home Page

To access this information:

1. Establish an Internet connection.

2. CHOOSE: Help, Microsoft on the Web

3. CHOOSE: *a menu option as shown at the right*

MOVING THE CELL POINTER

When you first open a new workbook, the **cell pointer** is positioned on cell A1 in Sheet1. For your convenience, Excel displays the current cell address in the Name box at the left-hand side of the Formula bar. In this section, you learn how to move the cell pointer around the worksheet using the mouse and keyboard. Although rudimentary, these skills are vital for efficiently creating and viewing worksheets.

Perform the following steps . . .

1. To move the cell pointer to cell G4 using the keyboard:
    PRESS: ➡ six times
        PRESS: ⬇ three times
    Notice that the cell address appears in the Name box and that the column and row headings are boldface.

2. To move to cell E12 using a mouse:
    CLICK: cell E12
    (*Hint*: Position the cross mouse pointer over cell E12 and click the left mouse button once.)

3. To move to cell E24 using the keyboard:
    PRESS: ⬇ 12 times
    You may notice that the first few rows scroll off the top of the screen.

4. To move to cell E124 using the keyboard, there is an easier method than pressing the ⬇ key 100 times. The PgUp and PgDn keys are used to move up and down a worksheet by as many rows as fit in the current document window. To move to cell E124, do the following:
    PRESS: PgDn until cell E124 is in view
        PRESS: ⬆ or ⬇ arrow keys to move to cell E124

5. To move back to cell E24 using the mouse:

CLICK: ▲ on the vertical scroll bar and hold down the left mouse button
CLICK: cell E24 when it appears after scrolling
(*Note:* You can also drag the scroll box on the vertical scroll bar.)

6. To move to cell AE24:
CLICK: ▶ on the horizontal scroll bar and hold down the left mouse button
CLICK: cell AE24 to move the cell pointer

7. To move back to cell E24:
DRAG: scroll box to the left on the horizontal scroll bar
Notice that a Scroll Tip appears showing the column letter as you drag the mouse. When you see "Column: E" in the Scroll Tip, stop dragging and proceed to Step 8.

8. CLICK: cell E24 to move the cell pointer

9. To move to the first cell (A1) in the worksheet using the keyboard:
PRESS: CTRL + HOME

10. To move the cell pointer in any direction until the cell contents change from empty to filled, filled to empty, or until a border is encountered, press CTRL with an arrow key. To move to column IV:
PRESS: CTRL + →

11. To move to row 65,536 (the last cell at the bottom of the worksheet):
PRESS: CTRL + ↓

12. You can also use the Name box to move directly to any cell in the worksheet. To move to cell AA100, for example:
CLICK: Name box with the I-beam mouse pointer
The cell address in the Name box will appear highlighted.

13. TYPE: **aa100**
PRESS: ENTER
You are taken immediately to cell AA100.

14. To move back to cell A1:
PRESS: CTRL + HOME

Now you're ready to start entering some information into the worksheet!

OVERVIEW OF DATA ENTRY

You create a worksheet by entering information into the individual cells. A worksheet can be as simple as a five-item household budget or as complex as an order-entry and invoicing application. The remainder of this session explores the basic building blocks for creating a worksheet from scratch, including entering, editing, and deleting cell information.

There are several types of information that may be entered into a worksheet cell: text, numbers, dates and times, formulas, and functions. To begin entering data, you must first move the cell pointer to the desired cell. Then, type the characters that you want to appear in the cell. And finally, you complete the entry by pressing **ENTER** or by clicking the mouse pointer on another cell.

To practice entering data, you will create the worksheet appearing in Figure 1.10 by the completion of this section.

FIGURE 1.10

SAMPLE WORKSHEET

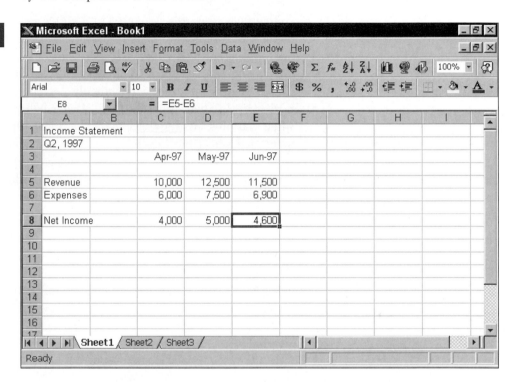

ENTERING TEXT

Text labels enhance the readability of a worksheet with headings, instructions, and descriptive information. Although a typical worksheet column is only eight or nine characters wide, a single cell in a worksheet can hold thousands of characters. With longer entries, the text spills over into the next cell, if it is empty. Later, you will learn how to emphasize important text using different fonts and alignment options.

Let's begin creating the worksheet.

Perform the following steps . . .

1. Move to cell A1. (*Hint*: **CTRL** + **HOME**)
For the remainder of this guide, you can use either the keyboard or mouse to move the cell pointer.

2. As you type the following text, watch the Formula bar. Enter the following heading for the worksheet:
TYPE: **Income Statement**
Notice that there is an ☒ and a ☐ to the left of the text in the Formula bar. Rather than pressing (ENTER) to accept the entry or (ESC) to cancel the entry, you can click the ☐ and ☒ symbols respectively.

3. To accept the entry and deposit it into the current cell:
PRESS: (ENTER)
Notice that the words do not fit in a single cell and must spill over into column B. This is acceptable as long as you do not want to place any information into cell B1. Otherwise, you would have to increase the width of column A. Session 2 discusses changing a column's width.
(*Note*: By default, Excel automatically moves the cell pointer down to the next row when you press (ENTER). If your cell pointer did not move to A2 when you pressed (ENTER), choose the Tools, Options command from the menu and select the *Edit* tab. From the resulting dialog box page, make sure that a "✓" appears in the *Move selection after Enter* check box and that "Down" is selected in the *Direction* drop-down list box. When finished, click the OK command button.)

4. Move the cell pointer into the following cells and type in the corresponding text. When you are finished typing a label, press (ENTER) or an arrow key. If you prefer using the mouse, you can click on the next cell after you have finished typing the label. If you make a mistake while typing, press the (BACKSPACE) key to delete the mistake and then type the correct information.

Enter the following text:

Move to Cell	TYPE:
A2	Q2, 1997
A5	Revenue
A6	Expenses
A8	Net Income

All the text data has now been entered into the worksheet.

ENTERING DATES

You enter dates as values in order to perform date arithmetic, such as calculating how many days have elapsed between two dates. Dates are typically entered into cells using one of the following formats: mm/dd/yy (for example, 12/31/96) or dd-mmm-yy (for example, 31-Dec-96). If you need to display monthly headings across the top of a column, you can enter a date as mmm-yy (for example, Dec-96).

You will now enter dates into the worksheet.

Perform the following steps . . .

1. Move to cell C3.

2. TYPE: **Apr-97**
   PRESS: ➡

3. Move the cell pointer into the following cells and type in the corresponding dates:

Move to Cell	*TYPE*
D3	**May-97**
E3	**Jun-97**

   With the cell pointer positioned on cell E3, you will notice that the Formula bar contains "6/1/1997" and not "Jun-97." This is one example of how the appearance of a cell can differ from its actual contents. You will encounter other examples later in this session.

All the dates have now been entered into the worksheet.

IN ADDITION ENTERING A DATE SERIES USING AUTOFILL

In Session 3, you learn how to use Excel's AutoFill feature for quickly entering a date series. This feature is especially useful for placing monthly headings at the top of your worksheet or listing consecutive dates (for example, 3/1/97, 3/2/97, and so on) down a column.

ENTERING NUMBERS

Numbers are entered into the worksheet for use in formulas and reports. Whereas text is initially left-aligned with the cell border, numbers and dates are right-aligned. When the cell pointer is positioned on a cell that contains a number, the raw form of the number usually appears in the Formula bar. In other words, the cell may read 8.50% in the worksheet but the value in the Formula bar reads .085. It is important to note that phone numbers, Social Security numbers, and zip codes are not considered numeric values, since they are never used in mathematical calculations.

Let's complete entering the static data into the worksheet.

Perform the following steps . . .

1. Move to cell C5.

2. TYPE: **10,000**
   PRESS: ➡
   (*Note*: When you start constructing formulas, you will enter values without any formatting (for example, 10000). In this step, you have entered a comma in the value to demonstrate an Excel formatting feature and to improve the readability of the worksheet.)

3. Move the cell pointer into the following cells and type in the corresponding numbers:

Move to Cell	TYPE
D5	**12,500**
E5	**11,500**

All the numeric data has now been entered into the worksheet. You are ready to enter formulas to calculate the remaining values.

QUICK REFERENCE
Entering Data

1. **Move the cell pointer to the desired cell location.**
2. **Type the information into the Formula bar. If you make a typing or spelling mistake, press the `BACKSPACE` key to erase the mistake.**
3. **To deposit the information into the cell, press `ENTER` or an arrow key, or click on a new cell using the mouse.**

ENTERING FORMULAS

A formula is a mathematical calculation that may contain numbers, cell references, and mathematical operators. The basic mathematical operators and rules of precedence apply to an Excel formula. These operators are similar to those found in most electronic spreadsheets (and high school algebra textbooks). For example, in the formula *(3+4)*5*, the *3+4* operation is performed before multiplying the sum by *5* because it appears in parentheses. Table 1.3 lists the common mathematical operators. As for the rules of precedence, Excel calculates what appears in parentheses first, multiplication and division operations (from left to right) second, and, lastly, addition and subtraction (again from left to right).

TABLE 1.3	Symbol	Description
Basic Mathematical Operators	( )	Parentheses
	*	Multiplication
	/	Division
	+	Addition
	—	Subtraction
	%	Percentage
	^	Exponentiation

You enter a formula into the worksheet by positioning the cell pointer where you want the result to appear and then typing an equal sign (=) to precede the expression. You can complete the expression either by typing or by pointing to the cell addresses. Newly introduced in Excel 97, you can use your own worksheet terminology (row and column headings) in constructing formulas rather than using cell references.

In the following exercise, you enter a formula that calculates Expenses as 60% of Revenue. Your first step is to move the cell pointer to where you want the result to appear and then enter the formula into the cell.

Perform the following steps . . .

1. Move to cell C6.

2. TYPE: =c5*60%
   PRESS: ➡
   In this expression, "c5" represents the cell address in the worksheet.

3. Move the cell pointer into the following cells and type in the corresponding formulas.

Move to Cell	TYPE
D6	=d5*60%
E6	=e5*60%

4. Let's create a second formula to subtract Expenses from Revenue, yielding Net Income. When constructing the formula, glance at the Formula bar to see the results of your mouse clicks and keystrokes.
   CLICK: cell C8

5. In this step, you build a formula by pointing:
TYPE: =
CLICK: cell C5
TYPE: –
CLICK: cell C6
CLICK: ▨ in the Formula bar
The answer 4,000 should now appear in the cell.

6. SELECT: cell D8

7. CLICK: Edit Formula button (▣) in the Formula bar
Notice that the equal sign is automatically entered in the Formula bar and that a display box called the Formula Palette appears.

8. If the Office Assistant appears asking to help create the formula, click the No option and then proceed with the following steps:
CLICK: cell D5 (12,500)
TYPE: –
CLICK: cell D6 (7,500)
Notice that the Formula Palette displays "Formula result = 5,000" as shown in Figure 1.11. This feature is useful for checking your work as you build a long formula.

FIGURE 1.11

EDIT FORMULA
DISPLAY BOX

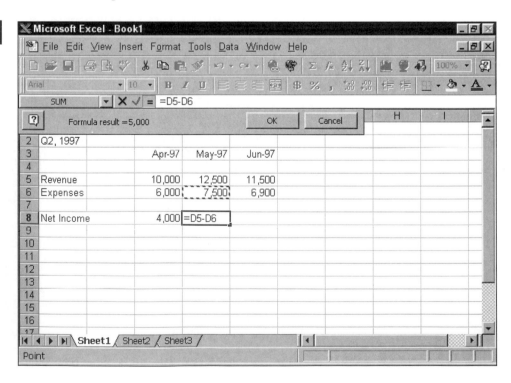

9. To complete the formula:
CLICK: OK command button in the display box

10. To demonstrate that Excel is paying attention, let's create a new *Natural Language Formula*:
CLICK: cell E8
TYPE: **=Revenue-Expenses**
PRESS: `ENTER`
Excel quickly reviews the worksheet, taking note of the column and row headings, and then calculates the formula and displays the result. Your worksheet should now appear similar to Figure 1.10.

QUICK REFERENCE	1. Select the cell to contain the formula.
Entering a Formula	2. TYPE: = (an equal sign)
	3. Enter the desired expression (for example, A4+B4) by typing or by pointing to the cells using the mouse.
	4. PRESS: `ENTER` or CLICK: ☐ in the Formula bar

EDITING A CELL

What if you type a label, a number, or a formula into a cell and then decide it needs to be changed? Novices and experts alike make data entry errors when creating a worksheet. Fortunately, Excel provides several options for editing information that has already been entered.

The primary methods for editing information are these:

- Before you press `ENTER` or click on another cell to deposit an entry, you can correct a typing or spelling mistake using `BACKSPACE`

- You can replace a cell's contents by typing over the original data. When you press `ENTER`, the new data overwrites the original contents.

- If a cell's entry is too long or complicated to retype, you can edit the entry by double-clicking the cell or by selecting the cell and pressing `F2`. A flashing vertical bar appears in the cell, advising you that the entry may be modified. After making the necessary changes, you press `ENTER` to overwrite the original cell or `ESC` to abort the modifications.

- You can also select a cell and then move the mouse pointer into the Formula bar area until it changes into an I-beam. At this point, click the left mouse button once to begin editing the contents of the Formula bar. Clicking ▣ performs the same function as pressing (**ENTER**) and clicking ☒ performs the same function as pressing (**ESC**).

Practice editing information in the worksheet.

Perform the following steps . . .

1. CLICK: cell A1

2. TYPE: **Profit/Loss Report**
   PRESS: (**ENTER**)

3. To modify the entry in cell A2 to read "Quarter 2" instead of "Q2":
   DOUBLE-CLICK: cell A2
   (*Note*: You can also press (**F2**) to enter Edit mode.)

4. Using the (◄) and (►) keys or the mouse, position the flashing vertical bar between the "Q" and the "2."

5. TYPE: **uarter**
   PRESS: Space bar
   PRESS: (**ENTER**)
   The cell entry should now read "Quarter 2, 1997."

6. DOUBLE-CLICK: cell C8
   Notice that the formula components in the cell are color-coded and that these colors correspond to the cell borders highlighted in the worksheet, as shown below. This feature, called *Range Finder*, is useful when you need to identify whether a calculation is drawing data from the correct cells.

	Apr-97	May-97	Jun-97
	10,000	12,500	11,500
	6,000	7,500	6,900
	=C5-C6	5,000	4,600

7. To cancel the Edit mode:
   CLICK: ☒ in the Formula bar

QUICK REFERENCE
Editing a Cell's Contents

1. **DOUBLE-CLICK: the cell that you want to edit (or PRESS: (F2))**

2. **Use the mouse and arrow keys to edit the entry.**

3. **PRESS: (ENTER) or CLICK: ▣**

ERASING A CELL

Excel allows you to quickly erase a single cell, a group of cells, or the entire worksheet with a few simple keystrokes. To erase a cell's contents, highlight the cell and press the (DELETE) key. If you would like to delete only the formatting of a cell, you choose Edit, Clear from the Menu bar to display further commands (listed in Table 1.4) on a cascading menu.

TABLE 1.4	*Command*	*Description*
Edit, Clear Commands	All	Removes the cell contents, formatting (for example, boldface and italic), and comments (reminders that are attached to a cell but do not appear when printed).
	Formats	Removes the cell formatting only, leaving the contents and attached cell comments intact.
	Contents	Removes the cell contents only, leaving the formatting and attached cell comments intact; same as (DELETE).
	Comments	Removes the cell comments only, leaving the cell contents and formatting intact.

In the next exercise, you practice erasing information from the worksheet.

Perform the following steps . . .

1. Move to cell A2.
2. PRESS: (DELETE) to remove the information from the cell
3. Move to cell A8.
4. CHOOSE: Edit, Clear
   CHOOSE: All from the fly-out menu
   Do not perform another command until proceeding to the next section, where you learn how to undo a command.

QUICK REFERENCE
Erasing a Cell

1. **SELECT: the cell that you want to erase**
2. **PRESS: (DELETE)**

USING THE UNDO COMMAND

The **Undo command** allows you to cancel up to the last 16 actions you performed in the worksheet. There are three methods for executing the Undo command. You can choose Edit, Undo from the menu, press the keyboard shortcut of CTRL +z, or click the Undo button ( ) on the Standard toolbar.

Let's practice two of these methods in the next exercise.

Perform the following steps . . .

1. To undo the last command that you executed in the previous section:
   CLICK: Undo button ( )
   Ensure that you click the main arrow portion of the toolbar button and not the drop-down triangle to the right. The words "Net Income" reappear in the worksheet.

2. SELECT: cell A1

3. PRESS: DELETE

4. CLICK: drop-down triangle on the Undo button ( )
   Your screen should now appear similar to Figure 1.12.

FIGURE 1.12

PERFORMING A MULTIPLE UNDO

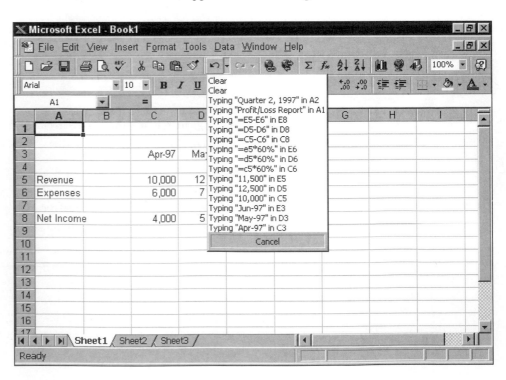

5. Move the mouse pointer downward in the Undo drop-down list until the first four items are highlighted.

6. To perform the multiple undo:
CLICK: mouse pointer on the fourth item in the drop-down list

SAVING AND CLOSING A WORKBOOK

When you are creating a workbook, it exists only in the computer's RAM (random access memory), which is highly volatile. To permanently store your work, you must save the workbook to the local hard disk, a network drive, or to a floppy diskette. Saving your work to a disk is similar to placing it into a filing cabinet. For important workbooks (ones that you cannot risk losing), you should save your work at least every 15 minutes, or whenever you're interrupted, to protect against an unexpected power outage or other catastrophe.

To save a workbook to a disk, click the Save button (💾) on the Standard toolbar or select the File, Save command from the menu. In the dialog box that appears, type a new filename using less than 255 characters, including spaces, and then press [ENTER] or click the Save command button. Do not use the following characters in filenames:

$$\backslash \quad / \quad : \quad * \quad ? \quad " \quad < \quad > \quad |$$

In the next few steps, you will save the current workbook to one of the following locations:

- *Advantage Files location* - This location may be on a diskette, a folder on your local hard drive, or a folder on a network server. The Advantage Files are the workbook files that have been created for you and that you will retrieve in the remaining exercises in this guide.

- *Data Files location* - This location may also be on a diskette, a hard drive folder, or a network folder. You will save the workbooks that you create or modify in the Data Files location.

> **IMPORTANT:** *Before continuing, ensure that you know the location of your Advantage Files and where to store your Data Files. If necessary, ask your instructor or lab assistant for additional information.*

Let's save the current workbook to your Data Files location.

1. Make sure that you have identified the location for storing your data files. If you require a diskette, place it into the diskette drive now.

2. CLICK: Save button (⊟)
    Excel displays a dialog box similar to the one shown in Figure 1.13; the filenames and directories may differ from your dialog box.

FIGURE 1.13

SAVE AS DIALOG BOX

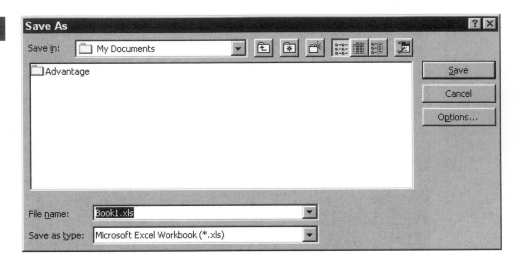

3. To specify a filename for the workbook:
    TYPE: **My First Workbook**

4. To specify where the workbook will be saved, do the following:
    CLICK: down arrow beside the *Save in* drop-down list box
    SELECT: *your Data Files location*
    PRESS: **ENTER** or CLICK: Save command button

    In this guide, we save workbooks to the "My Documents" folder on the hard disk and retrieve workbooks from the "Excel97" subfolder, which is located at the following path: \My Documents\Advantage\Excel97

5. When you are finished working with a workbook, you close the file to free up valuable RAM. To close the "My First Workbook" file:
    CHOOSE: File, Close

There are times when you'll want to save an existing workbook under a different filename. For example, you may want to keep different versions of the same workbook on your disk. Or, you may want to use one workbook as a template for future workbooks that are similar in style and format. Rather than retyping an entirely new workbook, you can retrieve an old workbook file, edit the information, and then save it under a different name using the File, Save As command. If you want to replace the old file instead, choose File, Save or click the Save button (▣).

QUICK REFERENCE
Saving a File

- **CLICK: Save button (▣), or**
- **CHOOSE: File, Save, or**
- **CHOOSE: File, Save As**

QUICK REFERENCE
Closing a File

- **CHOOSE: File, Close, or**
- **CLICK: Close button (☒) on the document window**

IN ADDITION USING LONG FILENAMES IN DOS (AND WINDOWS 3.1)

Because DOS can't understand filenames that are longer than eight characters, it changes a Windows filename when it tries to use a file with a long filename. For example,

the Windows filename "Multitasking Workbook" would be changed to "MULTIT~1.XLS" in DOS or when saved to a network drive that did not support long filenames.

IN ADDITION SAVING A WORKBOOK AS AN HTML DOCUMENT

To publish your Excel workbook on the Web, you must first save it as an HTML document using the File, Save as HTML command. *HTML* is an abbreviation for *Hypertext Markup*

Language, a convention used for marking textual documents with special formatting codes so that they display nicely in web browser software. For more information, ask the Office Assistant to search for information on "Publishing to HTML."

OPENING A WORKBOOK

Now that your workbook is stored in this electronic filing cabinet called a disk, how do you retrieve it for editing? To open a new workbook, you click the New button (▢) on the Standard toolbar. To modify or print an existing workbook, click the Open button (🗁) or choose the File, Open command from the menu. Once the Open dialog box appears, you select the file's location by clicking in the *Look in* drop-down list box. You then double-click the workbook's name appearing in the file list.

Perform the following steps . . .

1. Make sure that you have identified the location for retrieving the Advantage Files. If you require a diskette, place it into the diskette drive now.

2. To open a new workbook:
   CLICK: New button ( )
   (*Note*: You can also choose File, New from the menu and then double-click the blank Workbook template icon ( ) to load a new workbook.)

3. To practice using the Open dialog box:
   CLICK: Open button ( ) on the Standard toolbar

4. To view the Advantage Files:
   CLICK: down arrow beside the *Look in* drop-down list box
   SELECT: *your Advantage Files location*
   Your screen should now appear similar to Figure 1.14.

FIGURE 1.14

OPEN DIALOG BOX

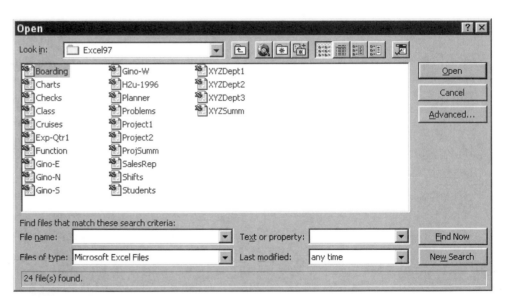

5. To change the display in the Open dialog box, try the following:
   CLICK: Detail button ( ) to see each workbook's file size and date
   CLICK: Properties button ( ) to see summary information
   CLICK: Preview button ( ) to see a workbook preview
   CLICK: List button ( ) to see a multiple-column format

6. Let's open a workbook:
   DOUBLE-CLICK: Students
   The "Students" workbook is loaded into memory and Sheet1 is displayed maximized in the application window.

QUICK REFERENCE
Opening a New Workbook

- **CLICK: New button (⬜), or**
- **CHOOSE: File, New**
  DOUBLE-CLICK: Workbook template icon (🖹)

QUICK REFERENCE
Opening an Existing
Workbook

1. **CLICK: Open button (📂), or**
   CHOOSE: File, Open from the Menu bar
2. **CLICK: down arrow beside the *Look in* drop-down list box**
3. **SELECT: a file location**
4. **DOUBLE-CLICK: the desired workbook**

IN ADDITION   OPENING AN OFFICE DOCUMENT FROM THE DESKTOP

You can open an existing document using one of the following methods:

- CHOOSE: **🏁Start**, Documents and then select the desired document from the 15 most recently-used files listed (if available)

- CHOOSE: **🏁Start**, Find, Files or Folders and then perform a search for the desired document name

- CHOOSE: **🏁Start**, Open Office Document and then select the desired document in the Open dialog box

---

IN ADDITION   EXCEL ON THE WEB

- *Excel as a Web browser:* You can open documents that are based on the Web's native Hypertext Markup Language (HTML). In the Open dialog box, select "HTML Documents" from the *Files of type* drop-down list box. Then, select a storage location and double-click the desired filename. Excel displays the document complete with hypertext links.

- *Excel reaches the Web:* With the appropriate connection, you can open and save Excel workbooks on the Internet. In the Open or Save dialog boxes, select an FTP Internet site location from the *Look in* or *Save in* drop-down list boxes, respectively. Once connected to a remote FTP server, you work with files the same as if they were on your local hard disk. This feature lets you share and update Excel workbooks with users from around the world.

LEAVING EXCEL

When you are finished using Excel, save your work and exit the program by clicking the Close button (✖) or by choosing the File, Exit command. If you have made modifications to a workbook and have not yet saved the changes, Excel asks whether the workbook should be saved or abandoned before exiting.

Perform the following steps . . .

1. To exit Excel:
   CHOOSE: File, Exit
   Assuming that no changes were made to the "Students" workbook, the application is closed and you are returned to the Windows desktop.

2. To exit Windows:
   CLICK: Start button (◼Start)
   CHOOSE: Shut Down
   SELECT: *Shutdown the computer?* option button
   CLICK: Yes command button

QUICK REFERENCE
Exiting Excel

- **CHOOSE: File, Exit or**
- **CLICK: Close button (✕) of the Excel application window**

SUMMARY

This session introduced you to using Microsoft Excel 97, an electronic spreadsheet program. We began the session exploring the advantages of electronic spreadsheets over manual worksheets, comparing the size of work areas and the speeds at which calculations and corrections are performed. The importance of planning the construction of a spreadsheet was also emphasized.

After you loaded Windows and Excel, this session presented an overview of Excel's major components, including the application and document windows. As well, you were introduced to data entry techniques for entering text, numbers, and formulas into the worksheet cells. Because even experts require some assistance now and then, this session also demonstrated some of Excel's Help features.

For easy reference, many of the commands and procedures appearing in this session are provided in Table 1.5, the Command Summary.

TABLE 1.5	*Command*	*Description*
Command Summary	Edit, Clear	Erases the contents and formatting of a cell.
	Edit, Undo (↶▾)	Reverses up to the last 16 actions performed.
	File, Close	Closes a workbook file.
	File, Exit (or ✕)	Leaves Excel.
	File, New (◻)	Opens a new workbook file.
	File, Open (📂)	Opens an existing workbook file.
	File, Save (💾)	Saves a workbook file to the disk.

TABLE 1.5	Command	Description
Continued	File, Save As	Saves a workbook file, specifying the filename.
	Help, Contents and Index	Displays the Help Topics window.
	Help, What's This?	Accesses context-sensitive help mouse pointer.
	Programs, Microsoft Excel	Launches Excel from the 🎨Start menu.

KEY TERMS

application window

In Microsoft Windows, each running application program appears in its own application window. These windows can be sized and moved anywhere on the Windows desktop.

cell

In an electronic spreadsheet program, this marks the intersection of a column and a row.

cell address

The location of a cell on a worksheet given by the intersection of a column and a row. Columns are labeled using letters. Rows are numbered. A cell address combines the column letter with the row number (for example, B9 or DF134).

cell pointer

The cursor on a worksheet that points to a cell. The cell pointer is moved using the arrow keys or the mouse.

context-sensitive help

A Help feature that provides a concise description for a particular menu option, toolbar button, or dialog box item.

document window

In Excel, each open workbook file appears in its own document window. These windows can be sized and moved anywhere within the Excel application window.

formulas

Mathematical expressions that define the relationships among various cells in a worksheet.

hyperlinks

In Microsoft Office 97, text or graphics that when clicked take you to another resource location, either within the same document or to a separate document stored on your computer, a network server, an Intranet resource, or onto the Internet.

Internet

A worldwide network of computer networks that are interconnected by standard telephone lines, fiber optics, and satellites.

Intranet

A local or wide area network that uses Internet protocols and technologies to share information within an institution or corporation.

Undo command

In Excel, a command that makes it possible to reverse up to the last 16 commands executed.

workbook

The Excel file where you create your work. A workbook appears in a document window and may contain worksheets and chart sheets.

World Wide Web (WWW)

A visual interface to the Internet based on *hyperlinks*. Using web browser software, you click on hyperlinks to navigate the resources on the Internet.

Exercises

SHORT ANSWER

1. Name two Office 97 Internet integration features.

2. List some of the advantages of using Excel over manual worksheets.

3. List the suggested planning steps for constructing a spreadsheet.

4. Explain the *context-sensitive help* features found in Excel.

5. Name the Help feature that provides a natural language interface for asking questions. What two areas of this feature can be customized?

6. How do you reverse the last three commands executed?

7. What is the fastest method for moving to cell DF8192?

8. What is the difference between a toolbar and a menu bar?

9. What is the significance of an ellipsis (...) after a menu option?

10. In Excel, how do you enter a formula into a cell? Provide an example.

HANDS-ON

(*Note*: Ensure that you know the storage location of your Advantage Files and your Data Files before proceeding.)

1. In this exercise, you will produce a worksheet for managing your personal credit cards. The tasks include entering text and numbers and then editing worksheet cells. Perform the following steps.

   a. Load Windows and Excel to begin working with a new workbook.

   b. Move the cell pointer to the following cells: (a) A21, (b) K50, (c) IV50, (d) IV16384, (e) AA1000, (f) A1

c. With your cell pointer in cell A1:
   TYPE: **Personal Financial Planner**
   PRESS: ENTER

d. Enter the following text labels:

Move to Cell	TYPE:
C3	**Budget**
D3	**Actual**
A6	**VISA**
A7	**Chevron**
A8	**AMEX**
A9	**M/C**

e. Enter the following numbers:

Move to Cell	TYPE:
C6	**1200**
C7	**500**
C8	**200**
C9	**75**
D6	**1200**
D7	**450**
D8	**215**
D9	**135**

f. Change the label in cell A6 from "VISA" to "Discover" by typing over the existing entry.

g. Change the label in cell A8 from "AMEX" to "AMEX Gold" using the mouse to edit the text in the cell.

h. Change the label in cell A9 from "M/C" to "Mastercard."

i. Change the budgeted value for Chevron in cell C7 to 400.

j. Reverse the change in the last step using the Undo button (🔄).

k. Change the Actual value for AMEX Gold in cell D8 to 210.

l. Reverse the change in the last step by pressing CTRL+z.

2. This exercise uses the same worksheet to practice entering formulas.

  a. Move to cell A11.

  b. TYPE: **Total Balances**

  c. Move to cell C11. Enter a formula that adds the Budget values in column C.

  d. Move to cell D11. Enter a formula that adds the Actual values in column D.

  e. Move to cell E3.

  f. TYPE: **Variance**

  g. In cell E6, enter a formula to subtract the actual Discover card balance from the budgeted value. (*Hint*: Budget − Actual.)

  h. In cell E7, enter a formula to subtract the actual Chevron balance from the budgeted value.

  i. Enter formulas to calculate the variance for the remaining cards.

  j. Using the Edit Formula button (▣), enter a formula to calculate the variance for the Total Balances.

  k. Save the workbook as "My Financial Plan" onto your Data Files diskette or into your Data Files folder. Your worksheet should now appear similar to Figure 1.15.

  l. Close the workbook before proceeding.

FIGURE 1.15

"MY FINANCIAL PLAN" WORKBOOK

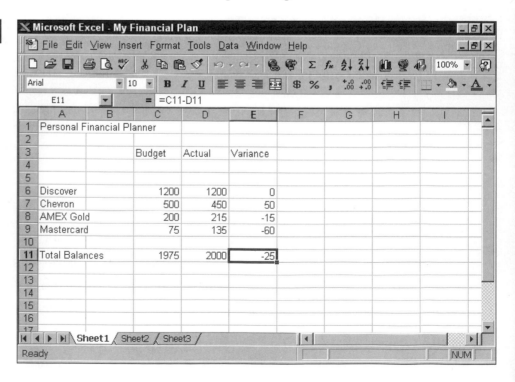

3. **On Your Own:** Your Personal Phone Book
Create a new workbook called "Personal Phone Book" that stores personal information for some of your closest friends. Include their given names in column A, surnames in column B, phone numbers in column C, and their age in column D. Add at least five entries and then create a formula that calculates the average age of your friends. Save the workbook to your Data Files location.

4. **On Your Own:** Explore a Microsoft Excel Help Topic
Pick a Microsoft Excel Help topic that interests you and write about it in a few paragraphs. Make sure to explain why you chose the topic and how to perform the procedures described. For example, you may be interested in learning how to publish a worksheet on the World Wide Web or how to customize the Office Assistant. You may want to look through the In Addition boxes in this session for more ideas.

CASE PROBLEMS   **THE BONDABLE GROUP**

(*Note*: In the following case problems, assume the role of the primary characters and perform the same steps that they identify. You may want to reread the session opening.)

1. Realizing that Pancho and Mackenzie need some help getting started on their spreadsheet, Jennifer calls a meeting for that afternoon. At 3:00 PM precisely, the three friends congregate in the boardroom around a small oval table. "Okay, let's review what our objectives are," Jennifer says, opening the meeting with her usual sentence. "First, we want to develop a spreadsheet that we can show to clients on the screen to help them better understand financial planning concepts. Second, we want to develop a single template that we can re-use for all of our clients. Is everyone with me so far?" The two gentlemen nod in agreement as Jennifer writes down the points on a flip chart. "Great, now let's brainstorm about what information we want to include." After more than an hour, the three partners emerge from the boardroom with a list of features that they want to appear in the spreadsheet.

The following list is a summary of the points written on the flip chart during the partners' afternoon meeting. Your job is to implement these points in an Excel spreadsheet.

- Enter the title of the worksheet "Your Guide to Financial Planning Success," in the top left-hand corner (cell A1).

- Enter the company's name, "The Bondable Group," immediately below the title of the worksheet.

- Leaving two blank lines after the company's name, enter the text label "Five Principles of Successful Investing:" in column A.

- Below this title, enter each of the five principles on a separate row:
  (1) Establish your goals.
  (2) Start early.
  (3) Make saving part of your regular routine.
  (4) Invest for the long term.
  (5) Diversify your portfolio.

- Leaving two more blank lines, enter the text label "Scoring Your Investment Objectives:"

- Below this title, enter the following information in columns A and B:

POINTS	QUESTION
	What is your age?
	What is your income?
	When will you need the money?
	How much risk can you take?
	TOTAL SCORE

- Save the workbook as "Bondable Plan" to your Data Files location.

2. On Friday morning, Pancho and Mackenzie receive their new notebook computers and immediately launch Microsoft Excel. They are very pleased with their new toys and don't even try to suppress their grins as they click away at the keyboards. "Hey Pancho, I've got a client meeting with Garrett Buggey before lunch. I'll try out the "Bondable Plan" workbook and let you know how it works." Pancho thanks Mackenzie and scurries from the office to make his own appointments.

Mackenzie arrives early at Garrett's office and is led to a small meeting room. While waiting for his client, Mackenzie opens the notebook computer and loads the "Bondable Plan" workbook. "Hiya Mac!" Garrett calls as he enters the room. "Hey, that's a nice system you've got there. When did you get it?" Mackenzie explains that the computer had arrived that morning and that he wants to show Garrett a new spreadsheet. Based on his personal information and a point-scoring system developed by Jennifer, Mackenzie enters the following information into the spreadsheet:

POINTS	QUESTION
5500	What is your age?
4320	What is your income?
1745	When will you need the money?
7500	How much risk can you take?
	TOTAL SCORE

After he enters the numbers into the spreadsheet, Mackenzie realizes that they forgot to create a formula for the TOTAL SCORE line. This is the most important figure in the entire spreadsheet! Fortunately, Mackenzie remembers how to total a column of numbers using an addition formula. With the total score displaying in the worksheet, Garrett changes his mind on how much risk he is prepared to take in his investments. Mackenzie changes the point score from 7500 to 6275, and they both watch as the TOTAL SCORE line changes instantaneously.

Perform the same steps Mackenzie did after loading the "Bondable Plan" workbook. Save the new workbook as "Garrett Buggey" and then close the workbook before proceeding.

3. Mackenzie returns to the office after a successful meeting with Garrett. After telling Pancho about the forgotten formula, they decide to review and revise the entire "Bondable Plan" workbook. Refer to the following list and implement the changes in your worksheet:

- Open the original "Bondable Plan" workbook.

- Edit the title "Your Guide to Financial Planning Success" to read "The Personal Guide to Financial Planning Success."

- Add a sixth principle to the "Successful Investing" list called "(6) Make adjustments over time." Make sure that you edit this area's title, as well.

- Edit the question about risk in the "Scoring Your Investment Objectives:" area to read "How much risk do you want to take?"

- Add a new area titled "Determining Your Asset Mix:" to the spreadsheet, two lines below the "Scoring Your Investment Objectives:" area.

- Enter the following information, in three columns, below this area's title.

ANSWER	RESULT	QUESTION
		What is your monthly salary?
		a. % of monthly salary for Investment
		b. % of investment for Savings
		c. % of investment for Income Funds
		d. % of investment for Growth Funds

- Pancho and Mackenzie will enter a client's information into the ANSWER column. You must create formulas for the RESULT column that will provide the proper calculation results. Looking at the example provided below, ensure that items b., c., and d. in the ANSWER column add up to 100%. Also, ensure that the same items in the RESULT column add up to the *monthly salary for investment* value (in this example, 500).

ANSWER	RESULT	QUESTION
$5,000		What is your monthly salary?
10%	**500**	a. % of monthly salary for Investment
30%	**150**	b. % of investment for Savings
30%	**150**	c. % of investment for Income Funds
40%	**200**	d. % of investment for Growth Funds

- Practice using the new table by inputting several combinations of figures into the ANSWER column. Manually check that the calculations in the RESULTS column are correct.

Save the revised "Bondable Plan" workbook, updating the existing version. Close the workbook and then exit Excel.

Microsoft Excel 97 for Windows

Working with Spreadsheets

SESSION

2

IRWIN

COMPUTER & INFORMATION TECHNOLOGY

SESSION OUTLINE

INTRODUCTION

Spreadsheets may look complicated, but even a new user can begin to construct one in a short period of time. With Microsoft's IntelliSense® technology, Excel provides several "Auto" features that can correct your spelling mistakes, format worksheet cells, and calculate formulas automatically. This session shows you how to set up a new workbook and enter data efficiently, and how to use AutoCalculate, AutoComplete, AutoCorrect, and AutoFormat. Once your spreadsheet is created, you can easily modify it and use it over and over.

CASE STUDY   **MADRID CLOTHING COMPANY**

Suriya Amin opened the first mall location for the Madrid Clothing Company in 1988. Since then the company has expanded into six locations across the Pacific Northwest, from the Alderwood Mall near Seattle to the Pacific Center in Vancouver, British Columbia. The Madrid Clothing Company supplies European casual wear for a middle- to upper-class clientele.

Suriya's younger brother Khalid, who is also one of her store managers, wants to expand the operation into California. Realizing that Suriya would never accept a serious proposal from her younger brother, Khalid decides to create and submit an anonymous "what-if" spreadsheet that compares the worst-case and best-case scenarios for such an expansion. To ensure that she takes the proposal seriously, Khalid must strive to give the report a very professional appearance. To this end, he must learn how to format a worksheet in Microsoft Excel and how to print the report with headers and footers.

In this session, you and Khalid will improve your efficiency working with Excel. You will create, proof, customize, enhance, save, and then print a workbook. By the end of this session, you will know how to apply these skills to any workbook you create.

CREATING A NEW WORKBOOK

When you first load Excel, an empty workbook called Book1 appears in the document window. To create a workbook, you simply enter information into the worksheets labeled from Sheet1 to Sheet3 and then save the workbook under a new filename. (*Note:* In Session 4, you learn how to add and delete sheets in a workbook.) If you've already entered information into Book1 and want to create a new workbook, choose the File, New command or click the New button ( ) on the Standard toolbar. Because each workbook that you open consumes memory, you should save your work and close all unnecessary documents before creating a new workbook.

In the next two sections, you will create the worksheet shown in Figure 2.1. You will use this worksheet throughout the session to practice several spreadsheet procedures.

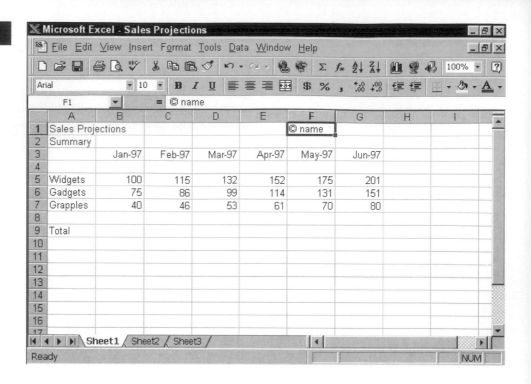

 **Perform the following steps . . .**

1. Make sure that you've loaded Excel and that a new workbook appears in the document window. Enter the following text labels for headings on the worksheet:

Move to Cell	TYPE:
A1	**Sales Projections**
A5	**Widgets**
A6	**Gadgets**
A7	**Grapples**
A9	**Total**

2. Enter the following dates as column headings:

Move to Cell	TYPE:
B3	**Jan-97**
C3	**Feb-97**
D3	**Mar-97**
E3	**Apr-97**
F3	**May-97**
G3	**Jun-97**

Before entering the numeric values for the spreadsheet, proceed to the next section to learn about cell ranges.

IN ADDITION USING TEMPLATES

Rather than creating a worksheet from scratch, you can open and then modify a *template*. A template is simply a worksheet that serves as the starting point for the creation of a new worksheet. You can create and save your own templates or access some of Excel's professionally designed built-in templates, including an Invoice, Expense Statement, and Purchase Order worksheet. To view the installed templates, choose the File, New command and select the *Spreadsheet Solutions* tab. For more information, ask the Office Assistant about "Using a Template."

INTRODUCING CELL RANGES

In most Windows programs, you select objects and then choose commands to act on the objects, such as a copy or format operation. To enhance an Excel worksheet, for example, you select a cell or group of cells—called a **cell range**—and then choose a formatting command. After executing the command, Excel leaves the selected range highlighted for you to choose additional commands. You can use either the keyboard or the mouse to select a cell range in a worksheet.

A cell range is a single cell or a rectangular block of worksheet cells. Each cell range has a beginning and an ending cell address. The top left-hand cell is the beginning cell and the bottom right-hand cell is the ending cell in a range. To specify a range in a worksheet formula, you enter the two cell addresses separated by a colon (for example, B4:C6). Figure 2.2 illustrates some cell ranges.

FIGURE 2.2

CELL RANGES

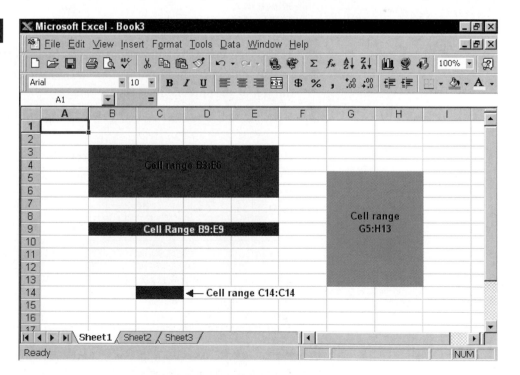

You will now practice selecting cell ranges.

Perform the following steps . . .

1. Move to cell B3.

2. To select the range of cells from B3 to G3 using the keyboard:
PRESS: (SHIFT) and hold it down
PRESS: (→) five times
If the highlight does not extend from cell B3 to G3, make sure that you are holding down the (SHIFT) key as you press (→).

3. When the range is highlighted, release the (SHIFT) key.

4. To remove the range selection, you can press any arrow key:
PRESS: (←)
(*Note:* You can also click on any cell to remove the highlighting from the cell range.)

5. To select the range of cells from B5 to G7 using a mouse:
CLICK: cell B5 and hold down the left mouse button
DRAG: the mouse pointer down and to the right until you reach G7

6. When the range is highlighted, release the mouse button. A selected range is highlighted in reverse (white text on a black background) from the rest of the worksheet. The exception is the active cell with the cell pointer, in this case cell B5 in the range B5:G7.

7. Using cell ranges makes your job of entering data easier and more accurate. As you type information into a highlighted cell range, the cell pointer is automatically moved to the next cell in the range when you press (ENTER). For example, do the following while the cell range remains selected:
TYPE: **100**
PRESS: (ENTER)
Notice that the cell pointer moves down to cell B6. When the cell pointer reaches the last cell at the bottom of the selected column, it will move to the top of the next column in the range.

8. With the cell range still highlighted, complete the data entry as follows:

	B	C	D	E	F	G
5	100	115	132	152	175	201
6	75	86	99	114	131	151
7	40	46	53	61	70	80

9. With the cell range still highlighted, practice moving from cell to cell:
PRESS: [ENTER] to move down one cell at a time; when you reach the bottom cell, the cell pointer moves to the top of the next column
PRESS: [SHIFT]+[ENTER] to move up one cell at a time; when you reach the top cell, the cell pointer moves to the previous column
PRESS: [TAB] to move right one cell; when you reach the rightmost cell in a row, the cell pointer moves to the next row
PRESS: [SHIFT]+[TAB] to move left one cell; when you reach the leftmost cell, the cell pointer moves to the previous row

10. To remove the highlighting and return to cell A1:
PRESS: [CTRL]+[HOME]

QUICK REFERENCE
Selecting a Range of Cells Using the Mouse

1. **Click once on the cell in the top left-hand corner of the range.**
2. **Hold down the left mouse button and drag the mouse pointer to the bottom right-hand corner of the range.**
3. **Release the mouse button.**

QUICK REFERENCE
Selecting a Range of Cells Using the Keyboard

1. **Position the cell pointer in the top left-hand corner of the cell range.**
2. **PRESS: [SHIFT] key and hold it down**
3. **Extend the highlight over the desired group of cells using the arrow keys ([←], [→], [↑], and [↓]).**
4. **Release the [SHIFT] key.**

SPELL-CHECKING A WORKSHEET

This section introduces the Spelling Checker for correcting typographical errors and misspellings. You can perform a spelling check on a particular cell range, a single sheet, several sheets, or the entire workbook. When a spelling check is requested, Excel begins scanning the cells with textual information. In addition to comparing each word to entries in Excel's main dictionary, you can create a custom dictionary that contains proper names, abbreviations, and technical terms.

Besides running a spelling check, Excel's **AutoCorrect** utility can automatically correct your typographical and capitalization errors as you type. You will find this feature extremely handy if you habitually misspell or mistype particular words. For example, people often type "thier" instead of "their"—making a simple but common typing mistake. Excel's AutoCorrect utility provides corrections for this word and hundreds of other commonly misspelled words. It also lets you easily insert complex symbols like © and ™ into your worksheet cells.

To start a spelling check, click the Spelling button ( ) on the Standard toolbar. When the Spelling Checker cannot identify a word and believes it to be misspelled, a dialog box appears allowing you to correct or ignore the entry, or to add the word to the custom dictionary or AutoCorrect list. The Spelling Checker also flags errors relating to repeated words (for example, "the ball was was red") and mixed case (for example, "the baLL was rEd"). An added benefit for users of Office 97 is that the terms you add to the custom dictionary and to AutoCorrect are shared by all applications.

Let's practice spell-checking a worksheet.

Perform the following steps . . .

1. Move to cell A2.

2. Enter a misspelled word:
   TYPE: **Summury**
   PRESS: ⌨ENTER

3. PRESS: ⌨CTRL + ⌨HOME to move to the top of the worksheet

4. To begin the spelling check:
   CLICK: Spelling button ( )
   (*Note:* You can also choose the Tools, Spelling command on the Menu bar to start a spelling check.) When Excel finds the first misspelled word, it displays the dialog box shown in Figure 2.3 and waits for further instructions:

FIGURE 2.3

SPELLING DIALOG BOX

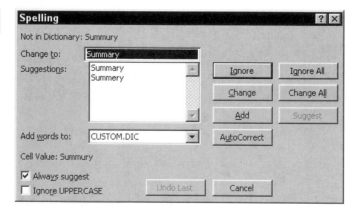

5. You have several options when the Spell Checker cannot find a word:

   • Select the correctly spelled word in the *Suggestions* list box and then click the Change command button.

   • Type the correct spelling of the word in the *Change to* text box and then click the Change command button.

   • If the word is spelled correctly and not frequently used, click the Ignore or Ignore All buttons to proceed to the next word.

   • If the word is spelled correctly and frequently used, click the Add button to add it to the custom dictionary.

> • If the word is one that you frequently mistype and the correct spelling appears in the *Change to* text, click the AutoCorrect command button to have Excel correct this mistake automatically in the future.

To correct the spelling of Summary and proceed:
CLICK: Change command button

6. Continue the spelling check for the remainder of the worksheet. A message box will appear notifying you when the spelling check is finished. To proceed:
PRESS: (ENTER) or CLICK: OK

7. To demonstrate using AutoCorrect:
CLICK: cell F1
TYPE: **(c)**
PRESS: Space bar
AutoCorrect replaces "(c)" with the proper copyright symbol "©" automatically when you press the Space bar.

8. To complete the cell entry:
TYPE: *your name*
PRESS: (ENTER)
(*Hint:* Do not take the above instruction literally. Enter your own name and not the text "your name.")

9. To review some of the other entries available in AutoCorrect:
CHOOSE: Tools, AutoCorrect
In the dialog box (Figure 2.4) that appears, notice the two columns in the list box: *Replace* and *With*. What you type into a worksheet cell is presented in the Replace column and what AutoCorrect replaces your typing with is presented in the *With* column. On your own, scroll through the list box and review the commonly misspelled words that AutoCorrect will automatically correct for you.

FIGURE 2.4

AUTOCORRECT DIALOG
BOX

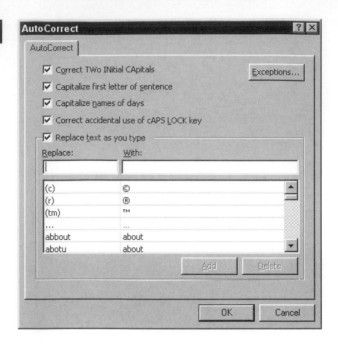

10. To proceed, ensure that all the check boxes are selected (as shown in Figure 2.4) and then do the following:
    CLICK: OK command button

11. PRESS: (CTRL) + (HOME) to move to the top of the worksheet

12. Make sure that you have identified the location for saving your Data Files. If you require a diskette, place it into the diskette drive now. Save your worksheet as "Sales Projections" and then close the workbook.

QUICK REFERENCE
Spell-Checking a Worksheet

1. **CLICK: Spelling button ( ), or**
   CHOOSE: Tools, Spelling

2. **When a misspelled word is located, Excel suggests alternative spellings. Select a suggestion and then click a command button to change the entry, add it to the dictionary, add it to AutoCorrect, or ignore the word for the remainder of the spelling check.**

DATA ENTRY USING AUTOCOMPLETE

Have you ever experienced a conversation with a person who insisted on finishing your sentences for you? Perhaps it was a friend, a business associate, or even your spouse. Although tremendously annoying in a social situation, this type of imposition proves to be an exceptional software feature—and it's called AutoComplete!

AutoComplete second-guesses what you are about to type into a worksheet cell by reviewing your past entries in that cell's column. Similar to the AutoCorrect feature, AutoComplete watches your keystrokes and then jumps in when it thinks it can help. While AutoCorrect at least lets you finish typing a word before correcting a mistake, AutoComplete lets only a few letters go by before completing a matching entry.

The following exercise illustrates using the AutoComplete feature.

Perform the following steps . . .

1. Open the workbook called "Problems" stored in the Advantage Files location. (*Remember:* This location may be on a diskette or in a folder on your hard disk or on a network drive.) The "Problems" workbook contains a single worksheet that is used to record problems in a computer lab. Notice that there are repeating entries beneath the columns labeled Shift, Supervisor, and Machine.

2. Let's add two new items to the worksheet. First, enter a date:
CLICK: cell A15
TYPE: **4/1/97**
PRESS: ➡

3. To add "Blue" in the Shift column:
TYPE: **b**
AutoComplete scans the existing entries in the column and then fills in the remaining letters in the word "blue." (*Note:* If "blue" does not appear, press ENTER and then choose the Tools, Options command. Click the *Edit* tab in the dialog box and then ensure that the *Enable AutoComplete for cell values* check box is selected. Click the OK command button to complete the dialog box.)

4. To move to cell C15 and accept the AutoComplete entry:
PRESS: ➡
Notice that the "b" is now capitalized in "Blue" so as to conform to the existing entries in the column.

5. Watch closely as you type each letter to add a new Supervisor to column C:
TYPE: **Brandon**
Notice that AutoComplete fills in "Bradley" as you type the "Bra" portion of the name. When you type the "n," AutoComplete realizes that you are entering a new Supervisor's name and removes the letters it had previously inserted for "Bradley."

6. To move to cell D15:
PRESS: ➡

7. An additional feature of AutoComplete is its ability to generate an up-to-date list of the unique entries from a column. To illustrate:
RIGHT-CLICK: cell D15

8. On the shortcut menu that appears:
CHOOSE: Pick From List
AutoComplete generates a list of items contained in the column and then displays its results in a pop-up list box.

9. SELECT: "Tower CPU" from the Pick List
Your screen should now appear similar to Figure 2.5.

10. To finish the line item:
RIGHT-CLICK: cell E15
SELECT: "15 - RAM parity error on boot" from the Pick List

11. Practice using the typing method and the Pick List to enter the following item to the Problem Report:

Move to Cell	Entry
A16	**5/15/97**
B16	**Green**
C16	**Kineshanko**
D16	**Laser printer**
E16	**13 - Low toner**

12. Save the workbook as "Problem Report" to your Data Files location. Then, close the workbook.

FIGURE 2.5

ENTERING DATA USING
A PICK LIST

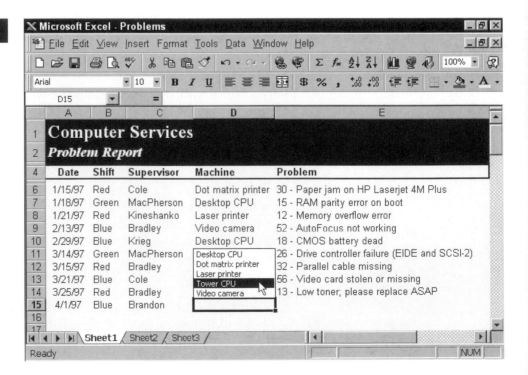

CALCULATING TOTALS

Adding together a few numbers on your worksheet is easy using a simple addition formula. Imagine the time it would take, however, to sum a column of 100 numbers with a formula such as =A1+A2+A3...+A99. Fortunately, Excel has anticipated many of these repetitive operations and provides a library of electronic shortcuts called **functions,** organized into the following categories:

- Database
- Date & Time
- Financial
- Information
- Logical

- Lookup & Reference
- Math & Trig
- Statistical
- Text

The mathematical and statistical functions are the most commonly used, enabling you to sum or average a range of numbers, count cell entries, and extract maximum and minimum results from a cell range. This section introduces the SUM function which is used as a replacement for long addition formulas. To enter the SUM function into a cell, you can type the expression or click the AutoSum button (Σ) on the Standard toolbar. Thanks to Excel's new **AutoCalculate** utility, you can view the sum of a selected cell range in the Status bar without even entering the SUM function!

THE SUM FUNCTION

The first step in using the SUM function is to move to the cell where you want the result to appear. Functions, like formulas, begin with an equal sign to inform Excel to expect a function name as opposed to a text label. The syntax for the SUM command is "=SUM(cell range)" where the cell range is the block of cells to be summed. You can enter the cell range by typing the cell addresses or by highlighting the block of cells using the mouse.

The objective of the following exercise is to demonstrate these two methods for entering the SUM function. Normally, you would not use a different method to sum each column. However, this example provides an opportunity to practice some important skills.

Perform the following steps . . .

1. Ensure that there are no open workbooks in the document area.

2. Open the "Sales Projections" workbook that you created earlier in this session.

3. Move to cell B9.

4. To calculate the total sales for the month of January, enter the SUM function by typing the cell addresses:
TYPE: **=sum(b5:b7)**
PRESS: ➡
The value 215 appears in the cell. (*Note:* You can enter the function name and cell range using uppercase or lowercase letters.)

5. To calculate the total sales for February, enter the SUM function into cell C9 by pointing to the cell range using the keyboard:
TYPE: **=sum(**
PRESS: ⬆ four times to move to cell C5
PRESS: **SHIFT** and hold down
PRESS: ⬇ twice to extend the range to cell C7
TYPE: **)** and release the **SHIFT** key
PRESS: ➡
The number 247 appears in cell C9.

6. To calculate the total sales for March, enter the SUM function into cell D9 by pointing to the cell range using the mouse:
TYPE: **=sum(**
CLICK: cell D5 and hold down the left mouse button
DRAG: mouse pointer to cell D7 and then release the mouse button
TYPE: **)**
PRESS: ➡
The number 284 appears in cell D9.

7. SELECT: cell range from E9 to G9

8. To calculate the total sales for April through June, enter the SUM function once and copy the formula to the remaining cells in the range using a keyboard shortcut:
TYPE: **=sum(e5:e7)**
PRESS: **CTRL**+**ENTER**
When you press **CTRL** + **ENTER**, Excel copies the entry in the active cell to the remaining cells in the highlighted range; in this case, F9 and G9.

9. To demonstrate using AutoCalculate:
CLICK: cell B9 and hold down the left mouse button

10. DRAG: mouse pointer to C9 and keep the mouse button depressed
The Status bar now displays "Sum=462", the sum of the selected cell range B9:C9. AutoCalculate provides an immediate summation of the selected cells without entering a formula or using a function.

11. DRAG: mouse pointer to G9 slowly, watching the Status bar as you move the cell pointer from D9 through to G9
The Status bar should now display "Sum=1881", the sum of the selected cell range B9:G9.

12. On your own, select other cell ranges using the mouse and watch the "Sum=" portion of the Status bar change to reflect the results.

IN ADDITION FORMULA AUTOCORRECT

Excel automatically corrects some common mistakes that novice users make when entering formulas and functions. For example, if you enter `==sum(b9:g9)` into a cell, Excel displays a dialog box with the proposed correction of `=sum(b9:g9)`. You simply click the Yes command button to have Excel edit the formula.

THE AUTOSUM BUTTON

Rather than entering an addition formula or the SUM function manually, you can use the AutoSum button ([Σ]) to automatically sum a cell range. To AutoSum a cell range, you position the cell pointer where you want the result to appear and click the AutoSum button ([Σ]) once. Excel enters the SUM function with its best guess of the desired cell range. If the range is correct, press (ENTER) to complete the entry. You can also bypass the need to press (ENTER) by double-clicking the AutoSum button ([Σ]) with the cell pointer in the desired cell.

Let's complete the "Sales Projections" workbook by calculating the total sales for each product.

Perform the following steps . . .

1. Move to cell H3.

2. TYPE: **Total**

3. Move to cell H9.

4. To calculate the total sales for all products:
   CLICK: AutoSum button ([Σ])
   Verify that the cell range appearing in the cell and in the Formula bar is correct before proceeding to the next step.

5. To proceed:
   CLICK: ▣ in the Formula bar
   (*Note:* You can also press (ENTER) or click the AutoSum button ([Σ]) a second time to accept the cell range.)

6. To calculate the total sales for each individual product, select the cell range from H5 to H7. Ensure that the entire range is highlighted.

7. CLICK: AutoSum button ([Σ])
   Because more than one cell is highlighted, the SUM function is automatically entered for all three cells. Your worksheet should now appear similar to Figure 2.6.

FIGURE 2.6

ENTERING THE SUM
FUNCTION AND USING
AUTOSUM

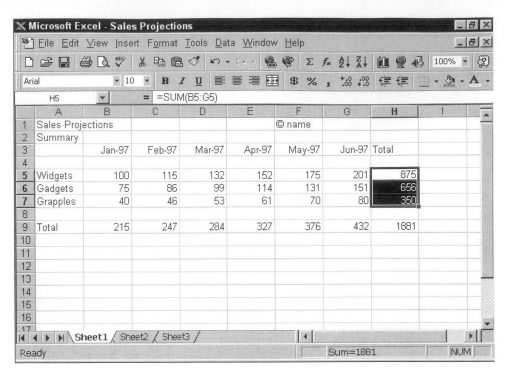

8. Using the mouse, click each of the cells H5, H6, and H7 and read the cell references in the Formula bar. Ensure that each SUM function sums the correct cell range.

9. Save the "Sales Projections" workbook to your Data Files location.

QUICK REFERENCE
AutoSum Button

1. **Move the cell pointer to where you want the result to appear.**
2. **CLICK: AutoSum button (Σ)**

Changing Column Widths

You can increase the **column width** of your worksheet columns to allow for long text labels, numbers, and date formats. To change a column's width from the default or standard width, move the cell pointer to any cell in the desired column and then choose the Format, Column, Width command from the Menu bar. In the *Column Width* text box, you type the desired width (up to 255) and then click on OK.

To change the width of more than one column at a time, you highlight cells within the columns (on any row) before you issue the command. You can also choose the Format, Column, AutoFit Selection command to have Excel calculate the best width for the column based on its entries. As with most procedures, there are keyboard and mouse methods for changing a column's width. Using the mouse, you can modify a column's width by dragging the column borders within the frame area.

You will now change the width of several columns in a *worksheet*.

Perform the following steps . . .

1. Move to cell A1.

2. To change the width of column A to 15 characters:
   CHOOSE: Format, Column, Width

3. In the *Column Width* text box, enter the number of characters:
   TYPE: **10**
   PRESS: [ENTER] or CLICK: OK
   The column's width is changed and you are returned to the worksheet.

4. To change the width of column B to 12 characters using the mouse, first move the mouse pointer into the column frame area where the column letters (A, B, and so on) appear.

5. Position the mouse pointer over the borderline between column B and column C. The mouse pointer changes shape from a cross to a black vertical line split by a horizontal double-headed arrow.

6. CLICK: the borderline and hold down the mouse button
   DRAG: the mouse pointer to the right to increase the width to 12
   (*Hint:* The width is displayed in a ToolTip. This method takes a very steady hand and good mouse control to get an exact width.)

7. Release the mouse button.

8. To concurrently change multiple columns to the same width, you must first select the columns by dragging the mouse pointer over the column letters in the frame area. For this step, select columns B through H using the mouse by clicking on the letter B and then dragging the mouse pointer to column H. The columns will appear highlighted.

9. To have Excel select the best width for each of the columns:
   CHOOSE: Format, Column, AutoFit Selection

10. Although the columns are adjusted to best fit their cell entries, most appear too narrow. With the columns still selected, drag any border (for example, the border between columns D and E) in the highlighted frame area to increase the width of all columns to 8 characters. When you release the mouse button, notice that all of the highlighted columns are sized to 8 characters wide.

QUICK REFERENCE
Changing a Column's Width

1. Select a cell in the column that you want to format.
2. CHOOSE: Format, Column, Width
3. Type the desired column width in the text box.
4. PRESS: [ENTER] or CLICK: OK

CHANGING ROW HEIGHTS

You can change the row height of any worksheet row to customize borders and line spacing. To change a row's height, move the cell pointer to any cell in the desired row and then choose Format, Row, Height from the Menu bar. In the *Row Height* text box, you type the desired height in points (where 72 points is equal to one inch) and then click on OK. Similar to changing a column's width, you can use a mouse to drag the row borders within the frame area to increase or decrease a row's height.

You will now change the height of several rows in a worksheet.

Perform the following steps . . .

1. Move to cell A1.

2. To change the height of row 1 to 25 points (approximately ⅜ inch), issue the formatting command:
   CHOOSE: Format, Row, Height

3. In the *Row Height* text box, enter a number for the height in points:
   TYPE: **25**
   PRESS: ENTER or CLICK: OK
   The row's height is changed, and you are returned to the worksheet.

4. To change the height of row 3 to 21 points using a mouse, first move the mouse pointer into the frame area where the row numbers appear.

5. Position the mouse pointer over the borderline between row 3 and row 4. The mouse pointer changes shape from a cross to a black horizontal line split by a vertical double-headed arrow.

6. CLICK: the borderline and hold down the mouse button
   DRAG: the mouse pointer down to increase the row height to 21
   (*Hint:* The height is displayed in a ToolTip.)

7. Release the mouse button.

8. To change multiple rows to the same height, you must first select the rows by dragging the mouse in the frame area. For this step, select the range from row 5 to row 9 by clicking on the number 5 and then dragging the mouse pointer to row 9.

9. To change the row height to 16 points:
   CHOOSE: Format, Row, Height
   TYPE: **16**
   PRESS: ENTER or CLICK: OK

10. Move to cell A1. Your worksheet should now appear similar to Figure 2.7.

FIGURE 2.7

CHANGING THE COLUMN
WIDTHS AND ROW
HEIGHTS

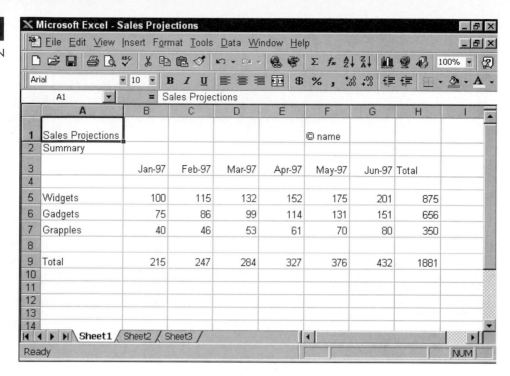

Unlike column widths, row heights are automatically adjusted to their best fit according to the font size of entries in the row. However, you can still modify the spacing in your worksheets by adjusting row heights manually. If you want to reset the row height back to the standard or default setting, choose the Format, Row, AutoFit command from the menu.

QUICK REFERENCE	
Changing a Row's Height	1. Select a cell in the row to format.
	2. **CHOOSE:** Format, Row, Height
	3. Type the desired row height in the text box.
	4. **PRESS:** ENTER or CLICK: OK

FORMATTING YOUR WORKSHEET

With Excel's spreadsheet publishing capabilities, you can enhance your worksheets with a variety of fonts, borders, and shading. You can also format numbers to display currency and percentage symbols and to specify the number of decimal places. The combination of these features enables you to produce professional-looking reports and presentations using Excel.

SELECTING CELL RANGES

To format your worksheet, select the cells that you want to enhance and then issue a formatting command. To this point in the guide, you've learned how to select a single cell and a block of cells called a range. There are several additional methods for selecting cells in a worksheet that will improve your productivity. For example, you can select multiple cell ranges in different areas of a worksheet and then apply a single command to format them all. Some common selection methods are provided below.

- To apply formatting changes to an entire worksheet, select the worksheet by pressing **CTRL**+**a** or by clicking once on the Select All button (□), located in the top left-hand corner of the frame area.

- To select multiple cell ranges, select the first cell range as usual and then hold down the **CTRL** key as you select the additional cell ranges using the mouse.

- To select a cell range that spans a large area of the worksheet (for example, A1:M300), select the first cell (top left-hand corner of the range) and then scroll to the last cell (bottom right-hand corner of the range) using the scroll bars. When the last cell is visible, press and hold down the **SHIFT** key and click the cell once. All the cells in between the first and last are highlighted.

Because a cell range remains highlighted after issuing a command, you can choose additional formatting commands without having to reselect cells. To remove the highlighting from a cell range, press an arrow key or click on any cell in the worksheet using the mouse.

USING FONTS

One of the most effective means of enhancing a worksheet is to vary the **fonts**—that is, the **typefaces** and point sizes—that are used in titles, column headings, row labels, and other worksheet cells. Although fonts are effective at drawing the reader's attention to specific topics, don't feel that you must use every font in each worksheet. Remember, a worksheet must be easy to read and understand—too many fonts are distracting.

To enhance your worksheet, select the cell or range of cells to format and then issue the Format, Cells command from the menu. (*Hint:* You can also select the Format Cells command from a shortcut menu.) For fonts and styles, select the *Font* tab (Figure 2.8) by clicking on it using the mouse. After making the desired selections from the dialog box, click the OK command button.

FIGURE 2.8

FORMAT CELLS DIALOG
BOX: *FONT* TAB

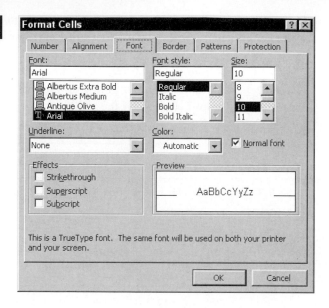

Rather than accessing the Format Cells dialog box from the menu, you can click buttons on the Formatting toolbar: Font (Arial ▼), Font Size (10 ▼), Bold (**B**), Italic (*I*), and Underline (U̲). These buttons provide single-step access to the most popular features found in the Format Cells dialog box.

You will now change fonts and styles in the worksheet.

**Perform
the
following
steps . . .**

1. SELECT: cell range from B3 to H3

2. To emphasize the column headings, make the dates bold:
CLICK: Bold button (**B**)

3. SELECT: cell range from A5 to A9

4. To italicize the product names:
CLICK: Italic button (*I*)

5. RIGHT-CLICK: cell A1
A shortcut menu appears.

6. To enhance the title:
CHOOSE: Format Cells
CLICK: *Font* tab

7. SELECT: Times New Roman from the *Font* list box
SELECT: Bold Italic from the *Font style* list box
SELECT: 18 from the *Size* list box
PRESS: **ENTER** or CLICK: OK

8. SELECT: cell A2

9. To enhance the sub-title using the Formatting toolbar:
SELECT: Times New Roman from the Font drop-down list box
(Arial ⌄)
SELECT: 14 from the Font Size drop-down list box (10 ⌄)
(*Hint:* To display the options in a drop-down list, click the down arrow beside the drop-down list on the toolbar.)

10. Save the "Sales Projections" workbook to your Data Files location.

QUICK REFERENCE Using Fonts	**1.** SELECT: the cell or cell range that you want to format
	2. CHOOSE: Format, Cells
	3. CLICK: *Font* tab
	4. SELECT: a font, font style, size, color, and effects
	5. PRESS: ENTER or CLICK: OK.

IN ADDITION USING CONDITIONAL CELL FORMATTING

New in Excel 97, you can flag results in your worksheet based on specific conditions. For example, you could highlight those salespeople who sell under 100 units by changing the font color of their name. To access this feature, choose the Format, Conditional Formatting command from the menu. For more information, ask the Office Assistant to search for help on "Conditional Formats."

FORMATTING VALUES

Numeric formats improve the appearance and readability of numbers in a worksheet by inserting dollar signs, commas, percentage symbols, and decimal places. Although the number appears differently on the worksheet when formatting is applied, the value in the Formula bar does not change—only the appearance of the number changes. In addition to dollar figures and percentages, Excel stores date and time entries as values and allows you to customize their display in the worksheet.

To enhance your worksheet with value formatting, select the desired cell range and then issue the Format, Cells command. When the dialog box appears, click the

Number tab to display a variety of numeric formatting options. Figure 2.9 provides an example of the Format Cells dialog box with the *Number* tab and the Currency category selected.

FIGURE 2.9

FORMAT CELLS DIALOG
BOX: *NUMBER* TAB

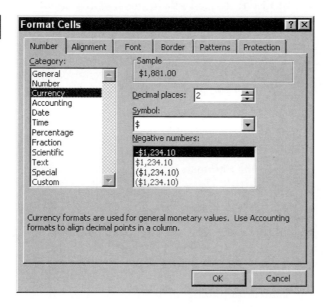

To format the values in your worksheet, select a *Category* from the list box and then make selections from that category's formatting options. You can also format values by clicking the following buttons on the Formatting toolbar: Currency Style ($), Percent Style (%), Comma Style (,), Increase Decimal (⌗), and Decrease Decimal (⌗). These buttons provide single-step access to the most popular features found in the dialog box. (*Note:* Although its name implies differently, the Currency Style ($) toolbar button formats values to the Accounting style, which lines up the dollar symbols and decimal points in a column.)

In this exercise, you change the visual appearance of several cells.

Perform the following steps . . .

1. SELECT: cell range from B9 to H9

2. To display the dialog box of numeric formatting options:
   RIGHT-CLICK: any cell in the highlighted cell range
   CHOOSE: Format Cells
   CLICK: *Number* tab

3. To view the currency formatting options:
   SELECT: Currency in the *Category* list box

4. To format the values with dollar signs, commas, and decimal places:
    SELECT: 2 in the *Decimal places* spin box
    SELECT: $ in the *Symbol* drop-down list box
    SELECT: ($1,234.00) in the *Negative numbers* list box (red option)
    PRESS: [ENTER] or CLICK: OK
    Notice that the value in H9 is unable to display in the cell. Instead, a series of "#" appears. This is Excel's way of informing you that the cell is not wide enough to display the value using the selected format. Your options are to either increase the column's width or select a different numeric format.

5. To increase the width of column H only to 10 characters:
    CLICK: cell H9
    CHOOSE: Format, Column, Width
    TYPE: **10**
    PRESS: [ENTER] or CLICK: OK

6. SELECT: cell range from B5 to H7

7. To select a number format with commas:
    CLICK: Comma Style button (,)

8. If there are no decimals displaying for the Comma style:
    CLICK: Increase Decimal button ( ) twice
    Otherwise, proceed to the next section.

QUICK REFERENCE	1.	**SELECT: the cell or cell range that you want to format**
Formatting Numbers and Dates	2.	**CHOOSE: Format, Cells**
	3.	**CLICK: *Number* tab**
	4.	**SELECT: a format from the *Category* list box**
	5.	**SELECT: formatting options for the selected category**
	6.	**PRESS: [ENTER] or CLICK: OK**

ALIGNING A CELL'S CONTENTS

Excel automatically aligns text against the left edge of a cell and values against the right edge. However, you can easily change the **cell alignment** for any type of information in the worksheet. You can even rotate text in a cell to any angle or orientation. Together with merging cells, you can create some interesting labels for your worksheet. Using the menu, choose the Format, Cells command and then make selections from the *Alignment* tab in the dialog box (Figure 2.10). Using the Formatting toolbar, click the Align Left ( ), Center ( ), Align Right ( ), and Merge and Center ( ) buttons to align cell information.

FIGURE 2.10

FORMAT CELLS DIALOG
BOX: *ALIGNMENT* TAB

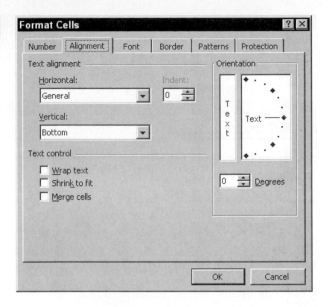

Let's change the alignment of some worksheet information.

Perform the following steps . . .

1. SELECT: cell range from B3 to H3

2. To center the date headings in their respective columns:
   CHOOSE: Format, Cells
   CLICK: *Alignment* tab
   SELECT: Center from the *Horizontal* drop-down list box
   SELECT: Center from the *Vertical* drop-down list box
   PRESS: **ENTER** or CLICK: OK

3. SELECT: cell range from A5 to A9

4. To right-align the product or row headings:
   CLICK: Align Right button (≡)

5. To center the sub-title in A2 across the width of the worksheet:
   SELECT: cell range from A2 to H2

6. CLICK: Merge and Center button (▦)
   Notice that the cells are merged into one cell and that the contents are centered. Your screen should now appear similar to Figure 2.11.

7. Save the "Sales Projections" workbook to your Data Files location.

FIGURE 2.11

THE "SALES
PROJECTIONS"
WORKSHEET AFTER
FORMATTING

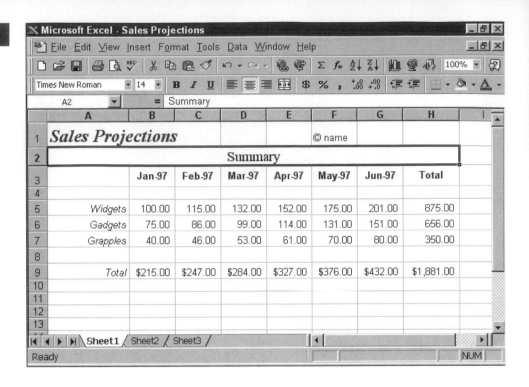

QUICK REFERENCE
Changing a Cell's
Alignment

1. **SELECT:** the cell or cell range that you want to format
2. **CLICK:** an alignment button on the Formatting toolbar, such as **Align Left** (▤), **Center** (▤), **Align Right** (▤), or **Merge and Center** (▦) buttons

---

IN ADDITION INDENTING TEXT IN A WORKSHEET CELL

New in Excel 97, you can indent text appearing in a worksheet cell up to 15 steps. To do so, select the desired cell and then click the Increase In-

dent button (▤) on the Formatting toolbar. To remove an indentation, you click the Decrease Indent button (▤).

ADDING BORDERS AND SHADING CELLS

The gridlines that appear in the document window are nonprinting lines, provided only to help you line up information in the worksheet. To enhance the readability of your printed worksheets, you can add borders, underlines, and shading to cells. Borders are used to separate data into logical sections and to emphasize titles. As well, these features allow you to create professional-looking invoice forms, memos, and tables.

To add borders and shaded patterns to your worksheet, select the desired cell or cell range and issue the Format, Cells command. In the dialog box that appears, select the *Border* tab or the *Patterns* tab. You can also click the Borders drop-down list (⬚▾) on the Formatting toolbar to quickly apply borders to a selection or use the Fill Color button (⬚▾) and the Font Color button (A▾) to change the background and font colors.

You will now practice creating borders and shading cells.

Perform the following steps . . .

1. SELECT: cell range from B3 to H3

2. To add a border to the worksheet:
   CLICK: down arrow beside the Borders drop-down list (⬚▾)
   Make sure that you click the down arrow and not the button itself. You should see a list of sample border formats appear.

3. SELECT: a thick outline border (in the bottom right-hand corner)
   The formatting is immediately applied to the selection.

4. To apply a color to the cells' background:
   CLICK: down arrow beside the Fill Color drop-down list (⬚▾)
   SELECT: a light yellow color

5. To change the text color:
   CLICK: down arrow beside the Font Color drop-down list (A▾)
   SELECT: a dark blue color

6. SELECT: cell range from B9 to H9

7. To add two different borders to this range:
   CHOOSE: Format, Cells
   CLICK: *Border* tab
   SELECT: a single line in the *Style* group
   SELECT: a top location (⬚) in the *Border* group
   SELECT: a double line in the *Style* group
   SELECT: a bottom location (⬚) in the *Border* group
   PRESS: **ENTER** or CLICK: OK
   Notice that you select a new line style before choosing the border group to which you want it applied.

8. In order to get a full appreciation of fonts and borders, Excel lets you temporarily remove the **gridlines** from the worksheet. This provides a more accurate view of how the worksheet will look when printed. To temporarily remove the gridlines from your worksheet:
   CLICK: cell A12
   CHOOSE: Tools, Options
   CLICK: *View* tab
   SELECT: *Gridlines* check box to remove the "✓"
   PRESS: **ENTER** or CLICK: OK
   (*Note:* This option provides a cleaner view of your worksheet on the screen, but it does not affect how the worksheet will print. The print options for gridlines and headings are specified in the Page Setup dialog box, described later in this session.)

Your worksheet should now appear similar to Figure 2.12.

FIGURE 2.12

APPLYING BORDERS AND
COLORS, AND
REMOVING THE
GRIDLINES

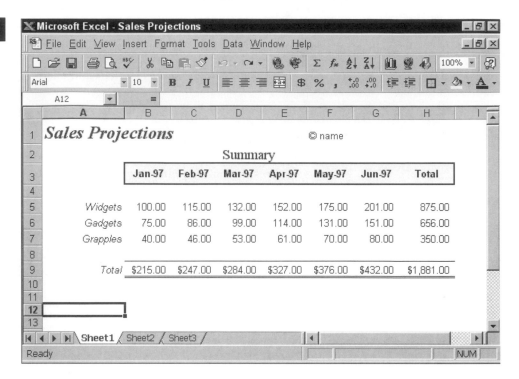

9. To return the display to normal:
CHOOSE: Tools, Options
CLICK: *View* tab (if it is not already selected)
SELECT: *Gridlines* check box so that a "✓" appears
PRESS: (ENTER) or CLICK: OK

10. Save the "Sales Projections" workbook to your Data Files location.

QUICK REFERENCE

Adding Borders, Colors,
and Patterns

1. **SELECT: the cell or cell range that you want to format**
2. **CHOOSE: Format, Cells**
3. **CLICK:** *Border* **tab to specify border lines**
4. **CLICK:** *Patterns* **tab to specify a shading level or color**
5. **PRESS:** (ENTER) **or CLICK: OK**

IN ADDITION ADDING A BACKGROUND BITMAP TO A WORKSHEET

Similar to specifying wallpaper for your Windows desktop, you can now add a texture or bitmap graphic image to an Excel 97 worksheet. To do so, choose Format, Sheet, Background from the Menu bar and then select a bitmap file. Excel will tile the selected graphic image across the entire worksheet.

COPYING FORMATTING OPTIONS

Excel's Format Painter button ( ) lets you copy the formatting styles from one area in your worksheet to another. To copy a cell's formatting, select the cell and click the Format Painter button ( ). To apply the formatting, you click on a single cell or drag the paintbrush mouse pointer to format an entire cell range. When you release the mouse button, the formatting styles are copied from the original selection to your new selection. Not only does this feature speed formatting operations, it ensures consistency among the cell formatting in your worksheet.

You will now practice using the Format Painter.

Perform the following steps . . .

1. To practice copying styles, let's format a cell with new options:
   SELECT: cell B5
   CLICK: Decrease Decimal button ( ) twice
   The entry in cell B5 will now appear as 100.

2. To copy this formatting change to the rest of the values:
   CLICK: Format Painter button ( )

3. Move the mouse pointer into the document window. Notice that the mouse pointer is now a cross with a paintbrush.

4. SELECT: the cell range from B5 to H9

5. Release the mouse button. Notice that all the values in the range are now formatted with the same features as cell B5.

6. To undo the last operation:
   CLICK: Undo button ( ) three times
   PRESS: ESC to remove the dashed marquee from around cell B5
   The cells now appear with their original formatting (two decimals).

7. PRESS: CTRL + HOME to move to cell A1

QUICK REFERENCE
Copying a Cell's Formatting

1. **SELECT: the cell whose formatting you want to copy**
2. **CLICK: Format Painter button ( ) on the Standard toolbar**
3. **SELECT: the cell range that you want to format**
4. **Release the mouse button to complete the operation.**

IN ADDITION COPYING FORMATTING TO SEVERAL RANGES

You can copy a cell's formatting to several cell ranges at the same time by double-clicking the Format Painter button ( ). After you apply the first coat to a cell range in the

worksheet, the mouse pointer remains a cross with a paintbrush so that you can paint other cell ranges. When you are finished, click the Format Painter button ( ) to return to the cross mouse pointer.

REMOVING FORMATTING OPTIONS

If you want to remove the formatting features applied to an area on your worksheet, select the cell or range of cells and then choose the Edit, Clear command from the menu. On the cascading menu that appears, select the Formats command. This command removes the formatting options only, not the contents of the cell or range of cells.

In this exercise, you practice removing formatting options.

Perform the following steps . . .

1. SELECT: cell A1

2. To remove the formatting for this cell:
CHOOSE: Edit, Clear, Formats
Notice that the cell's formatting is stripped while its contents are left intact.

3. To undo the last command:
CLICK: Undo button ( )

QUICK REFERENCE
Removing a Cell's Formatting

1. **SELECT: a cell or cell range**
2. **CHOOSE: Edit, Clear, Formats**

USING THE AUTOFORMAT COMMAND

The **AutoFormat** command lets you apply a predefined table format, complete with numeric formats, alignments, borders, shading, and colors, to a group of cells on your worksheet. This feature assumes that your data is organized in the worksheet as a table, with labels running down the left column and across the top row. To automatically format your worksheet, select a cell range and then choose the Format, AutoFormat command.

Let's apply a few different formats to our worksheet.

Perform the following steps . . .

1. SELECT: cell range from A3 to H9

2. To display the AutoFormat dialog box:
CHOOSE: Format, AutoFormat

3. In the *Table format* list box:
SELECT: Colorful 2
PRESS: (ENTER) or CLICK: OK

4. To remove the highlighting from the range:
SELECT: cell A12
Your screen should now appear similar to Figure 2.13.

FIGURE 2.13

APPLYING THE
AUTOFORMAT COMMAND

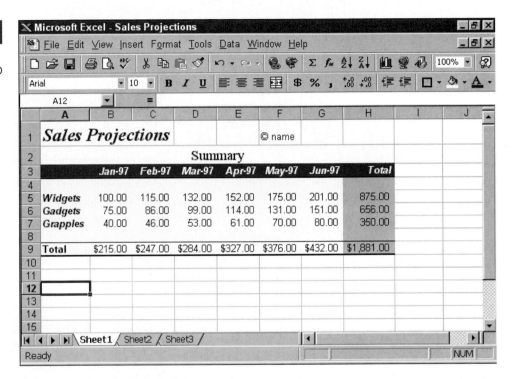

5. Practice choosing some of the other table format options from the AutoFormat dialog box. Before proceeding, reselect the Colorful 2.

6. Save the "Sales Projections" workbook to your Data Files location.

QUICK REFERENCE
Using AutoFormat

1. **SELECT: the cell or cell range that you want to format**
2. **CHOOSE: Format, AutoFormat**
3. **SELECT: an option from the *Table format* list box**
4. **PRESS: (ENTER) or CLICK: OK**

PRINTING THE WORKBOOK

This section introduces the commands for printing a workbook, including options for setting up the page and previewing the output.

DEFINING THE PAGE LAYOUT

You define the page layout settings for printing a workbook using the File, Page Setup command. In the dialog box that appears, you specify **margins, headers, footers,** and whether gridlines or row and column headings should appear on the final printed document. To make the process more manageable, Excel organizes the page layout settings under four tabs in the Page Setup dialog box (Figure 2.14):

- *Page* tab   The *Page* tab lets you specify the paper size, print scale, and the workbook's print orientation (for example, portrait or landscape).

- *Margins* tab   You specify the top, bottom, left, and right page margins in inches using this tab. Excel also lets you center the worksheet both horizontally and vertically.

- *Header/Footer* tab   You use a header and a footer to print static information at the top and bottom of each page, respectively.

- *Sheet* tab   Besides specifying the actual print area on this tab, you can tell Excel whether to print gridlines, titles, or row and column headings.

FIGURE 2.14

PAGE SETUP DIALOG BOX:
PAGE TAB DISPLAYED

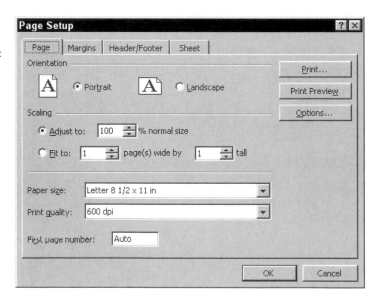

In this section, you define the page layout specifications for the "Sales Projections" workbook.

Perform the following steps . . .

1. Before changing options in the Page Setup dialog box, let's specify the print area for the worksheet:
   SELECT: cell range from A1 to H9
   CHOOSE: File, Print Area, Set Print Area
   PRESS: CTRL + HOME
   The print area on the worksheet is now surrounded by dashed lines.

2. To specify the page layout settings:
CHOOSE: File, Page Setup
CLICK: *Page* tab

3. Make the following selections:
SELECT: Portrait in the *Orientation* group
SELECT: Adjust to 100% normal size in the *Scaling* group
SELECT: "Letter 8½ × 11 in" in the *Paper Size* drop-down list box

4. To specify the margins:
CLICK: *Margins* tab

5. Make the following selections:
SELECT: 1.5 inches for the *Top* margin
SELECT: 1.5 inches for the *Bottom* margin
SELECT: 1 inch for the *Left* margin
SELECT: 1 inch for the *Right* margin
(*Hint:* To increase and decrease the margin values, you click the up and down triangles that appear to the right of each spin box.)

6. To center the worksheet between the left and right margins:
SELECT: *Horizontally* check box in the *Center on page* group

7. To specify a header and a footer:
CLICK: *Header/Footer* tab

8. To create a custom header:
SELECT: "(none)" at the top of the *Header* drop-down list box
CLICK: Custom Header command button
Figure 2.15 shows the Header dialog box and labels the buttons used for inserting information into the different sections.

FIGURE 2.15

CUSTOM HEADER DIALOG BOX

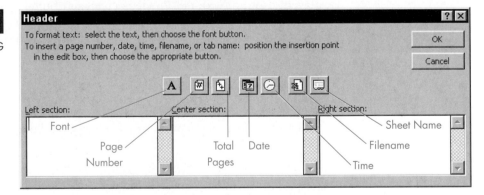

9. To create a header that prints the current date against the right margin:
CLICK: the mouse pointer in the *Right section* once
TYPE: **Printed on:**
PRESS: Space bar once
CLICK: Date button (as labeled in Figure 2.15)
CLICK: OK command button
You will see the custom header appear in the Page Setup dialog box.

10. To select a predefined footer:
    SELECT: "Sales Projections, Page 1" from the *Footer* drop-down list box

11. To confirm that the print area is correct and that no gridlines will appear on the printed worksheet:
    CLICK: *Sheet* tab

12. Confirm that the cell range from A1 to H9 appears in the *Print area* text box. Also, ensure that there are no check boxes selected in the *Print* group. (*Note:* By default, Excel does not print gridlines on your worksheet.)

13. To complete the Page Setup dialog box and return to the worksheet:
    PRESS: (ENTER) or CLICK: OK

14. Save the "Sales Projections" workbook to your Data Files location.

QUICK REFERENCE
Preparing to Print

1. **SELECT: the cell range that you want to print**

2. **CHOOSE: File, Print Area, Set Print Area**

3. **CHOOSE: File, Page Setup**

4. **In the Page Setup dialog box, specify options for page layout settings, margins, headers and footers, and whether to print gridlines or column and row headings.**

5. **PRESS: (ENTER) or CLICK: OK**

PREVIEWING THE OUTPUT

You can preview a workbook in a full-page display by choosing the File, Print Preview command or clicking the Print Preview button ([🔍]). Once the preview is displayed, use the Next and Previous command buttons near the top of the screen to move through the document page by page. Use the magnifying glass mouse pointer to zoom in and out on the page. If you need to modify some page layout options, click the Setup button to display the Page Setup dialog box or the Margins button to drag margin lines in the Preview window. You can also click the Page Break Preview button to adjust the page breaks in your worksheet and to resize the print area. A watermark appears in the background with "Page 1," "Page 2," and so on. This feature lets you visually arrange the print boundaries using the mouse.

Let's preview the worksheet.

Perform the following steps . . .

1. To preview how the "Sales Projections" workbook will print:
   CLICK: Print Preview button ([🔍])

2. To zoom in on the page:
   CLICK: Zoom command button

3. To zoom out, move the mouse pointer over the preview page and then click the left mouse button once.

4. When you are finished previewing the worksheet:
PRESS: (ESC) or CLICK: Close

PRINTING THE SELECTED RANGE

When you are satisfied with your worksheet in the Preview mode, choose the File, Print command to display the Print dialog box (Figure 2.16) or click the Print button (🖨) to send it directly to the printer. In the Print dialog box, you can specify what to print (a selected cell range or the entire workbook, for example) and how many copies.

FIGURE 2.16

PRINT DIALOG BOX

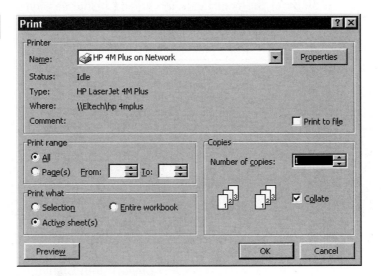

Let's print your worksheet.

Perform the following steps . . .

1. To send the worksheet to the printer and bypass the Print dialog box:
CLICK: Print button (🖨)
The document is printed using the default settings. This produces the same result as choosing the File, Print command and then clicking the OK command button, without changing any settings in the dialog box.

2. Save the "Sales Projections" workbook to your Data Files location.

3. Close the workbook and then exit Excel.

QUICK REFERENCE	1.	**CLICK: Print button (🖨)**
Printing a Worksheet	2.	**SELECT: additional print options, as desired**
	3.	**PRESS:** (ENTER) **or CLICK: OK**

SUMMARY

This session introduced you to the everyday procedures required to effectively work with Microsoft Excel. You created a workbook from scratch and then practiced entering formulas and using the SUM function. You also learned to use some of Excel's "Auto" features, including AutoCalculate, AutoComplete, AutoCorrect, and AutoFormat. The majority of the session, however, dealt with Excel's formatting capabilities. Column widths, row heights, fonts, numeric formats, cell alignments, borders, colors, and shading were all modified in customizing the sample workbook. Toward the end of the session, you concentrated on setting up and previewing a workbook for printing.

Many of the commands introduced in the session are provided in Table 2.1, the Command Summary.

TABLE 2.1	*Command*	*Description*
Command Summary	Edit, Clear, Formats	Removes formatting from the selected cell range.
	File, Page Setup	Sets the print area, margins, headers, and footers.
	File, Print (🖨)	Prints the workbook.
	File, Print Preview (🔍)	Previews the workbook before printing.
	Format, AutoFormat	Formats the selected range using predefined styles.
	Format, Cells	*Font* tab: Applies fonts, styles, and point sizes to cells. *Number* tab: Changes the appearance of values. *Alignment* tab: Changes the alignment of a cell. *Border* tab: Applies borders to cells. *Patterns* tab: Applies shading to cells.
	Format, Column, AutoFit Selection	Changes the column width to the best fit.
	Format, Column, Width	Changes the column width.
	Format, Row, Height	Changes the row height.
	Tools, Options	Removes gridlines from the screen display.
	Tools, Spelling (🔤)	Spell-checks a cell range, worksheet, or a workbook.

KEY TERMS

AutoCalculate

In Excel, a software feature that sums the selected range of cells and displays the result in the Status bar.

AutoComplete

In Excel, a software feature that assists you in entering data into a worksheet by filling in letters from existing entries in the column as you type.

AutoCorrect

In Excel, a software feature that corrects common typing and spelling mistakes automatically as you type. It also enables you to enter complex symbols quickly and easily.

AutoFormat

In Excel, a software feature that applies professionally designed formatting styles to your worksheet tables.

cell alignment

The positioning of data entered into a worksheet cell in relation to the cell borders.

cell range

One or more cells in a worksheet that together form a rectangle.

column width

The width of a worksheet column measured in characters. Because the actual width of a group of characters changes depending on the font size, it is often used only as a relative measure.

font

All the characters of one size in a particular *typeface;* includes numbers, punctuation marks, and upper- and lowercase letters.

footer

Descriptive information (such as page number and date) that appears at the bottom of each page of a document.

functions

Shortcuts that can be used in formulas to perform calculations.

gridlines

The lines on a worksheet that assist the user in lining up the cell pointer with a particular column letter or row number.

header

Descriptive information (such as page number and date) that appears at the top of each page of a document.

margins

Space between the edge of the paper and the top, bottom, left, and right edges of printed text.

row height

The height of a worksheet row measured in points. Points are the measurement unit for type—there are 72 points to the inch.

SUM function

Function used to add values stored in a range of spreadsheet cells.

typeface

The shape and appearance of characters. There are two categories of typefaces: serif and sans serif. Serif type (for example, Times Roman) is more decorative and, some say, easier to read than sans serif type (for example, **Arial**).

EXERCISES

SHORT ANSWERS

1. Why use the SUM function rather than a simple addition formula?

2. What is meant by a "best fit" or "AutoFit" column width?

3. How do you apply formatting changes to an entire worksheet?

4. How do you select multiple cell ranges in a worksheet?

5. What does "#########" in a cell indicate?

6. What unit of measure is used to specify the height of a row?

7. What unit of measure is used to specify the width of a column?

8. How does AutoCorrect differ from AutoComplete?

9. Name the tabs in the Page Setup dialog box.

10. Does turning the gridlines off for the screen display affect the way the document prints? Explain.

HANDS-ON

(*Note:* Ensure that you know the storage location of your Advantage Files and your Data Files before proceeding.)

1. This exercise retrieves an existing workbook, edits the information, and saves the workbook under a new filename. You also send a copy of the updated file to the printer.

   a. Open the "Exp-Qtr1" workbook that is stored in the Advantage Files location.

   b. Modify the worksheet to reflect the second quarter's expenses by editing the following cells listed.

Move to Cell	TYPE
D1	*your name*
B2	Apr-97
C2	May-97
D2	Jun-97
B6	43.44
C4	39.65
C7	119
D6	83.91
D8	98.60

c. Save this workbook to your Data Files location under the name "Exp-Qtr2". (*Hint*: Use the File, Save As command.)

d. Specify a header that prints only the current date in the top left-hand corner of the page.

e. Specify a footer that prints only the page number in the bottom right-hand corner of the page.

f. Review the worksheet in Print Preview mode.

g. Select the cell range from A1 to E10 and then set the print area.

h. Print the workbook.

i. Save the workbook, replacing the old version of the file.

2. This exercise uses the formatting commands covered in this session to enhance the "Exp-Qtr2" workbook.

a. If the workbook is not already loaded into memory, open the "Exp-Qtr2" workbook.

b. Make the following changes to column widths:

Column	Width
A	15
B	10
C	10
D	10
E	12

c. Make the following changes to row heights:

Row	Height
1	25
2	20
3	6
9	6
10	18

d. Make the headings from cell B2 to E2 bold and italic.

e. Center the headings horizontally and vertically in their columns.

f. Make the Expense items (the row labels) from A4 to A10 bold.

g. Right-align the Expense items.

h. Increase the size of the font for the title (in cell A1) to 18 points.

i. Select the cells from B2 to E2.

j. Place an outline border around these cells and then shade the interior a light green color.

k. Select the cells from B4 to E8.

l. Place a border grid around each of these cells and then shade the interior a light yellow color.

m. Change the screen display by removing the column and row headers and the gridlines. Then, clear the print area using the File, Print Area, Clear Print Area command.

n. Delete the word "Type" in cell A2.

o. Save the workbook as "Expenses - Formatted" to your Data Files location. Your screen should now appear similar to Figure 2.17.

p. Set the print area again and then print the workbook.

q. Close the workbook.

FIGURE 2.17

"EXPENSES - FORMATTED" WORKBOOK

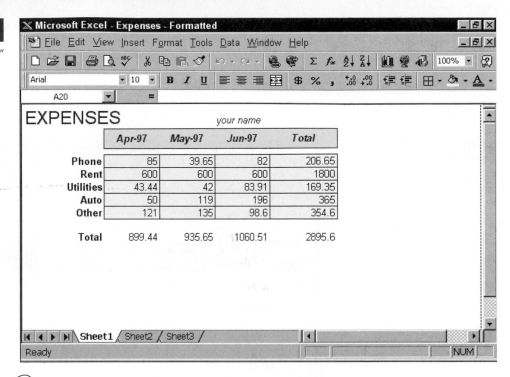

3. This exercise provides a step-by-step approach for using the formatting commands covered in this session to create a memo or fax form.

   a. Open a new workbook.

   b. Move to cell A1.

   c. TYPE: **Memorandum**

   d. Center the title between columns A and E.

   e. Choose an interesting font with boldface and a size of at least 24 points for the title.

   f. Make columns A through E at least 12 characters wide.

   g. Enter the following information:

Move to cell	TYPE
A3	**DATE:**
A4	**TO:**
A5	**FROM:**
A6	**SUBJECT:**

   h. Increase the row height to 30 points for rows 3 through 6.

   i. Right-align, italicize, and make bold each of the row headings in column A.

   j. Select an interesting font and a size of at least 12 points.

   k. Color the cell range from A1 to E1 and then change the font color.

l.   Color the cell range from A8 to E8 with the same fill color.

m.   Move to cell A1.

n.   Save this workbook as "Memorandum" to your Data Files location. Your worksheet should appear similar to Figure 2.18.

o.   Print and then close the workbook.

FIGURE 2.18

"MEMORANDUM" WORKBOOK

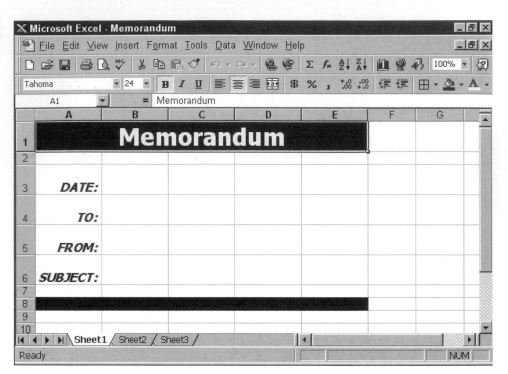

4.   **On Your Own:** Creating a Custom Invoice Form
For this exercise, you are to create a custom invoice form for your home-based business. The form should include your company name and address at the top of the form, an area for the customer's name and address, and then the following column headings:

Quantity   Item #   Description   Unit Price   Total Price

Outline the columns with borders to visually separate the itemized information. As desired, apply additional formatting to make the invoice professional and attractive. Save the workbook as "My Invoice Form" to your Data Files location and then print a copy of the worksheet. Finally, close the workbook before proceeding.

5.   **On Your Own:** Formatting Your Personal Phone Book
Retrieve the "Personal Phone Book" workbook that you created at the end of Session 1. Format the worksheet using the commands learned in this session and then print a copy of your phone book for review. When you are satisfied with the output, save the workbook back to your Data Files location. Close the workbook and then exit Excel.

CASE PROBLEMS **MADRID CLOTHING COMPANY**

(*Note:* In the following case problems, assume the role of the primary characters and perform the same steps that they identify. You may want to re-read the session opening.)

1. It's 10 o'clock on a Sunday morning and Khalid's one day off will be spent in front of his computer. He must create, format, and print the spreadsheet for his expansion proposal today. He will venture to the company's main office tomorrow and place the proposal strategically on Suriya's desk before anyone else arrives. With the caffeine from a fourth cup of coffee tingling through his veins, Khalid opens his folder of handwritten notes. His first task is to create the basic spreadsheet layout.

From the following table that Khalid has drawn by hand, create a spreadsheet called "Lucky 7" and then save it to your Data Files location.

California Expansion	Q1/98	Q2/98	Q3/98	Q4/98
Best-Case Scenario:				
Sales Revenue	22,500	38,000	52,800	85,700
Cost of Goods Sold				
Gross Margin				
Variable Expenses				
Fixed Expenses	6,000	6,000	6,000	6,000
Net Profit				
Worst-Case Scenario:				
Sales Revenue	15,800	18,900	26,500	36,000
Cost of Goods Sold				
Gross Margin				
Variable Expenses				
Fixed Expenses	7,500	7,500	7,500	7,500
Net Profit				

2. Looking over the spreadsheet, Khalid realizes how much work is still ahead of him. But instead of diving into the spreadsheet haphazardly, he contemplates the steps that he needs to perform. First of all, he must complete the missing information. For example, the Cost of Goods Sold and Variable Expenses for the Best-Case Scenario are 55 percent and 10 percent of the Sales Revenue, respectively. For the Worst-Case Scenario, the Cost of Goods Sold and Variable Expenses are 60 percent and 15 percent of the Sales Revenue. He must also enter a formula for each quarter to calculate the Gross Margin (Sales Revenue minus Cost of Goods Sold) and the Net Profit (Gross Margin minus Variable and Fixed Expenses). Lastly, Khalid decides to add a column called YTD that totals the figures from the four quarters.

Complete the "Lucky 7" spreadsheet following the steps that Khalid has outlined and then save the file to the Advantage Diskette.

3. Knowing that the presentation style is sometimes as important as the information itself, Khalid decides to format the "Lucky 7" worksheet to give it a professional appearance. Having worked through the examples in this session, Khalid applies fonts, styles, and numeric formats to the worksheet, aligns the cell contents of the column headings, applies some border lines and colors, and changes column widths and row heights. When satisfied with its appearance, Khalid checks the spelling in the spreadsheet and then prints it with the current date and page number appearing in the footer of the page.

Following Khalid's lead, format, spell-check, and print the workbook, and then save the file to the Advantage Diskette. Make sure that you test the accuracy of the spreadsheet's formulas using the AutoCalculate feature. You should also insert some new values for the Sales Revenue and watch the Net Profit result adjust. Check at least one of the columns manually using a calculator before saving and then closing the workbook. When finished, exit Excel and shut-down Windows.

Microsoft Excel 97 for Windows

Increasing Your Productivity

SESSION

3

IRWIN

COMPUTER & INFORMATION TECHNOLOGY

INTRODUCTION

Electronic spreadsheets are timesavers compared to the old pencil-and-paper spreadsheets. Now let us demonstrate some timesavers for the timesaver. Instead of building a worksheet cell by cell, Excel provides you with some data entry and command shortcuts that work with cell ranges. You will also learn how to enter built-in functions for performing complex calculations.

RIVERSIDE FORD, INC.

Riverside Ford is one of New Jersey's largest car dealerships. Located near the Meadowlands Arena, Riverside has always maintained a high profile in the community and has easily met Ford's contractual obligations for selling new cars and trucks. One of Zachary Rempel's duties as a business manager with Riverside is to generate the month-end summary report that must be submitted to Ford's regional office.

Just last week, the owner, Jackson L. Davies, purchased a new computer for Zachary and made him personally responsible for generating all of the dealership's reports. With an increased workload, Zachary knew that he would have to streamline operations and find a more efficient method for summarizing the data he received. Fortunately, the computer came with Microsoft Excel installed and, after only a few days, Zachary is now creating, formatting, and printing worksheets. However, Zachary has also become a little frustrated with Excel. He doesn't like entering long and complex formulas to perform standard calculations, like finding the average value for a column of numbers, picking the highest salesperson's commission in the month, or showing the monthly payment for a financed vehicle. And though he knows that there must be a better way, he doesn't have time to figure out these other methods on his own.

In this session, you and Zachary learn to improve your productivity in creating and editing worksheets. In addition to learning how to copy and move information and how to insert and delete columns and rows, you are introduced to Excel's built-in functions for performing standard calculations. This session provides you with some of the most powerful productivity tools that Excel has to offer.

ABSOLUTE AND RELATIVE CELL ADDRESSES

This section adds a new twist to referencing cells in formulas. In previous sessions, you typed the cell address or clicked on the cell that you wanted to include in a formula. You should be aware, however, that there are two types of cell addresses that can be entered into formulas: *relative* and *absolute*. The differences between the two types become important when you start copying and moving information in your worksheet.

When a formula is copied from one worksheet location to another, Excel automatically adjusts the cell references in the copied formula to reflect their new location. This adjustment spares you from having to type many similar formulas into the worksheet and thus saves a tremendous amount of time. A cell reference that adjusts when it is copied is referred to as a **relative cell address.** On the other hand, there are times when you don't want a cell reference to automatically adjust when it is copied. A cell reference that refers to an exact location on the worksheet and does not adjust is called an **absolute cell address.**

By default, formulas that you enter in Excel use relative cell references. To use an absolute cell reference, you must precede the column letter and the row number of the cell address with a dollar sign. For example, to make cell B5 an absolute cell reference in a formula, you would type dollar signs before the B and before the 5, such as B5. If you wanted to have the cell reference automatically adjust the row number when it was copied but not the column letter, then you would use *mixed cell addressing* and type a dollar sign before the column letter only, such as $B5. You will practice using these types of cell references in the next section on copying and moving worksheet information.

COPYING AND MOVING INFORMATION

To efficiently construct a worksheet, you need tools that reduce the number of repetitive entries you are required to make. For example, once you have created a formula that adds figures in one column, why not copy that formula to sum the adjacent column as well? Two of the most common editing activities in a worksheet are copying and moving data.

There are several different methods for copying and moving information in a worksheet. Similar to most Windows applications, Excel provides the **Clipboard** for sharing information within a workbook, among workbooks, and among applications. For quick "from-here-to-there" copy and move operations, Excel provides the **drag and drop** method where you use the mouse to drag cell information in a worksheet. This section provides examples using both methods for copying and moving information.

USING THE CLIPBOARD

If the drag and drop method is quicker and easier, why use the Clipboard to copy and move information? The Clipboard provides greater flexibility, allowing you to copy information to multiple locations in a worksheet. To use this method, you first select the cell range that you want to copy or move and then cut or copy the selection to the Clipboard. After moving the cell pointer to the desired destination, you paste the data from the Clipboard into the worksheet. You can then repeat the paste operation multiple times, if required.

The Clipboard commands, toolbar buttons, and keyboard shortcuts for copying and moving information appear in Table 3.1.

TABLE 3.1

Copying and Moving
Information Using the
Clipboard

Task Description	Menu Command	Toolbar Button	Keyboard Shortcut
Moves the selected cell range from the worksheet to the Clipboard	Edit, Cut	✂	CTRL +x
Copies the selected cell range to the Clipboard	Edit, Copy	▥	CTRL +c
Inserts the contents of the Clipboard at the cell pointer	Edit, Paste	▤	CTRL +v

FIGURE 3.1

THE "SALESREP"
WORKBOOK

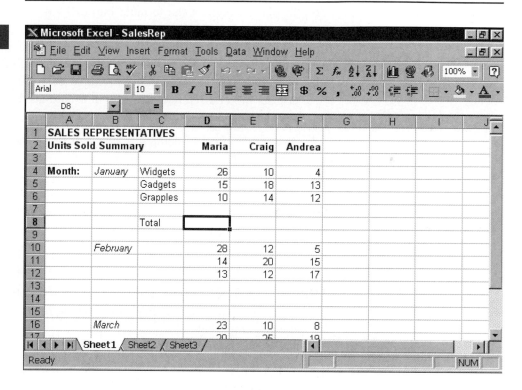

To practice using the Clipboard, you will open and then modify the "SalesRep" workbook (Figure 3.1). This workbook provides an incomplete summary for three sales representatives.

Perform the following steps . . .

1. Make sure that you know the storage location of your Advantage Files and your Data Files before proceeding. Open the "SalesRep" workbook, located in your Advantage Files location.

2. Let's cancel Excel's option for moving the cell pointer down one row each time you press (ENTER). Do the following:
   CHOOSE: Tools, Options
   CLICK: *Edit* tab
   SELECT: *Move selection after Enter* check box so that no "✓" appears
   PRESS: (ENTER) or CLICK: OK

3. The first step in completing this worksheet is to sum the January data for each salesperson. Do the following:
CLICK: cell D8

4. TYPE: **=d4+d5+d6**
PRESS: [ENTER]
The cell should now include the sum of the figures in column D (51).

5. To copy this formula onto the Clipboard:
CLICK: Copy button ([icon])
A dashed marquee now surrounds the cell range.

6. To place a copy of the formula into cell E8:
CLICK: cell E8
PRESS: [ENTER]
Notice that the result of the formula is the sum of the figures in column E (42). Because the formula uses relative cell addresses, it automatically adjusts the cell references to the new column. Look in the Formula bar to see the new formula (=E4+E5+E6).

7. To see the effect of using absolute cell references, let's edit the formula in cell E8:
DOUBLE-CLICK: cell E8
You will see the formula appear in the cell ready for editing and the color-coded borders around the appropriate cells.

8. PRESS: [HOME]
PRESS: [→] once
The cursor now appears to the right of the equal sign.

9. To make a cell address absolute, you type a dollar sign in front of the column letter and row number. However, there is a shortcut method, as demonstrated below:
PRESS: [F4] (Absolute key)
PRESS: [→]
PRESS: [F4] (Absolute key)
PRESS: [→]
PRESS: [F4] (Absolute key)
PRESS: [ENTER]

10. To copy this new formula onto the Clipboard using the shortcut menu:
RIGHT-CLICK: cell E8
CHOOSE: Copy

11. To place a copy of the Clipboard's contents into cell F8:
CLICK: cell F8
PRESS: [ENTER]
Notice that the result of the formula is still the sum of the figures in column E. The formula did not automatically adjust because it uses absolute cell references.

12. Now let's clean up the Total line. You are going to enter a new formula in cell D8 and then copy it to columns E and F. To begin:
CLICK: cell D8
PRESS: (**DELETE**)

13. DOUBLE-CLICK: AutoSum button (⟮Σ⟯)

14. To copy and then paste the formula:
CLICK: Copy button (⟮🗋⟯)
SELECT: cell range from E8 to F8
PRESS: (**ENTER**)

QUICK REFERENCE
Copying and Moving
Cell Information

1. Select the source cell or cell range.

2. To copy or move information:
CLICK: Copy button (⟮🗋⟯)
CLICK: Cut button (⟮✂⟯)

3. Select the destination cell or cell range.

4. PRESS: (**ENTER**) or CLICK: Paste button (⟮🗋⟯)

USING DRAG AND DROP

One of Excel's most popular features is drag and drop. This method uses the mouse to copy and move information from one location to another without using the Clipboard. Although you cannot perform multiple pastes, it is by far the easiest method for copying and moving information short distances. You can even use drag and drop to copy information between sheets in a workbook by holding down the (**ALT**) key and dragging the selection over a sheet tab.

You will now practice using drag and drop.

Perform the following steps . . .

1. To demonstrate how you can move cells using drag and drop:
SELECT: cell range from D2 to F2

2. Position the mouse pointer over a border of the selected cell range until a white arrow appears.

3. CLICK: left mouse button and hold it down
DRAG: mouse pointer downward one row until a shaded outline appears around cells D3 to F3

4. Release the left mouse button. The contents are moved to the newly high-lighted cell range.

5. To undo the last move operation:
CLICK: Undo button (⟮↺ ▾⟯)

6. To copy cells using drag and drop:
SELECT: cell range from C4 to C8

7. Position the mouse pointer over a border of the selected cell range until a white arrow appears.

8. PRESS: `CTRL` and hold it down
CLICK: left mouse button and hold it down
DRAG: mouse pointer downward until a shaded outline appears around cells C10 to C14
(*Note*: When you hold down the `CTRL` key, a plus sign appears at the tip of the mouse pointer to inform you that dragging and dropping the selection will result in a copy operation.)

9. Release the left mouse button. Using the same process, copy the cell range from C10 to C14 to the cell range C16 to C20. Your screen should appear similar to Figure 3.2.

FIGURE 3.2

THE "SALESREP" WORKBOOK AFTER COPYING AND MOVING CELL INFORMATION

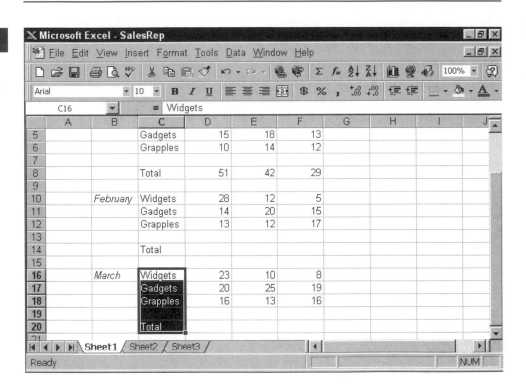

QUICK REFERENCE
Move and Copy Cells
Using Drag and Drop

1. Select the cell or cell range to copy or move.

2. Position the mouse pointer (a white arrow) over any border of the selected cells. (To copy the cells, hold down the `CTRL` key.)

3. Drag the selected cells to their destination. (To move between sheets in a workbook, hold down the `ALT` key.)

4. Release the mouse button and, if necessary, `CTRL` and/or `ALT`.

USING FILL RIGHT AND FILL DOWN

Excel provides two commands specially designed for copying formulas: Edit, Fill, Right and Edit, Fill, Down. These commands are used when you have entered a single formula or function that needs to be extended across a row (Fill Right) or down a column (Fill Down). Rather than choosing the menu commands, you can select the cell range and press the keyboard shortcuts CTRL +r for Fill Right or CTRL +d for Fill Down. If you prefer using the mouse, you can select a cell to copy and then drag the cell's **fill handle,** which is the black square that appears in the lower right-hand corner of a cell or cell range. This copies the formula across or down the selected range. You will practice using the fill handle in the next section.

Let's demonstrate the Fill Right command.

Perform the following steps . . .

1. To begin, let's create the first formula:
   CLICK: cell D14
   DOUBLE-CLICK: AutoSum button (Σ)

2. To copy the formula in cell D14 to the remaining cells:
   SELECT: cell range from D14 to F14
   CHOOSE: Edit, Fill, Right
   (*Note*: Ensure that the cell with the formula appears in the top left-hand corner of the selected range.)

3. You will now copy the formulas to the cell range D20 to F20. Before proceeding, ensure that cells D14 to F14 remain highlighted:
   CLICK: Copy button ( )
   CLICK: cell D20
   PRESS: ENTER

4. Save the workbook as "Sales Rep Report" to your Data Files location.

QUICK REFERENCE
Using Fill Right and Fill Down

1. Select the cell that contains the information to copy.

2. Extend the cell range downward or to the right, depending on where you want to place the copies. (*Hint:* The cell to copy always appears in the top left-hand corner of the cell range.)

3. CHOOSE: Edit, Fill, Right or Edit, Fill, Down, depending on where you want to place the copies.

CREATING A SERIES WITH AUTOFILL

With Excel's AutoFill feature, you can quickly enter a series into a worksheet. A **series** is simply a sequence of data that follows a pattern, typically mathematical (1, 2, 3,...) or date (Jan, Feb, Mar,...). From the menu, you enter a series using the Edit, Fill, Series command. If you prefer using the mouse, you can drag a cell's fill handle.

You will now practice using AutoFill.

Perform the following steps . . .

1. In this exercise, we move to a blank area of the worksheet to demonstrate some uses for the fill handle. To begin, do the following:
CLICK: Name box in the Formula bar
TYPE: **a50**
PRESS: **ENTER** or CLICK: OK

2. Move the cell pointer up to cell A40.

3. TYPE: **Jan**
PRESS: **ENTER**
You have to type in at least one cell entry as the starting point for a series. Make sure that your cell pointer remains on cell A40.

4. Position the mouse over the small black square in the bottom right-hand corner of the cell pointer. The mouse pointer will change to a black cross hair.

5. CLICK: left mouse button and hold it down
DRAG: the cell range outline to cell F40
Notice the yellow ScrollTip that appears when you drag the range.

6. Release the mouse button to complete the AutoFill operation. Since Jan was the starting entry for the series, Excel increments the series by one month for each column.

7. Move to cell A42.

8. TYPE: **Quarter 1**
PRESS: **ENTER**

9. DRAG: fill handle for A42 to cover the range to F42

10. Release the mouse button. Notice that Excel understands that the word "Quarter" refers to one in four. After Quarter 4, Excel begins again with Quarter 1.

11. Move to cell A44.

12. To create a custom data series:
TYPE: **Jan-97**
PRESS: **→**
TYPE: **Apr-97**
PRESS: **ENTER**
You must enter values into the first two cells so that Excel can extrapolate the value needed to increment the series further.

13. SELECT: cell range from A44 to B44
Make sure that both cells are selected before proceeding. Notice that there is only one fill handle for the range even though two cells are selected.

14. DRAG: fill handle to cover the cell range from A44 to F44

15. Release the mouse button.

16. Move to cell A46. Your worksheet should now appear similar to Figure 3.3.

17. Save the "Sales Rep Report" workbook to your Data Files location.

FIGURE 3.3

USING AUTOFILL TO COMPLETE A SERIES

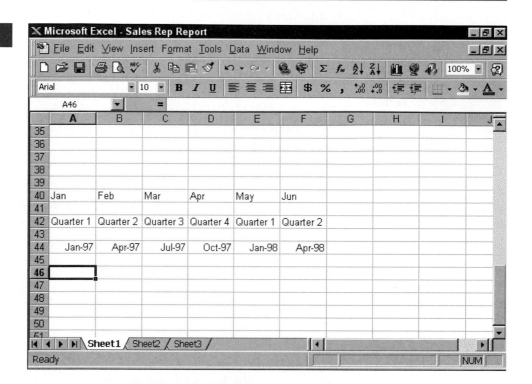

QUICK REFERENCE
Using AutoFill

1. **Select the cell that contains the data to continue in a series.**
2. **Position the mouse on the cell's fill handle, a small black square in the bottom right-hand corner of the cell, until it changes to a black cross hair mouse pointer.**
3. **Drag the fill handle to extend the series.**
4. **Release the mouse button to complete the operation.**

INSERTING AND DELETING ROWS AND COLUMNS

One way that you can quickly modify the layout of a worksheet is to add or delete rows and columns. As we mentioned in Session 1, people often create worksheets or design a report without fully understanding the problem that they are trying to solve. Therefore, worksheets must evolve as needs change and as the initial objectives become better defined. The ability to reorganize a worksheet by inserting and deleting rows and columns is an important part of this evolution.

To add a row or column to the worksheet, you choose the Insert, Rows or Insert, Columns command. To delete a row or column, you select a row or column and then choose the Edit, Delete command. The easiest method for selecting a row or column is to click its row number or column letter in the frame area. And the easiest method for choosing the Insert or Delete command is by right-clicking the row number or column letter in the frame area to display the shortcut menu.

You will now practice modifying the "Sales Rep Report" workbook.

Perform the following steps . . .

1. To view the top of the worksheet page:
   PRESS: CTRL + HOME

2. To add a blank column, move the cell pointer into the column frame area and do the following:
   RIGHT-CLICK: column E
   Notice that the entire column is highlighted and a shortcut menu appears.

3. CHOOSE: Insert
   The new column is inserted and the original information is moved one column to the right.

4. To insert another column:
   RIGHT-CLICK: G in the column frame
   CHOOSE: Insert
   The column is immediately inserted into the worksheet.

5. To delete a column:
   RIGHT-CLICK: B in the column frame
   CHOOSE: Delete

6. To undo the last command issued:
   CLICK: Undo button (↶ ▾)

7. To delete a row between the product figures and the total monthly sales lines, do the following:
   RIGHT-CLICK: 7 in the row frame
   CHOOSE: Delete
   RIGHT-CLICK: 12 in the row frame
   CHOOSE: Delete
   RIGHT-CLICK: 17 in the row frame
   CHOOSE: Delete
   Your worksheet should now appear similar to Figure 3.4.

8. Close the "Sales Rep Report" workbook without saving the changes.

FIGURE 3.4

INSERTING AND
DELETING COLUMNS
AND ROWS

	A	B	C	D	E	F	G	H	I	J
2	Units Sold Summary			Maria		Craig		Andrea		
3										
4	Month:	January	Widgets	26		10		4		
5			Gadgets	15		18		13		
6			Grapples	10		14		12		
7			Total	51		42		29		
8										
9		February	Widgets	28		12		5		
10			Gadgets	14		20		15		
11			Grapples	13		12		17		
12			Total	55		44		37		
13										
14		March	Widgets	23		10		8		
15			Gadgets	20		25		19		
16			Grapples	16		13		16		
17			Total	59		48		43		

QUICK REFERENCE
Inserting and Deleting
Rows and Columns

1. **RIGHT-CLICK: column letter or row number in the frame area**
2. **CHOOSE: Insert to insert a row or column**
   CHOOSE: Delete to delete a row or column

FUNCTIONS

This section introduces you to some very useful functions that can save you a tremendous amount of time in creating worksheets. And don't let the word *function* conjure up visions of your last algebra or calculus class; Excel's 300 or so functions are substitutes for entering lengthy formulas. Using functions, you can create formulas that calculate mortgage payments or analyze variances without having to first take a Finance or Statistics course.

For easy access, Excel groups its functions into the following categories: Database, Date & Time, Financial, Information, Logical, Lookup & Reference, Math & Trig, Statistical, and Text. You can enter a function by clicking the Paste Function button (f_x) on the Standard toolbar or by accessing the Formula Palette with the Edit Formula button (=). You can also enter a function like any other formula. First, type an equal sign followed by the function name. Then, depending on the type of function, you enter numbers, cell references, or range names within parentheses after the function name. In the next section, you learn how to name a cell range.

CREATING RANGE NAMES

A **range name** is a label that you give to a group of cells on the worksheet. This label or name can be used in formulas and functions to refer to a cell or cell range. As demonstrated in Session 1, Excel lets you create *Natural Language Formulas* by reviewing your worksheet headings and implementing range names on the fly. For example, with named ranges, you can enter a self-explanatory function like "=SUM(widgets)" rather than "=SUM(B3:B7)." Not only do named ranges make it easier to construct a worksheet, they make a worksheet easier to understand.

To create a range name, select the cell range and then click once on the Name box in the Formula bar. When the existing information appears highlighted in the Name box, type a new name and press ENTER. To display a drop-down list of all the named ranges in a workbook, you can click the down arrow beside the Name box. This list is useful for entering range names into formulas and for moving quickly to a particular range.

QUICK REFERENCE
Naming a Cell Range

1. Select a cell or cell range to name.
2. CLICK: Name box in the Formula bar
3. Type a name for the selected range.
4. PRESS: ENTER or CLICK: OK

USING MATH AND STATISTICAL FUNCTIONS

Mathematical and statistical functions are among the most commonly used categories of functions in spreadsheets. They are also the easiest functions to learn how to use. As described in Table 3.2, the SUM, AVERAGE, MAX, and MIN functions provide a great deal of flexibility and power for the typical application.

TABLE 3.2

Math and Statistical Functions

Function	Description
=SUM(range)	Adds together a range of cells.
=AVERAGE(range)	Determines the average value in a range of cells.
=MAX(range)	Determines the maximum value in a range of cells.
=MIN(range)	Determines the minimum value in a range of cells.

Let's practice using statistical functions.

Perform the following steps . . .

1. Open the "Function" workbook, located in your Advantage Files location. This workbook uses tabs to separate the exercises for Statistical, Financial, and Miscellaneous functions.
2. CLICK: Statistical sheet tab (if it is not already selected)
   (*Hint*: Using the mouse, click the worksheet tab named Statistical, located at the bottom of the document window.)

3. Let's start by assigning a name to the range of cells containing the student grades. To begin:
SELECT: cell range from B3 to B12

4. CLICK: Name box in the Formula bar
(*Note*: When selected properly, the "B3" appears highlighted.)

5. TYPE: **grades**
PRESS: ENTER
You can now reference this cell range as GRADES, using uppercase or lowercase letters.

6. CLICK: cell F4

7. To sum the column of results, use the SUM function:
TYPE: **=sum(grades)**
PRESS: ENTER
The answer 756 appears in cell F4.

8. To enter a function using the Formula Palette:
CLICK: cell F6
CLICK: Edit Formula button (=)
The Formula Palette appears under the Formula bar.

9. To display a list of the most commonly used functions:
CLICK: down arrow adjacent to the Name box

10. To select the AVERAGE function:
CLICK: AVERAGE
The Formula Palette now displays helpful information for the AVERAGE function.

11. With the information in the Number1 text box highlighted:
TYPE: **grades**
Notice that the actual cell contents appear at the right of the text box and that the result is calculated near the bottom of the Formula Palette. Your worksheet should now appear similar to Figure 3.5.

FIGURE 3.5

ENTERING THE AVERAGE
FUNCTION USING
THE FORMULA PALETTE

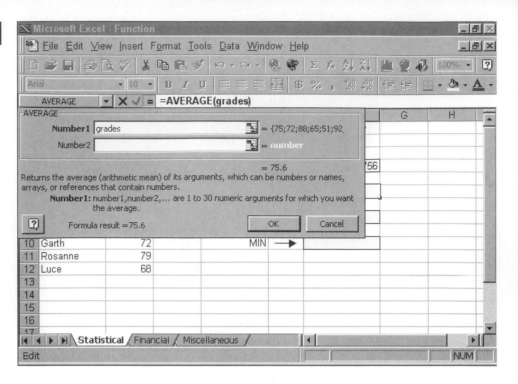

12. To complete the entry:
CLICK: OK command button

13. To enter a function using the Paste Function tool:
CLICK: cell F8
CLICK: Paste Function button (![fx]) on the Standard toolbar

14. In the Paste Function dialog box (Figure 3.6):
SELECT: Statistical in the *Function category* list box
SELECT: MAX in the *Function name* list box
CLICK: OK command button
Notice that the Formula Palette appears, similar to using the Edit Formula button (![=]).

FIGURE 3.6

PASTE FUNCTION
DIALOG BOX

Paste Function

Function category:	Function name:
Most Recently Used	LOGINV
All	LOGNORMDIST
Financial	MAX
Date & Time	MAXA
Math & Trig	MEDIAN
Statistical	MIN
Lookup & Reference	MINA
Database	MODE
Text	NEGBINOMDIST
Logical	NORMDIST
Information	NORMINV

MAX(number1,number2,...)

Returns the largest value in a set of values. Ignores logical values and text.

OK   Cancel

15. With the information in the Number1 text box highlighted:
TYPE: **grades**
CLICK: OK command button
The answer 94 appears in cell F8.

16. Using the Paste Function button (f_*), complete the entry in cell F10 for the MIN function. The answer 51 should appear in the cell before proceeding.

17. Let's use AutoCalculate to find some statistical results. As you may remember from Session 2, you selected a cell range and AutoCalculate displayed the sum of the range in the Status bar. You can also display a count of the values in a selected range, or the average, minimum, and maximum values. To demonstrate:
SELECT: cell range from B3 to B12
Notice that "Sum=756" appears in the Status bar.

18. To display a count of the values in the selected range:
RIGHT-CLICK: on the "Sum=756" AutoCalculate display area
CHOOSE: Count from the pop-up menu
The answer "Count=10" appears in the Status bar. Also, notice the other options that are available on the Shortcut menu.

19. Let's reset the AutoCalculate display area:
RIGHT-CLICK: on the AutoCalculate display area
CHOOSE: Sum

20. On your own, change some of the numbers in the grades column (column B) to see the effects on the statistical functions in column F. When ready to move on to the next section, save the workbook as "Completed Functions" to your Data Files location.

USING FINANCIAL FUNCTIONS

Excel's financial functions enable you to confidently use complex financial formulas in your worksheets. And the best part is that you don't even need to understand the difference between a stock and a bond! Some of the more popular financial functions, listed in Table 3.3, are devoted to making investment decisions and solving **annuity** problems. An annuity is a series of equal cash payments over a given period of time, such as an investment contribution or a loan payment.

TABLE 3.3 Financial Functions	*Function*	*Description*
	=PV(rate,periods,payment)	Calculates the **present value** (the principal) of a series of equal cash payments made at even periods in the future and at a constant interest rate.
	=FV(rate,periods,payment)	Calculates the **future value** of a series of equal cash payments made at even periods in the future and at a constant interest rate.
	=NPV(rate,cell range)	Calculates the **net present value** of a series of investments and returns (cash flows) appearing in a cell range, given a constant discount or interest rate.
	=IRR(cell range,guess)	Calculates the **internal rate of return** for a series of periodic investments and returns (cash flows) appearing in a cell range.
	=PMT(rate,periods,pv)	Calculates the payment amount for a loan or mortgage, given a constant interest rate and number of periods.

Let's practice using financial functions. The worksheet that you will use includes a loan payment calculation, an annuity, and an investment scenario.

Perform the following steps . . .

1. CLICK: Financial sheet tab of the "Completed Functions" workbook

2. CLICK: cell F3

3. As an example of a payment calculation, you will now calculate the monthly payments for a $20,000 car loan. The payments are made over three years (36 periods) at an annual interest rate of 8.5 percent. In other words, the *Present Value* or PV for the calculation is $20,000; the periods are 36 (3 years × 12 months); and the rate is 8.5 percent divided by 12 months (in order to change the annual rate to a monthly rate.) Let's use the Formula Palette to help us enter this equation:
TYPE: **=pmt**
CLICK: Edit Formula button (▣)

4. You should see the flashing insertion point in the *Rate* text box. If you don't know the cell address, you can click the Dialog Collapse button (▥) at the right and then click the desired cell in the worksheet. Let's practice selecting a cell using this method. Do the following:
CLICK: Dialog Collapse button (▥) to withdraw the dialog box
CLICK: cell B4
CLICK: Dialog Expand button (▤) to re-display the Formula Palette
Notice that the cell address B4 appears in the text box with its value appearing to the right.

5. Now you must ensure that the rate is calculated on a monthly basis:
TYPE: **/12**

6. To complete this function, you must provide values for all the text box labels that appear in boldface. Therefore, the next item to enter is the number of periods. Do the following:
SELECT: *Nper* text box
CLICK: Dialog Collapse button (▣)
CLICK: cell B5
CLICK: Dialog Expand button (▣)

7. To enter the present value:
SELECT: *Pv* text box
CLICK: Dialog Collapse button (▣)
CLICK: cell B3
CLICK: Dialog Expand button (▣)
Notice that the worksheet values that correspond to the cell references appear in the dialog box along with the function's result. Your screen should appear similar to Figure 3.7.

FIGURE 3.7

FORMULA PALETTE:
PMT FUNCTION

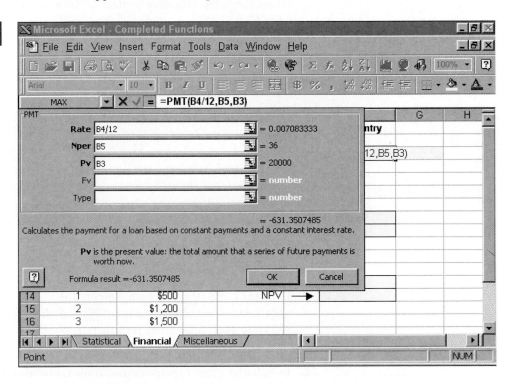

8. To complete the entry:
CLICK: OK command button
The answer ($631.35) appears in cell F3. The payment appears in parentheses to indicate it is a negative number, since it is a cash outflow from yourself to the bank.

9. In this scenario, an altruistic stranger offers you a choice between receiving a flat $6,000 at the end of five years or an annuity of $1,000 per year for the next five years. With an interest rate of 8 percent per year, you must determine which would be the better offer? This problem requires that you enter a future value calculation using the following syntax: FV(rate,periods,payment). Do the following:
CLICK: cell F8
TYPE: **=fv(b9,b10,b8)**
PRESS: **ENTER**
The better offer is $6,000 at the end of five years, since the future value of the annuity is only worth $5,866.60. With the majority of these calculations, you are concerned with the absolute or positive value for the number. Therefore, you can ignore the negative sign or parentheses.

10. Now, picture this: The same stranger offers you a choice between receiving $4,000 today or an annuity of $1,000 per year for the next five years. With an interest rate of 8 percent per year, you must determine which would be the better offer. This problem requires that you enter a present value calculation using the following syntax: PV(rate,periods,payment). Do the following:
CLICK: cell F9
TYPE: **=pv(b9,b10,b8)**
PRESS: **ENTER**
The better offer is $4,000 today, compared to receiving $3,992.71 in today's dollars over the next five years.

11. Some friends have just asked you to invest in a wonderful opportunity! The deal is simple. You give them $2,000 now and they will pay you $500 at the end of the first year, $1,200 in the second year, and $1,500 in the third year. In total, you are receiving $3,200 for your $2,000 investment. But is this a good investment? The *net present value* and *internal rate of return* are two profitability measures for such investments. Let's use the Formula Palette to help us in entering these functions:
CLICK: cell F13
TYPE: **=irr**
CLICK: Edit Formula button (■)

12. To specify the range of cash flow figures:
CLICK: Dialog Collapse button (▥) for the *Values* text box
SELECT: cell range from B13 to B16
CLICK: Dialog Expand button (▣)

13. To calculate the internal rate of return, you should also enter an estimate of your expected rate of return. Do the following:
SELECT: *Guess* text box
TYPE: **20%**
CLICK: OK command button
Not a bad deal at all! This calculation shows that you would make a return of over 23 percent on your investment.

14. Another test for the profitability of an investment is the net present value. We will use 10 percent as the expected interest rate:
CLICK: cell F14
TYPE: **=npv**
CLICK: Edit Formula button (▣=▣)

15. To specify the parameters for this function:
TYPE: **10%** in the *Rate* text box
SELECT: *Value1* text box
CLICK: Dialog Collapse button (▣) for the *Value1* text box
SELECT: cell range from B13 to B16
CLICK: Dialog Expand button (▣)
CLICK: OK command button
This calculation confirms that it is a wise investment opportunity. An investment is profitable if the net present value result is a positive number. Your worksheet should now appear similar to Figure 3.8.

FIGURE 3.8

"COMPLETED FUNCTIONS" WORKBOOK: *FINANCIAL* TAB

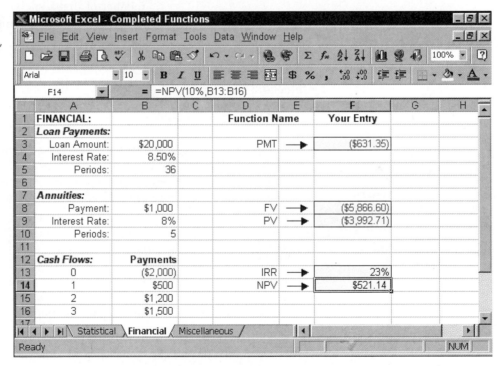

16. Change some numbers in the loan payments, savings account, and cash flow sections to see their effects on the functions that you entered. For example, what would the monthly payment be for a $15,000 car loan over four years? What if your friends needed $2,500 for their startup capital in Step 11? Would it still be a wise investment?

USING MISCELLANEOUS FUNCTIONS

This section describes some miscellaneous functions that you may find quite useful. Although often considered an intermediate-to-advanced topic, the IF function is one of the most useful available. With this function, you can evaluate a cell's value and then perform a calculation based on its contents. The miscellaneous functions covered in this section are described in Table 3.4.

TABLE 3.4

Miscellaneous Functions

Function	Description
=NOW( )	Provides the current date and time.
=TODAY( )	Provides the current date only.
=ABS(cell)	Provides the **absolute value** of a cell. For example, =ABS(−4.5) returns 4.5.
=ROUND(cell,digits)	Provides the **rounded value** of a cell to the number of digits specified. For example, =ROUND(3.9275,2) returns 3.93.
=INT(cell)	Provides the **integer value** of a cell. For example, =INT(3.75) returns 3.
=IF(condition,true,false)	Performs a calculation based on the condition being met.

In this exercise, you practice using some additional functions.

Perform the following steps . . .

1. CLICK: Miscellaneous sheet tab of the "Completed Functions" workbook

2. CLICK: cell E3

3. TYPE: =now()
   PRESS: ENTER
   (*Note:* This cell is formatted to display the date in a d-mmm-yy format. You can apply a different format to the cell, including one that displays the current time, without changing the function.)

4. In this scenario, you want cell E4 to display a commission rate that is based on a salesperson's unit sales. If sales are less than 10,000 units, the commission is 5 percent; otherwise, the commission is 6 percent. To enter this function, let's use the Formula Palette. Do the following:
   CLICK: cell E4
   TYPE: =if
   CLICK: Edit Formula button (=)

5. To specify the test condition:
   CLICK: Dialog Collapse button for the *Logical_test* text box
   CLICK: cell B4 ($15,000)
   TYPE: <10000
   CLICK: Dialog Expand button

6. To complete the other parameters for this function:
SELECT: *Value_if_true* text box
TYPE: **5%**
SELECT: *Value_if_false* text box
TYPE: **6%**
CLICK: OK command button
You should see the result 6 percent appear in cell E4.

7. Copy the expression in cell E4 to cells E5 and E6 using the fill handle.

8. Let's enter the ROUND function:
CLICK: cell E11
TYPE: **=round(**
CLICK: cell A11
TYPE: **,2)**
PRESS: ENTER

9. You will now learn to *nest* a function, meaning to place a function within a function. In this step, you enter a formula that returns the absolute, rounded value for the number in cell A13. Do the following:
TYPE: **=abs**
CLICK: Edit Formula button (=)

10. In the Formula Palette:
CLICK: down arrow adjacent to the Name box
SELECT: More Functions from the drop-down list
The Paste Function dialog box should now appear.

11. To enter the ROUND function:
SELECT: Math & Trig from the *Function category* list box
SELECT: ROUND from the *Function name* list box
CLICK: OK command button
Your worksheet should appear similar to Figure 3.9.

FIGURE 3.9

FORMULA PALETTE:
ROUND FUNCTION
NESTED IN THE ABS
FUNCTION

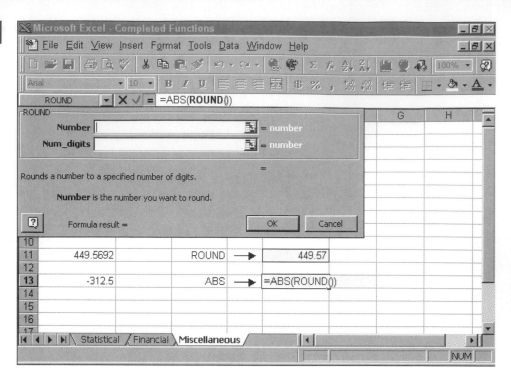

12. To complete the ROUND function:
CLICK: Dialog Collapse button (🔣) for the *Number* text box
                              CLICK: cell A13 (−312.5)
CLICK: Dialog Expand button (🔲)
SELECT: *Num_digits* text box
TYPE: **0**
CLICK: OK command button
The value 313 appears in cell E13.

13. Change some numbers in the worksheet to see the effects on the functions that you entered. You can also edit a function that you've entered by double-clicking the cell or by selecting the cell and clicking the Edit Formula button (▣).

14. Save the workbook as "Completed Functions" to your Data Files location.

USING GOAL SEEK

The Goal Seek command is a powerful "what-if" tool that lets you find questions for answers—similar to playing Jeopardy on television. For example, you can state exactly what you need as a bottom line profit and Goal Seek automatically calculates the sales required to meet this goal. How does Goal Seek work? Since profit is dependent on sales (*Sales* less *Expenses* equals *Profit*), Goal Seek quickly substitutes values into the sales variable until the desired profit is achieved.

To use Goal Seek, you choose the Tools, Goal Seek command from the menu. In the dialog box that appears, you enter the cell that contains the formula for calculating the target value (for example, *Profit*) and then enter the target value itself. You also need to tell Goal Seek what variable it is allowed to change in order to achieve this target value (for example, *Sales*). Once completed, you press $\boxed{\text{ENTER}}$ or click on OK.

Let's practice using Goal Seek.

Perform the following steps . . .

1. CLICK: Financial sheet tab in the "Completed Functions" workbook

2. If you changed any of the original values on this page, ensure now that the Loan Amount is $20,000 (in cell B3), the Interest Rate is 8.50 percent (in cell B4), and the Periods is 36 (in cell B5) before proceeding.

3. Let's use Goal Seek to calculate the maximum loan amount that we can afford with monthly payments of $500. To start Goal Seek:
   CLICK: cell F3
   CHOOSE: Tools, Goal Seek

4. In the *Set cell* text box, make sure that the cell address is F3.

5. To enter the monthly payment that we can afford:
   SELECT: *To value* text box
   TYPE: −500
   Notice that we enter −500, since it is a cash outflow to the bank.

6. To specify that the loan amount is the variable to change:
   SELECT: *By changing cell* text box
   CLICK: cell B3
   If the dialog box is covering cell B3, use the Dialog Collapse (⬛) and Expand (⬛) buttons. Your screen should now appear similar to Figure 3.10.

FIGURE 3.10

ENTERING VALUES INTO
THE GOAL SEEK
DIALOG BOX

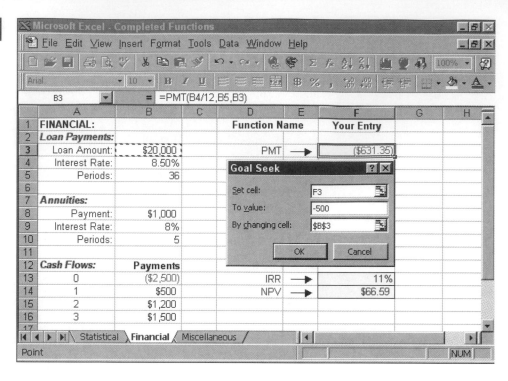

7. To solve the equation:
CLICK: OK to accept the Goal Seek dialog box
CLICK: OK to bypass the Goal Seek Status dialog box
When you return to the worksheet, the Loan Amount has been changed to
$15,839 in cell B3 and the payment in cell F3 is now $500.

8. Save the workbook as "Completed Functions" to your Data Files location.

9. Close the workbook and exit Excel.

QUICK REFERENCE
Using Goal Seek

1. **CHOOSE: Tools, Goal Seek**
2. **Specify the formula or expression which contains the target value.**
3. **Enter the desired target value.**
4. **Specify the variable to change.**
5. **PRESS:** (ENTER) **or CLICK: OK**

IN ADDITION SOLVING MORE COMPLEX "WHAT-IF" SCENARIOS

For more complex problems, Excel provides the **Solver** tool which allows you to specify more than one variable to change in order to meet multiple goals and constraints. For more information, ask the Office Assistant for help on "Using Solver for What-Ifs."

Summary

This section explored several new commands for increasing your productivity. After a discussion on absolute and relative cell addresses, you were introduced to the commands and shortcut keys for copying and moving information around your worksheet. Some final formatting commands were also introduced for inserting and deleting columns and rows in your worksheet.

The latter half of the session introduced several of Excel's built-in functions. The Statistical and Financial categories were emphasized with the SUM, AVERAGE, MAX, MIN, PV, FV, IRR, NPV, and PMT functions. Several miscellaneous functions were also introduced, including the IF function for calculating an expression based on a set of conditions.

Many of the commands used in the session are provided in Table 3.5, the Command Summary. See Tables 3.2 to 3.4 for the Function summaries.

TABLE 3.5 Command Summary	*Command*	*Description*
	Edit, Copy or (▣)	Places a copy of a cell or cell range onto the Clipboard.
	Edit, Cut or (✂)	Moves a cell or cell range from the worksheet to the Clipboard.
	Edit, Delete	Deletes a column or row from the worksheet.
	Edit Formula (=)	Opens the Formula Palette for creating and editing a formula.
	Edit, Fill, Down	Copies a cell to adjacent cells down the worksheet.
	Edit, Fill, Right	Copies a cell to adjacent cells across the worksheet.
	Edit, Paste or (▣)	Pastes the contents of the Clipboard into the active cell or selected cell range.
	Insert, Column/Row	Inserts a column or row in the worksheet.
	Paste Function (*fx*)	Displays the Paste Function dialog box for selecting a function for use in an equation.
	Tools, Goal Seek	Launches the Goal Seek tool for performing "what-if" analysis.

KEY TERMS

absolute cell address

Cell reference in a worksheet that does not adjust when copied to other cells.

absolute value

The value of a real number, disregarding its sign. For example, the absolute value of the number −5 is 5.

annuity

A series of equal cash payments over a given period of time.

Clipboard

In Windows, the Clipboard is a program that allows you to copy and move information within an application or among applications. The Clipboard temporarily stores the information in memory before you paste the data in a new location.

drag and drop

An Excel feature that allows you to copy and move information by dragging cell information from one location to another using the mouse.

fill handle

The small black square that is located in the bottom right-hand corner of a cell or cell range. You use the fill handle to create a series or to copy cell information.

future value

The value in future dollars of a series of equal cash payments.

integer value

The value of a number to the left of the decimal point. For example, the integer of 125.978 is the number 125.

internal rate of return

The rate of return at which the net present value is 0.

net present value

A calculation used to determine whether an investment provides a positive or negative return, based on a series of cash outflows and inflows.

present value

The value in present-day dollars of a series of equal cash payments made sometime in the future.

range name

A name that is given to a range of cells in the worksheet. This name can then be used in formulas and functions to refer to the cell range.

relative cell address

Cell reference in a worksheet that automatically adjusts when copied to other cells.

rounded value

The value of a number rounded to a specific number of decimal places. For example, the number 2.378 rounded to a single decimal returns the number 2.4.

series

A sequence of numbers or dates that follows a mathematical or date pattern.

Solver

An Excel tool that facilitates "what-if" analysis. Although similar to Goal Seek, Solver enables you to specify more than one variable to modify and more than one goal to attain.

EXERCISES

SHORT ANSWER

1. What is the difference between an absolute cell address and a relative cell address? How is this difference expressed in an Excel formula?

2. What is the primary difference between using the Edit, Copy command and the drag and drop method to copy information?

3. Explain the fastest way to put semi-annual headings at the top of your worksheet (i.e., Jan-97, Jul-97, Jan-98,...).

4. Why would you want to name a range of cells?

5. List the function categories in Excel.

6. Describe four statistical functions.

7. Describe five financial functions.

8. What is the purpose of the NOW function?

9. What is the purpose of the IF function?

10. How do you access the Paste Function dialog box from within the Formula Palette?

HANDS-ON

(*Note:* Ensure that you know the storage location of your Advantage Files and your Data Files before proceeding.)

1. The objective of this exercise is to create a new workbook, reorganize its layout, construct formulas, and then practice copying and moving information. Perform the following steps.

   a. Ensure that Excel is loaded and that a blank worksheet appears on the screen.

   b. Set column A's width to 20 characters.

   c. Set columns B through E to 10 characters wide.

  d. Type the text and numbers as displayed in Figure 3.11 into the appropriate cells. Make sure that you type your name into cell C1.

  e. Perform a spelling check and then save the workbook as "Income Statement" to your Data Files location.

FIGURE 3.11

"INCOME STATEMENT" WORKBOOK

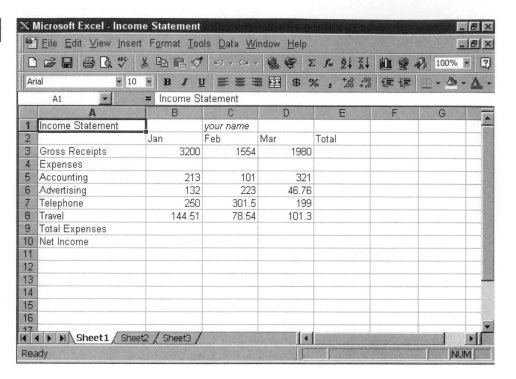

  f. Insert one row between each of the following:

- the "Income Statement" line and the month headings

- the month headings and the "Gross Receipts" line

- the "Total Expenses" line and the "Net Income" line

  g. Select the cell range from B3 to E3.

  h. Center the range and then make it bold and italic.

  i. Select the cell range from A7 to A10.

  j. Indent the entries by clicking the Increase Indent button (⏸) on the Formatting toolbar twice.

  k. Make the primary headings—Gross Receipts, Expenses, Total Expenses, and Net Income—bold.

  l. Make the title in cell A1 bold and assign a font of 14 points in size.

  m. Use the AutoSum button to sum the expenses for each month and then display the sum of the Gross Receipts in cell E5.

  n. Copy the function in cell E5 to cells E7 through E11 using the Copy (🗐) and Paste (📋) toolbar buttons.

o.   Enter a formula into cell B13 that subtracts the Total Expenses for January from the Gross Receipts.

p.   Copy the formula from cell B13 through cell E13 using the fill handle.

q.   Select the cell range from B5 to E13.

r.   Apply a numeric format to insert commas and two decimal places.

s.   Select the cell range from B3 to E3.

t.   Place a border around these cells and then apply a background fill color and font color.

u.   Select the cell range from B11 to E11.

v.   Add a single line for the top border of this range.

w.   Select the cell range from B13 to E13.

x.   Add a single line for the top border and a double line for the bottom border.

y.   Set the print area and then print the workbook centered horizontally on the page.

z.   Save the workbook as "Income Statement" to your Data Files location.

2.   This exercise uses the "Income Statement" workbook created in exercise 1. You modify the worksheet contents, apply names to cell ranges, and then create statistical functions.

a.   If it's not already displayed, open the "Income Statement" workbook located in your Data Files location.

b.   Select the cell range from B5 to D5.

c.   Name this cell range "Receipts" using the Name box.

d.   Name the following cell ranges:

Select the Range	Name the Range
B7 to D7	Accounting
B8 to D8	Advertising
B9 to D9	Telephone
B10 to D10	Travel
B11 to D11	Expenses

e.   Move to cell F3 and create a heading called "Average."

f.   Change the width of columns E and F to 12 characters.

g.   Move to cell F5.

h.   To average the Gross Receipts:
     TYPE: =average(receipts)
     PRESS: ENTER

i.   Complete the column as follows:

Move to cell	TYPE:
F7	=average(accounting)
F8	=average(advertising)
F9	=average(telephone)
F10	=average(travel)
F11	=average(expenses)

j.   Copy cell E13 to F13 using drag and drop.

k.   Copy the formatting characteristics from column E to column F.

l.   Set a new print area and then preview the worksheet. Your screen should now look similar to Figure 3.12.

m.   Print the worksheet.

n.   Save the workbook as "Income Statement" to your Data Files location and then close the workbook.

FIGURE 3.12

PREVIEWING THE
"INCOME STATEMENT"
WORKBOOK

X Microsoft Excel - Income Statement

Next   Previous   Zoom   Print...   Setup...   Margins   Page Break Preview   Close   Help

Income Statement   *your name*

	Jan	Feb	Mar	Total	Average
Gross Receipts	3,200.00	1,554.00	1,980.00	6,734.00	2,244.67
Expenses					
Accounting	213.00	101.00	321.00	635.00	211.67
Advertising	132.00	223.00	46.76	401.76	133.92
Telephone	250.00	301.50	199.00	750.50	250.17
Travel	144.51	78.54	101.30	324.35	108.12
Total Expenses	739.51	704.04	668.06	2,111.61	703.87
Net Income	2,460.49	849.96	1,311.94	4,622.39	1,540.80

Preview: Page 1 of 1   NUM

3.   In this exercise, you create a workbook from scratch for computing a loan or mortgage table.

a. To begin, ensure that you have an empty worksheet.

b. Enter the textual information:

Move to cell	TYPE:
A1	MORGAGE TABLE
D1	*your name*
A3	Principal Amount:
A4	Interest Rate:
A5	Years:
C4	Monthly Rate:
C5	Months:
C6	Payment:
A8	Payment #
B8	Principal
C8	Interest
D8	Balance

c. Change the column widths as follows:

Column	Width
A	18
B	15
C	15
D	15

d. Select the cell range from A3 to D8.

e. Right-align the entire range.

f. Select the cell range from A8 to D8.

g. Use bold and italic for the range and then apply an outline border with a background fill color and font color.

h. Enter the numeric information:

Move to cell	TYPE:
B3	150,000
B4	7.5%
B5	30
A9	0

i. Enter the formulas:

Move to cell	TYPE:
D4	=b4/12
D5	=b5*12
D6	=pmt(d4,d5,b3)
D9	=b3
A10	=a9+1

j. To calculate the amount of interest paid during each period (column C), move to cell C10 and enter the following formula:
    TYPE: **=d9*d4**
    PRESS: [ENTER]
    Notice that the monthly interest rate is an absolute cell reference. Since the formula will be copied down the worksheet, you must enter the formula with an absolute reference to ensure that the expression always refers to cell D4.

k. To calculate the amount of principal paid during each period (column B), move to cell B10 and enter the following formula:
    TYPE: **=abs(d6)-c10**
    PRESS: [ENTER]
    Again, the formula will always refer to the total payment amount when copied, so an absolute cell address is used in the expression.

l. To calculate the amount of principal left (the Balance for column D), move to cell D10 and enter the following:
    TYPE: **=d9-b10**
    PRESS: [ENTER]

m. Select the cell range from A10 to D10.

n. Format the numbers to appear with commas and no decimal places.

o. Select the cell range from A10 to D189.

p. CHOOSE: Edit, Fill, Down

q. Return to cell A1.

r. Change the loan principal amount from 150,000 to 175,000. Watch the worksheet recalculate the payments for each period.

s. Change the number of years to 25. Note the change in the ratio between the principal being paid back each period and the interest paid on the money borrowed.

t. Save the workbook as "Mortgage" to your Data Files location. Your worksheet should now look similar to Figure 3.13.

u. Print the worksheet.

v. Close the workbook and then exit Excel.

FIGURE 3.13

"MORTGAGE"
WORKBOOK

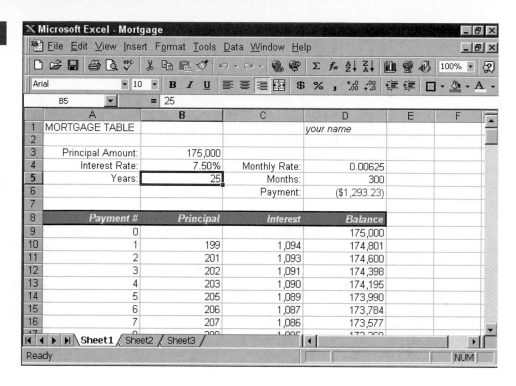

4. **On Your Own:** Your Personal Budget

Create a worksheet that contains your monthly budget information. Start by placing the months of the year across the top of the worksheet using the AutoFill feature. Create budget categories for each row, such as Food, Rent, Tuition, Loan, and Entertainment. At the far right of the worksheet, include a "Year-To-Date" column and an "Average" column. Enter the appropriate formulas for summing each month's total budget allowance and for calculating the summary columns. When finished, enter some sample figures to test your worksheet and then save it as "My Personal Budget" to your Data Files location.

5. **On Your Own:** Using Statistical Functions

Create a worksheet that contains a table of figures that spans four rows and three columns. Below this table, enter the name of each statistical function used in this session on a separate row. Beside the function name, enter the function equation using the entire table as the range value. Change numbers in the table to ensure that the figures flow through to the function equations correctly. Save the worksheet as "Using Functions" to your Data Files location.

CASE PROBLEM	RIVERSIDE FORD, INC.

(*Note:* In the following case problems, assume the role of the primary characters and perform the same steps that they identify. You may want to re-read the session opening.)

1. Zachary Rempel graduated from college in 1993 with a master's degree in economics. While his friends interviewed for entry-level jobs with larger companies, Zachary accepted the first position offered to him, as business manager for Riverside. Some of the reasons for Zachary's success at Riverside are that he willingly accepts new challenges and constantly looks for better ways of doing things. This was Zachary's attitude when Mr. Davies handed him the responsibility of generating all of the dealership's reports by computer.

Upon reviewing the previous month's reports, Zachary identifies an opportunity for moving one particular report written in Microsoft Word to Microsoft Excel. The SOFIT report, which is Riverside's own abbreviation for a Summary of Finance and Insurance Totals, summarizes the number of new and used cars that are sold in a given month, including the number of financing, insurance, warranty, and rust protection packages. Currently, the report is manually typed into a Word document and then printed. All of the calculations are performed using a handheld calculator; so if one number changes, the entire report must be recalculated. Zachary decides that this report deserves his immediate attention.

Assume the role of Zachary and convert the following SOFIT report for September into an Excel worksheet, complete with formulas for summing the columns. Save the document as "SOFIT - September" to your Data Files location.

Product Category	New Cars	New Dollars	Used Cars	Used Dollars
Retail Sales	20	492,000	15	138,000
Financing Packages	8	4,500	4	2,500
Life Ins. Policies	4	1,250	2	600
Option Packages	5	2,150	0	0
Ext. Warranties	3	1,800	0	0
Rust Protection	1	375	1	340
Totals				

2. Now that the original report has been converted into an Excel worksheet, Zachary decides to enhance the report and make better use of Excel's summary and reporting features. Perform the following modifications to the worksheet.

- Extend the report by two columns for "Total Cars" and "Total Dollars." Enter formulas on the Retail Sales row that add the New and Used values together for both the unit and dollar values. Copy these two formulas into the remaining rows of the table.

- Insert a row for "Accident & Health Ins." between "Life Ins. Policies" and "Option Packages." There are no sales figures for the month of September, so enter "0" in the appropriate cells.

- Insert two rows at the top of the worksheet for the name of the dealership and the name of the report. The first row of the worksheet should contain "Riverside Ford, Inc." and the second row should contain "SOFIT for September 1997."

- Format the worksheet by applying fonts, numeric styles, borders, fill colors, and font colors.

- Below the table, leave three blank lines and then enter the following information:

Packages:	Average	Total
New Cars		
Used Cars		
Total Cars		

- In the new table, calculate the average and total dollar value of all packages sold with vehicles. (*Hint:* Use the AVERAGE and SUM functions on the values extending from financing packages to rust protection.)

3. Zachary decides to enhance the report by adding the budget figures for Finance and Insurance to the worksheet. That way, Mr. Davies will be able to compare the actual results against the budget estimates on the same report. Having gone through this session, Zachary knows that the easiest method for copying a group of cells on a worksheet is using the drag and drop method. To prepare, he selects the entire cell range (including the titles at the top of the worksheet). He then presses the **ALT** key and holds it down as he drags the selection over top of the Sheet2 tab. Once the cell pointer is positioned at the top of Sheet 2, he releases the **ALT** key and the mouse button. He clicks the Sheet2 tab and then edits the title to read "Budget Estimates" instead of "Riverside Ford, Inc."

Complete the budget area on the worksheet for Zachary by editing the table to contain the figures shown in the table below. As a final step, print the report without gridlines, headers, or footers, and ensure that it appears centered horizontally on a single page. Save the workbook as "SOFIT - September" back to your Data Files location.

Product Category	New Cars	New Dollars	Used Cars	Used Dollars
Retail Sales	15	300,000	20	200,000
Financing Packages	10	5,000	8	2,500
Life Ins. Policies	5	1,500	4	1,200
Accident & Health Ins.	1	360	2	900
Option Packages	5	2,500	0	0
Ext. Warranties	5	1,800	0	0
Rust Protection	2	750	2	750

4. After explaining the finer points of Excel to Robyn Lombardi, a salesperson at Riverside, Zachary finishes the last bite of his sandwich. "Zak, what you've just finished describing sounds like something we can use on the floor," said Robyn excitedly. "Just imagine, we could calculate loan payments for customers while they are standing right in front of us! Can you design an attractive on-screen form if I provide you with a rough outline?" Zachary thought about what was involved in the project and ended up agreeing to create a simple form. At 4:30 PM, Robyn drops a handwritten form onto Zachary's desk with the following note. "Thanks, Zak. By the way, I mentioned our idea to Mr. Davies and he wants to see a sample of the form by tomorrow. Good luck!"

Create an on-screen form from the design sample that Robyn provided below. (*Hint:* Use the PMT function to perform the calculation.) Save your workbook as "Loan Form" to your Data Files location.

Riverside Ford, Inc.   **Loan Calculation**

Salesperson:	*Robyn Lombardi*	**List Price:**	*$30,000*
Customer:	*Mr. Smith*	**Negotiated Price:**	*$25,000*
Year/Make/Model:	*97 Ford Explorer*	**Ann. Interest Rate:**	*10%*
Serial Number:	*XLT1001-880801*	**Term in Months:**	*48*

Your monthly payment is: \$###.##

(Zak, this needs to be a formula!)

Microsoft Excel 97 for Windows

Managing a Workbook

SESSION OUTLINE

INTRODUCTION

What you've already learned to do with spreadsheets is quite sophisticated. Now we introduce some more commands to help you better manage your work. In this session, you will learn how to freeze titles on the screen, open windows to view different parts of a workbook, filter your data, create multiple-sheet workbook files, consolidate worksheets, and create simple macros. All of these features help you manage your workbooks more efficiently.

CASE STUDY GINO'S KITCHEN

Gino Lerma is the owner of four pizza restaurants in the Boston metropolitan area. Starting with one restaurant 15 years ago, Gino was able to open a new restaurant every few years through hard work and careful planning. Gino now considers himself semiretired, even though he still works around the clock and requires a full-time assistant, Larry Ingla. Although he is no longer part of the daily activities, Gino fondly remembers his many years of working in the kitchens.

Each month, Gino's managers use Microsoft Excel and a custom-developed worksheet to report on their restaurants' activities. Each manager sends his or her workbook file to Larry Ingla for consolidation. To date, Larry has been printing each workbook separately and then manually consolidating a report for Gino's review. Hearing much about the consolidation capabilities of Excel, Larry wants to use the computer to combine each individual workbook into a summary workbook. From this one summary workbook, he could then print a monthly consolidated report. It would also be nice if the summary workbook contained a separate sheet for each month and a Year-to-Date sheet at the end. That way, Larry could analyze and compare sales and costs on a month-to-month basis. Unfortunately, Larry has only heard about Excel's capabilities and doesn't know how to create his dream workbook.

In this session, you and Larry will learn how to manage and extract information from worksheets. In addition, you learn how to consolidate data using formulas that link separate worksheets and workbooks. To improve the reliability and consistency of your daily procedures, this session also shows you how to compose macros that you can play back in the future.

FREEZING TITLES

Most worksheets display row and column titles to serve as a frame of reference for information contained in the worksheet. In a worksheet that stores address information, the column headings might be first name, last name, address, city, and phone number. Unfortunately, these titles can scroll off the screen as you move the cell pointer around the worksheet. Using the Window, Freeze Panes command, you can freeze specific rows and columns on the screen so that they appear at all times, regardless of where you move the cell pointer in the worksheet. Let's demonstrate.

Perform the following steps . . .

1. Make sure that you've loaded Excel and know the storage location of your Advantage Files and your Data Files.

2. Open the "Planner" workbook, located in your Advantage Files location.

3. CLICK: cell B5

4. To quickly move to the end of the row:
PRESS: CTRL + ➡
The cell pointer moves to the end of the row, cell N5. Notice that you can no longer see the row titles in column A—they have scrolled off the screen. Assuming that you do not memorize your worksheets, you must return to column A to see what each row represents.

5. PRESS: CTRL + HOME
The cell pointer moves back to cell A1.

6. By freezing the window **panes,** you can lock the employee names in the first column no matter how far you move to the right. First, you position the cell pointer below the row and to the right of the column that you want to freeze. For this step, move the cell pointer to cell B7.

7. CHOOSE: Window, Freeze Panes

8. Position the tip of the mouse pointer below the scroll box on the vertical scroll bar and click once to move down the worksheet. Notice that the worksheet window scrolls down but leaves the top six rows visible.

9. Position the tip of the mouse pointer to the right of the scroll box on the horizontal scroll bar and click once to move across the worksheet. Again, notice that the worksheet scrolls but leaves the leftmost column of employee names visible. Your worksheet should now look similar to Figure 4.1.

10. To return to your starting screen position and unfreeze the panes:
PRESS: CTRL + HOME
CHOOSE: Window, Unfreeze Panes

FIGURE 4.1

THE "PLANNER"
WORKSHEET DIVIDED
INTO PANES

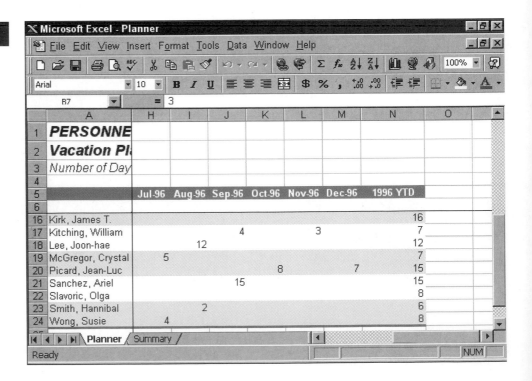

QUICK REFERENCE
Freezing Titles
1. **Position the cell pointer below and to the right of the row and column that you want to freeze.**
2. **To freeze the horizontal and vertical worksheet panes:**
    CHOOSE: Window, Freeze Panes
3. **To unfreeze the horizontal and vertical worksheet panes:**
    CHOOSE: Window, Unfreeze Panes

When a worksheet is relatively large and is organized under row and column headings, you freeze window panes to make it easier to work with your data. For a worksheet that is not grouped neatly into blocks or sections, you can use another tool. The next section explores the process of dividing a worksheet's document window into independent panes.

SPLITTING THE WINDOW INTO PANES

Similarly to freezing titles, you can manually split a worksheet's document window into two or four panes. This makes it easier to view and manage worksheets that cannot fit in a single window. You split the document window using the Split command or by dragging the **horizontal split box** or **vertical split box** at the end of each scroll bar (both are shown below).

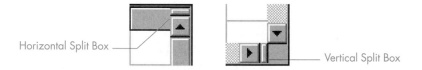

Horizontal Split Box

Vertical Split Box

To use the Window, Split command, you first position the cell pointer below or to the right of the column and row where you want the split to occur—as you would setting titles. If you prefer using the mouse, drag the split boxes to the desired window location. Once in place, you can finalize the positioning of panes by dragging the actual split bars that appear in the document window. To move between two panes or among four panes, you simply click the mouse pointer in the desired pane.

In this exercise, you practice splitting the window into panes.

Perform the following steps . . .

1. Position the mouse pointer over the horizontal split box (above the vertical scroll bar) until the pointer changes to a black horizontal double line split by a two-headed arrow.
2. CLICK: left mouse button and hold it down
    DRAG: the split box downward to split the window in half

3. Release the mouse button. Notice that you now have two vertical scroll bars for controlling both panes independently.

4. Position the tip of the mouse pointer below the scroll box on the bottom vertical scroll bar and click once to move down the worksheet.

5. Position the tip of the mouse pointer below the scroll box on the top vertical scroll bar and click twice to move the viewing area in the top pane. As opposed to freezing titles, notice that you can change the viewing area in both panes.

6. Position the mouse pointer over the vertical split box (to the right of the horizontal scroll bar) until the pointer changes to a black vertical double line split by a two-headed arrow.

7. CLICK: left mouse button and hold it down
DRAG: the split box to the left to split the window in half

8. Release the mouse button. Notice that you have divided the current worksheet window into four panes with four separate scroll bars.

9. CLICK: anywhere in the bottom left-hand window pane
PRESS: CTRL + HOME

10. CLICK: anywhere in the bottom right-hand window pane
PRESS: CTRL + HOME

11. CLICK: anywhere in the top right-hand window pane
PRESS: CTRL + HOME

12. CLICK: anywhere in the top left-hand window pane
PRESS: CTRL + HOME
This example demonstrates that you must click in the pane before moving the cell pointer in the pane. Your worksheet should now appear similar to Figure 4.2.

13. To quickly remove panes from the window:
CHOOSE: Window, Remove Split
(*Note*: You can also double-click each split box to remove the panes.)

14. Save the workbook as "Vacation Planner" to your Data Files location.

FIGURE 4.2

DIVIDING THE
WORKSHEET'S
DOCUMENT WINDOW
INTO PANES

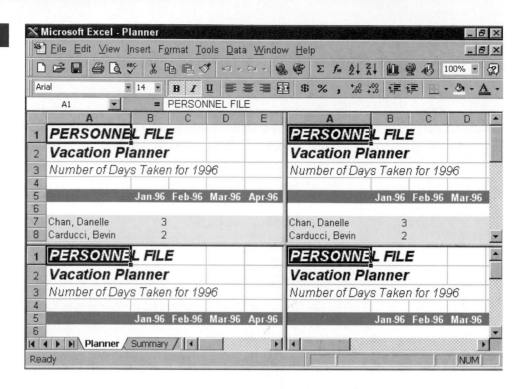

QUICK REFERENCE
Splitting the Window
into Panes

- **DRAG: horizontal and vertical scroll boxes to divide the current worksheet's document window into two or four panes**
- **To remove panes from the current window:**
  CHOOSE: Window, Remove Split

FILTERING WORKSHEET DATA

Excel's **AutoFilter** feature lets you find and retrieve data quickly from a worksheet list. Before you can use this feature, you must arrange your data in a particular way when constructing a worksheet. For example, you should leave several blank columns and rows between the data list and any other information in the worksheet. In the first row of a list, enter column headings or labels and then separate these headings from the data using a border. Finally, you need to design the list so that all columns contain the same type of information, such as text or numbers.

To start AutoFilter, select the desired cell range including the column heading labels and data and then choose the Data, Filter, AutoFilter command from the menu. When executed, AutoFilter analyzes the data and then displays a drop-down list arrow next to each column heading that contains its filtering options. To quickly filter and display data, you select a single criterion for a column from the drop-down list or choose to view a range of data, such as the top ten sales representatives based on units sold.

Let's practice filtering worksheet information.

Perform the following steps . . .

1. Ensure that the "Vacation Planner" workbook appears in the application window.

2. To start the AutoFilter command:
SELECT: cell range from A5 to N24
CHOOSE: Data, Filter, AutoFilter

3. To return to the top of the worksheet:
PRESS: CTRL + HOME
Notice that there are drop-down list arrows attached to each of the column headings in row 5.

4. To freeze the column headings in the worksheet window:
CLICK: cell B7
CHOOSE: Window, Freeze Panes

5. To move to the Year-to-Date column quickly:
CLICK: cell B5
PRESS: CTRL + →
Notice that the employee names in column A are still visible.

6. To select a filtering criterion:
CLICK: down arrow (▼) beside cell N5 to display its drop-down list
Your screen should now appear similar to Figure 4.3.

FIGURE 4.3

USING THE AUTOFILTER COMMAND

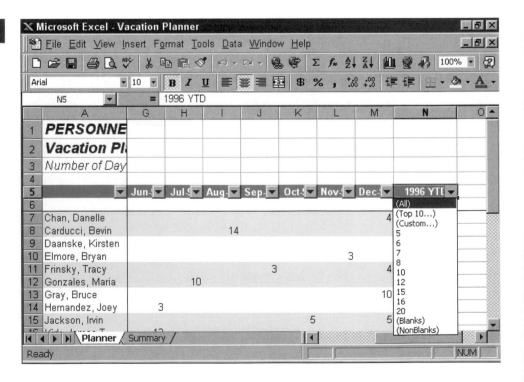

7. To display the three employees with the highest Year-to-Date figures for vacation days taken in 1996, do the following:
SELECT: (Top 10...) from the drop-down list
(*Note*: You can filter the list by two or more values, or apply more complex filtering options, by selecting the Custom option from a column's drop-down list box.)

8. In the dialog box that appears, specify that only the top three items (in this case, Year-to-Date vacation days) need to be displayed. Do the following:
SELECT: 3 in the *Show* spin box (Figure 4.4)

FIGURE 4.4

AUTOFILTER'S TOP 10
DIALOG BOX

9. To proceed with the filter operation:
PRESS: (ENTER) or CLICK: OK
The worksheet should now display only the following employees: Bevin Carducci, Maria Gonzales, and James T. Kirk. Also notice that the row numbers and drop-down arrow appear blue, as a reminder that you are currently viewing a subset of the total records.

10. To display all of the records once again:
CLICK: down arrow ([▼]) beside cell N5 to display its drop-down list
SELECT: (All) appearing at the top of the drop-down list
All of the records reappear in the worksheet window.

11. To remove the AutoFilter drop-down lists from the worksheet:
CHOOSE: Data, Filter, AutoFilter

12. To remove the window panes and return to the top of the worksheet:
CHOOSE: Window, Unfreeze Panes
PRESS: (CTRL) + (HOME)

QUICK REFERENCE
Filtering Data Using the
AutoFilter Command

1. **Create a worksheet with column headings and ensure that each column contains the same type of information (i.e., sales units).**
2. **Select the cell range to be filtered, including the column headings.**
3. **CHOOSE: Data, Filter, AutoFilter**
4. **CLICK: down arrow ([▼]) beside the column or cell to display a drop-down list box of filtering options.**
5. **Select a value from the drop-down list box to filter the list.**

IN ADDITION MANAGING A DATABASE USING EXCEL

Microsoft Excel is an excellent tool for storing and managing simple lists, especially ones requiring statistical or graphical analysis. In addition to using Excel for sorting and filtering data, you can link Excel with the Microsoft Access database program for sharing data, forms, and reports. For more information, ask the Office Assistant about "Managing an Access database."

WORKING WITH MULTIPLE WINDOWS

Using multiple document windows, you can load and display different workbook files at the same time or open different views of the same workbook. Multiple window views are useful when you have related information scattered in distant areas or across several worksheets in a large workbook, or perhaps stored in different workbooks. This section explains how to display and organize multiple windows in the Excel application window.

Before you can issue commands to affect a worksheet, its document window must be active. You activate a window by clicking on it in the document area or by choosing its name from the Window pull-down menu. If there is only one workbook open in the document area, it is active by default. To close a document window, you click its Close button (❌) in the upper right-hand corner of the window.

To automatically organize all the open windows in the document area, you can choose the Window, Arrange command to display the dialog box in Figure 4.5. The Arrange dialog box offers several options for arranging windows in the document area. The *Tiled* option lets you maximize the space for each window in a pattern similar to floor tiles. The *Horizontal* option places each worksheet in a horizontal strip in the document area while the *Vertical* option employs vertical strips. The *Cascade* option layers or fans the windows just as you would spread a deck of cards. Once you have selected an option, press (ENTER) or click on OK.

FIGURE 4.5

ARRANGE DIALOG BOX

You will now practice working with multiple windows.

Perform the following steps . . .

1. Before proceeding, ensure that the "Vacation Planner" workbook is the only open document window. Do the following:
   CHOOSE: Window
   One entry should appear at the bottom of this pull-down menu called "1 Vacation Planner." If there are more entries, choose each additional workbook option on the menu and click its Close button ([×]).

2. Let's practice working with document windows. A document window can be displayed as a window or it can be maximized to cover the entire document area. You can tell the difference by looking at the Title bar. If the name of the worksheet appears next to the words "Microsoft Excel" in the application's Title bar, then the document window has been maximized. If the name of the worksheet appears in its own Title bar within the document area, then the worksheet is displayed as a window. In this step, you practice manipulating the "Vacation Planner" worksheet window.
   To tile the worksheet window, do the following:
   CHOOSE: Arrange command from the Window pull-down menu
   SELECT: *Tiled* option button
   PRESS: (ENTER) or CLICK: OK

3. To maximize the worksheet window:
   CLICK: document window's Maximize icon ([□])
   (*Hint*: If you accidentally click the Minimize icon ([_]), you can restore the document window by clicking its Restore icon ([⊟]) or Maximize icon ([□]) in the Title bar that appears along the bottom of the document area.)

4. To minimize the worksheet window:
   CLICK: document window's Minimize icon ([_])
   (*Hint*: Make sure that you do not click Excel's Minimize icon. The worksheet window's icons will appear on the second row from the top of the screen.) When minimized, the Title bar for the window appears along the bottom of the document area, as follows:

5. To restore the worksheet window:
   CLICK: document window's Restore icon ([⊟])

6. Practice changing the worksheet between a windowed view, a minimized view, and a maximized view.

7. CHOOSE: Window, Arrange
   SELECT: *Tiled* option button
   PRESS: (ENTER) or CLICK: OK

8. To open a second window on this worksheet:
   CHOOSE: Window, New Window

9. The new document window appears over the top of the original window. To view both windows at the same time:
CHOOSE: Window, Arrange
SELECT: *Tiled* option button
PRESS: (ENTER) or CLICK: OK
Notice that the windows are identical, except for their Title bars. There are now two views of the "Vacation Planner" worksheet: "Vacation Planner:1" and "Vacation Planner:2" (Figure 4.6).

FIGURE 4.6

THE "VACATION PLANNER" WORKSHEET WITH TWO WINDOWS DISPLAYED

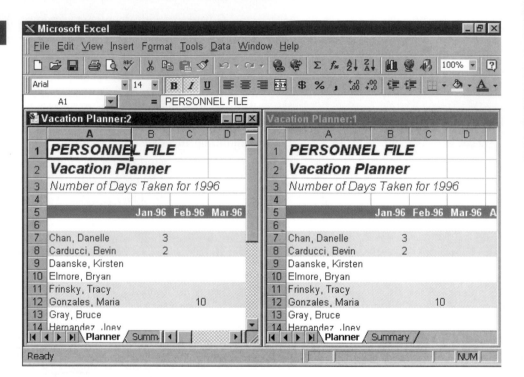

10. For a different window arrangement:
CHOOSE: Window, Arrange
SELECT: *Horizontal* option button
PRESS: (ENTER) or CLICK: OK

11. Practice switching between the two open windows using a mouse. Do the following:
CLICK: any part of a window in the document area to make it active
SELECT: each open window several times
With the possibility of having multiple windows open in the document area, it is important to be able to switch among them efficiently. You can execute commands or type information only in the active window, which is set apart from the rest by its solid or dark Title bar.

12. To switch to a worksheet window that is covered by another window, perform the following menu command:
CHOOSE: Window
CHOOSE: the window name that you want to make active

13. To make the first cell of the first window active:
CHOOSE: Window, 1
PRESS: [CTRL] + [HOME]

14. To make the second window active:
CHOOSE: Window, 2

15. The "Vacation Planner" workbook has a summary section located on the second worksheet tab. To move to this worksheet:
CLICK: Summary sheet tab (at the bottom of the document window)

16. Move back to the first window ("Vacation Planner:1") and then select cell B7.

17. In this step, you will change the number in cell B7 to see the effects of the change on the Summary section in the "Vacation Planner:2" window. Do the following:
TYPE: **5**
PRESS: [ENTER]
The Average Vacation Days for Jan-96 changes from 3.00 to 3.67. Your screen should now appear similar to Figure 4.7.

18. To clean up the document area:
CHOOSE: File, Close
CLICK: No when asked to save changes

FIGURE 4.7

VIEWING TWO
WORKSHEETS IN THE
SAME WORKBOOK

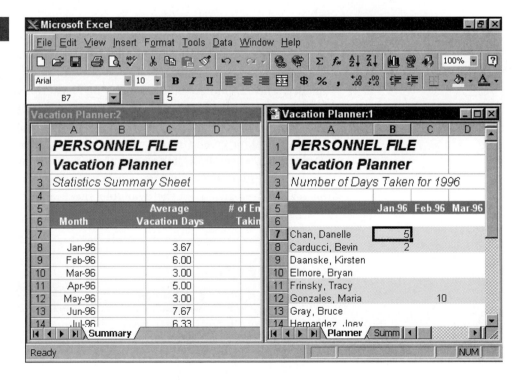

CREATING MULTIPLE-SHEET WORKBOOKS

In this section, you learn how to create and navigate a multiple-sheet workbook file. Multiple-sheet workbooks enable you to separate related information onto different pages in a single disk file. For example, imagine that you manage the advertising budgets for ten different brands of coffee. In addition to having individual reports for each brand, you need to produce a summary report that consolidates the budgets for the entire product line. Using a workbook, you can place the product summary report on the first worksheet and then each brand report on a subsequent worksheet. This three dimensional (3-D) capability enables you to easily manage and **consolidate** your information.

To access these additional sheets in a workbook, Excel provides tabs at the bottom of the document window. In a new workbook, Excel provides three worksheets by default. It may help you to think of a worksheet as a tear-off page on a notepad—the notepad representing the workbook. Although initially labeled Sheet1, Sheet2, and Sheet3, you can enter descriptive names for each worksheet. However, keep your sheet names under 30 characters, including spaces, for easy reference. You cannot use the asterisk (*), question mark (?), forward slash (/), backslash (\), or colon (:) in a worksheet's name. To move quickly to a particular worksheet, you scroll the tabs using the tab scroll buttons (shown below) and then click the desired sheet tab. You can also right-click any of the tab scroll buttons for a pop-up menu list of the available sheets in the current workbook.

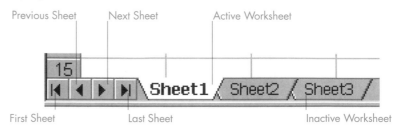

Excel's sheet tabs share the document window with the horizontal scroll bar. You can adjust how much room is devoted to each by dragging the tab split bar that is sandwiched between the two. Similar to creating window panes using the vertical split bar, the mouse pointer changes shape and color when positioned properly over the bar. You drag the tab split bar back and forth to increase and decrease the share of real estate given to each component. If you are working in a single-sheet workbook, you would normally drag the tab split bar to the far left. In this section, you will practice navigating worksheets and executing simple commands.

Let's create a multiple-sheet workbook.

Perform the following steps . . .

1. The document area in the Excel application window should be empty. To create a new workbook:
   CLICK: New Workbook button (🗋)

2. If the worksheet's document window is not maximized:
   CLICK: Maximize button (🗖)

3. To practice moving between the default worksheets:
   CLICK: Sheet2 tab
   CLICK: Sheet3 tab
   If you had multiple sheets in the workbook, you could click the Next Sheet button (▶) to scroll through the worksheet tabs. The active worksheet would remain highlighted as you scrolled.

4. To move to Sheet1 and rename the tab:
   DOUBLE-CLICK: Sheet1 tab
   Notice that the "Sheet1" text is highlighted on the worksheet tab.

5. TYPE: **Australia**
   PRESS: [ENTER]

6. To rename Sheet2:
   DOUBLE-CLICK: Sheet2 tab
   TYPE: **New Zealand**
   PRESS: [ENTER]
   (*Note*: You can also right-click a tab and then choose Rename from the shortcut menu that appears.)

7. Position the mouse pointer over the tab split bar until it changes to a black vertical double line split by a two-headed arrow.

8. DRAG: tab split bar to the left so that it rests to the right of the New Zealand tab (as shown below)

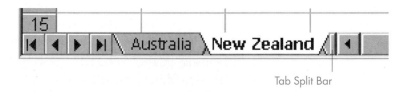

Tab Split Bar

9. Although not so important with only two worksheets in the file, let's practice selecting a worksheet using the shortcut menu:
   RIGHT-CLICK: any one of the tab scroll buttons (⏮, ◀, ▶, or ⏭)
   Notice that the first two menu choices are the new tabs, Australia and New Zealand.

10. To move to the Australia worksheet:
CHOOSE: Australia from the shortcut menu

11. To delete a worksheet in a workbook:
RIGHT-CLICK: any one of the tab scroll buttons
CHOOSE: Sheet3
RIGHT-CLICK: Sheet3 tab
CHOOSE: Delete from the shortcut menu
PRESS: `ENTER` or CLICK: OK to confirm the operation
The worksheet is permanently removed from the workbook.

12. To insert a new worksheet between Australia and New Zealand:
RIGHT-CLICK: New Zealand tab
CHOOSE: Insert
The Insert dialog box in Figure 4.8 appears. Notice that you can insert different types of sheets into the workbook, including worksheets and charts.

FIGURE 4.8

INSERT DIALOG BOX

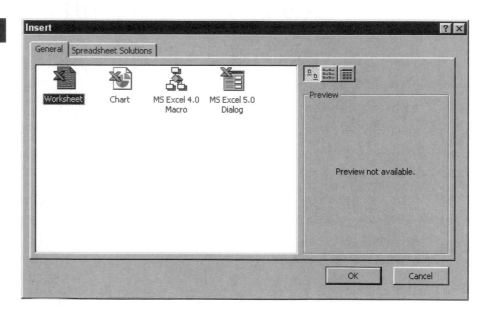

13. To insert a new worksheet:
DOUBLE-CLICK: Worksheet icon in the Insert dialog box
A new sheet, called Sheet4, appears next to the Australia tab.

14. To rename this worksheet:
DOUBLE-CLICK: Sheet4 tab
TYPE: **Japan**
PRESS: `ENTER`

15. Close the workbook and do not save the changes.

- Use the tab scroll buttons (⏮, ◀, ▶, or ⏭) to move through the available worksheets in a workbook file.
- Use the tab split bar to adjust the shared space for the sheet tabs and the horizontal scroll bar.
- RIGHT-CLICK: any one of the tab scroll buttons to display a pop-up menu showing all of the sheet names
- RIGHT-CLICK: a sheet tab to display a pop-up menu for inserting, deleting, and renaming sheets in a workbook
- DOUBLE-CLICK: a sheet tab to edit the tab name

CONSOLIDATING YOUR WORK

Whether you need to combine revenues from several regions or calculate productivity statistics for several departments, Excel's consolidation tools allow you to better manage, organize, and present your information. In this section, you learn how to consolidate data using two methods. First, you use a single workbook file to summarize information. Second, you consolidate the results of individual workbooks to produce a new summary workbook. To begin our discussion, you are introduced to the Group mode for working more efficiently with multiple-sheet files.

USING GROUP MODE

In a multiple-sheet workbook, the subsidiary sheets typically have a similar, if not identical, layout to the primary or summary worksheet. Therefore, you can copy the layout of the first worksheet to the remaining subsidiary worksheets and then enter the specific figures for each. Excel provides the **Group mode** to assist you in creating and formatting identical subsidiary worksheets. When you select more than one sheet tab, Group mode is automatically turned on and all the commands that you issue affect all the selected worksheets. For example, Group mode enables you to change a column's width in one worksheet and have that same modification made to all sheets in the workbook file. To understand the effects of Group mode, let's format a multiple-sheet file.

Perform the following steps to practice using Group mode.

Perform the following steps . . .

1. Close any workbooks that are currently open.

2. Open the "Shifts" workbook located on the Advantage Files diskette or in the Advantage Files folder. This workbook summarizes the production results for three shifts in a woodworking operation. The workbook file consists of four worksheets: one summary sheet and three detail sheets for each shift.

3. Let's start by renaming the sheet tabs:
DOUBLE-CLICK: Sheet1 tab
TYPE: **Summary**
PRESS: (ENTER)

4. To name the Sheet2 tab:
DOUBLE-CLICK: Sheet2 tab
TYPE: **Shift 1**
PRESS: (ENTER)

5. To name the Sheet3 tab:
DOUBLE-CLICK: Sheet3 tab
TYPE: **Shift 2**
PRESS: (ENTER)

6. To name the Sheet4 tab:
DOUBLE-CLICK: Sheet4 tab
TYPE: **Shift 3**
PRESS: (ENTER)

7. To select more than one worksheet at a time for Group mode:
CLICK: Summary tab
PRESS: (SHIFT) and hold it down
CLICK: Shift 3 tab
Notice that all four sheet tabs are highlighted and the word "[Group]" appears in the Title bar. (*Note*: To select multiple worksheet tabs that do not appear next to each other in a workbook, hold down the (CTRL) key and click the tabs individually.)

8. Release the (SHIFT) key.

9. With Group mode turned on, you can issue commands in the active worksheet which will carry through to the last selected worksheet in the workbook file. To begin, let's format the date headings to make them bold and italic:
SELECT: cell range from C4 to I4 on the Summary sheet

10. CLICK: Bold button (B)
CLICK: Italic button (I)
CLICK: Center button (≡)
These formatting commands are applied to all the sheets.
(*CAUTION*: Although the Group mode feature is very handy, it can also be quite dangerous. Remember that you can see the effects of the command only on the current worksheet. Without realizing, you can easily erase or reformat information on other sheets unintentionally. Make sure that selected sheets have a similar, if not identical, layout to the sheet in which you are making changes.)

11. To turn Group mode off:
RIGHT-CLICK: Summary tab
CHOOSE: Ungroup Sheets
Notice that there is no longer the word "[Group]" in the Title bar.

12. Browse through the worksheets to see the effects of the last few steps:
CLICK: Shift 1 tab
CLICK: Shift 2 tab
CLICK: Shift 3 tab
CLICK: Summary tab

QUICK REFERENCE
Turning Group
Mode On and Off

- **To turn Group mode on, select multiple worksheets by clicking their tabs while holding down the** (SHIFT) **or** (CTRL) **keys.**
- **To turn Group mode off, right-click any tab and then choose the Ungroup Sheets command from the shortcut menu.**

CONSOLIDATING A MULTIPLE-SHEET WORKBOOK

One of the nicest features of working with a multiple-sheet workbook is that information in one sheet can automatically update information in another sheet. The "Shifts" workbook, for example, contains three subsidiary sheets for each shift. In the next section, you will create formulas that sum the values from each subsidiary worksheet into the first summary worksheet. Thereafter, any changes to values in the subsidiary sheets are immediately reflected in the summary.

Perform the following steps . . .

1. Move to cell C5 in the Summary sheet.

2. As discussed in past sessions, you can enter formulas by directly typing into a cell or by accessing the Formula Palette. The following steps show you how to use several different methods for summarizing data. In a real-world application, however, you would create the first formula and then copy it to the remaining cells. Do the following:
TYPE: **=sum**
CLICK: Edit Formula button (=)
The Formula Palette appears for the SUM function.

3. To select the cell range to sum:
CLICK: Dialog Collapse button (▉) for the *Number1* text box
CLICK: Shift 1 tab
CLICK: cell C5 (20)
PRESS: (SHIFT)
CLICK: Shift 3 tab
Notice that we are grouping the worksheets from Sheet 1 to Sheet 3.

4. In Step 3, you selected a 3-D range for cell C5 on Sheet 1, Sheet 2, and Sheet 3. Let's see how Excel refers to this cell range in the Formula Palette. Do the following:
CLICK: Dialog Expand button (▥)
Your screen should now appear similar to Figure 4.9.

FIGURE 4.9

SELECTING A 3-D CELL
RANGE

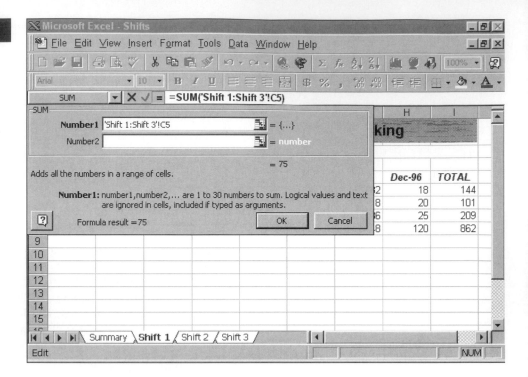

5. To complete the entry:
CLICK: OK command button
The answer of 75 appears in cell C5 on the Summary sheet.

6. Move to cell C6 in the Summary sheet.

7. To enter the SUM equation by typing, do the following:
TYPE: =sum('Shift 1:Shift 3'!c6)
PRESS: ENTER
An answer of 30 appears in the cell. Notice that you surround the tab range with single quotes and then separate the tabs from the cell address with an exclamation mark (!). If the tab names did not contain any spaces (for example, Shift1 instead of Shift 1), you could leave out the single quotes in the formula.

8. Move to cell C7 in the Summary sheet.

9. Let's create a formula by pointing to the cells without using the Formula Palette:
TYPE: =sum(
CLICK: Shift 1 tab
CLICK: cell C7
PRESS: SHIFT and hold it down
CLICK: Shift 3 tab
TYPE:)
PRESS: ENTER
An answer of 109 appears in the cell.

10. Let's copy the formula in cell C7 to cell C8 in the Summary worksheet. With cell C7 still selected, do the following:
CLICK: Copy button (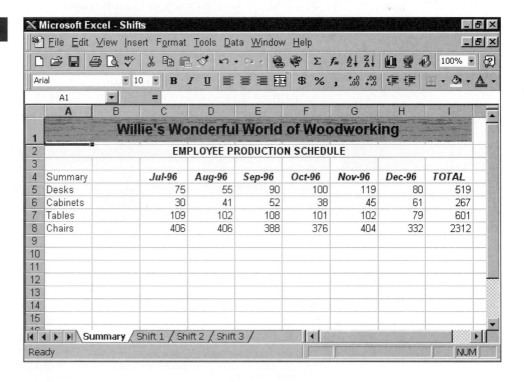)
CLICK: cell C8
PRESS: ENTER
An answer of 406 appears in the cell. Notice how the cell addressing changes *relative* to where it is copied.

11. Let's copy these formulas across the remainder of the worksheet:
SELECT: cell range from C5 through I8 on the Summary tab
CHOOSE: Edit, Fill, Right
PRESS: CTRL + HOME
Your worksheet should appear similar to Figure 4.10.

12. For practice, change some numbers in the subsidiary worksheets and then watch their effects on the Summary worksheet. Use your knowledge of arranging windows to best see the results of your changes. When finished, save the workbook as "Shift Summary" to your Data Files location and then close the workbook.

FIGURE 4.10

CONSOLIDATING A
MULTIPLE-SHEET
WORKBOOK

	Willie's Wonderful World of Woodworking							
	A	B	C	D	E	F	G	H	I
2	EMPLOYEE PRODUCTION SCHEDULE							
3								
4	Summary		Jul-96	Aug-96	Sep-96	Oct-96	Nov-96	Dec-96	TOTAL
5	Desks		75	55	90	100	119	80	519
6	Cabinets		30	41	52	38	45	61	267
7	Tables		109	102	108	101	102	79	601
8	Chairs		406	406	388	376	404	332	2312

Summary / Shift 1 / Shift 2 / Shift 3 /

Ready

CONSOLIDATING MULTIPLE WORKBOOKS

In addition to consolidating a multiple-sheet workbook, you can link separate workbook files. Linking workbooks has two major advantages over using one large workbook. First, the subsidiary workbooks are smaller in size and therefore easier to manage on a daily basis. Second, subsidiary workbooks are not restricted to the same computer as the summary workbook. For example, each department may control its own workbook and submit the file once a month for consolidation, perhaps on a diskette, across the network, or via the Internet. To create a consolidated workbook, you open each subsidiary workbook in the document area, along with the summary workbook, and then create formulas as you did in the previous section.

In this example, you compile three departmental workbooks from XYZ Corporation into a single summary workbook.

Perform the following steps . . .

1. Close any workbook files that are currently open in the document area.

2. To open four workbook files in one command:
CLICK: Open button ()

3. SELECT: your Advantage Files location
The workbook files should appear sorted by name.

4. In the file display area of the dialog box:
CLICK: XYZDept1
PRESS: **SHIFT** and hold it down
CLICK: XYZSumm
The four files should all appear highlighted, as shown in Figure 4.11.

FIGURE 4.11

SELECTING MULTIPLE
WORKBOOK FILES IN
THE OPEN DIALOG BOX

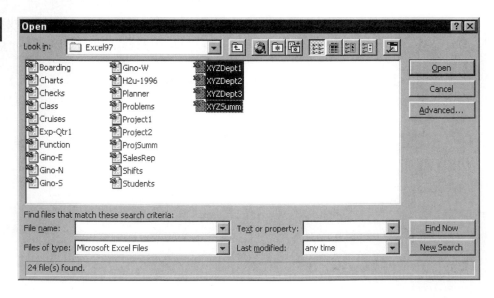

5. To open the selected files:
CLICK: Open command button
After a few seconds, the four files are loaded into Excel's document area.

6. To organize the windows within the document area:
   CHOOSE: Window, Arrange
   SELECT: *Tiled* option button
   PRESS: (**ENTER**) or CLICK: OK
   Your screen should now look like Figure 4.12.

FIGURE 4.12

WORKING WITH XYZ
CORPORATION'S
DEPARTMENTAL
WORKBOOKS

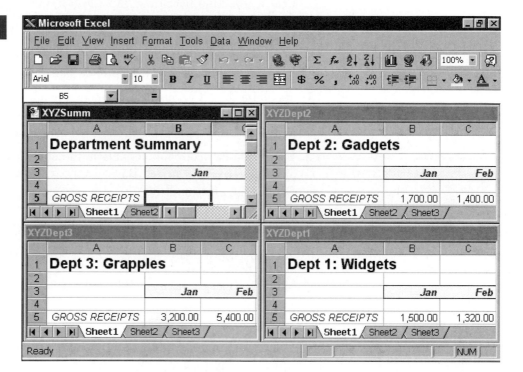

7. To move among the open windows in the document area, you position the mouse pointer on a visible part of the worksheet and click once. To practice, click the Title bars of the four worksheets. Notice that the solid or dark-colored Title bar represents the active worksheet window. When you are ready to proceed, ensure that the "XYZSumm" worksheet is active.

8. Before you consolidate the departmental workbooks into a consolidated workbook, notice that they share the same worksheet structure and layout. Although this is not necessary, it provides an instantaneous familiarity with each worksheet and makes entering the consolidation formulas much easier. To begin entering the first linking formula:
   SELECT: cell B5 in the "XYZSumm" workbook

9. A formula that links subsidiary workbooks is entered the same as any other formula. To inform Excel that you are entering a formula:
   TYPE: =
   CLICK: the Title bar of the "XYZDept1" workbook
   CLICK: cell B5 in the active workbook
   (*Hint*: After selecting the "XYZDept1" workbook, you may have to use the scroll bars to move the worksheet window so that cell B5 is visible.) Notice the formula being constructed in the Formula bar.

10. To complete the formula:
TYPE: +
CLICK: the Title bar of "XYZDept2" workbook
CLICK: cell B5 in this workbook
TYPE: +
CLICK: the Title bar of the "XYZDept3" workbook
CLICK: cell B5 in this workbook
PRESS: (ENTER)
The summary worksheet calculates the answer to be 6,400.00. Notice the equation that appears in the Formula bar.

11. Maximize the "XYZSumm" document window. If the Maximize button (☐) is covered by the expression in the Formula bar, you can click a cell in the active worksheet and then click the Maximize button (☐).

12. Before you can copy this formula to the other cells, you need to remove the absolute references to cell B5:
DOUBLE-CLICK: cell B5

13. Use the arrow keys or the I-beam mouse pointer to highlight a dollar sign ($) and then press (DELETE). Perform this step for each dollar sign that appears in the formula and then press (ENTER). When finished, the formula should read as follows:
=[XYZDept1.xls]Sheet1!B5+[XYZDept2.xls]Sheet1!B5+[XYZDept3.xls]Sheet1!B5

14. Ensure that cell B5 is selected and then copy the formula to the Clipboard:
CLICK: Copy button (▥)

15. To paste the formula into all the remaining cells at the same time:
SELECT: cell range from B5 to D5
PRESS: (CTRL) and hold it down
SELECT: cell range from B8 to D11
RELEASE: (CTRL)
PRESS: (ENTER)
The formula is pasted to all the highlighted cells. Your worksheet should now appear similar to Figure 4.13.

16. To save and then close all of the open workbooks, do the following:
PRESS: (SHIFT)
CHOOSE: File, Close All from the menu
CLICK: Yes to All command button, if it appears

FIGURE 4.13

COPYING THE
CONSOLIDATION
FORMULA TO THE
REMAINING CELLS

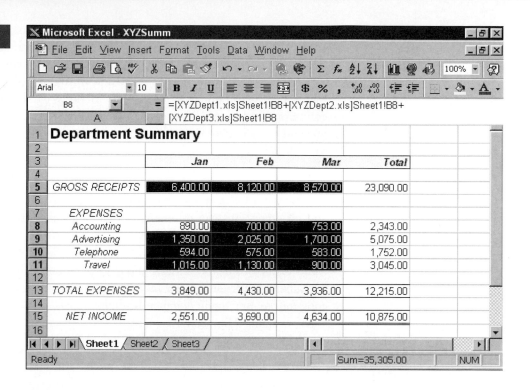

```
X Microsoft Excel - XYZSumm
```

| | File | Edit | View | Insert | Format | Tools | Data | Window | Help |

B8 = =[XYZDept1.xls]Sheet1!B8+[XYZDept2.xls]Sheet1!B8+
[XYZDept3.xls]Sheet1!B8

	A	Jan	Feb	Mar	Total
1	Department Summary				
2					
3		Jan	Feb	Mar	Total
4					
5	GROSS RECEIPTS	6,400.00	8,120.00	8,570.00	23,090.00
6					
7	EXPENSES				
8	Accounting	890.00	700.00	753.00	2,343.00
9	Advertising	1,350.00	2,025.00	1,700.00	5,075.00
10	Telephone	594.00	575.00	583.00	1,752.00
11	Travel	1,015.00	1,130.00	900.00	3,045.00
12					
13	TOTAL EXPENSES	3,849.00	4,430.00	3,936.00	12,215.00
14					
15	NET INCOME	2,551.00	3,690.00	4,634.00	10,875.00
16					

Sheet1 / Sheet2 / Sheet3

Ready   Sum=35,305.00   NUM

QUICK REFERENCE
Consolidating Workbooks

1. **Open the summary workbook and the subsidiary workbooks.**
2. **Organize the workbooks in the document area using the Window, Arrange command.**
3. **Enter a formula in the summary workbook that references cells in the subsidiary workbooks.**

IN ADDITION USING EXCEL'S CONSOLIDATE COMMAND

Excel provides a Consolidate command for consolidating worksheets. This command was not covered in this section because it introduces new concepts. The formula method

for consolidating your workbooks is simply an extension of the skills you already possess. For more information, ask the Office Assistant for help on "Data Consolidation."

WHAT IS A MACRO?

Many spreadsheet tasks are repetitive, such as enhancing titles with fonts and borders, formatting numbers, or printing cell ranges. For our benefit, Excel has assigned many of these monotonous tasks to toolbar buttons and "Auto" commands. However, there are still specific tasks that you may have to perform time and time again, such as entering and formatting your company name and address, that are not included as buttons on a toolbar. To save you time and improve the consistency of these operations, Excel enables you to store and play back keystrokes and commands in a **macro.** Using a special utility called the Macro Recorder, Excel writes the instructions for each task in the Visual Basic for Applications programming language. Using a macro, you can execute a series of instructions by pressing only two keys, clicking a toolbar button, or choosing a custom command from the Menu bar. You can even create custom command buttons and place them directly on a worksheet!

By incorporating macros into a worksheet, you make it easier to use for yourself and for others. Instead of having to remember all of the commands and keystrokes required to perform a procedure, you only have to remember a few simple keystrokes or which toolbar button to click. Furthermore, you can automate complicated tasks for co-workers or temporary personnel who are not familiar with using spreadsheets. If you are so inclined, you can even write your own Visual Basic code for creating menu commands, dialog boxes, and custom applications that don't even resemble Microsoft Excel.

CREATING MACROS

After planning the steps that you want performed in a macro, you simply record your keystrokes. The results are stored in a Visual Basic module. You can specify that macros be stored in the current workbook or in a special file called a **Personal Macro Workbook.** The Personal Macro Workbook is managed by Excel (you don't have to open or close this file) and provides a common area for storing macros that you will use with all your workbooks.

RECORDING A MACRO

The quickest method for creating a macro is to record the keystrokes that you press and the mouse clicks that you make while performing a procedure. Once recorded, the procedure may be executed again and again by selecting the macro. You turn on the Macro Recorder by choosing the Tools, Macro, Record New Macro command. When executed, the dialog box in Figure 4.14 appears.

FIGURE 4.14

RECORD NEW MACRO
DIALOG BOX

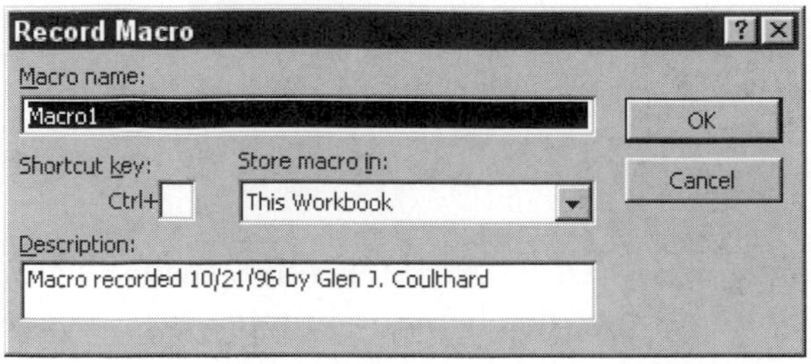

After entering a name for the macro, you select a shortcut key for implementing the macro and a location for storing the macro. After you click the OK command button, the recorder turns on and you perform the actions that you want included in the procedure. Once finished, you turn off the recorder by clicking the Stop button (■) or by choosing the Tools, Macro, Stop Recording command. Excel automatically writes the macro for you and stores it in a Visual Basic module.

You will now create a macro that automatically enters a company name and address into the worksheet and then formats the cells.

Perform the following steps . . .

1. Close any workbooks that may be open in the document area.

2. CLICK: New Workbook button (D)

3. To create a macro, you must first turn on the Macro Recorder:
CHOOSE: Tools, Macro, Record New Macro
The Record Macro dialog box appears, as shown in Figure 4.14.

4. In the dialog box, type the name (without spaces) that you want to assign to the macro:
TYPE: **CompanyName**

5. From the *Store macro in* drop-down list box:
SELECT: This Workbook
PRESS: (ENTER) or CLICK: OK
Notice that the word "Recording" appears in the Status bar and that the Stop Recording button floats above the application window.

6. As the first recorded step in the macro:
PRESS: (CTRL) + (HOME)

7. Now enter the company name and address information:
TYPE: **Sam's Superior Sailboats**
PRESS: ⬇
TYPE: **Suite 100, 2899 Seashore Drive**
PRESS: ⬇
TYPE: **Seattle, WA 98004**
PRESS: (ENTER)

8. To format this information:
SELECT: cell range from A1 to A3
CLICK: Bold button (B)
CLICK: Italic button (I)
SELECT: Times New Roman from the Font drop-down list (Arial ▾)
SELECT: 12 from the Font Size drop-down list (10 ▾)

9. SELECT: cell A1
SELECT: 14 from the Font Size drop-down list (10 ▾)

10. To stop the recording:
CLICK: Stop button (■)
And that's all there is to recording a macro! In the next section, you will get an opportunity to play back a macro.

QUICK REFERENCE
Recording a Macro

1. **CHOOSE: Tools, Macro, Record New Macro**
2. **Enter a name for the macro.**
3. **PRESS:** ENTER **or CLICK: OK**
4. **Perform the procedure to be recorded.**
5. **CLICK: Stop button** (■)

PLAYING BACK A MACRO

There are several methods for playing back a macro. You can execute a macro by selecting it from a dialog box, by pressing a keystroke combination, by clicking a toolbar button, or by selecting a custom command from the menu. In this section, you learn how to run a macro from the Macro dialog box.

Perform the following steps . . .

1. CLICK: Sheet2 tab
2. To enter the company name and address at the top of this worksheet:
CHOOSE: Tools, Macro, Macros
The dialog box in Figure 4.15 appears.

FIGURE 4.15

MACRO DIALOG BOX

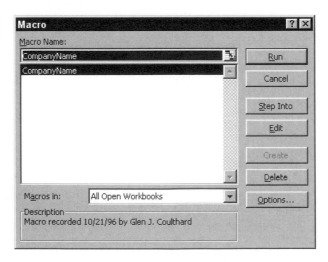

3. To run a macro from the *Macro Name* list box:
    SELECT: CompanyName macro
    CLICK: Run command button
    The company information is automatically entered and formatted in the proper range of the worksheet. (*Note*: You can also double-click a macro name in the list box area to execute the macro.)

QUICK REFERENCE
Playing Back a Macro

1. **CHOOSE: Tools, Macro, Macros**
2. **SELECT: the desired macro from the list box**
3. **PRESS: ENTER or CLICK: Run**

REVIEWING YOUR MACROS

You can easily review and edit a macro using the Visual Basic Editor. In this section, you learn how to modify Excel's code and play back the new version of your macro.

Perform the following steps . . .

1. To view the Visual Basic module:
    CHOOSE: Tools, Macro, Macros
    SELECT: CompanyName macro
    CLICK: Edit command button
    The Visual Basic Editor loads into memory and displays the macro module.

2. To see more of the macro:
    CHOOSE: Window, Tile Horizontally
    Your screen should now appear similar to Figure 4.16.

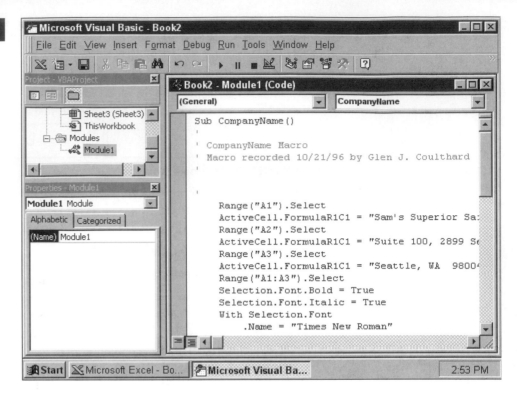

3. You edit the Visual Basic code as you would work with a word processing software program. For example, position the I-beam mouse pointer over the word "Suite" in the company's address. Do the following:
   DOUBLE-CLICK: "Suite"
   TYPE: **Room**
   DOUBLE-CLICK: "Drive"
   TYPE: **Road**

4. To see the results of our editing:
   CHOOSE: File, Close and Return to Microsoft Excel

5. To run the macro:
   CLICK: Sheet3 tab
   CHOOSE: Tools, Macro, Macros
   DOUBLE-CLICK: CompanyName macro in the list box
   Notice that the new information is entered into the cells. This example demonstrates how quick and easy it is to edit the code created by Excel's Macro Recorder.

6. Save the workbook as "My Macros" to your Data Files location.

7. Close the workbook and then exit Microsoft Excel.

QUICK REFERENCE Editing a Macro	1. CHOOSE: Tools, Macro, Macros
	2. SELECT: macro name from the list box
	3. CLICK: Edit command button
	4. Edit the Visual Basic code using basic wordprocessing keystrokes.
	5. CHOOSE: File, Close and Return to Microsoft Excel.

Summary

This session introduced you to several commands and procedures that increase your efficiency and productivity when working in Excel. The first part of the session concentrated on dividing the document window into panes for freezing titles on the screen. This technique is useful when your worksheet is organized under static column and row headings. When your application consists of separate but related areas, separating the workbook into multiple window views helps you keep track of the workbook's relationships. You also learned how to filter data and produce "top-ten" lists in your worksheet.

For consolidating worksheets or workbooks into a summary worksheet, the ability to organize and tile multiple windows in the document area is an incredible time-saver. The latter half of the session explored different methods for consolidating worksheet information. You also learned to use macros for automating common tasks and procedures. Excel's easy-to-use Macro Recorder gives everyone the ability to become a programmer using the Visual Basic for Applications language.

The Command Summary in Table 4.1 provides a list of the commands and procedures covered in this session.

TABLE 4.1	*Command*	*Description*
Command Summary	Data, Filter, AutoFilter	Analyzes a column's data and produces a filter method that enables you to limit the display of information.
	File, Close All	Closes all open documents in the document area.
	Tools, Macro, Macros	Displays a dialog box for executing or editing macros.
	Tools, Macro, Record New Macro	Records keystrokes, commands, and procedures and saves them as a macro.
	Tools, Macro, Stop Recording	Turns off the recorder to finish creating the macro; you can also click the Stop button (■).
	Window, Arrange	Arranges the open windows in the document area using square, horizontal, and vertical tiling options.
	Window, Freeze Panes	Lets you lock or freeze rows and columns on the screen so that they appear at all times.
	Window, New Window	Opens a new window in the document area for another view of the active workbook.
	Window, Remove Split	Removes panes created by choosing Window, Split or by dragging the horizontal and vertical split boxes.
	Window, Split	Splits the window into horizontal and vertical panes at the cell pointer.
	Window, Unfreeze Panes	Unfreezes the area that has been locked using the Window, Freeze Panes command.

KEY TERMS

AutoFilter

In Excel, a software feature that makes it easy for you to select, filter, and display worksheet information quickly and easily.

consolidate

The process of combining smaller worksheet files into a single summary worksheet, making it easier to manage large amounts of data.

Group mode

A special mode for working with multiple-sheet workbooks; enables you to perform commands on a single sheet and have those commands reflected in all other sheets in the file.

horizontal split box

A small box located at the top of the vertical scroll bar; used to divide a window into panes.

macro

A collection of keystrokes, commands, or procedures that can be executed using two keystrokes, a mouse click, or a menu selection. Macros are recorded or written by the user, saved to the disk, and then repeatedly used to perform frequent tasks or commands.

panes

When a document window has been divided into separate areas using the Window, Freeze Panes command or the Window, Split command, these areas are called *window panes* or *panes*. A worksheet can have a maximum of four panes at any one time.

Personal Macro Workbook

A special workbook file, managed by Excel, for storing macros that you want made available to all your workbooks.

vertical split box

A small box located at the far right of the horizontal scroll bar in a document window; used to divide a window into panes.

EXERCISES

SHORT ANSWER

1. What is the main difference between freezing titles on a worksheet and dividing a window into panes?

2. What options are available using the Window, Arrange command?

3. Name some advantages of linking workbooks.

4. What is the significance of a solid Title bar in a window?

5. How do you change the name of a sheet tab?

6. What is a macro?

7. How do you create a macro?

8. How are macros commonly played back?

9. How can you view or edit the macros that you have recorded?

10. Name two examples of when you might want to use a macro.

HANDS-ON

(*Note*: Ensure that you know the storage location of your Advantage Files and your Data Files before proceeding.)

1. In this exercise, you retrieve a workbook and practice freezing titles and viewing the worksheet using panes.

    a. Load Excel and close all of the open windows in the document area.

    b. Open the "Checks" workbook located in your Advantage Files location. This worksheet is an incomplete cash disbursements journal.

    c. CLICK: cell A8

    d. To see how many checks have been posted in the first quarter:
       PRESS: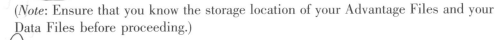
       Notice how the column text headings have scrolled out of view.

    e. Return to the top of the worksheet.

    f. Your objective is to freeze the titles in Rows 1 through 6 at the top of the screen. Then, when you move to the bottom of the column to enter new checks, you will still be able to see the column headings. The first step is to move to cell A8.

    g. CHOOSE: Window, Freeze Panes

    h. To enter more checks into the journal:
       PRESS: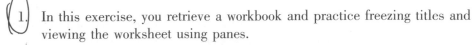
       The titles remain at the top of the screen as the cell pointer is repositioned at the bottom of the column.

    i. Enter the following checks into the journal:

Check	Date	Amount
51	17–Mar–97	550.45
52	24–Mar–97	300.95
53	31–Mar–97	750.25

Your worksheet should now appear similar to Figure 4.17.

FIGURE 4.17

THE "CHECKS"
WORKBOOK

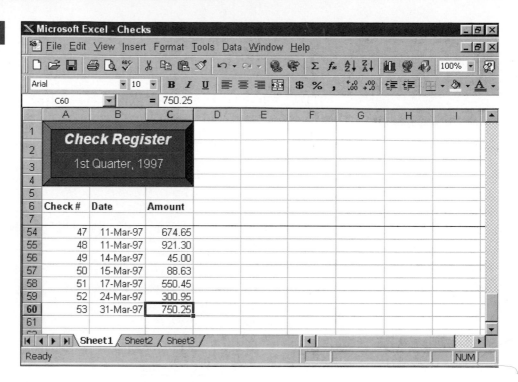

j. PRESS: CTRL + HOME

k. Unfreeze the row titles.

l. To create a new window onto the "Checks" workbook:
CHOOSE: Window, New Window

m. Arrange the open windows horizontally in the document area.

n. Arrange the open windows vertically in the document area.

o. Close the window titled "Checks:2" by clicking its Close button (☒).

p. Tile the single "Checks" window in the document area.

q. Save the workbook as "Check Register" to your Data Files location.

r. Close the workbook.

2. This exercise allows you to practice consolidating separate subsidiary work-book files into a summary workbook. The company, XYZ Developments, is currently working on two projects. Each project has a project manager responsible for hiring subcontractors and consultants. Fortunately, XYZ's project managers are experienced in using Excel and have set up tracking workbooks. Your objective is to complete a summary workbook that adds together the data from each project manager's file. (*Hint*: You will use link-ing formulas to consolidate these workbooks.)

a. Close all of the open windows in the document area.

b. Open the "Project1," "Project2," and "ProjSumm" workbooks that are stored in your Advantage Files location. Enter your name in cell E2 of the "ProjSumm" workbook.

c. Arrange the windows using the Tiled option.

d. Move to "Project1" and select cell B7.

e. Move to "Project2" and select cell B7.

f. Move to "ProjSumm" and select cell B7.
The last three steps ensure that cell B7 is visible in each worksheet.

g. Construct a formula to add together data from the two workbooks:
TYPE: =
CLICK: the Title bar of the "Project1" window
CLICK: cell B7
TYPE: +
CLICK: the Title bar of the "Project2" window
CLICK: cell B7
PRESS: `ENTER`

h. Modify the cell addresses to contain relative cell addresses rather than absolute cell addresses. (*Hint*: Remove the "$" symbols from the formula.)

i. Copy the formula in B7 to the cell range from B7 to M16.

j. PRESS: `CTRL` + `HOME`
CLICK: cell B7
Your screen should appear similar to Figure 4.18.

k. Save the workbook as "Project Summary" to your Data Files location.

l. Close all of the open windows.

FIGURE 4.18

"PROJECT SUMMARY" WORKBOOK

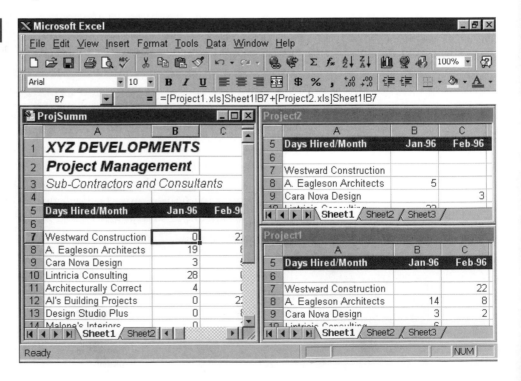

3. **On Your Own:** An Entertainment Review
Create a workbook that contains the following sheets: Music, Movies, and Books. For the Music sheet, add column titles for Title, Artist, Year, Producer, Label, and Rating. For the Movies sheet, add column titles for Title, Actors, Year, Director, Producer, and Rating. For the Books sheet, add column titles for Title, Author, Year, ISBN, Publisher, and Rating. Format all the worksheets using Group mode, and then add or edit the worksheet information as desired. When finished, enter some fictitious or real information with your personal rating system. Save the workbook as "Entertainment" to your Data Files location.

4. **On Your Own:** Macro Recordings
Open a new workbook and then create the following:

- a macro that enters your name into a worksheet cell and then assigns a Times New Roman font that is 12 points in size with a Bold and Italic style;

- a macro that enters the NOW function into two adjacent cells and then assigns one a date format and the other a time format;

- a macro that enters the following notice "© Copyright *Your Name, 1997*" and then assigns an Arial font that is 8 points in size with a Bold style.

Save the workbook as "More Macros" to your Data Files location and then close the workbook and exit Excel.

CASE PROBLEMS	GINO'S KITCHEN

(*Note*: In the following case problems, assume the role of the primary characters and perform the same steps that they identify. You may want to re-read the session opening.)

1. After a relaxing Christmas holiday, Larry arrives at the office to find the following note on his desk: "Larry, I trust you had a wonderful time on Nantucket Island. Sorry to be a pain, but I'd like the monthly restaurant report ASAP. Thanks. Gino." With his favorite mug in tow, Larry heads directly for the coffee machine, planning his strategy along the way. When he returns to his desk, Larry turns on the computer, launches Excel, and then locates the four managers' workbooks that are stored on the Advantage Diskette. These files are named "Gino-N", "Gino-S", "Gino-W", and "Gino-E". He loads all four workbooks into memory and then arranges the windows in a tiled pattern on the screen.

Leaning back in his chair, Larry ponders the task before him and then writes down the process on a piece of scrap paper. Before proceeding any further, Larry makes sure that the four restaurant workbooks appear tiled on the screen and then he performs the steps outlined in his list.

- Create a new workbook that contains a skeleton copy of the standard restaurant template. In other words, copy the contents of one restaurant's workbook to the new workbook and then delete the specific information. (*Hint*: Make sure that you leave the formulas in the new worksheet and delete only the financial information for the restaurant.)

- Edit the title in the new worksheet to read "Gino's Kitchen - All Restaurants."

- Consolidate the financial information from the four subsidiary workbooks.

- Format and print the new workbook for Gino's approval.

- Save the workbook as "Gino's Restaurants" to your Data Files location.

2. Having completed Gino's summary report, Larry decides to get a fresh start on 1996's year-end and create a summary workbook for his monthly reports. Using the same process as described in the previous case problem, Larry creates a new workbook with a skeleton copy of the standard restaurant template. Then, he renames and adds tabs in the workbook for Jan, Feb, Mar, and so on. He also inserts a new sheet at the very beginning of the workbook called "YTD" which he will use to sum the contents of the Jan through Dec sheets.

Using Group mode, Larry copies the skeleton template to the other sheets in the workbook. Still in Group mode, he makes some formatting enhancements to the worksheet that flow through to all the worksheets in the stack. After previewing the formatting enhancements, Larry ungroups the worksheets. Moving to the YTD worksheet, Larry creates formulas for consolidating the values from Jan through Dec. Pleased with his new summary, Larry saves the workbook as "Gino's YTD 1996" to the Data Files location.

3. It's 5:30 PM and Larry is getting ready to leave the office after a productive day. Just as he closes his briefcase, Gino strolls into his office to share a few ideas. "Larry, you did a good job on that summary report. Marvelous, just marvelous. But Larry, I'm troubled by the numbers that some of our establishments are reporting. I'd like you to develop and print a first-quarter budget for me using these figures." Gino hands Larry a piece of paper with handwritten notes. "I think that I might have to visit our accountant tomorrow. Can you have this ready for me by 9:00 AM?" Larry assures Gino as he strolls back down the hallway that he'll finish the budget by tomorrow morning.

Larry returns to his desk and turns on his computer once again. He loads the "Gino's YTD 1996" workbook and then saves it as "Gino's Budget 1997" to the Data Files location. Using Gino's information (provided below), he enters the budget estimates, groups the first four sheets (YTD, Jan, Feb, and Mar), and then prints the sheets centered horizontally. Lastly, he saves the worksheet and exits Excel.

All Restaurants	Jan	Feb	Mar
Food Sales	75,000	90,000	110,000
Beverage Sales	95,000	120,000	145,000
Food Costs	40,000	54,000	65,000
Beverage Costs	32,000	40,000	52,000
Manager's Salary	16,000	16,000	16,000
Wages & Benefits	26,500	30,000	36,000
Administration	2,500	4,500	5,000
Laundry & Misc.	9,500	12,000	10,500
Occupancy Costs	15,000	15,000	15,000

Microsoft Excel 97 for Windows

Creating Charts

SESSION OUTLINE

INTRODUCTION

Most businesspeople recognize the benefit of using graphics to improve the effectiveness of their presentations. Clearly, a visual display is quicker in conveying information than rows and columns of tiny numbers. This session demonstrates how you can use Excel to produce visually stunning charts and data maps from basic worksheet information.

CASE STUDY	H2 UNDERSCAPING LTD.

In 1989 Chip Yee started H2 Underscaping Ltd. (H2U), a landscaping operation that specializes in the installation of underground sprinkler systems. Since that time, H2U has grown from annual sales of $30,000 to its current year's projection of over $700,000. This tremendous growth is due in large part to Chip's sound financial and marketing analysis of the landscaping industry. Just the previous year, Chip purchased a competing business, called Xeriscaping, Inc. (*xeriscaping* is a special form of landscaping for desert or low fresh-water areas), that was losing money and turned it around into a profitable business unit at H2U. One of the other keys to Chip's success is his ability to closely monitor the seasonal trends of his industry.

Having just completed entering a full year's information into an Excel worksheet, Chip wants to take advantage of his slow time this January to analyze the results and trends for 1996. In particular, he wants to compare the dollar sales from his sprinkler installations against his new xeriscaping business. He also wants to plot his combined sales revenues against his expenses for the year to get a feeling for the seasonal trends. Although most of these numbers appear next to each other in the worksheet, Chip feels that he could better understand the results if they appeared in a chart. Ever since he can remember, Chip has been a visual learner and understands charts and pictures better than text or numbers. Unfortunately, Chip's experience with Excel has been limited to entering information into worksheets, formatting cells, using functions, and linking workbooks.

In this session, you and Chip learn about the different charting formats available in Excel and how to create basic charts and data maps using worksheet information.

FORMS OF BUSINESS GRAPHICS

A graphic representation of worksheet data is far more effective than the numbers alone for the same reason that road maps are easier to follow than written directions. The majority of people are visual learners and seem to remember what they see better than what they hear or read. Everybody has seen some sort of business graphic used at one time or another, depicting everything from interest rate trends to unemployment statistics.

Graphics are produced in a variety of formats to suit the specific needs of the business professional. For example, microcomputer images can be displayed on a monitor, photographed, plotted on paper (black and white or color), or made into transparencies to be used with an overhead projector. There are several types of charts available for presenting information to different audiences such as engineers, statisticians, medical researchers, and business professionals. This section describes some of the most popular business graphics, namely line charts, column charts, pie charts, and XY or scatter plot diagrams.

LINE CHARTS

When you need to plot trends or show changes over a period of time, the **line chart** is the perfect tool. The angles of the line reflect variations in a trend, and the distance of the line from the horizontal axis represents the amount of the variation. An example of a line chart appears in Figure 5.1.

FIGURE 5.1

A LINE CHART SHOWING CHANGES IN TELEVISION VIEWERSHIP OVER A FIVE-YEAR PERIOD

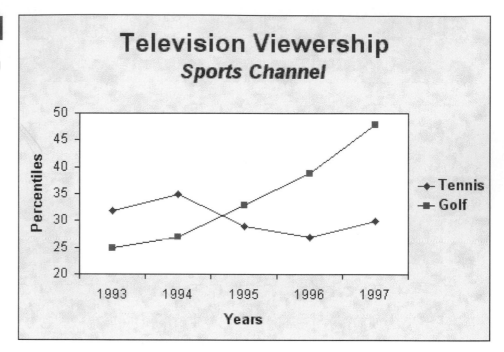

BAR OR COLUMN CHARTS

When the purpose of a chart is to compare one data element with another data element, a **column chart** is the appropriate form to use. A column chart also shows variations over a period of time, similarly to a line chart, and is one of the most commonly used graphs in business. An example appears in Figure 5.2. A *bar chart* also uses rectangular images, but they run horizontally rather than vertically.

FIGURE 5.2

A COLUMN CHART
COMPARING GOLF
VERSUS TENNIS
VIEWERSHIP OVER A
FIVE-YEAR PERIOD

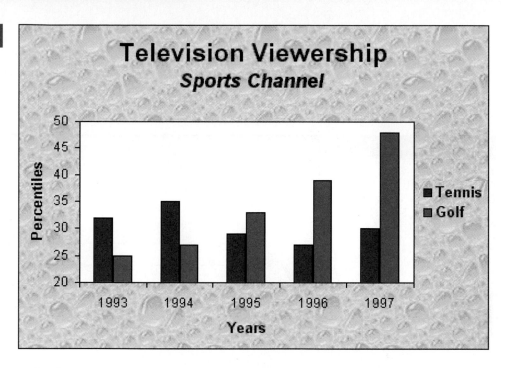

PIE CHARTS

A **pie chart** shows the proportions of individual components compared to the total. Similar to a real pie (the baked variety), a pie chart is divided into slices. An example of a pie chart appears in Figure 5.3.

FIGURE 5.3

A PIE CHART SHOWING
THE BREAKDOWN OF
EXPENSES FOR XYZ
COMPANY

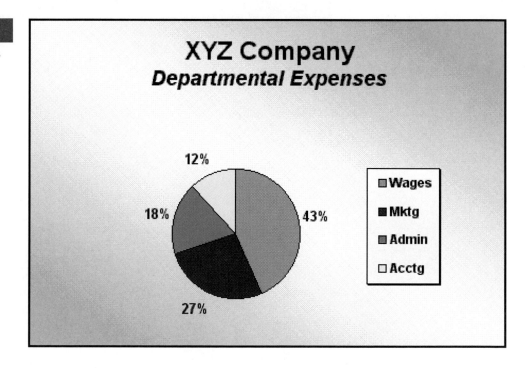

SCATTER PLOT CHARTS

XY charts, which are commonly referred to as *scatter plot diagrams,* show how one or more data elements relate to another data element. Although they look much like line charts, XY charts include a numeric scale along both the X and Y axes. Figure 5.4 shows an XY chart.

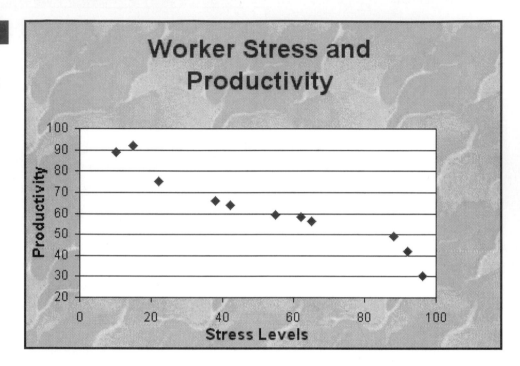

Principles of Business Graphics

With graphics programs, there is often a tendency to overindulge in the various formatting and customizing options available. Although a picture may be worth a thousand words, it is probably wise not to test this adage with business graphics. Regardless of the sophistication of your graphics program, do not attempt to tell an entire history using a single chart. To assist your planning of when and how to apply business graphics, there are certain basic principles to follow:

- *Simplicity*   Do not put too much information and formatting onto a single chart. If you include too much detail, the visual aspects become muddled and the symbols become difficult to understand.

- *Unity*   A chart must clearly relate the data elements it contains—that is, it must appear as a unit. For instance, if you use too much space between the variables (such as between columns in a column chart), you will probably destroy the unity of your chart.

- *Emphasis*   Use emphasis sparingly and correctly. Emphasis is used to draw one's attention to certain data elements or trends.
- *Balance*   Your graph should look balanced—both as a unit and in the context of the rest of the page. Changing the position of text affects the balance of the graph, as does changing the shading, color, and thickness of the lines used in a graph.

These four principles will assist you in developing charts that are easily read and interpreted. The next section introduces the methods for creating charts using Microsoft Excel. The concepts presented in this past section should be applied in the following sections.

CHART METHODS AND TYPES

There are two methods for creating a chart in Excel, differing primarily in the way the chart is printed and stored.

- You can create a new chart as a separate sheet in a workbook. This method works well for creating computer-based presentations and electronic slide shows.
- You can also create an **embedded chart** that is layered on an existing worksheet. An embedded chart can be printed and saved alongside related or clarifying information in the worksheet.

Regardless of the above methods, you create a new chart by choosing the Insert, Chart command or by clicking the Chart Wizard button (▦) on the Standard toolbar. The **Chart Wizard** guides you through the process of selecting a cell range to plot, choosing a chart type, adding elements to the chart, and, finally, selecting either a new sheet or an existing worksheet as the storage location for the new chart.

Excel's default chart type is a column chart. However, there are many additional chart types available in the gallery. Table 5.1 describes each type of chart. Many of these chart types have several formats, including three-dimensional (3-D) variations.

TABLE 5.1	*Chart Type*	*Description*
Chart Types	Area	Compares the amount or magnitude of change in data elements over a period of time.
	Bar	Compares data elements by value or time.
	Bubble	Plots the relationships between different sets of data like an XY chart, but includes a third variable whose value is shown by the size of the bubble.
	Column	Compares data elements over a period of time.
	Line	Shows trends in data over equal intervals of time.
	Pie	Shows the proportion of each individual element when compared to the total.
	Doughnut	Shows the proportion of each individual element when compared to the total; differs from pie chart in that you can display more than one data series.
	Radar	Shows each category as an axis or spoke from the center point, with lines connecting values in the same series.
	Stock	A high-low-close chart shows value ranges with a finite value, typically used for quoting stocks.
	Surface	Shows various combinations between two sets of data.
	XY (Scatter plot)	Plots the relationships between different sets of data, usually for scientific numerical analysis.

In the next section, you will create, print, and save a chart as a separate chart sheet in a workbook. Later, you will learn how to embed a chart on a worksheet and then print it with the worksheet data.

CREATING A CHART

You create a chart by selecting a range of cells to plot and issuing a menu command or by clicking the Chart Wizard button (⟦⟧). How does Excel know how to plot the information? What values does it place on the horizontal or **X-axis**? What values does it place on the vertical or **Y-axis**? Excel's decision process is examined in this section, along with the steps for creating a chart as a separate sheet in a workbook.

CHARTING A SINGLE RANGE

When you select a cell range to plot, Excel examines the shape of the highlighted area to determine which cells contain data and which cells contain headings or labels. If Excel finds text or dates in the left-hand column or in the top row, it then uses this information for the category and data labels. In other words, you should include the column headings and row labels when selecting a cell range so that Excel can automatically generate the labels for the X-axis and the legend.

In determining which information appears where, Excel counts the rows and columns in the selected range and plots the smaller dimension as the **data series** on the Y-axis. Excel always creates a chart based on the assumption that you want fewer data series than points along the X-axis. However, you can change this initial or default assumption in one of the dialog boxes displayed by the Chart Wizard.

Let's demonstrate using the Chart Wizard.

Perform the following steps . . .

1. Make sure that you've loaded Excel and know the storage location of your Advantage Files and your Data Files.

2. On the blank workbook that appears in the document window, create the worksheet appearing in Figure 5.5. Format cell A1 and then the table using the Table, AutoFormat command and Colorful 2 option. Then, change the column widths to 9.00 characters. When finished, save the workbook as "Employee" to your Data Files location.

FIGURE 5.5

"EMPLOYEE" WORKBOOK

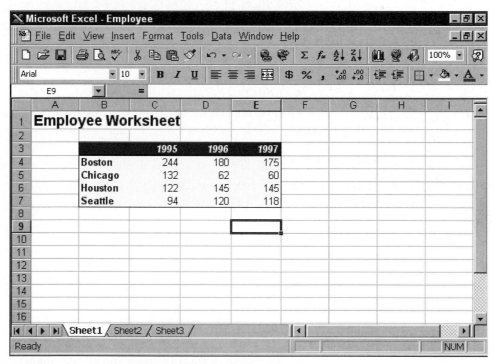

3. SELECT: cell range from B3 to E7
Notice that there are more cities (4) than years (3) in this selection. Therefore, Excel will place the cities on the horizontal or X-axis and will plot the years on the vertical or Y-axis.

4. To plot the selected range as a new chart sheet in the workbook:
CHOOSE: Insert, Chart
The Chart Wizard displays the first dialog box in a series of four, as shown
in Figure 5.6.

FIGURE 5.6

CHART WIZARD:
STEP 1 OF 4 - CHART
TYPE

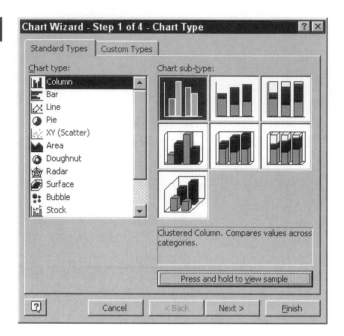

5. In the first dialog box, you select the type of chart that you want displayed
from either the *Standard Types* tab or the *Custom Types* tab. Notice that the
default type is a Column chart and that the first sub-type is selected. To
see a sample of how the worksheet data will appear using this chart type:
CLICK: "Press and hold to view sample" command button and hold it down

6. The *Chart sub-type* area is temporarily replaced by a *Sample* area for viewing a chart with your data. Release the mouse button to stop viewing the
sample chart.

7. With the Column option selected in the *Chart type* list box:
SELECT: "Clustered column with a 3-D visual effect" sub-type
(*Note*: A description of the selected option appears below the list when you
click on a chart sub-type.)

8. To continue to the next step:
CLICK: [Next >]
The Chart Wizard displays the second dialog box.

9. In Step 2 of 4, you select or modify the data range (Figure 5.7). You can
also specify the desired data elements to display (on the *Series* tab) and the
appropriate column and row orientation. The preview area helps you make
the right decision. To accept the defaults and proceed:
CLICK: [Next >]

FIGURE 5.7

CHART WIZARD:
STEP 2 OF 4 - CHART
SOURCE DATA

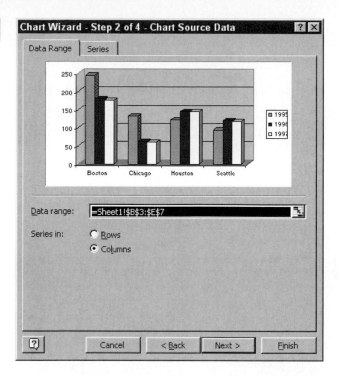

10. The Step 3 of 4 dialog box appears with a variety of formatting options, including tabs for adding and adjusting *Titles*, *Axes*, *Gridlines*, *Legend*, *Data Labels*, and *Data Table*. To add a title to this chart:
    CLICK: *Titles* tab

11. Position the I-beam mouse pointer in the *Chart title* text box and then click once to position the cursor.

12. TYPE: **Employee Levels**
    After waiting a few moments, you will notice that the title appears in the sample preview area. Your worksheet should now appear similar to Figure 5.8.

FIGURE 5.8

CHART WIZARD:
STEP 3 OF 4 - CHART
OPTIONS

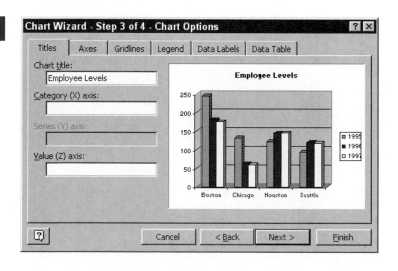

13. Since you will place this chart on a separate sheet in the workbook, let's include the table of worksheet numbers near the bottom of the chart. Do the following:
CLICK: *Data Table* tab
SELECT: *Show data table* check box so that a "✓" appears

14. You may notice that the sample preview looks crowded. Since we are displaying the table of numbers, let's delete the legend:
CLICK: *Legend* tab
SELECT: *Show legend* check box so that no "✓" appears

15. To proceed to the next step:
CLICK: Next >
The last dialog box appears (Figure 5.9).

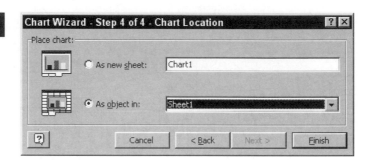

16. In the Chart Location dialog box, you specify where you want Excel to create and store the new chart. Do the following:
SELECT: *As new sheet* option button
TYPE: **Levels Chart** as the sheet tab's name
CLICK: Finish
The chart is displayed in a new sheet, called Levels Chart, in the same workbook file as the selected data.

17. To ensure that you are viewing all of the chart:
CLICK: down arrow beside the Zoom (100%) drop-down list box
CLICK: Selection option
(*Note*: Your zoom factor may appear differently than the icon shown above.)

18. Ensure that the Chart toolbar appears docked below the Formatting toolbar. If not, drag it into place using the mouse.

19. Let's demonstrate the link between the worksheet data and the chart. First, take note of Seattle's 1995 bar in the chart. Then, do the following:
CLICK: Sheet1 sheet tab
CLICK: cell C7
TYPE: **300**
PRESS: ENTER

20. To review the chart:
CLICK: Levels Chart sheet tab
Notice that the change in the worksheet data is immediately reflected in the chart. Your chart should now appear similar to Figure 5.10.

21. Save this workbook as "Employee" to your Data Files location and then close the workbook.

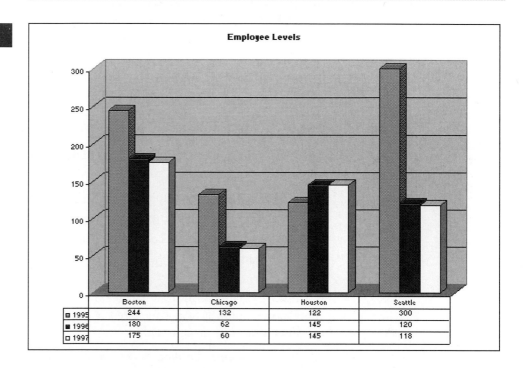

	Boston	Chicago	Houston	Seattle
1995	244	132	122	300
1996	180	62	145	120
1997	175	60	145	118

QUICK REFERENCE
Creating a Chart

1. **SELECT: the cell or range of cells to plot in a chart**
2. **CHOOSE: Insert, Chart or**
   CLICK: Chart Wizard button ( )
3. **Respond to the dialog boxes displayed by the Chart Wizard.**

CHARTING MULTIPLE RANGES

You can improve your productivity in Excel by reducing unnecessary keystrokes and commands. One method for reducing keystrokes is to select multiple cell ranges prior to formatting, deleting, or charting worksheet information. This allows you to place information anywhere in a workbook and still select it for charting. Because most worksheets are not as structurally perfect as the example in the last section, you must learn how to take advantage of this flexibility.

Perform the following steps . . .

1. Open the "XYZDept1" workbook located in your Advantage Files location.

2. To practice selecting multiple cell ranges, let's format the GROSS RECEIPTS line, TOTAL EXPENSES line, and NET INCOME line to display a currency format. Do the following:
   SELECT: cell range from B5 to E5

3. To select the range of cells from B13 to E13:
   PRESS: CTRL and hold it down
   CLICK: cell B13 and hold down the mouse button
   DRAG: mouse pointer from B13 to E13
   Notice that the original cell selection of B5 to E5 remains highlighted.

4. Release the mouse button and the CTRL key.

5. To select the range of cells from B15 to E15:
   PRESS: CTRL and hold down
   CLICK: cell B15 and hold down the mouse button
   DRAG: mouse pointer from B15 to E15

6. Release the mouse button and the CTRL key.

7. CLICK: Currency Style button ($)
   Each of the highlighted cells is formatted to the accounting format.

8. Now, we'll select some ranges for charting. To highlight the cell range for the horizontal or X-axis:
   SELECT: cell range from A3 to D3
   (*Note*: Column E is not included because it is a summed value and we want to compare the months only.)

9. When selecting the data ranges to plot, you must ensure that they are the same shape (for example, same number of rows and columns) so that they will contain the same number of items:
   PRESS: CTRL and hold it down
   SELECT: cell range from A5 to D5
   SELECT: cell range from A13 to D13

10. Release the CTRL key.
    At this point, there should be three cell ranges selected on the worksheet as shown in Figure 5.11.

FIGURE 5.11

SELECTING MULTIPLE
RANGES TO CHART

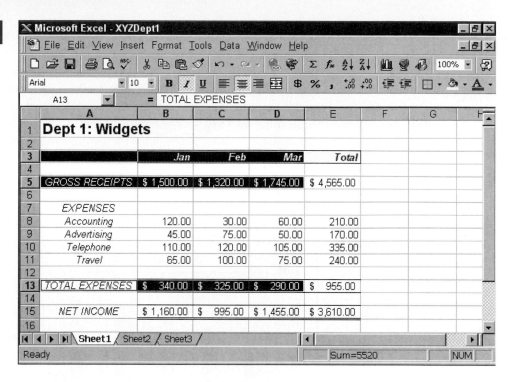

11. To produce a quick chart using the selected cell ranges:
    CLICK: Chart Wizard button (⬛)

12. When the first Chart Wizard dialog box appears:
    CLICK: Next > three times to move to Step 4 of 4

13. To complete the Chart Wizard:
    SELECT: *As new sheet* option button
    CLICK: Finish
    A new chart sheet appears in the workbook. Notice that the Y-axis is formatted with dollar signs because of your earlier formatting of the GROSS RECEIPTS and TOTAL EXPENSES lines.

14. Let's rename the chart sheet's tab:
    DOUBLE-CLICK: Chart1 tab
    TYPE: **Widgets**
    PRESS: (ENTER)

15. Save the workbook as "XYZ Chart" to your Data Files location.

The next section explains some general features of charts. Do not close the chart or workbook as they are referred to in the following sections.

WORKING WITH CHARTS

When the chart sheet is active, Excel modifies your work area slightly. In addition to the appearance of the Chart toolbar, you will find additional menu commands specific to formatting and manipulating charts. Because chart sheets are quite different from worksheets, you may find that it takes some time to adjust. For example, you no longer have the familiar rows and columns to guide your entry of information. Before learning how to format and enhance charts in the next sections, take a few moments to study the parts of a chart labeled in Figure 5.12 and described in Table 5.2.

FIGURE 5.12

PARTS OF A CHART

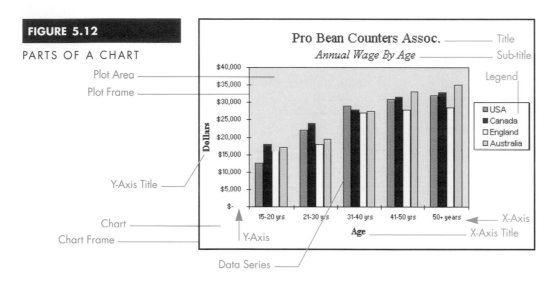

TABLE 5.2	*Component*	*Description*
Parts of a Chart Window	Chart and Chart Frame	The area inside a chart, including the **plot area,** titles, axes, legend, and other objects.
	Plot Area and Plot Frame	The area for plotting values from the worksheet. The plot area contains the axes and data series.
	Axes (X and Y) and Axes Titles	Most charts have a horizontal category axis (X) and a vertical value axis (Y) for plotting values.
	Data Marker	A single dot, bar, or symbol that represents one number from the worksheet.
	Data Series	A series of related values from the worksheet. A data series consists of related data markers.
	Legend	A key for deciphering the different data series appearing in the plot area.

SELECTING A CHART TYPE

By default, Excel selects a two-dimensional column chart for plotting your worksheet information. However, there are many different chart types and formats to choose from in the gallery, as summarized in Table 5.1. This section shows you how to access these different chart formats.

Perform the following steps . . .

1. First, ensure that the chart sheet is the active sheet:
   CLICK: Widgets sheet tab

2. To select a different chart type:
   CHOOSE: Chart, Chart Type
   Notice that the first four menu items on the Chart menu correspond to the dialog boxes in the Chart Wizard.

3. In the Chart Type dialog box, you select a primary chart type and then a sub-type. You can also select from a list of custom types:
   SELECT: Cylinder in the *Chart type* list box
   SELECT: "Bar with a cylindrical shape" as the *Chart sub-type*
   CLICK: "Press and hold to view sample" command button
   The dialog box should appear similar to Figure 5.13.

FIGURE 5.13

CHART TYPE
DIALOG BOX

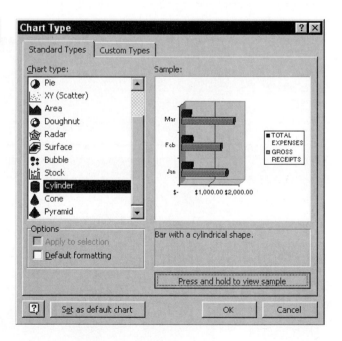

4. Release the mouse button to stop viewing the sample.

5. On your own, select the other chart types and then preview their sub-types using the "Press and hold to view sample" command button.

6. To proceed:
SELECT: Column in the *Chart type* list box
SELECT: "Clustered column with a 3-D visual effect" sub-type
PRESS: (**ENTER**) or CLICK: OK

7. Use the Chart Objects (Chart Area ▾) drop-down list box on the Chart toolbar to select individual chart objects. To demonstrate:
CLICK: down arrow adjacent to the Chart Objects (Chart Area ▾) box
SELECT: Chart Area
Notice that small black selection boxes appear around the chart area.

8. To ensure that you are viewing the maximum area of the chart:
CLICK: down arrow beside the Zoom (100% ▾) drop-down list box
CLICK: Selection option
This command tells Excel to display all of the selected object, in this case the Chart Area, in the document area. Your screen should now appear similar to Figure 5.14.

9. Save the workbook as "XYZ Chart" to your Data Files location.

FIGURE 5.14

WIDGETS CHART SHEET

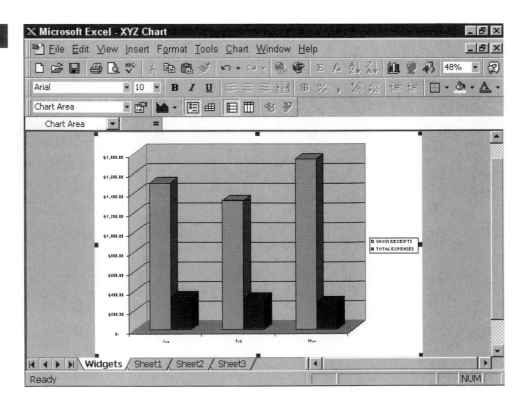

QUICK REFERENCE	1. **CHOOSE: Chart, Chart Type**
Selecting a Chart Type	2. **In the dialog box, select the chart type and sub-type.**
	3. **CLICK: "Press and hold to view sample" command button and hold it down to preview the format**
	4. **Release the mouse button to proceed.**
	5. **PRESS: ENTER or CLICK: OK**

CUSTOMIZING AND FORMATTING A CHART

Customizing a chart involves adding titles, legends, annotations, and arrows which emphasize certain aspects of the chart and improve its overall readability. Formatting a chart refers to setting the display options for each element of a chart. For example, if you are working on a color system, Excel differentiates each data series in a chart by assigning them different colors. When you print the chart to a non-color printer, however, the various colors appear as black or white. Therefore, you need to format the columns using patterns or shades of gray to differentiate the series. This section explores several methods for enhancing your chart.

To customize or format a chart, you must first select the chart object that you want to format. As demonstrated in the previous section, you can select objects using the Chart Objects (Chart Area) drop-down list box on the Chart toolbar. You can also select an object by clicking on it using the mouse. The following sections demonstrate how to add titles, legends, free-form text, arrows, fonts, patterns, and backgrounds to your chart.

ATTACHING TITLES

Titles are used to state the purpose of the chart and to explain the scales used for the axes. After adding titles, you can format the text using a variety of fonts, styles, and shading. You will now add a title to the Widgets graph.

 **Perform the following steps . . .**

1. Ensure that the chart sheet is active.

2. To add titles to the chart:
   CHOOSE: Chart, Chart Options
   CLICK: *Titles* tab

3. In the Chart Options dialog box:
   SELECT: *Chart title* text box
   TYPE: **Receipts vs. Expenses**
   SELECT: *Category (X) axis* text box
   TYPE: **Months**
   SELECT: *Value (Z) axis* text box
   TYPE: **Dollars**
   Your dialog box should now appear similar to Figure 5.15.

FIGURE 5.15

CHART OPTIONS
DIALOG BOX: *TITLES*
TAB

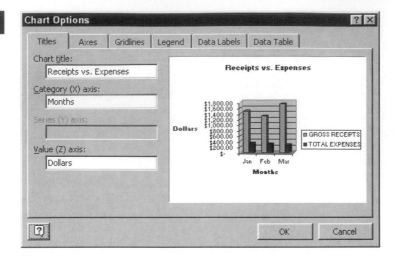

4. To accept the modifications:
    PRESS: (ENTER) or CLICK: OK

5. Let's format the "Dollars" entry for the Value Axis title:
    CLICK: Value Axis title once
    Notice that it is surrounded by small black selection boxes.

6. To display the formatting options for this object:
    CLICK: Format Object button (⊞) in the Chart toolbar
    (*Note*: The name of the Format Object button changes according to the
    chart object that is selected. For example, the ToolTip will now read "For-
    mat Axis Title.")

7. To change the alignment or orientation of the title:
    CLICK: *Alignment* tab
    CLICK: the leftmost "Text" box in the *Orientation* group (displaying text
    running down a single column)
    PRESS: (ENTER) or CLICK: OK

QUICK REFERENCE
Attaching Titles

1. **CHOOSE: Chart, Chart Options**
2. **CLICK:** *Titles* **tab**
3. **Type the desired titles into the** *Chart title, Value (X) axis,* **and** *Category (Z)*
    axis **text boxes.**
4. **PRESS:** (ENTER) **or CLICK: OK**

MODIFYING THE CHART LEGEND

A legend provides a key for the data series plotted in the chart. If you didn't specify a legend in the Chart Wizard dialog box, you can add one later using the Chart, Chart Options command. Although Excel places the legend at the right-hand side of the chart window by default, you can easily move the legend by dragging it using the mouse.

Perform the following steps . . .

1. To modify the legend:
   CHOOSE: Chart, Chart Options
   CLICK: *Legend* tab

2. To change the legend's location on the chart sheet:
   SELECT: *Top* option button
   Your screen should now appear similar to Figure 5.16.

FIGURE 5.16

CHANGING THE
LEGEND PLACEMENT

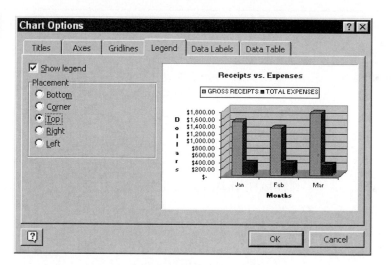

3. To accept the modifications:
   PRESS: [ENTER] or CLICK: OK

4. To move the legend to the bottom right-hand corner of the sheet, position the mouse pointer on the legend:
   CLICK: legend once and hold down the left mouse button
   DRAG: legend to the bottom right-hand corner

5. Release the mouse button. Notice that this method for moving the legend does not result in the rest of the chart objects being resized.

6. Let's finalize the legend's position on the chart sheet using a shortcut pop-up menu:
   RIGHT-CLICK: anywhere on the legend
   CHOOSE: Format Legend
   CLICK: *Placement* tab
   SELECT: *Right* option button
   PRESS: [ENTER] or CLICK: OK

QUICK REFERENCE
Modifying the Legend

- **To add or delete a legend:**
  CHOOSE: Chart, Chart Options
  CLICK: *Legend* **tab**
- **To format the legend:**
  RIGHT-CLICK: on the legend
  CHOOSE: Format Legend

ENTERING FREE-FORM TEXT

Using a text box, you can place free-form text anywhere in the chart area. You use free-form text to emphasize or draw attention to important areas of a chart or to add subsidiary information, such as copyright notices. Once text is entered, you can easily apply fonts and styles.

Perform the following steps . . .

1. For the next two sections, we access buttons on the Drawing toolbar. To display the Drawing toolbar:
    RIGHT-CLICK: on any toolbar
    CHOOSE: Drawing
    The Drawing toolbar should now appear on your screen. (*Note:* For a complete listing of the Excel toolbars and their buttons, refer to the Appendix at the end of this guide.)

2. If the Drawing toolbar appears in its own window, floating above the chart sheet:
    DRAG: Drawing toolbar downward to dock it near the Status bar

3. To provide a better view of your chart:
    CLICK: down arrow beside the Chart Objects (Chart Area ▼) box
    SELECT: Chart Area
    CLICK: down arrow beside the Zoom (100% ▼) box
    SELECT: 100%

4. Scroll the window to view the upper-right quadrant of the chart.

5. To enter free-form text, do the following:
    CLICK: Text Box button (▨) on the Drawing toolbar

6. Move the cross-hair mouse pointer into the chart area and drag a rectangle that is similar to the screen graphic in Figure 5.17.

FIGURE 5.17

CREATING A TEXT BOX

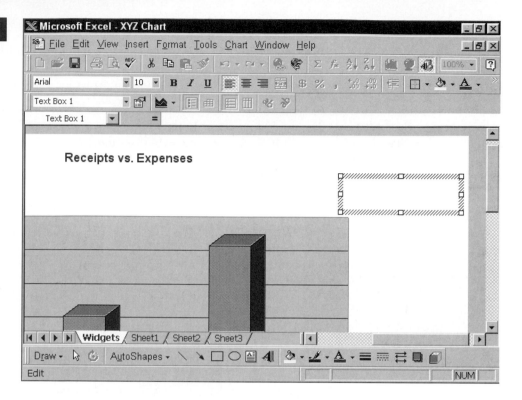

7. When you release the mouse button, you will notice a flashing insertion point. To enter the free-form text:
TYPE: **After Training**

8. To remove the insertion point and deselect the text box:
CLICK: on the white chart area surrounding the text box

QUICK REFERENCE
Adding Free-Form Text

1. **CLICK: Text Box button (** 🖻 **) on the Drawing toolbar**
2. **DRAG: a rectangle in the chart sheet**
3. **TYPE: any free-form text**

USING ARROWS FOR EMPHASIS

Besides free-form text, you can use other types of objects to direct the reader's attention. Arrows are the most common means for focusing a viewer on certain locations in your chart. Let's add an arrow for emphasis.

Perform the following steps . . .

1. To add an arrow to the chart:
    CLICK: Arrow button ( ) on the Drawing toolbar

2. Position the cross-hair mouse pointer below and to the left of the letter A in the word "After."

3. DRAG: the cross-hair mouse pointer toward the March GROSS RECEIPTS column (see below)

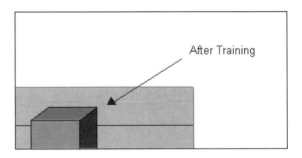

After Training

4. Release the mouse button. Your text box and arrow should appear similar to the above example.

5. To remove the selection boxes:
    CLICK: on the white chart area surrounding the arrow

6. Let's return to a full chart view:
    RIGHT-CLICK: Drawing toolbar
    CHOOSE: Drawing to remove the toolbar from view
    CLICK: down arrow beside the Zoom (100%) box
    SELECT: Selection

QUICK REFERENCE	1.	CLICK: Arrow button ( ) on the Drawing toolbar
Adding an Arrow	2.	DRAG: cross-hair mouse pointer in the chart sheet

CHOOSING FONTS AND TEXTURES

Formatting a chart involves changing its background color and texture, choosing fonts for headings and other text, and selecting patterns for data series. Although most commands are available in the Menu bar, you will find that using the Format Object button (📑) and shortcut pop-up menus are much easier and more convenient.

Perform the following steps . . .

1. Position the mouse pointer over the chart title and click the right mouse button to display its pop-up menu.

2. To enhance the text:
   CHOOSE: Format Chart Title

3. Let's change the font and style for the title:
   CLICK: *Font* tab
   SELECT: Bold Italic from the *Font style* list box
   SELECT: 24 from the *Size* list box
   PRESS: **ENTER** or CLICK: OK

4. To format the free-form text in the text box, move the I-beam mouse pointer over the word "After" and then do the following:
   DOUBLE-CLICK: the word "After" continuing to hold down the mouse button as you drag the pointer to highlight "Training" as well

5. CLICK: Format Object button (📑)
   SELECT: Italic from the *Font style* list box
   SELECT: 14 from the *Size* list box
   PRESS: **ENTER** or CLICK: OK

6. To format the Category axis:
   CLICK: down arrow beside the Chart Objects (Chart Area ▼) box
   SELECT: Category Axis
   CLICK: Format Object button (📑)
   CLICK: *Font* tab
   SELECT: 14 from the *Size* list box

7. To format the Category axis title:
   CLICK: down arrow beside the Chart Objects (Chart Area ▼) box
   SELECT: Category Axis Title
   CLICK: Font Size (10 ▼) box on the Formatting toolbar
   SELECT: 14

8. On your own, format the Value Axis and its Title using the same options as chosen in Steps 6 and 7.

9. To apply a background color for the legend box:
RIGHT-CLICK: on the legend
CHOOSE: Format Legend
CLICK: *Patterns* tab
SELECT: *Shadow* check box
SELECT: a light yellow color in the *Area* group

10. To change the font and point size:
CLICK: *Font* tab
SELECT: Regular in the *Font style* list box
SELECT: 12 in the *Size* list box
PRESS: (ENTER) or CLICK: OK

11. To format the plot area background:
CLICK: down arrow beside the Chart Objects (Chart Area ▼) box
SELECT: Walls
CLICK: Format Object button (🖻)
CLICK: Fill Effects command button
CLICK: *Texture* tab
SELECT: a marble texture
CLICK: OK command button twice to save your choices

12. Save the workbook as "XYZ Chart" to your Data Files location. Your chart is now ready for printing and should look similar to Figure 5.18.

FIGURE 5.18

A FORMATTED AND
CUSTOMIZED CHART

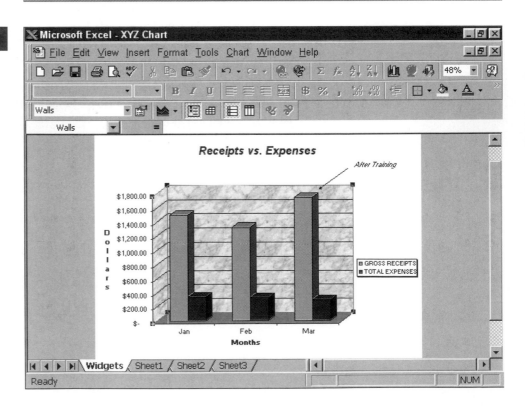

QUICK REFERENCE	1.	RIGHT-CLICK: a chart object
Choosing Fonts and Textures	2.	CHOOSE: Format *object*
	3.	Complete the dialog box entries.
	4.	PRESS: ENTER or CLICK: OK

Printing a Chart

When a chart is created as a separate chart sheet, you print it directly from the sheet using the File, Print command. For the most part, the general print options are identical to printing a worksheet. However, there is one additional set of layout options for scaling the chart to fit on a page. Like a worksheet, remember to preview your charts prior to printing.

Perform the following steps to print the Widgets chart.

Perform the following steps . . .

1. Ensure that the chart sheet is active.

2. To adjust the page layout options:
   CHOOSE: File, Page Setup
   CLICK: *Chart* tab
   The Page Setup dialog box appears.

3. In this dialog box, you select the appropriate size option for printing the chart. The *Scale to fit page* option prints the chart using the current height to width ratio, and the *Use full page* option adjusts the ratio to maximize the print area. Try the following option on your printer:
   SELECT: *Scale to fit page* option button
   CLICK: Print Preview command button
   Your screen should now appear similar to Figure 5.19.

FIGURE 5.19

PRINT PREVIEWING THE
WIDGETS CHART SHEET

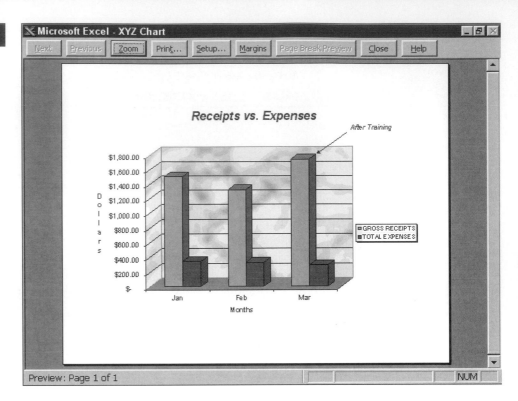

4. When finished viewing the chart, send it to the printer:
    CLICK: Print command button (at the top of the window)
    PRESS: ENTER or CLICK: OK

5. Save the workbook as "XYZ Chart" to your Data Files location, replacing
    the existing version.

6. Close the workbook.

QUICK REFERENCE
Printing a Chart

1. Ensure that the chart sheet is active.
2. CHOOSE: File, Page Setup
3. CLICK: *Chart* tab
4. SELECT: sizing options for printing the chart
5. CLICK: Print Preview command button to view the chart
6. CLICK: Print command button
7. PRESS: ENTER or CLICK: OK

EMBEDDING A CHART

This section explains how to embed a chart into a worksheet. An embedded chart is placed over—not entered into—a cell range. All of the customizing and formatting for embedded charts is the same as for chart sheets. However, the method for printing the chart differs slightly from the previous section.

To create an embedded chart, you select the *As object in* option button during the fourth step of the Chart Wizard and then specify a particular destination worksheet. The worksheet is displayed with the embedded chart appearing in the middle of the worksheet window. You can then drag the chart to where you want it positioned. To remove an embedded chart, you select the chart by clicking on it and then press DELETE . To print worksheet information along with the chart, you select a range that covers both areas of the worksheet and chart and then set the print area. To edit an embedded chart, you simply click the chart to make it active.

Let's practice embedding a chart in a worksheet.

Perform the following steps . . .

1. Open the "Cruises" workbook located in your Advantage Files location.

2. SELECT: cell range from A2 to D5

3. To use the Chart Wizard:
   CLICK: Chart Wizard button ( )

4. In the first step of the Chart Wizard dialog box:
   SELECT: Column from the *Chart type* list box
   SELECT: "Stacked Column" (two dimensional) sub-type
   CLICK: Next >

5. Since the cell range was selected prior to launching the Chart Wizard, let's bypass Step 2 of 4:
   CLICK: Next >

6. In Step 3 of 4 of the Chart Wizard:
   CLICK: *Titles* tab
   SELECT: *Chart title* text box
   TYPE: **Demographics**
   SELECT: *Value (Y) axis* text box
   TYPE: **Passengers**
   CLICK: Next >

7. You'll now accept the default options for placing the chart as an object in Sheet1. Do the following:
   CLICK: Finish
   The embedded chart appears in the middle of the worksheet window. Notice that the Chart toolbar also appears.

8. To move the chart below the worksheet information, first select the chart by clicking in the middle of it and then drag it to a new location:
CLICK: embedded chart once and hold down the mouse button
DRAG: chart to line up the top left-hand corner with cell A7

9. To size the chart, position the mouse pointer over one of the boxes on the embedded chart's borders. The mouse pointer should change to a black double-headed arrow. Now drag the bottom right-hand corner's sizing box to stretch the chart down to cell F20. (*Note*: If you wanted to retain a constant height to width ratio, you would hold down the (**SHIFT**) key as you drag the mouse. If you wanted to align the chart with worksheet cells, you would hold down the (**ALT**) key.)

Your screen should appear similar to Figure 5.20 when completed.

FIGURE 5.20

MANIPULATING AN
EMBEDDED CHART

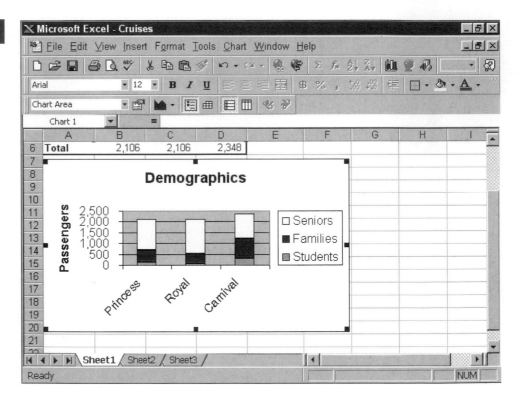

10. To return the focus to the worksheet:
CLICK: any visible worksheet cell
Notice that the selection boxes around the embedded chart and the Chart toolbar both disappear.

11. To edit or format the chart:
CLICK: on any part of the embedded chart once
Notice that it is now surrounded by the selection boxes and that the Chart toolbar reappears. All of the commands and procedures that you learned in previous sections (for example, adding titles, free-form text, and arrows) are available for use in formatting the embedded chart.

12. To print the worksheet along with the embedded chart:
SELECT: the entire cell range from A1 to the bottom right-hand corner of the embedded chart, F20
CHOOSE: File, Print Area, Set Print Area
CLICK: Print Preview command button

13. When you are satisfied with the preview:
CLICK: Print command button
PRESS: (ENTER) or CLICK: OK

14. Save the workbook as "Cruise Demographics" to your Data Files location.

15. Close the workbook.

QUICK REFERENCE
Creating an
Embedded Chart

1. **SELECT: the cell or range of cells to plot in a chart**
2. **CLICK: Chart Wizard button (▦)**
3. **Respond to the dialog boxes in the Chart Wizard. For Step 4 of 4, select the *As an object* option button and then specify a worksheet.**

USING MICROSOFT DATA MAP

Using a specialty charting tool called **Microsoft Data Map,** you can create a map to analyze your worksheet information geographically. For example, you could plot the number of UFO sightings by state or by country, assuming that you had a worksheet containing this information. Data Map also enables you to quickly analyze trends relative to a region's demographic breakdown. Existing demographic information is provided by Excel and is accessible from a special workbook called "Mapstats" located in the Datamap folder.

CREATING A DATA MAP

To use Data Map with Excel, you need to organize your worksheet data into columns. One column must contain geographic data such as the names of states or countries. This column determines the type of map that will be displayed (for example, a map of the United States, Canada, or the world.) To map your worksheet information, select the cell range that includes the geographic data and then click the Map button () on the Standard toolbar. You then drag the cross-hair mouse pointer on the worksheet to set the size and location of the map. When you release the mouse button, the selected cell range is analyzed and a map is displayed.

You will now practice creating a data map.

Perform the following steps . . .

1. Open the "Boarding" workbook, stored in your Advantage Files location. This worksheet provides a fictitious marketing report for a U.S. snowboarding manufacturer that wants to sell its products in the Canadian market.

2. To create a map showing the relative amount of money spent on snowboarding by each province, do the following:
   SELECT: cell range from A4 to B16
   Notice that you are including the column headings in the selection and that column A contains geographical information.

3. CLICK: Map button ( )
   (*Note*: If you do not see the Map button ( ) on the Standard toolbar, you may not have this feature installed on your computer. If this is the case, you must re-install Microsoft Excel and select the Data Map utility before performing the steps in the remainder of this session.)

4. To place the map to the right of the worksheet information, first move the cross-hair mouse pointer to the middle of cell C4 and then click the left mouse button once. This method for embedding a map provides a "best-fit" size for the map.

5. If a dialog box appears with the title Multiple Maps Available, you must do the following:
   SELECT: Canada
   CLICK: OK command button
   The map will now appear embedded in the worksheet.

6. Scroll the document window so that you can view the entire map and move the Microsoft Map Control dialog box by dragging its Title bar. Notice that the map shows provinces with higher sales using a darker shade of gray. Your screen should now appear similar to Figure 5.21.

FIGURE 5.21

CREATING A MAP
FROM WORKSHEET
INFORMATION

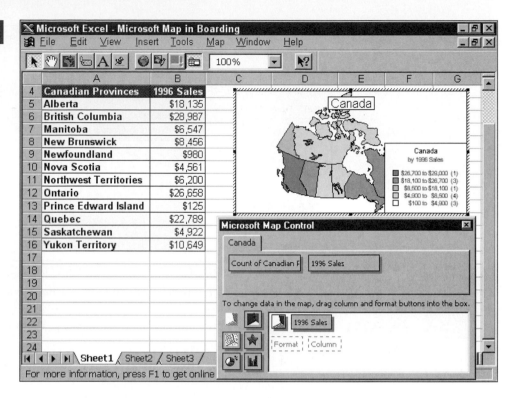

If the selected cell range contains ambiguous data or misspellings of geographic regions (states, provinces, or countries), a dialog box appears asking you for assistance. For the proper spellings and abbreviations of geographic regions, review the "Mapstats" workbook located in the "Program Files\Common Files\Microsoft Shared\Datamap\Data" folder. If you cannot locate the "Mapstats" workbook, choose the START, Find, Files or Folders command and perform a search of your hard disk.

QUICK REFERENCE
Embedding a
Data Map on a
Worksheet

1. **Create a worksheet with at least one column containing geographic data such as names or abbreviations of states, provinces, and countries.**
2. **Select the cell range to include in the data map.**
3. **CLICK: Map button ( ) on the Standard toolbar**
4. **CLICK: cell where you want to place the top-left corner of the map**

FORMATTING A DATA MAP

After embedding a data map on your worksheet, you can customize its appearance using the menu, toolbar, and Microsoft Map Control dialog box (shown in Figure 5.22). For example, you can color-code the geographic regions and change the way data is displayed on the map by simply dragging and double-clicking buttons in the Microsoft Map Control dialog box. However, be careful when dragging buttons in the work area. When you drag a new button onto an empty area, you are adding new formatting. When you drag a new button on top of an existing button, you are replacing the current formatting. In this section, you practice using some of the tools available for formatting a data map.

FIGURE 5.22

MICROSOFT MAP
CONTROL DIALOG BOX

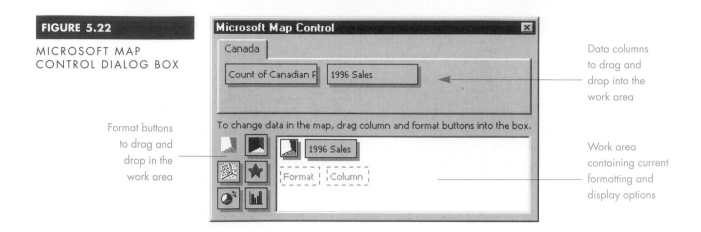

Data columns
to drag and
drop into the
work area

Format buttons
to drag and
drop in the
work area

Work area
containing current
formatting and
display options

**Perform
the
following
steps . . .**

1. Ensure that the data map appears with a hatched border, indicating that it is active and ready for formatting. If no border appears, double-click the data map object. If the data map appears with a hatched border but the Microsoft Map Control dialog box shown in Figure 5.22 does not appear, do the following:
   CLICK: Show/Hide Microsoft Map Control button (⊞) on the toolbar

2. To color-code the map of Canada:
   DRAG: Category Shading button (▨) over the existing format button in the work area
   (*Note*: You will know that you have positioned the mouse correctly when the row with the 1996 Sales button appears highlighted.)

3. Release the mouse button. Notice that the shades of gray are replaced by a color-coded map.

4. DRAG: Graduated Symbol button (★) over the existing format button in the work area

5. Release the mouse button. Now the map of Canada shows dots of varying sizes for each province, with each dot representing the relative dollar volume of 1996 Sales.

6. DRAG: Value Shading button (◣) over the existing format button in the work area

7. Release the mouse button to display the default map format.

8. To hide the Microsoft Map Control dialog box:
   CLICK: Show/Hide Microsoft Map Control button (⊞) in the toolbar

9. To change the gray-scale shading in the map:
   CHOOSE: Map, Value Shading Options from the menu
   CLICK: *Value Shading Options* tab
   The dialog box in Figure 5.23 appears.

FIGURE 5.23

FORMAT PROPERTIES
DIALOG BOX

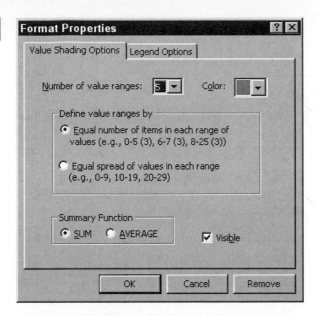

10. SELECT: 2 in the *Number of value ranges* drop-down list box
    PRESS: [ENTER] or CLICK: OK
    Notice that the map now displays the provinces using only two shading groups.

11. To display four shading categories:
    CHOOSE: Map, Value Shading Options
    SELECT: 4 in the *Number of value ranges* drop-down list box
    PRESS: [ENTER] or CLICK: OK

12. Let's display some additional features:
    RIGHT-CLICK: on any province in the map
    CHOOSE: Features from the shortcut menu

13. In the Map Features dialog box that appears:
    SELECT: *Canada Major Cities* check box in the *Visible* area
    PRESS: [ENTER] or CLICK: OK
    Now the map displays the locations of Canada's major cities (for example, Vancouver, Edmonton, Calgary, Toronto, and Montreal).

14. Position the mouse pointer over the black square appearing on the border in the bottom right-hand corner of the embedded map. To resize the map object, drag the border, with the mouse pointer on this black square, to cell G16.

15. To move the map to the left side, do the following:
CLICK: Grabber button (🖐) in the toolbar
CLICK: on any province in the map and hold down the mouse button
DRAG: the map to appear flush against the left and bottom borders

16. Release the mouse button.

17. DRAG: the legend to the top right-hand corner
DRAG: the title "CANADA" to the left slightly (if required)
Ensure that you can see the entire map of Canada and the title.

18. To finish editing the map and return to the worksheet:
CLICK: any cell in the worksheet
You are now ready to print the worksheet and data map.

QUICK REFERENCE
Customizing a Data Map

- Use the **Microsoft Map Control** dialog box to change the way data is displayed in the map.
- CHOOSE: **Map, Value Shading Options** to change the number of categories displayed in the map
- CHOOSE: **Features** from the map shortcut menu to add landmarks to the data map such as cities, highways, and lakes

---

PRINTING A DATA MAP

You print a data map as you would print any other embedded chart on your worksheet.

Perform the following steps . . .

1. To print the worksheet with the data map:
SELECT: the entire cell range from A1 to the bottom right-hand corner of the embedded map, approximately cell H17
CHOOSE: File, Print Area, Set Print Area

2. Let's print this worksheet with a landscape orientation:
CHOOSE: File, Page Setup
CLICK: *Page* tab
SELECT: *Landscape* option button in the *Orientation* group
CLICK: Print Preview command button
Your screen should now appear similar to Figure 5.24.

FIGURE 5.24

PREVIEWING THE
COMPLETED DATA
MAP

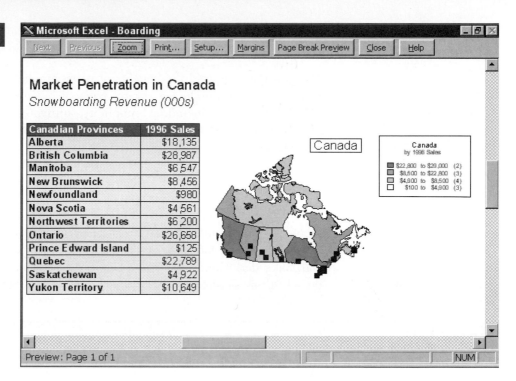

3. To send the worksheet to the printer:
CLICK: Print command button (at the top of the window)

4. When the Print dialog box appears:
PRESS: (ENTER) or CLICK: OK
The worksheet and data map are sent to the printer.

5. Move to cell A1 to remove the highlighting.

6. Save the workbook as "Snowboarding" to your Data Files location.

7. Close the workbook and then exit Excel.

QUICK REFERENCE
Printing a Data Map
with Worksheet Information

1. Select the cell range containing the worksheet information and the embedded data map.

2. CHOOSE: File, Print Area, Set Print Area

3. CHOOSE: File, Print

4. PRESS: (ENTER) or CLICK: OK

SUMMARY

This session discussed the benefits of using graphics to present worksheet information. Besides introducing several types of business graphics, the basic principles of graphing, including simplicity, unity, emphasis, and balance, were explained. In Excel, there are two methods for creating charts from worksheet information. A chart can be created, printed, and saved as a separate sheet in a workbook or embedded into an existing worksheet. In this session, you practiced both methods for creating a chart.

Excel provides several customizing and formatting options for enhancing a chart, including fonts, patterns, textures, titles, legends, and annotations. With over 90 different charting formats, it is guaranteed you will find the perfect tool to help you make that winning presentation! Table 5.3 summarizes the commands introduced in this session.

TABLE 5.3 Command Summary	*Command*	*Description*
	Chart, Chart Options	Displays a dialog box for modifying the selected chart's titles, legend, gridlines, and data labels. Same as the third step in the Chart Wizard.
	Chart, Chart Type	Selects the type and format of chart to display. Same as the first step in the Chart Wizard.
	Insert, Chart	Launches the Chart Wizard for creating a chart as a separate chart sheet or as an embedded object. Same as clicking the Chart Wizard button (🏛).
	Map, Value Shading Options	Displays a dialog box for changing the number of categories displayed on a data map.

KEY TERMS

Chart Wizard
A collection of dialog boxes that leads you through creating a chart in a workbook.

column chart
A chart that compares one data element with another data element and can show variations over a period of time.

data series
A series of values from the worksheet that are related.

embedded chart
A chart that is placed over worksheet cells and printed and saved along with the worksheet.

graphics

The pictorial representation of words and data.

legend

A key for deciphering the data series appearing in the plot area of a chart.

line chart

A chart that plots trends or shows changes over a period of time.

Microsoft Data Map

A special charting utility that enables you to create an embedded map from geographic data stored in a worksheet.

pie chart

A chart that shows the proportions of individual components compared to the whole.

plot area

The area for plotting values from the worksheet. The plot area contains the axes and data series.

X-axis

The horizontal or Category axis that shows the categories for which the chart is making comparisons.

XY charts

Charts that show how one or more data elements relate to another data element. Also called *scatter plot diagrams*.

Y-axis

The vertical or Value axis in a two-dimensional chart that shows the value or measurement unit for making comparisons among the various categories. The value axis in a three-dimensional chart is called the Z-axis.

EXERCISES

SHORT ANSWER

1. Describe the basic principles of using graphics.

2. Describe the four steps in creating a chart using the Chart Wizard.

3. List the different types of charts found in the Chart Type dialog box.

4. How do you select multiple ranges in a worksheet?

5. What are some placement options for a chart's legend?

6. Describe the process of adding free-form text to a chart.

7. Describe the process of adding an arrow to a chart.

8. How do you move an arrow once it has been placed on a chart?

9. How do you print an embedded chart without the worksheet data?

10. How must you organize a worksheet if you want to create a data map?

HANDS-ON

(*Note*: Ensure that you know the storage location of your Advantage Files and your Data Files before proceeding.)

1. The objective of this exercise is to create a worksheet and an embedded pie chart that show the breakdown of your total monthly expenses.

   a. Ensure that you have an empty workbook.

   b. Enter your name in cell A1.

   c. Create a worksheet that lists the following expense headings on separate rows within a column: RENT, FOOD, GAS, and FUN.

   d. Enter your monthly expense amounts in the column to the right of the row headings. (You may enter any values, not necessarily your own.)

   e. Select the row headings and values to produce an embedded chart.

   f. CLICK: Chart Wizard button (▥)

   g. Following the steps for each dialog box, select a 3-D pie chart that displays the names beside each pie wedge. Add a title to the chart that has the words "Monthly Expenses" on the first line. Delete the legend, if one appears.

   h. Once the chart appears on the worksheet, move it to the right of the present worksheet information and size it to cover fifteen rows by five columns.

   i. Select different textures, not just colors, for the various pie wedges.

   j. Print the worksheet and chart on the same page.

   k. Save the workbook as "My Pie Chart" to your Data Files location.

2. In this exercise, you retrieve a workbook and then create a line chart, stacked column chart, and a 3-D column chart.

   a. Close all of the open windows in the document area.

   b. Open the "Charts" workbook located on the Advantage Files diskette or in the Advantage Files folder. This worksheet is a planning tool used by XYZ Company to project sales and production. (Make sure to type your name into cell A3.)

   c. Create one line chart, in a separate chart sheet, showing the number of units sold for each product over the five-year period.

   d. Add an appropriate title to the chart.

   e. Name the sheet's tab LINE.

   f. Print the chart using the *Scale to Fit Page* option.

   g. Create one stacked column chart, in a separate chart sheet, that displays the revenue for each product over the five-year period. A stacked chart displays each product's portion of the total revenue in a single column for each year.

h. Add an appropriate title to the chart.

i. Name the sheet's tab STACK.

j. Print the chart using the *Use Full Page* option.

k. Create one 3-D column chart, in a separate chart sheet, to compare the Total Revenue versus the Total Costs over the five-year period.

l. Add an appropriate title to the chart.

m. Name the sheet's tab COLUMN.

n. Print the chart using the *Scale to Fit Page* option.

o. Save the workbook as "Charting" to your Data Files location.

p. Close all of the open windows in the document area.

q. Exit Excel.

3. **On Your Own**: Charting Your Personal Budget
Open the workbook called "Your Personal Budget" that you created in Hands-On Exercise 4 in Session 3. If you did not create this workbook, do so before proceeding. On a separate sheet, create a pie chart that shows the distribution of your expense categories using the Year-to-Date column as the data series. Create a stacked column chart, also on a separate sheet, that compares your total monthly expenses. Save this workbook as "Personal Budget Charts" to your Data Files location.

4. **On Your Own**: Creating a Population Data Map
Using the "Mapstats" workbook mentioned in this session, create and then format a data map of the United States showing the population per state. Use the Graduated Symbol format. Save the new workbook as "US Data Map" to your Data Files location.

CASE PROBLEMS | **H2 UNDERSCAPING LTD.**

(*Note*: In the following case problems, assume the role of the primary characters and perform the same steps that they identify. You may want to re-read the session opening.)

1. Chip finishes his conversation with Kayla Parker at the local bank and then places the phone gently into its cradle. He glances down at the notes that he scrawled on the borders of the Canadian *Globe and Mail* newspaper. Although thinking to himself, Chip shakes his head and speaks aloud, "So, Kayla wants a financial plan after seven years of doing business." Chip isn't really *that* surprised with Kayla's request; but, perhaps, he's just a little annoyed with his longtime friend and business advisor. Kayla has been there for him since his company's inception and has helped guide him through complicated financing issues, debtor problems, and investment opportunities. But with his latest acquisition of Xeriscaping, Inc., even Kayla must watch Chip and his company's performance with a lot closer scrutiny than before.

Fortunately, Chip just completed entering his past year's results into an Excel workbook called "H2U-1996," stored with the Advantage Files. He loads the worksheet and then decides to perform some additional formatting, wanting to ensure that it looks its best for Kayla. After customizing the page setup to a landscape orientation and inserting the current date in the footer, he prints the worksheet on a single page.

Upon reviewing the printout, Chip decides to impress Kayla even further by embedding a column chart, on the same page, showing comparative sales for the sprinkler installations versus the xeriscaping projects. He adds a title and legend to the chart and then prints the entire worksheet and chart onto a single page. Finally, Chip saves the workbook as "H2 Underscaping 1996" to his Data Files location.

2. Impressed with his first printout for Kayla, Chip decides to create a new chart (on a separate sheet in the workbook) and attach it to the first page. Wanting to inform Kayla of the seasonal trend lines for his business, Chip creates a line chart showing the Total Sales, Cost of Sales, and Total Expenses for the entire year. Chip annotates the chart with an arrow and text box pointing out the high and low seasons, in addition to adding titles and a legend to the chart. When finished, Chip prints the chart to fit on a single landscape page and then saves the workbook back to his Data Files location.

3. Arriving quite early the next morning, Chip notices that the answering machine's message indicator light is flashing at the receptionist's desk. Hitting the appropriate button, Chip plays back the following message: "Hi Chip, this is Kayla, down at the bank. I received your financial analysis yesterday and just wanted to commend you on your work. This report is far better than I've seen from most accountants, let alone business owners. I don't see a problem with your seasonal business trends, but I would like you to break down your Total Expenses into a pie diagram for me. That way, I can suggest ways for you to cut your fixed costs during the low period. Thanks again for the report. Bye for now."

Chip is glad to hear that Kayla approved of his analysis and decides to tackle the expense breakdown right away. After loading the "H2 Underscaping 1996" workbook, Chip enters the following year-to-date expense information into the worksheet:

Administration	25,000
Marketing	60,000
Rent	36,000
Wages	24,000
Total Expenses	**145,000**

After looking through the available chart formats, Chip decides to create a 3-D pie chart with percentages appearing beside each wedge. He adds a title to the chart and a legend, and then prints the chart to a single landscape page. When finished, he saves the workbook back to his Data Files location.

Appendix

Microsoft Excel 97 Toolbar Summary

STANDARD

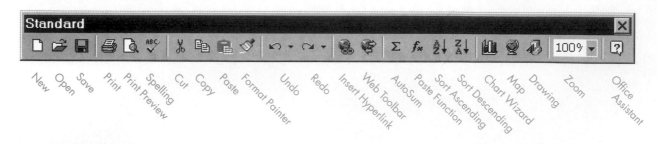

New   Open   Save   Print   Print Preview   Spelling   Cut   Copy   Paste   Format Painter   Undo   Redo   Insert Hyperlink   Web Toolbar   AutoSum   Paste Function   Sort Ascending   Sort Descending   Chart Wizard   Map   Drawing   Zoom   Office Assistant

FORMATTING

Font   Font Size   Bold   Italic   Underline   Align Left   Center   Align Right   Merge and Center   Currency Style   Percent Style   Comma Style   Increase Decimal   Decrease Decimal   Decrease Indent   Increase Indent   Borders   Fill Color   Font Color

CHART

Chart Objects   Format Selected Object   Chart Type   Legend   Data Table   By Row   By Column   Angle Text Upward   Angle Text Downward

DRAWING

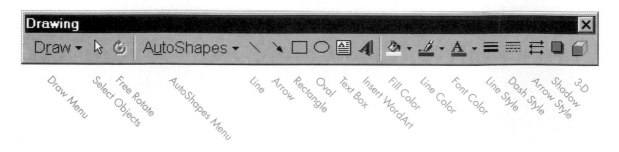

Draw Menu   Select Objects   Free Rotate   AutoShapes Menu   Line   Arrow   Rectangle   Oval   Text Box   Insert WordArt   Fill Color   Line Color   Font Color   Line Style   Dash Style   Arrow Style   Shadow   3-D

WEB

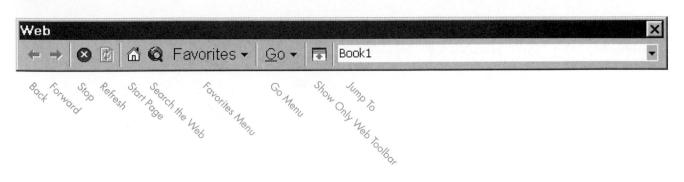

Index

The page numbers in boldface indicate Quick Reference procedures.

Microsoft® Access® 97 for Windows®

Sarah E. Hutchinson

Glen J. Coulthard

THE IRWIN/MCGRAW-HILL ADVANTAGE SERIES FOR COMPUTER EDUCATION

Boston, Massachusetts Burr Ridge, Illinois Dubuque, Iowa
Madison, Wisconsin New York, New York San Francisco, California St. Louis, Missouri

Irwin/McGraw-Hill

A Division of The **McGraw·Hill** Companies

MICROSOFT® ACCESS® 97 for WINDOWS®

This book is printed on acid-free paper.

3 4 5 6 7 8 9 0 WC/WC 9 0 9 8 7

ISBN 0-256-26000-1

Publisher: *Tom Casson*
Sponsoring editor: *Garrett Glanz*
Developmental editor: *Kristin Hepburn*
GTS production coordinator: *Cathy Stotts*
Marketing manager: *James Rogers*
Senior project supervisor: *Denise Santor-Mitzit*
Production supervisor: *Pat Frederickson*
Art director: *Keith McPherson*
Prepress buyer: *Heather D. Burbridge*
Compositor: *GTS Graphics, Inc.*
Typeface: *11/13 Bodoni Book*
Printer: *Webcrafters, Inc.*

http://www.mhcollege.com

WELCOME TO THE IRWIN ADVANTAGE SERIES

The Irwin Advantage Series has evolved over the years to become one of the most respected resources for software training in the world—to date, over 200,000 students have used one or more of our learning guides. Our instructional methodologies are proven to optimize the student's ability to learn, yet we continually seek ways to improve on our products and approach. To this end, all of our learning guides are classroom tested and critically reviewed by dozens of learners, teachers, and software training experts. We're glad you have chosen the Irwin Advantage Series!

KEY FEATURES

The following features are incorporated into the new Microsoft Office 97 student learning guides to ensure that your learning experience is as productive and enjoyable as possible:

CASE STUDIES

Each session begins with a real-world **case study** that introduces you to a fictitious person or company and describes their immediate problem or opportunity. Throughout the session, you obtain the knowledge and skills necessary to meet these challenges. At the end of the session, you are given an opportunity to solve **case problems** directly related to the case scenario.

CONCEPTS, SKILLS AND PROCEDURES

Each learning guide organizes and presents its content in logically structured session topics. Commands and procedures are introduced using **hands-on examples in a step-by-step format,** and students are encouraged to perform the steps along with the guide. These examples are clearly identified by the text design.

PERFORM THE FOLLOWING STEPS

Using this new design feature, the step progression for all hands-on examples and exercises are clearly identified. Students will find it surprisingly easy to follow the logical sequence of keystrokes and mouse clicks. No longer do you have to worry about missing a step!

END OF SESSION EXERCISES

Each session concludes with **short answer questions** and **hands-on exercises.** These comprehensive and meaningful exercises are integrated with the session's objectives; they were not added as an afterthought. They serve to provide students with opportunities to practice the session material. For maximum benefit, students should complete all the exercises at the end of each session.

IN ADDITION BOXES

These content boxes are placed strategically throughout the guide and provide information on related topics that are beyond the scope of the current discussion. For example, there are three typical categories that are visually identified by the following icons:

Integration

The key to productive and efficient use of Office 97 is in the integration features for sharing data among the applications. With a few mouse clicks, for example, you can create a PowerPoint presentation from a Word document, copy an Access database into an Excel workbook, and incorporate professional Office Art into your annual report. Under this heading, you will find methods for sharing information among the Microsoft Office 97 applications.

Advanced

In a 200+-page learning guide, there are bound to be features that are important but beyond the scope of the text. Therefore, we call attention to these features and offer suggestions on how to apply techniques or to search for more information.

Internet

The Internet is fast becoming a standard tool for gathering and exchanging information. Office 97 provides a high level of Internet connectivity, allowing the user to draw upon its vast resources and even publish documents directly on the World Wide Web. Although not every student will have a persistent Internet connection, you can review the content under this heading to learn about Office's Internet features.

Real life situations
introduce the topics

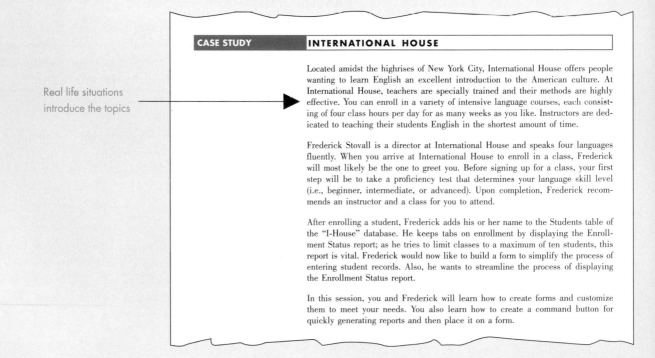

CASE STUDY	INTERNATIONAL HOUSE

Located amidst the highrises of New York City, International House offers people wanting to learn English an excellent introduction to the American culture. At International House, teachers are specially trained and their methods are highly effective. You can enroll in a variety of intensive language courses, each consisting of four class hours per day for as many weeks as you like. Instructors are dedicated to teaching their students English in the shortest amount of time.

Frederick Stovall is a director at International House and speaks four languages fluently. When you arrive at International House to enroll in a class, Frederick will most likely be the one to greet you. Before signing up for a class, your first step will be to take a proficiency test that determines your language skill level (i.e., beginner, intermediate, or advanced). Upon completion, Frederick recommends an instructor and a class for you to attend.

After enrolling a student, Frederick adds his or her name to the Students table of the "I-House" database. He keeps tabs on enrollment by displaying the Enrollment Status report; as he tries to limit classes to a maximum of ten students, this report is vital. Frederick would now like to build a form to simplify the process of entering student records. Also, he wants to streamline the process of displaying the Enrollment Status report.

In this session, you and Frederick will learn how to create forms and customize them to meet your needs. You also learn how to create a command button for quickly generating reports and then place it on a form.

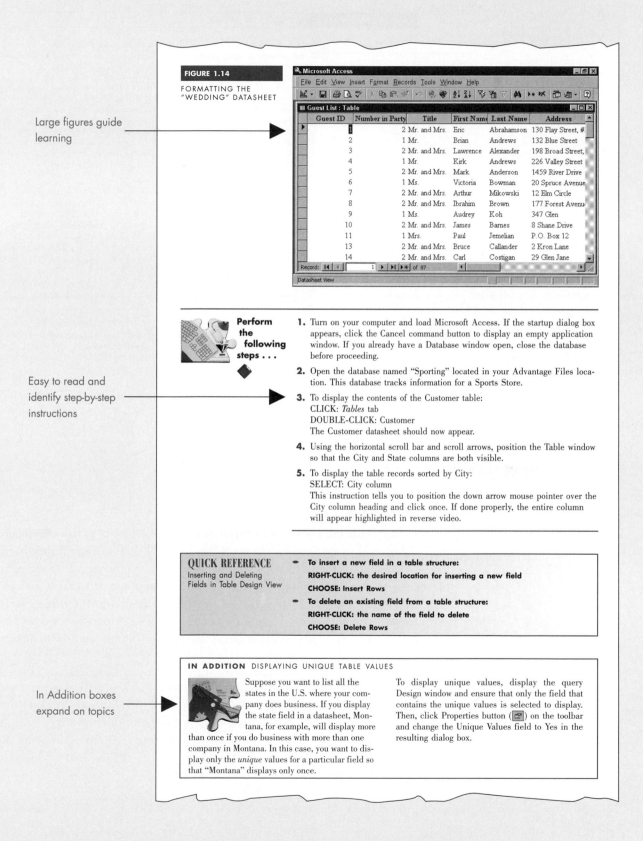

FIGURE 1.14

FORMATTING THE "WEDDING" DATASHEET

Large figures guide learning

Perform the following steps . . .

1. Turn on your computer and load Microsoft Access. If the startup dialog box appears, click the Cancel command button to display an empty application window. If you already have a Database window open, close the database before proceeding.

2. Open the database named "Sporting" located in your Advantage Files location. This database tracks information for a Sports Store.

3. To display the contents of the Customer table:
   CLICK: *Tables* tab
   DOUBLE-CLICK: Customer
   The Customer datasheet should now appear.

4. Using the horizontal scroll bar and scroll arrows, position the Table window so that the City and State columns are both visible.

5. To display the table records sorted by City:
   SELECT: City column
   This instruction tells you to position the down arrow mouse pointer over the City column heading and click once. If done properly, the entire column will appear highlighted in reverse video.

Easy to read and identify step-by-step instructions

QUICK REFERENCE
Inserting and Deleting Fields in Table Design View

- **To insert a new field in a table structure:**
  RIGHT-CLICK: the desired location for inserting a new field
  CHOOSE: Insert Rows
- **To delete an existing field from a table structure:**
  RIGHT-CLICK: the name of the field to delete
  CHOOSE: Delete Rows

IN ADDITION DISPLAYING UNIQUE TABLE VALUES

In Addition boxes expand on topics

Suppose you want to list all the states in the U.S. where your company does business. If you display the state field in a datasheet, Montana, for example, will display more than once if you do business with more than one company in Montana. In this case, you want to display only the *unique* values for a particular field so that "Montana" displays only once.

To display unique values, display the query Design window and ensure that only the field that contains the unique values is selected to display. Then, click Properties button ( ) on the toolbar and change the Unique Values field to Yes in the resulting dialog box.

Students practice with
real life projects →

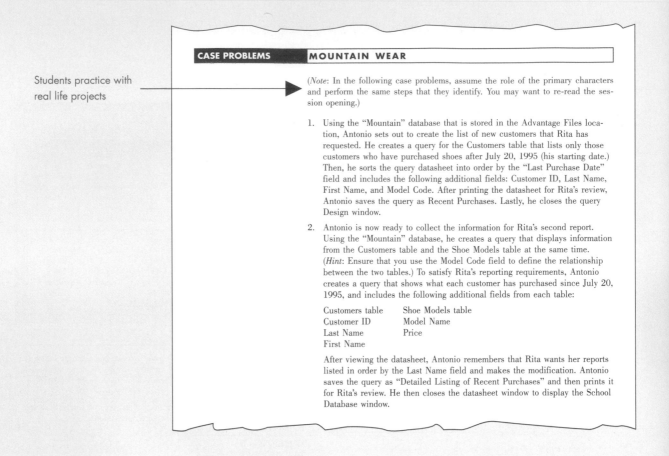

CASE PROBLEMS   MOUNTAIN WEAR

(*Note*: In the following case problems, assume the role of the primary characters and perform the same steps that they identify. You may want to re-read the session opening.)

1. Using the "Mountain" database that is stored in the Advantage Files location, Antonio sets out to create the list of new customers that Rita has requested. He creates a query for the Customers table that lists only those customers who have purchased shoes after July 20, 1995 (his starting date.) Then, he sorts the query datasheet into order by the "Last Purchase Date" field and includes the following additional fields: Customer ID, Last Name, First Name, and Model Code. After printing the datasheet for Rita's review, Antonio saves the query as Recent Purchases. Lastly, he closes the query Design window.

2. Antonio is now ready to collect the information for Rita's second report. Using the "Mountain" database, he creates a query that displays information from the Customers table and the Shoe Models table at the same time. (*Hint*: Ensure that you use the Model Code field to define the relationship between the two tables.) To satisfy Rita's reporting requirements, Antonio creates a query that shows what each customer has purchased since July 20, 1995, and includes the following additional fields from each table:

Customers table	Shoe Models table
Customer ID	Model Name
Last Name	Price
First Name	

After viewing the datasheet, Antonio remembers that Rita wants her reports listed in order by the Last Name field and makes the modification. Antonio saves the query as "Detailed Listing of Recent Purchases" and then prints it for Rita's review. He then closes the datasheet window to display the School Database window.

TEXT SUPPLEMENTS

ADVANTAGE FILES

Certain hands-on examples and exercises are marked with a disk ◆ icon, indicating the need to retrieve a document file from the **Advantage Files location.** These document files may be provided to you in a number of ways: packaged on a diskette accompanying this text, or on the computer network at your school. You may also download the files from the ***Advantage Online*** Web site (http://www.irwin.com/cit/adv). *These document files are extremely important to your success.* Check with your instructor or lab advisor for details on how to acquire the Advantage Files.

In addition to identifying the Advantage Files location, you will also need to specify a **Data Files location.** This location is used to save the documents that you create and may either be a blank diskette or a folder on the network server. Again, your instructor or lab advisor will specify the proper locations. More information on the file locations and the proper techniques for retrieving and saving information is provided inside the back cover of this book.

CD-ROM INTERACTIVE TUTORIALS

In addition to using this book, you may have access to our *Advantage Interactive* software. These interactive multimedia tutorials are fully integrated with the material from each session and make effective use of video clips, screen demonstrations, hands-on exercises, and quizzes. You will enjoy the opportunity to explore these tutorials and learn the software at your own pace. For ordering information, please refer to the coupon inside the front cover.

INSTRUCTOR'S RESOURCE KIT

For instructors and software trainers, each learning guide is accompanied by an **Instructor's Resource Kit (IRK).** This kit provides suggested answers to the short-answer questions, hands-on exercises, and case problems appearing at the end of each session. Furthermore, the IRK includes a comprehensive test bank of additional short-answer, multiple-choice, and fill-in-the-blank questions, plus hands-on exercises. You will also find a diskette copy of the Advantage Files which may be duplicated or placed on your network for student use.

SUPPORT THROUGH THE WWW

The Internet, and more specifically the World Wide Web, is an important component in our approach to software instruction for the Office 97 application series. The *Advantage Online* site at http://www.irwin.com/cit/adv is a tremendous resource for all users, providing information on the latest software and learning guide releases, download options for the Advantage Files, and supplemental files for the Instructor Resource Kits. We also introduce new methods for you to communicate with the authors, publisher, and other users of the series. As a dynamic venture, *Advantage Online* will evolve and improve over time. Please visit us to see the latest developments and contribute your valuable feedback.

NETWORK TESTING

Evaluation and assessment are important components of any instructional series. We are committed to providing quality alternatives to traditional testing instruments. With our Irwin Network Test Interactive software, instructors can select questions, create and administer tests, and then calculate grades—all on-line! Visit the *Advantage Online* site for more information on how we are progressing in this exciting area.

Before you begin

As with any software instruction guide, there are standard conventions that we use to indicate menu options, keystroke combinations, and command instructions.

MENU INSTRUCTIONS

In Office 97, all Menu bar options and pull-down menu commands have an underlined or highlighted letter in each option. When you need to execute a command from the Menu bar—the row of menu choices across the top of the screen—the tutorial's instruction line separates the Menu bar option from the command with a comma. Notice also that the word "CHOOSE" is always used for menu commands. For example, the command for quitting Windows is shown as:

CHOOSE: File, Exit

This instruction tells you to choose the File option on the Menu bar and then to choose the Exit command from the File pull-down menu. The actual steps for choosing a menu command are discussed later in this guide.

KEYSTROKES AND KEYSTROKE COMBINATIONS

When two keys must be pressed together, the tutorial's instruction line shows the keys joined with a plus (+) sign. For example, you can execute a Copy command in Windows by holding down CTRL and then pressing the letter **c**.

The instruction for this type of keystroke combination follows:

PRESS: CTRL +c

COMMAND INSTRUCTIONS

This guide indicates with a special typeface and color the data that you are required to type in yourself. For example:

TYPE: **Income Statement**

When you are required to enter unique information, such as the current date or your name, the instruction appears in italic. The following instruction directs you to type your name in place of the actual words: "your name."

TYPE: *your name*

ACKNOWLEDGMENTS

This series of learning guides is the direct result of the teamwork and heart of many people. We sincerely thank the reviewers, instructors, and students who have shared their comments and suggestions with us over the past few years. We do read them! With this valuable feedback, our guides have evolved into the product you see before you. We also appreciate the efforts of the instructors and students at Okanagan University College who classroom tested our guides to ensure accuracy, relevancy, and completeness.

We also give many thanks to Garrett Glanz, Kristin Hepburn and Tom Casson from Irwin for their skillful management of this text. In fact, special recognition goes to all of the individuals mentioned in the credits at the beginning of this guide. And finally, to the many others who weren't directly involved in this project but who have stood by us the whole way, we appreciate your encouragement and support.

WRITE TO US

We welcome your response to this book, for we are trying to make it as useful a learning tool as possible. Write to us in care of Garrett Glanz, Richard D. Irwin, 1333 Burr Ridge Parkway, Burr Ridge, IL 60521. Thank you.

Sarah E. Hutchinson
sclifford@mindspring.com

Glen J. Coulthard
current@junction.net

Contents

SESSION 1
Fundamentals

SESSION 2
Working with Tables

SESSION 3
Retrieving Information

SESSION 4
Presenting Your Data

SESSION 5
Working with Forms

Microsoft Access 97 for Windows

Fundamentals

SESSION OUTLINE

Introducing Microsoft Office 97
Working with Microsoft Access
Starting Access
The Guided Tour
Opening a Database
Working in Datasheet View
Manipulating Table Data
Getting Help
Closing a Database
Leaving Access
Summary
Key Terms
Exercises

INTRODUCTION

Modern database management systems for micro-computers enable you to store and manage large amounts of data. Whether you want to use a computer to track inventory products, issue invoices, manage personnel records, or store phone numbers, a computerized database management system will be a welcome addition to your business. This session introduces you to the fundamentals of working with Microsoft Access for Windows, a powerful database management application for personal computers.

CASE STUDY **SPRINGS COLLEGE, CO**

Isabel Oller has been looking for a job in the Colorado Springs area for over 18 months. And until today, she had been contemplating a move to another city in order to find steady employment. One of her prospects, the Springs College Seminar Services (SCSS), just called to inform Isabel that she made the short-list for a secretarial position and that they would be making a final decision in the next few days. In the past two weeks, Isabel has interviewed with three different people in the SCSS department. She really likes the people at Springs College and is genuinely excited by the idea of working for such a respected institution. SCSS offers one- to four-day courses, covering a broad range of topics.

After an anxious day and a half, Isabel receives a call from Max Weingold, the director of SCSS, offering her the position. He asks her to arrive to work at 8:00 AM sharp on the following Monday for an orientation and to complete the necessary paperwork. He finishes the conversation with a hearty "Welcome aboard!"

From the interviews, Isabel knows that she is expected to answer phones, write and edit letters, and organize meetings for the department. However, her first meeting with Max enlightens her about some additional expectations: "Now this may come as a surprise, Isabel, but you will be using Microsoft Access to store basic information on our instructors and students. We've given your phone number to all the instructors, in case they have a problem or need to modify the database for any reason. You will mostly use the database to look up student phone numbers to inform them when a seminar is canceled." Isabel is understandably concerned— she has never heard of Microsoft Access and doesn't know the first thing about managing a database!

In this session, you and Isabel learn about databases, the different components and features of Microsoft Access, how to display and edit the information, and how to use the Microsoft Access Help system.

INTRODUCING MICROSOFT OFFICE 97

Microsoft Office for Windows combines the most popular and exciting software programs available into a single suite of applications. In the Professional edition, Office 97 includes Microsoft Word, Microsoft Excel, Microsoft PowerPoint, Microsoft Access, and the all-new Microsoft Outlook, an integrated desktop information tool that manages your e-mail, calendar, contacts, to do lists, journal, and Office documents. Office 97 also provides shared applications (sometimes called "server applications") that let you create and insert clip art, organizational charts, and mathematical equations into your word processing documents, electronic spreadsheets, and presentations.

In addition to enjoying performance improvements over its predecessor, Office 97 offers integration with the Internet and World Wide Web (WWW) and benefits from many usability enhancements. For example, Office 97 lets you do the following:

- name your documents and databases using up to 250 characters,

- place shortcuts to files directly on the Windows desktop,

- use the Windows Briefcase program to compare and synchronize files,

- multitask applications with single-click functionality from the taskbar,

- save documents and reports in the Web's Hypertext Markup Language (HTML) format, and

- post documents and databases to your internal Intranet or to the Web.

All of Office's primary applications use Intellisense technology, helping users to focus on their work and not on their software. Examples of Intellisense are automatic spell and grammar checking and wizards that lead you through performing basic and complex tasks. Office 97 offers additional Help features, including an animated character called the Office Assistant who provides helpful tips and suggestions as you work.

INTEGRATION FEATURES

Many would say that the essence of Office 97 is its ability to share data among the suite of applications. For example, you can place an Excel chart in a report that you write using Word, a Word document in a PowerPoint presentation, an Access database in an Excel worksheet, and so on. You can also create and insert objects using shared applications—such as Microsoft Office Art and Microsoft Organization Chart—without ever leaving the current application. Using Microsoft Binder, you can assemble Word, Excel, and PowerPoint documents into a single file for distribution. Binder also allows you to print a collection of documents with consistent headers and footers and with consecutive page numbering.

INTERNET FEATURES

One of the most exciting innovations in Office 97 is its ability to take advantage of the World Wide Web and the Internet. For those of you new to the online world, the **Internet** is a vast collection of computer networks that spans the entire planet, made up of many smaller networks connected by standard telephone lines. The term **Intranet** is used to refer to a local or wide area network that uses Internet technologies to share information within an organization. To access the Internet, you need a network or modem connection that links your computer to an account on the university's network or to an independent Internet Service Provider (ISP).

Once connected, you use web browser software, such as Microsoft Internet Explorer or Netscape Navigator, to access the **World Wide Web (WWW).** The WWW provides a visual interface for the Internet and lets you search for information by simply clicking on highlighted words and images, known as **hyperlinks.** When you click a link, you are telling your web browser to retrieve and then display a page from a web site. Each web page has a unique location or address specified by its *Uniform Resource Locator* or URL. One example of a URL is: http://www.microsoft.com. For more information on the Internet and World Wide Web, visit your local bookstore, campus computing center, or computer users group.

Microsoft Office 97 provides a consistent set of tools for publishing documents, spreadsheets, presentations, and databases to the web and for accessing help directly from Microsoft's web site. Specifically, each Office application includes a Web toolbar that lets you quickly open, search, and browse documents on your local computer, Intranet, and the Internet. Furthermore, you can create your own hyperlinks and share your documents with the entire world after publishing it to a web server. As you proceed through this manual, look for the Internet integration features found in the *In Addition* boxes.

WORKING WITH MICROSOFT ACCESS

Picture a sales office with a row of filing cabinets that cover an entire wall—and you're responsible for managing them! Each cabinet stores multiple folders containing customer-related information, organized in alphabetical order by surname. Because everything is perfectly organized, you can always find a customer's folder in a matter of seconds.

It's now Friday afternoon and your supervisor has just asked you to retrieve the folders for all of your Boston customers. Furthermore, she wants you to list those customers who haven't made a purchase in the past six months. Your alphabetical filing scheme is not going to help you now! What you really need is a way to create, maintain, and summarize an information database quickly. The software tool you need is called a **database management system (DBMS).**

DATABASE TERMINOLOGY

This is not a course in database theory, but you should be familiar with some basic database concepts. To illustrate, we will use the analogy of a personal address or phone book. Make sure that you are comfortable with the following terms:

- *Database:* A **database** is collection of related information. For example, a phone book is a database of names and phone numbers. A single Access database can store millions of entries, called *records.*

- *Table:* A **table** is the primary element for collecting data that relates to a particular subject. In Access, tables are organized into columns and rows similar to an electronic worksheet. For example, all of the entries in your phone book would be stored in a single table in a database. All the tables in an Access database, as well as their associated objects, are stored in a single file that can consume up to 1 gigabyte of disk space.

- *Record:* A **record** is an individual entry in a table. For example, each person's information (for example, name, address, and phone number) would be stored in a single record in the phone book table. A single record of data represents a horizontal row in a table.

- *Field:* A **field** is piece of information in a record. For example, you can divide a person's record in the phone book table into fields for last name, first name, address, city, and phone number. Each record in a table is composed of fields. A field is a vertical column in a table.

ACCESS DATABASE OBJECTS

Although the term *database* often refers to individual data files, in Microsoft Access a database is a collection or family of **objects**—data tables, queries, reports, forms, macros, and modules. This section describes the objects you will find in an Access database.

- *Table object:* You use tables to store and manipulate information. If you build a single database that contains several tables, you will likely want to share information amongst them. To do so requires carefully planning the structure and design of your database.

- *Query object:* A **query** is a question you ask of your database. For example, when using a database that stores customer data, you might query the database for a list of those individuals who live in Chicago. The answer, which may draw data from more than one table in the database, typically displays a list of records called a **dynaset.**

- *Form object:* Unlike a table's grid-like layout, a **form** lets you view one record at a time and customize the display of that record. For example, you can apply formatting enhancements to emphasize important data and display error messages when incorrect data is entered. The different elements on a form are called **controls.** Using a control, you can display data from a field, the result of a calculation, text for a title or message, a graph, or other object.

- *Report object:* **Reports** are used to present, summarize, and print table data. Using a report, you can calculate totals, subtotals, and grand totals across a set of records and tables. Like form objects, reports also use controls to display, calculate, and emphasize information.

- *Macro and Module objects:* Using an Access **macro** object, you can automate frequently performed procedures. For example, you can create a command button that you place on a form for compiling and printing a report. For even more control of your database, you can develop code modules using Visual Basic for Applications. Although not discussed in this guide, Visual Basic plays an important role in the development of complete database applications. Refer to the Total Advantage series for Microsoft Office 97 for additional information.

If you are new to database management software, you may not understand all of the terms and concepts used in the above discussion. Don't despair—you'll definitely understand their importance and application by the end of this guide. Let's begin our exploration in the next section by starting Access and then taking the guided tour.

STARTING ACCESS

This session assumes that you are working on a computer with Windows 95 (or Microsoft Windows NT 4.0) and Microsoft Access 97 loaded on the hard disk drive.

Before you load Windows and Access, let's look at how to use the mouse and keyboard.

USING THE MOUSE AND KEYBOARD

Microsoft Access 97 for Windows is a complex yet easy-to-learn program. As you proceed through this guide, you will find that there are often three methods for performing the same command or procedure in Access:

- Menu bar   Select a command or procedure from the Menu bar positioned at the top of the screen or window.

- Shortcut menu   Point to and right-click an object to display a menu and then make a selection.

- Mouse   Point to and click a toolbar button.

Although this guide concentrates on the easiest methods, we recommend that you try the others and decide which you prefer. *Don't memorize all of the information in this guide! Be selective and find your favorite methods.*

Although you can use Access with only a keyboard, much of the program's basic design relies on using a mouse. Regardless of whether your mouse has two or three buttons, you will use the left or primary mouse button for selecting database objects and menu commands and the right or secondary mouse button for displaying shortcut menus.

The most common mouse actions used in Access are these:

- Point   Slide the mouse on your desk to position the mouse pointer over the desired object on the screen.

- Click   Press down and release the left mouse button quickly. Clicking is used to position the insertion point and to choose menu commands.

- Right-Click   Press down and release the right mouse button. Right-clicking the mouse on text or an object displays a context-sensitive shortcut menu.

- Double-Click   Press down and release the mouse button twice in rapid succession. Double-clicking is used in Access to select text.

- Drag   Press down and hold the mouse button as you move the mouse pointer across a field. When the mouse pointer reaches the desired location, release the mouse button. Dragging is used to select a block of text or to move objects or windows.

You may notice that the mouse pointer changes shape as you move it over different parts of the screen. Each mouse pointer shape has its own purpose and may provide you with important information. There are five primary mouse shapes you should be aware of:

↖	left arrow	Used to choose menu commands and toolbar buttons.
⧗	hourglass	Informs you that Excel is occupied and requests that you wait.
I	I-beam	Used to position the insertion point and edit text.
➡	horizontal arrow	Used to select a horizontal row in a table (Datasheet view).
⬇	vertical arrow	Used to select a vertical column in a table (Datasheet view).

Aside from being the primary input device for including text in a database, the keyboard offers shortcut methods for performing commands and procedures. For example, several menu commands have shortcut key combinations listed to the right of the command in the pull-down menu. Therefore, you can perform a command by simply pressing the shortcut keys rather than accessing the Menu bar. Many of these shortcut key combinations are available throughout Windows applications.

LOADING WINDOWS

Because Windows is an operating system, it is loaded automatically into the computer's memory when you turn on the computer. If you haven't already turned your computer on, perform the following steps.

Perform the following steps . . .

1. Turn on the power switches to the computer and monitor. After a few seconds, the Windows desktop will appear (Figure 1.1). (*Note:* The desktop interface on your computer may look different from Figure 1.1.)

FIGURE 1.1

THE WINDOWS DESKTOP

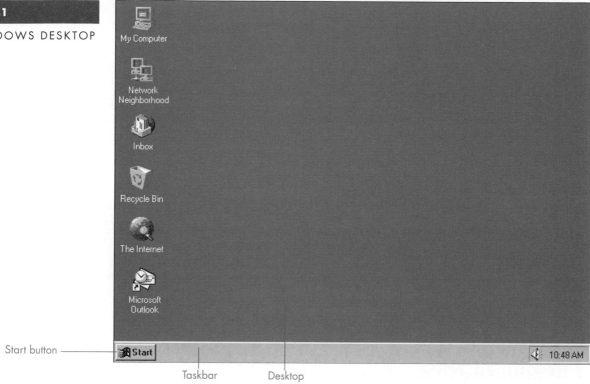

Start button ——

Taskbar   Desktop

2. If a Welcome to Windows dialog box appears, do the following:
CLICK: Close button ([**X**]) in the top corner of the dialog box window

---

QUICK REFERENCE
Loading Windows

Turn on your computer to automatically load Microsoft Windows 95 (or Microsoft Windows NT 4.0).

LOADING MICROSOFT ACCESS 97

Using the Start button ([Start]), you can readily access your favorite programs, documents, and system management tools. In this section, you load Microsoft Access 97.

Perform the following steps . . .

1. Position the mouse pointer over top of the Start button ([Start]) and then click the left mouse button once. The Start pop-up menu appears.

2. Point to the Programs command using the mouse. Notice that you do not need to click the left mouse button to display the list of programs in the fly-out or cascading menu.

3. Move the mouse pointer horizontally to the right until it highlights an option in the Programs menu. You can now move the mouse pointer up and down the Programs menu. Notice that you still haven't clicked the left mouse button.

4. Point to the Microsoft Access menu item and then click the left mouse button once to execute the command. After a few seconds, the Microsoft Access screen appears.

5. If the Office Assistant window (shown at the right) appears:
CLICK: Close button ([✕]) in its top right-hand corner

In Figure 1.1, the Windows taskbar is located at the bottom of the screen. Each application that you are currently working with is represented by a button on the taskbar. Switching between open applications on your desktop is as easy as clicking the appropriate taskbar button, like switching channels on a television set. At this point, you should see a button for Microsoft Access on the taskbar.

QUICK REFERENCE	**1.** **CLICK: Start button** ([🏁 Start])
Loading Microsoft Access 97	**2.** **CHOOSE: Programs, Microsoft Access**

THE GUIDED TOUR

Software programs designed for Microsoft Windows have many similarities in screen design and layout. Each program operates in its own **application window,** while the spreadsheets, letters, and database tables you create appear in separate **document windows.** Access uses these windows for presenting and managing data. Later in this session, you will learn about the *Database window* and the Datasheet view.

APPLICATION WINDOW

When you first load Microsoft Access, the application window and the startup dialog box appear, as shown in Figure 1.2. The application window contains the Title bar, Menu bar, Database toolbar, and Status bar. You use the startup dialog box to open an existing database or to create a new database. To make your choice even easier, the startup dialog box displays a list box with the last database files that you have opened.

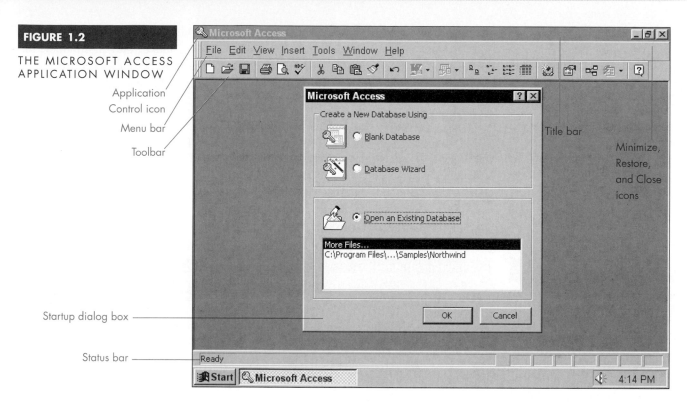

FIGURE 1.2

THE MICROSOFT ACCESS
APPLICATION WINDOW

Application
Control icon

Menu bar

Toolbar

Title bar

Minimize,
Restore,
and Close
icons

Startup dialog box

Status bar

The primary components of the application window are:

Application Control icon (🔑)	Used to identify the application. You can double-click the Control icon to close Microsoft Access.
Minimize (☐) and Maximize (☐), Restore (☐), and Close (☒) icons	Located in the top right-hand corner, these icons control the display of the application window using the mouse. (*Note:* Since the window is already maximized, the Maximize icon does not appear in Figure 1.2.)
Title bar	The Title bar contains the name of the program or database file. Using a mouse, you can move a window by dragging its Title bar.
Menu bar	Contains the Access menu commands.
Toolbar	The toolbars in Access are dynamic. Depending on the activity, Access displays the toolbar and buttons that you're most likely to use.
Status bar	Located at the bottom of the application window and above the taskbar, the Status bar displays the status or mode and other helpful information.

Although the application window is usually maximized, you can reduce it to a window that appears on the desktop. You can then size, move, and manipulate the application window to customize your work environment in Windows. In this guide, we assume that the Access application window is always maximized.

DATABASE WINDOW

When you open a database, Microsoft Access also opens a Database window. The Database window is your command center; it provides the means to create, view, and edit database objects such as tables, forms, and reports. Until you create or open a database, no Database window appears in the application window. When you open an existing database, its name appears in the Title bar of the Database window. Figure 1.3 shows the screen after opening the "Wedding" database.

Object tabs are provided along the top of the Database window. You click these tabs to display the different types of objects contained in the database. The *Tables* tab is shown selected in Figure 1.3. If you clicked the *Queries* tab, a list of query objects would appear in the dialog box. The Database window also provides you with three *processing buttons*. The New command button is used to create a new database object. You click the Open command button to call up the selected database object, or double-click the desired object. The Design command button lets you modify the specifications for an existing database object.

The Database window contains the Database Control icon (⊞) in the top left-hand corner and the Minimize (▬), Maximize (□), and Close (✕) buttons in the top right-hand corner. To close a database (along with its Database window), choose File, Close from the menu or simply click the Close (✕) button using the mouse. You can customize the view of the object icons in the Database window by clicking the Large Icons (⊞), Small Icons (⊞), List (⊞), and Details (⊞) buttons on the toolbar.

MENU BAR

Access commands are grouped together on the Menu bar (Figure 1.4), as shown in the following example.

FIGURE 1.4

ACCESS MENU BAR

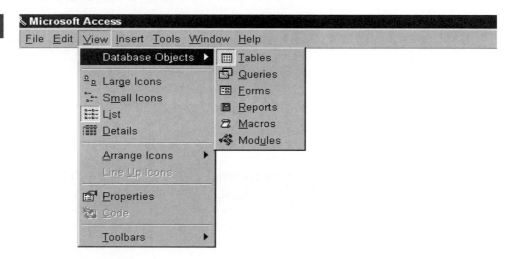

Commands in this guide are written in the following form:

CHOOSE: View, Database Objects, Tables

where View is the Menu bar option, Database Objects is the command on the pull-down menu, and Tables is the command on the fly-out menu. To execute a command, click once on the Menu bar option and then click once on the desired menu commands. Commands that are not available for selection appear dimmed. Commands that are followed by an ellipsis require further information to be collected in a dialog box.

In the following exercise, you practice accessing the Menu bar.

Perform the following steps . . .

1. To remove the startup dialog box without making a selection:
   CLICK: Cancel command button

2. To access the Help command, position the tip of the mouse pointer on the word Help in the Menu bar and click the left mouse button once. A pull-down menu appears below the Help option.

3. To see the pull-down menus associated with other menu options, drag the mouse pointer slowly to the left over the additional options on the Menu bar. (*Note:* You need not hold down the left mouse button as you move the mouse pointer.)

4. To leave the Menu bar without making a command selection, position the pointer in a blank area of the Title bar and click once.

5. To display the pull-down menu for the File option:
CHOOSE: File
This instruction tells you to click the left mouse button once with the pointer on the File option in the Menu bar. (*Note:* All menu commands that you execute in this guide begin with the word "CHOOSE.")

6. To leave the Menu bar without making a selection:
CLICK: an empty area on the Access Title bar

SHORTCUT MENUS

Access uses context-sensitive shortcut menus for quick access to menu commands. Rather than searching for commands in the Menu bar, you position the mouse pointer on text or an object, such as a table or a graphic, and click the right mouse button. A pop-up menu appears with the most commonly selected commands for the text or object.

To practice accessing a shortcut menu, perform the following steps.

Perform the following steps . . .

1. To display a shortcut or pop-up menu, position the mouse pointer over any button on the toolbar and click the right mouse button. A shortcut menu should appear.

2. To remove the shortcut menu from the screen:
PRESS: ESC
The shortcut menu disappears.

QUICK REFERENCE
Using Shortcut Menus

1. Position the mouse pointer over an item, such as a toolbar button.

2. CLICK: the right mouse button to display a shortcut or pop-up menu

3. CHOOSE: a command from the menu, or
PRESS: ESC to remove it

TOOLBARS

A **toolbar,** called the Database toolbar, appears immediately below the Menu bar. Access provides several toolbars and hundreds of buttons, sometimes called *icons*, for quick and easy mouse access to its more popular commands and features. Using the mouse, you can point at any toolbar button until a yellow ToolTip appears with the button name. We will describe the buttons on the toolbar as they become relevant.

When working with an open database, the Database toolbar appears as labeled in Figure 1.5.

FIGURE 1.5

DATABASE TOOLBAR

New Database
Open Database
Save
Print
Print Preview
Spelling
Cut
Copy
Paste
Format Painter
Undo
OfficeLinks
Analyze
Large Icons
Small Icons
List
Details
Code
Properties
Relationships
New Object
Office Assistant

With no open database objects in the application window, many of the toolbar buttons on your screen will appear dimmed and unavailable.

IN ADDITION MOVING TOOLBARS

- To un-dock a toolbar, position the mouse pointer over the Move bar (▐) appearing at the left of the docked toolbar. Click the left mouse button and drag the toolbar into the application

window. The toolbar turns into a floating window, complete with a Title bar and Close box.

- To re-dock a floating toolbar, position the mouse pointer over its Title bar and drag it toward one of the borders. Release the mouse button when the toolbar snaps into place.

STATUS BAR

When Access is ready for you to perform an action, the Status bar displays the text "Ready." In general, the **Status bar** displays messages depending on what you are doing in Access. When Access doesn't perform an operation as expected, check the Status bar for error messages relating to the current processing task. Also, the Status bar informs you of the *toggle* status (on or off) of the CAPS LOCK and NUM LOCK keys and other keyboard keys.

DIALOG BOX

A dialog box is a common mechanism in Windows applications for collecting information before processing a command or instruction (Figure 1.6). An ellipsis (. . .) following a command on a pull-down or pop-up menu informs you that Access will present a dialog box when the command is selected. In a dialog box, you indicate the options you want to use and then click the OK command button when you're finished. Dialog boxes are also used to display messages or to ask for confirmation of commands.

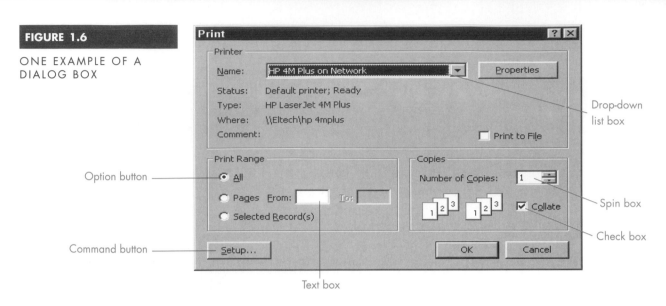

A **dialog box** uses several methods for collecting information, as shown in Figure 1.6 above and described in Table 1.1 below.

TABLE 1.1

Parts of a Dialog Box

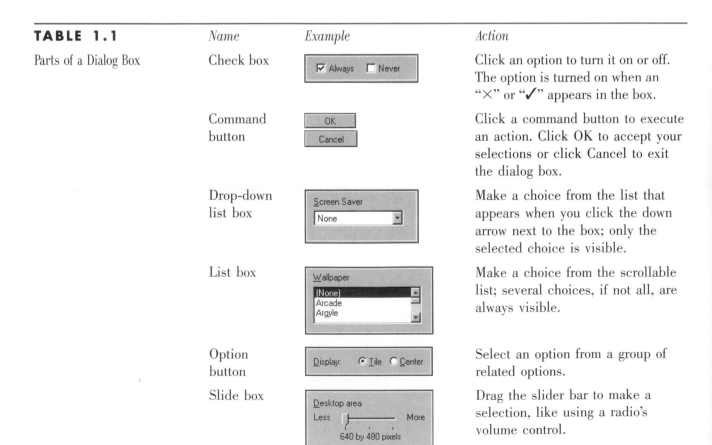

Name	Example	Action
Check box	☑ Always ☐ Never	Click an option to turn it on or off. The option is turned on when an "×" or "✔" appears in the box.
Command button	OK / Cancel	Click a command button to execute an action. Click OK to accept your selections or click Cancel to exit the dialog box.
Drop-down list box	Screen Saver / None	Make a choice from the list that appears when you click the down arrow next to the box; only the selected choice is visible.
List box	Wallpaper / (None) / Arcade / Argyle	Make a choice from the scrollable list; several choices, if not all, are always visible.
Option button	Display: ⦿ Tile ○ Center	Select an option from a group of related options.
Slide box	Desktop area / Less — More / 640 by 480 pixels	Drag the slider bar to make a selection, like using a radio's volume control.

	Name	Example	Action
TABLE 1.1 **Continued**	Spin box	Wait: 6 ↕ minutes	Click the up and down arrows to the right of the box until the number you want appears.
	Tab	Contents Index Find	Click a named tab at the top of the window to access other pages of options in the dialog box.
	Text box	File name: untitled	Click inside the text box and then type the desired information.

Most dialog boxes also provide a question mark icon (**?**) near the right side of the Title bar. If you have a question about an item in the dialog box, click the question mark and then click the item to display a pop-up help window. To remove the help window, click on it once.

OPENING A DATABASE

Before you can manipulate or view the objects in an Access database, you must first open the database file. The quickest way to open a database is to make a selection from the startup dialog box that appears when you first load Access. To open a database using the Database toolbar, click the Open Database button (🖙). You can also choose the File, Open Database command from the Menu bar. Once the Open dialog box appears, you select the file's location by clicking in the *Look in* drop-down list box. You then double-click the database's name appearing in the file list area.

Throughout this guide, you will open and save databases to one of the following locations:

- *Advantage Files location* - This location may be on a diskette, a folder on your local hard drive, or a folder on a network server. The Advantage Files are the database files that have been created for you and that you will retrieve in the remaining exercises in this guide.

- *Data Files location* - This location may also be on a diskette, a hard drive folder, or a network folder. You will save the databases that you create or modify in the Data Files location.

> **IMPORTANT:** *Before continuing, ensure that you know the location of your Advantage Files and where to store your Data Files. If necessary, ask your instructor or lab assistant for additional information.*

In this exercise, you practice opening a database file named "School" from the Advantage Files location.

Perform the following steps . . .

1. CLICK: Open button ( ) on the Database toolbar
    The dialog box in Figure 1.7 appears. (*Note:* You will have different file-names displaying in your dialog box than those shown in Figure 1.7. These filenames may also appear as icons in the file list area, but don't worry about their appearance right now. You will learn how to change the display of filenames in Step 3.)

FIGURE 1.7

THE OPEN DIALOG BOX

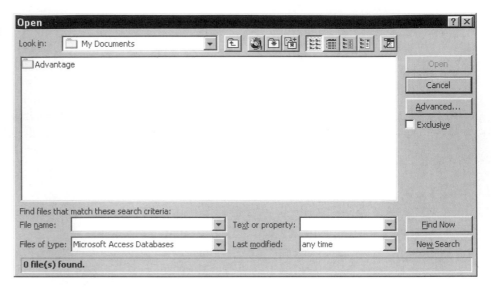

2. To display a list of the Advantage database files:
    CLICK: down arrow beside the *Look in* drop-down list box
    SELECT: *your Advantage Files location*
    In this guide, we will assume that you save your work to the "My Documents" folder on the hard disk and retrieve database files from the "Access97" sub-folder, located at the following path:
    \My Documents\Advantage\Access97

3. To customize the display for the file list area in the Open dialog box, try the following:
    CLICK: Details button ( ) to see each database's file size and last modification date
    CLICK: Properties button ( ) to see summary information for the selected database
    CLICK: Preview button ( ) to see a preview of the selected file (*Note:* Although this feature is used extensively for previewing word processing or spreadsheet files, database files do not typically provide previewing capability.)
    CLICK: List button ( ) to see database icons and names in a multiple-column format

4. In the file list area:
    DOUBLE-CLICK: School
    The "School" database opens into a Database window.

5. To display a list of the data tables stored in the "School" database, ensure that the *Tables* tab is selected by clicking on it once with the mouse.

6. To see a list of the forms that have already been created and are stored in the "School" database:
CLICK: *Forms* tab
You will now see the "Course Entry Form" in the Database window.

7. To see a list of the reports stored in the "School" database:
CLICK: *Reports* tab
You will see entries for "Course Offerings" and "Instructor Listing" in the Database window.

8. To display the instructor information that is stored in this database:
CLICK: *Tables* tab
DOUBLE-CLICK: Instructors
The Instructors data table is loaded into the computer's memory and displayed in **Datasheet view.** Much like a worksheet in Microsoft Excel, the data appears in rows and columns called a **datasheet** (Figure 1.9). This view lets you see multiple records on the screen at once. (*Note:* Depending on your screen size, you may see more or fewer records than shown in Figure 1.8.)

FIGURE 1.8

THE INSTRUCTORS TABLE
DISPLAYED IN DATASHEET
VIEW

Instructor ID	First Name	Last Name	Address	City	Stat
abre	Eric	Abrahamson	9450 Middleton Wa	Seattle	WA
andb	Brian	Andrews	132 Blue Street	San Francisco	CA
alel	Lawrence	Alexander	Box 4403	Chicago	IL
andk	Kirk	Andrews	226 Valley Street	Vancouver	BC
andm	Mark	Anderson	1459 River Drive	Houston	TX
boww	Victoria	Bowman	70 Brookesfield Rd	San Mateo	CA
mika	Arthur	Mikowski	12 Elm Circle	Alexandria	VA
broi	Ibrahim	Brown	Box 117, Yonge St.	Toronto	ON
koha	Audrey	Koh	347 Glencoe Dr	Alta Dena	CA
barj	James	Barnes	8 Shane Drive	Boston	MA
jemp	Paul	Jemelian	P.O. Box 12	Burlingame	CA
calb	Bruce	Callander	2 Kron Lane	Markham	ON
cosc	Carl	Costigan	#10-Riverside Way	Ventura	CA
forj	Jorges	Forneau	Apt. 115, Tillicum R	Thousand Oaks	CA
calj	John	Callus	P.O. Box 312	Mississauga	ON

Record: 1 of 26

Datasheet View

QUICK REFERENCE
Opening a Database

1. **CLICK: Open button (⊞), or**
2. **CLICK: down arrow beside the *Look in* drop-down list box**
3. **SELECT: a file location**
4. **DOUBLE-CLICK: the desired database**

IN ADDITION OPENING AN OFFICE DOCUMENT FROM THE DESKTOP

You can open an existing document using one of the following methods:

- CHOOSE: ⊞Start, Documents, and then select the desired document from the 15 most recently used files listed (if available)

- CHOOSE: ⊞Start, Find, Files or Folders and then perform a search for the desired database

- CHOOSE: ⊞Start, Open Office Document and then select the desired database in the Open dialog box

---

IN ADDITION OPENING A DATABASE USING THE WORLD WIDE WEB

With the appropriate connection, you can open and save Access databases on the Internet. In the Open or Save dialog boxes, select an FTP Internet site location from the *Look in* or *Save in* drop-down list boxes, respectively. Once connected to a remote FTP server, you can work with files the same as if they were on your local hard disk. This feature lets you share databases with users from around the world.

WORKING IN DATASHEET VIEW

In this section, you learn to work in and customize the Datasheet view. In addition to moving around a datasheet efficiently, you will change the datasheet's font selection and apply special effects to enhance the datasheet's screen display and printed output.

MOVING AROUND A DATASHEET

In a datasheet, each row represents an individual record and each column represents field information. The intersection of a row and column is often called a **cell.** To properly manage a database, you must know how to efficiently move the **cursor** (sometimes called an *insertion point*) to view all parts of a table. Table 1.2 provides a summary of the cursor-movement keys available in Datasheet view mode.

TABLE 1.2	*Keystroke*	*Task Description*
Moving the Cursor	⬆, ⬇	Moves to the previous or next record, respectively
	⬅, ➡	Moves cursor to the left or to the right
	CTRL + ⬅	Moves one field to the left
	CTRL + ➡	Moves one field to the right
	PgUp, PgDn	Moves up or down one screen
	HOME	Moves to first (leftmost) field in a record
	END	Moves to last (rightmost) field in a record
	CTRL + HOME	Moves to the top (first record and first field)
	CTRL + END	Moves to the bottom (last record and last field)

Let's practice moving around the datasheet.

Perform the following steps . . .

1. To move to the last field in the record, one field at a time:
   PRESS: ➡ repeatedly
   If you're working with a table that is wider than the screen, the screen will automatically scroll horizontally. After the cursor reaches the last field, it will move to the first field of the second row.
   (*CAUTION:* If your cursor is flashing inside a field, pressing ➡ positions the cursor at the next character in the field and does not move it to the next field. Therefore, to perform the above instruction, you would press **ENTER** first to complete Edit mode and then press ➡.)

2. To move to the first field in a record:
   PRESS: **HOME**

3. To move down a screen:
   PRESS: **PgDn**

4. To move to the last field in the database table:
   PRESS: **CTRL** + **END**

5. To move to the beginning of the database table:
   PRESS: **CTRL** + **HOME**

6. Let's practice moving the cursor using the navigation buttons located in the bottom left-hand corner of the datasheet window. To move to the next record in the column using the mouse:
   CLICK: Next Record button (▶)

7. To move to the last record at the bottom of the column:
   CLICK: Last Record button (▶|)

8. To move to the first record at the top of the column:
CLICK: First Record button (⏮)

9. To move the cursor to a specific cell in the datasheet:
CLICK: on any cell in the Last Name column using the I-beam mouse pointer
Notice that the cursor is now flashing in the selected field. This means that you have entered Edit mode, which we will discuss further in the next section.

10. To move to the beginning of the database table:
PRESS: (ENTER) to complete Edit mode
PRESS: (CTRL) + (HOME)

CUSTOMIZING DATASHEET VIEW

By default, Access displays a datasheet in a window. You can maximize, minimize, and close this window just as you would any other window. In addition, you can customize a datasheet by changing its display font and by sizing, moving, freezing, and hiding its columns. All of the customizing options for changing the display of a datasheet are also reflected in its printed output.

In this section, you learn to change basic display options. In Session 2, you will adjust the width and position of columns in the datasheet window.

Perform the following steps . . .

1. To maximize your view of the datasheet:
CLICK: Maximize button (☐) on the datasheet window
The datasheet expands to fill the entire application window.

2. To minimize the datasheet:
CLICK: Minimize button (▁) for the datasheet window
Refer to the diagram below to ensure that you are clicking the right button. The datasheet window is minimized to display only its Title bar near the bottom of the application window.

Application window icons ⎯⎯⎯⎯⎯⎯ [_][⧉][X]
Datasheet window icons ⎯⎯⎯⎯⎯⎯ [_][⧉][X]

3. To restore the datasheet window:
CLICK: Restore button (⧉) on the Title bar, which should appear as shown below

4. The datasheet window returns to its maximized state. To restore the datasheet window to a window, do the following:
CLICK: Restore button (⧉) again

5. Position the mouse pointer over the datasheet window's sizing corner and then drag the mouse to size the window to resemble Figure 1.9.

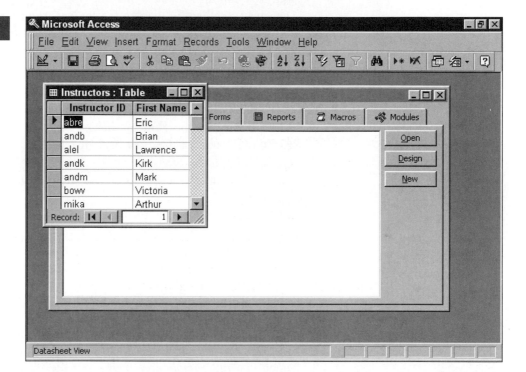

6. Move the datasheet window by positioning the mouse pointer on a blank area in the window's Title bar and then dragging the mouse. On your own, practice dragging the datasheet window around the work area in the application window.

7. Using the mouse and the sizing corner, size the datasheet window back to its original size and position. (Refer to Figure 1.8.)

8. To change the display font for the datasheet:
CHOOSE: Format, Font from the menu

9. In the dialog box that appears, you can change the font's typeface, style, and size. In addition, you can select a display color for the table data. To illustrate, do the following:
SELECT: Times New Roman in the *Font* list box
SELECT: Italic in the *Font Style* list box
SELECT: 12 in the *Size* list box

10. To change the display color for text in the datasheet:
CLICK: down arrow beside the *Color* drop-down list box
SELECT: Blue
CLICK: OK command button
The datasheet window is displayed immediately using the new selections.
Hint: You can also select formatting options using buttons on the Formatting (Datasheet) toolbar. To display the toolbar, right-click the Table Datasheet toolbar and then choose Formatting (Datasheet) from the shortcut menu. To remove the toolbar, right-click it and then choose Formatting (Datasheet) once again.

11. Let's select a more practical font for viewing table data:
CHOOSE: Format, Font
SELECT: Arial in the *Font* list box
SELECT: Regular in the *Font Style* list box
SELECT: 10 in the *Size* list box
CLICK: down arrow beside the *Color* drop-down list box
SELECT: Black
CLICK: OK command button

12. To apply some special display effects to the datasheet:
CHOOSE: Format, Cells

13. In the Cell Effects dialog box that appears, you can choose to display or hide the gridlines, change the color of the gridlines, and apply special effects. To illustrate, do the following:
SELECT: *Horizontal* check box so that no "✓" appears
SELECT: *Vertical* check box so that no "✓" appears
Notice that the *Sample* area shows you the results of the selections you have made in this dialog box.

14. To proceed:
CLICK: OK command button
The datasheet window now appears without gridlines separating the cells.
(*Hint:* Remember that your selections in the Font and Cell Effects dialog boxes also affect the way a datasheet is printed.)

15. Let's apply some special display effects to the datasheet:
CHOOSE: Format, Cells
SELECT: *Raised* option button in the *Cell Effect* area
CLICK: OK command button
Your datasheet window should now appear similar to Figure 1.10.

FIGURE 1.10

APPLYING FONTS AND
CELL EFFECTS TO THE
DATASHEET WINDOW

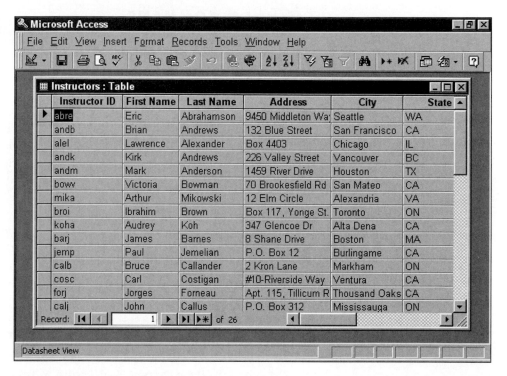

16. To return to a plain white background with gridlines for the datasheet window:
CHOOSE: Format, Cells
SELECT: *Flat* option button in the *Cell Effect* area
SELECT: *Horizontal* check box so that a "✓" appears
SELECT: *Vertical* check box so that a "✓" appears
CLICK: OK command button

QUICK REFERENCE
Customizing the Display of
a Datasheet Window

- **To change the display font for a datasheet:**
  CHOOSE: Format, Font
  SELECT: options from the Font dialog box
  CLICK: OK command button
- **To apply special effects to cells in a datasheet:**
  CHOOSE: Format, Cells
  SELECT: options from the Cell Effects dialog box
  CLICK: OK command button

Manipulating table data

In this section, you learn to use the Undo command and then practice editing, deleting, and inserting information in a datasheet window.

THE UNDO COMMAND

Before learning how to modify table information, you should be familiar with the **Undo command** for reversing mistakes made during editing. Unlike other Office 97 products, Access does not offer a multiple undo capability. To undo the most recent change you made to a field's contents, you choose the Edit, Undo Typing command. To undo all the changes you made to the current field, you choose Edit, Undo Current Field/Record. When you move the cursor to another record, your changes are saved automatically. However, you can undo the saved changes by choosing Edit, Undo Saved Record. Your changes become permanent as soon as you begin editing another record or move to another window.

Instead of choosing commands from the menu, you can undo your changes in the current field or record by pressing the `ESC` key once. Pressing `ESC` again will undo all of the changes made to the current record. Another keyboard short-cut for the Undo command is `CTRL` + z which lets you undo the changes to the last saved record. You will practice using the Undo command in the next section.

QUICK REFERENCE Undo command	• **CHOOSE: Edit, Undo Typing to reverse the most recent change you made to data** • **CHOOSE: Edit, Undo Current Field/Record to reverse all the changes you made to the current field or record** • **CHOOSE: Edit, Undo Saved Record to reverse any changes you made to a previous record**

EDITING TABLE DATA

In Datasheet view, you edit data by first selecting the existing data or cell and then performing a command or typing new information. When you open a table, the first field in the first record of the table is selected automatically. Other important points to keep in mind when working with an Access table in Datasheet view include:

- If you start typing while data is selected (highlighted), what you type will replace the selection.
- If the flashing cursor is positioned in a cell but no data is selected, what you type will be inserted in the field.
- Press `BACKSPACE` to delete the character to the left of the cursor and press `DELETE` to delete the character to the right of the cursor.

In the following steps, you practice selecting and editing field and record data in the Instructors table (stored in the "School" database.)

Perform the following steps . . .

1. Ensure that the Instructors table appears on the screen and then move to the first field in the first record. The "abre" in the first column should appear highlighted. (*Note:* You may want to maximize the datasheet window to view more of the table data.)

2. To position the cursor ready for editing, move the I-beam mouse pointer to the right of the name "Brian" in the First Name column of record 2 and then click the left mouse button once. The flashing cursor should appear to the right of the letter "n" in "Brian."

3. To change the spelling of Brian's name to Bryan, do the following:
   PRESS: ◀ twice
   PRESS: BACKSPACE
   TYPE: **y**
   Notice that a pencil icon (✏), called the *pencil indicator*, appears in the row frame area near the left side of the record. The pencil indicator appears when editing changes haven't been saved yet and then disappears when you move to another record; the act of moving to another record saves the changes to the previous record automatically.

4. To complete the editing process:
   PRESS: ENTER
   The contents for the Last Name column now appear highlighted. Notice that the pencil indicator still appears since you are still in the current record.

5. To save the changes to the current record:
   PRESS: ▼ to move to the next record
   The changes made to Bryan Andrew's record are saved and the pencil indicator disappears.

6. To replace the contents of an entire cell in the datasheet, you select the entire cell's contents and then type the new entry. To illustrate, position the mouse pointer over the gridline appearing to the left of the City column for the fifth record, as shown below. Notice that the mouse pointer changes to a plus sign or cross shape.

Street	Vancouver	BC
Drive	Houston	TX
sfield Rd	San Mateo	CA

Position mouse pointer here →

7. With the cross mouse pointer, click the gridline once to select the entire cell's contents. If done correctly, the cell will appear highlighted.

8. To replace "Houston" with "Dallas":
TYPE: `Dallas`
PRESS: `ENTER`

9. To practice deleting a cell's contents and then using the Undo command, let's select a new cell in the datasheet window:
SELECT: the cell with "Bowman" as the Last Name (record 6)
(*Hint:* This instruction tells you to position the cross mouse pointer over the gridline appearing to the left of the Last Name "Bowman" and then to click the left mouse button once.)

10. To delete the cell's contents:
PRESS: `DELETE`

11. To undo this last change and bring the data back:
PRESS: `ESC`
(*Note:* You could have also chosen the Edit, Undo Delete command from the menu.) The field should now contain the original data.

12. To edit Audrey Koh's last name so that it appears as "Moh," position the I-beam mouse pointer over Audrey Koh's Last Name field. The I-beam pointer marks where you can place the cursor and begin editing once you click with the mouse. In this step, position the I-beam to the left of the "K" in "Koh" and then click once with the left mouse button. A flashing cursor appears to the left of the letter "K."

13. If you press ➡ and ⬅, the cursor will move right and left within the field. To practice:
PRESS: ➡ twice
PRESS: ⬅ until the cursor returns to the left of "K"

14. To delete the "K":
PRESS: `DELETE`
TYPE: M
"Moh" should now be displaying in the Last Name field.

15. To move the cursor and update the record:
CLICK: any field in another record
Remember, by moving the cursor to another record, the changes you make to a record are saved onto the disk.

16. If you decide now that you shouldn't have changed Audrey Koh's record, you reverse the change by doing the following:
CHOOSE: Edit, Undo Saved Record
"Koh" should now reappear in the Last Name field.

17. To position the cursor at the top of the table:
PRESS: `ENTER` to complete Edit mode
PRESS: `CTRL` + `HOME`

QUICK REFERENCE Modifying a Table's Field Information	**To edit field data:** 1. **Position the cursor in a cell by pointing to the cell with the I-beam mouse pointer and clicking once with the mouse.** 2. **Make your changes.** 3. **Select another record to save the changes.** **To delete field data:** 1. **Select a cell by pointing to the gridline appearing to the left of the cell and clicking once with the cross mouse pointer.** 2. **PRESS: [DELETE] to delete the selected cell's contents** 3. **If necessary, choose the Undo command to reverse the action.**

IN ADDITION PROOFING YOUR WORK

Similar to Microsoft Word, Access provides a full-featured Spell Checker that allows you to check spellings in Text and Memo fields.

The AutoCorrect utility, another new feature of Access 97, automatically corrects frequently mistyped words as you type. Ask the Office Assistant for more information on using these powerful proofing tools.

WHEN DOES ACCESS SAVE YOUR CHANGES?

As you learned in the last section, Access automatically saves your editing changes when you select or click in a different record in the table. Therefore, you don't have to explicitly choose the Save command to save table records. When you edit a record, the indicator at the left side of the record changes to a pencil indicator. When you move to another record, the pencil indicator disappears, which means that your changes to that record have been saved. To save the changes you make to a record without moving to a different record, press (SHIFT) + (ENTER) as a keyboard shortcut.

ADDING AND DELETING RECORDS

In Datasheet view, you delete a record by selecting the record and then pressing (DELETE). You can also delete a record by positioning the cursor in any field of the record and then clicking the Delete Record button (▶✕) on the toolbar. Before removing the record permanently, Access displays a dialog box that lets you reconsider your choice. You click the Yes command button to delete the record or the No command button to restore the record. You can also delete a group of selected records by first dragging the mouse in the **record selection area,** which is to the left of the first column in the datasheet, and then pressing (DELETE). Refer to the diagram below for clarification.

Current or
Active Record

Field Column
Headings

Record
Selection Area

Similarly to how you select a field, you select an entire record by positioning the mouse pointer to the left of the record in the record selection area, until the pointer changes to a horizontal arrow (➡), and then clicking the left mouse button once. The entire row will appear highlighted when selected properly. (*Note:* To select an entire record using the menu, position the cursor in any field of the record and then choose the Edit, Select Record command.)

Let's practice selecting datasheet information.

Perform the following steps . . .

1. Using the mouse, select the following record from the table:
   SELECT: the second record (for Bryan Andrews)
   This instruction tells you to position the mouse pointer to the left of the first column of the second record, until a horizontal arrow (➡) appears, and click once with the mouse.

2. To delete the selected record:
   PRESS: (**DELETE**)
   A confirmation dialog box should appear, as shown in Figure 1.11.
   (*CAUTION:* Access always displays this dialog box when you try to delete a record. If you select the Yes button at this point, the record will be permanently deleted from the table. If you select the No button, the record will remain in the data table.)

FIGURE 1.11

DIALOG BOX
CONFIRMING A RECORD
DELETION

3. CLICK: Yes command button

4. To delete another record:
   CLICK: in any field of the fifth record (for Victoria Bowman)
   CLICK: Delete Record button (✖) on the Database toolbar

5. To confirm the deletion:
   CLICK: Yes command button

6. To add a new record to the Instructor's table:
CLICK: New Record button (▶✳) on the Database toolbar
(*Hint:* You can also click the ▶✳ button located beside the navigation buttons at the bottom of the datasheet window to add a new record.)

7. Let's enter the following information into the new record that appears at the bottom of the datasheet window:
TYPE: **joyj**
PRESS: ENTER
TYPE: **James**
PRESS: ENTER
TYPE: **Joyce**
PRESS: ENTER
TYPE: **123 Anywhere Street**
PRESS: ENTER
TYPE: **Portland**
PRESS: ENTER
TYPE: **OR**
PRESS: ENTER
TYPE: **97008**

8. To save the record and return to the top of the datasheet window:
PRESS: SHIFT + ENTER
PRESS: CTRL + HOME

9. To close the datasheet (but not the Database window):
CLICK: Close button (✗) for the "Instructors" datasheet window

10. If you are asked to save changes to the table layout:
CLICK: Yes command button
You should now see the Database window.

QUICK REFERENCE Deleting a Record	1. SELECT: the record you want to delete
	2. PRESS: DELETE or CLICK: Delete Record button (▶✗)
	3. CLICK: Yes button to permanently delete the record, or
	CLICK: No button to undelete the record

QUICK REFERENCE Adding a Record	1. CLICK: New Record button (▶✳)
	2. Type the desired information into the fields appearing at the bottom of the datasheet window.
	3. PRESS: SHIFT + ENTER to save the record

GETTING HELP

Access provides several **context-sensitive help** features and a comprehensive library of online documentation. Like many developers trying to minimize the retail price of software and maximize profits, Microsoft has stopped shipping volumes of print-based documentation in favor of online and web-based Help options. This section describes the Access help features and how to find more detailed information.

CONTEXT-SENSITIVE HELP

Context-sensitive help refers to a program's ability to present helpful information reflecting your current position in the program. In Access, you can retrieve context-sensitive help for menu options, toolbar buttons, and dialog box items. The help information is presented concisely in a small pop-up window that you can remove with the click of the mouse. This type of help lets you access information quickly and then continue working without interruption. Table 1.3 describes some methods for accessing context-sensitive help while working in Access.

TABLE 1.3	*To display...*	*Do this...*
Displaying Context-Sensitive Help Information	A description of a dialog box item	Click the question mark button ([?]) in a dialog box's Title bar and then click an item in the dialog box. A helpful description of the item appears in a pop-up window. Alternatively, you can often right-click a dialog box item and then choose the What's This? command from the shortcut menu.
	A description of a menu command	Choose the Help, What's This? command and then choose a command using the question mark mouse pointer. Rather than executing the command, a helpful description of the command appears in a pop-up window.
	A description of a toolbar button	Point to a toolbar button to display its ToolTip label. You can also choose the Help, What's This? command and then click a toolbar button to display more detailed help information.

In the following exercise, you will access context-sensitive help.

Perform the following steps . . .

1. To display help for the File, New Database command, you must first activate the question mark mouse pointer. Do the following:
    CHOOSE: Help, What's This?
    Your mouse pointer should now appear with an attached question mark.
    (*Note:* You can also press (SHIFT)+(F1) to activate this pointer.)

2. Using the question mark mouse pointer (and not the keyboard):
   CHOOSE: File, New Database
   Rather than executing the command, Access provides a brief description of the command in a pop-up window.

3. After reading the description, close the window by clicking on it once.

4. To display a ToolTip for a toolbar button, position the mouse pointer over the Details button (⊞) on the Database toolbar. After a second or two, a ToolTip will appear showing the button's name.

5. To display additional information for the Details button:
   PRESS: (SHIFT) + (F1)
   This command tells you to hold down the (SHIFT) + (F1) key and then tap the (F1) key. Then, release the (SHIFT) key.

6. CLICK: Details button (⊞)
   The following pop-up window appears:

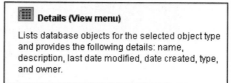

7. CLICK: the pop-up window once to remove it

QUICK REFERENCE Displaying Context-Sensitive Help	1. **CHOOSE: Help, What's This?**
	2. **Using the question mark mouse pointer, select the desired item for which you want to display a help pop-up window**

OFFICE ASSISTANT

The Office Assistant is your personal and customizable computer guru. When you need to accomplish a particular task, you call up the Assistant by clicking the Office Assistant button (🔲) on the Database toolbar. To conduct a search of the entire Help system, you simply type an English phrase in the form of a question. The Assistant analyzes your request and provides a resource list of suggested topics. Furthermore, the Assistant watches your keystrokes and mouse clicks as you work and can offer suggestions and shortcuts to make you more productive and efficient.

Let's put your Assistant to work.

Perform the following steps . . .

1. To display the Office Assistant:
CLICK: Office Assistant button (🔲)
The Office Assistant and its associated tip window appear as shown in Figure 1.12. The text in the tip window may already be selected. If not, select the text before you begin typing your question in the next step.

FIGURE 1.12

OFFICE ASSISTANT AND
TIP WINDOW

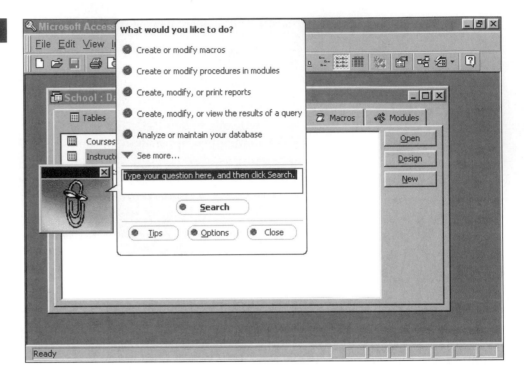

2. Type your request just as you would ask the question out loud. For this example, let's find out what a "module" is in an Access database.
TYPE: **What is a module?**
CLICK: Search button
(*Note:* You need not be concerned about typing your questions using perfect grammar or punctuation. However, spelling does count!)

3. A tip window appears with several topics displayed. You must now refine your search by selecting one of these topics. Do the following:
CLICK: Modules: What they are and how they work
A Help Topics window appears with the requested information. You will learn more about working with this window in the next section.

4. CLICK: Close button (❎) on the Help Topics window
CLICK: Close button (❎) on the Office Assistant window

Occasionally an illuminated light bulb will appear in the Office Assistant window. This light bulb informs you that the Assistant wants to share a new tip or suggestion with you. To view the tip, click the light bulb in the Office Assistant window. To close the window, click its Close button.

IN ADDITION CUSTOMIZING THE OFFICE ASSISTANT

- To customize your Assistant's appearance:
  RIGHT-CLICK: Office Assistant window
  CHOOSE: Choose Assistant from the pop-up menu

- To customize your Assistant's behavior:
  RIGHT-CLICK: Office Assistant window
  CHOOSE: Options from the pop-up menu

HELP TOPICS WINDOW

For a complete topical listing of the Help system, choose the Contents and Index command from the Help menu. This command displays the Help Topics window, as shown in Figure 1.13. You can think of the Help Topics window as the front door to the vast help resources in Access.

FIGURE 1.13

HELP TOPICS WINDOW: CONTENTS TAB

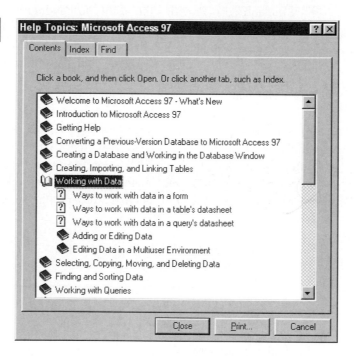

The Help Topics window provides three different tools, each on its own tab, to help you find the information you need quickly and easily. You point to and click a tab using the mouse to make the tab active in the window. Refer to the following tab descriptions to determine which tool you should use when requiring assistance:

- *Contents tab* Displays a list of help topics organized as a hierarchy of books and pages. This tab is your Table of Contents for the entire Help system. Notice in Figure 1.13 that there are three different types of icons displayed:

  represents a help category; double-click a book icon to view the books and topics it contains represents an open category that is currently displaying its contents; double-click an open book icon to close (or collapse) the book

? represents a help topic; double-click a topic icon to display a help window

- *Index* tab   Displays an alphabetical list of keywords and phrases, similar to a traditional book index. To search for a topic using this tab, type a word (or even a few letters) into the text box which, in turn, makes the list box scroll to the first matching entry in the index. Then, double-click the desired entry to display the help topic. If a keyword has more than one associated topic, a Topics Found window appears and you can select a further topic to narrow your search.

- *Find* tab   Provides the ability to conduct a full-text search of the Help system for finding a particular word or phrase. Although similar to the *Index* tab, this tab differs in its ability to look past indexed keywords and search the help text itself.

When you double-click a help topic, it is displayed in a secondary window. You may find that *secondary* windows include some unfamiliar buttons, like **≫** and **↰**, embedded in the help text. The **≫** symbol, which we'll called the Chiclet button, represents a "See Also" link that you can click to move to a related topic. The Show Me symbol (**↰**) actually initiates the command you're interested in. You may also notice that some words or phrases in the help window have a dotted underline. If you click such a word or phrase, a definition pop-up window appears.

You will now access the Help Topics window.

Perform the following steps . . .

1. To display the Help Topics window:
   CHOOSE: Help, Contents and Index

2. CLICK: *Contents* tab
   Your screen should now appear similar to Figure 1.13, except that your book categories will appear collapsed. (*Note:* The Help Topics window remembers the tab that was selected when it was last closed. It will automatically return to this tab the next time you access Help.)

3. To display the contents of a book:
   DOUBLE-CLICK: "📕 Working with Data" book
   (*Note:* You can double-click the book icon (📕) or the book's title. If you find it difficult to double-click using the mouse, you can also select or highlight the book by clicking it once and then click the Open command button.)

4. To further clarify the search:
DOUBLE-CLICK: "🕮 Adding or Editing Data" book
Notice that this book contains multiple topics.

5. To display a help topic:
DOUBLE-CLICK: "? Edit the data in a field" topic
The Help Topics window is removed from view and a secondary window appears with the topic information.

6. Place the mouse pointer over the green underlined word "Datasheet" in Step 1 and then click the left mouse button once. Notice that the pointer changes into a hand when positioned correctly. A definition pop-up window appears with more information on Datasheet view.

7. To remove the pop-up window that appears:
CLICK: the window once using the left mouse button

8. To close the help window and return to Access:
CLICK: Close button (❌)

QUICK REFERENCE
Searching for Help Using the Help Topics Window

1. **To display the Help Topics window:**
CHOOSE: Help, Contents and Index

2. **CLICK:** *Contents* **tab to navigate a hierarchical Help system**
CLICK: *Index* **tab to search for a word or phrase in a keyword index**
CLICK: *Find* **tab to conduct a full-text search of the Help system**

IN ADDITION ACCESSING HELP DIRECTLY FROM MICROSOFT

If you are connected to the Internet, you can keep current on product and company news by visiting Microsoft's Web site. You'll also find helpful productivity tips and online support for all the Office 97 products.

To access this information:

1. Establish an Internet connection.

2. CHOOSE: Help, Microsoft on the Web

3. CHOOSE: *a menu option as shown at the right*

🕸 Free Stuff
🕸 Product News
🕸 Developer Forum
🕸 Frequently Asked Questions
🕸 Online Support

🕸 Microsoft Office Home Page
🕸 Send Feedback...
🕸 Best of the Web
🕸 Search the Web...
🕸 Web Tutorial

🕸 Microsoft Home Page

Closing a Database

One of the more powerful features of working in Windows is your ability to open and share data among multiple application windows. For example, you can easily copy data from a Microsoft Access datasheet into a Microsoft Excel worksheet. However, your computer must be quite sophisticated and powerful to run multiple applications efficiently at the same time. In most cases, you should close a Database window and exit Access when you are finished working so as not to waste memory that may be needed by other applications. You close the current or active Database window by choosing File, Close from the menu or by clicking the Close button (☒) in the top right-hand corner of the Database window.

Perform the following steps . . .

1. Ensure that the "School" Database window appears on the screen.

2. To close this window:
   CLICK: Close button (☒) for the "School" Database window

QUICK REFERENCE
Closing a Database

- CHOOSE: File, Close, or
- CLICK: Close button (☒)

Leaving Access

When you are finished using Access, exit the program by clicking the Close button (☒) or by choosing the File, Exit command.

Perform the following steps . . .

1. To exit Access:
   CLICK: Close button (☒) of the Access application window
   The application is closed and you are returned to the Windows desktop.

2. To exit Windows:
   CHOOSE: 🏁Start, Shut Down
   SELECT: *Shutdown the computer?* option button
   CLICK: Yes command button

QUICK REFERENCE
Exiting Access

- CLICK: Close button (☒) on the application window, or
- CHOOSE: File, Exit

SUMMARY

Microsoft Access is a relational database management system for microcomputers. A database management system enables you to store and manipulate large amounts of data such as customer lists. You create a database application in Access using objects for tables, queries, forms, and reports. Information is gathered, stored, and manipulated in tables, the primary element of an Access database.

In this session, you learned to open a data table and view its information using Datasheet view mode. After using some keyboard shortcut keys for moving around a datasheet, you modified field information and added and deleted records. You also learned that once you begin to work on a different record in the table, any changes you made to the previous record are saved. The session concluded with an introduction to the Help system.

COMMAND SUMMARY

Many of the commands and procedures appearing in this session are provided in the command summary in Table 1.4.

TABLE 1.4 Command Summary	*Task Description*	*Menu Command*	*Keyboard Shortcut*
	Opens a database	File, Open Database	🖿
	Selects a display font for Datasheet view	Format, Font	
	Applies special formatting enhancements to a datasheet	Format, Cells	
	Reverses the most recent changes	Edit, Undo	ESC
	Deletes the current or active record from a datasheet		✗
	Adds a new record to a datasheet		▶* or ▶✳
	Displays the Access Help system	Help, Contents and Index	?
	Closes the Database window	File, Close	✗
	Exits Microsoft Access	File, Exit	✗

KEY TERMS

application window
In Microsoft Windows, each running application program appears in its own application window.

cell
In a datasheet, this marks the intersection of a column and a row.

context-sensitive help
A Help feature that provides a concise description for a particular menu option, toolbar button, or dialog box item.

controls
The different elements on a form or report.

cursor
The vertical flashing bar that indicates your current position on the screen. The cursor shows where the next typed characters or spaces will appear. Also called an *insertion point*.

database
A collection of related data stored for a variety of business purposes. In Access, a database includes a collection of *objects*—data tables, queries, reports, forms, and other objects.

database management system (DBMS)
A software tool that lets you create and maintain an information database. You also use a DBMS software tool to summarize and produce reports based on the data.

datasheet
When table data is displayed in horizontal rows and vertical columns, it is called a datasheet.

Datasheet view
In this mode, the table data is displayed in rows and columns and is referred to as a datasheet.

dialog box
A box that displays messages or asks for confirmation of commands.

document window
In Microsoft Windows, each open document appears in its own document window. These windows can be sized and moved anywhere within the document area. (A document window represents your workspace.)

dynaset
The result of a query.

field
A piece of information in a record.

form

A form enables you to view one record on the screen at a time and to customize the display of that record.

hyperlinks

In Microsoft Office 97, text or graphics that when clicked take you to another resource location, either within the same document or to a separate document stored on your computer, a network server, an Intranet resource, or onto the Internet.

Internet

A worldwide network of computer networks that are interconnected by standard telephone lines, fiber optics, and satellites.

Intranet

A local or wide area network that uses Internet protocols and technologies to share information within an institution or corporation.

macro

Using a macro, you can automate frequently performed procedures.

object

Something that you can select and manipulate as a unit.

query

A question you ask of your database.

record

An individual entry, or row, in a table.

record selection area

An area to the left of the first column in the datasheet.

reports

Used to present table data in a polished format on the printed page.

Status bar

Located at the bottom of the application window, the Status bar displays messages depending on what you are doing in Access.

table

An Access object that is used to collect data relating to a particular subject.

toolbar

The toolbar is located beneath the Menu bar and provides quick and easy mouse access to the more popular features of Access.

Undo command

In a software application, a command that reverses, or cancels, the last command executed.

World Wide Web (WWW)

A visual interface to the Internet based on *hyperlinks*. Using web browser software, you click on hyperlinks to navigate the resources on the Internet.

EXERCISES

SHORT ANSWER

1. Research the names of two other popular database software packages for personal computers.

2. Define the following terms: *table, record,* and *field.* Explain their relationships to each other.

3. What is the primary element of a Microsoft Access database?

4. What is an *object* in Microsoft Access? Provide examples.

5. What is the procedure for deleting a record in Datasheet view?

6. What is the procedure for adding a record in Datasheet view?

7. How do you close a Database window?

8. In Microsoft Access, what is a datasheet and when would you use it?

9. In Microsoft Access, what is a form and when would you use it?

10. In Microsoft Access, what is a query and when would you use it?

HANDS-ON

(*Note:* Ensure that you know the storage location of your Advantage Files and your Data Files before proceeding.)

1. In this exercise, you practice using the Help system in Microsoft Access.

  a. Ensure that Microsoft Access is loaded. If the startup dialog box appears, remove it from the screen.

  b. CHOOSE: Help, Contents and Index

  c. In the Help Topics window, search for information on "opening databases."

  d. Display information on converting a database from Access 95 to Access 97.

  e. Print the topic.

  f. In the Help Topics window, search for information on keyboard shortcuts.

  g. Display Help information on using shortcuts keys to navigate in Datasheet view.

  h. Print the topic.

  i. Close the Help window.

2. In this exercise, you will open an existing database from the Advantage Files location and practice moving around a table.

  a. Open the "Wedding" database.

  b. Open the Guest List table.

  c. Maximize the Guest List table.

d. Move to the last record in the table.

e. Move to the first record in the table.

f. Move to the second record.

g. Move to the last field in the second record.

h. Move to the first field in the second record.

i. Restore the datasheet to a window.

j. Close the datasheet window using the Close button ([✕]).

3. In this exercise, you will practice formatting and making editing changes to the "Wedding" database.

a. Ensure that the "Wedding" Database window appears.

b. Open the Guest List table.

c. Size the datasheet window to fill the work area by dragging the sizing corner and the window's Title bar.

d. Apply a display font of Times New Roman, 12-point, and Maroon in color.

e. Remove the horizontal and vertical gridlines from the datasheet. Your window should now appear similar to Figure 1.14.

FIGURE 1.14

FORMATTING THE "WEDDING" DATASHEET

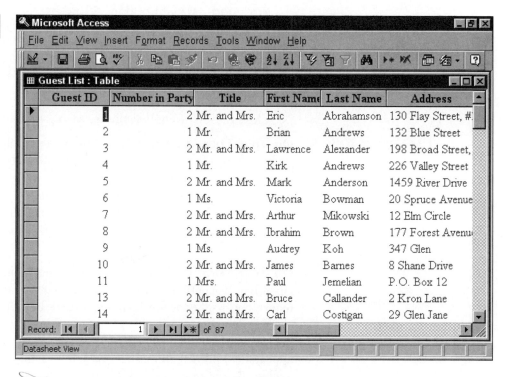

f. Re-apply a display font of Arial, Regular, 10-point, and Black in color.

g. Turn on the horizontal and vertical gridlines.

h. Select the entire First Name field for Mark Anderson.

i. Change Mark's name to Robert.

j. PRESS: (SHIFT) + (ENTER) to save the record

4. In this exercise, you will practice deleting and adding a record.

a. Ensure that the "Wedding" Database window appears and that the Guest List table is open.

b. Move the cursor downwards in the table until you see Mr. and Mrs. James Barnes' record.

c. Select the entire record using the mouse pointer and the record selection area.

d. Delete Mr. and Mrs. James Barnes' record permanently.

e. Add a new record to the datasheet.

f. PRESS: (ENTER) where it says (AutoNumber)

TYPE: **2** for the number in the party

Notice that the AutoNumber field automatically increments to 130.

g. Enter the following information for the Sigalets, who have requested to be seated on the Groom's side and have already accepted the invitation:

Mr. and Mrs. Gordon Sigalet
999 Mockingbird Lane
Smith Falls, CA 94110

h. PRESS: (SHIFT) + (ENTER) to save the record

i. Move to the top of the datasheet.

j. Close the "Wedding" database, saving the layout changes.

5. **On Your Own:** Explore a Microsoft Access Help Topic
Pick a Microsoft Access Help topic that interests you and write about it in a few paragraphs. Make sure to explain why you chose the topic and how to perform the procedures described. For example, you may be interested in learning how to retrieve help from Microsoft's site on the World Wide Web or how to customize the Office Assistant. Use the Access Help system for researching your topic.

6. **On Your Own:** Customizing Your Datasheet View
Open the "School" database stored in your Advantage Files location. Customize the display of the Instructors table by trying various font typefaces, sizes, styles, and colors. Then, use the Format, Cells command to change the display of the datasheet background. Once you are satisfied with its appearance, print the datasheet by clicking the Print button () on the toolbar. Before proceeding, ensure that you change the settings back to the standard font and background, and then close the database.

CASE PROBLEMS   **THE EXPERT HANDYMAN, INC.**

(*Note:* In the following case problems, assume the role of the primary characters and perform the same steps that they identify. You may want to re-read the session opening.)

1. Isabel has been working at SCSS for three days now and is very happy so far. She especially likes her co-workers, Jack, Alicia, and Raymond, and feels comfortable with the types of tasks she is performing, such as writing letters and answering the phone. Although Max Weingold intimidates her a little bit, she notices that he treats everyone in the office with the same manner and tone.

    Midway through the morning, Isabel receives a phone call from an excited instructor. "Hello Isabel? My name is Consuelo Agueda and I teach the tax courses for SCSS. Due to a family emergency, I can't make my TX101 course tomorrow. It's only a one-day course, and it is offered again in two weeks. Perhaps you can ask the students to transfer into that section. Sorry, I've got to run."

    Isabel has to put her newly acquired Microsoft Access knowledge to work right away. She loads the "Springs" database and then opens the Instructors table to view the courses that Consuelo teaches for SCSS. Isabel confirms that Consuelo does teach the TX101 course and then closes the Instructors table. Next, she opens the Students table and moves the cursor to each record that has "TX101" in the Course field. She writes down the phone number for each student so that she can call them later to inform them that the course is canceled. In total, she collects three phone numbers. Having completed her first task using Access, Isabel closes the Students table.

2. Marcel Rafat, one of the students in the original TX101 course, calls later that day thanking Isabel for the cancellation message. Unfortunately, he cannot take the TX101 course that is being held in two weeks. After apologizing to Marcel, Isabel hangs up the phone and displays the Students table once again. After selecting Marcel Rafat's record, she deletes it from the table, closes the Students table and the "Springs" database, and then minimizes Microsoft Access.

3. Not long after closing the "Springs" database, she receives a call from another student, named Jonathan Hull, who is interested in changing the SCSS course for which he is already registered. Isabel opens the "Springs" database and then the Students table. After finding Jonathan's record, Isabel learns that he wants to take C100 instead of C150. However, he only wants to take the course if Dominick Soldano is the instructor. Isabel asks Jonathan to hold the line while she finds out who is instructing the C100 course.

    Isabel minimizes the Students table and opens the Instructors table. After scanning the list of records, she sees that Dominick Soldano is indeed teaching the C100 course and then closes the Instructors table. She communicates the news to a grateful Jonathan and proceeds to modify his record in the Students table that she has just restored. When finished, she closes the table and the "Springs" database, and then exits Microsoft Access.

Microsoft Access 97 for Windows

Working with Tables

SESSION

2

IRWIN
COMPUTER & INFORMATION TECHNOLOGY

SESSION OUTLINE

INTRODUCTION

Not too long ago, computerized databases were created and maintained by computer scientists and were only found in large organizations and government agencies. With the advent of database management software for microcomputers, even novice computer users can now manage vast amounts of information on their home computers. Microsoft Access, for example, allows you to perform complex database procedures with only a few mouse clicks. This session shows you how to create, modify, and customize data tables, the most important objects in an Access database.

LAKELAND GYM

Although conveniently located in the downtown core of St. Paul, Minnesota, few people visit Lakeland Gym outside of the morning and evening peak hours. But thanks to a recent marketing campaign, Lakeland Gym's membership is finally on the rise. The manager, Peter Iverrson, has instituted a special midday rate to attract business people to the club during their lunch hour. So far the idea is working well, with over 55 new members joining at the "Midday Special" rate of $59.99 per month. As a "Midday Special" member, you get unlimited access to the club's facilities between the hours of 11:00 AM and 2:00 PM.

Josephine Kendall, Peter's assistant, currently uses a word processing application to keep track of the membership—including each member's name, address, and phone number—but believes that a dedicated database application, such as Microsoft Access, would help her manage the data more efficiently. For starters, she finds it tedious to type in data for each new member. She also finds it difficult to find and display a member's record once it has been created. In the future, Josephine wants to use the advanced reporting features found in database applications like Access. After presenting her case to Peter, they both agree that she should create a new database to manage Lakeland Gym's membership data. But there's just one small hitch—Josephine doesn't know how to create an Access database from scratch.

In this session, you and Josephine learn how to create a new database. Specifically, you will design and create a data table, work with indexes, add records to a table, modify a table's structure, and then print a datasheet.

DESIGNING A DATABASE

Many people who have worked with databases can attest to the "90/10 rule" of database design. It reads something like this: Spend 90 percent of your time designing a database properly in order to spend only 10 percent of your time maintaining it. As you can probably infer from this rule, many problems arising in database management are traceable to a faulty database design. This section provides tips for designing a database.

1. *Determine your output requirements.* State your expectations of the database in terms of the queries and reports desired from the system.

2. *Design your database application on paper.* Transfer your database concept onto paper to prove that you understand the design. This step also ensures that you have a working document for future reference.

3. *Divide information into separate fields.* Determine what to include in the database and then divide the information into separate fields for flexibility in searching, sorting, and manipulating the data.

4. *Divide information into separate data tables.* Avoid occurrences where the same information is typed into the same fields in different records. Instead, try to divide redundant information into separate tables, in a process called normalizing, and then establish relationships amongst them for sharing information on forms and reports. Access 97 provides the Table Analyzer Wizard to help you in this process.

5. *Identify each record with a unique code.* You should always have a unique code or field that identifies a particular record, especially when attempting to establish relationships between tables. This code does not need to contain information related to the subject or record—a numeric field that is automatically incremented works fine.

6. *Place the most important fields at the top of the table structure.* Because of the way databases are stored, you should place the most important fields at the top of a table structure to improve performance. Important fields are ones you use in sorting and querying the table.

7. *Test your database.* Add several records to the table and then produce a few queries and reports to see whether the data is easily accessible.

CREATING A DATABASE

Microsoft Access makes it easy to get started creating and using a database. In this section, we describe some of the tools provided in Access that help you create new databases and tables. To fully appreciate the following discussion, make sure that you understand the difference between a *database* and a *table.* A table is a single object within a database; its primary function is to store information. A database exists on a much grander scale and often consists of many objects, including tables, queries, forms, and reports.

After the planning process, you have two options for implementing a database using Access. First, you can create a blank database and then populate it with the required objects. For example, in an inventory control system, you could create a blank database and then add tables for Products, Suppliers, Tax Codes, and Customers. Once completed, you must then create the data entry forms, product catalogs, costing sheets, and other reports, not to mention any other objects that you need to make the database system useful for your business. A second option for implementing a database is to use the **Database Wizard.** This wizard provides over 20 different designs for business and personal database applications, complete with tables, queries, forms, reports, and a main menu or switchboard to make accessing the database easier.

It is not necessary to understand all the ins and outs of using the Database Wizard. It is important, however, to know that there are several professionally designed databases already available and easily accessible. Some of these database templates are shown in Figure 2.1. You can access this dialog box by selecting the *Database Wizard* option button in the startup dialog box and then clicking the OK command button. If you are already working in Access, choose the File, New Database command or click the New Database button () on the toolbar. Once the dialog box appears, you click the *Databases* tab to see the wizard's templates.

FIGURE 2.1

DATABASE DESIGN
TEMPLATES

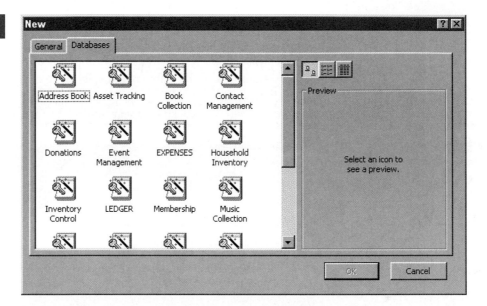

In this section, you create a new database based on a template provided by the Database Wizard.

Perform the following steps . . .

1. Make sure that you've loaded Microsoft Access. If the startup dialog box appears, click the Cancel command button to display an empty application window. If you already have a Database window open, close the database before proceeding.

2. To create a new database using the Database Wizard:
   CHOOSE: File, New Database
   CLICK: *Databases* tab in the New dialog box
   Your screen should now appear similar to Figure 2.1. (*Note:* If you haven't installed any database design templates, you will not be able to perform the steps in this section.)

3. Let's create an Inventory Control system:
   DOUBLE-CLICK: Inventory Control template icon ()

4. In the File New Database dialog box that appears, you must now specify a location to save the file. The file may be too large (over 600KB) to store onto an existing data diskette. Therefore, you should store it on your hard disk or in a network folder:
CLICK: down arrow beside the *Save in* drop-down list box
SELECT: desired location on your hard disk
CLICK: Create command button
(*Note:* In this step, you accept the default filename as "Inventory Control1" and direct the database file to be stored on the hard disk. If your disk does not have enough free disk space, the wizard displays an error message and will not create the database properly.)

5. The first dialog box of the wizard appears with a description of the Inventory Control system. After reading its contents, do the following:
CLICK: Next >
Your screen should now appear similar to Figure 2.2.

FIGURE 2.2

INVENTORY CONTROL
DATABASE WIZARD

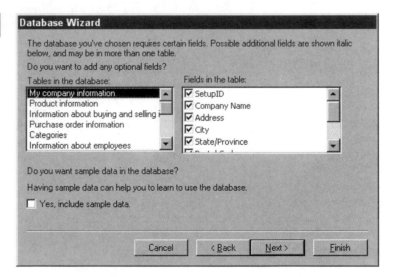

6. In this step, you specify the fields that you want included in each table. You can also choose to have the wizard add some preliminary data to the database. For practice, let's add the sample data:
CLICK: *Yes, include sample data* check box so that a "✓" appears
CLICK: Next >

7. In this step, you specify the desired screen appearance for the database.
CLICK: each option in the list box to see its preview
SELECT: Colorful 2
CLICK: Next >

8. In this step, you specify the desired style for your printed reports.
CLICK: each option in the list box to see its preview
SELECT: Bold
CLICK: Next >

9. You now have the opportunity to name your database and to select a corporate logo or other picture to print on your reports. Accept the default name of "Inventory Control" and then proceed to the next step:
CLICK: Next >

10. In the final step of the Database Wizard, ensure that the *Yes, start the database* check box is selected and then do the following:
CLICK: Finish
The wizard creates the database from your selections in the previous five dialog boxes and then launches the database system for your review. Depending on the speed of your computer and disk drive, this process can take several minutes. Once displayed, your screen should appear similar to Figure 2.3.

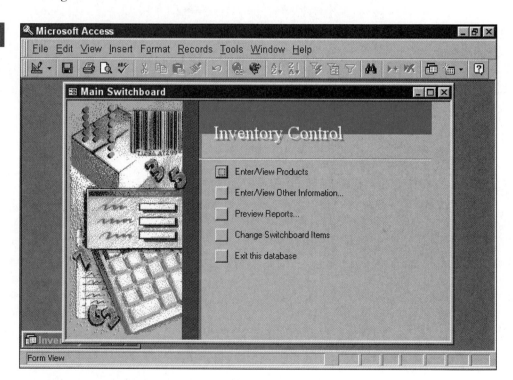

FIGURE 2.3

COMPLETED INVENTORY CONTROL DATABASE SYSTEM

11. Every database system created using the Database Wizard provides a switchboard or form object that acts as a main menu. Let's take this new database system for a spin:
CLICK: *Enter/View Products* button on the switchboard
A new window appears displaying details for the first product. Notice at the bottom of this window that the table has five records of sample data. You can scroll through these records using the navigation buttons.

12. To close the product information window:
CLICK: its Close button ([X])
You are immediately returned to the main switchboard.

13. To preview a report generated in real-time from the database system:
CLICK: *Preview Reports...* button to display a sub-menu
CLICK: *Preview the Product Summary Report* button
A Preview window appears showing the Product Summary Report. You will learn how to use the Preview window later in this session.

14. To close the Preview window and then return to the main switchboard:
CLICK: its Close button (☒)
CLICK: *Return to Main Switchboard* button

15. To exit the Inventory Control database system:
CLICK: *Exit this database* button

QUICK REFERENCE Using the Database Wizard Templates	**1.** CHOOSE: File, New Database, or CLICK: New Database button (▢) **2.** CLICK: *Databases* tab **3.** DOUBLE-CLICK: a database template icon (⬚) **4.** Respond to the wizard's questions.

CREATING A TABLE

If all of your database needs are satisfied by the templates found in the Database Wizard, you can stop working through this guide and start exploring the templates on your own. To unlock the real power behind Access, however, you must read and study the methods presented in this section for creating tables from scratch. Because most of us have specific objectives and requirements for our database applications, it is often quicker to create a blank database and then add the appropriate objects than it is to edit objects that have been created by the Database Wizard.

When you first load Microsoft Access, you create a blank database by selecting the *Blank Database* option button in the startup dialog box and then clicking the OK command button. If you are already working in Access, choose the File, New Database command or click the New Database button (▢) on the toolbar. In the New dialog box that appears, click the *General* tab and then double-click the Blank Database template icon (⬚). You must then specify the database's name and storage location in the File New Database dialog box. When you click the Create command button, Access creates and saves the database file and then presents its Database window.

Once you have created a blank database, you are presented with a clean slate in the Database window and an almost eerie silence from Access. No dialog boxes or wizards appear to tell you what your next move should be. Although intimidating at first, this silence indicates the unrestricted freedom you possess for creating new database objects. Most commonly, you begin by creating tables to store information.

There are three primary methods for creating tables in Access, as described below:

- *Using the Table Wizard*

  You create a table structure using this wizard much like you created a complete application using the Database Wizard. Rather than creating a new table from scratch, you compile it by picking and choosing fields from existing business and personal table structures. This method lets you quickly populate an empty Database window with reliable and usable table objects.

- *Using Datasheet View*

  You create a table by typing information into a blank datasheet, just as you would in creating a worksheet in Excel. When you save the table, Access creates the structure and assigns the proper data types to each field based on the information you've entered. This method lets novice users create tables without an in-depth understanding of table structures and data types.

- *Using Design View*

  Get down to the nuts and bolts of creating a table using the Design view. In table Design view, you create the table structure manually, specifying the field names, data types, and indexes. This method requires the greatest understanding of database design and how Access stores data.

Now let's create a database for MediaSport Incorporated, a fictional company based in Chicago that sells personalized sporting items to companies throughout North America. MediaSport's primary business involves printing corporate logos on sporting items such as baseball hats and football jerseys. These items are typically distributed by MediaSport's customers to their clients, employees, and other business associates.

Perform the following steps . . .

1. Ensure that Microsoft Access is loaded and that no Database window appears in the work area.

2. To create a new database for MediaSport.:
   CLICK: New Database button (⬛) on the Database toolbar
   CLICK: *General* tab in the New dialog box
   DOUBLE-CLICK: Blank Database template icon (🔑)

3. In the File New Database dialog box that appears:
TYPE: **MediaSport** in the *File name* text box, replacing "db1"
CLICK: down arrow beside the *Save in* drop-down list box
SELECT: *your Data Files location*
CLICK: Create command button
After a few moments, you are presented with an empty Database window
with "MediaSport: Database" appearing in its Title bar, as shown in
Figure 2.4.

FIGURE 2.4

THE "MEDIASPORT"
DATABASE WINDOW

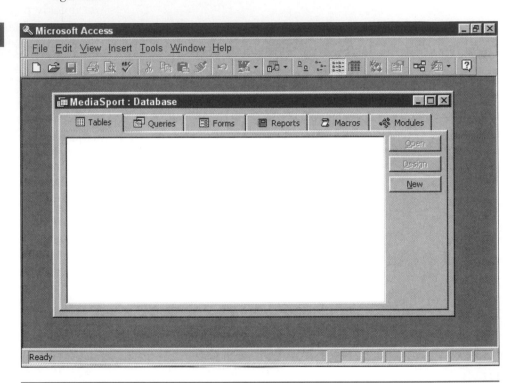

Because tables are the foundation for all your queries, forms, and reports, you need
to create at least one table before creating any other database object. In the next
section, you design the structure for a table that will store information on each of
MediaSport's customers.

QUICK REFERENCE
Creating a New Database

1. **CHOOSE: File, New Database, or**
   CLICK: New Database button (▯)
2. **CLICK:** *General* **tab**
3. **DOUBLE-CLICK: Blank Database template icon (⬚)**
4. **Type a name for the database and select its storage location.**
5. **CLICK: Create command button**

CREATING A TABLE STRUCTURE

You create a new table for a database by defining its structure using one of the three methods described in the previous section. To begin, click the *Tables* tab in the Database window and then click the New command button. The New Table dialog box appears as shown in Figure 2.5. From this dialog box, you select a method to use in creating the table: Datasheet View, Design View, or Table Wizard. Importing and linking tables is covered at the end of this session.

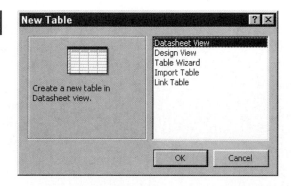

FIGURE 2.5

NEW TABLE DIALOG BOX

You will now create a new table structure named "Customer."

Perform the following steps . . .

1. Ensure that the "MediaSport" Database window appears on the screen. Do the following to create a new table:
   CLICK: *Tables* tab
   CLICK: New command button
   The New Table dialog box appears as shown in Figure 2.5.

2. Before showing you how to use the Table Wizard and Datasheet View methods, let's create a table from scratch using table Design view. After completing this section, you will understand the various data types and terminology necessary to take full advantage of the other methods. To begin:
   DOUBLE-CLICK: Design View
   The Table window appears in **Design view,** as shown in Figure 2.6. You use this grid-like view to define or modify Access database objects; the Design view screen will look different depending on the object you are designing (e.g., table, form, or report). In table Design view, you can add, delete, and rename fields; set a field's data type; specify a field's properties or characteristics; and choose a primary key for organizing and sorting a database.

FIGURE 2.6

DEFINING A TABLE'S
STRUCTURE IN TABLE
DESIGN VIEW

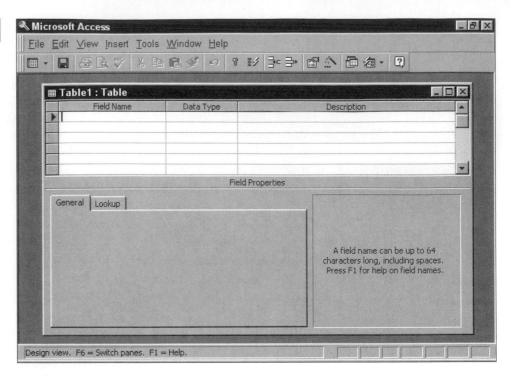

3. Using the grid, you enter a unique name for each field in the table. Field names must start with a letter and, like all database objects, can include letters, numbers, spaces, and punctuation. With the insertion point in the *Field Name* column:

   TYPE: **Company ID**

   PRESS: TAB to move to the *Data Type* column

   By default, Access inserts Text as the data type for the Company ID field. You may also notice that entries in the Field Properties portion of the dialog box now appear for the Company ID field. Notice that Access has set the *Field Size* property to 50 characters. Because Access stores only the data you enter into the field, it's fine to leave the width at 50 even if you require only a few characters. (*Note:* We describe the Field Properties tabs, *General* and *Lookup*, in more detail later when you modify the database structure.)

4. Even though you won't change the data type for the Company ID field, let's view the options available in the drop-down list.

   CLICK: down arrow beside the *Data Type* field

   Your screen should now appear similar to Figure 2.7.

FIGURE 2.7

DATA TYPES DROP-DOWN
LIST BOX

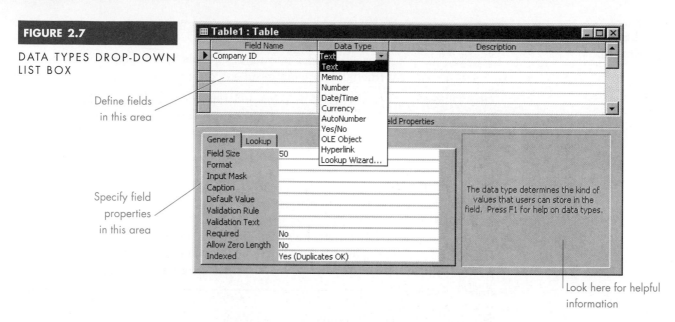

Define fields
in this area

Specify field
properties
in this area

Look here for helpful
information

Now is the perfect time to summarize the available data types, described in Table 2.1. In this exercise, every field that you will enter uses the Text data type, including the phone number and fax number fields. But that may not always be the case. When creating table structures, it is important that you choose the correct data type before adding records. The data type you select determines the kind of values you can enter. You can change the data type after you've entered data; however, if the data types aren't compatible, you may lose some data.

TABLE 2.1	*Type*	*For Storing What Information*
Data Types	Text	Store up to 255 characters of alphanumeric data, including letters, numbers, spaces, and punctuation. Use this data type when the data doesn't need to be used for calculations.
	Memo	Store up to 64,000 characters of alphanumeric data. Use this data type when you need to type several sentences or paragraphs.
	Number	Numeric data that can be used in calculations.
	Date/Time	Dates and times.
	Currency	Numeric data with a leading dollar sign. Use this data type for currency values such as dollars, francs, or yen. (*Note:* This data type also works well for storing numbers with less than four decimal places.)
	AutoNumber	A numeric value that Access automatically increments by 1 for each record you add to a table.

TABLE 2.1
Continued

Type	For Storing What Information
Yes/No	Logical or Boolean values. Use this field to store yes/no, true/false, or on/off results.
OLE Object	OLE (Object Linking and Embedding) objects, graphics, or other binary data. Field capacity is up to one gigabyte (GB) or limited by available disk space.
Hyperlink	Text or numbers stored as a hyperlink address, such as a Uniform Resource Locator (URL) or a Universal Naming Convention (UNC) network path name.
Lookup Wizard	When the value that you need exists in another table or in a list of static values, you use the Lookup Wizard to help you establish a link to the table or to define the combo box that will display the list of values on a form or report.

5. Let's view the field properties available for the Number data type:
   SELECT: Number
   Notice that "Number" is now displaying in the *Data Type* column. The field properties have also changed, as they will for each data type you select.

6. To change the data type back to Text:
   CLICK: down arrow beside the *Data Type* field
   SELECT: Text

7. Although optional, you should enter a short description of the field. This description will display on the status line when you select the field in a form. To enter a description:
   PRESS: TAB
   TYPE: Unique identification code based on the company name

8. To define a second field in the table:
   PRESS: TAB

9. Immediately below the Company ID field, add the fields shown in Figure 2.8 to the table. The grid portion of the Table window should appear similar to Figure 2.8 before proceeding.

FIGURE 2.8

COMPLETED TABLE
DESIGN VIEW GRID

Field Name	Data Type	Description
Company ID	Text	Unique identification code based on the company name
Company Name	Text	
Company Contact	Text	Contact person at the customer's location
Sales Representative ID	Text	Unique four-letter code based on the sales rep's name
Address	Text	
City	Text	
State	Text	
Zip	Text	
Phone	Text	Direct phone line of contact person
Fax	Text	Direct fax line of contact person

<table>
<tr><td>QUICK REFERENCE
Defining a New Table
Structure Using Design View</td><td>1. **CLICK:** *Tables* tab in the Database window
2. **CLICK: New command button**
3. **DOUBLE-CLICK: Design View**
4. **Enter the field names in the *Field Name* column**
5. **Select data types in the *Data Type* column**
6. **Enter optional descriptions in the *Description* column**</td></tr>
</table>

IN ADDITION USING THE HYPERLINK DATA TYPE

Use an Access table to store addresses (URLs) for accessing Internet sites based on the HTTP and FTP protocols. Once you've defined a field as a Hyperlink data type, you can enter three pieces of information in the following format: *displaytext#address#subaddress*. You can also use the Insert, Hyperlink command, rather than typing the information directly.

For example, to place Microsoft's web site into a Hyperlink field:

TYPE: `Microsoft's Site#http://www.microsoft.com#`

With the proper connection, you can now access Microsoft's web site by clicking the blue-underlined display text that appears in the field.

SETTING A PRIMARY KEY

Before saving the new table, you should specify a **primary key,** which is a field that uniquely identifies each record in the table. A primary key is used by Access for searching and finding data stored in tables and for defining relationships between tables. Once a field is defined as the primary key for a table, its datasheet is automatically indexed (as illustrated in the tables below), or sorted, into order by that field.

Natural Order (as entered)

ID	Name	Age
1	Harry	84
2	Maria	56
3	Charles	32
4	Jenna	45

Indexed by Name

ID	**Name**	Age
3	**Charles**	32
4	**Jenna**	45
1	**Harry**	84
2	**Maria**	56

Indexed by Age

ID	Name	**Age**
3	Charles	**32**
4	Jenna	**45**
2	Maria	**56**
1	Harry	**84**

Keep the following in mind when working with primary keys:

- The primary key is the main index for the data table and determines the order in which data is displayed in the datasheet.

- Two records cannot have the same data in the primary key field. You must either remove the duplicate values, define a different primary key, or include an additional field in the primary key.

- There are three types of primary keys: AutoNumber, single-field, and multiple-field. The AutoNumber primary key is the easiest to maintain since Access takes care of it for you. A single-field key uses data from only one field, while a multiple-field key is based on data from a combination of fields.

- If you don't specify a primary key, Access will define one for you by creating an ID field that contains the AutoNumber data type. This simple primary key works fine for most tasks.

To set a primary key, select the field you want to sort by and then click the Primary Key button (🔑) on the toolbar or choose the Edit, Primary Key command. To set a multiple-field primary key, you select multiple rows by holding down the (CTRL) key and clicking in the row selection area to the left of each field name and then click the Primary Key button (🔑).

You will now create a primary key for the table.

Perform the following steps . . .

1. To define the Company ID field as the primary key field:
SELECT: Company ID field by clicking in the row selection area to the left of the field name (similar to selecting a record in Datasheet view)
CLICK: Primary Key button (🔑)
A key image should now appear to the left of the Company ID field name. Also, you may notice in the Field Properties area that "Yes (No Duplicates)" is displaying opposite the Indexed option; this tells you that duplicate field data are not allowed in this primary key field. In other words, two customers cannot have the same Company ID.

2. Now that you've defined the structure and have set a primary key, you must save the table as part of the "MediaSport" database.
CLICK: Save button (🖫)
TYPE: **Customer**
PRESS: (**ENTER**) or CLICK: OK

3. To close the Table window and display the Database window:
CLICK: Close button (☒) on the Table window

QUICK REFERENCE	**1.**	**SELECT: the desired field by clicking in the row selection area**
Setting a Primary Key	**2.**	**CLICK: Primary Key button (🔑) on the toolbar, or**
		CHOOSE: Edit, Primary Key from the menu

DEFINING AND REMOVING INDEXES

Access lets you create indexes that are used in addition to a primary key. An **index,** like the primary key, is stored with the table and contains pointers that determine the display order of records. If you want to display records in an order that isn't based on the primary key field, you need to first create an index. When you add records to a table that has a primary key and associated indexes, the primary key and indexes are automatically updated. For this reason, many indexes can slow down data entry.

In this section, you create a new index for the Customer table and then practice deleting indexes.

 **Perform the following steps . . .**

1. Ensure that the "MediaSport" Database window appears. To create an index, display the Customer table structure in Design view.
SELECT: Customer table name (it should already be selected)
CLICK: Design command button
The Customer table structure appears in the Table window.

2. Let's assume that you want to sort the database by the contents of the City field. To create an index for this field:
SELECT: City field by clicking in the row selection area

3. You will now specify an option in the Field Properties area to create a new index. Do the following:
CLICK: *Indexed* text box once to position the cursor
CLICK: down arrow beside the *Indexed* text box
The indexing options in Table 2.2 appear. (*Note:* You will learn more about Field Properties later in this session.)

TABLE 2.2

Indexing Options

Indexed Property Setting	Description
No	Do not create an index on this field. You can also use this option to delete an index.
Yes (Duplicates OK)	Create an index on this field; fields can contain the same data. For example, a City field should be indexed using this option since more than one record will likely pertain to the same city.
Yes (No Duplicates)	Create an index on this field; like primary key fields, no two fields can contain the same data. For example, you may want a Part Numbers field to be indexed with this option, since no two part numbers are the same.

4. CLICK: Yes (Duplicates OK)

5. To view the indexes you have defined so far:
CLICK: Indexes button (⟨🗎⟩)
A window appears displaying a list of the current indexes, as shown in Figure 2.9. Notice that there are two additional indexes appearing besides the Primary Key entry and the City index that you just defined. Access automatically creates indexes for fields that contain the letters "ID" in their names. For example, Access proceeded to define indexes for the Company ID field and the Sales Representative ID field. You learn how to delete these additional indexes in the next step.

FIGURE 2.9

THE INDEXES WINDOW

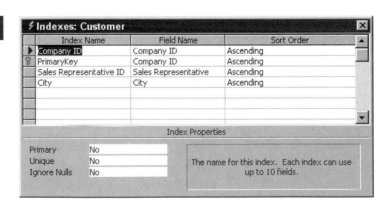

6. To delete the Company ID index in the Indexes window:
RIGHT-CLICK: the row selection area for the Company ID field
CHOOSE: Delete Rows from the pop-up menu
(*Note:* You can also remove an index by setting its Indexed property to "No" in the Field Properties box.)

7. To delete the Sales Representative ID index:
RIGHT-CLICK: the row selection area for the Sales Representative ID field
CHOOSE: Delete Rows from the pop-up menu

8. To close the Indexes window:
   CLICK: Close button (☒) on the Indexes window

9. To close the Table window and save your changes:
   CLICK: Close button (☒) on the Table window
   CLICK: Yes command button
   You should now see the Database window.

QUICK REFERENCE
Defining an Index in
Design View

1. **SELECT: the field you want to use as an index**
2. **SELECT:** *Indexed* **text box in the Field Properties area**
3. **CLICK: down arrow now appearing beside the** *Indexed* **text box**
4. **SELECT: an indexing option**

QUICK REFERENCE
Removing an Index in
Design View

1. **CLICK: Indexes button (▦) on the toolbar**
2. **RIGHT-CLICK: row selection area for the index you want to delete**
3. **CHOOSE: Delete Rows**

ADDING RECORDS

Now that you've learned to design the structure for a table, you will put the table to work storing information. One of the easier methods for adding records to a table is using the table's datasheet. After populating the table with a few records, you will then learn how to create a form.

Let's use the Customer table for practicing these skills.

Perform the following steps . . .

1. Ensure that the Database window appears for the "MediaSport" database and that the *Tables* tab is selected.

2. To display the datasheet for the Customer table:
   DOUBLE-CLICK: Customer
   The Customer datasheet appears on the screen. The cursor is positioned in the Company ID field and the field description (that you typed when creating the table structure) is displayed in the Status bar.

3. Don't worry if some data is too wide to display in the column; you will learn how to widen the columns later in this session. For now, let the text scroll in the field window as you type. Do the following:
   TYPE: ROSI
   PRESS: TAB
   (*Note:* The code "ROSI" is derived from the first four letters of the company name, which you will type in next.) The cursor should now be positioned in the Company Name field.

4. Enter the remaining information for the record:
TYPE: **Rosie's Cookie Company**
PRESS: `TAB`
TYPE: **Jean Arston**
PRESS: `TAB`
TYPE: **VTRI**
PRESS: `TAB`
TYPE: **2200 Main Street**
PRESS: `TAB`
TYPE: **Bloomington**
PRESS: `TAB`
TYPE: **IN**
PRESS: `TAB`
TYPE: **47405**
PRESS: `TAB`
TYPE: **812-936-7750**
PRESS: `TAB`
TYPE: **812-936-5591**

5. To move to the next record in the datasheet:
PRESS: `TAB`
The cursor should move to the first field in the second record. When the cursor left the first record, it was automatically saved onto the disk. You don't need to do anything else to save the data. Also, while entering a record, Access places the pencil indicator symbol (🖉) to the left of the record you're working on. The pencil is displayed when you've made changes to the current record, but haven't yet saved the changes. If the cursor is in a record that hasn't been changed, the record indicator looks like a right-pointing triangle (▶). Once you start entering a new record, an asterisk (✳) will display one record below, marking the empty record at the bottom of the table.

6. Use the following information to enter data for the next two records:

Record 2	*Record 3*
ABCM	SILV
ABC Metals	Silver Spring Toyota
Frances Hillman	Steve Yap
PVIE	RHEU
550 Montgomery Street	Box 1440
Minneapolis	Silver Spring
MN	WA
55402	98004
612-330-9780	206-462-8002
612-330-9781	206-462-8119

7. After data has been entered into a table, you can easily modify a field's information using the techniques described in Session 1. You can also view fields that aren't currently in view by clicking the scroll arrows and by dragging the scroll box back and forth on the horizontal scroll bar. On your own, practice using the scroll arrows and scroll box to move around the datasheet. Then, try some of the datasheet editing techniques listed in Table 2.3.

TABLE 2.3	*Procedure*	*Description*
Datasheet Editing Techniques	`TAB`	Moves to the next field in a record; when the cursor is positioned on the last field, `TAB` moves to the next record.
	`SHIFT` + `TAB`	Moves to the previous field in a record.
	`HOME`, `END`	Moves to first or last field in a record. In Edit mode, these keys move the insertion point to the first and last characters in a field, respectively.
	`F2`	Enters and exits Edit mode for the current field.
	`ESC`	Lets you undo changes you've made to the current field or record.
	`CTRL` + "	Replaces the value in a field with the value of the same field in the previous record.

8. You may have noticed that the records aren't displaying in the primary key order by Company ID. You must first leave the datasheet and then return to view them in keyed order. To illustrate, let's move to Design view and then back to Datasheet view:
   CLICK: View button ( )
   CLICK: View button ( )
   Notice that the icon displayed on the View button changes depending on the currently selected view mode. You can also click the down arrow to the right of this button to display a list of all the available views. As for the datasheet, the records are now displayed in keyed order, sorted by the Company ID, as shown in Figure 2.10.

9. To close the datasheet for the Customer table:
   CLICK: Close button (**X**)
   CLICK: Yes, if asked to save the changes to the layout of the datasheet

FIGURE 2.10

THE CUSTOMER
DATASHEET DISPLAYED IN
SORTED ORDER

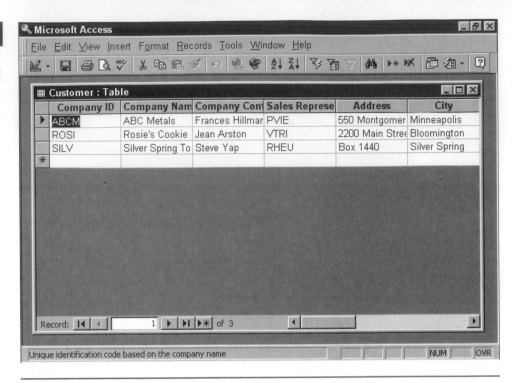

QUICK REFERENCE
Switching Between
Datasheet View and
Design View

When working with a table, you click the View button on the toolbar to switch between the available view modes. The icon displayed on the View button determines the default selection. For example, clicking this View button (☑ ▾) switches to Design view, while clicking this View button (▦ ▾) switches to Datasheet view.

CREATING A SIMPLE FORM

When you create a table, the data is automatically displayed in rows and columns using a datasheet. The advantage of working in the Datasheet view mode is that you can see more than one record and field on the screen at the same time. There may be times, however, when you would prefer to view a single record on the screen. In Access, this singular view of a record is accomplished using a **form.** Many people find it easier to focus on a single record using **Form view,** as opposed to Datasheet view.

USING THE AUTOFORM WIZARD

In this section, you learn to use the **AutoForm Wizard.** This wizard creates a form for you automatically and without asking you any questions! The form is displayed immediately and includes all the fields from the selected table. There is not an easier method for creating a form.

Perform the following steps . . .

1. Ensure that the Database window is displayed for the "MediaSport" database and that the *Tables* tab is selected.

2. To create a form using the AutoForm Wizard, you must first select the desired table from the Database window:
   SELECT: Customer
   (*CAUTION:* Make sure the table name is highlighted. Do not double-click the table name mistakenly.)

3. To create your first form object:
   CLICK: down arrow attached to the New Object button (☒▾)
   A drop-down list appears with options for creating new objects. Your screen should appear similar to Figure 2.11

FIGURE 2.11

NEW OBJECT BUTTON'S DROP-DOWN MENU

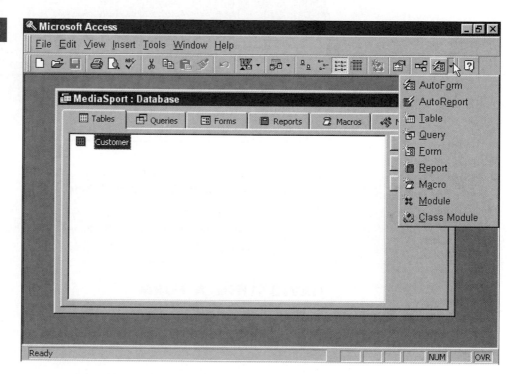

4. To access the AutoForm Wizard:
   CLICK: AutoForm from the New Object button's (☒▾) menu
   After a few moments, a new form appears in front of the Database window as shown in Figure 2.12

5. Before continuing, let's save the form specifications. Do the following:
   CLICK: Save button (🖫)
   TYPE: **Customer AutoForm**
   PRESS: **ENTER** or CLICK: OK

FIGURE 2.12

A NEW FORM CREATED
USING THE AUTOFORM
WIZARD

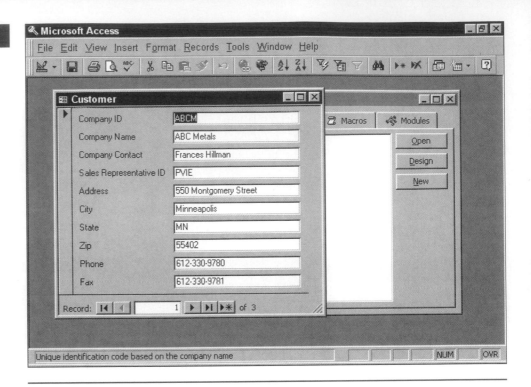

QUICK REFERENCE
Creating a Form Using the
AutoForm Wizard

1. **CLICK:** *Tables* tab in the Database window
2. **SELECT:** a table name
3. **CLICK:** down arrow attached to the New Object button (🖼️▾)
4. **CLICK:** AutoForm from the drop-down list

NAVIGATING A FORM

While displaying the form, you can move from record to record using the buttons
along the bottom of the Form window. Table 2.4 summarizes these buttons. The
methods for editing information in Form view are similar to editing in Datasheet
view.

TABLE 2.4

Form Window Buttons

Button	Description
◄◄	Displays the first record in the table
◄	Displays the previous record in the table
►	Displays the next record in the table
►►	Displays the last record in the table
►✳	Adds a record to the end of the table

In this exercise, you practice navigating within the form and adding records to the
table.

Perform the following steps . . .

1. To go to the last record in the database:
CLICK: ▶|

2. To move to the previous record:
CLICK: ◀

3. To add a new record to the database:
CLICK: ▶✳

4. Add the following information to your table using the Form. As you did when entering data using Datasheet view, press **TAB** to move to the next field in the current record. When the last field is reached on the form, the next record will be displayed when you press **TAB**.

Company ID	Company Name	Company Contact	Sales Rep ID	Address	City	State	Zip	Phone	Fax
BREW	Brewery Supplies, Inc.	Randy Brewski	PVIE	9999 River Forest Drive	Houston	TX	77079	713-649-6060	713-649-6061
COMP	Computers, Intl.	Cecilia Adams.	KCLI	7771 Shannon Square	Clackamas	OR	97015	503-990-2222	503-990-2221
DISC	Discount Glass	Moira Walsh	KAND	2222 50th Street	Northfield	IL	60093	708-256-3950	708-256-3951
FARM	Farming Equipment, Inc.	Bruce Towne	JAZA	14499 3rd Avenue	Walnut Grove	CA	95690	916-776-1332	913-776-1333
FLOW	Flowers Anywhere	Kela Henderson	JAZA	80 Rockford Square	Bushland	TX	79012	806-313-9651	806-313-9652
NATI	National Dentistry	Camilla Edsell	RHEU	101 6th Street, S.E.	Vancouver	BC	V6T 1Z1	604-774-0011	604-774-0012
PAPE	Paper Supplies, Etc.	Tessa Huberty	VTRI	111 Glen Vista	Ventura	CA	93003	805-912-3500	805-912-3512
PUBL	Publishing Etc.	Rich Williams	KAND	2000 Hilltop Way	Truckee	NV	89450	702-888-4590	702-888-4591
SCHU	Schuler and Co.	Presley Schuler, Jr.	KCLI	1000 Tower Plaza	Stockton	CA	95204	209-597-8616	209-597-8626

5. When you're finished typing in the Customer data, press **SHIFT** + **ENTER**. This keyboard shortcut ensures that the current record is saved before proceeding.

6. To display the data in a datasheet:
CLICK: |◀ to move to the first record
CLICK: down arrow attached to the View button (▨ ▾)
CHOOSE: Datasheet View
Notice that a bullet appears next to the currently selected option in the drop-down list.

7. To get a better view of the datasheet:
CLICK: Maximize button (□) on the Table window
Your screen should now appear similar to Figure 2.13.

FIGURE 2.13

A MAXIMIZED VIEW OF
THE CUSTOMER
DATASHEET

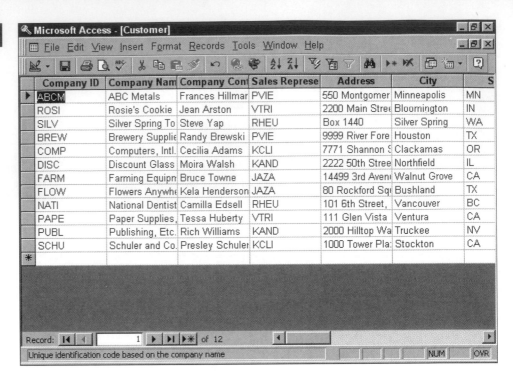

8. To display the data in a form:
   CLICK: down arrow attached to the View button ()
   CHOOSE: Form View

9. CLICK: Restore button () for the Form window

10. To close the current window so that only the Database window appears in
    the work area:
    CLICK: its Close button ()

11. To view the new form in the Database window:
    CLICK: *Forms* tab
    You should now see an object for "Customer AutoForm."

12. To return to the previous view:
    CLICK: *Tables* tab

In the next section, you learn to customize the Datasheet view by changing the
datasheet's column widths, row heights, and field order.

CUSTOMIZING THE DATASHEET VIEW

You have numerous options for customizing the appearance, or layout, of a datasheet. We've already introduced techniques in Session 1 for changing the display font and adding special effects to cells. Because a datasheet is only an image of the underlying table data, you can also manipulate the datasheet's column widths, row height, and field order without affecting the table structure itself. On the other hand, you can modify a table's structure by renaming a column's heading in the Datasheet view mode. Just remember to save your layout changes by clicking on the Save button (🖫) before closing a datasheet window.

ADJUSTING COLUMN WIDTHS

To change the width of a column in Datasheet view, you point to the column border between the field names at the top of the window, and then drag the border left or right to decrease and increase the width. To have Access calculate the best width for a column, try double-clicking the border line rather than dragging it. Access scans the column for the longest entry and then adjusts the column automatically. If you prefer using the menu, you can choose Format, Column Width and then type in the desired column width.

In this exercise, you practice changing column widths.

Perform the following steps . . .

1. Ensure that the Database window is displayed for the "MediaSport" database and that the *Tables* tab is selected.

2. To display the Customer datasheet:
   DOUBLE-CLICK: Customer

3. Let's maximize the window to see more of the datasheet:
   CLICK: Maximize button (🗖) on the Table window

4. Position the pointer between the Company Name and Company Contact field names. Notice that the mouse pointer changes to a vertical bar, crossed by a horizontal two-headed arrow (✛).

5. Drag the column border to the right until you can see all the text in the Company Name column.

6. To have Access calculate the best width for the Company Contact and Address columns, do the following:
   DOUBLE-CLICK: the border line between the Company Contact and Sales Representative ID column headings
   DOUBLE-CLICK: the border line between the Address and City column headings

7. You can also use the menu to widen a column. Position the cursor in any record of the Sales Representative ID field column.

8. CHOOSE: Format, Column Width

9. In the dialog box that appears:
TYPE: 10 into the *Column Width* text box
PRESS: [ENTER] or CLICK: OK
Notice that you can click the Best Fit command button in this dialog box rather than double-clicking the border lines between columns to have Access calculate the best width.

ADJUSTING ROW HEIGHTS

By default, the current display font that you've selected determines the row height for a datasheet. Row height is measured in **points,** which are typographical measurement units equal to 1/72 inch. To change the height of all rows in a datasheet, you point to any border between two rows in the record selection area, and then drag the border up or down. You can also choose the Format, Row Height command from the Menu bar and type in the desired height.

Let's practice changing the row height in the datasheet.

Perform the following steps . . .

1. To change the row height using the mouse, position the mouse pointer between any two rows in the record selection area. Notice that the pointer changes to a horizontal line crossed by a vertical two-headed arrow (⬍).When you change the height of a row using the mouse, all the rows in the datasheet are affected.

2. DRAG: the row border downwards slightly
When you release the mouse button, all rows are adjusted to the new row height.

3. To change the rows back to their standard height:
CHOOSE: Format, Row Height
SELECT: *Standard Height* check box so a "✓" appears
PRESS: [ENTER] or CLICK: OK

REORDERING FIELDS

In Datasheet view, field columns are displayed in the same order in which they appear in the table structure. For a different view of your data, you can reposition the columns in a datasheet. You move a column by selecting it using the mouse and then dragging it to its new location.

In this section, you will move the Company Contact field so that it displays before the Company Name field.

Perform the following steps . . .

1. To select the Company Contact column, point to the Company Contact field name. The mouse pointer becomes a downward-pointing arrow (↓). Click the left mouse button once to select the entire column.

2. To move the column to the left, click and drag the field name to the left, over the Company Name field. When the pointer is in the correct position, release the mouse button. The columns should be reordered as shown in Figure 2.14.

FIGURE 2.14

REORDERING FIELDS IN THE CUSTOMER DATASHEET

Microsoft Access - [Customer : Table]

File Edit View Insert Format Records Tools Window Help

Company ID	Company Contact	Company Name	Sales Re	Address	
ABCM	Frances Hillman	ABC Metals	PVIE	550 Montgomery Street	Minn
BREW	Randy Brewski	Brewery Supplies, Inc.	PVIE	9999 River Forest Drive	Hous
COMP	Cecilia Adams	Computers, Intl.	KCLI	7771 Shannon Square	Clacl
DISC	Moira Walsh	Discount Glass	KAND	2222 50th Street	North
FARM	Bruce Towne	Farming Equipment, Inc.	JAZA	14499 3rd Avenue	Walr
FLOW	Kela Henderson	Flowers Anywhere	JAZA	80 Rockford Square	Bush
NATI	Camilla Edsell	National Dentistry	RHEU	101 6th Street, S.E.	Vanc
PAPE	Tessa Huberty	Paper Supplies, Etc.	VTRI	111 Glen Vista	Vent
PUBL	Rich Williams	Publishing, Etc.	KAND	2000 Hilltop Way	Truck
ROSI	Jean Arston	Rosie's Cookie Company	VTRI	2200 Main Street	Bloo
SCHU	Presley Schuler, Jr.	Schuler and Co.	KCLI	1000 Tower Plaza	Stoc
SILV	Steve Yap	Silver Spring Toyota	RHEU	Box 1440	Silve

Record: 14 ◄ 1 ► ►I ►* of 12

Contact person at the customer's location   NUM   OVR

QUICK REFERENCE
Moving a Field

1. Select the column (field) that you want to move by pointing to the field name and then clicking once. The entire column will appear highlighted.

2. To move the column, drag the selected column by its field name to the desired location and then release the mouse button.

SAVING THE DATASHEET LAYOUT

After manipulating the Datasheet view to suit your needs, you can save your changes to the column widths, row height, font selection, and column ordering using the Save button (💾) or by choosing the File, Save command. Otherwise, all the changes that you made in the last few sections are temporary and Access will discard the settings when you close the window.

Perform the following steps . . .

1. To save the changes that you've made in the last few sections:
   CLICK: Save button (💾)

2. To close the datasheet:
   CLICK: its Close button (❌)
   The Database window will appear maximized.

QUICK REFERENCE
Saving the Datasheet Layout

1. **Ensure that the datasheet is active.**
2. **CLICK: Save button (💾), or**
   CHOOSE: File, Save

MODIFYING THE TABLE STRUCTURE

After working with a data table, you may find that you need an additional field or that one of the existing fields needs to be wider. Modifying a structure in Access is as simple as editing a table. After switching to table Design view, you can add fields, delete fields, and modify data types. However, you should not perform structural changes carelessly. When you modify a table's structure, you also affect the forms and reports that are based on the table.

INSERTING AND DELETING FIELDS

In the Database window, you select the table that you want to work with and then click the Design command button to display its structure in Design view. To insert or delete a row, position the mouse pointer in the desired location and then right-click the mouse to display a pop-up menu. From the menu, choose Insert Rows or Delete Rows to insert or delete a row in the table structure.

You will now practice modifying a table's structure.

Perform the following steps . . .

1. Ensure that the Database window is displayed for the "MediaSport" database and that the *Tables* tab is selected.

2. To modify the structure of the Customer table:
   SELECT: Customer
   CLICK: Design command button
   The Customer table appears in table Design view.

3. To insert a new field beneath the Company ID field, position the mouse pointer over the Company Name field (second row).

4. To insert a new field called "Company Size":
RIGHT-CLICK: Company Name in the *Field Name* column
CHOOSE: Insert Rows
Refer to Figure 2.15 for an example of the pop-up menu that appears.

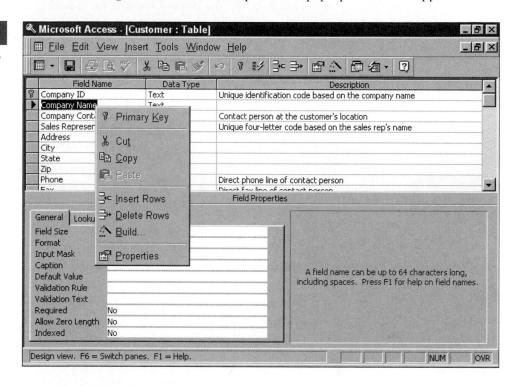

5. TYPE: **Company Size**
PRESS: **TAB**
CLICK: down arrow beside the *Data Type* field
SELECT: Number
PRESS: **TAB**
TYPE: **Number of employees**

6. To save the new structure for the Customer table:
CLICK: Save button (■)

7. To view the Customer datasheet:
CLICK: View button (▦ ▾)
Notice that the Company Size field now appears in the datasheet.

8. To return to table Design view:
CLICK: View button (▨ ▾)

9. To delete the Company Size field:
RIGHT-CLICK: Company Size in the *Field Name* column
CHOOSE: Delete Rows from the pop-up menu
CLICK: Yes command button to confirm the deletion
The Company Size field no longer appears in the structure.

10. To save the table structure:
CLICK: Save button (⊟)

QUICK REFERENCE
Inserting and Deleting
Fields in Table Design View

- **To insert a new field in a table structure:**
  RIGHT-CLICK: the desired location for inserting a new field
  CHOOSE: Insert Rows
- **To delete an existing field from a table structure:**
  RIGHT-CLICK: the name of the field to delete
  CHOOSE: Delete Rows

IN ADDITION CHANGING DATA TYPES FOR FIELDS THAT CONTAIN DATA

At some point you may need to change a field's data type. Depending on the change you make, Access may not be able to convert the existing data into the new format. You should always make a backup copy of your database before changing field types! For more information, ask the Office Assistant for help on "data type conversions."

SETTING FIELD PROPERTIES

Every field in a table has a set of properties. A field property is a specific characteristic of a field or data type that enables you to provide greater control over how your data is stored, displayed, and printed. You set field properties in the lower portion of the Design window.

- Field Size — Allows you to define the maximum length of a text or numeric field. Use this option if you know that all of the entries in a particular field are less than a certain length.

- Format — Allows you to specify how numbers, dates, times, and text are displayed and printed. For example, you can format the display of a part number entered as A100B123 to appear as A-100-B-123.

- Decimal Places — Allows you to specify the number of places to display to the right of the decimal; for numeric and currency fields only.

- Input Mask — Allows you to simplify data entry for fields that have the same format, such as phone number fields, by creating an input mask. For example, an input mask of "(000)000-0000" lets you enter "8005551111" and have Access display the number as (800)555-1111. This property comes with its own wizard to help you make selections.

- Caption — Allows you to define a default field label to appear on forms and reports, instead of the field name specified in the table structure.

- Default Value — Allows you to enter a value or expression that is automatically entered when fields are created. For example, if most of the addresses in a table are local, you might set a default value for the City and State fields.

- Validation Rule — Allows you to enter an expression that defines the rules for entering data into a specific field. For example, if you specify the Validation Rule of ">3" in a restaurant's Reservation field, Access will display an error message if you attempt to type 1, 2, or 3 into the field.

- Validation Text — Allows you to define the text that displays if you enter invalid data into a field. For example, in the Validation Rule example above, the text "We only accept reservations for 4 or more people" might display when the user types a number that is less than 4.

- Required — Allows you to specify whether a value is required in a field. If a value is required, Access displays an error message if you attempt to skip entering data into the field.

- Allow Zero Length — By default, Access stores a null value in an empty field. This property allows you to store a zero-length string of text. Type " " into the field after changing the Allow Zero Length field property to Yes. Zero length strings behave differently than null values. For example, if a query is based on a field with a null value, the record isn't included in the resulting dynaset.

- Indexed — Use this field to specify whether the table should be indexed on this field in order to speed searches.

In this section, you learn how to set field properties.

Perform the following steps . . .

1. Ensure that the Customer table appears in table Design view.

2. To set up an input mask for the Phone field:
   SELECT: Phone in the *Field Name* column
   For this step, you simply click the I-beam mouse pointer in the Phone field to display its properties.

3. CLICK: *Input Mask* text box in the Field Properties area
CLICK: Build button ([**...**]) that appears to the right of the text box
The Input Mask Wizard launches and displays its first dialog box (shown in Figure 2.16).

FIGURE 2.16

INPUT MASK WIZARD

4. At the top of the list box:
CLICK: Phone Number in the *Input Mask* side of the list box
PRESS: [**TAB**]
The cursor moves to the *Try It* text box.

5. TYPE: **7085551000**
Notice that the entry appears as (708) 555-1000 in the *Try It* text box.

6. To proceed in the wizard:
CLICK: [**Next >**]

7. In this step, you can customize the way the input mask works. Let's proceed to the next step:
CLICK: [**Next >**]

8. In this step, you decide whether to store the additional symbols used in the input mask with your data. If you are working with thousands of phone numbers, the extra space consumed by these symbols may become significant. Therefore, most people prefer to only store the raw information in the table. To proceed:
CLICK: [**Next >**]

9. Now that the wizard is finished asking its questions:
CLICK: [**Finish**]

10. To complete the structural changes to the Customer table:
CLICK: Save button ([🖫])
CLICK: Close button ([✖])

<table>
<tr><td>**QUICK REFERENCE**
Selling Field Properties</td><td>1. **Enter table Design view to modify a table's structure.**
2. **SELECT: the desired property in the Field Properties area**
3. **Set the desired property's value.**
4. **CLICK: Save button (⊟) to save the structure**</td></tr>
</table>

IN ADDITION MORE ON FIELD PROPERTIES

Field properties provide you, the database developer, with tremendous power at the design stage. Using these properties, you can specify the complete characteristics of a particular field before any reports or forms are created.

Because field properties are inherited by other database objects automatically, you can control how the fields on your forms will behave when designing the table structure. For more information, ask the Office Assistant about "Setting Field Properties."

Printing a Datasheet

Now that you've created and populated a table, you should know how to print its contents. The quickest way to print a table is to select it in the Database window and then click the Print button (🖨) on the toolbar. You can also choose the File, Print command from the Menu bar.

Access prints a datasheet as it appears on the screen. For datasheets that are too large to print on a sheet of paper, Access prints them from left to right and then from top to bottom. For example, if your datasheet is four pages wide and two pages long, Access prints the top four pages first and then the bottom four pages. To print a datasheet in Landscape mode (across the length of the paper), which is often used for printing wide datasheets, open the table into Datasheet view and then choose File, Page Setup from the menu. You can then select the *Landscape* option button on the *Page* tab and click OK to continue.

Let's print the Customer table.

Perform the following steps . . .

1. Ensure that the Customer table appears in the Database window.

2. DOUBLE-CLICK: Customer
   The table is opened into a datasheet window.

3. To set a landscape print orientation for the datasheet:
   CHOOSE: File, Page Setup
   CLICK: *Page* tab
   CLICK: *Landscape* option button in the *Orientation* area
   PRESS: (ENTER) or CLICK: OK

4. To preview the worksheet:
   CLICK: Print Preview button (🔍) on the toolbar
   Your screen should now appear similar to Figure 2.17.

FIGURE 2.17

PREVIEWING THE
CUSTOMER DATASHEET

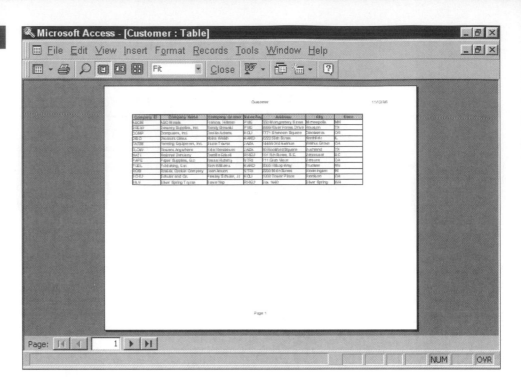

5. Assuming that you are pleased with the preview:
   CLICK: Print button (🖨) on the toolbar
   Notice that the Print dialog box does not appear when you click the toolbar button.

6. To close the Preview window:
   CLICK: Close command button in the toolbar
   CLICK: Close button (❌) to close the Datasheet window

7. To restore the Database window:
   CLICK: Restore button (🗗)

QUICK REFERENCE
Printing a Datasheet

1. Open the datasheet that you want to print.

2. CHOOSE: File, Page Setup to set the margins and orientation

3. PRESS: (ENTER) or CLICK: OK when you are ready to proceed

4. CLICK: Print Preview button (🔍)

5. CLICK: Print button (🖨)

MORE ON CREATING TABLES

Now that you've gone through the process of creating a table structure step-by-step, it is time to show you how to use some productivity tools. In addition to importing data directly into a database, you will learn to use the Table Wizard and Datasheet View methods to simplify the process of creating a table structure. The Table Wizard feature provides you with sample table structures from which you can pick and choose fields to build your own tables. Using the Datasheet View method, you don't even have to think about creating a table. You simply enter information into the datasheet cells and then let Access create the appropriate structure.

USING THE TABLE WIZARD

In this section, we lead you through using the Table Wizard to create a simple table.

Perform the following steps . . .

1. Ensure that the Database window is displayed for the "MediaSport" database and that the *Tables* tab is selected.

2. To create a table structure for storing recipes, do the following:
   CLICK: New command button
   DOUBLE-CLICK: Table Wizard
   The Table Wizard dialog box appears as shown in Figure 2.18.

FIGURE 2.18

TABLE WIZARD DIALOG BOX

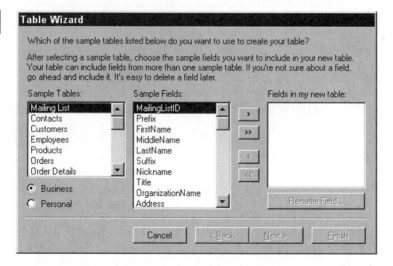

3. By default, the *Business* option button is chosen in the bottom-left corner of the Table Wizard dialog box. And as a result, only business-related table structures appear in the *Sample Tables* list box. To view the Personal tables that are available:
   SELECT: *Personal* option button
   Notice that different table names now appear in the list box.

4. To create a table structure that stores recipes:
SELECT: Recipes in the *Sample Tables* list box

5. To include all of the suggested fields for Recipes in your table:
CLICK: Include All button (>>)
(*Note:* You use the Include One button (>) to select one field at a time for the *Fields in my new table* list box. You can also select a different table from the *Sample Tables* list box and then add fields from that table to your new table.)

6. CLICK: Finish
After a few seconds, the Recipes datasheet appears.

7. To see what you've accomplished using the Table Wizard:
CLICK: View button ( )

8. Scroll through the fields and then return to the Database window:
CLICK: Close button (X)
You should see a table object called "Recipes" appear in the window.

QUICK REFERENCE
Using the Table Wizard
to Create a Table

1. **CLICK:** *Tables* tab in the Database window
2. **CLICK: New command button**
3. **DOUBLE-CLICK: Table Wizard**
4. **SELECT: a sample table that fits your requirements**
5. **SELECT: fields from the sample table that you want to include in your new table**
6. **CLICK:** Finish

USING THE DATASHEET VIEW METHOD

You will now learn how to create a table structure using the Datasheet View method.

Perform the following steps . . .

1. Ensure that the Database window is displayed for the "MediaSport" database and that the *Tables* tab is selected.

2. To create a table structure, do the following:
CLICK: New command button
DOUBLE-CLICK: Datasheet View
A blank datasheet window appears with 30 blank records and 20 field columns named Field1, Field2, and so on.

3. To rename the fields in your table structure, double-click the column headings and then type over the existing entries. Do the following:
   DOUBLE-CLICK: Field1
   TYPE: **Title**
   DOUBLE-CLICK: Field2
   TYPE: **Author**
   DOUBLE-CLICK: Field3
   TYPE: **ISBN**
   DOUBLE-CLICK: Field4
   TYPE: **In Stock**
   DOUBLE-CLICK: Field5
   TYPE: **On Order**

4. Complete three records in the datasheet with the following information:

Title	Author	ISBN	In Stock	On Order
My Cat, My Friend	Mew, Nancy	0-256-17574-1	24	132
Gardening With Ron	Weedman, Ron	1-321-32525-5	85	0
Ten Tips for Travel	Jackson, Miles	0-656-78931-6	12	40

5. To complete the process:
   CLICK: Save button (▣)
   TYPE: **Books**
   PRESS: **ENTER** or CLICK: OK

6. To let Access create a primary key for the table:
   CLICK: Yes command button in the dialog box that appears
   After a few moments, Access displays the datasheet for the Books table with a new AutoNumber field.

7. To see what you've accomplished:
   CLICK: View button (⬓▾)
   Notice that Access correctly analyzed the existing data and identified the In Stock and On Order fields as numeric data types and the ISBN field as a text data type (Figure 2.19).

FIGURE 2.19

CREATING A TABLE
STRUCTURE USING
DATASHEET VIEW

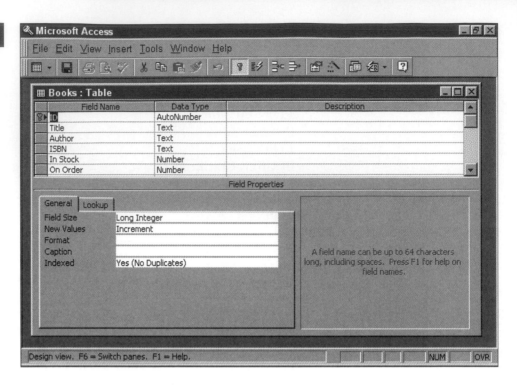

8. After you are finished perusing the details of the new table structure, return to the Database window:
CLICK: Close button (☒)

QUICK REFERENCE
Using Datasheet View to
Create a Table

1. **CLICK:** *Tables* **tab in the Database window**
2. **CLICK: New command button**
3. **DOUBLE-CLICK: Datasheet View**
4. **Enter data into the datasheet that appears.**
5. **CLICK: Save button (🖫)**

REMOVING DATABASE OBJECTS

So as not to consume disk space unnecessarily, let's delete the Recipes and Books tables.

Perform the following steps . . .

1. Ensure that the Database window is displayed for the "MediaSport" database and that the *Tables* tab is selected.

2. To delete the Recipes table:
RIGHT-CLICK: Recipes
CHOOSE: Delete from the pop-up menu
CLICK: Yes command button

3. To delete the Books table:
   RIGHT-CLICK: Books
   CHOOSE: Delete from the pop-up menu
   CLICK: Yes command button

4. Close the Database window.

QUICK REFERENCE
Deleting an Object in the
Database Window

1. **CLICK: the desired tab, such as *Tables***
2. **RIGHT-CLICK: the object that you want to delete**
3. **CHOOSE: Delete from the pop-up menu**
4. **CLICK: Yes command button to confirm**

LINKING AND IMPORTING DATA

In addition to creating a database structure from scratch, you can import or link data from a variety of external sources, including other Access database tables, Excel and Lotus spreadsheets, text files, and other database file formats. You can even import a table that has been created using HTML, the Web's native Hypertext Markup Language. When you *import* data, Access creates a new copy of the information and stores it in your Access database. If you are importing a table from another Access database, you can also import its form and report objects. When you *link* data, Access works with the original data file to retrieve and modify information. A linked table or file is never stored in your Access database.

To demonstrate linking and importing data, let's create a new database and populate it with external data tables.

Perform the following steps . . .

1. Having completed the previous exercises, you should now have a blank work area in the Access application window. If not, close the Database window that appears.

2. To create a new database for this exercise:
   CLICK: New Database button (⬚) on the Database toolbar
   CLICK: *General* tab in the New dialog box
   DOUBLE-CLICK: Blank Database template icon (⬚)

3. In the File New Database dialog box that appears:
   TYPE: **External** in the *File name* text box
   CLICK: down arrow beside the *Save in* drop-down list box
   SELECT: *your Data Files location*
   CLICK: Create command button
   After a few moments, you are presented with an empty Database window with "External: Database" appearing in its Title bar.

4. In the next few steps, you will import data that is stored in a dBASE III database. Ensure that the *Tables* tab is selected and then do the following:
   CHOOSE: File, Get External Data, Import

5. In the Import dialog box that appears:
SELECT: *your Advantage Files location* from the *Look in* drop-down list
SELECT: dBASE III from the *Files of type* drop-down list box
DOUBLE-CLICK: Customer.dbf
Access begins immediately importing your data.

6. When Access is finished the process, a dialog box appears:
CLICK: OK command button for confirmation
CLICK: Close command button to close the Import dialog box
You should now see a table object called "Customer" in the Database window.

7. DOUBLE-CLICK: Customer table to display its datasheet window
Your screen should look similar to Figure 2.20.

FIGURE 2.20

IMPORTING DATA FROM
A DBASE III FILE

	CUSTNUM	TITLE	FIRSTNAME	LASTNAME	ADDRESS	CITY
▶	3906	Mr.	Frank	Chihowski	4111 Beach Sid	San Francisco
	3909	Ms.	Rosalie	Skears	9504 Wellington	San Mateo
	4500	Ms.	Joellen	Baldwin	2729 Glen Ellen	San Francisco
	4809	Ms.	Veronica	Visentin	90 Spruce Stree	San Mateo
	4999	Mr.	Charles	Cattermole	18 Cameo Road	San Francisco
	5100	Ms.	Lynne	Morrow-Tabacch	11322 Overlook	San Mateo
	5410	Mr.	Sean	Dennis	132 Walnut Lan	San Francisco
	5807	Mr.	Samuel	Hussey	23 Linlew Drive,	San Mateo
	6211	Ms.	Heidi	Buehre	3255 S. Parker	San Mateo
＊						

Record: ◄◄ ◄ | 1 | ► ►► ►＊ of 9

8. CLICK: Close button (✖) on the datasheet window

9. Now, let's demonstrate linking your Access database to tables stored in other database file formats. Let's begin:
CHOOSE: File, Get External Data, Link Tables

10. First, let's establish a link to a second dBASE III file:
SELECT: dBASE III from the *Files of type* drop-down list box
DOUBLE-CLICK: Stock.dbf

11. A second dialog box now appears asking you to select a dBASE III index file. Since this database does not have an associated index:
CLICK: Cancel command button
CLICK: OK command button to confirm the link

12. To establish a link to a Paradox database file:
SELECT: Paradox from the *Files of type* drop-down list box
DOUBLE-CLICK: Dealers.db
CLICK: OK command button confirm this link
CLICK: Close command button to remove the dialog box
Your screen should now appear similar to Figure 2.21. Notice the icons used for the linked table objects.

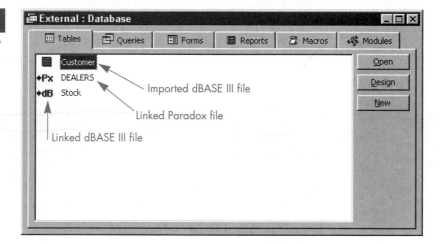

FIGURE 2.21

THE DATABASE WINDOW AFTER LINKING TABLE OBJECTS

13. DOUBLE-CLICK: DEALERS table to display its datasheet window
CLICK: Close button (☒) on the datasheet window

14. DOUBLE-CLICK: Stock table to display its datasheet window
CLICK: Close button (☒) on the datasheet window

15. Close the Database window and then exit Microsoft Access.

QUICK REFERENCE
Linking and Importing Data

1. **SELECT:** *Tables* tab in the Database window

2. **CHOOSE:** File, Get External Data

3. **CHOOSE:** Import or Link Tables from the cascading menu

4. **SELECT:** *the desired database file* and respond to the prompts

---

IN ADDITION MOVING DATA FROM AN EXCEL WORKBOOK TO AN ACCESS DATABASE

 Many people begin simple database applications by storing information in the rows and columns of an Excel worksheet. After a period of time, the amount of data stored in the worksheet may be better managed using Access. You can use the following methods to move data between these applications:

- In Excel, you move your data to an Access database by choosing the Data, Convert to MS Access command from the menu. If this command does not appear on your menu, ensure that you have installed the AccessLinks add-in program.

- In Access, you can import a worksheet using the Get External Data command and the Import Spreadsheet Wizard.

Summary

In this session, you learned how to design a database structure and add records to a table using Datasheet view and Form view. When creating a table using Design view, you learned to enter unique field names, select data storage types, and specify field properties. After entering some data to your new table, you modified its view by altering column widths and the row height and by reordering columns. To make data entry even easier, you learned to create a form using the AutoForm Wizard and then added some additional records. Several suggestions were also offered in this session to help you plan your database design and become more productive at creating tables.

COMMAND SUMMARY

Table 2.5 provides a summary of the commands introduced in this session.

TABLE 2.5	*Task Description*	*Menu Command*	*Toolbar Button*
Command Summary	Creates a new database	File, New Database	🗋
	Creates a blank database		
	Creates a database using the Database Wizard		
	Creates a new table by importing or linking data	File, Get External Data	
	Sets a primary key	Edit, Primary Key	
	Creates a new database object		
	Switches to Datasheet view		
	Switches to Design view		
	Displays the Indexes window	View, Indexes	

	Task Description	Menu Command	Toolbar Button
TABLE 2.5 *Continued*	Saves the datasheet layout	File, Save	
	Sets margins and page orientation	File, Page Setup	
	Previews a datasheet for printing	File, Print Preview	
	Prints a table	File, Print	

KEY TERMS

AutoForm Wizard
An Access tool that creates a form automatically, using all of the fields from the selected table in a Database window.

Database Wizard
An Access tool providing over 20 professionally designed database templates that you may use in creating your own database applications.

Design view
In this mode, you can design and make changes to the structure of a database.

form
A screen design for manipulating data in a table one record at a time.

Form view
The mode that Access is in when you view a form on the screen.

index
A field other than the primary key field that is used to put records in a desired order.

normalizing
The process of dividing redundant information into separate databases.

points
Typographical measurement of row height and fonts; one point is equal to $1/72$ inch.

primary key
A field that uniquely identifies each record in a table.

Table Wizard
An Access tool that simplifies the process of creating a table structure.

EXERCISES

SHORT ANSWER

1. What are the seven steps for planning a database, as discussed in this session?

2. What data storage types can be defined in a table structure?

3. Describe two ways you can customize the view of a datasheet.

4. What is the difference between Design view and Datasheet view?

5. When would you want to insert a row in a table structure?

6. What does it mean to "normalize a database"?

7. What is the procedure for printing a datasheet?

8. How does a primary key differ from an index?

9. When would you use the AutoForm Wizard?

10. Name three methods for creating a table in an Access database.

HANDS-ON

(*Note:* Ensure that you know the storage location of your Advantage Files and your Data Files before proceeding.)

1. In this exercise, you practice creating a new table structure and then populating the table with records.

   a. Open the "MediaSport" database that you created in this session.

   b. Create a new table for this database using the following structure:

Field Name	Data Type	Description (Optional)
Sales Representative ID	Text	Unique four-letter code based on the sales rep's name
Last Name	Text	
First Name	Text	
Middle Initial	Text	
Date Hired	Date/Time	
Vacation Days	Number	
Base Salary	Currency	

c. Define the Last Name field as the primary key.

d. Save the table structure as Sales Representatives.

e. Display the datasheet for the table and add the following records. (*Note:* International users may have to modify the way the Date Hired column is entered. For example, Canadians typically enter dates in the dd/mm/yy format, instead of mm/dd/yy.)

Sales Rep ID	Last Name	First Name	Middle Initial	Date Hired	Vacation Days	Base Salary
LMAT	Matson	Lisa	E.	4/15/84	25	45000
KAND	Andrews	Kirk	A.	11/1/89	10	22500
KCLI	Clifford	Karen	C.	10/25/76	30	62000
VTRI	Trimarchi	Valerie	M.	2/15/88	20	54000
TCHA	Chang	Thomas	R.	4/30/92	10	18000
JAZA	Azavedo	Jane	K.	9/24/91	10	16500
RHEU	Heurrera	Ricardo		6/28/65	30	39500
PVIE	Vieau	Pierre	T.	2/26/81	35	75000
RKEL	Keller	Roberta		3/31/90	15	29000

f. Change the column width of each column in the Sales Representatives table using the Best Fit option.

g. Decrease the column widths further for the Sales Representative ID and Middle Initial columns.

h. Close the Sales Representatives window and save the new layout.

i. Close the "MediaSport" Database window.

2. This exercise lets you practice creating a new table structure and adding records.

a. Open the "Wedding" database, stored in the Advantage Files location.

b. Create a new table using the following table structure.

Field Name	Data Type	Description (Optional)
Gift Number	AutoNumber	
Guest ID	Number	
Category	Text	i.e., Engagement Shower, Wedding, etc.
Gift Description	Text	
Where Purchased	Text	

c. Define the Gift Number field as the primary key field.

d. Save the table structure as Gifts.

e. Display the datasheet for the table and add the following records. (*Note: The Gift Number will be entered automatically. Just press* **TAB** *to bypass that field.*)

Gift Number	Guest ID	Category	Gift Description	Where Purchased
1	21	Kitchen Shower	Set of knives	Latham's
2	19	Kitchen Shower	Baking utensils	The Napa Kitchen
3	5	Engagement	Teacup - blue floral	Giordi's
4	3	Kitchen Shower	Set of mixing bowls	The Napa Kitchen
5	87	Engagement	Book - Getaways	Brian's Bookstore

f. Change the displayed font to 12 point.

g. Modify the column widths to fit, as necessary.

h. Increase the row height in the datasheet.

i. Close the Gifts window, but do not save the layout changes.

j. "Giordi's" has changed its name to "Monde Boutique." Display the Gifts datasheet and update the third record.

k. Close the Gifts window.

3. In the last exercise, you created a table in the "Wedding" database called Gifts. You will now create a form for this table.

a. Using the AutoForm Wizard, create a form for the Gifts table. When finished, the form should look similar to Figure 2.22.

FIGURE 2.22

CREATING A FORM
USING THE AUTOFORM
WIZARD

b. Save the form as Gift Entry Form.

c. Move the record pointer to the bottom of the Gifts table and then enter records 6–9, as shown below:

Gift Number	Guest ID	Category	Gift Description	Where Purchased
6	15	Wedding	China place setting	Monde Boutique
7	2	Engagement	Teacup - blue rim	Monde Boutique
8	15	Wedding	Wooden ice bucket	The Napa Kitchen
9	19	Engagement	Teacup - green rim	The Napa Kitchen

d. Close the Form window.

4. In this exercise, you practice customizing the layout of the Gifts datasheet that is stored in the "Wedding" database. (*Note:* You created the Gifts table in exercise 2 and added data to it in exercises 2 and 3.)

a. Display the Gifts datasheet.

b. Widen the Gift Description and Where Purchased columns to accommodate the data.

c. Move the Guest ID column so that it displays before the Gift Number column.

d. Print the Gifts datasheet.

e. Save the new datasheet layout.

f. Close the Gifts window and the "Wedding" Database window.

5. **On Your Own:** Creating a Library Database
Using the Access Database Wizard[1], create a database application for tracking your collection of books. Save the new database as "Book Collection" to your Data Files location. Select all of the fields suggested in the wizard's dialog box, including *ISBN Number* and *Place of Publication,* and then choose to include sample data. After the application is created and displayed, test the choices on the main switchboard. When you are comfortable with using the application, delete the existing sample records and then add your own book information to the database. Close the database application before proceeding.

6. **On Your Own:** Creating a Personal Address Book
Using the Datasheet View method, create a database and table for storing information about your personal friends and business contacts. Include fields for each person's first and last names, street address, city, state or province, country, zip or postal code, phone and fax numbers, and birthdate. Save the database as "My Phone Book" to your Data Files location. In table Design view, create an input mask for the phone and fax numbers. Then, create and use an AutoForm to add several new records to the table. Close the database before proceeding.

CASE PROBLEMS   **LAKELAND GYM**

(*Note:* In the following case problems, assume the role of the primary characters and perform the same steps that they identify. You may want to re-read the session opening.)

1. As each day passes, Josephine wishes she could find the time to create her membership database using Microsoft Access. The steady increase in the club's membership has increased her workload and she really feels the need to get this problem solved. In the past two days, another 15 people have joined the club at the "Midday Special" rate! Locking herself in her office, Josephine forces herself to make time to create the database. Fortunately, she had already written down the following notes about the kind of information to include in Lakeland's membership database.

---

[1] This exercise assumes that you have installed the complete set of database templates and wizards.

Lakeland Database Application

Table 1:   Last Name (Primary Key)
Membership   First Name
                 Address
                 City
                 State
                 Zip

Table 2:   Last Name (Primary Key)
Employees   First Name
                 Home Phone
                 Salary Amount

Using her notes, Josephine creates a new database called "Lakeland" with one table named Membership and another named Employees. She saves the database to her Data Files location. Just as she finishes saving, the phone rings. "Hi Josephine, this is Peter. Listen, I'm stuck in traffic. Would you mind covering for me at the Executive luncheon today? You need to be there around noon." Glancing at her watch, Josephine realizes that she only has ten minutes, so she hangs up the phone and closes the database. She will have to add records to the tables at another time.

2.   After the luncheon, Josephine returns to her office and, again, locks her door. She can now add records to the Membership table of the Lakeland database. She first uses the AutoForm Wizard to create a new form for the Membership table, which she saves as Membership Data Entry Form. She then uses the form to add the following five records.

Last Name	First Name	Address	City	State	Zip
McWilliams	Keith	1 Chapman Lane	Burlingame	CA	94010
Neumiller	Irving	16 Meadow Avenue	Stockton	CA	95207
McConnell	Britton	84 McClary Boulevard	Calistoga	CA	95450
Peck	Ozola	83 Yerming Way	Sacramento	CA	95828
Prioleau	Michelle	90 Ocean Street, #64	S.F.	CA	94109

As she is about to enter a sixth record, Peter buzzes her on the intercom. "Josephine, would you mind coming into my office to brief me on the luncheon?" Before leaving, Josephine saves and closes the Lakeland database.

3. On the way back to her office, Josephine is struck with an idea for modifying the Membership table. She decides to add a Member Status field in the table that will hold a "P" for a part-time midday member or an "F" for full-time member. Convincing herself that this is really a wonderful idea, Josephine proceeds to edit the structure of the Membership table to include the Member Status field. She defines the new field to contain text and then displays the updated table in datasheet mode. Her final task is to enter the Member Status types for the records that she has already typed in:

Last Name	First Name	Member Status
McWilliams	Keith	P
Neumiller	Irving	P
McConnell	Britton	F
Peck	Ozola	P
Prioleau	Michelle	P

She also decides to enter the following new members and then exits the Lakeland database to go to her afternoon aerobics class.

Last Name	First Name	Address	City	State	Zip	Member Status
Mueller	Peter	1223 Lombard #A	S.F.	CA	94109	F
Koulakis	Patrick	54 Sterling Place	Orinda	CA	94563	P
Moser	James	Box 46	Walnut Grove	CA	95690	F

Microsoft Access 97 for Windows

Retrieving Information

SESSION

HTTP WWW

3

IRWIN

COMPUTER & INFORMATION TECHNOLOGY

SESSION OUTLINE

INTRODUCTION

One of the primary advantages of a computerized database is the ability to retrieve and display specific information quickly and easily. Rather than searching through endless filing cabinets to compile a list of all your customers in Atlanta, for example, you simply enter an instruction and let Access do the work for you. In this session, you retrieve, organize, and summarize information from a database table.

| CASE STUDY | MOUNTAIN WEAR |

Antonio is a sales representative for Mountain Wear, a Texas manufacturer of rugged footwear. Although he has only worked for the company a short time, he enjoys the job and the challenges it presents. Antonio shares a small office with two other sales representatives and the district manager, Rita Bingham. Like all of the sales representatives at Mountain Wear, Antonio is responsible for keeping track of his sales and customer records using Microsoft Access.

On Monday morning, Antonio arrives at work to find a note attached to his computer monitor. The unmistakable handwriting belongs to Rita.

Antonio, I need to see a printout of all your customers. Also, can you provide a list of all your sales, including the items that were sold and who purchased them? Remember that I need you to print these reports at the end of each month. You obviously missed the deadline for today's reports. However, I still need this information to keep our records current. I'll be back in the office tomorrow morning—please have them ready and on my desk. Thanks.

Although Antonio knows how to add and modify records in a database, he doesn't know how to create the lists that Rita has requested. And, unfortunately, his two coworkers are out of the office on sales calls.

In this session, you and Antonio learn how to sort and find records in a table, use filters, create and save queries, and retrieve information from more than one table in a database.

SORTING A TABLE

Sorting a table's records into a particular order is the first step in making information out of raw data. Not only does sorting allow you to better organize and present data, it makes it much easier to scan a datasheet for a specific record. In this section, you learn how to perform a simple sort operation on records displayed in Datasheet view. You can also use the steps provided below to sort records displayed in Form view.

The general process for sorting a table is to first select the column or field whose contents you want to place into a particular order. To sort the records into ascending order (0 to 9, A to Z), click the Sort Ascending button ([↓]) on the toolbar. To sort the records into descending order (9 to 0, Z to A), click the Sort Descending button ([↓]). You can also sort a table by the contents of more than one column, if the columns are adjacent to one another, by selecting both columns before clicking the desired toolbar button. Access sorts the records starting with the leftmost selected column. To save the sort specification along with the datasheet layout, click the Save button ([⊟]) on the toolbar. The next time that you open the table, the sort order will be reapplied automatically.

You will now practice sorting a database table.

Perform the following steps . . .

1. Turn on your computer and load Microsoft Access. If the startup dialog box appears, click the Cancel command button to display an empty application window. If you already have a Database window open, close the database before proceeding.

2. Open the database named "Sporting" located in your Advantage Files location. This database tracks information for a Sports Store.

3. To display the contents of the Customer table:
CLICK: *Tables* tab
DOUBLE-CLICK: Customer
The Customer datasheet should now appear.

4. Using the horizontal scroll bar and scroll arrows, position the Table window so that the City and State columns are both visible.

5. To display the table records sorted by City:
SELECT: City column
This instruction tells you to position the down arrow mouse pointer over the City column heading and click once. If done properly, the entire column will appear highlighted in reverse video.

6. To perform the sort operation:
CLICK: Sort Ascending button ([↓]) on the toolbar
The table appears in sorted order by city name.

7. If you were to sort this table into ascending order by State, you would end up with three records for California grouped next to each other. Although not a terrible inconvenience for a table of this size, consider sorting a table containing thousands of records from across the nation. Imagine the futility in trying to find a specific company's record when the only sort order applied is by state. By further sorting this table into Company Name order, you would provide better information and easier access to information.

   To demonstrate, let's sort the Customer table by State and then by Company Name. Because Access requires that the sort columns be adjacent and that the leftmost column be sorted first, you must first move the State column to the left of the Company Name column. To begin, do the following:
SELECT: State column

8. DRAG: State column to the left of the Company Name column
CLICK: anywhere in the datasheet to remove the column highlighting

9. SELECT: State and Company Name columns by dragging the down arrow mouse pointer over the column headings
Your screen should now appear similar to Figure 3.1.

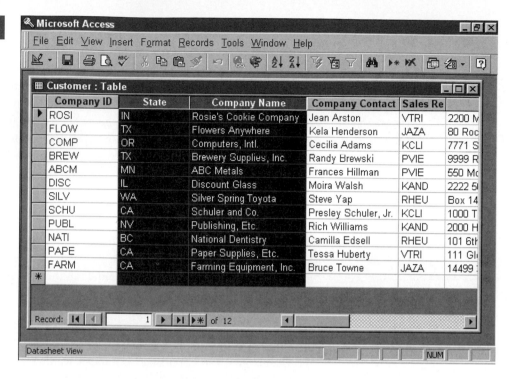

10. To perform the sort operation:
CLICK: Sort Ascending button (⬆) on the toolbar
Notice that the table records are sorted by State and, in the case of California and Texas, also by Company Name.

11. Although you could save this layout for later use, let's close the window without saving any changes. Do the following:
CLICK: Close button (❌) for the Table window

12. In the dialog box that appears:
CLICK: No command button when asked to save the design

QUICK REFERENCE
Sorting Records in a Table

1. **Display the datasheet for the table that you want to sort.**
2. **Select the column or columns whose contents you want to sort.**
3. **CLICK: Sort Ascending (⬆) or Sort Descending (⬇)**
4. **CLICK: Save button (💾) to save the layout and sort order**

FINDING INFORMATION

The Find command in Access lets you search an entire table for the existence of a few characters, a word, or a phrase. With large databases, this command is especially useful for moving the cursor to a particular record for editing. To use the Find command, you display a datasheet, select the field in which to perform the search, and then click the Find button ([🔍]) on the toolbar. If you prefer, you can also choose Edit, Find command from the menu. In the dialog box that appears, you type in the text you are searching for and then press (ENTER) or click the Find Next command button.

Wildcard characters, such as the ? to represent a single character and the *   to represent a group of characters, can be used if you are unsure of how to spell a search term. For example, the search entry Schuler* would find matches with "Schuler and Co.," "Schuler Inc.," and "Schuler and Associates." The search entry ??S? would find matches for "ROSI" and "DISC." In this section, you use the Find command to locate records in the Customer table.

Perform the following steps . . .

1. Ensure that the "Sporting" Database window appears in the work area and that the *Tables* tab is active.

2. To display the contents of the Customer table:
   DOUBLE-CLICK: Customer

3. To position the cursor in the Company Name field:
   PRESS: (TAB)

4. To find the record for Paper Supplies, Etc.:
   CLICK: Find button ([🔍]) on the toolbar
   TYPE: **Paper*** in the *Find What* text box
   CLICK: *Search Only Current Field* check box so that a "✓" appears
   Your dialog box should appear similar to Figure 3.2.

FIGURE 3.2

FIND DIALOG BOX

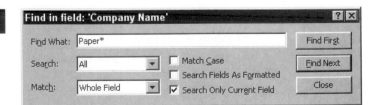

5. To proceed with the search:
   CLICK: Find Next command button
   The cursor moves down the column and stops on the "Paper Supplies, Etc." entry in the Company Name field. (*Note*: The Find dialog box may be covering the currently selected field. If necessary, drag the dialog window by its Title bar to another location.)

6. To continue the search:
CLICK: Find Next command button
A dialog box appears stating that no more matches were found.

7. To end the current search:
CLICK: OK command button
CLICK: Close command button

8. To begin a new search:
PRESS: CTRL + HOME

9. CLICK: Find button (🔍) on the toolbar
TYPE: **Vancouver** in the *Find What* text box
CLICK: *Search Only Current Field* check box so that no "✓" appears
(*Note*: A keyboard shortcut to clicking the Find button on the toolbar is to press CTRL + f.)

10. CLICK: Find Next command button

Notice that the Find command locates the entry with Vancouver, even though it is stored in a different column. Although quite responsive with this small table of records, the Find command becomes quite slow when asked to search all of the fields in a large table. Therefore, you should attempt to limit your searches to the current column or field whenever possible.

11. To close the Find dialog box:
CLICK: Close command button

12. To return to the top of the datasheet:
PRESS: CTRL + HOME

QUICK REFERENCE
Finding Specific Data in a Table

1. **Display the datasheet for the table that you want to search.**
2. **Position the cursor in the column you want to search.**
3. **CLICK: Find button (🔍) on the toolbar**
4. **TYPE: the text you want to search for into the *Find What* text box**
   SELECT: Find Next command button
5. **When you're finished with a search, respond to the command button prompts in the dialog boxes.**

USING FILTERS

A **filter** lets you limit the display of records in a table using a simple matching criterion, rather than having to create a new database object. Think of a filter as similar in function to a pasta strainer that lets water through but not the pasta. When you apply a filter to a table, some records are allowed to pass through for display while others are not. Only a subset of the table's records are displayed when a filter is applied.

In this section, you are introduced to several methods for filtering table information: **Filter For Input, Filter By Selection, Filter Excluding Selection, Filter By Form,** and the **Advanced Filter/Sort** command. You also learn how to save filters as query objects. Queries are discussed in the next section.

FILTERING FUNDAMENTALS

In applying a filter to a table, you are attempting to restrict the display of records to a subset that matches a particular value. The Filter For Input method lets you type this matching value or expression directly into a text box that appears on a shortcut menu. Using the Filter By Selection method, you select the desired value right from the datasheet and then click the Filter By Selection button (▼) on the toolbar. To display all records not containing the selected value, you choose the Records, Filter, Filter Excluding Selection command. The datasheet is immediately redisplayed showing only those records matching (or excluding) the selected value.

Here are some tips to keep in mind when using these filtering methods. You can apply more than one filter to a table; for example, all residents of Boston over the age of 20. If you want to filter a table based on a partial field entry, for example all surnames beginning with "Mc", you can use wildcards with the Filter For Input method or select a partial value before clicking the Filter By Selection button (▼). Once filtered, you can then sort the resulting subset of records using the Sort Ascending (↓) and Sort Descending (↓) toolbar buttons.

Let's practice applying a filter to the Customer table.

Perform the following steps . . .

1. Ensure that the Customer datasheet Table window appears.

2. Using the horizontal scroll bar, scroll the Table window so that the City and State columns are visible.

3. In the first row of the City field ("Minneapolis"):
   RIGHT-CLICK: the mouse pointer anywhere in the cell
   CHOOSE: Filter For: command
   After you click on the menu command, a flashing I-beam cursor appears in the shortcut menu's text box.

4. To limit the table display to those records that have cities beginning with the letter "s", do the following (as shown in Figure 3.3):
TYPE: s*
PRESS: **ENTER**
The table now displays only two records: Silver Spring and Stockton.

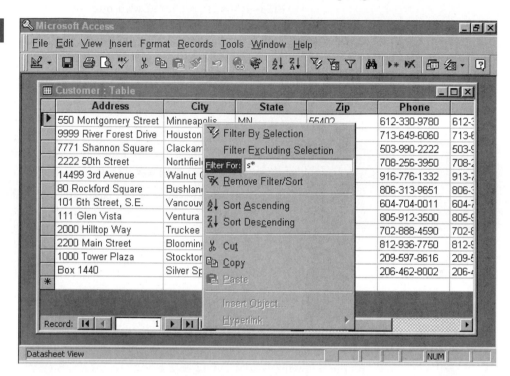

5. To remove the filter and display all of the records once again:
CLICK: Remove Filter button (🔽) on the toolbar
(*Hint*: The Apply Filter button on the toolbar is toggled on and toggled off. When a filter is active, the Apply Filter button is toggled on and is renamed temporarily to "Remove Filter.")

6. To filter the table so that only those records having "KCLI" as their sales representative are displayed, scroll the Table window so that the Sales Representative ID column is visible.

7. In the Sales Representative ID column of the third record:
DOUBLE-CLICK: KCLI

8. To apply the selected value as a filter:
CLICK: Filter By Selection button (🔽) on the toolbar
Notice that the total number of records appears as "of 2 (Filtered)" at the bottom of the Table window.

9. For demonstration purposes, let's apply a second filter to this table:
RIGHT-CLICK: any cell in the Company Name column
CHOOSE: Filter For: command
TYPE: s*
PRESS: (ENTER)
Although not a revelation with only two records displayed, this ability to apply multiple filters to a table is especially useful when you must deal with hundreds or thousands of records.

10. To remove the filter and display all of the records once again:
CLICK: Remove Filter button (🔽) on the toolbar

QUICK REFERENCE
Using Filter By Selection

1. **Display the datasheet for the table that you want to filter.**
2. **SELECT: all or part of an existing field entry**
3. **CLICK: Filter By Selection button (🔽) on the toolbar**

IN ADDITION USING EXPRESSIONS WITH THE FILTER FOR INPUT METHOD

You can build elaborate filters using field names. For example, to apply a filter that displays only those records containing zip codes with 79999 or less, do the following:

1. RIGHT-CLICK: any cell in the Table window
2. CHOOSE: Filter For: command

3. TYPE: [Zip] < 80000
4. PRESS: (ENTER)

Notice that (1) you can right-click any cell in the table and (2) you must enclose the field name in square brackets.

FILTERING BY FORM

For more detailed filtering operations, you use the Filter By Form method to specify multiple matching criteria. For example, in a table for storing client or contact information, you can limit the display to only those records containing "Dallas" in the City field, "Manager" in the Title/Position field, and "Active" in the Status field. You can also use "Or" logic in applying your filters. For example, you can limit the display to only those records containing "Dallas" or "Houston" in the City field; something that you cannot do using the Filter By Selection method.

To demonstrate, you will now use the Filter By Form method.

Perform the following steps . . .

1. Ensure that the Customer datasheet Table window appears.

2. Using the horizontal scroll bar, scroll the Table window so that the City and State columns are visible.

3. To display the Filter By Form window:
CLICK: Filter By Form button (🔲) on the toolbar
Notice that the previous filter condition appears in the grid.

4. To delete this filter specification:
CLICK: Clear Grid button (☒)

5. To display only those records from California or Texas:
CLICK: State field once
Notice that a down arrow appears next to the cell. This indicates that Access has compiled a drop-down list of the values currently appearing in this column.

6. To display the values available for selection:
CLICK: down arrow beside the State field
Your screen should now appear similar to Figure 3.4.

FIGURE 3.4

ENTERING A MATCHING CRITERION USING FILTER BY FORM

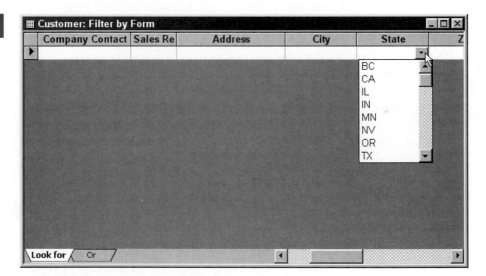

7. SELECT: CA from the drop-down list box
You should see "CA" appear in the field.

8. To select an additional state:
CLICK: *Or* tab at the bottom of Filter By Form window

9. SELECT: TX from the State drop-down list box
You should see "TX" appear in the field.

10. To apply this newly created filter:
CLICK: Apply Filter button (▽) on the toolbar

11. Scroll the window so that the State column is visible. You should now see only those records that contain either "CA" or "TX" in the column.

12. To remove the filter and display all of the records once again:
CLICK: Remove Filter button ([▽]) on the toolbar

QUICK REFERENCE
Using Filter By Form

1. **Display the datasheet for the table that you want to filter.**
2. **CLICK: Filter By Form button ([▥]) on the toolbar**
3. **Enter the filtering criteria using the Look For and Or tabs.**
4. **CLICK: Apply Filter button ([▽]) on the toolbar**

ADVANCED FILTER/SORT OPERATIONS

When you want to define a filter that uses multiple criteria, including "Or" logic, and sorts the resulting subset of records in the same step, choose the Records, Advanced Filter/Sort command from the Menu bar. In the design grid that appears, you specify the desired fields, criteria, and sort order. When you are satisfied, click the Apply Filter button ([▽]) on the toolbar to display the results.

In this exercise, you specify your filter criteria using the design grid.

Perform the following steps . . .

1. Ensure that the Customer datasheet Table window appears.

2. To display the design grid for entering more complicated filters:
CHOOSE: Records, Filter, Advanced Filter/Sort
The window shown in Figure 3.5 appears. In the top portion of the window, the Customer table structure appears with a list of its field names. In the bottom portion or design grid, you define your filter specification. Notice that the filter previously applied already appears in the grid area.

FIGURE 3.5

THE DESIGN GRID FOR
THE ADVANCED
FILTER/SORT COMMAND

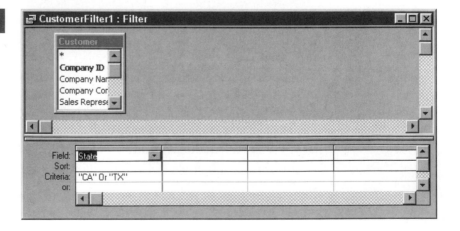

3. To remove the existing filter specification:
CLICK: Clear Grid button ([×]) on the toolbar

4. Let's forget about the top half of this window for now and concentrate on the design grid. To display only those records containing CA in the State field and VTRI in the Sales Representative field, you must define a new filter specification using the design grid. Do the following:
CLICK: I-beam mouse pointer in the first column of the *Field* row
CLICK: down arrow that appears beside the field

5. To define the State filter as CA:
SELECT: State from the drop-down field list
CLICK: I-beam mouse pointer in the *Criteria* row
TYPE: **CA**

6. To define the Sales Representative ID filter as VTRI:
CLICK: I-beam mouse pointer in the second column of the *Field* row
SELECT: Sales Representative ID from the drop-down field list
CLICK: I-beam mouse pointer in the *Criteria* row
TYPE: **VTRI**

7. To apply this filter:
CLICK: Apply Filter button (▽) on the toolbar
The record for Paper Supplies, Etc. is displayed in the datasheet.

8. To remove the filter and display all of the records:
CLICK: Remove Filter button (▽) on the toolbar

9. To close the datasheet:
CLICK: Close button (✕) for the Table window
CLICK: No command button when asked to save the layout

QUICK REFERENCE
Using Advanced Filters

1. **Display the datasheet for the table that you want to filter.**
2. **CHOOSE: Records, Filter, Advanced Filter/Sort from the menu**
3. **Specify the filtering criteria and sort order using the design grid.**
4. **CLICK: Apply Filter button (▽) on the toolbar**

SAVING A FILTER AS A QUERY

Once you have defined a filter using Filter By Form or by choosing the Advanced Filter/Sort command, you can save the criteria specifications as a query object in the Database window. With the filter form or design grid displayed, you click the Save As Query button (💾) on the toolbar and then type the desired name for the query object. To complete the save operation, press (**ENTER**) or click the OK command button. The new query object will now appear in the Database window. You will learn more about queries and how they differ from filters in the next section.

QUICK REFERENCE
Saving a Filter as a Query

1. **CLICK: Filter By Form button (▣) or**
   CHOOSE: Records, Filter, Advanced Filter/Sort
2. **Specify the desired filtering criteria.**
3. **CLICK: Save As Query button (▣)**
4. **TYPE: a name for the new query object**
5. **PRESS: ENTER or CLICK: OK**

QUERY FUNDAMENTALS

A query is a question you ask of your database, such as "How many customers live in Chicago?" or "What is the average age of employees in XYZ Corporation?" Using queries, you can view and analyze specific data in your tables. You can also use the results of a query in presenting data in forms and reports. In this section, you learn how to design queries using the **Simple Query Wizard.**

Although similar to filters, queries differ in several significant areas. While both filters and queries allow you to retrieve and display a subset of records, queries allow you to display data from multiple tables, control which fields display and in what order they display, and perform calculations on field values. Also, filters provide a temporary view of a subset of records while queries are saved as independent database objects.

TYPES OF QUERIES

There are two primary types of queries in Microsoft Access: *select queries* and *action queries*. A **select query** lets you ask questions of your database, retrieve data from multiple tables, sort the data, and display the results in a datasheet. Action queries, on the other hand, automatically perform an action on the retrieved data. The four types of action queries include (1) **update query,** which updates the data in a table, (2) **append query,** which adds data to another table, (3) **delete query,** which deletes records from one or more tables, and (4) **make table query,** which creates a new table from a query's results. In this session, we focus on select queries, the most common type of query.

CREATING A SIMPLE QUERY

Once you have determined the need to create a query, you proceed by clicking on the *Queries* tab in the Database window and then clicking the New command button. As an alternative, you can select the desired table name on the *Tables* tab and then select New Query from the New Object (▣ ▾) drop-down list button on the toolbar. Regardless of the method for starting a new query, you are presented with the dialog box in Figure 3.6.

FIGURE 3.6

THE NEW QUERY
DIALOG BOX

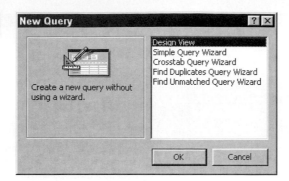

The easiest method for creating a query is to select the Simple Query Wizard. If you would rather design a query from scratch, double-click the Design View option in the dialog box. In this section, you will practice querying the Customer table using the Simple Query Wizard. The results of the query will display in a special table, called a **dynaset,** and will list only the Company Name, Company Contact, Phone, and Fax for each entry.

Perform the following steps . . .

1. Ensure that the "Sporting" Database window appears in the work area and that the *Tables* tab is active.

2. To create a new query:
   CLICK: *Queries* tab
   CLICK: New command button
   You should now see the dialog box that appears in Figure 3.6.

3. To demonstrate the query wizard:
   DOUBLE-CLICK: Simple Query Wizard
   After a few seconds, the first screen of the wizard appears.

4. Ensure that "Table: Customer" appears in the *Tables/Queries* drop-down list box.

5. To build a query that shows each record's Company Name, Company Contact, and phone numbers, do the following:
   DOUBLE-CLICK: Company Name in the *Available Fields* list box
   The Company Name field is transferred to the *Selected Fields* list box.

6. To complete the field selection:
   DOUBLE-CLICK: Company Contact
   DOUBLE-CLICK: Phone
   DOUBLE-CLICK: Fax
   Your screen should now appear similar to Figure 3.7.

FIGURE 3.7

SELECTING FIELDS IN
THE SIMPLE QUERY
WIZARD

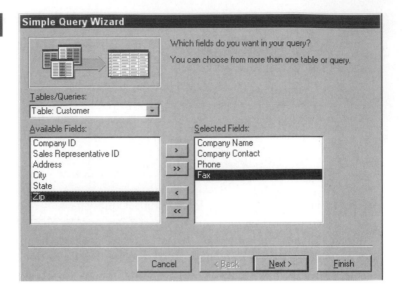

7. To proceed to the next screen:
CLICK: Next >

8. To rename the query:
TYPE: `Customer Phone Book Query`

9. If it is not already selected:
CLICK: *Open the query to view information* option button

10. To proceed:
CLICK: Finish

11. On your own, change the column widths to the best fit for each field by double-clicking the column borders. Your screen should appear similar to Figure 3.8 when completed. This resulting query table is sometimes called a *dynaset*.

12. To save the layout and close the datasheet:
CLICK: Save button (🖫)
CLICK: Close button (☒)
Notice that the "Customer Phone Book Query" query object now appears in the Database window.

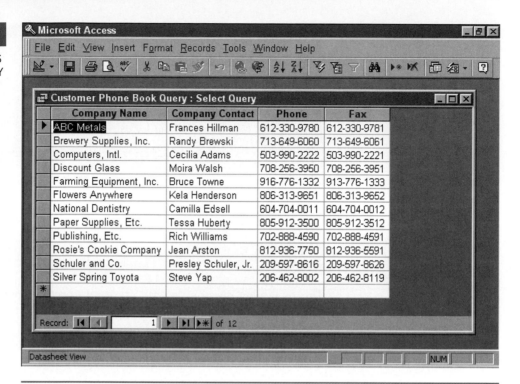

FIGURE 3.8

DISPLAYING THE RESULTS FROM THE SIMPLE QUERY WIZARD

QUICK REFERENCE
Create a Query Using the Simple Query Wizard

1. **CLICK: Queries tab in the Database window**
2. **CLICK: New command button**
3. **DOUBLE-CLICK: Simple Query Wizard**
4. **Proceed by selecting fields and defining the query in the wizard.**

USING THE QUERY DESIGN WINDOW

While the Simple Query Wizard provides an excellent way to get started, you will find that you need the Design window to tap the real power in using queries. The query Design window appears when you select the Design View option in the New Query dialog box or when you select a query in the Database window and then click the Design command button. The Design window is a graphical **query-by-example** tool. In other words, you provide an example of the desired results in the grid by choosing fields and typing the criteria.

Figure 3.9 shows the Customer Phone Book Query that you created in the last section as displayed in the query Design window. The top portion of the window displays the tables on which you've chosen to base your query. The bottom portion of the window contains the grid that you use to specify your criteria and sorting options. To add a field to the grid, you simply drag its name from the table list and drop it into the *Field* row.

FIGURE 3.9

QUERY DESIGN WINDOW

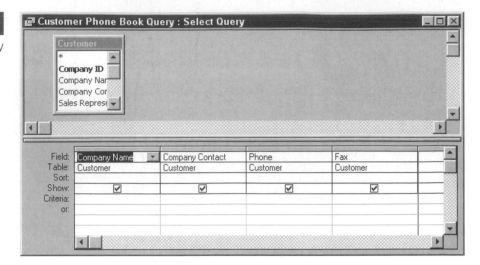

The remaining rows on the grid are used to refine your queries and are described below:

- *Table*   Used to clarify which table the field belongs to when dealing with a multiple-table query.

- *Sort*   Used to sort the resulting table into ascending or descending order by the field in this column.

- *Show*   Used to specify whether the field should be displayed in the resulting table.

- *Criteria*   Used to set criteria for selecting records to be displayed in the resulting table.

- *Or*   Used to specify a second criterion for selecting records to be displayed.

Notice that you can't see all the field names in the Customer table object shown in Figure 3.9. When using Access, you often have to size windows and objects to meet your needs. To resize an object, you position the mouse pointer over the object's border until the pointer changes to a two-headed arrow. You then click and hold down the mouse as you drag the object's border in the desired direction for sizing.

CREATING A NEW QUERY

In this section, you learn how to create a new query using the query Design window.

Perform the following steps . . .

1. Ensure that the "Sporting" Database window appears in the work area and that the *Queries* tab is active.

2. To create a new query using the Design View method:
    CLICK: New command button
    DOUBLE-CLICK: Design View

3. In the Show Table dialog box, you specify the tables (and existing queries) on which to base your new query. Do the following:
    SELECT: Customer
    CLICK: Add command button
    CLICK: Close command button
    The query Design window appears with the Customer table object in the top portion and a clean grid below.

4. Position the mouse pointer over the right border of the Customer table object until the pointer changes shape to a two-headed arrow.

5. DRAG: the mouse pointer to the right until you see the widest field name (Sales Representative ID) appear in the object's window

6. Notice that you can only see the first few field names. To see additional field names, drag the scroll box down the vertical scroll bar in the Customer table object.

7. Now drag the scroll box to the very top of the vertical scroll bar. The Customer table object should look similar to the following:

    Notice that an asterisk (*) appears at the top of the list box. The asterisk (*) provides a shortcut method for selecting fields to appear in a query. When the asterisk is dragged into the grid, all fields from the table are included automatically. However, you cannot specify a sort order or criteria in the column grid containing the asterisk. Also notice that "Company ID" is bold; this indicates that the Company ID field is the primary key for this table.

ADDING FIELDS AND WIDENING COLUMNS

In this section, you will add the Company Name, Company Contact, City, and Phone fields to the grid.

Perform the following steps . . .

1. Position the mouse pointer over the Company Name field name in the Customer table object and then drag the name into the *Field* box, located in the first column of the grid. When you release the mouse button, "Company Name" should display in the *Field* row.

2. To select another field name to appear in the grid:
   DOUBLE-CLICK: Company Contact field name in the table object
   The field name appears in the next available column automatically.

3. Let's try another shortcut method:
   CLICK: in the next available *Field* row cell
   CLICK: down arrow adjacent to the cell
   SELECT: City from the drop-down list

4. To add the last field name to the grid:
   DOUBLE-CLICK: Phone in the table object

5. To view the datasheet for the query:
   CLICK: View button ()
   The Company Name, Company Contact, City, and Phone fields should now appear in Datasheet view.

   (*CAUTION*: If you edit the field data in this datasheet, the underlying Customer table is changed also!)

6. On your own, change the column widths to the best fit for each field by double-clicking the column borders.

7. To return to the query Design window:
   CLICK: View button ()

QUICK REFERENCE
Adding Fields to the Grid in the Query Design Window

- **DRAG: the desired field name from the table object into the *Field* row of the grid, or**
- **DOUBLE-CLICK: the desired field name in the table object to add it to the next available column in the grid**

INSERTING AND DELETING FIELDS

Once you have created a query, you may decide later to modify it by inserting some additional fields. To accomplish this, drag a new field name into the *Field* row of the grid where you want it inserted. All existing fields are moved one position to the right. To delete a column from the grid, click in the column you want to delete and then choose the Edit, Delete Columns command from the menu. (*Note*: To keep a column in the grid without displaying it, make sure that no "✓" appears in that field column's *Show* check box.)

QUICK REFERENCE
Inserting and Deleting
Columns in the Grid

- **To insert a field:**

  DRAG: the field name into the grid where you want it to appear

- **To delete a column from the grid:**

  1. **SELECT: the column that you want to delete**

  2. **CHOOSE: Edit, Delete Columns**

SPECIFYING SEARCH CRITERIA

Querying a database involves more than limiting its display to specific fields. You usually want to extract records from the table that meet a given condition. Imagine being able to display a customer's entire purchase history with a few simple keystrokes. And doing this all while talking to them on the phone!

To limit the records that display in a datasheet, you enter a **conditional statement** in the *Criteria* row of the grid. A conditional statement can take one of several forms. First, you can enter an example of the value that you are looking for, such as Toronto in the City column. Second, you can use mathematical operators to limit records between a given range of values or dates. Lastly, you can use wildcards to retrieve information as you did earlier in this session when specifying filters. The question mark (?) is used to represent a single character, and the asterisk (*) is used to represent one or more characters.

The more common mathematical query operators and wildcard character examples are summarized in Table 3.1.

TABLE 3.1	*Command*	*Task*
Common Query Operators	>	Greater than; find values that are greater than the specified value. For example, >5000 finds all records where the field value is greater than 5,000. (*Note*: You don't enter commas in numeric queries.)
	<	Less than; find values less than the specified value. For example, <12/31/86 retrieves all records where the field value is less than December 31, 1986.
	>=	Greater than or equal to; find values greater than or equal to the specified value. For example, >=Moser retrieves all records where the field value starts with "Moser" and then continues to the end of the alphabet.
	<=	Less than or equal to; find values less than or equal to the specified value. For example, <=98000 retrieves all records where the field value (perhaps a zip code) contains 98000 or lower.
	Between V1 And V2	List those records that contain values between V1 and V2. For example, Between 21 And 65 in an Age field.
	V1 Or V2	List those records that have either V1 or V2 values.
	Not V1	List those records that don't have a V1 value.
	Wildcard Character Examples	
	Like Sm?th	List those records in which the field begins with "Sm", has a single character in the middle of the name, and ends with "th". Example: Smyth, Smith.
	Like Ch*ng	List those records in which the field begins with "Ch", has one or more characters in the middle of the name, and ends with "ng". Example: Chang, Chickering.
	Like *on*	List those records in which the field has "on" in the middle of the field. Example: Conditional, Conference, Monday.
	Like */*/93	List those records which end with 93 in the date field.

You have a bit of flexibility when entering expressions into the Criteria field. For example, to list your customers in Boise, you could type:

- Boise
- =Boise
- "Boise"
- ="Boise"

In the above example, Access would display "Boise" with the quotation marks in the grid. If the text you're searching for contains two words, such as Carson City, you would typically surround the text with quotation marks. After you've typed in search criteria, Access converts it to a standard format. For example, if you type ca* as the search criteria, Access displays Like "ca*" in the grid.

Let's practice specifying search criteria.

Perform the following steps . . .

1. At this point, we assume that you have completed the last section, and that the query Design window appears on your screen.

2. To specify Houston as the criterion for the City field:
CLICK: I-beam mouse pointer in the *Criteria* row for the City column
TYPE: **Houston**
PRESS: (ENTER)
Notice that the criterion becomes "Houston" when you press (ENTER).

3. To display the datasheet:
CLICK: View button (📼 ▾)
One record for Brewery Supplies, Inc. appears in the datasheet.

4. To return to the query in Design view:
CLICK: View button (📐 ▾)

5. In this step, you will type "v*" into the *Criteria* row for the City column. To begin, let's clear the Criteria row in the grid:
SELECT: *Criteria* box for the City column
CHOOSE: Edit, Delete Rows
TYPE: **v***
PRESS: (ENTER)
The criterion becomes Like "v*" when you press (ENTER).

6. To display the datasheet:
CLICK: View button (📼 ▾)
The screen should now look similar to Figure 3.10.

FIGURE 3.10

THESE RECORDS MEET THE CRITERIA SPECIFIED IN STEP 5, "V*"

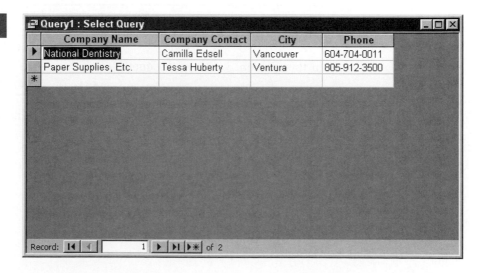

7. CLICK: View button ( )

8. To delete the criteria in the grid:
CHOOSE: Edit, Delete Rows

9. On your own, do the following:

a. Add the Sales Representative ID field to the grid.

b. Specify "VTRI" as the search criteria for the Sales Representative ID column.

c. Display the datasheet. Two records should match the criteria.

d. Display the query Design window.

e. Delete the contents of the *Criteria* row.

QUICK REFERENCE
Entering Search Criteria
in the Query Window

1. **SELECT: a column or field in the *Criteria* row of the grid**
2. **TYPE: a conditional query statement**
3. **CLICK: View button ( ) to view the results of the query**
4. **CLICK: View button ( ) to return to the Design window**

IN ADDITION DISPLAYING UNIQUE TABLE VALUES

Suppose you want to list all the states in the U.S. where your company does business. If you display the state field in a datasheet, Montana, for example, will display more than once if you do business with more than one company in Montana. In this case, you want to display only the *unique* values for a particular field so that "Montana" displays only once.

To display unique values, display the query Design window and ensure that only the field that contains the unique values is selected to display. Then, click Properties button ( ) on the toolbar and change the Unique Values field to Yes in the resulting dialog box.

SAVING THE QUERY FORM

In this section, you save the query form.

Perform the following steps . . .

1. Ensure that the query Design window appears before proceeding.

2. To save the query object:
CLICK: Save button ( )
TYPE: **Customer Listing**
PRESS: **ENTER** or CLICK: OK
(*Note:* A query can't have the same name as the table.)

3. To close the query Design window:
CLICK: Close button ([**X**])
You should now see two query objects in the Database window.

ADVANCED QUERY OPERATIONS

In this section, you enter conditional search criteria, sort the resulting query datasheet, and perform calculations on table data using the query Design window.

USING CONDITIONAL SEARCH CRITERIA

Using the query Design window, you can perform simple and complex query operations. A simple query usually involves extracting information based on a single criterion or condition. A complex query, on the other hand, involves more than one criterion and employs conditional logic. **Conditional logic** is the method by which criteria statements are joined and executed in a query statement. For example, you may want to list all of your Florida customers who deal with a particular sales agent. This query requires that you join the two criteria using a *logical and* statement and that the two entries exist in the same row of the query Design window.

As another example, you may want to find all your customers who live in either Sacramento or Phoenix. Obviously, this query requires a *logical or* statement. For a *logical or* relationship, you can use the *Criteria* row or the *Or* row in the grid. For example, in the City column, you can enter "Sacramento" or "Phoenix" on the *Criteria* row, or you can enter "Sacramento" on the *Criteria* row and "Phoenix" immediately below on the *Or* row. For each query, the resulting datasheet is the same.

To specify a range of values, you can use one of two methods. To retrieve all the records where an employee's salary is greater than $40,000 and less than $60,000, type >40000 and <60000 on the *Criteria* row for the Salary column. To retrieve those records where the salary is greater than or equal to $40,000 and less than or equal to $60,000, type between 40000 and 60000 on the *Criteria* row. Ensure that you don't enter commas or quotation marks when entering numbers that you want to use in calculations.

In this section, you create a query for the Sales Representatives table.

Perform the following steps . . .

1. Ensure that the "Sporting" Database window appears in the work area and that the *Queries* tab is active.

2. To create a new query:
   CLICK: New command button
   DOUBLE-CLICK: Design View

3. In the Show Table dialog box that appears:
   SELECT: Sales Representatives
   CLICK: Add command button
   CLICK: Close command button
   The query Design window appears with the Sales Representatives table object in the top portion and a clean grid below.

4. DRAG: the sizing border of the table object to fit the longest field name

5. Add the Last Name, First Name, Date Hired, Vacation Days, and Base Salary fields to the grid by double-clicking their field names.

6. To list the sales reps who have between 10 and 30 vacation days:
   SELECT: *Criteria* box of the Vacation Days column
   TYPE: **between 10 and 30**
   PRESS: (**ENTER**)

7. To perform the query and display the datasheet:
   CLICK: View button ([▦ ▾])
   Notice that the resulting datasheet (Figure 3.11) includes values between 10 and 30, including 10 and 30, in the Vacation Days column.

FIGURE 3.11

RESULTING DATASHEET AFTER PERFORMING A QUERY

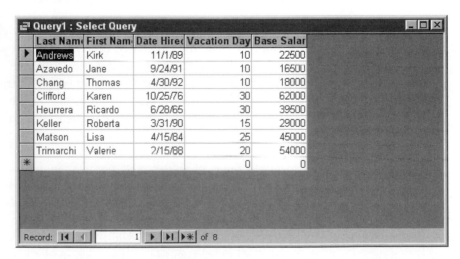

	Last Name	First Name	Date Hired	Vacation Day	Base Salary
▶	Andrews	Kirk	11/1/89	10	22500
	Azavedo	Jane	9/24/91	10	16500
	Chang	Thomas	4/30/92	10	18000
	Clifford	Karen	10/25/76	30	62000
	Heurrera	Ricardo	6/28/65	30	39500
	Keller	Roberta	3/31/90	15	29000
	Matson	Lisa	4/15/84	25	45000
	Trimarchi	Valerie	2/15/88	20	54000
*				0	0

Record: |◀| |◀| 1 |▶| |▶| |▶*| of 8

8. CLICK: View button ([✎ ▾])

9. To delete the current criteria:
   CHOOSE: Edit, Delete Rows

10. To save the query:
CLICK: Save button ( )
TYPE: **Sales Rep Listing**
PRESS: (**ENTER**) or CLICK: OK

11. On your own, enter criteria into the grid so that the records for the following sales representatives display in the datasheet:

   a. Sales reps who have a base salary that is less than $20,000

   b. Sales reps who have a base salary that is between $29,000 and $54,000

   c. Sales reps who have a base salary that is greater than $29,000 and less than $54,000

   d. Sales reps who have a base salary that is greater than $29,000 or less than $54,000

12. To close the query Design window without saving the changes:
CLICK: Close button (**X**)
CLICK: No command button

IN ADDITION RETURNING THE TOP VALUES ONLY

To display the top values from a query, display the query Design window and click the Top Values button (All ▾) on the toolbar. You can then specify a number of rows (for example, the top ten values) or a percentage of the matching table records (for example, the top five percent.) Ensure that only the field that contains the values is selected to display and then view the datasheet to see the results.

SORTING QUERY RESULTS

In this section, you create a new query and specify a sort order in the grid. Unless you specify a sort order explicitly, the resulting table displays in the same order that governs the underlying table, which may or may not be determined by a primary key field.

Perform the following steps . . .

1. Ensure that the "Sporting" Database window appears in the work area and that the *Queries* tab is active.

2. To create a new query:
CLICK: New command button
DOUBLE-CLICK: Design View

3. In the Show Table dialog box that appears:
SELECT: Customer
CLICK: Add command button
CLICK: Close command button

4. DRAG: the sizing border of the table object to fit the longest field name

5. Add the Company ID, Company Contact, and Sales Representative ID fields to the grid.

6. To perform the query and display the datasheet:
CLICK: View button (⊞ ▾)
Since the data table's primary key is the Company ID field, its contents govern the display order of the resulting table.

7. CLICK: View button (⬚ ▾)

8. To display the datasheet in order by the Sales Representative ID field:
CLICK: *Sort* box for the Sales Representative ID column
CLICK: down arrow that appears in the *Sort* row
SELECT: Ascending

9. Display the datasheet. The list should now appear in sorted order by the Sales Representative ID field, as shown in Figure 3.12.

10. Return to the query Design window.

FIGURE 3.12

SORTING A QUERY'S
RESULTS USING THE
DESIGN WINDOW

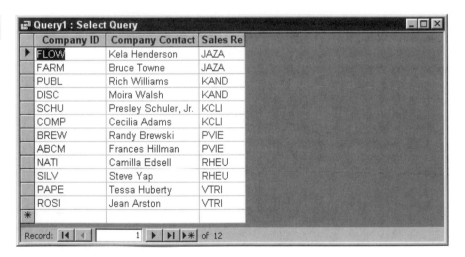

You can also define a secondary sort key so that the records for each sales representative display in order by the Company ID field. To do this, you must move the Sales Representative ID column so that it displays before the Company ID column. You can then specify an ascending sort for the Sales Representative ID field and an ascending sort for the Company ID field. The field that is the leftmost column becomes the primary sort key.

Let's institute a secondary sort key.

Perform the following steps . . .

1. Ensure that you are in query Design view.

2. To select the Sales Representative ID column so that you can move it, position the down arrow mouse pointer just above the field name and then click the left mouse button once. If done properly, the Sales Representative ID column will appear highlighted.

3. To move the column:
   DRAG: the frame area above the field name to the leftmost column of the grid and then release the mouse button

   (*CAUTION*: Ensure that the mouse pointer is an arrow before clicking and dragging the field column.)

4. CLICK: *Sort* box for the Company ID column
   CLICK: down arrow that appears in the *Sort* row
   SELECT: Ascending

5. Display the datasheet. Notice that the table is in order by the Sales Representative ID column; for each Sales Representative ID, the datasheet is sorted in order by the Company ID field.

6. Close the datasheet window without saving the query.

QUICK REFERENCE
Sorting a Query's Results

1. **CLICK: Sort box of the desired field or column**
2. **CLICK: down arrow that appears in the *Sort* row**
3. **SELECT: Ascending, Descending, or (not sorted)**

MODIFYING A QUERY

In this section, you modify a query named Customer Listing that you created earlier in this session. You will modify the query so that it is sorted into order by the City field.

Perform the following steps . . .

1. Ensure that the "Sporting" Database window appears in the work area and that the *Queries* tab is active.

2. To modify the Customer Listing query:
   SELECT: Customer Listing
   CLICK: Design command button
   The Customer Listing's Design window should appear.

3. To display the datasheet in sorted order:
   CLICK: *Sort* box for the City column
   CLICK: down arrow that appears in the *Sort* row
   SELECT: Ascending

4. CLICK: View button (▦▾)
   The datasheet appears, sorted in order by the City field.

5. To save the modified query:
   CLICK: Save button (🖫)

6. Close the datasheet window to display the Database window.

QUICK REFERENCE
Modify a Query

1. **Open the desired query in Design view.**
2. **Modify the grid in the query Design window.**
3. **CLICK: Save button (🖫) to save the query**

PERFORMING CALCULATIONS

Besides performing searches on table data, you can perform calculations on textual and numeric data to summarize all the records in a table or selected records. For example, you might want to determine the average number of vacation days earned by each sales rep. To perform a calculation, you must first display an additional row in the grid called *Total* by clicking the Totals button (∑) on the toolbar or by choosing the View, Totals command. Table 3.2 describes some of the calculations that you can perform using the *Total* row in the query Design window.

TABLE 3.2

Performing Basic Calculations

Calculation	Description
Sum	Displays the total of values stored in a field
Avg	Displays the average of values stored in a field
Min	Displays the lowest value stored in a field
Max	Displays the highest value stored in a field
Count	Returns the number of entries in a field
StDev	Displays the standard deviation of values
Var	Displays the variance of values
First	Returns the field value of the first record
Last	Returns the field value of the last record

You will now practice performing a calculation.

Perform the following steps . . .

1. Ensure that the "Sporting" Database window appears in the work area and that the *Queries* tab is active.

2. Using the Design View method, create a new query based on the Sales Representatives table.

3. Add the Vacation Days and Base Salary fields to the design grid.

4. To display the *Total* row in the grid:
CLICK: Totals button (Σ)

5. The "Group By" option in the *Total* row is used to perform calculations on subsets of records in the table. However, we want to perform a calculation using all of the records. To calculate the average for each of the fields, you will select "Avg" in the *Total* row for both Vacation Days and Base Salary. Do the following:
CLICK: *Total* box for the Vacation Days column
CLICK: down arrow that appears in the *Total* row
SELECT: Avg
CLICK: *Total* box for the Base Salary column
CLICK: down arrow that appears in the *Total* row
SELECT: Avg
Your query Design window should now appear similar to Figure 3.13.

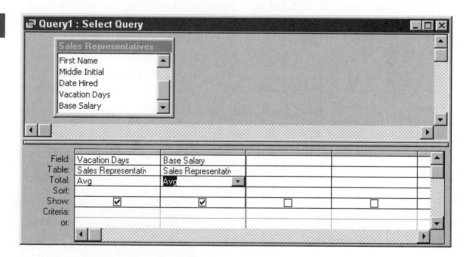

6. CLICK: View button (▦ ▾)
The result of the calculation appears below. Notice that the numbers are displaying with trailing decimal places; you will choose a new formatting option for these numbers shortly.

7. CLICK: View button (▨ ▾)

8. To control the display of trailing decimal places in a field, you modify its field properties. Do the following:
   CLICK: *Total* box for the Vacation Days column|
   CLICK: Properties button (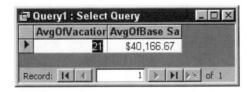) on the toolbar
   CLICK: *Format* field
   CLICK: down arrow that appears beside the *Format* field
   SELECT: Fixed
   CLICK: *Decimal Places* field
   CLICK: down arrow that appears beside the *Decimal Places* field
   SELECT: 0

9. With the Field Properties dialog box still displaying, you will now set the display format for the Base Salary field. If necessary, drag the dialog box out of the way so that the Base Salary field is visible. Do the following:
   CLICK: *Total* box for the Base Salary column
   CLICK: *Format* field
   CLICK: down arrow that appears beside the *Format* field
   SELECT: Currency
   CLICK: *Decimal Places* field
   CLICK: down arrow that appears beside the *Decimal Places* field
   SELECT: 2
   CLICK: Close button (❌) for the Field Properties dialog box

10. To display the results of the calculations:
    CLICK: View button (▦▾)
    The datasheet should now look like the following:

AvgOfVacatior	AvgOfBase Sa
21	$40,166.67

Query1 : Select Query — Record: 1 of 1

In the following steps, you perform calculations on selected records in a table; to accomplish this, you must use the "Group By" expression in the *Total* row. Your objective is to determine the average base salary of those individuals who receive ten vacation days per year.

Perform the following steps . . .

1. If you completed the last section, the datasheet should be displaying. Before proceeding, return to the query Design window.

2. To base your search on the Vacation Days column:
   CLICK: *Total* row for the Vacation Days column
   CLICK: down arrow that appears in the *Total* row
   DRAG: the scroll bar upwards
   SELECT: Group By

3. To determine the average Base Salary of those individuals who receive ten

vacation days per year:
CLICK: *Criteria* row for the Vacation Days column
TYPE: **10**
PRESS: [ENTER]

4. CLICK: View button ([▦ ▾])
The answer "$19,000.00" appears in the datasheet. That is, $19,000.00 is
the average salary for sales reps receiving 10 vacation days per year.

5. Close the datasheet window without saving the query.

QUICK REFERENCE
Performing Calculations

1. Display the query Design window.

2. CLICK: Totals button (Σ) to display the *Total* row in the grid

3. CLICK: Total row in the desired field column

4. CLICK: down arrow that appears in the *Total* row

5. SELECT: a calculation to perform

IN ADDITION USING CALCULATED FIELDS

To display the results of a calculation that draws its data from other columns, you must create a calculated field. For example, you can create an expression that multiplies the contents of an "In Stock" field by a "Unit Cost" field and then display the answer in a column entitled "Stock Value". Calculated fields are entered into the *Field* row of the design grid and their results are displayed in the dynaset. For the above example,

you would enter the following expression:
Stock Value: [In Stock]*[Unit Cost]

Notice that the table's field names must be enclosed by square brackets. When you run the query, the results of the calculation are displayed in the "Stock Value" column of the dynaset. For more information, ask the Office Assistant for help on "Calculated Fields."

QUERYING MULTIPLE TABLES

Microsoft Access is a relational database management system. In other words, Access provides the capability to relate or join separate tables in your database for the purpose of sharing information and reducing data redundancy. To establish a relationship or an association between tables, they must contain a common field. The most common type of relationship is the *one-to-many relationship*, where *one* record in Table A has *many* matching records in Table B. For example, let's say that Table A contains a single record for each sales representative in your organization and that Table B contains one record for each of your customers. Because each sales representative manages several customer accounts, there is a one-to-many relationship between these tables. Other types of relationships include *one-to-one* and *many-to-many*, but are far less common.

This section demonstrates how to work with multiple tables in the query Design window. In the exercise that follows, you must relate the Customer and Sales Representatives tables for the purpose of seeing the sales reps' full name beside each customer, rather than just the sales reps' ID codes.

Perform the following steps . . .

1. Ensure that the "Sporting" Database window appears in the work area and that the *Queries* tab is active.

2. To create a new multiple-table query:
CLICK: New command button
DOUBLE-CLICK: Design View

3. In the Show Table dialog box that appears:
DOUBLE-CLICK: Customer
DOUBLE-CLICK: Sales Representatives
CLICK: Close command button

4. DRAG: the sizing borders of the table objects in the query Design window to fit the longest field name
DRAG: the Title bars of the table objects to arrange them neatly

5. You must now define a relationship between these two tables. This relationship will be based on the common field, Sales Representative ID, between the two tables. To set the relationship:
DRAG: Sales Representative ID field from the Customer table over to the Sales Representative ID field in the Sales Representatives table

A line will appear, connecting the two Sales Representative ID fields, when you release the mouse button and drop the field (Figure 3.14).

FIGURE 3.14

JOINING THE CUSTOMER
AND THE SALES
REPRESENTATIVES TABLES

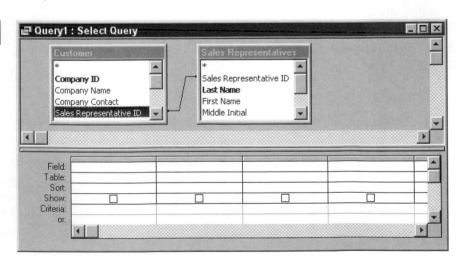

6. Add the Company Name and Company Contact fields from the Customer table to the grid.

7. Add the First Name and Last Name fields from the Sales Representatives table to the grid.

8. CLICK: View button (▣ ▾)
   Note that for each company you can see the full name of the sales representative.

9. Return to the query Design window.

10. To display the datasheet in order by the Company Name field:
    CLICK: *Sort* box for the Company Name column
    CLICK: down arrow that appears in the *Sort* row
    SELECT: Ascending

11. CLICK: View button (▣ ▾)
    The datasheet should now appear in sorted order, by the Company Name field, as shown in Figure 3.15.

FIGURE 3.15

THE RESULTING
DATASHEET WINDOW

Company Name	Company Contact	First Name	Last Name
ABC Metals	Frances Hillman	Pierre	Vieau
Brewery Supplies, Inc.	Randy Brewski	Pierre	Vieau
Computers, Intl.	Cecilia Adams	Karen	Clifford
Discount Glass	Moira Walsh	Kirk	Andrews
Farming Equipment, Inc.	Bruce Towne	Jane	Azavedo
Flowers Anywhere	Kela Henderson	Jane	Azavedo
National Dentistry	Camilla Edsell	Ricardo	Heurrera
Paper Supplies, Etc.	Tessa Huberty	Valerie	Trimarchi
Publishing, Etc.	Rich Williams	Kirk	Andrews
Rosie's Cookie Company	Jean Arston	Valerie	Trimarchi
Schuler and Co.	Presley Schuler, Jr.	Karen	Clifford
Silver Spring Toyota	Steve Yap	Ricardo	Heurrera

Query1 : Select Query

Record: ◀◀ ◀ 1 ▶ ▶▶ ▶* of 12

12. Close the datasheet window without saving the query.

13. Close the Database window.

14. Exit Microsoft Access.

QUICK REFERENCE
Querying Multiple Tables

1. **Create new query.**

2. **Select two or more tables on which to base your query.**

3. **DRAG: the common field from the first table object to the common field in the next table object to link the two tables**

4. **Add fields from each table to the grid.**

IN ADDITION RELATIONAL DATABASE CONCEPTS

When working with multiple tables, you should understand some fundamental relational database terms and concepts. For example:

- Primary Key: A field (or fields) containing unique values that is used to refer to specific records in one table from another table.

- Foreign Key: A field that refers to the primary key field in another table.

- Referential Integrity: The rules that must be followed to preserve the relationship between tables. For example, you cannot delete a sales representative record in Table A that still has customer assocations in Table B. To maintain referential integrity, you must remove the customer associations first in Table B before deleting the sales representative's record in Table A.

For more information, ask the Office Assistant for help on "Establishing relationships between tables."

SUMMARY

In this session, you learned how to sort, find, and filter table records in a database. You also created, customized, and modified simple and complex queries. Specifically, you added display fields and criteria to a grid in the query Design window. You also learned how to sort the results of a query and perform calculations on a table. Lastly, you linked two tables together and displayed their contents using a multiple-table query.

COMMAND SUMMARY

Table 3.3 provides a list of the commands and procedures covered in this session.

TABLE 3.3	*Task Description*	*Menu Command*	*Toolbar Button*
Command Summary	Sorts the contents of a column into ascending order	Records, Sort, Sort Ascending	
	Sorts the contents of a column into descending order	Records, Sort, Sort Descending	
	Finds records in a datasheet	Edit, Find	
	Filters records by selection	Records, Filter, Filter By Selection	
	Filters records excluding the selection	Records, Filter, Filter Excluding Selection	
	Filters records by criteria entered into form	Records, Filter, Filter By Form	
	Filters records by criteria entered into a design grid	Records, Filter, Advanced Filter/Sort	
	Applies a filter created using Filter By Form or Advanced Filter/Sort		

TABLE 3.3 *Continued*	Task Description	Menu Command	Toolbar Button
	Creates a new query object		
	Saves a query	File, Save	
	Deletes the contents of a row in the grid portion of the query Design window	Edit, Delete Rows	
	Deletes the contents of a column in the grid portion of the query Design window	Edit, Delete Columns	
	Displays the *Total* row in the query Design window	View, Totals	Σ
	Displays the Field Properties dialog box	View, Properties	

KEY TERMS

action query

With this query type, you ask questions of a database and, depending on the results, Access performs an action that changes one or more objects in the database.

Advanced Filter/Sort

In Access, a command that returns a subset of records from a data table matching a filter and sort specification.

append query

A type of action query that adds data to a table.

conditional logic

The method by which criteria statements are joined and executed in a query statement.

conditional statement

A query statement that limits the number of records that display in the datasheet.

delete query

A type of action query that deletes records in a datasheet from one or more tables.

dynaset

The result of a query. A dynaset is usually displayed as a datasheet table of the records matching the query parameters.

filter

The process or method of temporarily restricting the display of records in a data table to those that match a particular search specification.

Filter By Form

In Access, a command that returns a subset of records from a table matching a filter specification.

Filter By Selection

In Access, a command that returns a subset of records from a table matching the selected value in the datasheet or form.

Filter Excluding Selection

In Access, a command that returns a subset of records from a table not matching the selected value in the datasheet or form.

Filter For Input

In Access, a command that returns a subset of records from a table matching a filter specification that you enter in a shortcut menu text box.

make table query

A type of action query that creates a new table.

query-by-example

The process of querying a table in a visual mode by choosing fields and typing in record criteria.

Simple Query Wizard

An Access tool that simplifies the process of creating a query.

select query

With this query type, you ask questions of your database and display the results in a datasheet.

update query

A type of action query that updates data in a table.

EXERCISES

SHORT ANSWER

1. When would you use the Find command rather than creating a Query?

2. When would you use a Filter rather than creating a Query?

3. What are the four methods for filtering records in a table?

4. What is the difference between a select query and an action query?

5. List the options available in the New Query dialog box.

6. List the calculations that you can perform in a query.

7. What is the purpose of the *Criteria* row in the grid?

8. In a query Design window, how would you ensure that the resulting datasheet is sorted into ascending order by the Company field?

9. How do you change between query Design view and Datasheet view?

10. How do you relate two tables together in the query Design window?

HANDS-ON

(*Note*: Ensure that you know the storage location of your Advantage Files and your Data Files before proceeding.)

1. In this exercise, you open the "School" database and then sort records and apply a filter.

   a. Open the "School" database stored in the Advantage Files location.

   b. Create a new query, based on the Students table, using the Simple Query Wizard.

   c. Include the following fields in the query: First Name, Last Name, Company, City, and Phone.

   d. Name the query Student Phone Book.

   e. Finish the wizard by displaying the datasheet for the query.

   f. Select the Last Name column in the datasheet.

   g. Sort the records into ascending order using the Sort Ascending button () on the toolbar.

   h. Before applying a filter to the City column, select the letters "San" in the entry "San Francisco" in any visible record.

   i. Apply the filter to the datasheet by clicking the Filter By Selection button (🏷) on the toolbar.

   j. Save the query by clicking the Save button (💾).

   k. Print the datasheet by clicking the Print button (🖨).

   l. Close the datasheet window by clicking the Close button (✖).

2. You will now modify the Student Listing query in the "School" database using query Design view.

   a. Display the Student Listing query in Design view.

   b. Change the field order in the grid to State, City, Last Name, First Name, Address, and Zip.

   c. Although still included in the grid, do not display the Address and Zip fields in the resulting datasheet.

   d. Modify the grid so that the datasheet is sorted by the State field and, for all like States, the datasheet is in order by the City field. Remove any other Sort options from the grid.

   e. Limit the display of records to those that contain the letters "san" anywhere in the City field. Your screen should now appear similar to Figure 3.16.

   f. Display the datasheet.

g. Save the query by clicking the Save button (⊞).

h. Print the datasheet by clicking the Print button (🖨).

i. Close the datasheet window by clicking the Close button (✕).

FIGURE 3.16

DATASHEET FOR THE
MODIFIED STUDENT
LISTING QUERY

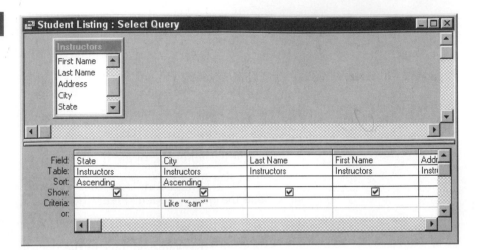

3. In this exercise, you create a multiple-table query for the "School" database.

a. Create a query that includes the Courses and Instructors tables.

b. If they are not already joined, relate the two tables using the Instructor ID field.

c. Include the Title and Location fields from the Courses table, and the First Name and Last Name fields from the Instructors table.

d. Display the datasheet.

e. Adjust the column widths to best fit the data.

f. Save the query as Related Instructor Summary.

g. Print the datasheet

h. Close the datasheet and then the Database window.

4. **On Your Own:** Performing Calculations in a Query
    Open the "School" database and create a new query using the Design View method. In the design grid, ask the following question of the database: "What is the average course length of all entries in the database?" After displaying the result in a datasheet, format your answer to fixed with two decimal places and then save the query as "Average Length in Days." Secondly, create a query that counts the number of courses that are greater than 1 day in length. Save this query as "Long-Term Courses." Close the "School" database window when you are finished.

5. **On Your Own:** Querying Your Personal Address Book
Earlier in this guide, you created a database called "My Phone Book" and saved it to your Data Files location. (*Note:* If you have not created this database, do so now by referring to the On Your Own exercises in Session 2.) Create a new query that lists each person's name and phone number. Sort the query using the Last Name field as the primary sort key and the First Name field as the secondary sort key. Save the query as "Alphabetical Phone Listing" and then print the resulting datasheet. When finished, close the Database window and exit Microsoft Access.

CASE PROBLEMS	MOUNTAIN WEAR

(*Note:* In the following case problems, assume the role of the primary characters and perform the same steps that they identify. You may want to re-read the session opening.)

1. Using the "Mountain" database that is stored in the Advantage Files location, Antonio sets out to create the list of new customers that Rita has requested. He creates a query for the Customers table that lists only those customers who have purchased shoes after July 20, 1995 (his starting date.) Then, he sorts the query datasheet into order by the "Last Purchase Date" field and includes the following additional fields: Customer ID, Last Name, First Name, and Model Code. After printing the datasheet for Rita's review, Antonio saves the query as Recent Purchases. Lastly, he closes the query Design window.

2. Antonio is now ready to collect the information for Rita's second report. Using the "Mountain" database, he creates a query that displays information from the Customers table and the Shoe Models table at the same time. (*Hint:* Ensure that you use the Model Code field to define the relationship between the two tables.) To satisfy Rita's reporting requirements, Antonio creates a query that shows what each customer has purchased since July 20, 1995, and includes the following additional fields from each table:

Customers table	Shoe Models table
Customer ID	Model Name
Last Name	Price
First Name	

After viewing the datasheet, Antonio remembers that Rita wants her reports listed in order by the Last Name field and makes the modification. Antonio saves the query as "Detailed Listing of Recent Purchases" and then prints it for Rita's review. He then closes the datasheet window to display the School Database window.

3. "Antonio, your reports look great!" Antonio smiled as Rita praised him in front of his co-workers. "I'd like you to show Jose and Wendy how you produced these reports so quickly. They typically spend the last three days of each month compiling their reports. Could you do me one last favor? I'd like a modified version of the second report you gave me. That is, I'd like to see a list of only those customers who live in San Mateo. Thanks again, Antonio." Antonio turned back to his computer, avoiding the eyes of his two new friends. From the next cubicle, he heard "Congratulations, Antonio. Not just anyone, nor any report for that matter, can impress Rita. You'll have to show us how you do it next month." Antonio was relieved that his two co-workers were pleased and not upset by his newfound status.

Antonio begins working on the new report immediately. Using the "Mountain" database, he displays the query Design window for the "Detailed Listing of Recent Purchases" query and then enters a criterion to list only those customers who live in San Mateo (without displaying the field in the dynaset.) He saves the query using the same name, prints the new result, and then places a copy of the printout in Rita's in-box. Lastly, he closes the database and exits Access.

Presenting Your Data

SESSION

HTTP://WWW

4

IRWIN
COMPUTER & INFORMATION TECHNOLOGY

INTRODUCTION

The purpose of a database management system is to turn data into information. To this end, a report can be used to summarize a thousand invoices into a customer sales history or an accounts receivable report. Each day, people make business decisions using reports obtained from database management systems. This session shows you how to create, modify, and customize reports for presenting data stored in your Access databases.

VACATION VISTAS, INC.

Frank Muldanno owns and operates a tour company in Memphis that specializes in Caribbean cruises. Because business has been rather slow lately, Frank has decided to move his store to the downtown core in hopes of generating more walk-in business. Finding his dream location, Frank contacts the landlord of the property to discuss terms. Although the rent for the storefront is more than Frank anticipated, he takes a risk that business will pick up and, on this faith, he signs the lease.

To ensure that he has enough cash to make it through his first six months in the new location, Frank decides to take out a bank loan. After that time, he is confident that the proceeds from the business will cover all of his monthly bills, including his salary. Frank must now focus on putting together a package for Nancy Moorehead, the loan officer at Washington Bank. To demonstrate his ability to pay back the loan, he wants to show her his current client list, which he maintains using Microsoft Access. However, to impress Nancy, he decides to improve the presentation format of his client list. Until now, he has simply been printing his datasheet. Frank knows that he must design and produce a report, but he hasn't created one before.

In this session, you and Frank will learn how to create columnar and tabular reports, print mailing labels, use the report Design view, and customize a report structure to meet your needs.

CREATING A NEW REPORT

You create **reports** in order to "dress up" or summarize your tables and query results for presentation purposes. Each report may contain a variety of design elements such as text, data, graphics (for example, a chart or picture), lines, borders, and colors. Some examples of typical reports generated using Microsoft Access include sales summaries, invoices, mailing labels, personal address books, and inventory listings.

Similar to creating any new database object, the process for creating a report is to first click the *Reports* tab in the Database window and then click the New command button. Alternatively, you can open a table or query (or simply select a table or query name in the Database window) and then click the down arrow attached to the New Object button (⬚▾) on the toolbar. If you select the New command button from the Database window, the dialog box shown in Figure 4.1 appears with options for creating a new report. These options are summarized in Table 4.1.

FIGURE 4.1

NEW REPORT DIALOG
BOX

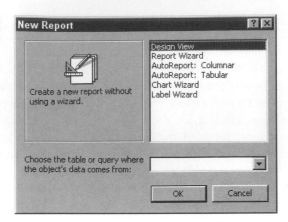

TABLE 4.1	Report Option	Purpose
Options for Creating a New Report	Design View	Creates a new report using report Design view
	Report Wizard	Creates a new report using the Report Wizard
	AutoReport: Columnar	Creates a new columnar report that includes all of the fields from the selected table or query displayed down a single column; each value displays on a separate line or row with the field label to the left
	AutoReport: Tabular	Creates a new tabular report that includes all of the fields from the selected table or query; field labels appear at the top of each column and each row represents a new record
	Chart Wizard	Using a report wizard, creates a new chart based on values in a table or query
	Label Wizard	Using a report wizard, creates a mailing label report; you choose the label format, paper size, number of labels per page, and the label size

In this section, you learn to create reports using the Access **report wizards.** Even experienced users should start creating their reports using a wizard and then complete them in Design view. Later in this session, you will use the report Design view to modify, format, and customize a report and its elements.

USING THE AUTOREPORT WIZARDS

An **AutoReport Wizard** is the easiest report wizard to use because Access performs all of the work without prompting you for any additional information. As mentioned in Table 4.1, there are actually two AutoReport wizards, Columnar and Tabular, accessible from the New Report dialog box. If, however, you choose the AutoReport option from the New Object button (🔳▼), Access generates a single-column report (Columnar) based on the open or selected table or query. To create any other type of report, you must access the *Reports* tab in the Database window.

Let's get started creating some reports.

Perform the following steps . . .

1. Turn on your computer and load Microsoft Access. If the startup dialog box appears, click the Cancel command button to display an empty application window. If you already have a Database window open, close the database before proceeding.

2. Open the database named "School" located in your Advantage Files location.

3. To display the contents of the Students table:
CLICK: *Tables* tab
DOUBLE-CLICK: Students
The Students datasheet should now appear.

4. To automatically generate a columnar report for this table:
CLICK: down arrow attached to the New Object button ([🗐 ▾])
CLICK: AutoReport
After a few seconds, a columnar report of the table's data appears in Print Preview mode.

5. Using the window's Title bar, sizing borders, and scroll bars, position the window to appear similar to Figure 4.2.

FIGURE 4.2

A COLUMNAR REPORT CREATED USING THE AUTOREPORT WIZARD

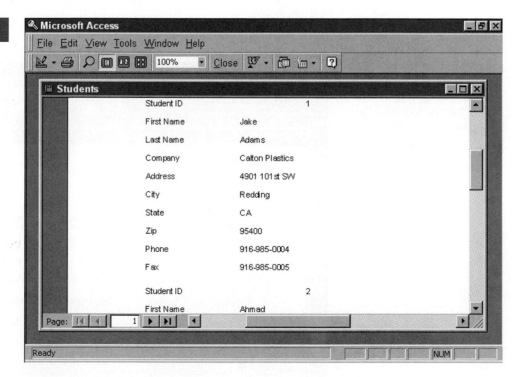

6. To zoom out so you can see more of the report:
CLICK: Zoom button ([🔎])

7. To zoom back in:
CLICK: Zoom button ([🔎])

8. On your own, try clicking the One Page (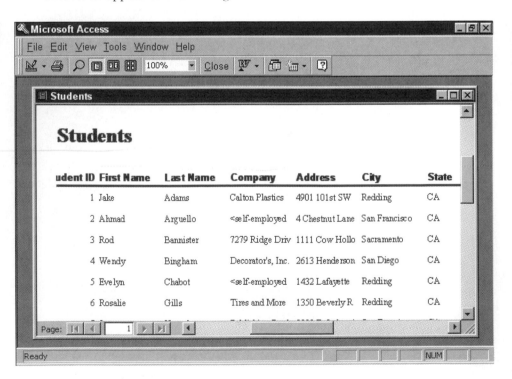), Two Pages (□□), Multiple Pages (□□), and Zoom menu (100% ▾) buttons to change the view perspective of your report. Before continuing, select One Page (□) with a zoom factor of 100%.

9. To close the Print Preview window without saving the report:
CLICK: its Close button (✕)
CLICK: No command button when asked to save the changes

10. To close the datasheet window:
CLICK: its Close button (✕)
The "School" Database window should now appear.

11. To create a tabular report using the AutoReport wizard:
CLICK: *Reports* tab
CLICK: New command button

12. In the New Report dialog box:
SELECT: AutoReport: Tabular
CLICK: down arrow beside the *Choose the table...* drop-down list box to display a list of table names and queries in the School database
SELECT: Students
CLICK: OK command button
After a few seconds, a tabular report appears in Print Preview mode.

13. Using the window's Title bar, sizing borders, and scroll bars, position the window to appear similar to Figure 4.3.

FIGURE 4.3

A TABULAR REPORT
CREATED USING THE
AUTOREPORT WIZARD

udent ID	First Name	Last Name	Company	Address	City	State
1	Jake	Adams	Calton Plastics	4901 101st SW	Redding	CA
2	Ahmad	Arguello	<self-employed	4 Chestnut Lane	San Francisco	CA
3	Rod	Bannister	7279 Ridge Driv	1111 Cow Hollo	Sacramento	CA
4	Wendy	Bingham	Decorator's, Inc.	2613 Henderson	San Diego	CA
5	Evelyn	Chabot	<self-employed	1432 Lafayette	Redding	CA
6	Rosalie	Gills	Tires and More	1350 Beverly R	Redding	CA

14. To display the entire report page:
CLICK: One Page (🔲) button

15. To zoom in on a particular area, move the magnifying glass mouse pointer over the bottom left-hand corner of the report and then click the left mouse button once. You should now see the current date appear in the page footer for this report. Also, the magnifying glass mouse pointer now contains a minus sign, indicating that the next click will cause the display to zoom out.

16. CLICK: magnifying glass mouse pointer anywhere on the report
The display should zoom out to view a single page.

17. To view this report using Design view:
CLICK: Close command button in the toolbar

18. On your own, move and size the report Design window and Toolbox window, if it appears, to look similar to Figure 4.4. You will learn how to create and modify reports in Design view later in this session.

FIGURE 4.4

A TABULAR REPORT DISPLAYED IN REPORT DESIGN VIEW

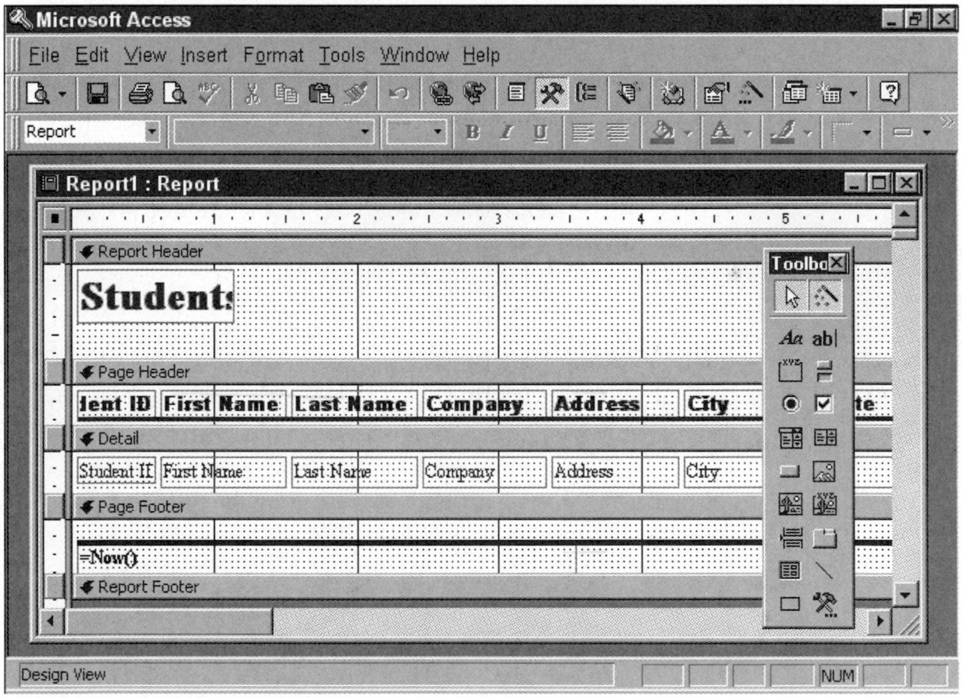

19. To save this report:
CLICK: Save button (🔲) on the toolbar
TYPE: **Students Tabular AutoReport**
PRESS: (ENTER)

20. To close the report Design window:
CLICK: its Close button (❌)
You should see the new report object listed in the Database window.

QUICK REFERENCE	1.	**CLICK:** *Reports* **tab**
Using the AutoReport Wizard	2.	**CLICK: New command button**
	3.	**SELECT: AutoReport: Columnar or AutoReport: Tabular**
	4.	**SELECT: a table or query upon which to base the report**
	5.	**PRESS:** (ENTER) **or CLICK: OK**

USING THE REPORT WIZARD

In this section, you use the Report Wizard to create a report that groups students by the City in which they live.

Perform the following steps . . .

1. Ensure that the "School" Database window appears in the work area and that the *Reports* tab is active.

2. To create a new report:
   CLICK: New command button

3. In the New Report dialog box:
   SELECT: Report Wizard
   CLICK: down arrow beside the *Choose the table...* drop-down list box
   SELECT: Students
   CLICK: OK command button
   The first dialog box for the Report Wizard appears.

4. In the *Available Fields* list box:
   DOUBLE-CLICK: City
   DOUBLE-CLICK: Last Name
   DOUBLE-CLICK: First Name
   DOUBLE-CLICK: Phone
   (*Note*: The order in which you select the fields is important. Rather than double-clicking the field names, you can select a field by clicking on it once and then move it to the *Selected Fields* list box using the buttons shown in Table 4.2.)

	Button	Purpose
TABLE 4.2	**>**	Adds the highlighted field to the report
Report Wizard dialog box buttons	**>>**	Adds all of the fields to the report
	<	Removes the highlighted field
	<<	Removes all of the fields
	Cancel	Cancels the current Report Wizard selections
	< Back	Displays the previous wizard dialog box
	Next >	Displays the next wizard dialog box
	Finish	Finishes the wizard and displays the report

5. To proceed to the next dialog box:
CLICK: **Next >**

6. In this dialog box, you specify the desired grouping options. To group records by the contents of a particular field, you double-click the field in the *Do you want to add any grouping levels?* list box. The layout preview area in the dialog box helps you visualize the grouping options you have selected. To group the students in our report by the city in which they live, do the following:
DOUBLE-CLICK: City
CLICK: **Next >**

7. You now specify the desired sorting options for the detail records. You can sort the report up to four levels deep. In other words, if you sort a report by a Country field, you could then choose to sort by Region, State, and City fields. For our exercise, you will sort the report's detail records by the contents of the Last Name and First Name fields. Do the following:
CLICK: down arrow beside the first sort option's drop-down list box
SELECT: Last Name
CLICK: down arrow beside the second drop-down list box
SELECT: First Name
Notice that Sort Ascending buttons appear beside the drop-down list boxes. To select a descending sort order, you would simply click this button. Your dialog box should now appear similar to Figure 4.5.

FIGURE 4.5

SPECIFYING A SORT
ORDER USING THE
REPORT WIZARD

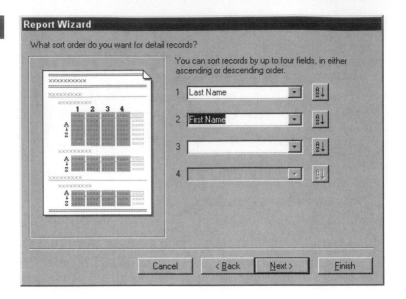

8. To proceed to the next dialog box:
CLICK: Next >

9. In this dialog box, you specify the desired layout and page orientation for the report. For grouped reports, the Report Wizard provides some nice layout options for separating and organizing information. Also, you can choose between a portrait and a landscape page orientation for viewing and printing the report. Do the following:
CLICK: *Outline 1* option button in the *Layout* area
CLICK: *Portrait* option button in the *Orientation* area
CLICK: Next >

10. In this dialog box, you specify the desired report style. On your own, click the style names appearing in the list box one at a time in order to preview their formats in the layout preview area. When you are ready to proceed, do the following:
SELECT: Soft Gray
CLICK: Next >

11. In the final dialog box, you enter a name for the report and then determine whether to preview it or conduct some further work in report Design view. For this exercise, do the following:
TYPE: **Student Listing By City**
CLICK: *Preview the report* option button
CLICK: Finish
After a few seconds, the report is created, saved, and then displayed in the Print Preview window.

12. On your own, move, size, and scroll the Print Preview window to appear similar to Figure 4.6.

FIGURE 4.6

THE COMPLETED REPORT
IN PRINT PREVIEW MODE

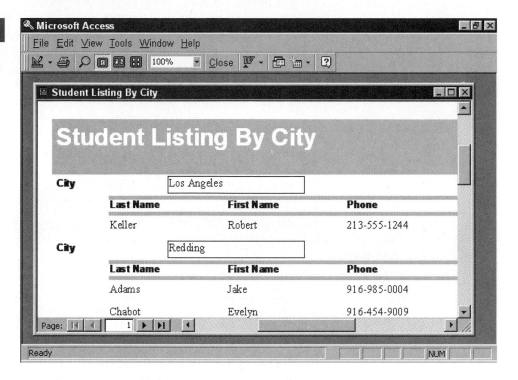

13. Using the magnifying glass mouse pointer, zoom in and out on different areas of the report.

14. To close the report:
CLICK: Close button (|X|)
You should see the new report's name listed in the Database window.

QUICK REFERENCE
Creating a Report Using
the Report Wizard

1. **CLICK:** *Reports* **tab in the Database window**
2. **CLICK: New command button**
3. **SELECT: Report Wizard**
4. **SELECT: a table or query upon which to base the report**
5. **Proceed through the dialog boxes to specify fields, grouping and sorting options, a report style, page layout, and a report name.**
6. **CLICK:** | Finish | **to generate the report based on your selections**

CREATING A FILTERED REPORT

To this point, you have experienced first-hand how quickly you can generate professional-looking reports using the Access report wizards. Although the previous examples used tables on which to base their reports, you can just as easily apply a filter or select a query. The advantage of using a query is that you will have already specified the desired fields and sort order for the data. Furthermore, you can both limit and extend the data displayed in a report using a query's ability to filter information and to perform calculations. For further information on designing queries, refer back to Session 3.

In this section, you create a report that uses the filters and sort order specified in a table's datasheet.

Perform the following steps . . .

1. Ensure that the "School" Database window appears in the work area.

2. To display the Instructors datasheet:
   CLICK: *Tables* tab
   DOUBLE-CLICK: Instructors
   The datasheet window appears in the work area.

3. In the City field for Instructor ID "abre", use the I-beam mouse pointer to select the letter "S" in "Seattle."

4. To filter the table so that only those records beginning with the letters "S" in the City field are displayed, do the following:
   CLICK: Filter By Selection button (⊠)
   Only four records should be displayed in the datasheet.

5. To sort the datasheet into descending order by the Last Name field:
   SELECT: Last Name column
   CLICK: Sort Descending button (⊠) on the toolbar

6. Before you can produce a report using this filter and sort order, you must save the datasheet. Do the following:
   CLICK: Save button (⊟)

7. To launch the AutoReport Wizard:
   CLICK: down arrow attached to the New Object button (⊠▾)
   CLICK: AutoReport
   The report inherits the filter and sort order and then displays the typical columnar report in Print Preview mode.

8. On your own, size and position the window and then scroll through the report. Notice that only those instructors starting with "S" in the City field are included in the report.

9. Close the Print Preview window, without saving the report, and then close the Table window.

1. **Display a table using Datasheet view.**

2. **Create and apply filters using Filter By Selection, Filter Excluding Selection, Filter By Form, or the Advanced Filter/Sort command.**

3. **Sort the filtered datasheet using the Sort Ascending ( ) or Sort Descending ( ) buttons on the toolbar.**

4. **CLICK: Save button ( ) on the toolbar**

5. **CLICK: down arrow attached to the New Object button ( )**

6. **CLICK: AutoReport**

IN ADDITION CREATING AN ACCESS REPORT FROM EXCEL DATA

If you need more reporting power than provided in Microsoft Excel, you can choose the Data, MS Access Report command on the Excel menu bar to launch the Access Report Wizard. If this command does not appear on the menu, you need to load the AccessLinks add-in program. For more information, ask the Microsoft Excel Office Assistant about the "AccessLinks" add-in program.

CREATING MAILING LABELS

In this section, you will learn how to create a mailing label report. The procedure for creating labels is very similar to the one you used in creating a report with the Report Wizard. Let's begin by creating mailing labels for the Instructors table, stored in the "School" database.

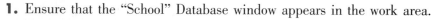

Perform the following steps . . .

1. Ensure that the "School" Database window appears in the work area.

2. To create a new report:
   CLICK: *Reports* tab
   CLICK: New command button

3. In the New Report dialog box:
   SELECT: Label Wizard
   CLICK: down arrow beside the *Choose a table...* drop-down list box
   SELECT: Instructors
   CLICK: OK command button
   The first dialog box for the Label Wizard appears, as shown in Figure 4.7.

FIGURE 4.7

SELECTING A LABEL SIZE
AND FORMAT

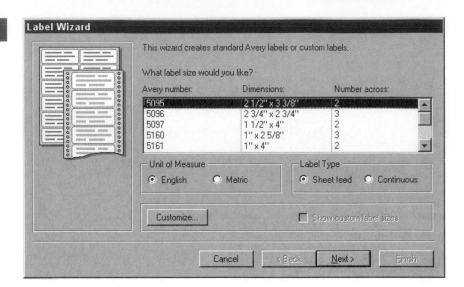

4. In this dialog box, you specify the label size and format. For mailing labels, the Avery 5160 format, which displays three labels across the page, is very common. You can also create other types of labels, including ones for file folders and diskettes. Do the following:
CLICK: *Sheet Feed* option button in the *Label Type* area
SELECT: Avery number 5160
CLICK: Next >

5. In the next dialog box that appears, you select the font used for the labels. Do the following to accept the default font size and color:
CLICK: Next >

6. You can now enter text and specify the layout of fields on your label. To build the mailing label for the Instructors table:
DOUBLE-CLICK: First Name in the *Available fields* list box
PRESS: Spacebar
DOUBLE-CLICK: Last Name
PRESS: ENTER
DOUBLE-CLICK: Address
PRESS: ENTER
DOUBLE-CLICK: City
TYPE: , (a single comma)
PRESS: Spacebar
DOUBLE-CLICK: State
PRESS: Spacebar
DOUBLE-CLICK: Zip
Your label should now appear similar to Figure 4.8.

FIGURE 4.8

SELECTING FIELDS FOR
THE LABEL PROTOTYPE

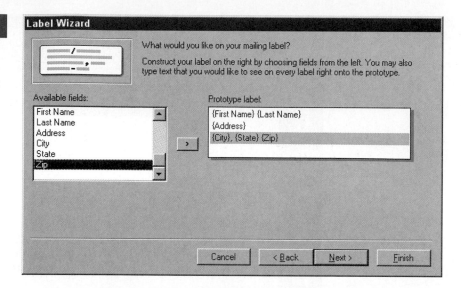

7. To continue designing the label:
   CLICK: [Next >]

8. In this dialog box, you specify the sort order for your labels. To sort our labels by the contents of the Last Name and First Name fields:
   DOUBLE-CLICK: Last Name
   DOUBLE-CLICK: First Name
   CLICK: [Next >]

9. To accept the default name and preview the labels:
   CLICK: [Finish]
   After a few seconds, the labels report is created, saved, and then displayed in the Print Preview window. Your screen should now appear similar to Figure 4.9.

10. To close the Print Preview window:
    CLICK: Close button ([X])
    You should now see the "Labels Instructors" report listed in the Database window.

FIGURE 4.9

THE MAILING LABEL
DESIGN IN PRINT
PREVIEW MODE

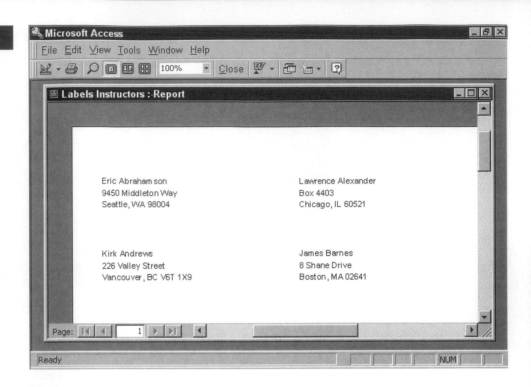

QUICK REFERENCE

Creating a Mailing Labels
Report

1. **CLICK:** *Reports* **tab in the Database window**
2. **CLICK: New command button**
3. **SELECT: Label Wizard**
4. **SELECT: a table or query upon which to base the report**
5. **Proceed through the dialog boxes to specify the label size and format, specify a font, select fields, and name the label report.**
6. **CLICK:** Finish **to generate the mailing label report based on your selections**

USING REPORT DESIGN VIEW

Although the Report Wizards let you create a variety of reports, you should also know how to create a report from scratch and how to modify a report that you created using a wizard. You may, for instance, want less space to display between the columns in a report. Or maybe you want to include a company logo or picture. Even experienced users should create their initial report layout using a Report Wizard and then modify it using the procedures described in the following sections. Before leading you through customizing a report, we need to describe the different components of an Access report structure.

UNDERSTANDING REPORTS

Reports consist of different sections or areas on a page. These sections contain **controls** that determine what displays in the report. Access reports use two kinds of controls: bound and unbound. A **bound control** is one whose source of data is a field in a table or query. An example of a bound control is one that causes the data to display in a report column; the displayed data is bound to data in a field stored in a table or query. An **unbound control** is a control that doesn't have a source of data. For example, a report title is an unbound control; you can type in the title directly. Most descriptive labels and decorative lines are also considered unbound controls.

To make the concept of controls easier to understand, let's compare a report displayed using Print Preview mode with one displayed using report Design view.

Perform the following steps . . .

1. Ensure that the "School" Database window appears in the work area and that the *Reports* tab is selected.

2. To preview the Instructor Listing report:
   DOUBLE-CLICK: Instructor Listing

3. Maximize the Print Preview window to see more of the report.

4. To zoom out:
   CLICK: Zoom button (🔍)
   The report should look similar to Figure 4.10. Although you can't read the data when it is zoomed out, you can see its four main sections:

   - *Report Header*. This section contains information, such as the report title, that appears only once at the beginning of a report.

   - *Page Header*. This section contains information repeated at the top of each page, such as the column headings in a tabular report.

   - *Detail*. This section contains the main body of the report. It typically contains the controls that are bound to fields in a table or query; these controls cause the detail data to display.

   - *Page Footer*. This section contains information repeated at the bottom of each page, such as the page number or copyright notice.

FIGURE 4.10

TABULAR REPORT IN
PRINT PREVIEW MODE

Report Header

Page Header

Detail (Body)

Page Footer

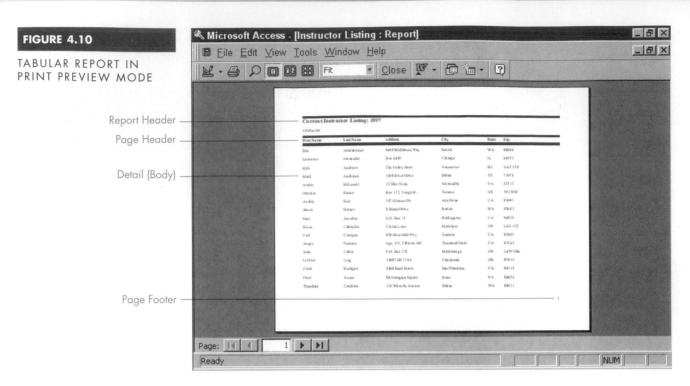

5. To display the report in Design view so that you can see the sections more clearly:
   CLICK: Close command button in the toolbar
   CLICK: Design command button in the Database window
   The screen should now appear similar to Figure 4.11. Notice that "*=Now( )*" appears in the Report Header. This unbound control displays the current date in the report. Also, there are no controls visible in the Page Footer or Report Footer sections.

6. After you're comfortable with your understanding of the different parts of a report, close the report Design window. To do so, you can click the Close button ([X]) or choose the File, Close command.

In the following sections, you will practice modifying some of the controls in the Instructor Listing report.

IN ADDITION INSERTING THE DATE, TIME, AND PAGE NUMBER

You can add a control to your report that displays the current date and time by choosing the Insert, Date and Time command. Also, you can place and align a page number con-

trol in the Page Header or Page Footer of a report using the Insert, Page Numbers command.

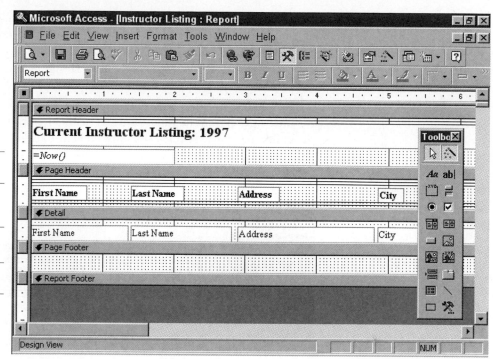

EDITING CONTROL TEXT

In this section, you edit the Report Header section of the Instructor Listing report. The Report Header currently includes the text "Current Instructor Listing: 1997." You are going to edit the heading to display "Maryland Community College: Instructors."

Perform the following steps . . .

1. Ensure that the "School" Database window appears maximized in the work area and that the *Reports* tab is selected.

2. To display the Instructor Listing report in report Design view:
   SELECT: Instructor Listing
   CLICK: Design command button

3. Before editing an unbound control, you must first select the control. Position the mouse pointer over the report title and then click the left mouse button once.

4. DRAG: the I-beam mouse pointer to select the entire title

5. To enter the new title:
   TYPE: `Maryland Community College: Instructors`
   The new text replaces the selected heading.

6. To save the new report design:
   CLICK: Save button (■) on the toolbar

7. To preview the report:
CLICK: down arrow attached to the View button (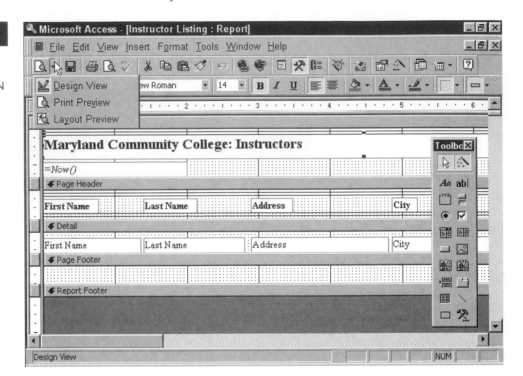)
Your screen should now appear similar to Figure 4.12. Notice that there are three views available for selection: Design View, Print Preview, and Layout Preview. Since you've already seen Design View and Print Preview, the only one left to explain is Layout Preview. This view mode is unique in that it lets you view your report quickly without retrieving all of the data from a table or query. It retrieves only enough data to illustrate what the report will look like when printed.

FIGURE 4.12

DISPLAYING THE THREE OPTIONS AVAILABLE FROM THE VIEW BUTTON

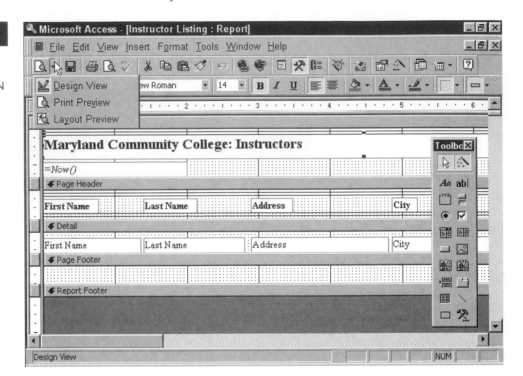

8. To view the report using Layout Preview:
CLICK: Layout Preview option from the drop-down list button

9. To return to report Design view:
CLICK: Close command button on the toolbar

QUICK REFERENCE
Editing Text in an Unbound Control

1. **SELECT: the unbound control you want to change**

2. **Edit the control text using the I-beam mouse pointer and standard editing keystrokes.**

RESIZING CONTROLS

You may have noticed that there is an abundance of white space appearing between the columns in the Instructor Listing report. To change the width of a control (column), you first select the control and then drag its border to the left or right. In this exercise, you will narrow the First Name control in the Detail section.

Perform the following steps . . .

1. If you completed the last section, the report Design view of the Instructor Listing report appears on the screen.

2. To select the First Name control in the Detail section, position the mouse pointer over the First Name control and click the left mouse button once. (*Note*: Make sure that you select the First Name control in the Detail section, not in the Page Header section.)

3. You change the size of controls as you would the size of any object. When you position the mouse pointer over one of the black selection boxes, the pointer changes to a horizontal, double-headed arrow. You can then click and drag the mouse in any direction to increase or decrease the size of the control. In this step, position the mouse pointer over the right border's selection box and drag the First Name control's right border to the left so that it becomes 1 inch wide, as shown on the ruler above the Report Header.

4. To preview the report:
   CLICK: Print Preview button ([◻])
   Notice that although the column is narrower, the columns to the right have remained in their original positions. Therefore, the report looks the same as before. In the next section, you learn to reposition the controls in the Page Header and Detail sections.

5. To return to the Design view of the report:
   CLICK: Close command button on the toolbar

6. On your own, narrow the Last Name and City controls in the Detail section by about ½ inch.

7. If you preview the report right now, you'll see that the report doesn't look any different. But never fear! Continue on to the next section to learn how to move controls.

QUICK REFERENCE
Resizing Controls in Report Design View

1. **SELECT: the desired control you want to change**
2. **Position the mouse pointer on the left or right border's selection box until the mouse pointer changes to a double-headed arrow.**
3. **DRAG: the border to the left or right to decrease or increase its size**

MOVING CONTROLS

After selecting a control by clicking on it once, you move the hand mouse pointer over its border and then drag the mouse to move the control. Make sure that you position the mouse pointer on the control's border line and not on one of its selection boxes. When positioned correctly, the hand mouse pointer becomes visible and you can drag the control in any direction: up, down, left, or right. Let's practice moving Last Name control in the report.

Perform the following steps . . .

1. Ensure that the report appears in report Design view.

2. SELECT: Last Name control in the Detail section

3. Position the mouse over the top border of the Last Name control, between two selection boxes, until a hand mouse pointer appears.

4. DRAG: the control to the left until it almost touches the First Name control

5. Using the procedure described in Steps 2 and 3, move the Address, City, State, and Zip fields to the left so that each is close to the field control on its left.

6. CLICK: Print Preview button ( )
   Notice that the Page Header controls are no longer displaying above their respective columns in the Detail section.

7. CLICK: Close command button in the toolbar

8. On your own, move each Page Header control to display above the corresponding Detail control field.

9. CLICK: Print Preview button ( )
   Your screen should now appear similar to Figure 4.13.

10. To return to the report Design view and save the new report design:
    CLICK: Close command button
    CLICK: Save button ( )

FIGURE 4.13

PREVIEWING THE REPORT
AFTER MOVING AND
SIZING CONTROLS

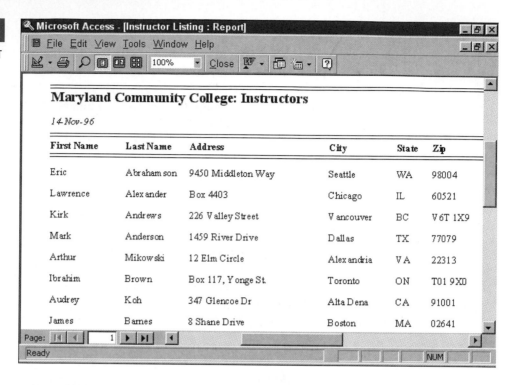

First Name	Last Name	Address	City	State	Zip
Eric	Abrahamson	9450 Middleton Way	Seattle	WA	98004
Lawrence	Alexander	Box 4403	Chicago	IL	60521
Kirk	Andrews	226 Valley Street	Vancouver	BC	V6T 1X9
Mark	Anderson	1459 River Drive	Dallas	TX	77079
Arthur	Mikowski	12 Elm Circle	Alexandria	VA	22313
Ibrahim	Brown	Box 117, Yonge St.	Toronto	ON	T01 9X0
Audrey	Koh	347 Glencoe Dr	Alta Dena	CA	91001
James	Barnes	8 Shane Drive	Boston	MA	02641

QUICK REFERENCE

Moving a Control in
Report Design View

1. **SELECT:** the desired control you want to change
2. **Position** the mouse pointer on the border, between its selection boxes, until the mouse pointer changes to a small black hand.
3. **DRAG:** the border frame up, down, left, or right

IN ADDITION EXPORTING A REPORT TO HTML FORMAT

You can export an Access report to HTML format using the File, Save As/Export command. You can even enhance the report's appearance, navigation, and formatting options by applying an HTML template file during the conversion. This command produces one HTML document for every page of the report, which you can then store on an Internet or Intranet website. With the File, Save As HTML command, you can launch the Publish to the Web Wizard to automate the process of creating HTML documents from your tables, forms, and reports. For more information on publishing reports on the Web, see "Publishing Objects For the Internet" in Session 5.

CUSTOMIZING A REPORT

To enhance the presentation of a report, you can customize and apply formatting to its various elements. For example, you can add a new field or control to a report, move and resize controls, change the formatting appearance of a control, and add unbound text and graphics to a report. In this section, you learn to use the Formatting toolbar and other techniques for enhancing a report.

FORMATTING A CONTROL

Similar to selecting and formatting text in a word processing document, you select a control in report Design view and then apply a formatting command using the Formatting toolbar. You can also use the Format Painter button ([⟨]) on the toolbar to copy the formatting characteristics from one control to another control. To apply the same formatting characteristics to several controls, you double-click the Format Painter button ([⟨]) to turn it on and then, once you are finished painting the desired controls, click it again to turn it off.

Let's practice formatting the Instructor Listing report.

Perform the following steps . . .

1. Ensure that the report appears in report Design view.

2. If the Toolbox window appears on your screen, do the following:
   CLICK: Toolbox button ([✸]) to remove the window

3. If you want to apply the same formatting characteristics to multiple controls, you must first select the desired controls. Do the following to format the entire Detail section of the report:
   CLICK: First Name control in the Detail section
   PRESS: (SHIFT) and hold it down
   CLICK: Last Name control
   CLICK: Address control
   CLICK: City control
   CLICK: State control
   CLICK: Zip control

4. Release the (SHIFT) key. All the controls should now appear selected in the Detail section.

5. To change the typestyle or font:
   CLICK: down arrow beside the Font Name ([Times New Roman ▾]) drop-down list box on the Formatting toolbar
   CLICK: Arial
   Notice that the control text is immediately updated to show the new font selection. Also, the controls remain selected in case you want to apply further formatting commands.

6. To remove the selection boxes from the controls, click the mouse pointer in an empty area near the bottom of the Design window.

7. SELECT: First Name control in the Detail section

8. To demonstrate the Format Painter:
CLICK: Format Painter button (⟨✐⟩) in the toolbar
Notice that the button now appears turned on or pressed in.

9. To apply the formatting characteristics of the First Name bound control to its column heading in the Page Header area:
CLICK: First Name label in the Page Header section
Notice that the button now appears turned off in the toolbar.

10. With the First Name control still selected:
DOUBLE-CLICK: Format Painter button (⟨✐⟩) in the toolbar
Again, the button appears turned on.

11. CLICK: Last Name label in the Page Header section
Notice that the button remains turned on and the mouse pointer still shows the attached paintbrush.

12. To apply the formatting to the remainder of the labels:
CLICK: Address label
CLICK: City label
CLICK: State label
CLICK: Zip label

13. To turn off the Format Painter:
CLICK: Format Painter button (⟨✐⟩)

14. On your own, select the First Name control in the Page Header area and then use the (**SHIFT**) and click method to select the remaining controls in this area.

15. To apply boldface to these label controls:
CLICK: Bold button (**B**) on the Formatting toolbar

16. To remove the selection boxes from the controls, click the mouse pointer in an empty area near the bottom of the Design window. Your screen should now appear similar to Figure 4.14.

FIGURE 4.14

FORMATTING A REPORT
IN REPORT DESIGN VIEW

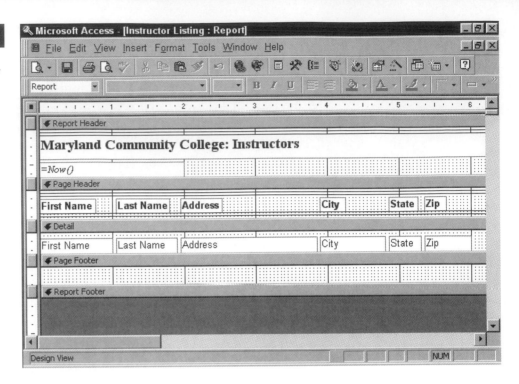

17. Let's preview the report:
CLICK: Print Preview button (🔍)

18. To return to report Design view:
CLICK: Close command button

QUICK REFERENCE
Using the Formatting Toolbar

1. **SELECT: the desired control or controls you want to format**
2. **CLICK: a toolbar button on the Formatting toolbar**

ADDING A GRAPHIC

In this section, you are going to place an unbound graphic image into the Instructor Listing report. The name of the graphic is "Books.bmp" and is stored in your Advantage Files location. You will insert the graphic into the Report Header so that it prints on the first page of the report (Figure 4.15). To have the graphic print on every page or with every record, you would instead insert it in the Page Header or Detail sections (Figure 4.16).

FIGURE 4.15

INSERTING A GRAPHIC
CONTROL IN THE REPORT
HEADER

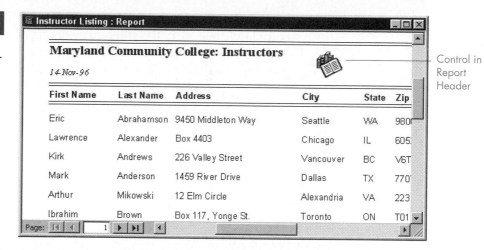

FIGURE 4.16

INSERTING A GRAPHIC
CONTROL IN THE DETAIL
SECTION

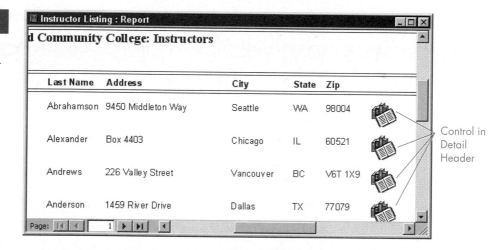

Let's practice inserting an unbound graphic control.

Perform the following steps . . .

1. Ensure that the report appears in report Design view.

2. If the Toolbox window is not present on your screen, do the following:
   CLICK: Toolbox button (🛠) on the toolbar

3. DRAG: the mouse pointer slowly over the toolbox buttons and notice that a description of each button displays as a yellow ToolTip

4. To place a graphic in your report, you must first create a frame for the image:
   CLICK: Image button (🖼)
   In the next step, you tell Access where to position the frame.

5. Let's place the image in the Report Header. Position the mouse pointer to the right of the text in the Report Header, at the 4-inch position and near the top border. This will become the upper left-hand corner of the frame. Click and drag the mouse pointer down and to the right (to the 5-inch position and near the bottom border of the Report header). To finish drawing the frame, release the mouse button.

6. The Insert Picture dialog box should now appear. Access is waiting for you to tell it more about the image you're about to insert. The graphic is stored in your Advantage Files location.
   CLICK: down arrow beside the *Look in* drop-down list box
   SELECT: *the disk and folder location of your Advantage Files*
   Your screen should now display two graphic files: Books and Phone.

7. To select the graphic:
   DOUBLE-CLICK: Books
   In report Design view, the report should look like Figure 4.17.

FIGURE 4.17

THE REPORT HEADER
WITH AN IMAGE
INSERTED

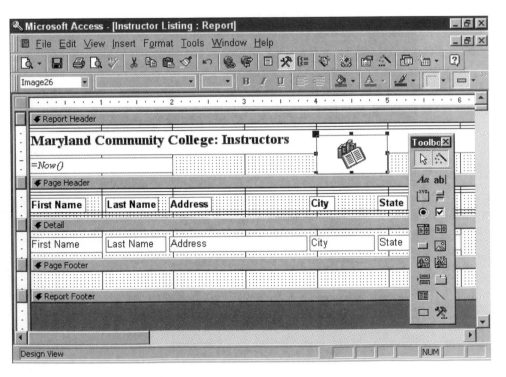

8. To view the report:
   CLICK: Print Preview button (🔍)
   The report should look similar to Figure 4.15. (*Note*: You can size and move graphics in the same way that you manipulate field controls.)

9. To return to report Design view and save the report:
   CLICK: Close command button
   CLICK: Save button (💾)

QUICK REFERENCE
Adding a Graphic Image
in Report Design View

1. **CLICK: Toolbox button (** ⚒ **) to display the Toolbox window**
2. **CLICK: Image button (** 🖼 **)**
3. **Point to the upper left-hand corner of where you want the graphic to be displayed and then drag down and to the right to create a frame.**
4. **Select the desired image from the Insert Picture dialog box.**

THE AUTOFORMAT WIZARD

If you want to impress your readers with a professionally designed report created in minutes, try using the **AutoFormat Wizard.** With this wizard, you apply a style template to an existing report layout displayed in Design view. To illustrate, let's use the wizard to format the Instructor Listing report.

Perform the following steps . . .

1. Ensure that the report appears in report Design view.

2. To delete the graphic image:
   SELECT: the Books image (📚)
   PRESS: DELETE
   CLICK: an empty area near the bottom of the Design window

3. To remove the Toolbox window:
   CLICK: Toolbox button (⚒)

4. To start the AutoFormat Wizard:
   CLICK: AutoFormat button (🖎) on the toolbar

5. To view the options available:
   CLICK: Options command button
   Notice that you can choose to apply the *Font*, *Color*, or *Border* attributes displayed in the selected template.

6. To select a new format for the Instructor Listing report:
   SELECT: Bold in the *Report AutoFormats* list box
   The dialog box should now appear similar to Figure 4.18.

FIGURE 4.18

SELECTING AN
AUTOFORMAT TEMPLATE

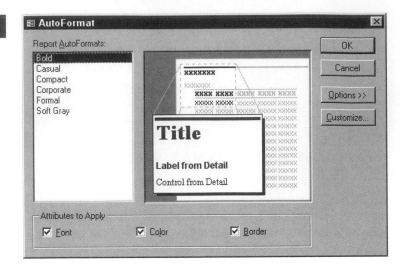

7. To apply the formatting:
   CLICK: OK command button
   Your report is formatted with the styles shown in the preview area of the AutoFormat dialog box.

8. On your own, resize the controls so that all the text is displayed.

9. To view the report:
   CLICK: Print Preview button (🔍)

10. To close the report and not save the changes:
    CLICK: Close button on the toolbar
    CHOOSE: File, Close from the menu
    CLICK: No command button when asked to save these last few changes to the report design

11. Restore the Database window.

12. Close the Database window and then exit Microsoft Access.

QUICK REFERENCE
Using the AutoFormat
Wizard

1. **CLICK: an empty area in the report Design window**
2. **CLICK: AutoFormat button (🖼)**
3. **Make a selection from the AutoFormat dialog box.**
4. **CLICK: OK command button to apply the selected template**

SUMMARY

In this session, you learned how to create reports using the Access report wizards. A report wizard simplifies the process of reporting your data from a table or query by making assumptions for you about the formatting and style of the completed report. The AutoReport Wizard is the fastest and easiest of the wizards to use. However, the Report Wizard and Label Wizard let you create sophisticated reports with minimal effort.

You also learned how to customize a report using report Design view. Reports are made up of different sections, including the Report Header, Page Header, and Detail sections. The Report Header prints at the very beginning of the report. For example, the report title is commonly displayed in the Report Header section. The Page Header prints at the top of each page. For example, the current date or page number might display in the Page Header. The Detail section displays the report data. Each report section contains controls which can be modified (deleted, resized, moved, and formatted) to meet your needs.

COMMAND SUMMARY

Table 4.3 provides a list of the commands and procedures covered in this session.

TABLE 4.3	*Task Description*	*Task Procedure*
Command Summary	Creates an AutoReport	CLICK: New Object button (⊞▾)
	Zooms in and out in Preview mode	CLICK: Print Preview button (🔍)
	Edits control text	SELECT: a control and click to position the I-beam pointer in the control
	Resizes a control	SELECT: a control and then drag its selection boxes
	Moves a control	SELECT: a control and then drag a border edge with the hand mouse pointer
	Copies the formatting from one control to another	CLICK: Format Painter button (🖌)
	Displays the Toolbox window	CLICK: Toolbox button (🛠)
	Adds a graphic to a report	CLICK: Image button (🖼)
	AutoFormats a report	CLICK: AutoFormat button (📋)

KEY TERMS

AutoFormat Wizard

Using this tool, you can apply professionally designed formatting templates to a report with the click of a toolbar button.

AutoReport Wizard

Using this tool, you can have Access create a single-column report without requesting any information from you. There are actually two types of AutoReport Wizards, Columnar and Tabular, accessible from the New Report dialog box.

bound control

In Access, a control whose source of data is a field in a table or query.

controls

Elements of a form and a report. Access uses two types of controls: bound and unbound.

reports

In Access, reports are used to present, summarize, or improve the appearance of data. Reports are often included in presentations.

report wizards

Access tools that simplify the process of creating a report. You select the type of report and then respond to prompts.

unbound control

In Access, a control that doesn't have a source of data; you can type the control information in directly.

EXERCISES

SHORT ANSWER

1. What are the two types of AutoReports that you can create?
2. List the report options available in the New Report dialog box.
3. What is the difference between columnar and tabular reports?
4. What is the difference between bound and unbound controls?
5. In a printed report, where would you find the report header, page header, and detail sections?
6. Describe the process of including a graphic image in a report.
7. How do you change text in an unbound control?
8. How do you move a control?
9. How to you resize a control?
10. How would you change the font and style of a control?

HANDS-ON

(*Note*: Ensure that you know the storage location of your Advantage Files and your Data Files before proceeding.)

1. To practice using the AutoReport Wizards, create two AutoReports for the Customer table that is stored in the "Sporting" database. When finished, print and then save the reports as "Customer AutoReport - Columnar" and Customer AutoReport - Tabular." Return to the Database window when finished.

2. Using the Label Wizard, you will now create mailing labels for the Customer table that is stored in the "Sporting" database.

   a. Ensure that the "Sporting" Database window appears.

   b. Create a new mailing label report based on the Customer table.

   c. Select the Avery 5160 label format.

   d. Select the default font and color settings.

   e. Make the field layout for the labels similar to the following:

      Company Contact
      Company Name
      Address
      City, State Zip

   f. Sort the labels by the Zip field.

   g. Save the labels as Customer Mailing Labels.

   h. Preview and then print the mailing labels.

   i. Close the mailing labels report.

3. To practice creating and editing a report, perform the following steps using the Customer table of the "Sporting" database.

   a. Using the Report Wizard, create a tabular report and include the following fields: Company Name, Company Contact, City, Phone, and Fax.

   b. Do not select a grouping, but sort the report on the City field.

   c. Assume the default layout and orientation settings.

   d. Select a "Corporate" style for the report.

   e. Save the report as "Corporate Customer Listing" and then preview the report before proceeding. After some adjustments to the preview window, your screen should appear similar to Figure 4.19.

FIGURE 4.19

"CORPORATE CUSTOMER
LISTING" REPORT
PREVIEW

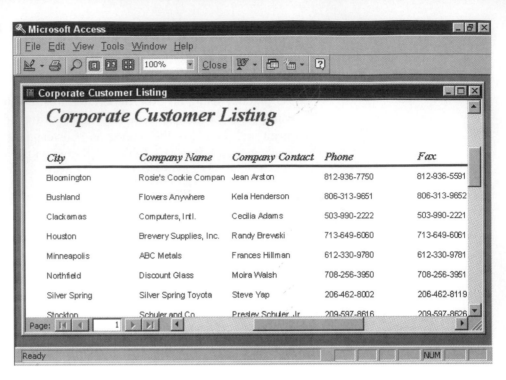

f. Return to report Design view.

g. Edit the report by resizing and moving the field controls in the Detail area.

h. Move the controls in the Page Header so that they are closer to their adjacent fields in the Detail area.

i. Edit the Report Header text to read "Preferred Customers By City."

j. Save the report.

k. Preview and then print the report.

l. Close the report to display the Database window.

4. **On Your Own:** Adding a Graphic to a Report
For this exercise, add the "Phone" picture that is stored in your Advantage Files location to the report you created in Exercise 3. The graphic should display in the Report Header section, immediately above the phone and fax columns. Save and print the report. Once completed, close the report and then close the database.

5. **On Your Own:** Your Personal Phone Report
In Sessions 2 and 3, you created and customized a database called "My Phone Book." (*Note*: If you have not created this database or query, do so now by referring to the On Your Own exercises in Sessions 2 and 3.) Now, create a report for this database called "My Phone Report" that is based on the "Alphabetical Phone Listing" query created in Session 3. Include all the fields from the query in the report and select your own style and formatting options. Add the "Phone" picture to the Report Header and then print out the report. After saving the report, close the Database window and exit Microsoft Access.

CASE PROBLEMS | **VACATION VISTAS, INC.**

(*Note*: In the following case problems, assume the role of the primary characters and perform the same steps that they identify. You may want to re-read the session opening.)

1. In preparation for his meeting with Nancy at Washington Bank, Frank prepares to create a few reports using the "Vistas" database that is stored in the Advantage Files location. In the first report, he wants to show the "Client List by Last Name" query in the form of a tabular report. He wants the data to be sorted into order by the City field and secondly by the Last Name field. He also wants the report to display in Portrait mode. He types in "Client Listing Report" as the title that will appear when the report is printed.

    To show Nancy how much business he has had recently, Frank creates a report that lists his clients in order by the Travel Period field. He uses the Report Wizard to display the data stored in the Client List by Travel Period query. He groups the report by the Travel Period field and sorts it by the Last Name field. Like the previous report he created, he wants this report to display in Portrait mode. He types in "Travel Period Report" as the title that will appear when the report is printed.

    Frank prints both reports so that he can review them prior to his meeting with Nancy.

2. After reviewing the printouts, Frank decides to make a few changes to the Client Listing Report that is stored in the "Vistas" database. First, he centers the main title of the report. He then changes the font of the Page Header row and the Detail row to Arial 8 point. Frank then saves, previews, and prints the report.

3. Frank got the loan! In one week, he moves into his new location! He decides to notify all of his existing clients that appear in the Client List table of the "Vistas" database. Not wasting any time, Frank creates mailing labels for each person in the Client List table. He wants the mailing labels to be sorted by the Last Name field and wants to display two mailing labels across on the page. When finished, he saves the report as "Client List Mailing Labels."

Microsoft Access 97 for Windows

Working with Forms

SESSION

5

IRWIN

COMPUTER & INFORMATION TECHNOLOGY

SESSION OUTLINE

INTRODUCTION

In this session, you learn how to create and modify a form using the Access form wizards and form Design view. You also learn how to create your own command buttons, which you can then place on custom forms to automate tasks and build complete database applications. Finally, you learn how to copy, rename, and delete objects in the Database window and set properties for the database. These procedures are invaluable as you continue to use and explore database management with Microsoft Access.

Located amidst the highrises of New York City, International House offers people wanting to learn English an excellent introduction to the American culture. At International House, teachers are specially trained and their methods are highly effective. You can enroll in a variety of intensive language courses, each consisting of four class hours per day for as many weeks as you like. Instructors are dedicated to teaching their students English in the shortest amount of time.

Frederick Stovall is a director at International House and speaks four languages fluently. When you arrive at International House to enroll in a class, Frederick will most likely be the one to greet you. Before signing up for a class, your first step will be to take a proficiency test that determines your language skill level (i.e., beginner, intermediate, or advanced). Upon completion, Frederick recommends an instructor and a class for you to attend.

After enrolling a student, Frederick adds his or her name to the Students table of the "I-House" database. He keeps tabs on enrollment by displaying the Enrollment Status report; as he tries to limit classes to a maximum of ten students, this report is vital. Frederick would now like to build a form to simplify the process of entering student records. Also, he wants to streamline the process of displaying the Enrollment Status report.

In this session, you and Frederick will learn how to create forms and customize them to meet your needs. You also learn how to create a command button for quickly generating reports and then place it on a form.

CREATING A NEW FORM

Throughout this guide, you have worked with and displayed table data and query results using Datasheet view. One alternative to displaying records in this grid-like layout is to display one record at a time using Form view. Similar to creating a new report, you create a new form using a form wizard or in Design view. Some examples of forms that you may want to create and use with a database include data entry forms that resemble their paper counterparts, switchboard forms that provide menus of choices, and custom dialog boxes. In fact, forms make it easier for all users, especially those who are less familiar with Access, to become more productive.

To create a new form, you click the *Forms* tab in the Database window and then click the New command button. Alternatively, you can open a table or query (or simply select a table or query name in the Database window) and then click the down arrow attached to the New Object button ( ) on the toolbar. From the drop-down list that appears, you can select either AutoForm or Form. If you select the New command button from the Database window, the dialog box shown in Figure 5.1 appears. These list box options are summarized in Table 5.1.

FIGURE 5.1

NEW FORM DIALOG BOX

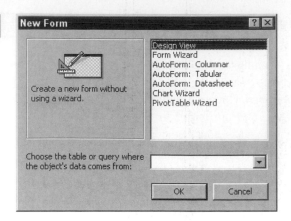

TABLE 5.1	*Form Option*	*Purpose*
Options for Creating a New Form	Design View	Creates a new form using report Design view
	Form Wizard	Creates a new form using the Form Wizard
	AutoForm: Columnar	Creates a new single-column form that includes all of the fields from the selected table or query; each value displays on a separate line with the field label to the left
	AutoForm: Tabular	Creates a new tabular form that includes all of the fields from the selected table or query; field labels appear at the top of each column and each row represents a new record
	AutoForm: Datasheet	Creates a new datasheet form that includes all of the fields from the selected table or query; resembles a table in Datasheet view
	Chart Wizard	Using a form wizard, creates a form with an embedded chart
	PivotTable Wizard	Using a form wizard, creates a form with a Microsoft Excel Pivot Table

In this section, you learn to create new forms using the Access **form wizards.** Later in this session, you will learn how to use the form Design view to modify, format, and customize a form and its elements. Many of the same editing techniques you used to edit reports can also be used to edit forms.

USING THE AUTOFORM WIZARDS

Like its cousin the AutoReport Wizard, an **AutoForm Wizard** offers the quickest and easiest way to create a new form. There are three AutoForm wizards accessible from the New Form dialog box: Columnar, Tabular, and Datasheet. If, however, you click the AutoForm option from the New Object button ( ), Access creates a single-column form (Columnar) based on the open or selected table or query.

You will now learn how to create an AutoForm.

Perform the following steps . . .

1. Turn on your computer and load Microsoft Access. If the startup dialog box appears, click the Cancel command button to display an empty application window. If you already have a Database window open, close the database before proceeding.

2. Open the database named "Wedding" located in your Advantage Files location.

3. To display the contents of the Guest List table:
CLICK: *Tables* tab
DOUBLE-CLICK: Guest List
The Guest List datasheet should now appear.

4. To automatically create a columnar form for this table:
CLICK: down arrow attached to the New Object button ( )
CLICK: AutoForm
After a few seconds, a columnar form appears (Figure 5.2.) Notice that each field is displayed on a separate line on the form and that each field label appears to the left of the *bound control*. Also, every form created by an Access wizard automatically provides the navigational buttons shown at the bottom of the form in Figure 5.2.

FIGURE 5.2

A COLUMNAR FORM
CREATED USING THE
AUTOFORM WIZARD

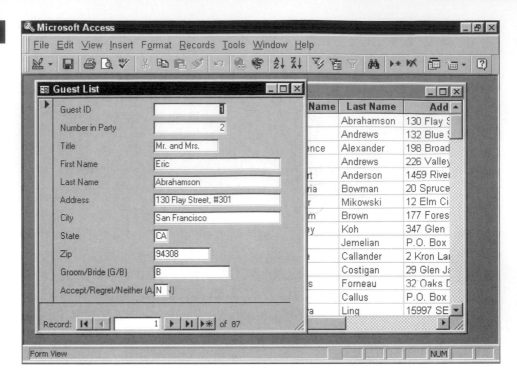

5. To close the form without saving the form design:
CLICK: its Close button (⊠)
CLICK: No command button when asked to save the changes

6. To close the datasheet window:
CLICK: its Close button (⊠)

7. To create a new form using the AutoForm: Tabular Wizard:
CLICK: *Forms* tab
CLICK: New command button
The dialog box in Figure 5.1 should be displayed.

8. To base the new form on the Gifts table:
SELECT: AutoForm: Tabular
CLICK: down arrow beside the *Choose the table…* drop-down list box to
display the table names and queries available in the database
SELECT: Gifts
CLICK: OK command button

A tabular form for the Gifts table appears as shown in Figure 5.3. (*Note:* The AutoFormat Wizards apply the formatting style last selected by the user. Therefore, your form may appear with different formatting characteristics than those shown in Figure 5.3.)

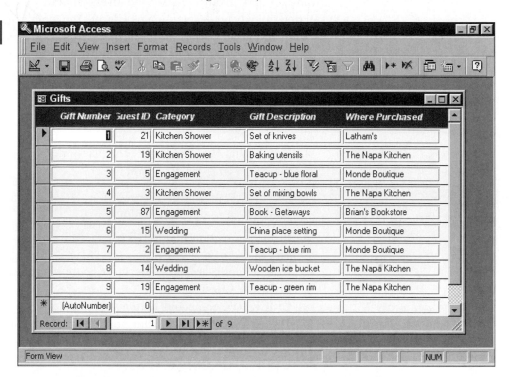

9. To save this form:
   CLICK: Save button (🖫) on the toolbar
   TYPE: **Gifts Tabular AutoForm**
   PRESS: (ENTER)

10. To close the form:
    CLICK: Close button (☒)
    The name of the new form should appear in the Database window.

QUICK REFERENCE
Using the AutoForm
Wizards

1. **CLICK:** *Forms* tab
2. **CLICK: New command button**
3. **SELECT: AutoForm: Columnar, Tabular, or Datasheet**
4. **SELECT: a table or query upon which to base the form**
5. **PRESS:** (ENTER) **or CLICK: OK**

USING THE FORM WIZARD

In this section, you use the Form Wizard to create a new form for the Wedding database. The Form Wizard provides a step-by-step approach to creating a form from scratch. Even experienced users should employ the Form Wizard to get started quickly on designing a new form. You simply select fields to display, choose a form layout and style, and then name the form. Once completed, you can then enter form Design view to add new fields or controls and to customize the appearance of the form.

Let's practice using the Form Wizard.

Perform the following steps . . .

1. Ensure that the "Wedding" Database window appears in the work area and that the *Forms* tab is active.

2. To create a new form:
   CLICK: New command button

3. In the New Form dialog box:
   SELECT: Form Wizard
   CLICK: down arrow beside the *Choose the table…* drop-down list box
   SELECT: Guest List
   CLICK: OK command button
   The first dialog box for the Form Wizard appears.

4. In the *Available Fields* list box:
   DOUBLE-CLICK: First Name
   DOUBLE-CLICK: Last Name
   DOUBLE-CLICK: Number in Party
   DOUBLE-CLICK: Groom/Bride (G/B)
   Your screen should now appear similar to Figure 5.4. (*Note:* You would not use this form for data entry since some of the fields in the table are missing from the form. However, you might use this form to provide a simple read-only view of the table information.)

FIGURE 5.4

SELECTING FIELDS IN THE
FORM WIZARD

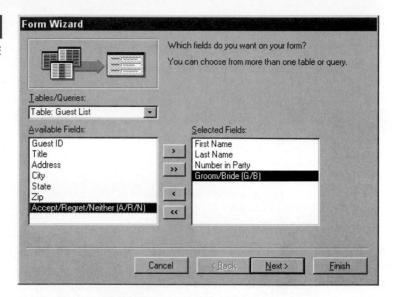

5. To proceed to the next dialog box:
CLICK: Next >

6. In this dialog box, you select the desired form layout. Notice that three of the four options (Columnar, Tabular, and Datasheet) mirror the AutoForm options in the New Form dialog box. On your own, click the layout options one at a time in order to preview their formats. When you are ready, do the following:
CLICK: *Tabular* option button before proceeding
CLICK: Next >

7. In this dialog box, you select the desired form style. On your own, click the style names appearing in the list box one at a time in order to preview their formats. When you are ready, do the following:
SELECT: Stone
CLICK: Next >

8. In the final dialog box, you enter a name for the form and then determine whether to preview it or to open it and continue working in form Design view. For this exercise, do the following:
TYPE: **Guest List Form Wizard**

CLICK: *Open the form to view or enter information* option button
CLICK: [Finish]
After a few seconds, the form is created, saved, and then displayed, as shown in Figure 5.5.

FIGURE 5.5

THE COMPLETED FORM

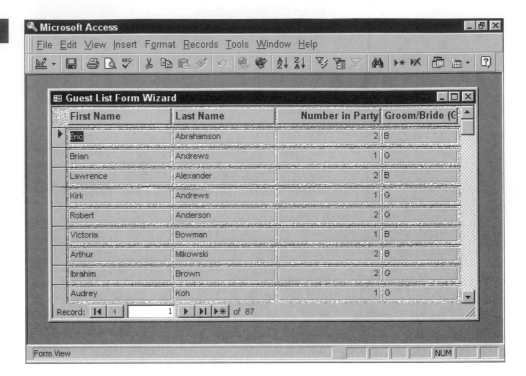

9. To close the form:
   CLICK: Close button ([X])
   You should now see the new form's name appearing in the Database window.

10. To close the Database window:
    CLICK: Close button ([X])

QUICK REFERENCE
Creating a Form Using the Form Wizard

1. **CLICK:** *Forms* tab in the Database window
2. **CLICK:** New command button
3. **SELECT:** Form Wizard
4. **SELECT:** a table or query upon which to base the form
5. Proceed through the dialog boxes to specify fields, a layout option and form style, and a form name.
6. **CLICK:** [Finish] to create and then display the form

CREATING A MULTIPLE-TABLE FORM

In this section, you learn how to display data from two different tables on the same form. If you can take yourself back to the beginning of Session 2 and the discussion on designing a database, you may remember the suggestion to *normalize* your database by dividing redundant information into separate tables. To reiterate, you should strive to reduce occurrences where the same information is typed into the same fields in different records. Although redundant data is best stored in two tables, Access lets you display the data on a single form.

To include data from more than one table on a form, you use a **subform,** which is a form within a form. In Access, the primary or background form is referred to as the Main form and the subform is the embedded form. We will illustrate these principles in the following exercise.

Perform the following steps . . .

1. Open the database named "Mountain" located in your Advantage Files location. This database contains two tables. The first table, Customers, contains address and purchase information for over 80 different customers. The second table, Shoe Models, contains descriptions and price information for ten models of shoes.

2. Before you design a form that displays data from more than one table, ensure that the tables can be related using a common field and then formalize the relationship. In this exercise, the database contains two tables which both contain a field called Model Code. Rather than entering the description and price for each shoe purchased, only the shoe's Model Code has been entered into the Customer table. To establish the intended relationship, do the following:
CLICK: *Tables* tab
CLICK: Relationships button ([⊡]) on the toolbar

3. In the Show Table dialog box that appears layered in front of the Relationships window, ensure that the *Tables* tab is selected and then do the following:
DOUBLE-CLICK: Customers
DOUBLE-CLICK: Shoe Models
CLICK: Close command button
The two table objects should now appear in the Relationships window.

4. On your own, size and move the two table objects so that all of the field names are displayed and some space exists between the objects. In other words, no scroll bars should appear in the table objects.

5. To establish the relationship:
DRAG: Model Code field name from the Shoe Models table object over top of the Model Code field name in the Customers table object

6. Release the mouse button. The Relationships dialog box in Figure 5.6 appears to confirm the operation. Ensure that the contents of your dialog box matches Figure 5.6 before proceeding.

FIGURE 5.6

ESTABLISHING A
RELATIONSHIP BETWEEN
TWO TABLE OBJECTS

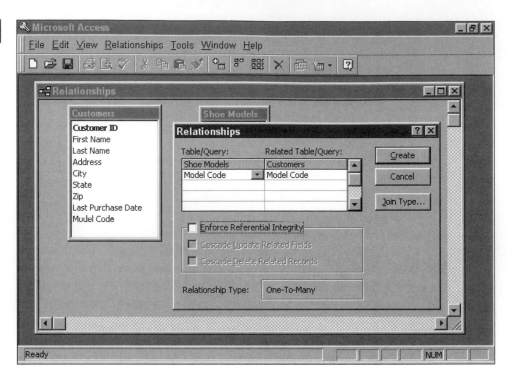

7. To accept the defaults and confirm the relationship:
CLICK: Create command button
You should now see a join line appear in the Relationships window that links the two table objects.

8. To save and then close the Relationships window:
CLICK: Save button (🖫)
CLICK: Close button (☒)

9. Now you are ready to create a new form:
CLICK: *Forms* tab
CLICK: New command button

10. In the New Form dialog box:
SELECT: Form Wizard
CLICK: down arrow beside the *Choose the table…*drop-down list box
SELECT: Shoe Models
CLICK: OK command button

11. In the first dialog box that appears, you specify the fields that you want to include from the two tables. Do the following:
CLICK: ⟩⟩ to move all the fields from the Shoe Models table to the *Selected Fields* list box

12. To display the fields in the Customers table:
CLICK: down arrow for the *Tables/Queries* drop-down list box
SELECT: Table: Customers
The *Available Fields* list box is populated with the Customers fields.

13. To select fields from the Customers table for display on the form:
DOUBLE-CLICK: First Name
DOUBLE-CLICK: Last Name
DOUBLE-CLICK: Last Purchase Date
CLICK: Next >

14. In this dialog box, you specify how you want to view your data. Do the following:
SELECT: by Shoe Models
CLICK: *Form with subform(s)* option button
CLICK: Next >

15. In this dialog box, you specify the desired layout for the subform. Do the following:
CLICK: *Datasheet* option button
CLICK: Next >

16. In this dialog box, you specify the desired style for the form. Do the following:
SELECT: Colorful 2
CLICK: Next >

17. In the final dialog box, accept the default names and display the form:
CLICK: *Open the form to view or enter information* option button
CLICK: Finish
The new form is displayed in the work area. For each shoe model displayed on the main form, there are a number of customers who have purchased the model and who will appear in the datasheet subform.

18. In the datasheet subform, let's increase the width of the Last Purchase Date column to its best fit width:
DOUBLE-CLICK: border line at the right side of the Last Purchase Date column header
Your form should now appear similar to Figure 5.7.

FIGURE 5.7

THE COMPLETED
MULTIPLE-TABLE FORM

Main Form:
Shoe Models

Subform:
Customers

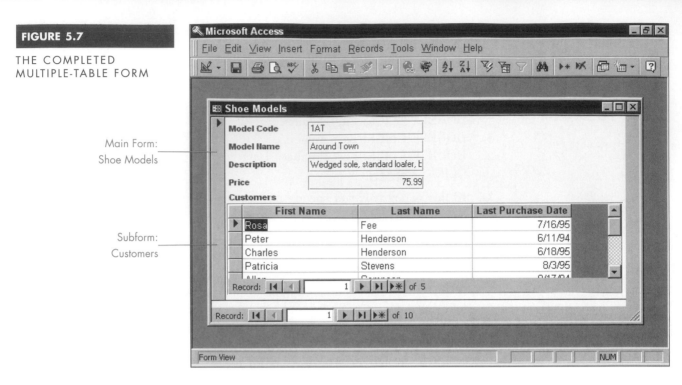

19. To demonstrate how the main form and subform are related, click the navigational buttons for the main form (bottom-most controls) and watch the contents of the datasheet change.

20. When you are ready to proceed, close the form:
CLICK: Close button (☒)

QUICK REFERENCE
Creating a Multiple-Table
Form Using the Form
Wizard

1. **Establish a relationship between the desired tables in database using the Relationships button ( ) on the toolbar.**
2. **Create a new form using the Form Wizard.**
3. **Select fields from more than one table for the form.**
4. **Specify a screen layout and style for the form.**
5. **CLICK:** Finish **to create and then display the form**

USING THE FORM DESIGN VIEW

Using form Design view, you can create new forms from scratch and tinker under the hood of forms that you create using the form wizards. Like report Design view, the primary elements of a form consist of *bound controls* and *unbound controls*. To refresh your memory, a bound control is one that relates to data stored in an underlying table or query. An example of an unbound control is a descriptive label or graphic element placed on the form to enhance its presentation.

SIZING AND FORMATTING CONTROLS

In this section, you size and apply formatting to the controls on a form.

Perform the following steps . . .

1. Ensure that the "Mountain" Database window appears in the work area and that the *Forms* tab is active. To perform the steps in this section, you must first successfully complete the previous section on creating a multiple-table form.

2. To display the Shoe Models Main form in the report Design view:
   SELECT: Shoe Models
   CLICK: Design command button

3. Maximize the view of the form by clicking the Maximize button (🔳). Your screen should now appear similar to Figure 5.8. Notice the area on the Main form that is labeled for the Customers subform.

FIGURE 5.8

DISPLAYING A FORM IN DESIGN VIEW

```
Microsoft Access - [Shoe Models : Form]                    _ 🗗 ✕
File  Edit  View  Insert  Format  Tools  Window  Help        _ 🗗 ✕

Form          ▼            ▼    ▼  B  I  U  ≡ ≡ ≡  🎨 ▼ A ▼ 🖊 ▼  ▢ ▼  ▢ ▼

  · · · · · 1 · · · · · · 2 · · · · · · 3 · · · · · · 4 · · · · · 5 · · · · · 6 ·
  ◄ Form Header
  ◄ Detail
    Model Code        Model Code
    Model Name        Model Name
    Description       Description
    Price             Price
    Customers
    Customers Subform
                            Label Control        Field Control
  ◄ Form Footer

Design View                                              NUM
```

4. In the next few steps, you will resize and format the controls appearing above the Customers subform. For your first task, the Description control needs to be extended to the right in order to display its long text entries. To resize a control, you must first select the control and then drag its border to the left or right. Position the mouse pointer over the Description *field control* (as opposed to the *label control* to its left) and then click the left mouse button once. If done properly, the control should appear surrounded by black selection boxes.

5. When you position the mouse pointer over a selection box, the pointer changes to a horizontal, double-headed arrow. You can now click and drag the mouse in any direction to increase or decrease the size of the control. In this step, position the mouse pointer over the right border's selection box and then, do the following:
DRAG: the Description control's right border to the right until it reaches the 4-inch mark on the ruler

6. To resize another control:
SELECT: Price field control
DRAG: the Price control's right border to the left until it reaches the 2-inch mark on the ruler

7. To better view the text on the form, let's change the appearance of the field controls. First, you need to select all the controls on the form:
SELECT: Model Code field control
PRESS: (SHIFT) and hold it down
CLICK: Model Name field control
CLICK: Description field control
CLICK: Price field control

8. Release the (SHIFT) key.

9. Although there is no need to use this command for the current form, let's demonstrate how you can adjust vertical spacing between fields:
CHOOSE: Format, Vertical Spacing, Decrease
Notice that the fields are positioned closer together.

10. To increase the spacing between the selected fields:
CHOOSE: Format, Vertical Spacing, Increase
The fields should now appear as they did before Step 9 was performed.

11. To format the selected field controls:
CLICK: down arrow attached to the Fill/Back Color button (🎨▾)
SELECT: light gray color
(*Note:* The field controls on the form should immediately display using the new color selection. If they do not, click on the button portion of the Fill/Back Color button (🎨▾).)

12. With the field controls still selected:
CLICK: down arrow attached to the Font/Fore Color button (🅰▾)
SELECT: a dark blue color
CLICK: an empty area on the yellow background of the form

13. Let's change the alignment of the label controls:
SELECT: Model Code label control
PRESS: (SHIFT) and hold it down
CLICK: Model Name label control
CLICK: Description label control
CLICK: Price label control

14. Release the (SHIFT) key.

15. To right-align the selected controls:
RIGHT-CLICK: one of the selected label controls
CHOOSE: Properties

16. In the Multiple selection properties dialog box:
CLICK: Text Align box (you may have to scroll down first)
CLICK: down arrow that appears to the right of the text box
SELECT: Right
You will notice that the text alignment in the label controls changes immediately, as shown in Figure 5.9.

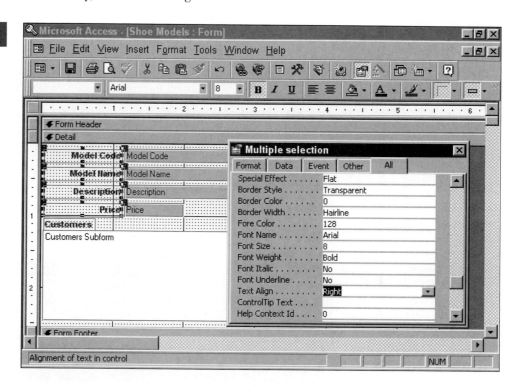

17. To close the dialog box:
CLICK: its Close button (☒)
CLICK: Print Preview button (🔍)

18. On your own, zoom in and out on the form for review. When satisfied, return to Design view and save the form design:
CLICK: Close command button on the toolbar
CLICK: Save button (💾)

QUICK REFERENCE
Resizing Controls

1. **SELECT: the desired control you want to change**
2. **Position the mouse pointer on the left or right border's selection box until the mouse pointer changes to a double-headed arrow.**
3. **DRAG: the border to the left or right to decrease or increase its size**

ADDING, DELETING, AND REPOSITIONING CONTROLS

Regardless of the wizard you may have selected to initially create a form, you can customize the form in Design view by adding and deleting field and label controls. Each bound field control on your form has an attached label control. If you delete a field control from a form, the associated label control is also deleted. On the other hand, you can delete a label control by itself without affecting the field control. The quickest way to delete a bound or unbound control from a form is to first select the control and then press DELETE.

In this section, you delete a label control, move a field control, add a new text label control, and then apply formatting enhancements to some of the controls. When finished, the form will look like Figure 5.10.

FIGURE 5.10

MANIPULATING CONTROLS ON THE SHOE MODELS FORM

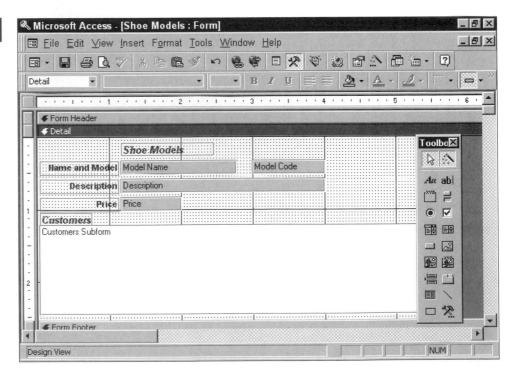

Perform the following steps . . .

1. Ensure that the Shoe Models form appears in form Design view.

2. If the Toolbox window is not present on your screen, do the following:
   CLICK: Toolbox button (⚒) on the toolbar

3. To delete a control:
   CLICK: an empty area on the yellow background of the form
   SELECT: Model Code label control (not the field control)
   PRESS: (DELETE)

4. To move a control:
   SELECT: Model Code field control
   DRAG: Model Code field control so that the left border aligns with the 3-inch mark on the ruler; align the control with the Model Name field control as shown in Figure 5.10

5. To size the control:
   SELECT: Model Code field control
   DRAG: the Model Code control's right border to the left until it reaches the 4-inch mark on the ruler

6. To edit the contents of a label control:
   SELECT: Model Name label control
   DOUBLE-CLICK: the I-beam mouse pointer on the word "Model" to select it and then hold the left mouse button down
   DRAG: the I-beam mouse pointer to the right to select the entire label

7. To enter the new label text:
   TYPE: **Name and Model**
   The new text replaces the selected label.

8. To add a new text label control:
   CLICK: Label tool (**Aa**) in the Toolbox window
   DRAG: a small rectangle on the form for the title "Shoe Models" as shown in Figure 5.10

9. When you release the mouse button, a text box appears. Do the following:
   TYPE: **Shoe Models**
   PRESS: (ENTER)
   The "Shoe Models" label control should now appear selected. If it is not surrounded by selection boxes, click on the label control once.

10. To format the new text label control:
    CLICK: down arrow beside the Font Size (8 ▾) drop-down list box
    CLICK: 10
    CLICK: Italic button (***I***)

11. To copy this formatting style to the "Customers" label control, ensure that the "Shoe Models" label control still appears selected and then do the following:
    CLICK: Format Painter button (🖌)

12. To apply the formatting characteristics:
CLICK: Customers label control

13. On your own, size and position the controls to appear similar to Figure 5.10.

14. To preview how the form will look when printed:
CLICK: Print Preview button (🔍)

15. On your own, zoom and position the Print Preview window to appear similar to Figure 5.11.

16. To return to Design view and save the form design:
CLICK: Close command button on the toolbar
CLICK: Save button (💾)

FIGURE 5.11

DISPLAYING THE FORM
ONCE AGAIN IN PRINT
PREVIEW MODE

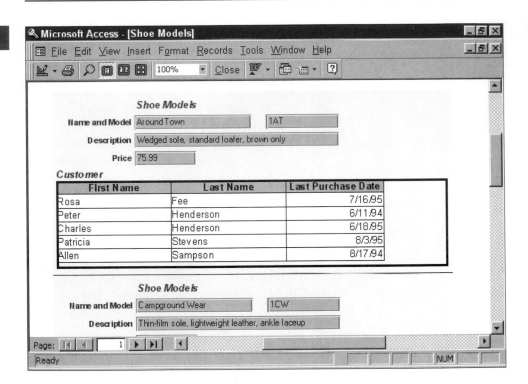

QUICK REFERENCE
Deleting Controls

1. **SELECT: the desired control or controls you want to delete**
2. **PRESS:** `DELETE`

QUICK REFERENCE
Adding a Label Control

1. **Display the Toolbox window by clicking the Toolbox button (🔧).**
2. **CLICK: Label button (Aa) in the Toolbox window**
3. **DRAG: a box on the form that will contain the label**
4. **Type in the desired text label.**
5. **PRESS:** `ENTER`

CHANGING TAB ORDER

If you have completed all of the steps in this lesson, you already have a complex form displayed on the screen. Your next step will be to make this form easier to use. To this end, you will tell Access where to move the cursor when you press the (**TAB**) key in Form view. Currently, the cursor starts in the Model Code field when you open a form; Access still views this field control as if it were the first field on the form. Having moved the Model Code field in the last section, the Model Name field now appears first. To inform Access that the field order has changed in the form, you will complete the following exercise.

Perform the following steps . . .

1. Ensure that the Shoe Models form appears in form Design view.

2. To switch to Form view:
   CLICK: View button (⊞ ▾)
   Notice that the cursor appears in the Model Code field.

3. PRESS: (**TAB**)
   Notice that the cursor moves to the left to the Model Name field. This is not very intuitive!

4. PRESS: (**TAB**)
   Notice that the cursor moves down to the Description field.

5. You will now change this tab order to start in the Model Name field and then proceed to the Model Code and Description fields. To return to Design view:
   CLICK: View button (☑ ▾)
   CHOOSE: View, Tab Order
   The Tab Order dialog box appears as shown in Figure 5.12. Notice that the Model Code field appears before the Model Name field in the *Custom Order* list box.

FIGURE 5.12

THE TAB ORDER DIALOG BOX

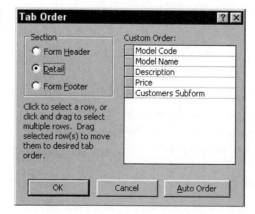

6. SELECT: the button to the left of Model Name to select the entire row (*Note:* Make sure that the row is highlighted before continuing.)

7. DRAG: the row button for Model Name upwards so that it displays above the Model Code field, and then release the mouse button

8. To proceed and display the form:
   CLICK: OK to accept the dialog box
   CLICK: View button (⊞ ▾)

9. With the cursor now starting in the Model Name field:
   PRESS: TAB to move to the Model Code field
   PRESS: TAB to move to the Description field
   Now the cursor reacts intuitively when you press the TAB key.

10. To return to Design view and save the form:
    CLICK: View button (⬛ ▾)
    CLICK: Save button (💾)

QUICK REFERENCE
Changing the Tab Order

1. **CHOOSE: View, Tab Order in form Design view**
2. **SELECT: the row button for the field you want to move**
3. **DRAG: the row button for the selected field to the desired position**
4. **PRESS: ENTER or CLICK: OK**

SETTING FIELD PROPERTIES

When adding table records, you may find that you type the same data repeatedly into a particular field. For example, you may have to enter data into a customer database where all of the customers live in the same city. Wouldn't it be nice if Access automatically filled in City and State fields every time a record was added to the table? Then, you would only need to type an entry into the fields if a customer lived in a different city or state.

In this exercise, you set a default value for a field.

Perform the following steps . . .

1. Ensure that the Shoe Models form appears in form Design view.

2. RIGHT-CLICK: Price field control
   (*Hint:* Position the mouse pointer over the control and then click the right mouse button once.)

3. CHOOSE: Properties from the pop-up menu
   The properties dialog box for the Price field control now appears. As you can see, using the Properties box, you can control almost every aspect of a field. Not only can you establish a default value for a field, you can also control such things as what happens when the user makes a data entry mistake and what happens when you press ENTER.

4. To change the display format of information in the field control:
   CLICK: *All* tab at the top of the dialog box
   CLICK: *Format* text box
   CLICK: down arrow that appears to the right of the text box
   SELECT: Currency option

5. To establish a default value for the Price field:
   CLICK: *Default Value* text box
   TYPE: **95.00**

6. To close the Properties window:
   CLICK: Close button (☒)

7. To display the form:
   CLICK: View button (▦ ▾)
   Notice that the contents of the Price field are displayed using a Currency format.

8. To display a new blank record:
   CLICK: New Record button (▸*) on the toolbar
   Notice that "$95.00" appears in the Price field as the default value.

9. To return to Design view and save the form:
   CLICK: View button (▨ ▾)
   CLICK: Save button (▤)

QUICK REFERENCE Setting Properties for a Field Control	1. **RIGHT-CLICK: a field control in form Design view**
	2. **CHOOSE: Properties from the shortcut menu**
	3. **CLICK: a property text box**
	4. **Select or type the desired value into the text box.**
	5. **CLICK: Close button (☒)**

CREATING A COMMAND BUTTON

In this section, you create a **command button** for a form. You may be asking why place a button on a form? Most commonly, you link a macro to a button that performs an action or command sequence when clicked. For example, suppose you have a custom form for entering data into the Shoe Models table. You can place a command button on this form to display a report in Print Preview mode when it is clicked. In the following steps, you create the command button pictured in Figure 5.13.

FIGURE 5.13

A "PREVIEW REPORT"
COMMAND BUTTON THAT
DISPLAYS ON THE SHOE
MODELS FORM

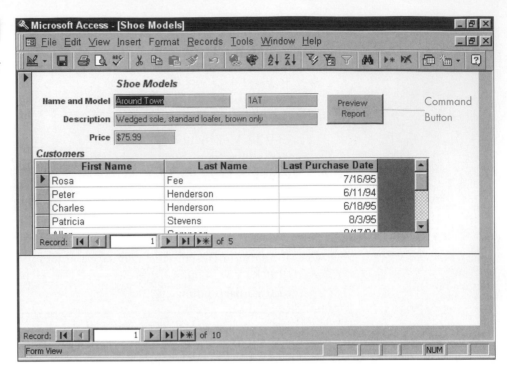

 **Perform the following steps . . .**

1. Ensure that the Shoe Models form appears in form Design view.

2. To return to the Database window:
CLICK: Database Window button (⊡) on the toolbar
The Database window appears in the foreground and the Shoe Models form Design window is rotated to the background.

3. To create a quick tabular report for the Shoe Models table using the AutoReport Wizard:
CLICK: *Reports* tab
CLICK: New command button

4. In the New Report dialog box:
SELECT: AutoReport: Tabular
CLICK: down arrow beside the *Choose the table...* drop-down list box
SELECT: Shoe Models
CLICK: OK command button

5. To return to the report Design view and save the report:
CLICK: Close command button in the toolbar
CLICK: Save button (🖫) on the toolbar
TYPE: **Shoe Models Tabular AutoReport**
PRESS: **ENTER**

6. To close the report Design window:
CLICK: Close button (☒)
You should now see the new report appearing in the Database window.

7. To redisplay the form Design window:
CHOOSE: Window, Shoe Models: Form from the menu

8. Ensure that the window is maximized.

9. Ensure that the Toolbox window is displayed.

10. Ensure that the Control Wizards tool ([⬂]) in the Toolbox window is selected. The button should appear pressed in before continuing.

11. To create a command button:
CLICK: Command button tool ([⬛]) in the Toolbox window

12. CLICK: left mouse button once to the right of the Model Code control
(*Note:* Refer to Figure 5.13 for further clarification on placement.)

13. The first Command Button Wizard dialog box appears. In the *Categories* list box, do the following:
SELECT: Report Operations
Your screen should now appear similar to Figure 5.14.

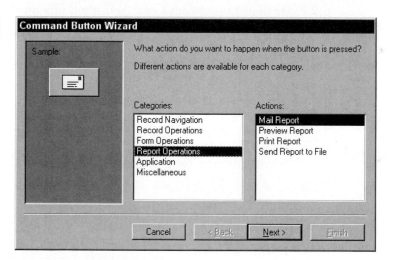

14. In the *Actions* list box:
SELECT: Preview Report
CLICK: [Next >]

15. In this dialog box, you specify the name of the report that you want to preview. Do the following:
SELECT: Shoe Models Tabular AutoReport (if not already selected)
CLICK: [Next >]

16. In this dialog box, you specify whether to display text or an icon graphic on the command button. Do the following:
CLICK: *Text* option button
CLICK: [Next >]

17. In this dialog box, you specify a name for the button control. This name is not displayed on the button, but you may refer to it in a macro or code module. Do the following:
TYPE: **Shoe Report**
CLICK: Finish

18. Now that you have returned to form Design view, you can size and move the command button control to match Figure 5.13. Use the mouse to drag the selection boxes surrounding the control to size it properly. To move a control, you drag it using the hand mouse pointer.

19. Let's see how this command button works:
CLICK: View button (⊞ ▾)
Again, your screen should appear similar to Figure 5.13.

20. CLICK: Preview Report command button
After a few seconds, the Shoe Models Tabular AutoReport displays on the screen in Print Preview mode.

21. On your own, zoom in and then scroll around the report using the horizontal and vertical scroll bars.

22. When you are ready to proceed:
CLICK: Close command button
CLICK: View button (▨ ▾)
CLICK: Save button (🖫)

23. To close the form Design view:
CLICK: its Close button (☒)
You should now see the Database window.

24. To restore the Database window to a window:
CLICK: its Restore button (🗗)

IN ADDITION LINKING TO THE INTERNET USING A COMMAND BUTTON

Rather than previewing a report or running a macro, you can use a command button to open an Internet address. After adding the command button to a report or form, right-click the object and choose the Properties command from its shortcut menu. In the dialog box that appears, click the Hyperlink Address text box and then type in the desired address, also called a "URL." For more information, ask the Office Assistant about "Hyperlink Addresses in Controls."

IN ADDITION CREATING A DATABASE APPLICATION

While this guide focuses mainly on teaching you how to create and manipulate database objects, this section demonstrates the potential for creating your own customized applications using Access. An application ties the objects you create together into a coherent system. Let's review the four levels in Microsoft Access application development:

1. Create database objects to store and present your data

2. Set field and control properties to customize data handling

3. Write Visual Basic modules that respond to specific user events

4. Extend Visual Basic by linking to external Microsoft Access library databases (MDAs) and dynamic-link libraries (DLLs).

For more information, ask the Office Assistant for help on "Creating a database application."

Managing Your Database

As you continue to use Access, you will create many databases and many different database objects, including table, query, form, and report objects, and it is important for you to know how to manage them.

WORKING WITH OBJECTS

In this section, you learn how to copy, rename, and delete database objects.

Perform the following steps . . .

1. Ensure that the "Mountain" Database window appears in the work area.

2. To display the two forms that you have recently created:
   CLICK: *Forms* tab

3. To display the shortcut menu for a database object:
   RIGHT-CLICK: Customers Subform
   Your screen should now appear similar to Figure 5.15.

FIGURE 5.15

DISPLAYING THE
SHORTCUT MENU FOR A
DATABASE OBJECT

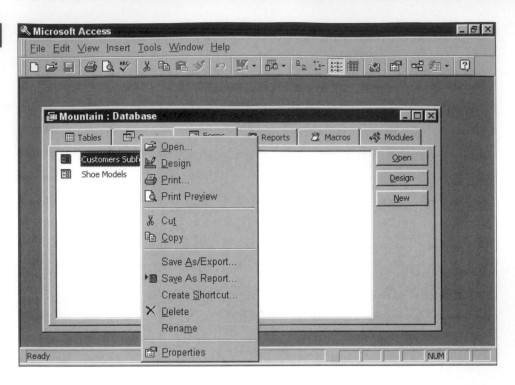

4. From the shortcut menu that appears, you can open, print, move, copy, delete, and rename a database object. To demonstrate how you would delete an object, do the following:
   CHOOSE: Delete
   CLICK: No command button to cancel this selection
   (*Note:* By deleting this subform, you would have critically affected the Shoe Models Main form.)

5. To copy a table structure:
   CLICK: *Tables* tab
   RIGHT-CLICK: Shoe Models
   CHOOSE: Copy
   The table is copied to the Windows Clipboard.

6. To paste an identical table structure, less the data:
   CLICK: Paste button (📋) on the toolbar

7. In the Paste Table As dialog box that appears:
   TYPE: **Future Shoe Models**
   CLICK: *Structure Only* option button
   CLICK: OK command button
   A new table appears in the Database window. This is an excellent way to get started quickly when creating a new table that is based on an existing table in the database.

8. To rename this new table:
RIGHT-CLICK: Future Shoe Models
CHOOSE: Rename
TYPE: **Proposed Shoe Models**
PRESS: (**ENTER**)

QUICK REFERENCE
Copying, Renaming, and
Deleting Objects

1. **RIGHT-CLICK: the desired database object**

2. **From the shortcut menu that appears:**

CHOOSE: Copy, or

CHOOSE: Rename, or

CHOOSE: Delete

3. **Proceed with the operation of pasting, renaming, or confirming the deletion of the selected object.**

PUBLISHING OBJECTS FOR THE INTERNET

In this section, you learn how to export your tables, forms, and reports to HTML documents for publishing on the Internet. As discussed in Session 1, Microsoft Office 97 provides Internet Assistants for saving documents in the Web's native Hypertext Markup Language (HTML). For Access, you must first create your database objects and then export them to HTML. Let's practice this simple procedure.

Perform the following steps . . .

1. Ensure that the "Mountain" Database window appears in the work area.

2. To display the two forms that you have recently created:
CLICK: *Forms* tab

3. To export the Shoe Models form for publishing on the Web:
RIGHT-CLICK: Shoe Models
CHOOSE: Save As/Export

4. In the Save As dialog box:
SELECT: *To an External File or Database* option button
CLICK: OK command button

5. In the Save Form dialog box, you specify the name and type of file to export. Do the following:
TYPE: **Shoes**
CLICK: down arrow beside the *Save as type* drop-down list box
SELECT: HTML documents
CLICK: Export command button
(*Note:* You can also specify a *Save in* location from the drop-down list box appearing at the top of the dialog box.)

6. In the HTML Output Options dialog box, leave the *HTML Template* text box blank and then, do the following:
CLICK: OK command button
Congratulations—you're now a webmaster! Well, maybe not quite yet, but that's all there is to publishing an Access object for the Internet. If you have access to a web server, contact the administrator for further directions on how to upload web pages. Figure 5.16 displays an example of what the "Shoes" HTML document might look like using Microsoft's Internet Explorer Web browser.

FIGURE 5.16

DISPLAYING THE
EXPORTED FORM IN
MICROSOFT'S INTERNET
EXPLORER

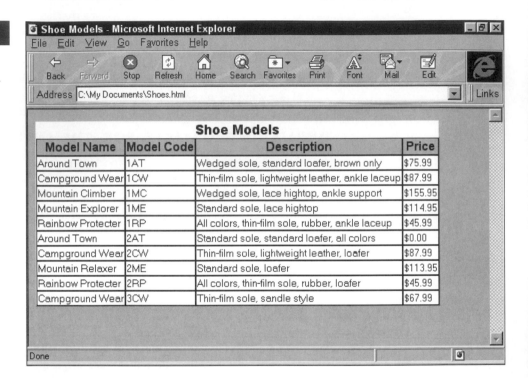

Shoe Models

Model Name	Model Code	Description	Price
Around Town	1AT	Wedged sole, standard loafer, brown only	$75.99
Campground Wear	1CW	Thin-film sole, lightweight leather, ankle laceup	$87.99
Mountain Climber	1MC	Wedged sole, lace hightop, ankle support	$155.95
Mountain Explorer	1ME	Standard sole, lace hightop	$114.95
Rainbow Protecter	1RP	All colors, thin-film sole, rubber, ankle laceup	$45.99
Around Town	2AT	Standard sole, standard loafer, all colors	$0.00
Campground Wear	2CW	Thin-film sole, lightweight leather, loafer	$87.99
Mountain Relaxer	2ME	Standard sole, loafer	$113.95
Rainbow Protecter	2RP	All colors, thin-film sole, rubber, loafer	$45.99
Campground Wear	3CW	Thin-film sole, sandle style	$67.99

QUICK REFERENCE
Exporting Database Objects
As HTML Documents

1. **RIGHT-CLICK: the desired database object**

2. **CHOOSE: Save As/Export**
   SELECT: *To an External File or Database* option button
   CLICK: OK command button

3. **Specify a location, filename, and a file type of "HTML Documents" and then click the Export command button.**

4. **Specify an HTML Template for customizing the document or simply click the OK command button to proceed.**

SETTING OBJECT AND DATABASE PROPERTIES

You will now learn how to store some detailed information about the objects and databases that you create using Access. In addition to descriptively naming a database object, you can input notes and comments about any object, including the database itself. You can also hide an object from displaying in the Database window by selecting the *Hidden* attribute in its Properties window.

In this section, you learn to manipulate the object and database properties.

Perform the following steps . . .

1. Ensure that the "Mountain" Database window appears in the work area and that the *Tables* tab is selected.

2. To display the properties for the Proposed Shoe Models table:
   RIGHT-CLICK: Proposed Shoe Models
   CHOOSE: Properties

3. In the Properties window that appears, type the following into the *Description* text box:
   TYPE: `This copy of the original Shoe Models table is used for inputting the future models that are not yet commercially available.`
   Notice the *Hidden* check box that appears at the bottom of this dialog box. If desired, you select this check box to hide a database object.

4. CLICK: OK command button

5. To set the global properties for the database:
   CHOOSE: File, Database Properties
   CLICK: *Summary* tab (if it is not already selected)

6. On your own, enter the information appearing in Figure 5.17.

FIGURE 5.17

FILLING IN THE DATABASE
PROPERTIES FOR
"MOUNTAIN"

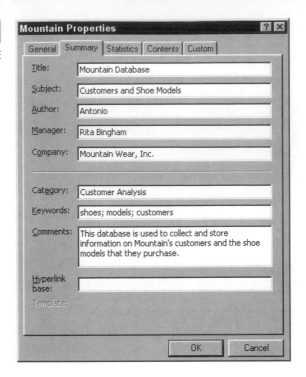

7. CLICK: *Statistics* tab

This tab, along with the *General* tab, displays information such as when the database was created, last modified, and last saved.

8. CLICK: *Contents* tab

This tab lists the objects appearing in each of the tabs of the Database window.

9. CLICK: *Custom* tab

This tab lets you define and manage any custom properties that you want to create.

10. CLICK: *Summary* tab

CLICK: OK command button

11. Close the Mountain database.

12. Exit Microsoft Access.

QUICK REFERENCE

Setting Database Properties

1.   **CHOOSE: File, Database Properties**

2.   **CLICK: *Summary* tab to enter general subject information**

3.   **CLICK: *Contents* tab to view the existing database objects**

4.   **CLICK: OK complete the dialog box**

IN ADDITION BACKING UP THE DATABASE

One of the most important tasks you can perform after creating and adding data to a database is to make a backup copy of it to another stor-age location. Back up a database using "My Computer" or the Windows Explorer, or using special-ized backup software.

IN ADDITION COMPACTING A DATABASE

When you make changes to a data-base, such as copying and deleting objects, the database can become fragmented and make inefficient use of disk space. Compacting a data-base packs the database more closely together, usu-ally resulting in a smaller disk file. To compact a database, you close the database and then choose Tools, Database Utilities, Compact Database from the Menu bar.

Summary

This session introduced you to some more advanced Access topics, including cre-ating forms and managing your database. In the first part of the session, you used a form wizard to create a form that contained a subform. You then edited the form to reposition the field controls and their labels, formatted the appearance of the controls, and then changed the tab order. You learned that by viewing the proper-ties for a field control, you can modify its characteristics or attributes.

You also learned to place a command button on a form. Command buttons are used to automate frequently used procedures and can save you much time when work-ing with Access. Finally, you learned some management techniques for copying, renaming, and deleting database objects and for setting object and database prop-erties.

COMMAND SUMMARY

Table 5.2 provides a list of the commands and procedures covered in this session.

TABLE 5.2	Task Description	Menu Command	Toolbar Button
Command Summary	Creates an AutoForm		New Object button ([⚄▾])
	Establishes a relationship between tables in database		[⊶]
	Changes the back color of an object or control		[⬥▾]
	Changes the fore color of an object or control		[A▾]
	Changes the vertical spacing between controls on a form	Format, Vertical Spacing	
	Displays the Toolbox window		[⚒]
	Adds a text label control to a form		[Aa]
	Changes a form's tab order	View, Tab Order	
	Displays a command button on a form		[▫]
	Lets you edit and view database summary information	File, Database Properties	

EY TERMS

AutoForm Wizard

Using this tool, you can have Access create a single-column form without requesting any information from you. There are actually three types of AutoForm Wizards accessible from the New Form dialog box.

command button

A button that you create and place onto forms to automate frequently used procedures.

form wizards

Access tools that simplify the process of creating a form. You select the type of form and then respond to prompts.

subform

A form within a form.

EXERCISES

SHORT ANSWER

1. What is the difference between a single-column form and a tabular form?

2. What is a subform?

3. Provide an example of when you might want to use a subform.

4. How do you delete an Access control in form Design view?

5. On a form, how do you change the display color in a text box?

6. What does it mean to change the tab order on a form?

7. What is a command button?

8. When would you want to give a field a default value?

9. What is the easiest method or process for managing objects in the Database window?

10. How would you hide a subform object that appears on the *Forms* tab?

HANDS-ON

(*Note:* Ensure that you know the storage location of your Advantage Files and your Data Files before proceeding.)

1. Using an AutoForm Wizard, create a single-column form for the Sales Representatives table of the "Sporting" database. Save the form as "Sales Rep AutoForm." Close the form window.

2. In form Design view, modify the Sales Rep AutoForm so that it looks like the one shown in Figure 5.18.

FIGURE 5.18

A FORM CREATED FOR THE "SPORTING" DATABASE

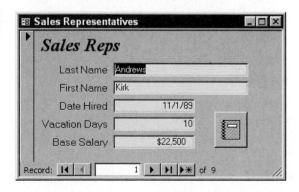

Be sure to perform the following steps.

a. Delete the unwanted field controls from the AutoForm.

b. Format the text as shown in Figure 5.18.

c. Format the display of the Base Salary field.

    d. Include a command button that previews the "Complete Customer Listing" report. Display the icon graphic shown in Figure 5.18.

    e. Test the command button and preview the report.

    f. Save the form.

    g. Print the form.

    h. Close all windows except for the Database window.

3. To practice editing a form, perform the following steps to edit the "Sports Store Customers" form in the "Sporting" database.

    a. Delete the "Sales Representative ID" control from the form.

    b. Change the vertical spacing of the controls so that they are spaced evenly.

    c. Include less vertical space between controls. You should now be able to view all fields in the form window without scrolling.

    d. Change the text of the form title to "Customer Information."

    e. Save the form.

    f. Print the form.

    g. Close all windows except for the Database window.

4. In this exercise, you will practice managing objects using the "Sporting" database.

    a. Make a copy of the Customer table structure and data. Name the copy "Copied Customer Table."

    b. Rename the "Copied Customer Table" object to "Backup Customer Table."

    c. Delete the "Backup Customer Table" object from the database.

    d. Close the database.

5. **On Your Own:** Your Personal Data Entry Form
In previous sessions, you created and customized a database called "My Phone Book." (*Note:* If you have not created this database or query, do so now by referring to the On Your Own exercises in Sessions 2, 3, and 4.) You must now create and customize a form for this database called "My Data Entry Form." Include all the fields from the table in the form and select your own style and formatting options. Save the form before continuing.

6. **On Your Own:** Customizing Your Data Entry Form
Continue customizing your form by adding a command button to run the report called "Alphabetical Phone Listing" that you created in Session 4. Test the form and preview the report using the command button. After returning to Design view, add the "Phone" picture image to the form. Print and then save the form. Lastly, close the Database window and exit Microsoft Access.

CASE PROBLEMS   **INTERNATIONAL HOUSE**

(*Note:* In the following case problems, assume the role of the primary characters and perform the same steps that they identify. You may want to re-read the session opening.)

1. Frederick wants to simplify the process of entering student records. He finds that his eyes get blurry when entering many records into the tiny rows and columns of the datasheet grid. Using the "I-House" database, he creates a single-column form for the Students table that includes all the fields. He places a title of "Data Entry" near the top of the form and then saves the form as "Student Data Entry Form."

2. Frederick wants to create a command button on the Student Data Entry Form that, when clicked, automatically displays the Enrollment Status report. Frederick decides to name the button "Enrollment Status" and position it at the top right-hand corner of the form window. After creating and positioning the button, he tests it to ensure that it works properly and then saves the form using its original name.

3. Feeling confident with creating forms, Frederick decides to make some additional changes to the Student Data Entry Form. First, he uses a command to reduce the amount of vertical space that displays on the form. He then formats the controls on the form. Lastly, he adds the "Book" graphic image to the form for presentation purposes. Frederick saves the form using its original name and then calls it a day.

Index

The page numbers in boldface indicate Quick Reference procedures.

Microsoft® PowerPoint® 97 for Windows®

Sarah E. Hutchinson

Glen J. Coulthard

THE IRWIN/MCGRAW-HILL ADVANTAGE SERIES FOR COMPUTER EDUCATION

Boston, Massachusetts Burr Ridge, Illinois Dubuque, Iowa
Madison, Wisconsin New York, New York San Francisco, California St. Louis, Missouri

Irwin/McGraw-Hill

A Division of The **McGraw·Hill** *Companies*

MICROSOFT® POWERPOINT® 97 for WINDOWS®

3 4 5 6 7 8 9 0 WC/WC 9 0 9 8 7

ISBN 0-256-26001-X

Publisher: *Tom Casson*
Sponsoring editor: *Garrett Glanz*
Developmental editor: *Kristin Hepburn*
GTS production coordinator: *Cathy Stotts*
Marketing manager: *James Rogers*
Senior project supervisor: *Denise Santor-Mitzit*
Production supervisor: *Pat Frederickson*
Art director: *Keith McPherson*
Prepress buyer: *Heather D. Burbridge*
Compositor: *GTS Graphics, Inc.*
Typeface: *11/13 Bodoni Book*
Printer: *Webcrafters, Inc.*

http://www.mhcollege.com

WELCOME TO THE IRWIN ADVANTAGE SERIES

The Irwin Advantage Series has evolved over the years to become one of the most respected resources for software training in the world—to date, over 200,000 students have used one or more of our learning guides. Our instructional methodologies are proven to optimize the student's ability to learn, yet we continually seek ways to improve on our products and approach. To this end, all of our learning guides are classroom tested and critically reviewed by dozens of learners, teachers, and software training experts. We're glad you have chosen the Irwin Advantage Series!

KEY FEATURES

The following features are incorporated into the new Microsoft Office 97 student learning guides to ensure that your learning experience is as productive and enjoyable as possible:

CASE STUDIES

Each session begins with a real-world **case study** that introduces you to a fictitious person or company and describes their immediate problem or opportunity. Throughout the session, you obtain the knowledge and skills necessary to meet these challenges. At the end of the session, you are given an opportunity to solve **case problems** directly related to the case scenario.

CONCEPTS, SKILLS AND PROCEDURES

Each learning guide organizes and presents its content in logically structured session topics. Commands and procedures are introduced using **hands-on examples in a step-by-step format,** and students are encouraged to perform the steps along with the guide. These examples are clearly identified by the text design.

PERFORM THE FOLLOWING STEPS

Using this new design feature, the step progression for all hands-on examples and exercises are clearly identified. Students will find it surprisingly easy to follow the logical sequence of keystrokes and mouse clicks. No longer do you have to worry about missing a step!

END OF SESSION EXERCISES

Each session concludes with **short answer questions** and **hands-on exercises.** These comprehensive and meaningful exercises are integrated with the session's objectives; they were not added as an afterthought. They serve to provide students with opportunities to practice the session material. For maximum benefit, students should complete all the exercises at the end of each session.

IN ADDITION BOXES

These content boxes are placed strategically throughout the guide and provide information on related topics that are beyond the scope of the current discussion. For example, there are three typical categories that are visually identified by the following icons:

Integration

The key to productive and efficient use of Office 97 is in the integration features for sharing data among the applications. With a few mouse clicks, for example, you can create a PowerPoint presentation from a Word document, copy an Access database into an Excel workbook, and incorporate professional Office Art into your annual report. Under this heading, you will find methods for sharing information among the Microsoft Office 97 applications.

Advanced

In a 200+-page learning guide, there are bound to be features that are important but beyond the scope of the text. Therefore, we call attention to these features and offer suggestions on how to apply techniques or to search for more information.

Internet

The Internet is fast becoming a standard tool for gathering and exchanging information. Office 97 provides a high level of Internet connectivity, allowing the user to draw upon its vast resources and even publish documents directly on the World Wide Web. Although not every student will have a persistent Internet connection, you can review the content under this heading to learn about Office's Internet features.

Real life situations introduce the topics →

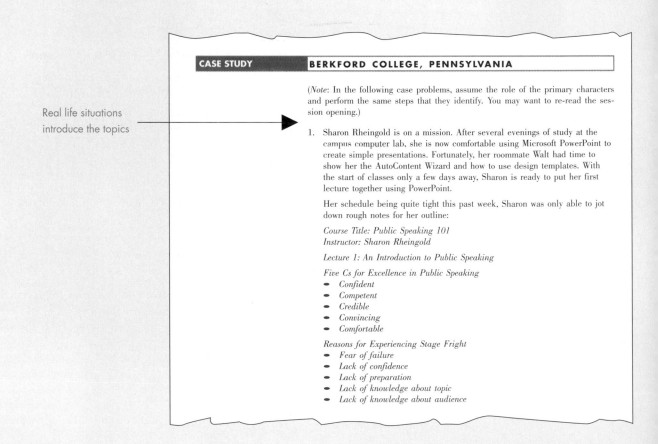

CASE STUDY   **BERKFORD COLLEGE, PENNSYLVANIA**

(*Note*: In the following case problems, assume the role of the primary characters and perform the same steps that they identify. You may want to re-read the session opening.)

1. Sharon Rheingold is on a mission. After several evenings of study at the campus computer lab, she is now comfortable using Microsoft PowerPoint to create simple presentations. Fortunately, her roommate Walt had time to show her the AutoContent Wizard and how to use design templates. With the start of classes only a few days away, Sharon is ready to put her first lecture together using PowerPoint.

   Her schedule being quite tight this past week, Sharon was only able to jot down rough notes for her outline:

   Course Title: Public Speaking 101
   Instructor: Sharon Rheingold

   Lecture 1: An Introduction to Public Speaking

   Five Cs for Excellence in Public Speaking
   - *Confident*
   - *Competent*
   - *Credible*
   - *Convincing*
   - *Comfortable*

   Reasons for Experiencing Stage Fright
   - *Fear of failure*
   - *Lack of confidence*
   - *Lack of preparation*
   - *Lack of knowledge about topic*
   - *Lack of knowledge about audience*

Large figures guide
learning

Easy to read and
identify step-by-step
instructions

In Addition boxes
expand on topics

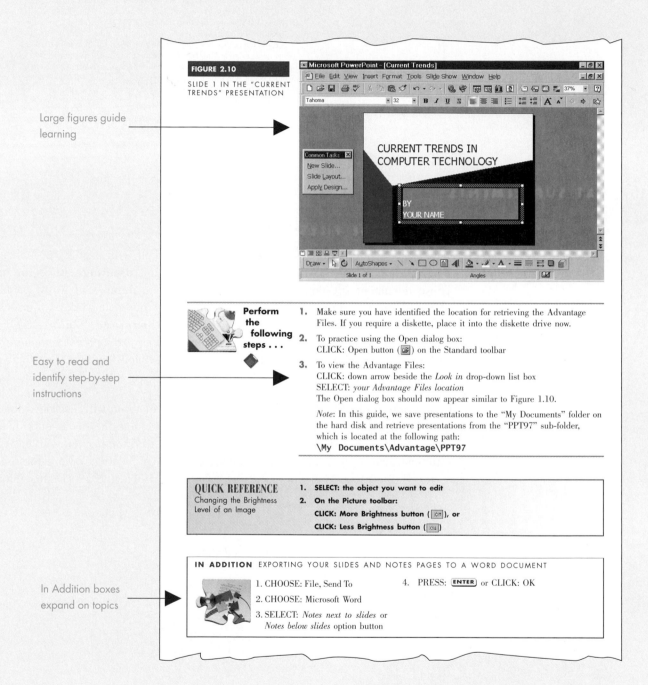

FIGURE 2.10

SLIDE 1 IN THE "CURRENT
TRENDS" PRESENTATION

Perform the following steps . . .

1. Make sure you have identified the location for retrieving the Advantage Files. If you require a diskette, place it into the diskette drive now.

2. To practice using the Open dialog box:
CLICK: Open button (📂) on the Standard toolbar

3. To view the Advantage Files:
CLICK: down arrow beside the *Look in* drop-down list box
SELECT: *your Advantage Files location*
The Open dialog box should now appear similar to Figure 1.10.

Note: In this guide, we save presentations to the "My Documents" folder on the hard disk and retrieve presentations from the "PPT97" sub-folder, which is located at the following path:
\My Documents\Advantage\PPT97

QUICK REFERENCE
Changing the Brightness
Level of an Image

1. SELECT: the object you want to edit
2. On the Picture toolbar:
CLICK: More Brightness button (🔆), or
CLICK: Less Brightness button (🔅)

IN ADDITION EXPORTING YOUR SLIDES AND NOTES PAGES TO A WORD DOCUMENT

1. CHOOSE: File, Send To
2. CHOOSE: Microsoft Word
3. SELECT: *Notes next to slides* or *Notes below slides* option button
4. PRESS: ENTER or CLICK: OK

Students practice with
real life projects

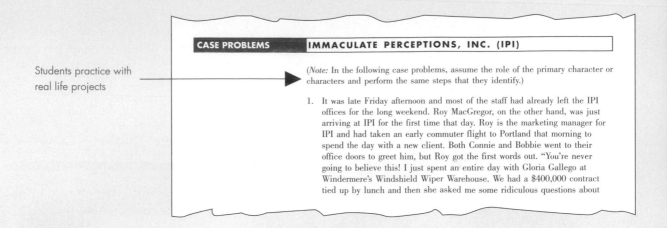

CASE PROBLEMS   **IMMACULATE PERCEPTIONS, INC. (IPI)**

(*Note:* In the following case problems, assume the role of the primary character or characters and perform the same steps that they identify.)

1. It was late Friday afternoon and most of the staff had already left the IPI offices for the long weekend. Roy MacGregor, on the other hand, was just arriving at IPI for the first time that day. Roy is the marketing manager for IPI and had taken an early commuter flight to Portland that morning to spend the day with a new client. Both Connie and Bobbie went to their office doors to greet him, but Roy got the first words out. "You're never going to believe this! I just spent an entire day with Gloria Gallego at Windermere's Windshield Wiper Warehouse. We had a $400,000 contract tied up by lunch and then she asked me some ridiculous questions about

TEXT SUPPLEMENTS

ADVANTAGE FILES

Certain hands-on examples and exercises are marked with a disk ◆ icon, indicating the need to retrieve a document file from the **Advantage Files location.** These document files may be provided to you in a number of ways: packaged on a diskette accompanying this text, or on the computer network at your school. You may also download the files from the ***Advantage Online*** Web site (http://www.irwin.com/cit/adv). *These documents files are extremely important to your success.* Check with your instructor or lab advisor for details on how to acquire the Advantage Files.

In addition to identifying the Advantage Files location, you will also need to specify a **Data Files location.** This location is used to save the documents that you create and may either be a blank diskette or a folder on the network server. Again, your instructor or lab advisor will specify the proper locations. More information on the file locations and the proper techniques for retrieving and saving information is provided inside the back cover of this book.

CD-ROM INTERACTIVE TUTORIALS

In addition to using this book, you may have access to our *Advantage Interactive* software. These interactive multimedia tutorials are fully integrated with the material from each session and make effective use of video clips, screen demonstrations, hands-on exercises, and quizzes. You will enjoy the opportunity to explore these tutorials and learn the software at your own pace. For ordering information, please refer to the coupon inside the front cover.

INSTRUCTOR'S RESOURCE KIT

For instructors and software trainers, each learning guide is accompanied by an **Instructor's Resource Kit (IRK).** This kit provides suggested answers to the short-answer questions, hands-on exercises, and case problems appearing at the end of each session. Furthermore, the IRK includes a comprehensive test bank of additional short-answer, multiple-choice, and fill-in-the-blank questions, plus hands-on exercises. You will also find a diskette copy of the Advantage Files which may be duplicated or placed on your network for student use.

SUPPORT THROUGH THE WWW

The Internet, and more specifically the World Wide Web, is an important component in our approach to software instruction for the Office 97 application series. The *Advantage Online* site at http://www.irwin.com/cit/adv is a tremendous resource for all users, providing information on the latest software and learning guide releases, download options for the Advantage Files, and supplemental files for the Instructor Resource Kits. We also introduce new methods for you to communicate with the authors, publisher, and other users of the series. As a dynamic venture, *Advantage Online* will evolve and improve over time. Please visit us to see the latest developments and contribute your valuable feedback.

NETWORK TESTING

Evaluation and assessment are important components of any instructional series. We are committed to providing quality alternatives to traditional testing instruments. With our Irwin Network Test Interactive software, instructors can select questions, create and administer tests, and then calculate grades—all on-line! Visit the *Advantage Online* site for more information on how we are progressing in this exciting area.

Before you begin

As with any software instruction guide, there are standard conventions that we use to indicate menu options, keystroke combinations, and command instructions.

MENU INSTRUCTIONS

In Office 97, all Menu bar options and pull-down menu commands have an underlined or highlighted letter in each option. When you need to execute a command from the Menu bar—the row of menu choices across the top of the screen—the tutorial's instruction line separates the Menu bar option from the command with a comma. Notice also that the word "CHOOSE" is always used for menu commands. For example, the command for quitting Windows is shown as:

CHOOSE: File, Exit

This instruction tells you to choose the File option on the Menu bar and then to choose the Exit command from the File pull-down menu. The actual steps for choosing a menu command are discussed later in this guide.

KEYSTROKES AND KEYSTROKE COMBINATIONS

When two keys must be pressed together, the tutorial's instruction line shows the keys joined with a plus (+) sign. For example, you can execute a Copy command in Windows by holding down CTRL and then pressing the letter **c**.

The instruction for this type of keystroke combination follows:

PRESS: CTRL +c

COMMAND INSTRUCTIONS

This guide indicates with a special typeface and color the data that you are required to type in yourself. For example:

TYPE: **Income Statement**

When you are required to enter unique information, such as the current date or your name, the instruction appears in italic. The following instruction directs you to type your name in place of the actual words: "your name."

TYPE: *your name*

ACKNOWLEDGMENTS

This series of learning guides is the direct result of the teamwork and heart of many people. We sincerely thank the reviewers, instructors, and students who have shared their comments and suggestions with us over the past few years. We do read them! With this valuable feedback, our guides have evolved into the product you see before you. We also appreciate the efforts of the instructors and students at Okanagan University College who classroom tested our guides to ensure accuracy, relevancy, and completeness.

We also give many thanks to Garrett Glanz, Kristin Hepburn and Tom Casson from Irwin for their skillful management of this text. In fact, special recognition goes to all of the individuals mentioned in the credits at the beginning of this guide. And finally, to the many others who weren't directly involved in this project but who have stood by us the whole way, we appreciate your encouragement and support.

WRITE TO US

We welcome your response to this book, for we are trying to make it as useful a learning tool as possible. Write to us in care of Garrett Glanz, Richard D. Irwin, 1333 Burr Ridge Parkway, Burr Ridge, IL 60521. Thank you.

Sarah E. Hutchinson
sclifford@mindspring.com

Glen J. Coulthard
current@junction.net

Contents

SESSION 1
Fundamentals 97

SESSION 2
Creating a Presentation

SESSION 3
Designing a Presentation

SESSION 4
Adding Visual Effects

SESSION 5
Notes, Handouts, and Printing

APPENDIX
Toolbar Summary 169

INDEX   173

Microsoft PowerPoint 97 for Windows

Fundamentals

SESSION OUTLINE

INTRODUCTION

Welcome to Microsoft PowerPoint 97 for
Windows, a software program that helps you
organize and present information to an audience.
You can use PowerPoint to create overhead transparencies, 35 mm slides, audience handouts and
speaker's notes, and computer-based slide presentations. PowerPoint also provides tools that
help you outline your thoughts, build a presentation quickly using professionally designed
templates, and enhance your presentation with
pictures, charts, sound, and video.

CASE STUDY   **VACATION VISTAS, INC.**

Owned by Frank Muldanno, Vacation Vistas of Memphis is a tour operation specializing in Caribbean cruises. For the past eight months, business has been extremely slow. To increase demand for their cruises, Frank believes that he and his staff must direct more of their marketing to the local seniors community.

One of Frank's new marketing tactics was to hire Juanita Gomez, a local computer consultant and graphic designer, to produce a 35 mm slide presentation that he could show at the neighborhood seniors' hall. Halfway through developing the presentation, Juanita accepted a job in Seattle but promised to send Frank the completed slides from the West Coast.

One week before the presentation, Frank receives a disk and a letter from Juanita with the following note: *"Dear Frank, please review the enclosed presentation and send the disk back to me for final production of the 35 mm slides. By the way, the presentation was created using Microsoft PowerPoint. Good luck, Juanita."* Fortunately, Frank has recently purchased Microsoft Office, which includes PowerPoint, for his new office computer. Although he hasn't used the program before, he is relatively comfortable using Windows.

In this session, you and Frank will learn how to load and exit Microsoft PowerPoint and how to open and close an existing presentation. You'll also take a guided tour of the screen and learn how to access the Help facility. Lastly, you will experiment with the different methods of viewing a presentation in PowerPoint.

INTRODUCING MICROSOFT OFFICE 97

Microsoft Office for Windows combines the most popular and exciting software programs available into a single suite of applications. In the Professional edition, Office 97 includes Microsoft Word, Microsoft Excel, Microsoft PowerPoint, Microsoft Access, and the all-new Microsoft Outlook, an integrated desktop information tool that manages your e-mail, calendar, contacts, to do lists, journal, and Office documents. Office 97 also provides shared applications (sometimes called "server applications") that let you create and insert clip art, organizational charts, and mathematical equations into your word processing documents, electronic spreadsheets, and presentations.

In addition to enjoying performance improvements over its predecessor, Office 97 offers integration with the Internet and World Wide Web (WWW) and benefits from many usability enhancements. For example, Office 97 lets you do the following:

- name your documents using up to 250 characters,
- place shortcuts to files directly on the Windows desktop,
- use the Windows Briefcase program to compare and synchronize files,

- multitask applications with single-click functionality from the taskbar,

- save documents in the web's Hypertext Markup Language (HTML) format, and

- post documents to your internal intranet or to the web.

All of Office's primary applications use Intellisense technology, helping users to focus on their work and not on their software. Examples of Intellisense are automatic spell and grammar checking and wizards that lead you through performing basic and complex tasks. Office 97 offers additional Help features, including an animated character called the Office Assistant who provides helpful tips and suggestions as you work.

INTEGRATION FEATURES

Many would say that the essence of Office 97 is its ability to share data among the suite of applications. For example, you can place an Excel chart in a report that you write using Word, a Word document in a PowerPoint presentation, an Access database in an Excel worksheet, and so on. You can also create and insert objects using shared applications—such as Microsoft Office Art and Microsoft Organization Chart—without ever leaving the current application. Using Microsoft Binder, you can assemble Word, Excel, and PowerPoint documents into a single file for distribution. Binder also allows you to print a collection of documents with consistent headers and footers and with consecutive page numbering.

INTERNET FEATURES

One of the most exciting innovations in Office 97 is its ability to take advantage of the World Wide Web and the Internet. For those of you new to the online world, the **Internet** is a vast collection of computer networks that spans the entire planet, made up of many smaller networks connected by standard telephone lines. The term **Intranet** is used to refer to a local or wide area network that uses Internet technologies to share information within an organization. To access the Internet, you need a network or modem connection that links your computer to an account on the university's network or to an independent Internet Service Provider (ISP).

Once connected, you use web browser software, such as Microsoft Internet Explorer or Netscape Navigator, to access the **World Wide Web (WWW).** The WWW provides a visual interface for the Internet and lets you search for information by simply clicking on highlighted words and images, know as **hyperlinks.** When you click a link, you are telling your web browser to retrieve and then display a page from a web site. Each web page has a unique location or address specified by its *Uniform Resource Locator* or URL. One example of a URL is: http://www.microsoft.com. For more information on the Internet and World Wide Web, visit your local bookstore, campus computing center, or computer users group.

Microsoft Office 97 provides a consistent set of tools for publishing documents, spreadsheets, presentations, and databases to the web and for accessing help directly from Microsoft's web site. Specifically, each Office application includes a

Web toolbar that lets you quickly open, search, and browse documents on your local computer, Intranet, and the Internet. Furthermore, you can create your own hyperlinks and share your documents with the entire world after publishing it to a web server. As you proceed through this manual, look for the Internet features found in the *In Addition* boxes.

CREATING PRESENTATIONS WITH POWERPOINT

Microsoft PowerPoint is a software program that enables you to produce high-quality output, such as overhead transparencies, 35 mm slides, and computer-based displays, for presentation to an audience. Even if you don't consider yourself a speechwriter or graphics designer, you can still create informative and attractive presentations using PowerPoint. In PowerPoint, a **presentation** is the collection of slides, handouts, speaker's notes, and outlines contained in a single disk file. Below we describe these presentation elements and some additional PowerPoint features:

- *Slides.* A PowerPoint **slide** is an individual page in your presentation. Figure 1.1 shows a sample slide. You can output the slides on your printer as overhead transparencies or send your presentation file on a diskette to an outside service bureau to develop 35 mm slides. A more fashionable option is to display your PowerPoint presentation on a computer monitor or use a projection unit (or LCD panel) and a large projection screen.

FIGURE 1.1

ONE EXAMPLE OF A
PRESENTATION SLIDE

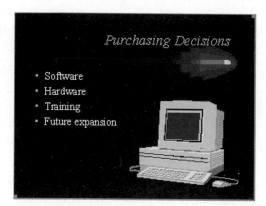

- *Handouts.* A **handout** consists of two to six slide images printed on a single page. Handouts help support your presentation by keeping the audience focused on what you are saying and by not requiring them to write down everything they see on the projection screen.

- *Speaker's notes.* To assist you in the actual delivery of a presentation, PowerPoint lets you enter and print a notes page for each slide.

- *Outlines.* For brainstorming and organizing your thoughts, PowerPoint's outline feature is extremely valuable. In outline form, the text of your presentation—that is, headings and main body text—appears without the slide's background, colors, or graphics.

- *Templates.* For those people who may question their creative and artistic talent, there is absolutely nothing to worry about—PowerPoint provides over 100 professionally designed templates containing proven layouts, color schemes, background textures, and typefaces. A **template** defines what your presentation will look like, where text and other objects will appear, and which foreground and background colors will be used.

- *"Auto" features.* Several "Auto" features make it easier for you to perform your work. For example, PowerPoint's AutoCorrect feature will automatically replace "teh" with "the" and "ast he" with "as the" and ensure that your sentences begin with an uppercase letter. Also, when automatic spell checking is enabled, misspelled words are marked with a red wavy underline. To correct the spelling mistake, you right-click the wavy underline and then choose an option from the shortcut menu. The AutoClipArt command provides suggestions on which pictures to include in your presentation to better convey your message.

- *Wizards.* As you will see in this learning guide, PowerPoint employs many **wizards** to help you get your work done. These software features make short order of the tasks that might otherwise be repetitive, time-consuming, or difficult.

- *The Office Assistant.* Think of the Office Assistant, a component of Power-Point's Help system, as your own personal computer guru. When you have a question about how to accomplish a task in PowerPoint, you can "talk" to the Office Assistant using typed English phrases. The Office Assistant analyzes your request and provides a resource list of potential help topics. The Assistant can also provide step-by-step instructions on how to complete a task and can even perform certain tasks for you.

- *PowerPoint Central.* PowerPoint Central is an online magazine, or electronic slide show, that is automatically installed on your computer as part of a typical PowerPoint 97 installation. In it, you can find suggestions and tips for using PowerPoint and creating effective presentations. Also, it provides an additional resource for templates, sounds, animation clips, and other types of objects that you might want to include in a presentation.

- *PowerPoint Viewer.* Microsoft PowerPoint includes a **run-time version** of the program called the PowerPoint Viewer. You can create a presentation on your computer and then send it along on a diskette with the PowerPoint Viewer to your employees, clients, students, or other recipients who do not own Microsoft PowerPoint. As long as they have Microsoft Windows installed on their computers, the recipients of your diskettes will be able to view (but not change) your presentation using the Viewer.

Now, let's begin our journey through Microsoft PowerPoint 97.

STARTING POWERPOINT

This session assumes that you are working on a computer with Windows and Microsoft PowerPoint 97 loaded on the hard disk drive. Before you load Windows and PowerPoint, let's look at how to use the mouse and keyboard.

USING THE MOUSE AND KEYBOARD

Microsoft PowerPoint 97 for Windows is a complex yet easy-to-learn program. As you proceed through this guide, you will find that there are often three methods for performing the same command or procedure in Word:

- Menu   Select a command or procedure from the Menu bar.

- Mouse   Point to and click a toolbar button or use the Ruler.

- Keyboard   Press a keyboard shortcut (usually CTRL +letter).

Although this guide concentrates on the quickest and easiest methods, we recommend that you try the others and decide which you prefer. *Don't memorize all of the methods and information in this guide! Be selective and find your favorite methods.*

Although you may use PowerPoint with only a keyboard, much of the program's basic design relies on using a mouse. Regardless of whether your mouse has two or three buttons, you use the left or primary mouse button for selecting text and menu commands and the right or secondary mouse button for displaying shortcut menus. The most common mouse actions used in PowerPoint are listed below:

- Point   Slide the mouse on your desk to position the tip of the mouse pointer over the desired object on the screen.

- Click   Press down and release the left mouse button quickly. Clicking is used to position the insertion point, choose menu commands, and make selections in a dialog box.

- Right-Click   Press down and release the right mouse button. Right-clicking the mouse on text or an object displays a context-sensitive shortcut menu.

- Double-Click   Press down and release the mouse button twice in rapid succession. Double-clicking is often used in PowerPoint to select and execute an action.

- Drag   Press down and hold the mouse button as you move the mouse pointer across the screen. When the mouse pointer reaches the desired location, release the mouse button. Dragging is used to select a block of text or to move objects or windows.

You may notice that the mouse pointer changes shape as you move it over different parts of the screen or during processing. Each mouse pointer shape has its own purpose and may provide you with important information. There are five primary mouse shapes you should be aware of:

↖	left arrow	Used to choose menu commands, access the toolbars, and make selections in dialog boxes.
⌛	Hourglass	Informs you that PowerPoint is occupied with another task and requests that you wait.
I	I-beam	Used to modify and edit text and to position the insertion point.
🖑	Hand	In a Help window, the hand is used to select shortcuts and definitions.

As you proceed through this guide, other mouse shapes will be explained in the appropriate sections.

Aside from being the primary input device for entering text in a presentation, the keyboard offers shortcut methods for performing commands and procedures. For example, several menu commands have shortcut key combinations listed to the right of the command in the pull-down menu. Therefore, you can perform a command by simply pressing the shortcut keys rather than accessing the Menu bar. Many of these shortcut key combinations are available throughout Windows applications.

LOADING WINDOWS

Because Windows is an operating system, it is loaded automatically into the computer's memory when you turn on the computer. In this section, you turn your computer on to load Windows.

Perform the following steps . . .

1. Turn on the power switches to the computer and monitor. After a few seconds, the Windows desktop will appear (Figure 1.2). (*Note:* The desktop interface on your computer may look different from Figure 1.2.)

2. If a Welcome to Windows dialog box appears, do the following:
CLICK: Close button (☒) in the top right-hand corner of the window

FIGURE 1.2

THE WINDOWS DESKTOP

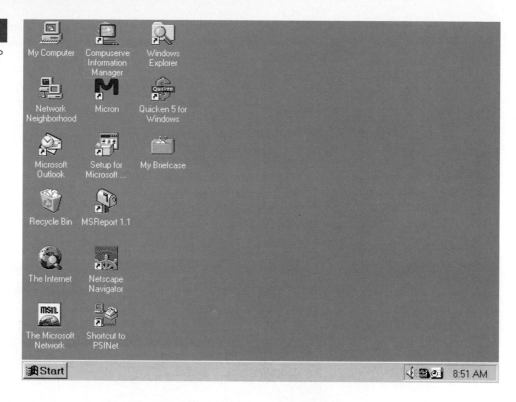

QUICK REFERENCE
Loading Windows

Turn on your computer to load Microsoft Windows (or Microsoft Windows NT 3.51 or later).

LOADING MICROSOFT POWERPOINT 97

In this section, you load Microsoft PowerPoint.

Perform the following steps . . .

1. Point to the Start button (Start) on the taskbar and then click the left mouse button once. The Start menu appears as a pop-up menu.

2. Point to the Programs command using the mouse. Notice that you do not need to click the left mouse button to display the list of programs in the fly-out or cascading menu.

3. Move the mouse pointer horizontally to the right until it highlights an option in the Programs menu. You can now move the mouse pointer up and down the Programs menu. Notice that you still haven't clicked the left mouse button.

4. Point to the Microsoft PowerPoint menu item and then click the left mouse button once to execute the command. After a few seconds, the Microsoft PowerPoint screen appears.

5. If the Office Assistant (shown at the right) appears:
CLICK: Close button ([✕]) in its top right-hand corner

6. The PowerPoint startup dialog box should appear on your screen (Figure 1.3). You use this dialog box to determine how you want to proceed when PowerPoint is first loaded.
(*Note:* You can turn this feature off using the Tools, Options command. For this guide, we leave the startup dialog box displayed.) As shown in Figure 1.3, the Common Tasks toolbar may also appear on your screen. We describe the Common Tasks toolbar shortly.

FIGURE 1.3

THE POWERPOINT
STARTUP DIALOG BOX
AND THE COMMON
TASKS TOOLBAR

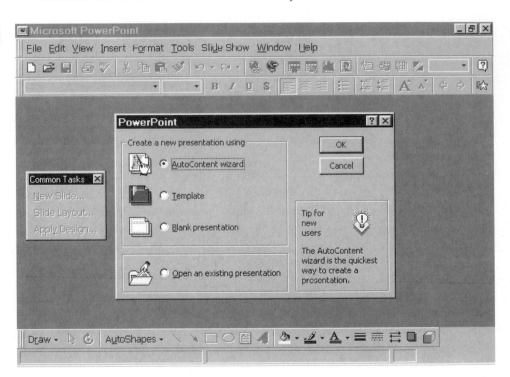

7. Before continuing, let's temporarily remove the startup dialog box so that we can describe the components of PowerPoint in the next section. We will return to the options available in the startup dialog box later. Do the following:
CLICK: Cancel command button
(*Note:* The word CLICK means to point to the command button and then click the left mouse button once.) The Common Tasks toolbar may still appear on your screen.

QUICK REFERENCE	1.	**CLICK:** Start button (start)
Loading Microsoft PowerPoint 97	2.	**CHOOSE:** Programs, Microsoft PowerPoint

THE GUIDED TOUR

Software programs designed for Microsoft Windows, such as PowerPoint, have many similarities in screen design and layout. Each program operates in its own application window, while the presentations, spreadsheets, and letters you create appear in separate document windows. In PowerPoint, the document window is referred to as the presentation window. This section explores the various parts of PowerPoint, including the tools for manipulating application and presentation windows.

APPLICATION WINDOW

The PowerPoint screen consists of the **application window** and the **presentation window.** The application window (Figure 1.4) contains the Title bar, Menu bar, Standard toolbar, Formatting toolbar, Drawing toolbar, Status bar, and Slide work area. Presentation windows contain the actual slide presentations that you create and store on the disk.

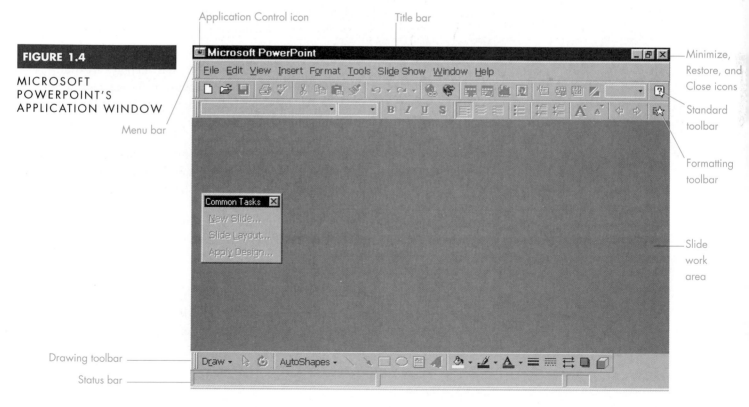

FIGURE 1.4

MICROSOFT POWERPOINT'S APPLICATION WINDOW

The primary components of the application window are listed below:

Application Control icon (🔲)	Used to size and position the application window using the keyboard. (*Note:* It is easier to use the mouse to perform the same options available in the Control menu.)
Minimize (🔲) and Maximize (🔲), Restore (🔲), and Close (🗙) icons	Located in the top right-hand corner of the application window, these icons are used to control the display of the application window using the mouse. (*Note:* The Maximize button doesn't appear in Figure 1.4.)
Title bar	The Title bar contains the name of the program or presentation file. Using a mouse, you can move a window by dragging its Title bar.
Menu bar	Contains the PowerPoint menu commands.
Standard toolbar	The Standard toolbar displays buttons for opening and saving presentations, editing text, and accessing special features using the mouse.
Formatting toolbar	The Formatting toolbar displays buttons for accessing character and paragraph formatting commands using a mouse.
Drawing toolbar	The Drawing toolbar displays buttons for drawing objects such as lines, circles, and boxes.
Status bar	Located at the bottom of the application window and above the taskbar, the Status bar displays the current slide number and a description of the current design template. The Status bar contains information once a presentation is opened.
Slide work area	The Slide work area is where your presentation windows appear. You can work on more than one presentation at the same time in this work area.

Although typically maximized, you can size, move, and manipulate the PowerPoint application window on the Windows desktop to customize your work environment.

PRESENTATION WINDOW

The presentation window provides the viewing and editing area for a presentation. Figure 1.5 shows an example of a presentation window that is not maximized, as it would appear in the Slide work area of PowerPoint's application window. You will open and display a presentation window shortly.

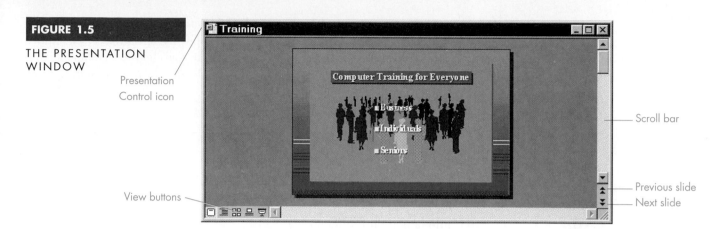

FIGURE 1.5

THE PRESENTATION
WINDOW

The primary components of the presentation window are listed below:

Presentation Control icon (⊞)	Used to size and position the application window using the keyboard. (*Note:* It is easier to use a mouse to perform the same options available in the Presentation Control menu.)
Scroll bar	Placed at the right border of the presentation window, the vertical scroll bar facilitates moving from slide to slide using the mouse. As you drag the scroll box or elevator up and down, the current slide number displays in a Slide number box along the scroll bar.
Previous slide (⯅), Next slide (⯆)	Use these buttons to display the previous slide or the next slide.
View buttons	Located at the bottom left-hand corner of the presentation window, the View buttons let you change the current view of the presentation.

You should recognize some familiar components in the presentation window that appear in all windows. For example, the Minimize and Maximize icons appear in the top right-hand corner of the presentation window. To restore a maximized presentation to a window, you click the Restore icon (⧉). To maximize the presentation window, you click the Maximize icon (☐). Before proceeding, make sure that your application and presentation windows are maximized.

MENU BAR

PowerPoint commands are grouped together on the Menu bar, as shown below.

File Edit View Insert Format Tools Slide Show Window Help

Commands in this guide are written in the following form: Edit, Copy, where Edit is the Menu bar option and Copy is the command to be selected from the pull-down menu. To execute a command, click once on the Menu bar option and then click once on the pull-down menu command. Commands that are not available for selection appear dimmed. Commands that are followed by an ellipsis (...) require further information to be collected in a dialog box. If you choose a command that is followed by a sideways triangle (▶), an additional pull-down menu will appear.

Now you will practice accessing the Menu bar.

Perform the following steps . . .

1. To choose the Help command, position the tip of the mouse pointer on the word Help in the Menu bar and click the left mouse button once. A pull-down menu appears below the Help option.

2. To see the pull-down menu associated with the File menu option, point to the File option on the Menu bar.

3. To leave the Menu bar without making a selection:
   CLICK: anywhere in the Slide work area
   (*Note:* Also, clicking the menu option again, clicking the Title bar, or pressing ESC removes the pull-down menu.)

4. To again display the pull-down menu for the File option:
   CHOOSE: File
   This instruction tells you to click the mouse pointer on File in the Menu bar. (*Note:* All menu commands that you execute in this guide begin with the word "CHOOSE.")

5. To again leave the Menu bar without making a selection:
   CHOOSE: File

SHORTCUT MENUS

PowerPoint uses context-sensitive shortcut menus for quick access to menu commands. Rather than searching for commands in the Menu bar, you position the mouse pointer on text or an object, such as a graphic, and click the right mouse button. A pop-up menu appears with the most commonly selected commands for the text or object.

Now you will practice accessing a shortcut menu.

Perform the following steps . . .

1. To display a shortcut or pop-up menu, position the mouse pointer over any button on the Standard toolbar and click the right mouse button. The shortcut menu at the right should appear.

2. To remove the shortcut menu from the screen, move the mouse pointer into the Slide work area and click the left mouse button. The shortcut menu disappears.

QUICK REFERENCE
Using Shortcut Menus

1. **Position the mouse pointer over an item, such as a toolbar button.**
2. **CLICK: the right mouse button to display a shortcut or pop-up menu**
3. **CHOOSE: a command from the menu, or**

   CLICK: the left mouse button in the Slide work area to remove it

TOOLBARS

Assuming that you haven't yet customized your PowerPoint screen, you will see the Standard and Formatting toolbars appear below the Menu bar. You may also see the Common Tasks toolbar appear somewhere in the Slide work area and the Drawing toolbar appear at the bottom of the application window.

PowerPoint provides eleven toolbars and hundreds of buttons and drop-down lists for quick and easy mouse access to its more popular commands and features. Don't worry about memorizing the button names appearing in the following graphics— the majority of these buttons are explained in subsequent sessions and all toolbars and their buttons are summarized in the Appendix. You can also point at any toolbar button and pause until a yellow ToolTip appears with the button name. With the ToolTip displayed, an extended description for the button appears in the Status bar.

Below we identify the buttons on the Standard and Formatting toolbars. (*Note:* On your computer, many of the buttons on these toolbars appear dimmed, currently unavailable for use. Many will become available once you open a presentation.)

The Standard toolbar provides access to file management and slide editing commands.

The Formatting toolbar lets you access formatting commands.

To display additional toolbars, you point to an existing toolbar and click the right mouse button. From the shortcut menu that appears, you can display and hide toolbars by clicking their names in the pop-up menu. If a toolbar is currently being displayed, a check mark appears beside its name. You can also choose the View, Toolbars command to display the Toolbars menu.

In this section, you practice displaying and hiding toolbars.

Perform the following steps . . .

1. Position the mouse pointer over any button on the Standard toolbar.

2. CLICK: right mouse button to display the shortcut menu

3. To display the Animation Effects toolbar:
   CHOOSE: Animation Effects
   The new toolbar appears in the Slide work area.

4. To remove the Animation Effects toolbar:
   RIGHT-CLICK: Animation Effects toolbar
   This instruction tells you to position the mouse pointer over the Animation Effects toolbar and click the right mouse button.

5. You will notice that the Animation Effects command on the shortcut menu has a check mark. To remove the Animation Effects toolbar:
   CHOOSE: Animation Effects
   The Animation Effects toolbar disappears from the application window.

STATUS BAR

The Status bar provides status information for a presentation, including the current slide number and template description. The Status bar shows that "FANS" is the name of the current template.

| Slide 1 of 3 | FANS | |

To correct all of your spelling errors at once, use the book icon on the Status bar. If your presentation is free of spelling errors, a check mark will appear on the book icon. Otherwise, an "✗" will appear. To jump through the spelling errors in a presentation, double-click the book icon.

DIALOG BOX

A dialog box is a common mechanism in Windows applications for collecting information before processing a command or instruction (Figure 1.6). In a dialog box, you indicate the options you want to use and then click the OK button when you're finished. Dialog boxes are also used to display messages or to ask for confirmation of commands.

A dialog box uses several methods for collecting information, as shown in Figure 1.6 and described in Table 1.1.

FIGURE 1.6

A DIALOG BOX

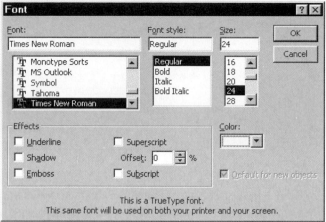

TABLE 1.1	*Name*	*Example*	*Action*
Parts of a dialog box	Check box	☑ Always ☐ Never	Click an option to turn it on or off. The option is turned on when an "✓" appears in the box.
	Command button	OK / Cancel	Click a command button to execute an action. You accept or cancel the selections in a dialog box by clicking the OK or Cancel command buttons, respectively.
	Drop-down list box	Screen Saver / None	Make a choice from the list that appears when you click the down arrow next to the box; only the selected choice is visible.
	List box	Wallpaper / (None) / Arcade / Argyle	Make a choice from the scrollable list; several choices, if not all, are always visible.
	Option button	Display: ⦿ Tile ○ Center	Select an option from a group of related options.
	Slide box	Desktop area / Less — More / 640 by 480 pixels	Drag the slider bar to make a selection, like using a radio's volume control.
	Spin box	Wait: 6 minutes	Click the up and down arrows to the right of the box until the number you want appears.

TABLE 1.1	*Name*	*Example*	*Action*
Continued	Tab	General | Letters & Faxes	Click a named tab at the top of the window to access other pages of options in the dialog box.
	Text box	File name: untitled	Click inside the text box and then type the desired information.

Most dialog boxes provide a question mark button ([?]) near the right side of the Title bar. If you have a question about an item in the dialog box, click the question mark and then click the item to display some helpful information. You should also know that dialog boxes have a memory. For example, the tab that appears when you exit the dialog box will be selected the next time you open the dialog box.

THE WINDOWS TASKBAR

The Windows taskbar is usually located on the bottom of your screen below the Status bar. (*Note:* We say "usually" because you can move the taskbar on your desktop.) Each application that you are currently working with is represented by a button on the taskbar. To switch between applications, click the appropriate application button on the taskbar. At this point, you should see a button for Microsoft PowerPoint on the taskbar.

GETTING HELP

PowerPoint provides several **context-sensitive help** features and a comprehensive library of online documentation. Like many developers trying to minimize the retail price of software and maximize profits, Microsoft has stopped shipping volumes of print-based documentation in favor of disk-based Help systems. However, a Help system is only as good as the search tools that it provides. Fortunately for us, Windows gives developers the tools and capability to create consistent and easy-to-use Help systems. This section describes the context-sensitive help features found in PowerPoint and then describes where to find more detailed information using the Help Topics window.

CONTEXT-SENSITIVE HELP

Context-sensitive help refers to a software program's ability to retrieve and present helpful information reflecting your current position in the program. In PowerPoint, you can access context-sensitive help for menu options, toolbar buttons, and dialog box items. The help information is presented concisely in a small pop-up window that you can remove with a click of the mouse. This type of help lets you access information quickly and then continue working without interruption. Table 1.2 describes some methods for accessing context-sensitive help while working in PowerPoint.

TABLE 1.2	To display...	Do this...
Displaying context-sensitive Help information	A description of a dialog box item	Click the question mark button (⟦?⟧) in a dialog box's Title bar and then click an item in the dialog box. A helpful description of the item appears in a pop-up window. Additionally, you can often right-click a dialog box item to display its description.
	A description of a menu command	Choose Help, What's This? from the Menu bar and then choose the desired command using the question mark mouse pointer. Rather than executing the command, a helpful description of the command appears in a pop-up window.
	A description of a toolbar button	Point to a toolbar button to display its ToolTip label. You can also choose Help, What's This? from the Menu bar and then click a toolbar button to display more detailed help information in a pop-up window.

In this section, you access context-sensitive help.

Perform the following steps . . .

1. Let's practice choosing Help, What's This? to access Help for the File, New command and one of the toolbar buttons. Let's start with the File, New command.
   CHOOSE: Help

2. To activate the question mark mouse pointer:
   CHOOSE: What's This?

3. CHOOSE: File, New
   Rather than executing the command, Word provides a description of the command.

4. After reading the description, close the window by clicking on it once.

5. To display information about a toolbar button:
   CHOOSE: Help, What's This?
   CLICK: Open button (⟦🖝⟧) on the Standard toolbar
   The following pop-up window appears:

Open (File menu)
Opens or finds a file.

6. CLICK: the pop-up window once to remove it

7. Word also provides a special Help tool called the Office Assistant. The Office Assistant watches your keystrokes as you work and offers suggestions and shortcuts. The Office Assistant may appear as a paperclip (by default) or as another character. At this point, if the Office Assistant already appears on your screen, as it does in Figure 1.7, skip to Step 8. To display the Office Assistant:

CLICK: Office Assistant button ([?])

The Office Assistant and its associated tip window appear. Your screen should appear similar to Figure 1.7.

FIGURE 1.7

OFFICE ASSISTANT AND
TIP WINDOW

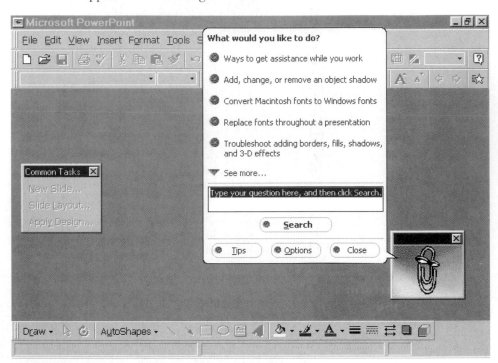

8. To type in a question about using clip art in a presentation:
TYPE: **use clip art**

9. To display information about your topic, click the Search button.
CLICK: Search button in the tip window
A list of related topics appears.

10. To close the tip window:
CLICK: Close button
The Office Assistant box, without the tip window, now appears in the presentation window. By simply clicking the animated character, the Office Assistant will display information about the procedure you are performing. Occasionally an illuminated light bulb will appear in the Office Assistant box. This is the Office Assistant's way of telling you it has a new tip or suggestion. You tell the Office Assistant that you want to view the tip by clicking the light bulb.

11. To remove the Office Assistant:
CLICK: Close button ([X]) in its top right-hand corner

QUICK REFERENCE
Displaying Context-
Sensitive Help

1. **CHOOSE: Help, What's This?**

2. **Using the question mark mouse pointer, select the desired item for which you want to display a help pop-up window:**

    - **CHOOSE: a menu command, or**
    - **CLICK: a toolbar button, or**
    - **CLICK: a dialog box item**

IN ADDITION CUSTOMIZING THE OFFICE ASSISTANT

To customize the Office Assistant, you do the following:

1. Ensure that the Office Assistant box appears.

2. RIGHT-CLICK: the Office Assistant character in the box

3. CHOOSE: Choose Assistant from the menu

4. Use the Gallery tab to select your favorite Office Assistant.

5. Select or remove features in the Options tab.

6. When finished, press ENTER or CLICK: OK

HELP TOPICS WINDOW

The primary way that you access PowerPoint's Help system is by choosing the Help, Contents and Index command from the menu. This command displays the Help Topics window, as shown in Figure 1.8. You can think of the Help Topics window as the front door to PowerPoint's vast help resources.

FIGURE 1.8

HELP TOPICS WINDOW:
CONTENTS TAB

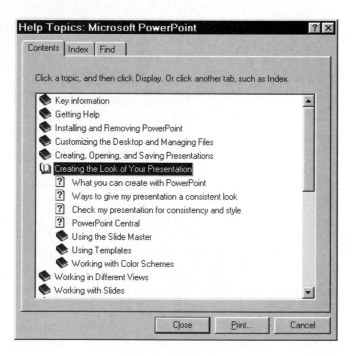

The Help Topics window provides three different tools, each on its own tab, to help you find the information you need quickly and easily. You point to and click a tab using the mouse to make the tab active in the window. Refer to the following tab descriptions to determine which tool you should use when requiring assistance:

- *Contents* tab   Displays a list of help topics organized as a hierarchy of books and pages. Think of this tab as the Table of Contents for the entire Help system. You navigate through categories by double-clicking book icons (📖) until reaching the desired help topic (❓). Notice in Figure 1.8 that there are three different types of icons displayed:

      📖   represents a help category; double-click a book icon to view the books and topics it contains

      📖   represents an open category that is currently displaying its contents; double-click an open book icon to close (or collapse) the book

      ❓   represents a help topic; double-click a topic icon to display a help window

- *Index* tab   Displays an alphabetical list of keywords and phrases, similar to a traditional book index. To search for a topic using this tab, you type a word (or even a few letters) into the text box which, in turn, makes the list box scroll to the first matching entry in the index. When the desired entry appears in the list box, double-click it to display the help topic. If a keyword has more than one associated topic, a Topics Found window appears and you can select a further topic to narrow your search.

- *Find* tab   Provides the ability to conduct a full-text search of the Help system for finding a particular word or phrase. Although similar to the *Index* tab, this tab differs in its ability to look past indexed keywords and search the help text itself.

When you double-click a help topic, it is displayed in a *secondary* window. You may find that secondary windows include some unfamiliar buttons, like ⏩ and ↰, embedded in the help text. The ⏩ symbol, which we'll call the Chiclet button, represents a "See Also" link that you can click to move to a related help topic. The ↰ symbol, called the Show Me button, initiates the command you're interested in. You may also notice that some words or phrases in the help window have a dotted underline. If you click such a word or phrase, a definition pop-up window appears.

In this section, you access the Help Topics window.

Perform the following steps . . .

1. CHOOSE: Help, Contents and Index

2. CLICK: *Contents* tab
   Your screen should now appear similar to Figure 1.8, except that your book categories will appear collapsed. (*Note*: The Help Topics window remembers the tab that was selected when it was last closed. It will automatically return to this tab the next time you access the Help system. For example, if you close the Help Topics window with the *Index* tab active, it will appear active the next time you display the window.)

3. To display the contents of a book:
   DOUBLE-CLICK: "📘 Creating the Look of Your Presentation" book
   (*Note*: You can double-click the book icon (📘) or the book's title. If you find it difficult to double-click using the mouse, you can also select or highlight the book by clicking it once and then click the Open command button.) This particular book contains four topic pages and three additional book categories.

4. To further clarify the search:
   DOUBLE-CLICK: "📘 Using Templates" book
   Notice that this book contains three topics.

5. To display a help topic:
   DOUBLE-CLICK: "❓ Create my own template" topic
   The Help Topics window is removed from view and a secondary window appears with the topic information.

6. To print the help topic:
   RIGHT-CLICK: anywhere in the help text of the secondary window
   CHOOSE: Print Topic (as shown in Figure 1.9)
   (*Note*: You can also print help information directly from the *Contents* tab. If you select a book by clicking on it once and then click the Print command button, the entire book—including the additional book categories that may be contained within the book—is sent to the printer. If you select an individual topic and click Print in the Help Topics window, only the highlighted topic is sent to the printer.)

FIGURE 1.9

DISPLAYING A HELP
TOPIC AND A SHORTCUT
MENU

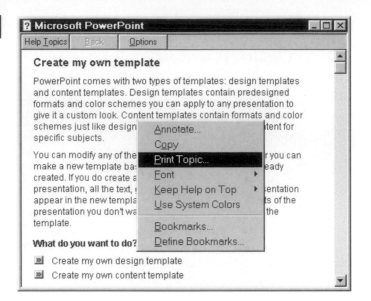

7. In the Print dialog box that appears:

- CLICK: OK command button to print the topic, or

- CLICK: Cancel command button if you do not have a printer

Whatever your selection, you are returned to the secondary window. (*Note*: If you selected to print the topic and your computer does not have a printer connected, you may be returned to Word with an error message. In this case, choose Help, Contents and Index to redisplay the Help Topics window and then proceed to Step 10.)

8. To close the secondary window and return to the Help Topics window:
CLICK: Help Topics button (immediately under the Title bar)

9. To close the current book:
DOUBLE-CLICK: "📖 Creating the Look of Your Presentation" book
Notice that the list of books and topics is collapsed under the book icon.

10. Let's search for some information using the keyword index:
CLICK: *Index* tab

11. To find the topics related to Word's AutoFormat feature:
TYPE: **autoclipart**
The list automatically scrolls to the "AutoClipArt command" topic.

12. To display a sub-topic located beneath one of the "AutoClipArt command" headings:
DOUBLE-CLICK: AutoClipArt command
A secondary window appears with a few related topics.

13. DOUBLE-CLICK: "Ways to insert pictures in a presentation" topic

14. Since this window contains so much information, let's maximize it to fill the presentation window.
CLICK: Maximize button (🗖) in the secondary window

15. You may have noticed that a term in this secondary window appears with a dotted underline. To view the definition of this term, do the following:
CLICK: "bitmaps" with the hand mouse pointer (🖑)
A pop-up window appears with a definition.

16. After reading the help text, remove the definition pop-up window:
CLICK: the pop-up window once

17. To return to the Help Topics window:
CLICK: Help Topics button

18. Let's close the Microsoft Word Help system. To do so:
CLICK: Cancel command button (in the lower right-hand corner)
The Help Topics window is removed. (*Remember*: The next time you open the Help Topics window, the *Index* tab will be selected.)

QUICK REFERENCE Searching for Help Using the Help Topics Window	**1.** **To display the Help Topics window:** **CHOOSE: Help, Contents and Index** **2.** **CLICK:** *Contents* **tab to navigate a hierarchical Help system** **CLICK:** *Index* **tab to search for a word or phrase in a keyword index** **CLICK:** *Find* **tab to conduct a full-text search of the Help system**

OPENING A PRESENTATION

In this section, you open a presentation that we've created for you. You will find this presentation file at your *Advantage Files location*. In this learning guide, we refer to the following two locations when saving and opening files:

- *Advantage Files location*—This location may be on a diskette, in a folder on your local hard drive, or in a folder on a network server. The Advantage Files are the presentation files that have been created for you and that you will retrieve in the remaining exercises in this guide.

- *Data Files location*—This location may also be on a diskette, in a hard drive folder, or in a network folder. You will save the presentations that you create or modify to the Data Files location. This location may be the same disk or folder where you keep the Advantage Files; however **if you are using diskettes we recommend you keep the Advantage Files and Data Files on separate diskettes.** Otherwise, you will run out of storage space.

> **IMPORTANT:** *Before continuing, ensure that you know the location of your Advantage Files and where to store your Data Files. If necessary, ask your instructor or lab assistant for additional information.*

When opening a presentation, your first step is to display the Open dialog box by clicking the Open button () on the Standard toolbar or choosing File, Open from the Menu bar. Once the Open dialog box appears, you select where the file is stored by clicking in the *Look in* drop-down list box and then selecting a file location. To load the presentation, you double-click the file's name appearing in the file list.

Next you open a file from your Advantage Files location.

Perform the following steps ...

1. Make sure you have identified the location for retrieving the Advantage Files. If you require a diskette, place it into the diskette drive now.

2. To practice using the Open dialog box:
   CLICK: Open button () on the Standard toolbar

3. To view the Advantage Files:
   CLICK: down arrow beside the *Look in* drop-down list box
   SELECT: *your Advantage Files location*
   The Open dialog box should now appear similar to Figure 1.10.

   Note: In this guide, we save presentations to the "My Documents" folder on the hard disk and retrieve presentations from the "PPT97" sub-folder, which is located at the following path:
   \My Documents\Advantage\PPT97

FIGURE 1.10

THE OPEN DIALOG BOX

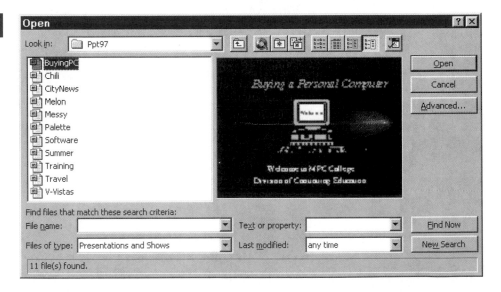

4. To change the display in the Open dialog box, try the following:
   CLICK: Detail button (▦) to see each presentation's file size and date
   CLICK: Properties button (▦) to see summary information
   CLICK: Preview button (▦) to see a presentation preview
   CLICK: List button (▦) to see a multiple-column format

5. Let's open a presentation:
DOUBLE-CLICK: BuyingPC
The presentation is loaded into PowerPoint's presentation window. Your screen now should now appear similar to Figure 1.11.

FIGURE 1.11

THE "BUYINGPC"
PRESENTATION FILE

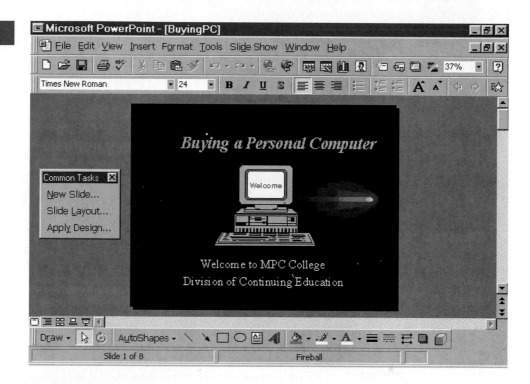

QUICK REFERENCE
Opening a Document

1. **CLICK: Open button (****), or**
   CHOOSE: File, Open from the Menu bar
2. **CLICK: down arrow beside the *Look in* drop-down list box**
3. **SELECT: a file location**
4. **DOUBLE-CLICK: the desired presentation**

IN ADDITION OPENING A PRESENTATION FROM THE WINDOWS DESKTOP

From the Windows desktop, you can open a presentation that you've worked with recently. Click the Start button on the taskbar and then choose the Documents command.

Then, choose the document's name. The application you used to create the document loads automatically.

IN ADDITION OPEN AN INTERNET PRESENTATION

If your computer has an Internet connection, you can open presentations located on the World Wide Web or at an FTP site directly from the Open dialog box. In the Open dialog box, you click the Search the Web button () to launch your Web browser program. Using the procedure specific to your browser, you type in a *URL* (*Uniform*

Resource Locator), an address that points to a specific location on the Internet. All Web URLs begin with "http://". All FTP URLs begin with "ftp://".

For more information about opening Internet documents, choose Help, Contents and Index from the Menu bar. Then click the Index tab and type **Internet, opening files on.**

Viewing a Presentation

PowerPoint provides five different views of a presentation: Slide view, Outline view, Slide Sorter view, Notes Page view, and Slide Show view. You switch among these views using the View command on the Menu bar or by clicking the View buttons located in the bottom left-hand corner of the presentation window. The active view of your presentation before being saved or closed becomes the default view when it is subsequently opened. Each view is described and illustrated in the following section.

SLIDE VIEW

The most common view to use for building or finalizing a presentation is Slide view. Similar to Page Layout view in Word for Windows, this view shows you how the slide will appear when printed or displayed. All text, graphics, and other media elements in your presentation appear in Slide view. You can perform the following tasks in Slide view:

- Insert, edit, and delete text
- Draw lines, squares, ovals, polygons, or other objects
- Add clip art, scanned photographs, or other media objects
- Add graphs, charts, or data from other applications
- Change the appearance of text and objects
- Change a template's style or color scheme

To select the Slide view, click the Slide view button (▣) or choose View, Slides from the menu. There are three toolbars, by default, that are available in Slide view—Standard, Formatting, and Drawing. As mentioned previously, you can add or remove toolbars using the shortcut menu, accessed by clicking the right mouse button over any toolbar button.

OUTLINE VIEW

Outline view is especially useful for organizing your thoughts and developing the textual content for a presentation. You can also use Outline view much as you would a word processor to enter, arrange, and edit textual information. You perform the following tasks in Outline view:

- Insert, arrange, and edit textual content (titles and main body text)
- Promote and/or demote textual content in your outline
- Display a slide's text with or without formatting
- Show a slide's titles only, or show titles and full text

To select the Outline view, click the Outline view button () or choose View, Outline from the menu. In Outline view, the Outlining toolbar replaces the Drawing toolbar that is usually displayed in Slide view.

SLIDE SORTER VIEW

The Slide Sorter view provides a light table for viewing multiple slides. When selected, this view arranges thumbnail representations of your slides, complete with text and graphics, in rows and columns. Slide Sorter view gives you an immediate feeling for the continuity or flow of a presentation. You perform the following tasks in Slide Sorter view:

- Manipulate the order of slides
- Add transitional effects from one slide to another
- Incorporate special "build effects" for a particular slide, such as highlighting each point in turn
- Hide slides from being displayed in a computer-based slide show
- Set timing options for rehearsing your presentation

To select the Slide Sorter view, click the Slide Sorter view button (▦) or choose View, Slide Sorter from the menu. In Slide Sorter view, the Slide Sorter toolbar replaces the Formatting toolbar.

NOTES PAGE VIEW

The Notes Page view allows you to insert, edit, and delete reminder notes for yourself on each slide. You can also use a slide's notes page for creating extended notes as an audience handout. Whatever the purpose, this view lets you enter text and graphics in a Notes placeholder located below the image of the slide.

To select the Notes Page view, click the Notes Page view button (▣) or choose View, Notes Page from the menu.

SLIDE SHOW VIEW

In Slide Show view, the presentation is displayed as an electronic computer-based slide show, complete with slide transitions and timing effects. The ability to switch quickly among the different views allows you to modify a slide's content in Slide or Outline view and receive immediate feedback in Slide Show view. This view is also called an *on-screen presentation*.

To select the Slide Show view, click the Slide Show view button (⬛) or choose View, Slide Show from the menu. The most common methods for controlling a presentation in Slide Show view appear in Table 1.3.

TABLE 1.3 Controlling a Slide Show Presentation	*Task Description*	*Keyboard and Mouse Methods*
	Go to the next slide	CLICK: left mouse button, or PRESS: `PgDn`, `→`, `↓`, `ENTER`, Spacebar, or TYPE: **N**
	Go to the previous slide	PRESS: `PgUp`, `←`, `↑`, or TYPE: **P**
	Go to a specific slide	TYPE: **desired slide number,** and then PRESS: `ENTER`
	Go to the first slide	PRESS: `HOME`
	Blank the screen to black	PRESS: **b** to blank screen to black PRESS: **b** again to unblank screen
	Blank the screen to white	PRESS: **w** to blank screen to white PRESS: **w** again to unblank screen
	Exit the slide show	PRESS: `ESC`

If you click the right mouse button in Slide Show view, a shortcut menu appears that provides options that are similar to those described in Table 1.3.

FOR PRACTICE

Let's practice switching among the views using the "BuyingPC" presentation.

Perform the following steps . . .

1. First, let's remove the Common Tasks toolbar from view.
   RIGHT-CLICK: Common Tasks toolbar
   CHOOSE: Common Tasks

2. To display the "BuyingPC" presentation in Outline view:
   CLICK: Outline View button (⬛)
   Your screen should now appear similar to Figure 1.12.

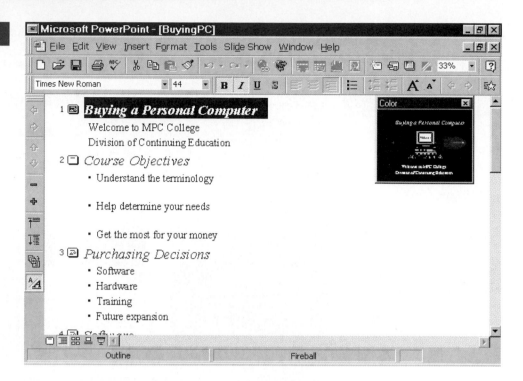

FIGURE 1.12

OUTLINE VIEW

3. To display the "BuyingPC" presentation in Slide Sorter view:
CLICK: Slide Sorter view button (⊞)
Your screen should now appear similar to Figure 1.13.

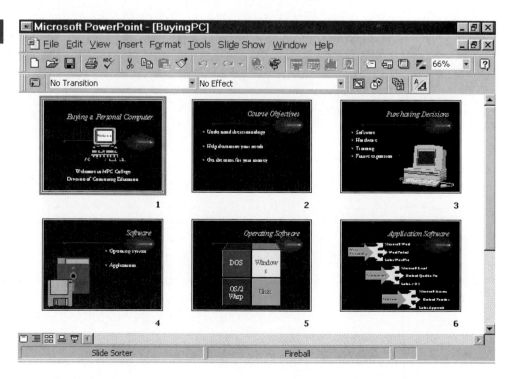

FIGURE 1.13

SLIDE SORTER VIEW

4. To display the presentation in Notes Page view:
CLICK: Notes Page view button (⬛)
Your screen should now appear similar to Figure 1.14.

FIGURE 1.14

NOTES PAGE VIEW

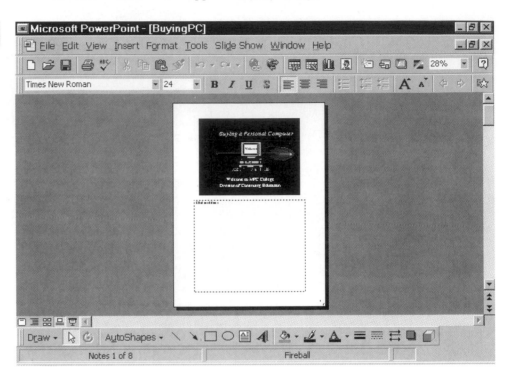

5. To display the presentation in Slide Show view:
CLICK: Slide Show view button (⬛)
Your screen should now appear similar to Figure 1.15.

6. To proceed to the next slide in the presentation:
CLICK: left mouse button once

7. To display the next slide using the keyboard:
PRESS: Spacebar

8. To return to the previous slide using the keyboard:
PRESS: ⬆

9. To return to the first slide in the presentation:
PRESS: HOME

10. To exit the Slide Show view:
PRESS: ESC

11. Return to Slide view.
CLICK: Slide view button (▱)

12. Before continuing to the next section, redisplay the Common Tasks toolbar.
RIGHT-CLICK: the Standard toolbar
CHOOSE: Common Tasks

QUICK REFERENCE
Changing the View
for a Presentation

- CLICK: ▱ to change to Slide view
- CLICK: ≣ to change to Outline view
- CLICK: ▦ to change to Slide Sorter view
- CLICK: ▣ to change to Notes Page view
- CLICK: ▤ to change to Slide Show view

CLOSING A PRESENTATION

When you are finished working with a presentation, you should close the file to free up valuable computer memory. To close a presentation window, choose File, Close from the Menu bar or click the Close icon (☒) in the presentation window. If you've made changes to your presentation since you last saved it, you should save the presentation before you close the window.

Let's now close the "BuyingPC" presentation.

Perform the following steps . . .

1. Since you haven't made any changes to the presentation:
   CHOOSE: File, Close

2. If there are any other presentations appearing in the slide area, repeat Step 1 to clear them from memory.

LEAVING POWERPOINT

When you are finished using PowerPoint, save your work and exit the program by clicking the Close button (☒) that is located in the Title bar of the application window or choose File, Exit from the Menu bar. If you have made modifications to the presentation and have not saved the changes, PowerPoint asks whether the presentation should be saved or abandoned before exiting the program.

Now you will end the current working session.

Perform the following steps . . .

1. CLICK: Close button (☒) of the application window
   Assuming that no changes were made to the document, the application is closed and you are returned to the Windows desktop.

2. To exit Windows:
   CHOOSE: Start, Shut Down
   SELECT: *Shutdown the computer?* option button
   CLICK: Yes command button

QUICK REFERENCE	• CLICK: Close button ([X]) of the application window, or
Exiting PowerPoint	• CHOOSE: File, Exit

SUMMARY

PowerPoint provides you with powerful tools for creating presentations. A presentation can include one or more of the following: slides, handouts, speaker's notes, and outlines. In this session, after loading Microsoft Windows and PowerPoint, you were led on a guided tour of the program's major components. We also used the Help facility to retrieve information on menu commands and toolbar buttons.

Near the end of the session, you opened an existing presentation and practiced using the View buttons—located at the bottom of the presentation window—to display the presentation in five different views. These views included Slide view, Outline view, Slide Sorter view, Notes Pages view, and Slide Show view. The session concluded when you closed the presentation and exited PowerPoint.

COMMAND SUMMARY

Many of the commands and procedures appearing in this session are provided in Table 1.4 below.

TABLE 1.4	*Task Description*	*Menu Command*	*Alternative Method*
Command Summary	Access the PowerPoint Help facility	Help, Contents and Index	
	Access the Office Assistant	Help, Microsoft PowerPoint Help	[?]
	Access context-sensitive descriptions	Help, What's This?	
	Open an existing presentation file	File, Open	[open]
	Close a presentation file	File, Close	[X]
	Leave PowerPoint	File, Exit	[X]

KEY TERMS

application window
In Microsoft Windows, each running application program appears in its own application window. These windows can be sized and moved anywhere on the Windows desktop.

handout

In PowerPoint, a handout which is given to audience members with two to six small images of the actual slides on each printed page.

hyperlinks

Highlighted words or phrases that appear when viewing information on the World Wide Web. You click the hyperlink to view a different document.

Internet

A collection of computer networks that spans the globe.

Intranet

A local or wide area network that uses Internet technologies to share information.

presentation

In PowerPoint, a presentation is a collection of slides, handouts, speaker's notes, and outlines, all in one disk file.

presentation window

In PowerPoint, each open presentation appears in its own presentation window. These windows can be sized and moved anywhere within the Slide work area. (A presentation window represents your workspace.)

run-time version

A scaled-down version of the original software that includes a "player" for the application's data files, but does not usually allow the user access to any editing features.

slide

In PowerPoint, a slide is an individual page of a presentation.

template

A template defines how slide text will look, where the text and other objects will be positioned, and what colors will be used.

wizards

Wizards lead you through creating presentations and performing other tasks in PowerPoint.

World Wide Web (WWW)

A visual interface for the Internet.

EXERCISES

SHORT ANSWER

1. What does the term *integration* mean as it relates to Microsoft Office?
2. What is the purpose of *PowerPoint Central*?
3. What are some of the output options for a presentation?
4. What is a dialog box?
5. How do you display the Help Topics window?

6. How do you open a presentation?

7. Describe the five different views that are available in PowerPoint.

8. In Slide Show view, how do you proceed to the next slide?

9. In Slide Show view, how do you return to the previous slide?

10. In Slide Show view, how do you return to the first slide?

HANDS-ON

(*Note*: Ensure that you know the location of your Advantage Files and where to store your Data Files. If necessary, ask your instructor or lab assistant for additional information.)

1. In this exercise, you practice accessing PowerPoint's Help facility.

   a. Load Microsoft PowerPoint.

   b. Remove the PowerPoint dialog box when it appears.

   c. Using the Help, What's This? command, retrieve help for the Open button (🖼).

   d. After reading the contents of the Help window, close the window.

   e. In the Help Topics window, display the *Index* tab.

   f. Search for information on "opening presentations."

   g. Display the *Contents* tab.

   h. Browse through the Help topics by pressing the ⬇ key repeatedly.

   i. Close the Help Topics window.

   j. Using the Office Assistant, display help for "using color in presentations."

   k. Close the Office Assistant and tip window before proceeding.

2. In this exercise, you open the presentation named "Training" from the Advantage Files location.

   a. Open the "Training" presentation from the Advantage Files location.

   b. If the presentation isn't maximized in the presentation window, click its Maximize button (🔲).

   c. Display the presentation in Slide Sorter view.

   d. Display the presentation in Outline view.

   e. Display the presentation in Notes Page view.

   f. Display the presentation in Slide Show view.

   g. Let the slide show run on its own. (*Note*: You don't have to click the mouse button to display the next slide because transitions have been built into this presentation.) If you need to exit from the presentation before you've viewed all the slides, press (ESC).

   h. Close the "Training" presentation.

3. In this exercise, you open the presentation named "Summer" from the Advantage Files location.

   a. Open the "Summer" presentation from the Advantage Files location.

   b. Display the presentation in Slide Show view.

   c. Practice navigating through the presentation using the keyboard and mouse methods.

   d. Move directly to slide number 3.

   e. Display the first slide in the presentation.

   f. Blank the presentation to a black screen.

   g. Unhide the presentation.

   h. Blank the presentation to a white screen.

   i. Unhide the presentation.

   j. Return to Slide view.

   k. Close the "Summer" presentation.

4. On your own, learn more about giving presentations by reviewing one of PowerPoint's presentations. To begin, choose File, New from the Menu bar and then click the *Presentations* tab. Then double-click the "Presentation Guidelines-Dale Carnegie Training" presentation template. (*Note*: You must click the template name to see its full name.) Display the presentation in Slide view and review its contents. When you're finished, close the presentation.

CASE PROBLEMS   **VACATION VISTAS, INC.**

(*Note*: In the following case problems, assume the role of the primary characters and perform the same steps that they identify. You may want to re-read the session opening.)

1. Frank stares intently at the opened courier package in front of him. The letter from Juanita, which he has already read and is still digesting, has been placed neatly upon his desk. He now reads the sticky note in his left hand. *Frank, the presentation file at the Advantage Files location is called "V-Vistas." I recommend that you proof the textual and graphical content in the presentation. Bye for now, Juanita.*

   Not one to waste too much time sulking, Frank plans his approach. He loads the presentation into PowerPoint and gets an overall feel for the product using the Slide Sorter view. To proof the textual content, Frank switches to Outline view and finds two blatant mistakes. He writes down the two mistakes on a notepad that will later become his review letter to Juanita. To proof the graphical content, Frank uses the Slide view and again finds two obvious mistakes in the graphics that Juanita chose for the presentation. As before, Frank copies down the two mistakes on his note pad.

Having closed the presentation, Frank must now write a letter to Juanita Gomez specifying the two textual errors and the two graphical errors in the "V-Vistas" presentation. He addresses it to her Seattle home at 1500 Country Club Lane, Seattle WA 98004. He'll include this review letter when he sends the disk back to Juanita for final production.

2. With only one week to go before his presentation at the local seniors' hall, Frank is getting a little nervous. As the expected attendance exceeds 100 seniors, he has rented a speaker's podium, a 35 mm slide projector, and a large screen. Unfortunately, Frank isn't used to speaking in front of large groups and truly wanted some time to practice before the actual presentation.

Having learned the fundamentals of PowerPoint, Frank remembers that he can use the Slide Show view to display and work through the presentation. He loads the "V-Vistas" presentation into PowerPoint and switches to Slide Show view. After progressing through four slides, Frank notices one of his staff passing by his office door with a client. Not wanting the client to see the unfinished presentation, Frank blanks the screen to black temporarily. When he unhides the presentation, he backs up a couple of slides to refocus his attention. With his train of thought interrupted, he decides to return to the first slide and start again. This time, he makes it all the way through the presentation.

3. Having finished practicing, Frank decides to close the "V-Vistas" presentation file and exit Microsoft PowerPoint. He doesn't save any changes that he may have made in the presentation. Before leaving his office for the evening, Frank writes down a summary of the five views and the primary methods for navigating a presentation in Slide Show view. He places the summary beside his monitor for easy reference.

Microsoft PowerPoint 97 for Windows

Creating a Presentation

SESSION

HTTP://WWW

2

IRWIN
COMPUTER & INFORMATION TECHNOLOGY

SESSION OUTLINE

INTRODUCTION

Compare electronic slide presentations with hand-written or typed overheads and you can immediately appreciate the value and impact of using presentation software like PowerPoint. But not only are electronic presentations more effective, they can take less time and effort to create. In this session, you learn how to improve the quality of your presentations while dramatically reducing your production timelines and budgets.

CASE STUDY	BERKFORD COLLEGE, PENNSYLVANIA

Sharon Rheingold is a second-year law student at Berkford College in Pennsylvania. As a credit component toward her studies this semester, Sharon accepted a job teaching Public Speaking 101 to first-year business students. Given her goal of one day becoming a successful trial lawyer, Sharon saw this job as an opportunity to hone her communication skills on a captive audience. Little did she realize that Dr. Kirsten Antoski, the dean of Business Administration, had personally developed the course and expects each of her instructors to hand out professional presentation materials for each lecture. With an already suffocating course load, Sharon wonders how she can possibly meet Dr. Antoski's expectations and complete her own studies.

While discussing the situation with her roommate Walt, the two students thought of an especially good idea. Walt, a fourth-year student in the Faculty of Education, recommended Sharon use Microsoft PowerPoint to develop her lesson plans and course notes. Walt assured Sharon that with only a few tips she would be producing professional-looking handouts in hours instead of days. Furthermore, she could use PowerPoint to help teach her students some of the principles of public speaking.

In this session, you and Sharon learn how to use the AutoContent Wizard to create new presentations quickly and easily. You also learn how to use a design template, modify a slide's information, save a presentation to the disk, and print a presentation.

CREATING A PRESENTATION: AN OVERVIEW

Even if you haven't had much experience using PowerPoint, creating a new presentation is easy. You'll be amazed at how quickly you can organize content, select an output medium, and design the look of your slides. Though you may initially believe otherwise, the most time-consuming task involves gathering and writing the content for a presentation. It is important that you have a clear understanding of a presentation's objectives and can verbalize the information that you want to communicate to an audience. Anybody can choose background colors, apply fonts and styles, and insert graphics on a slide. Your goal is to create a presentation that communicates a message effectively—and that takes work.

USING POWERPOINT TO CREATE A PRESENTATION

The following steps provide an overview of the process for creating a presentation using Microsoft PowerPoint:

1. *Select a starting point for your presentation.*
   In the startup dialog box (Figure 2.1) that appears when you first load PowerPoint, the *AutoContent Wizard* and *Template* options can help you get started creating a new presentation. The **AutoContent Wizard** provides the quickest and easiest method for creating a presentation by presenting you with a series of questions about the subject, type of output for your presentation, and presentation style. If you just want to pick a subject or a visual style for a presentation, choose the *Template* option. For the greatest flexibility, you can create a presentation from scratch using the *Blank Presentation* option.

FIGURE 2.1

THE POWERPOINT
STARTUP DIALOG BOX

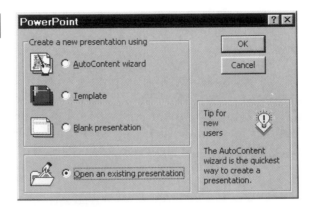

2. *Create the individual slides for your presentation.*
   After you select the starting point for your slide presentation, you must create the individual slides by adding, editing, and deleting text and graphics for each slide page. You typically use the Outline view to enter a slide's textual content and the Slide view to finalize the colors, typefaces, and placement of graphics, charts, and other objects. If you started creating a presentation using the AutoContent Wizard or by picking a presentation template, many of the slides for your presentation are automatically added to the presentation file. You simply edit the titles and body text on the slides to ensure their appropriateness for the topic. When you create a blank presentation, PowerPoint provides you with the first slide; you must create any additional slides from scratch.

3. Review and refine your presentation in its entirety.
   Once you've created the individual slides, you use Slide Sorter view and Slide Show view to review the presentation. While working in Slide Sorter view, you can manipulate the linear order of the slides, set the timing for rehearsing a presentation, hide slides, and add special effects to your presentation. For example, PowerPoint provides you with the ability to create **build slides** for computer-based presentations. On a build slide, you can make bullets appear on the screen one at a time and even dim previous points on the slide to draw further attention to the current bullet. Also, in Slide Sorter view you can incorporate transitions into your presentation. A **transition** is the visual effect you see when you go from one slide to the next in a computer-based presentation. For the acid test of previewing your work as it would be presented live, you use the Slide Show view.

4. *Save and print your presentation.*

   Not to tempt fate, you should save your presentation regularly as you work. Also, print your presentation for others to review. It's always wise to let your friends and co-workers find the errors before your audience has the opportunity! A second benefit of printing a presentation is that you will have a paper copy in case your computer files are deleted accidentally or become corrupted by a virus.

REACHING FOR THE DICTIONARY

Before you create a presentation in the next section, let's introduce and define some important terms:

Object
Your slides will typically contain one or more different elements, or objects. An object can be text, a graphic, a picture, a shape, and so on.

Design Template
Defined briefly in the last session, a design template is a presentation whose background, color scheme, typefaces, and other formatting options can be applied to another presentation. By using templates, you need not reinvent the wheel each time you create a presentation. PowerPoint provides 17 professionally designed templates from which you can choose. You can also design your own custom templates, using your corporate or school colors, for example, and then apply them to the new presentations you create.

Presentation Template
A presentation template is a presentation whose subject outline can be applied to another presentation. PowerPoint provides over 32 presentation templates that you can choose from to match your subject.

Default presentation format
PowerPoint provides a default presentation format—complete with a background design, color scheme, typefaces, and so on—that is applied when you choose the *Blank Presentation* option from the startup dialog box.

Masters
Each presentation you create contains a master for each output option in the presentation; that is, one for slides, one for the outline, one for the notes pages, and one for the audience handouts. Whatever you place on a master page will print on each page in the presentation, whether a slide page or a notes page. For example, to have a graphic of your company or school logo appear on each slide in the presentation, you place it on the Slide Master.

These terms will be explained further in later sections, but now we move on to learning by doing rather than by reading!

USING THE AUTOCONTENT WIZARD

If you're finding it difficult to organize and write down your thoughts, select the *AutoContent Wizard* option button from the startup dialog box or after choosing File, New from the Menu bar. After progressing through six dialog boxes, you'll have a skeletal framework for building a complete presentation.

In this section, you practice using the AutoContent Wizard.

Perform the following steps . . .

1. Make sure that you've loaded Microsoft PowerPoint and that you've identified the location for storing your Data Files. If you require a diskette, place it into the diskette drive now.

2. If the Office Assistant (shown at the right) appears:
CLICK: Close button (☒) in its top right-hand corner

3. If the PowerPoint startup dialog box appears on your screen, do the following (otherwise, proceed to Step 4):
SELECT: *AutoContent Wizard* option button
PRESS: **ENTER** or CLICK: OK
Now proceed to Step 5.

4. If the startup dialog box does not appear on your screen and you are certain that Microsoft PowerPoint is loaded, do the following to initiate the AutoContent Wizard:
CHOOSE: File, New from the Menu bar
CLICK: *Presentations* tab
DOUBLE-CLICK: AutoContent Wizard icon

   (*CAUTION*: A message may appear warning you that the wizard you are about to open may contain a *macro virus*. This is just a warning message and doesn't mean that a virus exists. Because a virus can harm your data and program files, ensure that the files you open come from reputable sources. If you don't want this message to display the next time you activate a wizard, clear the *Always ask before opening presentations with macros* check box. For now, click the Enable Macros button.)

5. The AutoContent Wizard is launched and presents the initial AutoContent Wizard screen. Your screen should now appear similar to Figure 2.2. On the left side of the dialog box, you see the steps the AutoContent Wizard will go through in order to format the final presentation. To skip to a particular step, you click its associated box. Otherwise, if you click Next, the next step will occur.

FIGURE 2.2

AUTOCONTENT WIZARD:
INITIAL SCREEN

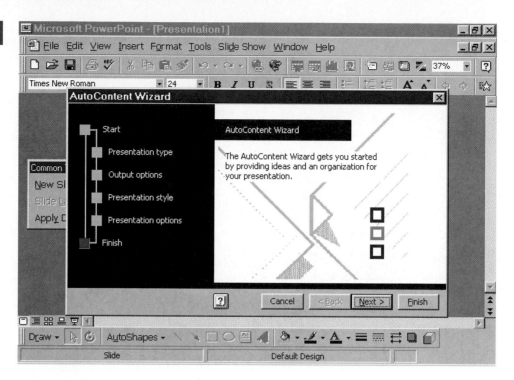

6. To proceed to the next screen (Presentation Type):
CLICK: Next button
Your screen should now appear similar to Figure 2.3.

FIGURE 2.3

AUTOCONTENT WIZARD:
CHOOSING THE TYPE
OF PRESENTATION

7. In this step you select the type of presentation you want to give. PowerPoint presents seven categories of presentations. When you click a category, a list of related presentations appears in the list box to the right. Make the following selections.
CLICK: Corporate button
SELECT: Company Meeting in the list box

8. To define the output options for the presentation.
CLICK: Next button

9. SELECT: *Presentations, informal meetings, handouts* option

10. To define the presentation style:
CLICK: Next button

11. Make the following selections.
SELECT: *On-screen presentation* option button
SELECT: No in the *Will you print handouts?* area

12. To proceed to the next screen:
CLICK: Next button

13. In this step, you enter the information you want to appear on the opening slide such as the title of your presentation, your name, and any personal information such as your company name. Use the mouse to move the cursor and to select text. (*Note:* You can also press TAB to move the cursor to the next text box and SHIFT + TAB to move to the previous text box.) After positioning the cursor, type the text you want to appear in the text box.

Before continuing to the next step:
SELECT: the text in the *Presentation title* text box, if necessary
TYPE: **Effective Communication Skills** in the *Presentation title* text box
SELECT: the text in the *Your name* text box, if necessary
TYPE: ***your name*** into the *Your name* text box
SELECT: the text in the *Additional information* text box, if necessary
TYPE: ***your school or company name*** into the *Additional information* text box
If you prefer fictitious information, refer to Figure 2.4.

FIGURE 2.4

AUTOCONTENT WIZARD:
CREATING THE TITLE
SLIDE

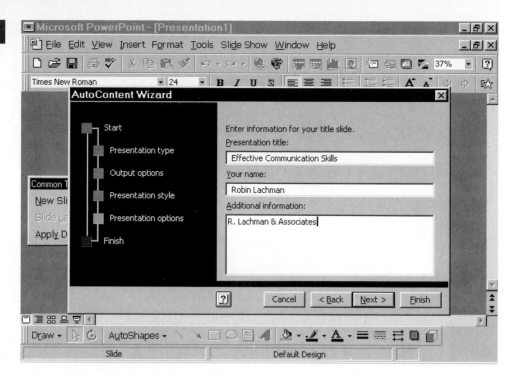

14. To continue:
CLICK: Next button

15. If you wish, review your selections by clicking the Back button. Otherwise:
CLICK: Finish button
The presentation is compiled and your presentation appears in Outline view
(Figure 2.5). In this view, you see the text of your presentation and a slide
miniature of the current slide. You can easily edit the text of your presenta-
tion in Outline view. We describe this view in more detail in Session 3.

FIGURE 2.5

YOUR PRESENTATION IN
OUTLINE VIEW

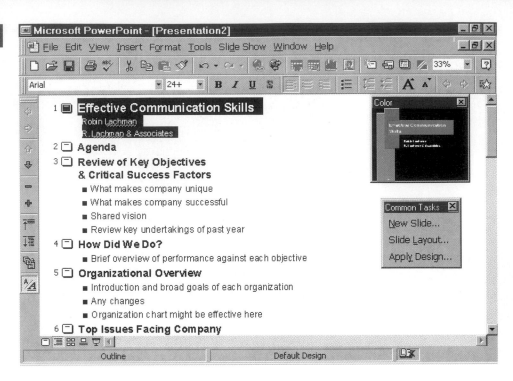

16. To display the presentation in Slide Show view:
CLICK: Slide Show view button ([🖳])

17. To advance through the presentation:
CLICK: left mouse button continuously until you reach the end of the presentation and are returned to Outline view

18. Let's close the presentation and move on to the next section, where you will learn more about design templates. Do the following:
CHOOSE: File, Close
CLICK: No when asked whether you want to save the presentation

QUICK REFERENCE
Using the AutoContent
Wizard

1. SELECT: *AutoContent Wizard* option button in the startup dialog box
PRESS: ENTER or CLICK: OK
(*Note:* You can also choose File, New and select the AutoContent Wizard from the *Presentations* tab.)

2. Proceed through the AutoContent Wizard dialog boxes, replying to questions and clicking the Next button.

3. When you reach the last slide:
CLICK: Finish button

USING A DESIGN TEMPLATE

One of the problems with the advent of presentation software like PowerPoint is that the presentation author has been hurled into the role of graphic designer. Many people who are highly skilled writers and content researchers find it difficult to take on the additional role of art director. Fortunately, PowerPoint provides 17 design templates to help those of us who consider themselves artistically challenged.

In this section, you create a presentation entitled "The Future of Computer and Communications Technology" for a class project. The objective of the presentation is to inform your classmates of three primary technology trends: connectivity, online information access, and interactivity.

Now you practice picking a design template.

Perform the following steps . . .

1. If the PowerPoint startup dialog box appears on your screen, click its Cancel button.

2. Your first step is to display the New Presentation dialog box:
    CHOOSE: File, New

3. To select a design template:
    CLICK: *Presentation Designs* tab

4. To view the design templates in a list:
    CLICK: List button (▦)
    Your screen should now appear similar to Figure 2.6. (*Note:* You may not have the same design templates stored on your hard drive as those shown in Figure 2.6.)

FIGURE 2.6

NEW PRESENTATION
DIALOG BOX:
PRESENTATION
DESIGNS TAB

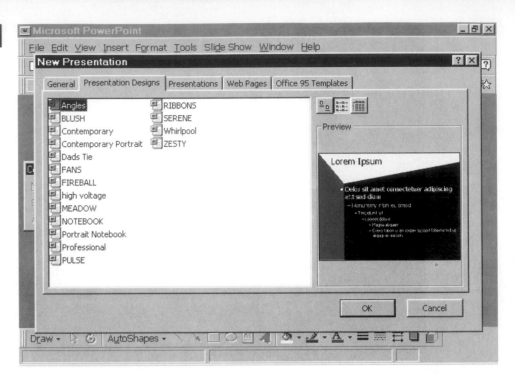

5. To preview a design template, you single-click the template name. An example of the design will appear in the Preview window. On your own, preview at least five design templates.

6. In this step, you will pick the "angles" design template:
DOUBLE-CLICK: angles

7. PowerPoint needs to know what layout you want to use for the first slide (Figure 2.7). Notice that the name of the AutoLayout appears below the command buttons in the dialog box. Do the following:
SELECT: Title Slide layout (located in the upper-left corner)
PRESS: (ENTER) or CLICK: OK
Your screen should now appear similar to Figure 2.8.

8. Before you modify this new presentation, let's continue to the next section to learn how to save it to disk.

FIGURE 2.7

NEW SLIDE DIALOG BOX

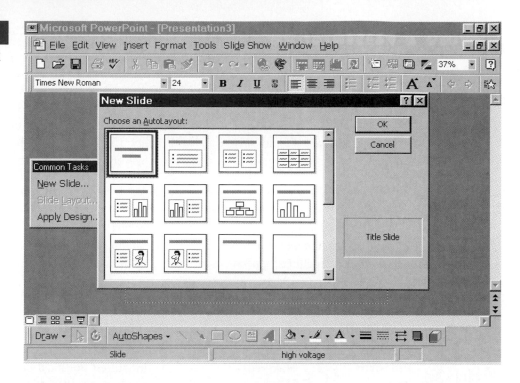

FIGURE 2.8

A TITLE SLIDE

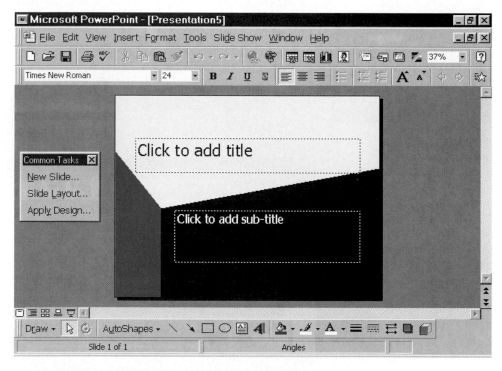

Saving a Presentation

When you work on a presentation, it exists only in the computer's RAM (random access memory) which is highly volatile. To permanently store your work, you must save the presentation to the hard disk, a network drive, or to a floppy diskette. Saving your work to a disk is similar to placing it into a filing cabinet. To be safe, you should save your work every 15 minutes, or whenever you're interrupted, to protect against an unexpected power outage or other catastrophe.

To save a presentation to a disk, you click the Save button (🖫) on the Standard toolbar or you select the File, Save command from the menu. If you haven't saved the presentation before, a dialog box appears where you specify the save location and name for the file. When naming a file, you can use up to 255 characters, including spaces. You can't use the following characters in filenames:

$$\backslash \quad / \quad : \quad * \quad ? \quad " \quad < \quad > \quad |$$

Now you will save the current presentation.

Perform the following steps . . .

1. Make sure that you have identified the location for storing your data files. If you require a diskette, place it into the diskette drive now.

2. CLICK: Save button (🖫)
   Your screen should now appear similar to Figure 2.9.

FIGURE 2.9

THE FILE SAVE DIALOG BOX

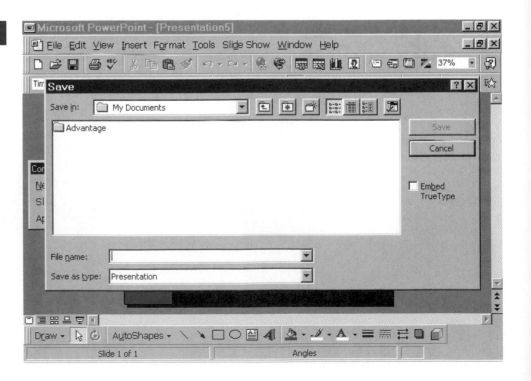

3. To specify a filename for the presentation:
TYPE: **Current Trends**

4. To specify where the presentation will be saved, do the following:
CLICK: down arrow beside the *Save in* drop-down list box
SELECT: *your Data Files location*
PRESS: (**ENTER**) or CLICK: Save command button

There are times when you'll want to save an existing presentation under a different filename. For example, you may want to keep different versions of the same presentation on your disk. Or, you may want to use one presentation as a template for future presentations that are similar in style and format. Rather than creating an entirely new presentation, you can retrieve an old presentation file, edit the information, and then save it under a different name using the File, Save As command. If you want to update or replace an existing file, you use File, Save or click the Save button (🖫).

QUICK REFERENCE
Saving a File

- CLICK: Save button (🖫) on the Standard toolbar, or
- CHOOSE: File, Save, or
- CHOOSE: File, Save As to save a file under a different name

---

IN ADDITION SAVE A PRESENTATION TO AN FTP SITE

If you want your presentation to be accessible to others on the Internet, consider saving it to an FTP site. *FTP (File Transfer Protocol)* makes it possible for users to transfer presentations over the Internet. You can save to an FTP site if your computer has an Internet connection that supports saving files. To save to an FTP site:

1. CHOOSE: File, Save As

2. SELECT: Internet Connections (FTP) from the Save in drop-down list

3. DOUBLE-CLICK: the site you want to save to (*Note:* You can add FTP sites to the list by selecting Add/Modify FTP Locations in the file area.)

4. TYPE: a name for your presentation

5. PRESS: (**ENTER**) or CLICK: Save command button

IN ADDITION SAVE AS HTML

To publish your PowerPoint presentation on the Web, you must save it in an HTML format first. *HTML (Hypertext Markup Language)* is a system for marking up documents so that they can be viewed on the World Wide Web. To save a presentation as an HTML document:

CHOOSE: File, Save as HTML

(*Note:* It is a good idea to choose File, Save to save your presentation in a PowerPoint format before saving it in an HTML file format. Then you can make changes to your presentation later.)

Adding Slides

It's not just what you say, it's *how* you say it. As the old Chinese proverb has it, "Tell me and I'll forget; show me and I may remember; involve me and I'll understand." Involving an audience in your presentation means making it visually interesting, aesthetically pleasing, and relevant. Although we won't teach you writing skills in this guide, we will provide some pointers for communicating effectively using PowerPoint. To begin, your presentations should include some, if not all, of the following slides in addition to the body of the presentation:

- Use a *Title slide* to act as the backdrop for people entering the room or auditorium at the beginning of your presentation

- Use an *Introduction slide* to set the stage for your presentation and convince the audience that it will be a worthwhile use of their time

- Use an *Agenda* or *Objectives slide* to prepare the audience for what's coming up ahead in the presentation

- Use a *Closing slide* to reiterate and summarize your main ideas, to draw conclusions, and to revisit the presentation's objectives

Now that the "look" is defined for your presentation, let's create some slides. It's very easy; the instructions are right on the slide! As you proceed, you'll see that PowerPoint automatically creates **placeholders** on new slides for your text and graphics. There are three primary types of placeholders: Title or Sub-title, Text, and Object. While the first two are self-explanatory, an Object placeholder contains such items as clip art, graphs, and organizational charts. To edit a Title or Text placeholder, you click the mouse once in the placeholder and then type the desired text. To edit an Object placeholder, you double-click the mouse in the placeholder and create or pick the desired object.

When you add a new slide to your presentation, PowerPoint displays a dialog box with several **AutoLayout** options that are formats for positioning text and graphics using placeholders. These AutoLayouts include slide formats for title slides, bulleted lists, graphs, two-column text slides, tables, and slides with clip art or graphics. AutoLayouts provide a great starting point for creating new slides in your presentation.

ADDING TEXT TO A SLIDE

The slides you create in this section contain text only. You will edit the layout of the slides so that you can add graphics later in the session. In this section, you create the first two slides in the "Current Trends" presentation.

Perform the following steps . . .

1. Position the mouse pointer over the Title placeholder (appearing as "Click to add title" on the slide) and click the left mouse button once.

2. TYPE: **CURRENT TRENDS IN COMPUTER TECHNOLOGY**
Notice that the text automatically wraps to the next line in the placeholder box. Do not press (**ENTER**) when you are finished typing.

3. CLICK: the Sub-title placeholder (appearing as "Click to add sub-title" on the slide)
PRESS: (**ENTER**) to begin typing on the second line
TYPE: **by**
PRESS: (**ENTER**)
TYPE: *your name*
Notice that "Slide 1 of 1" appears in the Status bar. Your screen should now appear similar to Figure 2.10.

FIGURE 2.10

SLIDE 1 IN THE "CURRENT TRENDS" PRESENTATION

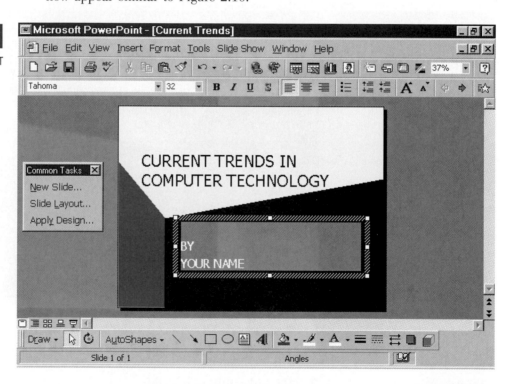

4. Let's add a second slide to the presentation. The easiest way to add a new slide is to use the Common Tasks toolbar, shown to the right. If the Common Tasks toolbar already appears in your application window, proceed with Step 5.

Otherwise, point to an existing toolbar and then:
RIGHT-CLICK: to display the shortcut menu
CHOOSE: Common Tasks
The Common Tasks toolbar should appear on your screen.

5. To add a new slide:
CHOOSE: New Slide from the Common Tasks toolbar
PowerPoint adds the new slide immediately following the currently active slide.

6. The New Slide dialog box appears, showing you the AutoLayout options for creating a new slide.
SELECT: Bulleted List
(*Note*: The Bulleted List may already be selected.)
PRESS: (ENTER) or CLICK: OK
Your screen should now appear similar to Figure 2.11. A new slide with a Title placeholder and a Text placeholder (appearing as "Click to add text" on the slide) is displayed in the presentation window. These placeholders correspond to the AutoLayout option that you just selected.

FIGURE 2.11

SLIDE 2 IN THE "CURRENT TRENDS" PRESENTATION

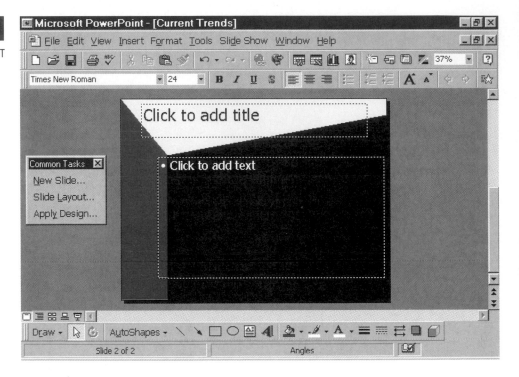

7. To add a title to the slide:
CLICK: Title placeholder
TYPE: **The Leading Trends**

8. To add content to the slide:
CLICK: Text placeholder
TYPE: **Connectivity**
PRESS: (ENTER)
TYPE: **Interactivity**
Your screen should now appear similar to Figure 2.12.

FIGURE 2.12

SLIDE 2: TEXT HAS BEEN
ENTERED

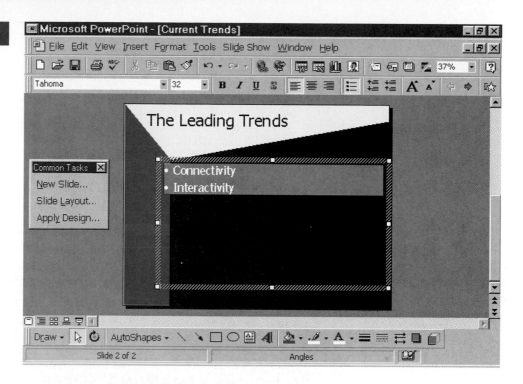

QUICK REFERENCE
Creating a Slide with Text

1. **To create a new slide:**
    CHOOSE: New Slide from the Common Tasks toolbar
    SELECT: an AutoLayout option in the New Slide dialog box
    PRESS: ENTER or CLICK: OK
2. **CLICK: a Title or Text placeholder in the slide**
    TYPE: *the desired text content*

MANIPULATING BULLETS

In the last section, PowerPoint automatically inserted bullets in the Text place-holder when you pressed the ENTER key. In this section, you learn how to manipulate bullets on a slide to group information. People remember information better when it is "chunked" together, so try to organize your slide text hierarchically. To illustrate the effect of chunking information, consider phone numbers and how much easier they are to remember in the form 708-555-1212 as opposed to 7085551212. You can apply this same principle to your slides using hierarchical bullets.

To promote a point and move it up one level in importance, you indent it to the left using the Promote (Indent Less) button ([←]). To demote a point and move it down one level in importance, you indent it to the right using the Demote (Indent More) button ([→]). The Promote ([←]) and Demote ([→]) buttons appear on the Formatting toolbar.

Now you practice promoting and demoting bullets.

Perform the following steps . . .

1. Position the insertion point in the text area of "Interactivity."

2. To demote this point:
CLICK: Demote button (➡️) on the Formatting toolbar
Notice that the characteristics of the text change. Not only is the text indented but the font size has changed.

3. To return this point to its original position:
CLICK: Promote (Indent Less) button (⬅️)

4. Practice promoting and demoting the two bullets on this slide.

5. Before proceeding to the next section, return both bullets to their original positions.

QUICK REFERENCE
Changing the Indent
Level of Bulleted Items

- CLICK: Promote button (⬅️) to indent text to the left
- CLICK: Demote button (➡️) to indent text to the right
- Using the keyboard, press TAB to demote text and SHIFT + TAB to promote text.

ADDING THE REMAINING SLIDES

In this section, you will add the remaining slides to the "Current Trends" presentation.

Perform the following steps . . .

1. To add a third slide to the presentation:
CHOOSE: New Slide from the Common Tasks toolbar

2. Pick a layout for the new slide from the New Slide dialog box:
SELECT: Bulleted List
PRESS: ENTER or CLICK: OK

3. CLICK: Title placeholder
TYPE: **CONNECTIVITY**

4. CLICK: Text placeholder
TYPE: **Current Trends:**
PRESS: ENTER

5. To type text at a new indent level:
CLICK: Demote (Indent More) button (➡️)
TYPE: **Voice mail and e-mail**
PRESS: ENTER
TYPE: **Telecommuting**
PRESS: ENTER
TYPE: **Internet-based information**
Your screen should now appear similar to Figure 2.13.

FIGURE 2.13

SLIDE 3 IN THE
"CURRENT TRENDS"
PRESENTATION

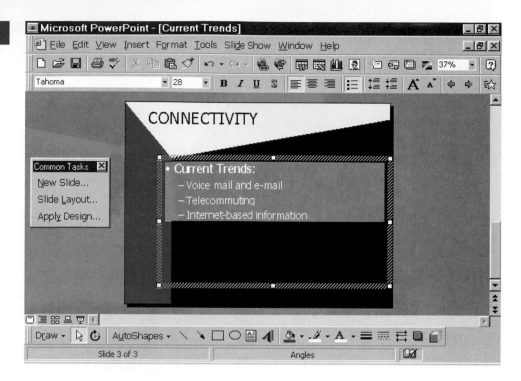

6. To add a fourth slide to the presentation:
CHOOSE: New Slide from the Common Tasks toolbar

7. Pick a layout for the new slide from the New Slide dialog box:
SELECT: Bulleted List
PRESS: **ENTER** or CLICK: OK

8. CLICK: Title placeholder
TYPE: **INTERACTIVITY**

9. CLICK: Text placeholder
TYPE: **Current Trends:**
PRESS: **ENTER**

10. To type text at a new indent level:
CLICK: Demote (Indent More) button (➡)
TYPE: **Multimedia Computers**
PRESS: **ENTER**
TYPE: **Personal Digital Assistants**
PRESS: **ENTER**
TYPE: **"Internet appliances"**
Your screen should now appear similar to Figure 2.14.

FIGURE 2.14

SLIDE 4 IN THE "CURRENT TRENDS" PRESENTATION

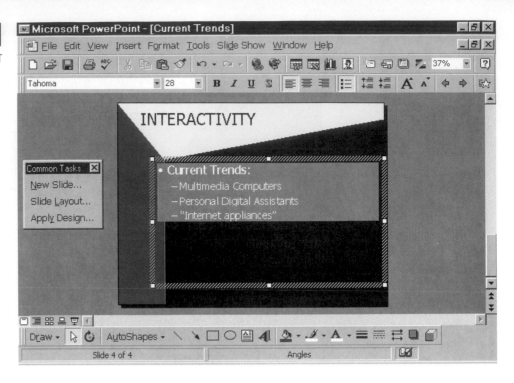

11. To save the presentation:
    CLICK: Save button (🖫)

To modify the content of slides you've already created, use the elevator scroll box on the vertical scroll bar (or the double arrows, ⬇ and ⬆, appearing at the bottom of the scroll bar) to move through the presentation. You will practice using the elevator scroll box and arrows later in this session.

Reviewing Your Presentation

To view a presentation as it will appear in its completed form, you use the Slide Show view. To access the Slide Show view, choose View, Slide Show from the Menu bar or click the Slide Show view button (🖳). The presentation fills the entire screen with the current slide, that is, the slide that appears in the presentation window. To view a slide show from the beginning, you must remember to first drag the elevator scroll box to the top of the vertical scroll bar. After you view the last slide in your presentation, the presentation window reappears.

In this section, you view the "Current Trends" presentation.

Perform the following steps . . .

1. DRAG: the elevator scroll box to the top of the vertical scroll bar
    Notice that, as you drag the scroll box, the current slide number and first few words of the title appear in the presentation window.

2. CLICK: Slide Show view button (🖳)
    The first slide fills the entire screen.

3. To display the next slide:
CLICK: left mouse button

4. To display the previous slide:
PRESS: ⬆

5. Continue by clicking the left mouse button to view the entire presentation. When finished, you are returned to the presentation window where you left off.

Now, let's add some pizzazz to this presentation by inserting some additional graphics to the slides!

EDITING A PRESENTATION

When installing PowerPoint, you have the option of installing the **Clip Gallery,** a collection of images that you can select to include in your presentations. You can also use the Clip Gallery to organize any pictures, sounds, and video clips that you collect. If you choose AutoClipArt from the Tools menu, PowerPoint will analyze the words in your presentation and provide suggestions about which clip art images to use. In this section, you will edit slide 2 of the "Current Trends" presentation to include a picture from the Clip Gallery. You will then resize and move the inserted picture so that it is proportional to the text on the slide. When you are finished, slide 2 will look like Figure 2.15.

FIGURE 2.15

SLIDE 2 WITH THE
INSERTED CLIP ART

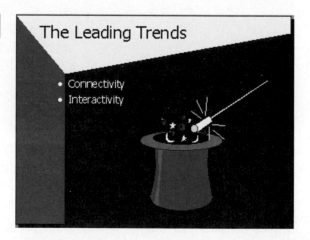

CHANGING THE LAYOUT OF A SLIDE

The easiest way to add clip art or a graphic to an existing slide is to select a new AutoLayout for the slide. First, you make the desired slide active by displaying it in the presentation window. Second, you choose the Slide Layout command from the Common Tasks toolbar. When the Slide Layout dialog box appears, you select a new AutoLayout that includes a clip art or graphic object placeholder and then press ENTER or click the Apply command button.

In this section, you practice changing the layout of a slide.

Perform the following steps . . .

1. Ensure that the "Current Trends" presentation appears in the presentation window.

2. To move to slide 2 in the "Current Trends" presentation:
DRAG: the elevator scroll box downward to display slide 2
Remember that you can also click the Next Slide (▼) and Previous Slide (▲) buttons on the vertical scroll bar to move through a presentation one slide at a time.

3. To modify the slide's layout to accommodate a clip art image:
CHOOSE: Slide Layout from the Common Tasks toolbar
SELECT: Text & Clip Art as the AutoLayout option
PRESS: [ENTER] or CLICK: Apply
Your screen should appear similar to Figure 2.16.

FIGURE 2.16

APPLYING THE TEXT & CLIP ART AUTOLAYOUT

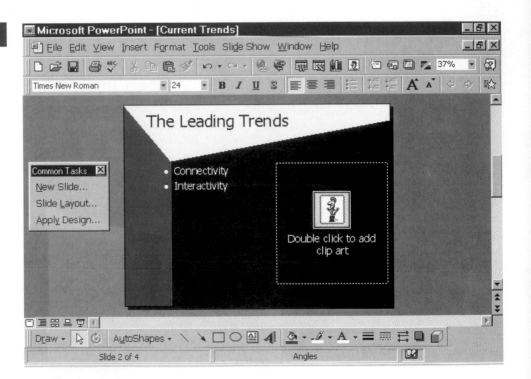

QUICK REFERENCE
Changing the Layout of an Existing Slide

1. Display the slide you want to modify in the presentation window.
2. CHOOSE: Slide Layout from the Common Tasks toolbar
3. SELECT: a new layout in the Slide Layout dialog box
4. PRESS: [ENTER] or CLICK: Apply

INSERTING CLIP ART

In this section, you add a picture from the Clip Gallery to slide 2 of the "Current Trends" presentation. You will then resize and reposition the art to fit nicely on the slide.

Perform the following steps . . .

1. To add clip art to the slide:
    DOUBLE-CLICK: clip art placeholder
    (*Remember*: You double-click Object placeholders to modify their content.)
    The Clip Gallery window appears (Figure 2.17). If this is the first time that you've used the Clip Gallery, it must first gather and categorize the images before you see the dialog box appearing in Figure 2.17. This is a one-time process only. (*Note*: If you do not have the Clip Gallery installed on your computer, contact your instructor or refer to the Microsoft PowerPoint *User's Guide* for further assistance.)

FIGURE 2.17

THE CLIP GALLERY

2. Let's select a picture from the Entertainment category:
    SELECT: Entertainment from the list of categories
    SELECT: the picture shown in Figure 2.18 from the list of pictures in the dialog box
    (*Note*: You may have to drag the scroll box downward to see this picture.)

3. To add the picture to your slide:
PRESS: **ENTER** or CLICK: Insert
Your screen should now appear similar to Figure 2.18. The clip art image is inserted and is currently selected. You know the object is selected because it is surrounded by selection handles, which look like small boxes. Notice also that the Picture toolbar now appears on your screen. You can use this toolbar to perform tasks such as changing the shape and color of the selected image. The Picture toolbar only appears when you select a picture object.

FIGURE 2.18

ADDING A CLIP ART
IMAGE TO THE
"CURRENT TRENDS"
PRESENTATION

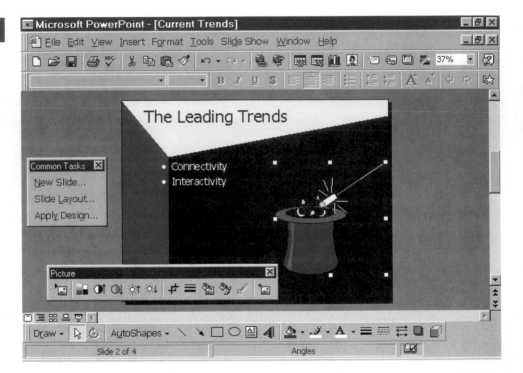

4. To resize a picture, you select it by clicking once on the object and then dragging its selection handles inward or outward. You use the corner handles to size an object larger or smaller, while maintaining its relative proportions. To move the picture, you position the mouse pointer in the center of the object and drag the object to another location on the slide.

5. Practice sizing and moving the picture to make it appear as similar to Figure 2.15 as possible.

6. To save your editing changes:
CLICK: Save button (🖫)

QUICK REFERENCE
Inserting Clip Art

1. **In the presentation window, display the slide you want to modify.**
2. **CHOOSE: Slide Layout from the Common Tasks toolbar**
3. **SELECT: an AutoLayout option with a clip art placeholder**
4. **PRESS: ENTER or CLICK: Apply**
5. **DOUBLE-CLICK: clip art placeholder**
6. **SELECT: a clip art image from the Clip Gallery**
7. **PRESS: ENTER or CLICK: OK**

QUICK REFERENCE
Resizing and Moving
Clip Art

1. **SELECT: clip art object by clicking the mouse pointer once over the object (handles appear around the picture when properly selected)**
2. **DRAG: a handle on the object to size the picture, or**
   DRAG: the center of the object to move the picture

USING THE STYLE CHECKER

Before you print a presentation, review it using PowerPoint's **Style Checker.** The Style Checker studies your presentation for spelling errors, visual clarity, and the proper use of punctuation. You respond to the Style Checker's suggestions by clicking the Change or Ignore buttons. Figure 2.19 shows the Style Checker dialog box. The Options command button enables you to further customize what the Style Checker checks for in order to match your company's particular style. For example, let's say that you always want your presentations to use a 32-point size for the text on a Title slide, no more than two fonts or five bullets on any given slide, and all bulleted text to end without a period. You can establish each of these style rules, as well as many others, using the Options button.

FIGURE 2.19

THE STYLE CHECKER
DIALOG BOX

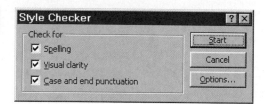

In this section, you use the Style Checker to review the "Current Trends" presentation.

Perform the following steps . . .

1. Ensure that slide 1 of the "Current Trends" presentation appears in the presentation window.

2. To activate the Style Checker:
   CHOOSE: Tools, Style Checker

3. Before starting the Style Checker, let's look at some of the options that are available to you. Do the following:
   CLICK: Options command button
   CLICK: *Case and End Punctuation* tab and review the options
   CLICK: *Visual Clarity* tab and review the options
   Figure 2.20 shows the contents of the two tabs.

FIGURE 2.20

THE STYLE CHECKER
DIALOG BOX: OPTIONS

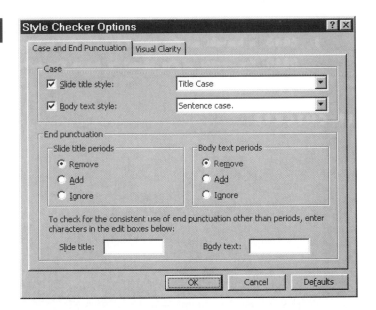

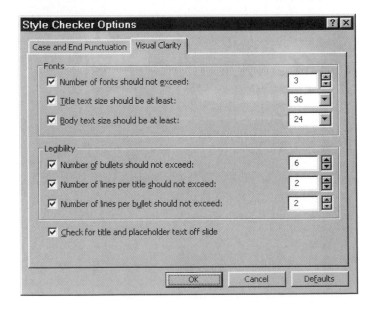

4. To return to the Style Checker dialog box and start the process:
CLICK: Cancel button
CLICK: Start button

5. Proceed by clicking the Ignore button if the Style Checker finds any spelling suggestions and style inconsistency remarks.

QUICK REFERENCE
Using the Style Checker

1. **CHOOSE: Tools, Style Checker**

2. **Use the Options button to customize style settings, as desired.**

3. **Respond to the Style Checker's suggestions by clicking the Ignore or Change buttons.**

PRINTING A PRESENTATION

Now that you've created a presentation, this section explains how to send it to the printer. This section provides only a brief glimpse at the tools available.

The quickest method for sending a presentation to the printer is to click the Print button ( ) on the Standard toolbar. When you click this button, no dialog boxes appear asking you to confirm your choice, so ensure that the printer is online and has sufficient paper. You can also use the File, Print command to print a document, which causes the Print dialog box to display (Figure 2.21). After making selections, you press ENTER or click OK to proceed.

FIGURE 2.21

PRINT DIALOG BOX

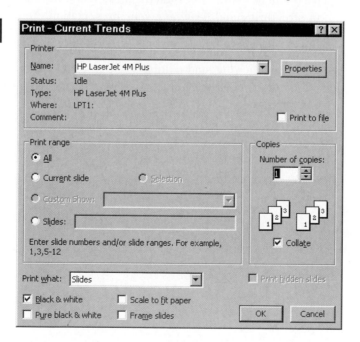

Now you will print a presentation.

Perform the following steps . . .

1. To print the "Current Trends" presentation:
   CHOOSE: File, Print
   The Print dialog box appears. (*Note*: You can also press the CTRL +p shortcut key to display the Print dialog box.)

2. At this point, PowerPoint assumes that you want to print the slides in the current presentation window. To see the other options:
   CLICK: down arrow beside the *Print what* drop-down list box

3. To print all of the slides in the presentation:
   SELECT: Slides (the default selection)
   PRESS: ENTER or CLICK: OK

4. Close the presentation window and exit PowerPoint. (*Note*: Do not save the changes to the presentation file.)

QUICK REFERENCE
Printing a Presentation

1. **CHOOSE: File, Print from the menu**
2. **SELECT: what you want to print in the *Print what* drop-down list box**
3. **PRESS: ENTER or CLICK: OK**

SUMMARY

This session introduced you to the fundamentals of creating a presentation. You used one of PowerPoint's intelligent helpers, the AutoContent Wizard, to assist you in structuring and designing your presentation. You then created another presentation by picking a design template and added slides to the presentation by choosing New Slide from the Common Tasks toolbar. This session also introduced you to saving, viewing, and editing a slide presentation. You manipulated the text and bullets on a slide in addition to changing its layout and adding clip art. Finally, you performed a style check on a presentation and learned how to print a slide presentation.

COMMAND SUMMARY

Many of the commands and procedures appearing in this session are provided in Table 2.1.

TABLE 2.1	Task Description	Menu Command	Alternative Method
Command Summary	Create a new presentation	File, New	
	Save a presentation to the disk	File, Save	
	Save a presentation to a new location or to a different name	File, Save As	
	Select all the text in a placeholder	Edit, Select All	ENTER +a
	Change the layout of a slide	Format, Slide Layout	Choose Slide Layout from the Common Tasks toolbar
	Use the Style Checker	Tools, Style Checker	
	Print a presentation	File, Print	

KEY TERMS

AutoContent Wizard

A PowerPoint tool that leads you through creating the structure for your presentation.

AutoLayout

In PowerPoint, a slide format with text and graphic placeholders. You select an AutoLayout for a head start when adding a new slide to a presentation.

build slides

In PowerPoint, a slide in which the bullet points are displayed one at a time.

Clip Gallery

A collection of professionally designed images that you can include in your presentations.

default presentation format

The design template that is in effect when you start by choosing the Blank Presentation option.

design template

A design template is a presentation whose background, color scheme, typefaces, and other formatting options can be applied to another presentation.

masters

The slide, outline, and notes page templates that determine how the standard slides, outlines, and notes pages are formatted and will appear in a presentation. Any visuals that you include on a master will print on every page in the presentation.

object

In PowerPoint, an object is an individual element on a slide. It can be text, a graphic, a picture, a shape, a video clip, and so on.

placeholders

In PowerPoint, slide locations where you enter titles, sub-titles, main text, clip art, graphs, and organizational charts.

presentation template

A presentation template is a presentation whose subject outline can be applied to another presentation.

Style Checker

Using this PowerPoint tool, you can review your presentation for spelling errors, clarity of visual style, and use of punctuation.

transition

In PowerPoint, an effect used in computer-based presentations to dissolve or wipe one slide from the screen before the next appears.

EXERCISES

SHORT ANSWER

1. What are the basic steps for creating a presentation?

2. What elements of your presentation does the AutoContent Wizard help you define?

3. Provide some specific examples of how you might customize the Style Checker to your needs.

4. How do you insert a new slide in a presentation?

5. How would you go about changing the font size of the text in a text box all at once?

6. What is the procedure for printing a presentation using the menu?

7. How do you change a slide's AutoLayout?

8. How do you manipulate bullet levels on a slide?

9. What is the procedure for resizing a clip art image?

10. When would you want to use the File, Save As command rather than the File, Save command?

HANDS-ON

(*Note*: Ensure that you know the location of your Advantage Files and where to store your Data Files. If necessary, ask your instructor or lab assistant for additional information.)

1. Perform the following steps to create a three-slide presentation named "Using Color." The objective of your presentation is to describe some guidelines for using color in on-screen presentations.

   a. Load Microsoft PowerPoint.

   b. Create a new on-screen presentation using a design template.
   CHOOSE: File, New
   CLICK: *Presentation Designs* tab

   c. Select the Contemporary Portrait template design.

   d. Select the Title Slide AutoLayout from the New Slide dialog box.

   e. The title of your presentation is:
   Using Color Wisely

   f. The sub-title of your presentation is:
   By
   your name

   g. Add a second slide to the presentation, based on the Bulleted List layout, with the following information.

   Title:
   Keep it Simple
   Bullet 1: **Choose colors properly to make powerful statements**
   Bullet 2: **Too many colors or unnecessary colors can dilute the effect**

   h. Add a third slide to the presentation, based on the Bulleted List layout, with the following information.

   Title:
   Target Your Output Needs
   Bullet 1: **For 35 mm slides, pick dark backgrounds**
   Bullet 2: **For overhead transparencies, pick light backgrounds**

   i. Display the presentation using Slide Show view.

   j. Return to the Slide view.

   k. Save the presentation as "Using Color" to your Data Files location.

2. In this exercise, you edit slide 3 of the "Using Color" presentation that you created in the last exercise to look like Figure 2.22. Make sure to do the following:

    a. Change the layout of slide 3 to the Text & Clip Art layout.

    b. Add the picture of a target to the slide. (*Hint*: The target is located in the Sports & Leisure category of the Microsoft Clip Gallery).

    c. In Slide view, resize the clip art image so it appears similar to Figure 2.22.

FIGURE 2.22

SLIDE 3 OF THE "USING COLOR" PRESENTATION

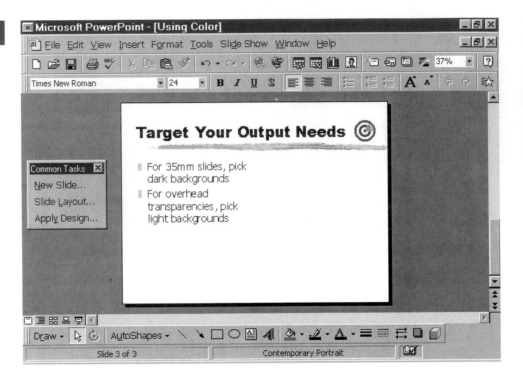

d. Display the presentation using Slide Show view.

e. Return to Slide view.

f. Print the entire presentation.

g. Save the "Using Color" presentation back to your Data Files location.

h. Close the presentation.

3. Create a presentation for the five slides shown in Figure 2.23. Save the presentation to your Data Files location as "Advertising."

FIGURE 2.23

SLIDE 1

SLIDE 2

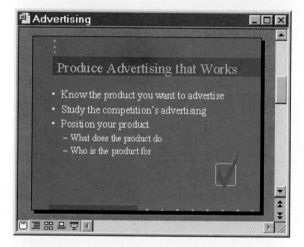

SLIDE 3

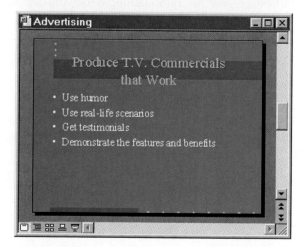

SLIDE 4

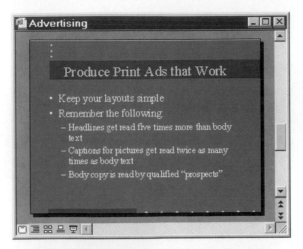

SLIDE 5

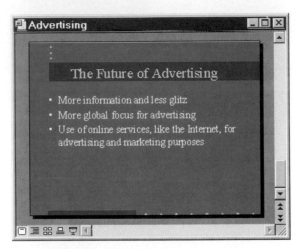

4. In this exercise, you create a presentation that contains the information shown below. On your own, decide which design template and layouts to use to best present the information. When you are finished, save the presentation as "Storage" to your Data Files location.

Harold Harvey's Self-Storage
You can't beat our prices!
1- 800-HAR-VEYS

Full range of sizes and features:
Choose from small, medium, and large storage units. We will even customize the interior of your unit to meet your unique requirements.

Climate controlled:
Worried about weather extremes? Don't bother! All storage units are climate controlled.

Protected environment

- *All of our locations are fenced and lighted, and use 24-hour video surveillance.*

- *A resident manager is present at each location. If you have questions or concerns, just pick up the phone.*

Rental trucks available free:
If you're just moving in to Harold Harvey's Self-Storage, we'll provide you with a rental truck—FREE.

CALL US!
Your name
Sales representative

5. On your own, create the contents of your own personal web site using PowerPoint's "Personal Home Page (Online)" presentation template. Begin by choosing File, New from the Menu bar. Then select the "Personal Home Page (Online)" template from the *Presentations* tab. Proceed by filling in the information requested on each slide. When you're finished, save the presentation as "On Your Own-1" to your Data Files location.

6. On your own, create a presentation on a topic you're interested in (e.g., hiking, traveling, or reading.) Include between five and eight slides and at least one clip art picture. Save the presentation as "On Your Own-2" to your Data Files location.

CASE STUDY　　　　**BERKFORD COLLEGE, PENNSYLVANIA**

(*Note*: In the following case problems, assume the role of the primary characters and perform the same steps that they identify. You may want to re-read the session opening.)

1. Sharon Rheingold is on a mission. After several evenings of study at the campus computer lab, she is now comfortable using Microsoft PowerPoint to create simple presentations. Fortunately, her roommate Walt had time to show her the AutoContent Wizard and how to use design templates. With the start of classes only a few days away, Sharon is ready to put her first lecture together using PowerPoint.

   Her schedule being quite tight this past week, Sharon was only able to jot down rough notes for her outline:

   Course Title: Public Speaking 101
   Instructor: Sharon Rheingold

   Lecture 1: An Introduction to Public Speaking

   Five Cs for Excellence in Public Speaking
   - *Confident*
   - *Competent*
   - *Credible*
   - *Convincing*
   - *Comfortable*

   Reasons for Experiencing Stage Fright
   - *Fear of failure*
   - *Lack of confidence*
   - *Lack of preparation*
   - *Lack of knowledge about topic*
   - *Lack of knowledge about audience*

   Methods for Overcoming Stage Fright
   - *Be positive*
   - *Practice often*
   - *Prepare thoroughly*
   - *Research your topic*
   - *Research your audience*

   Now Sharon has to enter these notes into PowerPoint in order to create color overhead transparencies. Since her content is fairly well organized, she decides to use one of PowerPoint's presentation design templates. In addition to an opening slide introducing the course and herself, Sharon calculates that the presentation only requires one outline slide for the lecture and three content slides for each of her main discussion topics. At the last minute, she decides to add a closing slide that thanks the students for attending the presentation and wishes them luck for the coming semester. Sharon saves the presentation as "Public Speaking 101" to her Data Files location and prints the six slides for review.

2. An experienced public speaker herself, Sharon knows the importance of practicing her presentation before she has to deliver it in front of an audience. She uses PowerPoint's Slide Show view to go through the "Public Speaking 101" presentation and then reviews it again in the Slide Sorter view. "Almost there!" she thinks to herself.

Although she feels comfortable with the presentation, Sharon notices that the lecture may be too short. After not much deliberation, Sharon decides to add one more slide to the presentation. Using Slide view, she displays the last content slide titled "Methods for Overcoming Stage Fright" and then clicks the New Slide button on the Status bar. She adds a slide with the following content and then revises her outline slide at the beginning of the presentation.

Types of Presentations
- *Technical (for technical specifications)*
- *Instructional (for communicating a process)*
- *Illustrative (with anecdotal stories)*
- *Demonstrative (with live demonstration)*
- *Discussion (for informal group meetings)*

Again, Sharon practices the presentation using the Slide view and then saves it and prints it out on the laser printer for Walt to review.

3. Walt returned late from his part-time job after three hours of overtime and was not in the best of moods to review Sharon's presentation. "Why is there so much text here?" exclaimed Walt, rubbing his eyes and trying to focus on the pages Sharon had handed to him. "Can't you put a couple of pictures in this thing to liven it up a little?" Walt walked slowly across the living room and then looked up, "You should have used the Clip Gallery to add some pictures. I know there's one picture in there of a person standing at a podium. You can use that one for this "Five Cs" slide. And for the last slide, don't just say "Thank You". Insert a fun graphic to let them know that they're in the best public speaking section on campus!"

Sharon thought about Walt's comments and took each to heart. She would add some pictures to her presentation using the Clip Gallery, perform one more practice run, and then print out the final presentation for her students.

Save Sharon's presentation as "Public Speaking 101" to the Data Files location.

4. During morning coffee, Dr. Tomas Ritchie, the law faculty's premier authority on Canadian business law, listened intently to Dr. Antoski's enthusiastic recount of Sharon Rheingold's first class. Since Tomas had known Sharon for two years, he was not surprised with Kirsten's glowing report of his star pupil. However, he was quite surprised that Sharon was a skilled computer user and could prepare such high-quality materials. He would definitely keep this fact in mind for future projects!

Two weeks later, Dr. Ritchie approached Sharon to ask her help in preparing a lecture he was conducting for the American Business Association. The presentation, "Understanding Canadian Business Law," was to be delivered the next day at the association's annual general meeting. The original speaker had canceled at the last moment, due to a family emergency, and Dr. Ritchie was contacted as her replacement. Fortunately, the original speaker had already arranged the equipment and room for a computer-based presentation. The only item Dr. Ritchie was missing was the presentation!

Dr. Ritchie showed Sharon a quick outline and asked her to prepare a "computerized slide show." He didn't have any details for content and would most likely have to "wing it" at the podium. However, he wanted her to produce an introductory slide with his name and the name of the presentation, along with a separate slide for each topic he was going to discuss. The topics included:

The Law of Torts in Canada
- *The tort concept*
- *Elements of a tort*
- *Burden of proof*
- *Professional liability*

Types of Contracts
- *Contract of sale*
- *Contract of employment*

Formation of a Contract
- *Offer and acceptance*
- *Consideration*
- *Intention to enter into a contract*
- *Capacity to contract*
- *Requirement of writing*

Effects of and Remedies for a Breach of Contract
- *What is a breach?*
- *Express repudiation*
- *Damages*
- *Quantum meruit*

Forms of Business Organization
- *Sole proprietorship*
- *Partnership*
- *Corporation*

Knowing that Dr. Ritchie would be a great ally in coming years, Sharon wanted to do everything she could to impress her advisor. She created and printed the presentation in less than an hour, handing it to him just as he was about to leave for home. Sharon would have to remember to thank Walt for introducing her to Microsoft PowerPoint!

Save this presentation as "Canadian Law" to your Data Files location.

Microsoft PowerPoint 97 for Windows

Designing a Presentation

SESSION

3

IRWIN
COMPUTER & INFORMATION TECHNOLOGY

SESSION OUTLINE

INTRODUCTION

In this session, you learn to use some of Power-Point's more productive features, including methods that help you take control of your presentations. You soon discover that when it comes to designing a presentation in PowerPoint, you have endless options at your fingertips. Rather than show you every design and productivity feature, this session concentrates on the most commonly used tools.

H2 UNDERSCAPING LTD.

In 1989 Chip Yee started H2 UnderScaping Ltd. (H2U), a landscaping operation that sells and installs underground sprinkler systems. Since that time, H2U has grown from annual sales of $30,000 to its current year's projection of over $700,000. Now that his employees perform most of the administrative duties and manual labor, Chip has more time on his hands to get involved in the community.

Chip is an active member in both the local Chamber of Commerce and the Downtown Business Association. The Chamber's president, Mrs. Vi Krieg, recently approached Chip to ask him to act as spokesperson at this year's Business Show. Specifically, Vi asked Chip to prepare an electronic presentation for the evening banquet and emphasized that there would be representatives from neighboring Chambers in the audience. Obviously the president wants to impress her peers with their group's professionalism and technical proficiency!

Fortunately, Chip is familiar with Microsoft Office and has become quite good at using Microsoft Word. Although he has created only one or two simple presentations in PowerPoint, Chip has discovered that the programs in Microsoft Office work alike in many ways, making them easy to learn and use. But this presentation would be challenging. In addition to creating a content-rich presentation, Chip will have to pull off an Oscar-winning performance to satisfy Mrs. Krieg.

In this session, you and Chip learn about some features for making your Power-Point presentations stand out from the crowd. Rather than relying on PowerPoint's stock designs, you learn to enhance the design templates, edit the Slide Master, and utilize color. In addition, you customize bullets, manipulate text in Outline view, and learn to position text anywhere on a slide. Good luck to you both!

APPLYING TEMPLATES

Using templates is like having the fastest graphics design specialist as part of your staff. Fortunately for you, PowerPoint's graphics design specialist knows over 100 different designs and lets you apply any one of them to your presentations. Just think of the time savings—after typing the content for a presentation in Outline view, you simply pick and choose from multiple design templates to finalize the look and feel of your presentation for a particular audience. You could even deliver the same presentation to two different groups using two different design templates.

If you can remember back to Session 2, you chose a design template named "angles." This template uses red, black, and white to divide the slide into three visual areas. All of PowerPoint's templates, including the "angles" template, are stored in separate files on the hard disk. Actually, a template is defined as any presentation whose design and format specifications you want to apply to another presentation.

Not only can you pick from the templates provided by PowerPoint, any presentation you create can serve as a template for another presentation. The advantage of using PowerPoint's templates is that they were all created by professional artists and presentation designers. To apply a template, choose Format, Apply Design from the menu or choose Apply Design from the Common Tasks toolbar. In the Apply Design dialog box that appears, you select the desired template and then click the Apply command button.

In this section, you apply a different template to a presentation.

Perform the following steps . . .

1. Make sure that you have identified the location for retrieving your Advantage Files and for saving your Data Files. If you require a diskette, place it in the diskette drive now.

2. Open the "Chili" presentation from the Advantage Files location. The first slide of the "Chili" presentation should appear in the presentation window (Figure 3.1).

FIGURE 3.1

"CHILI" PRESENTATION

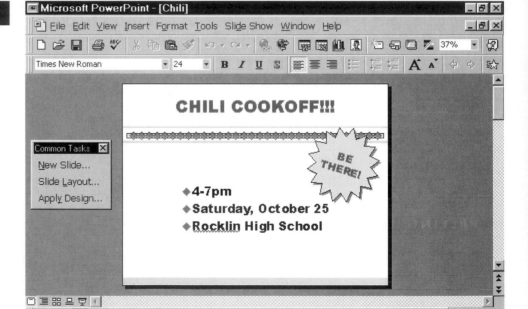

3. Review the contents of this presentation. Do the following:
    CLICK: Slide Show view button
    CLICK: left mouse button repeatedly, until you've run through the entire presentation
    When you have viewed all the slides, PowerPoint will display the first slide of your presentation in Slide view.

4. To select a new template for the presentation:
   CHOOSE: Apply Design from the Common Tasks toolbar
   (*Note:* If the Common Tasks toolbar doesn't appear, right-click one of the
   currently displayed toolbars and then choose Common Tasks from the toolbar menu.) The Apply Design dialog box appears, as shown in Figure 3.2.

FIGURE 3.2

APPLY DESIGN TEMPLATE
DIALOG BOX

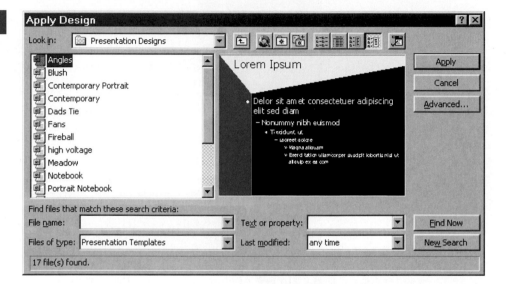

5. The templates are listed in alphabetical order. Using the mouse, click on
   several templates in the template list box. You will notice that a representation of the selected template appears in the area to the right. Before proceeding to the next step:
   SELECT: "Dads Tie" from the list of templates
   PRESS: ENTER or CLICK: Apply
   The new template will be applied to every slide in your presentation. When
   finished, your screen should appear similar to Figure 3.3.

FIGURE 3.3

THE "CHILI"
PRESENTATION USING
THE DAD'S TIE DESIGN
TEMPLATE

6. To get a better feel for how the template actually looks:
   CLICK: Slide Show view button (⬚)
   CLICK: left mouse button repeatedly, until you've run through the entire presentation

7. After being returned from Slide Show view to Slide view in the presentation window, save the presentation as "Chili Cookoff" with the new template:
   CHOOSE: File, Save As
   TYPE: **Chili Cookoff** in the *File name* text box
   CLICK: down arrow beside the Look in drop-down list box
   SELECT: *your Data Files location*
   PRESS: (**ENTER**) or CLICK: Save command button

QUICK REFERENCE
Applying a New Template
to an Existing Presentation

1. **Open the desired presentation and switch to Slide view.**

2. **CHOOSE: Apply Design from the Common Tasks toolbar, or**
   CHOOSE: Format, Apply Design from the Menu bar

3. **SELECT: a template from the Apply Design dialog box**

4. **PRESS: (ENTER) or CLICK: Apply**

IN ADDITION DOWNLOADING ADDITIONAL TEMPLATES FROM THE WEB

If you have access to the World Wide Web, you can download additional templates and wizards from Microsoft's Web site. To do this:

1. CHOOSE: Help, Microsoft on the Web
2. CHOOSE: Free Stuff

Then follow the instructions on the Web page to download the files you want.

EDITING MASTERS

PowerPoint provides a master page for each element of your presentation: slides, handouts, and notes pages. Any text, graphic, or other object that you place on a master page appears on every page of that type in the presentation. For example, you can place your company's logo on the Handout Master so that it prints out on every handout page automatically. PowerPoint lets you edit the following types of masters:

- *Slide Master*   The Slide Master holds the formatting for all the titles, main text, and background placeholders in your presentation. To edit the Slide Master, hold down **SHIFT** and click the Slide view button (▢). Or choose View, Master, Slide Master from the Menu bar.

- *Title Master*   The Title Master holds the formatting for any slides in your presentation that use the Title Slide layout. Unless you edit the Title Master, title slides conform to the Slide Master. To edit the Title Master, choose View, Master, Title Master from the Menu bar.

- *Handout Master*   The Handout Master holds the formatting for the appearance of headers and footers on handout pages. To edit the Handout Master, hold down **SHIFT** and click the Outline View button (▤) or the Slide Sorter View button (▦). Or choose View, Master, Handout Master from the Menu bar.

- *Notes Master*   The Notes Master holds the formatting for your Notes pages. To edit the Notes Master, hold down **SHIFT** and click the Notes Page view button (▣). Or choose View, Master, Notes Master from the Menu bar.

In this section, you edit the Slide Master for the "Chili Cookoff" presentation. The slides in this presentation use two different design layouts. Slides 2, 3, and 5 use the *Title Slide* layout and slides 1 and 4 use the *Bulleted List* layout. If you were to edit the Title Master, only slides 2, 3, and 5 would be affected. However, in the following section, you edit the Slide Master which will affect all slides in the presentation.

EDITING THE SLIDE MASTER

To help you imagine the contents of an actual slide, PowerPoint inserts Title and Text placeholders on the Title and Slide Masters. However, you do not type text into the placeholders—they are there only to show you the formatting specifications. If you want text to appear on every slide in your presentation, you must use the Drawing toolbar, described later in this session.

You will now change the appearance of all the titles in your presentation by editing the Slide Master.

Perform the following steps . . .

1. Assuming that you just completed the last section, slide 1 of the "Chili Cookoff" presentation should appear in the presentation window. If it doesn't appear, retrieve it from your Data Files location. Ensure that you are viewing slide 1 in Slide view before proceeding.

2. To practice changing the Slide Master:
   CHOOSE: View, Master, Slide Master
   Your screen should now appear similar to Figure 3.4.

FIGURE 3.4

THE SLIDE MASTER FOR THE "CHILI COOKOFF" PRESENTATION

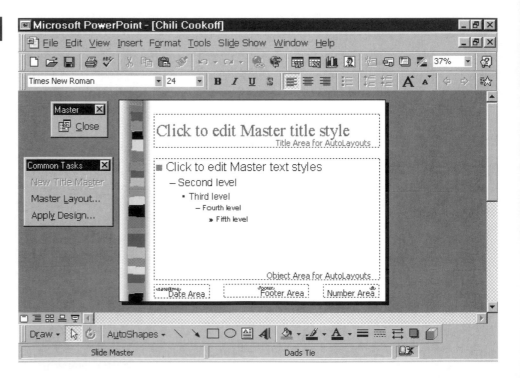

3. Currently, the titles of the slides in this presentation are displayed using Times New Roman. To include italic formatting in the title:
   CLICK: Master title placeholder (which appears as "Click to edit Master title style")
   CLICK: Italic button (*I*) on the Formatting toolbar
   Notice that you do not need to select the text in the placeholder to change its formatting characteristics. You simply position the insertion point in the placeholder.

4. To preview the slides using the new format:
CLICK: Slide view button (🖼)
Notice that the title of slide 1 is italicized.

5. To view the next slide:
CLICK: Next Slide button (⯯) on the vertical scroll bar
Notice that the title of slide 2 is also italicized.

6. View the remaining slides in the presentation and notice that all the main titles are italicized.

In this and subsequent sessions, as you learn more about designing a presentation and adding visuals, you will periodically make changes to the Slide Master. In general, however, you should edit the Slide Master only when you want to change the format of the entire presentation.

QUICK REFERENCE
Editing the Title and Slide Masters

1. **Open the desired presentation and switch to Slide view.**

2. **CHOOSE: View, Master, Title Master to edit all Title slides**
CHOOSE: View, Master, Slide Master to edit all other slides

3. **Edit the Title and Text placeholders on the Title and Slide Masters, add text boxes, insert graphics and charts, and add other objects as desired.**

4. **CHOOSE: View, Slides to return to Slide view**

EDITING AN INDIVIDUAL SLIDE

As you learned in the last section, if you want to format more than one slide at once, change the Title or Slide Master. Otherwise, modify individual slides. It is important to note that any changes you make to individual slides are considered *exceptions* to the Slide Master. If you later change the Slide Master or apply a design template, PowerPoint applies the new format but retains your exceptions. In this section, you learn to edit an individual slide in the "Chili Cookoff" presentation.

You will now remove the italic attribute from the first slide of the "Chili Cookoff" presentation and add the bold attribute.

Perform the following steps . . .

1. Ensure that you are viewing slide 2 in Slide view before proceeding.

2. Unlike formatting the Master title placeholder in the last section, formatting a single title requires that you first select all the text in the Title placeholder. To do so:
CLICK: in the Title placeholder
CHOOSE: Edit, Select All
(*Hint:* You can also drag the I-beam mouse pointer across the text or press CTRL +a to quickly select all the text in a placeholder.)

3. To remove the italic attribute and apply boldface to the selection:
CLICK: Italic button (**I**) to turn off the italic attribute
CLICK: Bold button (**B**) to turn on the bold attribute

4. To remove the active selection from the placeholder:
CLICK: anywhere outside the placeholder area (e.g., click near the top right-hand corner of the slide)
Slide 2 should now look similar to Figure 3.5. Slide 2 no longer conforms to the Slide Master. If you make a formatting change in the Slide Master, for example, all the slides in your presentation will change *except* for slide 2.

FIGURE 3.5

SLIDE 2 AFTER
FORMATTING THE TITLE

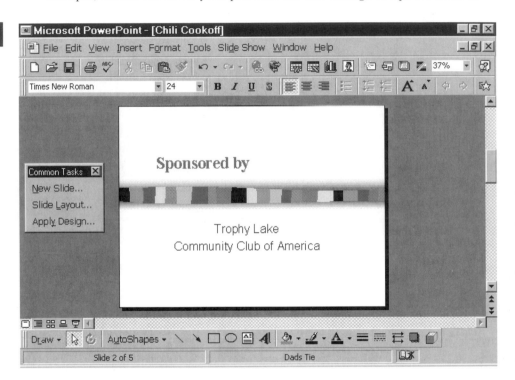

5. But what if you want slide 2 to reinherit the Slide Master attributes so that it will change along with the other slides? To do so, perform the following:
CHOOSE: Slide Layout from the Common Tasks toolbar
CLICK: Reapply button
The text now conforms to the Slide Master once again.

QUICK REFERENCE
Reapplying the Slide Master
Format to a Slide

1. **Make the desired slide active in the presentation window.**

2. **CHOOSE: Slide Layout from the Common Tasks toolbar, or**
   CHOOSE: Format, Slide Layout

3. **CLICK: Reapply command button**

THE IMPORTANCE OF COLOR

The colors used in a presentation can influence how an audience responds to your message. Colors not only bring emotion to a presentation, they communicate its formality. For example, a presentation that uses deep blues and grays better suits IBM's serious image than Apple's flamboyant image. Used improperly, colors can also undermine your presentation's theme and distract the audience. You would not want to use red, the internationally recognized color for "stop," as the background color for a presentation on entrepreneurship. You should also be aware that a significant portion of your audience—especially adult males—may be colorblind and not perceive the differences between two or more colors. Keeping all these points in mind, you are best advised to keep your color selection simple and restrained.

Fortunately for us, Microsoft hired professional artists to compile PowerPoint's numerous color schemes. A **color scheme** is a set of eight colors that you can apply to individual slides, notes pages, and audience handouts. The eight main colors include a background color, text and line color, shadows color, title text color, fill color, and three colors for accents. By using color schemes, you ensure that all the colors in your presentation are balanced and will work well together. Also, color schemes make it easy to apply a new set of colors to your presentation, just as using templates makes it easy to change its overall design.

To experiment with the colors that are available, you can choose Format, Slide Color Scheme from the menu to display the Color Scheme dialog box (shown in Figure 3.6). Using the *Standard* tab, you can choose one of six preset color schemes that change the way colors are used for all the objects on your slides. These schemes include a mixture of light and dark backgrounds and colors for the slide objects. As a general rule of thumb, you should pick darker backgrounds for 35 mm slides and on-screen presentations, and light background colors for overhead transparencies.

The *Custom* tab gives you control over individual slide objects. When you are satisfied with your color selections, you select the Apply command button to apply the new color scheme to the current slide or the Apply to All command button to change the entire presentation. It is important to note that the Apply to All option changes the color scheme for the Slide Master as well.

FIGURE 3.6

COLOR SCHEME DIALOG
BOX: STANDARD TAB

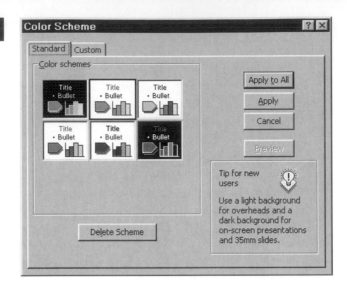

EDITING THE CURRENT COLOR SCHEME

In this section, you change the colors used in the "Chili Cookoff" presentation.

Perform the following steps . . .

1. Ensure that you are viewing slide 1 in Slide view before proceeding.

2. CHOOSE: Format, Slide Color Scheme
   The dialog box in Figure 3.6 should appear. The scheme shown in the center of the top row is currently applied to your presentation.

3. Experiment with how your slides would look with a few of the other schemes by doing the following:
   SELECT: a color scheme
   CLICK: Preview button
   DRAG: Color Scheme dialog box to reveal more of the preview image

4. DRAG: Color Scheme dialog box back to its original position

5. Repeat steps 3 and 4 to view a few more color schemes.

6. To pick the original color scheme:
   SELECT: the color scheme in the center of the first row
   You may find that a standard color scheme works well for you. If not, you will want to create a color scheme that is customized to your needs.

7. To change the color for individual slide objects, do the following:
   CLICK: *Custom* tab
   The Color Scheme dialog box should appear similar to Figure 3.7.

FIGURE 3.7

COLOR SCHEME DIALOG
BOX: CUSTOM TAB

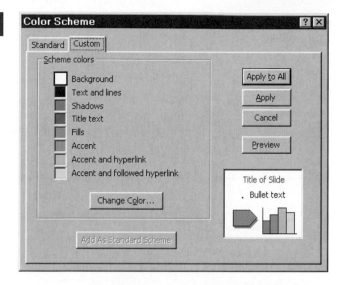

FIGURE 3.7

COLOR SCHEME DIALOG
BOX: CUSTOM TAB

8. To modify the foreground or text color for the Title placeholder:
CLICK: *Title Text* color box (in the *Scheme Colors* area)
CLICK: Change Color command button
The Title Text Color dialog box appears (Figure 3.8). The default color
palette appears. You select different colors by pointing to them in the
palette and then clicking. (*Note:* You can mix your own colors using the
Custom tab.)

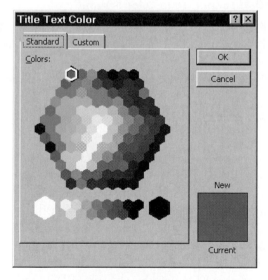

FIGURE 3.8

TITLE TEXT COLOR
DIALOG BOX

9. Black is the currently selected color for title text.
SELECT: a different color in the color palette
CLICK: OK command button

10. To apply the new color to the current slide only:
CLICK: Apply command button
Notice that the new color has been incorporated into the current slide.

11. On your own, display the other slides in the "Chili Cookoff" presentation. You'll notice that they still conform to the Slide Master's color scheme. When you are done, return to viewing slide 1 in Slide view.

12. To reapply the original color scheme to slide 1:
CHOOSE: Format, Slide Color Scheme
CLICK: *Standard* tab
SELECT: the original color scheme (top row, center)
CLICK: Apply command button
Slide 1 should now conform to the original color scheme.

QUICK REFERENCE Changing an Individual Color	1. **CHOOSE: Format, Slide Color Scheme** 2. **CLICK: *Custom* tab** 3. **SELECT: a slide object (in the Scheme Colors area)** 4. **CLICK: Change Color command button** 5. **SELECT: a new color in the color palette** 6. **CLICK: Apply to change the color on the current slide, or** **CLICK: Apply to All to change the color for all slides**

QUICK REFERENCE Reapply the Slide Master Colors	1. **Make the desired slide active in the presentation window.** 2. **CHOOSE: Format, Slide Color Scheme** 3. **CLICK: *Standard* tab** 4. **SELECT: the master color scheme (in the Color Schemes area)** 5. **CLICK: Apply command button**

VIEWING SLIDES IN BLACK AND WHITE

Depending on how you plan to output your presentation, you may at some point want to see how your presentation looks in black and white. This feature is especially relevant if you plan to print slides, handouts, or notes pages on a black and white laser printer. To view your presentation in black and white, click the Black and White view button (⬛) on the Standard toolbar or choose View, Black and White from the Menu bar. PowerPoint will automatically convert your on-screen colors to black, white, and shades of gray. In this view mode, you can also change how selected objects appear by choosing Black and White from the shortcut menu and then choosing a display option.

In the following steps, you view the "Chili Cookoff" presentation in Black and White View.

Perform the following steps . . .

1. Ensure that you are viewing slide 3 of the "Chili Cookoff" presentation before continuing.

2. To display the presentation in black and white:
   CLICK: Black and White view button (⬛)
   The slide has been converted to shades of black and white. Notice that PowerPoint also displays a color miniature of the current slide.

3. Point to the Title placeholder in the top of the window and then right-click to display the shortcut menu.

4. CHOOSE: Black and White
   Your screen should appear similar to Figure 3.9. Using the options on the shortcut menu, you can change the appearance of the selected object or choose "Don't Show" to remove the object from view.

FIGURE 3.9

BLACK AND WHITE
SHORTCUT MENU

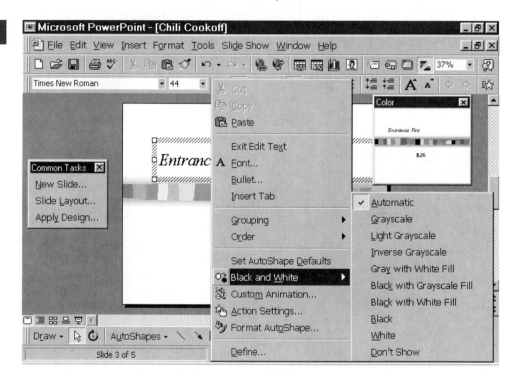

5. To remove the shortcut menu, click anywhere in the presentation window.

6. To switch back to color mode:
   CLICK: Black and White view button (⬛)

QUICK REFERENCE
Viewing a Presentation in Black and White

1. **CLICK: Black and White view button (⬛), or**
   CHOOSE: View, Black and White

2. **Change the way objects appear by choosing Black and White from the shortcut menu and then choosing an available option.**

WORKING MORE WITH TEXT

After completing the following sections, you will be able to take full control over the display of text in your presentations. Specifically, you learn how to customize the use of bullets, edit and organize textual content using the Outline view, and position text on the slide using the Text tool. In terms of formatting guidelines for text, keep in mind the following points as you work through this section:

- Strive for visible and readable text
- Strive for consistency in formatting
- Strive for simplicity and less as more
- Do not mix case (e.g., This Is Difficult To Read On A Slide)
- Do not use too many typefaces
- Avoid writing sentences on your slide; use phrases and summaries
- Ensure parallelism (e.g., consistent use of passive or active voice)

TEXT BULLETS

A bulleted list, as a format, is one technique for controlling and organizing the amount of text displayed on a slide. Bulleted lists are also used to emphasize certain points on a slide. A **bullet** is the graphic (usually a circle) that precedes an item in a list. As you've seen in this learning guide, PowerPoint adds bullets to some placeholders; that is, when you press (ENTER) after typing a line of text, a bullet is inserted automatically on the next line.

PowerPoint lets you control the display of bullets and also lets you select custom bullet symbols. You can remove or add bullets to a Text placeholder using the Bullets tool (▦) on the Formatting toolbar. You can also insert custom bullets using the Format, Bullet command. For review, you may want to refer back to Manipulating Bullets in the Adding Slides section of Session 2 before proceeding.

In this section, you change the way bullets appear in the "Chili Cookoff" presentation.

Perform the following steps . . .

1. Display slide 1 of the "Chili Cookoff" presentation in Slide view before proceeding.

2. To use a custom bullet symbol for all slides in your presentation, let's edit the Slide Master. Specifically, let's change the main-level bullets from ■ to ➜. Do the following:
   CHOOSE: View, Master, Slide Master

3. CLICK: Master text placeholder (it appears as "Click to edit Master text styles" on the slide)

4. To change the ■ bullet symbol, do the following:
   CHOOSE: Format, Bullet
   CLICK: down arrow beside the *Bullets from* drop-down list box
   SELECT: Wingdings
   (*Note:* You may have to scroll downward to find Wingdings near the bottom
   of the list.) The Bullet dialog box should look like Figure 3.10.

FIGURE 3.10

BULLET DIALOG BOX,
SHOWING THE
WINGDINGS SYMBOLS

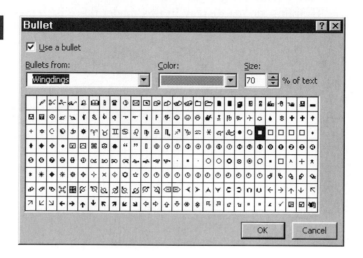

5. To specify a new symbol for the bullet:
   SELECT: ➜
   PRESS: (ENTER) or CLICK: OK

6. To view the slides:
   CLICK: Slide view button (▣)
   Notice that arrows are now used for the major bullet points.

7. To save your changes:
   CLICK: Save button (▣)

QUICK REFERENCE
Changing a Bullet Symbol

1. **Display the Slide Master, or an individual slide.**

2. **Position the insertion point in the line that contains the bullet you want to change.**

3. **CHOOSE: Format, Bullet**

4. **SELECT: a symbol font from the *Bullets from* drop-down list box**

5. **SELECT: a symbol from the Bullet dialog box**

6. **PRESS: (ENTER) or CLICK: OK**

MANIPULATING TEXT IN OUTLINE VIEW

The majority of our time so far has been spent in Slide view and Slide Show view. Many of the tasks you have performed, including changing indent levels and bullets, can also be accomplished using the Outline view. In Outline view, you can apply formatting and reorder your slides. Many people prefer working in Outline view because it lets you see the textual content from more than one slide at a time. Graphics do not display in this mode; there is, however, an icon beside each slide number that indicates whether graphics appear on that slide. The Outlining toolbar, labeled below, appears in Outline view. (*Note:* By default, the Outlining toolbar appears along the left side of the application window.)

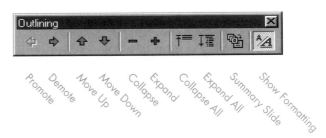

Now you will practice using Outline view to move a paragraph and an entire slide.

Perform the following steps . . .

1. Display slide 1 of the "Chili Cookoff" presentation in Slide view.

2. To change the view mode to Outline view:
   CLICK: Outline view button (▦)

3. If the viewing area isn't maximized, maximize the presentation window by clicking its Maximize button (▢). Your screen should now appear similar to Figure 3.11.

FIGURE 3.11

OUTLINE VIEW

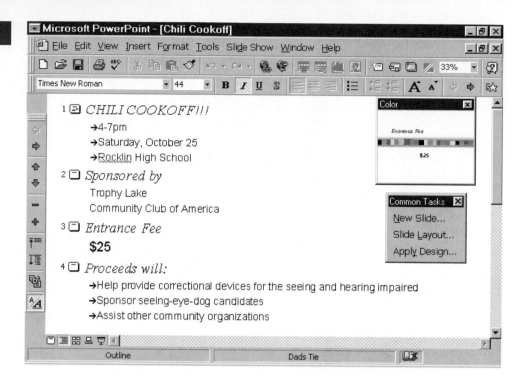

4. To get an overview of the presentation, display the slide titles only:
CLICK: Collapse All button (⬚) on the Outlining toolbar

5. To redisplay all of the text:
CLICK: Expand All button (⬚) on the Outlining toolbar

6. In Outline view, if you find the text format distracting, you can easily remove it. Do the following:
CLICK: Show Formatting button (⬚) on the Outlining toolbar
Your screen should now appear similar to Figure 3.12.

FIGURE 3.12

OUTLINE VIEW WITHOUT
FORMATTING

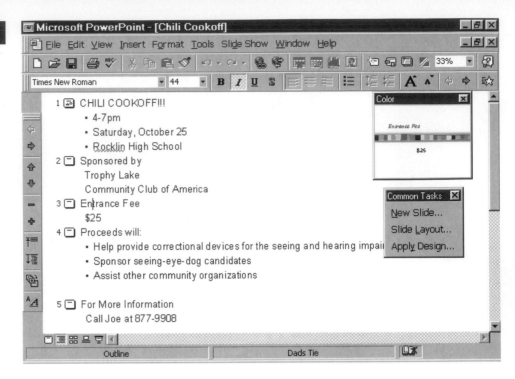

7. To redisplay the formatting:
CLICK: Show Formatting button (🄰) again

8. To select all the text on the first slide so that you can apply additional formatting, do the following:
CLICK: slide icon for slide 1
When you move the mouse pointer over the icon, it changes to a four-headed arrow (✛).

9. To display the text in bold letters:
CLICK: Bold button (🄱) on the Formatting toolbar

10. To select an individual line or bullet of text on a slide, you position the four-headed arrow (✛) mouse pointer over the associated bullet and click the left mouse button once. To practice moving a paragraph:
SELECT: "Saturday, October 25" on slide 1

11. To move this item so that it displays first in the list:
CLICK: Move Up button (⬆) on the Outlining toolbar
(*Note:* You can also drag the bullet up or down in the list using the mouse.)

12. Using the mouse:
DRAG: "Rocklin High School" bullet above "4-7pm" on slide 1

13. On your own, move the bulleted items to their original positions (i.e. time, date, location)

14. To move slide 3 so that it displays after slide 1, you must first select the slide by clicking its slide icon:
SELECT: slide 3

15. DRAG: slide 3 icon to after slide 1
(*Note:* A horizontal line marks where the slide will be positioned. Ensure that this line is below slide 1 before you release the mouse button. If you make a mistake, choose Edit, Undo and then retry.)

16. On your own, move slide 2 back to its original position after slide 3.

17. Return to Slide view before proceeding to the next section.

IN ADDITION EXPORTING A POWERPOINT OUTLINE TO WORD

1. CHOOSE: File, Send To
   CHOOSE: Microsoft Word

2. SELECT: Outline only in the
   Write-Up dialog box

3. PRESS: ENTER or CLICK: OK

USING THE TEXT BOX TOOL

The Title and Text placeholders are great for entering textual content that flows in a consistent and regular fashion. For those other times when you need more flexibility in positioning text on a slide, you use the **Text Box button** (▣) on the Drawing toolbar. Also, you must use the Text Box tool if you want to place text on the Slide Master so that it appears on every slide. You cannot use the Title and Text placeholders on the Slide Master to hold text; they are visible only for changing formatting characteristics.

In this section, you insert free-form text in the bottom right-hand corner of a slide. When you finish, slide 3 of the "Chili Cookoff" presentation will look like Figure 3.13.

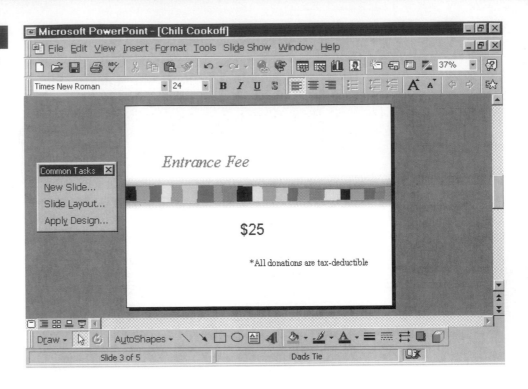

FIGURE 3.13

FREE-FORM TEXT PLACED
ON SLIDE 3 OF THE
"CHILI COOKOFF"
PRESENTATION

**Perform
the
following
steps . . .**

1. In Slide view, display slide 3 of the "Chili Cookoff" presentation.

2. To enter free-form text using the Text Box tool:
   CLICK: Text Box button (📄) on the Drawing toolbar

3. By referring to Figure 3.13:
   CLICK: where you want to type your first character (*)

4. An insertion point appears and starts blinking inside the box. The box will expand as you type. Do the following:
   TYPE: *All Donations are tax-deductible

5. CLICK: outside the text box
   Your screen should now appear similar to Figure 3.13. (*Note:* By default, the text that you type using the Text Box tool doesn't automatically wrap to the next line. If you want text to wrap automatically, you must first draw a text box by dragging with the mouse and then type in its contents.)

6. Save the "Chili Cookoff" presentation to your Data Files location.

QUICK REFERENCE
Inserting Text Using the
Text Box Tool

1. **Make the desired slide active in the presentation window.**

2. **CLICK: Text Box button (📄) located on the Drawing toolbar**

3. **CLICK: the left mouse button once to position the insertion point, or**
   DRAG: the mouse pointer on the slide to create a text box

WORKING WITH AUTOSHAPES

When your objective is to emphasize important points or promote audience interest in your presentation, consider adding drawings to your slides from PowerPoint's library of AutoShapes. An **AutoShape** is a ready-made shape that you can insert in your document and then resize and move as necessary. PowerPoint provides the following categories of AutoShapes: (1) lines, (2) connectors, (3) basic shapes, (4) block arrows, (5) flowcharting symbols, (6) stars and banners, and (7) callouts. Next you insert an AutoShape in the "Chili Cookoff" presentation and then edit it to meet your needs.

INSERTING AN AUTOSHAPE

You display a menu of AutoShapes by clicking the AutoShape button (AutoShapes ▾) on the Drawing toolbar. After selecting a shape from the AutoShapes menu, you can do one of two things to insert the AutoShape on a slide.

- If you click on your slide, the AutoShape is inserted in its default size.

- If you drag with the mouse to create an outline for the AutoShape, the AutoShape is inserted according to your specifications.

In either case, selection handles appear around the object. At this point, you can further size and move the AutoShape. You use the same procedure to size and move AutoShapes as you do to edit other types of objects.

Now you will insert an AutoShape on slide 3 of the "Chili Cookoff" presentation.

Perform the following steps . . .

1. Display slide 3 of the "Chili Cookoff" presentation in the presentation window.

2. Before continuing, ensure that the Drawing toolbar appears in the application window.

3. In the next few steps, you insert an arrow on the current slide.
   CLICK: AutoShapes button (AutoShapes ▾) on the Drawing toolbar
   CHOOSE: Block Arrows from the menu
   Your screen should now appear similar to Figure 3.14.

FIGURE 3.14

THE BLOCK ARROWS
AUTOSHAPE MENU

4. CHOOSE: the arrow positioned in the fourth row, second column
   The mouse pointer now appears as a cross hair.

5. In this step, you'll insert the AutoShape in its default size.
   CLICK: about 1½ inches to the right of "Entrance Fee" title
   The arrow now appears on your slide, surrounded by selection handles.
   Your screen should now appear similar to Figure 3.15. Don't worry if your
   AutoShape is in a different position than the one in Figure 3.15; you resize
   and move the AutoShape next.

FIGURE 3.15

A SHAPE WAS INSERTED
IN ITS DEFAULT SIZE

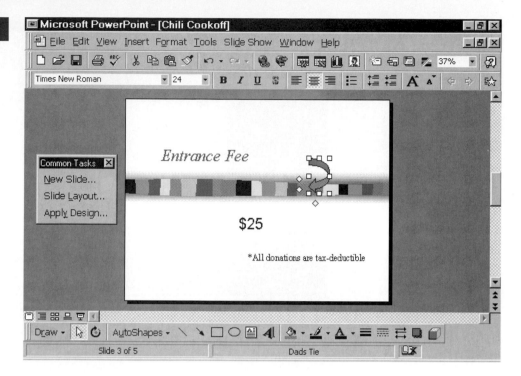

6. If you recall, you resize an object by dragging its sizing handles. You move an object by positioning the mouse pointer over the object until a four-headed arrow (↔) appears. You then drag the object to its new position. On your own, move and resize the object so that your slide appears similar to the one in Figure 3.16.

7. Save the "Chili Cookoff" presentation to your Data Files location.

FIGURE 3.16

THE SHAPE WAS MOVED
AND RESIZED

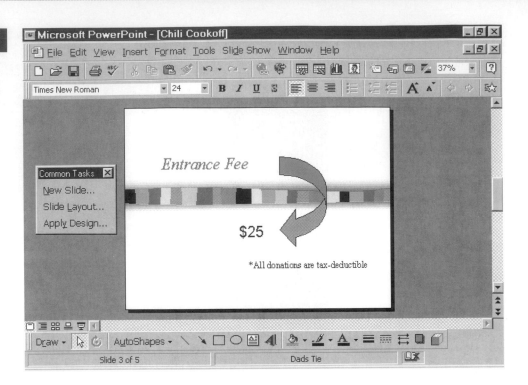

QUICK REFERENCE
Inserting an AutoShape

1. **CLICK: AutoShapes button (AutoShapes) on the Drawing toolbar**
2. **SELECT: an AutoShape category**
3. **SELECT: an AutoShape**
4. **To insert the AutoShape in its default size:**
   CLICK: on the slide, where you want to position the AutoShape
   To insert the AutoShape in the size you specify:
   DRAG: on the slide to create an outline for the AutoShape

EDITING AN AUTOSHAPE

In this section, you replace the shape you inserted in the last section with a different shape. You do this by clicking the Draw button (Draw) on the Drawing toolbar, choosing Change AutoShape, and then selecting a different shape. You will then rotate the shape using the Free Rotate button (⟳) on the Drawing toolbar and change the color of the shape using the Fill Color button (◇·). Remember that the shape must be selected before you can edit it.

Perform the following steps . . .

1. Ensure that the shape you inserted in the last section is selected.
2. To pick a different shape:
   CLICK: Draw button (Draw)
   CHOOSE: Change AutoShape from the menu
   CHOOSE: Block Arrows
   CHOOSE: the arrow positioned in the first row, fourth column
   Your screen should now appear similar to Figure 3.17.

FIGURE 3.17

CHANGING THE CURRENT
SHAPE

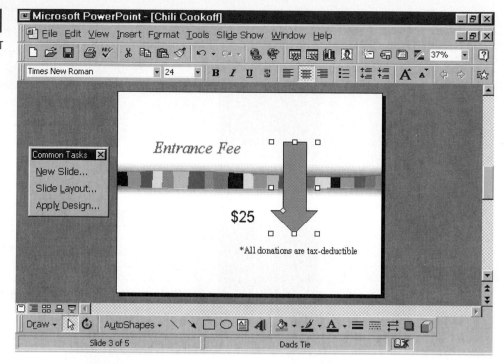

3. Now you will use the Free Rotate button (⟳) to rotate the shape to the left.
CLICK: Free Rotate button (⟳)
A round dot appears at each corner of the shape.

4. To rotate the shape, point to the dot on the bottom-left corner of the shape
and then drag to the left and up. Use Figure 3.18 as your reference. (*Note:*
After rotating the shape, you may find it necessary to move the shape further away from the dollar amount.)

FIGURE 3.18

ROTATING THE CURRENT
SHAPE

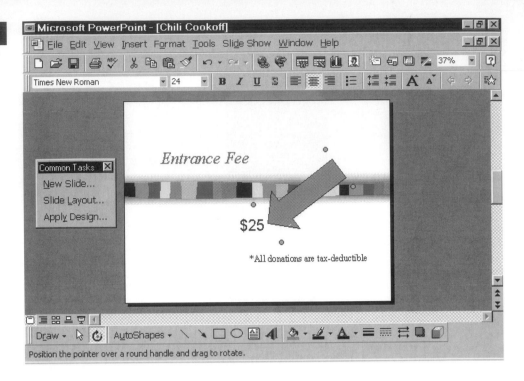

5. Now let's change the color of the arrow.
   CLICK: the arrow on the Fill Color button (🪣▾)
   CLICK: purple (or the color of your choice)
   The shape should appear with the new color.

6. Save the "Chili Cookoff" presentation to your Data Files location.

7. As you can see, you have significant control over how shapes appear in your presentation. On your own, practice using some of the other buttons on the Drawing toolbar. When you're finished, close the "Chili Cookoff" presentation without saving.

QUICK REFERENCE
Selecting a Different
AutoShape

1. **SELECT: the current AutoShape on the slide**
2. **CLICK: Draw button (Draw ▾) on the AutoShapes toolbar**
3. **CHOOSE: Change AutoShape**
4. **SELECT: a different AutoShape**

SUMMARY

In this session, you learned how to add your own design flair to a presentation. The session began by describing PowerPoint's templates, which you can use to define how text will appear on a slide, where objects will be positioned, and which colors will be used. You also edited the Slide Master, which holds the formatting specifications for the Title and Text placeholders and the background for the entire presentation. In the second half of the session, you learned the importance of selecting colors for a presentation and how to choose and apply a color scheme. The session concluded by leading you through selecting a custom bullet, manipulating text in the Outline view, and inserting free-form text on a slide using the Text Box tool. You also practiced inserting and editing AutoShapes.

COMMAND SUMMARY

Many of the commands and procedures appearing in this session are provided in Table 3.1 below.

TABLE 3.1	*Task Description*	*Menu Command*	*Alternative Methods*
Command Summary	Apply a new design template	Format, Apply Design Template	Choose Apply Design on the Common Tasks toolbar
	Edit the Title Master	View, Master, Title Master	
	Edit the Slide Master	View, Master, Slide Master	**SHIFT** + ⬜
	Reapply the Slide Master attributes	Format, Slide Layout	Choose Slide Layout on the Common Tasks toolbar
	Change the color scheme	Format, Slide Color Scheme	
	Select a custom bullet symbol	Format, Bullet	
	Reverse the last command executed	Edit, Undo	↶
	Insert an AutoShape	Insert, Picture, AutoShapes	Click AutoShapes button (AutoShapes ▾) on the Drawing toolbar
	Change the AutoShape		Click Draw button (Draw ▾) on the Drawing toolbar and then choose Change AutoShape
	Rotate an AutoShape		↻ (Drawing toolbar)
	Change the color of an AutoShape		⬧▾ (Drawing toolbar)

KEY TERMS

AutoShape

In PowerPoint, a ready-made shape that you can customize to meet your needs.

bullet

A graphic that precedes an item in a list.

color scheme

In PowerPoint, a set of eight colors that are used as the main colors in your presentation.

Handout Master

In PowerPoint, this slide holds the formatting specifications for the headers and footers of all Handout pages.

Notes Master

In PowerPoint, this slide holds the formatting specifications for the placeholders and background of all Notes pages.

Slide Master

In PowerPoint, this slide holds the formatting specifications for the placeholders and background of all slides except Title slides.

Title Master

In PowerPoint, this slide holds the formatting specifications for the placeholders and background of all Title slides.

Text Box button

This button is available on the Drawing toolbar and lets you enter text on a slide without using the placeholders.

EXERCISES

SHORT ANSWER

1. For what reason might you want to use Black and White view?

2. What is the procedure for typing text outside the current placeholders on a slide?

3. What are the advantages of working in Outline view?

4. How is your presentation affected when you choose Apply Design from the Common Tasks toolbar and then select a design?

5. Why is it significant that changes you make to individual slides are considered *exceptions* to the Slide Master?

6. In Outline View, how do you select all the text on a slide?

7. In Outline View, how do you move a slide?

8. When would you use the Bullet On/Off button?

9. When would you want to use the Title Master instead of the Slide Master?

10. What procedure would you use to change the color of an AutoShape?

HANDS-ON

(*Note:* Ensure that you know the location of your Advantage Files and where to store your Data Files. If necessary, ask your instructor or lab assistant for additional information.)

1. In this exercise, you retrieve the "CityNews" presentation from your Advantage Files location and then edit the Slide Master, change the design template, insert a clip art image, and apply a different color scheme.

    a. Retrieve "CityNews" from the Advantage Files location.

    b. Using the Slide Master, modify the presentation so that the title and main text of every slide appear bold.

    c. Using the Slide Master, select a new custom bullet symbol (■) to replace the main bullet symbol (●).

    d. Apply the "Zesty" design template to the presentation.

    e. Edit slide 5 of the presentation to look like Figure 3.19. (*Hint:* The clip image was resized and moved, and the text placeholder on the left was enlarged.)

FIGURE 3.19

SLIDE 5 OF THE "CITYNEWS" PRESENTATION

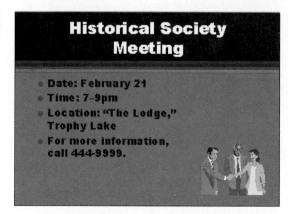

f. Edit the current color scheme. Select a color scheme that uses a white background. Apply the new color scheme to the entire presentation.

g. Display the presentation using Slide Show view.

h. Return to Slide view.

i. To reverse the color change you made in Step f, choose Edit, Undo from the Menu bar.

j. Save the presentation as "Trophy Lake News" to your Data Files location.

k. Close the presentation.

2. In this exercise, you edit the "Trophy Lake News" presentation that you saved in exercise 1.

   a. Ensure that slide 6 of the "Trophy Lake News" presentation appears on your screen.

   b. Using the Text Box button (), insert the following text in the bottom right-hand corner of slide 6:
   *All pets must be leashed

   c. Change the size of the newly inserted text to 20 points.

   d. Change the font of the newly inserted text to Arial, if this font exists on your computer.

   e. Display the presentation in Outline view.

   f. On slide 2, move the "Historical Society" bullet after the "Jazz Festival" bullet.

   g. Move slide 5 (Historical Society) to after slide 6 (Jazz Festival).

   h. Display the presentation using Slide view.

   i. Edit slide 4 to look like Figure 3.20. (*Hint:* Insert the shapes from the "Stars and Banners" AutoShape category. Use their default size. Drag the shapes into position.)

FIGURE 3.20

SLIDE 4 OF THE "TROPHY LAKE NEWS" PRESENTATION

   j. Display the entire presentation, beginning with slide 1, in Slide Show view.

   k. Save the presentation as "Trophy Lake News" to your Data Files location.

   l. Close the presentation.

3. In this exercise, you open a presentation called "Messy" from the Advantage Files location and improve its design. In its current form the presentation contains too many elements, thus confusing the message.

   a. Open "Messy" from the Advantage Files location.

   b. Delete all the AutoShapes on slide 1.

c. Change the bullets from ➜ to ● on slides 2 and 3. (*Hint:* Use the Slide Master.)

d. Apply the Bulleted List layout to slide 3.

e. Change the font size of the bulleted text on slides 2 and 3 to 28 point.

f. Choose a different design for the presentation.

g. Save the presentation as "Tidy" to your Data Files location.

4. On your own, create a presentation that contains the information and topics we describe below. Keep the following in mind as you proceed:

a. We've underlined the suggested title for each slide. However, feel free to modify or add to the topics we describe below.

b. Decide which design template and layouts to use to best present the information.

c. Enhance your presentation with one or more AutoShapes and clip art images.

d. Ensure that your name and the current date appear on the bottom of each slide. (*Hint:* Use the Slide Master and the Text Box tool.)

e. When you are finished, save the presentation as "On Your Own-3" to your Data Files location.

<u>The Structure of the United States Government</u>
by
your name

<u>The Three Branches of Government</u>
Executive Branch
Legislative Branch
Judicial Branch

<u>Executive Branch</u>
The President
The Vice President

<u>Legislative Branch</u>
Congress
- *Senate*
- *House*

<u>Judicial Branch</u>
The Supreme Court of the United States

5. On your own, create a presentation that tries to convince your audience (a relative, business associate, or other individual) why you need a vacation. Use your experience with PowerPoint to make the most compelling case possible. When you're finished, save the presentation as "On Your Own-4" to your Data Files location. (Bon Voyage!)

CASE PROBLEMS   **H2 UNDERSCAPING LTD.**

(*Note:* In the following case problems, assume the role of the primary characters and perform the same steps that they identify. You may want to re-read the session opening.)

1. By his next lunch meeting with Vi Krieg, Chip had already developed a storyboard for his presentation. "A storyboard," he explained to Vi, "reduces the amount of wasted time typically spent brainstorming around the computer. I simply jot down everything that I want to show on each slide in these little boxes. It's a great way to organize my thoughts for a presentation." Vi was very impressed with the page Chip handed to her (an example of which appears below.)

Title: Business Show, 1996 **#1** **Sub-title:** Presented by Chip Yee H2 UnderScaping Ltd.	**Title:** Evening's Agenda **#2** **Bullets:** • Chamber's mission • Benefits of membership • Community affairs • Member profile • Summary
Title: Chamber's Mission **#3** **Bullets:** • To lobby for changes in law to promote economic prosperity for all • To work for opportunity and education for small businesses nationwide • To promote the policies and initiatives of the National Chambers of Commerce	**Title:** Benefits of Membership **#4** **Bullets:** • Business-to-business directory • Monthly luncheon meetings • Monthly newsletter • Corporate library • Special events and guest speakers
Title: Community Affairs **#5** **Bullets:** • High-school career prep program • Organizer of celebrity auction for children's charities • Organizer of downtown Easter parade • Fund-raiser for local women's center	**Title:** Member Profile **#6** **Bullets:** Donna Osaki, M.D., is off to Saudi Arabia to set up the country's first community health center. Donna accepted this position immediately when approached by the Surgeon General. We wish Donna the very best overseas!
Title: Summary **#7** **Bullets:** • Our Chamber is true to its ideals • Our Chamber works for its members • Our Chamber works for its community • Our Chamber has the best people!	**Title:** Closing **#8** **Sub-title:** Thank you for attending this evening!

"Are you sure we can pull this off using a computer-based presentation?" asked Vi, wondering if Chip realized the actual time and effort it would involve. Chip nodded confidently. "You see, Vi, I've already planned out how this will work on the computer. First, I'll take my storyboard and create an on-screen presentation using the Contemporary template since it communicates a dignified and professional image for the Chamber. Next, I'll position your name as our Chamber president in the bottom right-hand corner of each slide using the Text Box button on the Slide Master. Everything will look just stunning!"

Vi was getting excited about Chip's plans for the presentation. She couldn't wait to see the final product and begged Chip to send her a printed copy of his work as soon as he was finished. Chip agreed, and they departed from their lunch feeling well-nourished and anticipating a wonderful Business Show!

Save this presentation as "Business Show" to your Data Files location.

2. Two weeks before he was to make his Chamber presentation, Chip received a letter from Ms. Paula Deviq, a business administration teacher at the local high school. The letter read, *"Dear Mr. Yee, I understand that you are preparing a presentation for the Chamber at this year's Business Show banquet. I have a proposition for you. I would like you to deliver your presentation to my senior class in business administration early next week. In return, you would enjoy an opportunity to practice your speech and receive constructive criticism from my class. Please consider this invitation and reply to me as soon as possible. Sincerely, Paula Deviq."* Chip called Paula immediately after reading the letter and accepted her polite, and timely, invitation.

Thinking about the presentation for Paula's class that evening, Chip decided that he should change the look and feel of the presentation to better suit high school students. Instead of using the look of the Contemporary template, he decided to pick something much livelier and more colorful to keep their attention. Also, he would look through the Clip Gallery to find some relevant pictures. Specifically, he wanted to add three different pictures—on each of slides 4, 5, and 6. Another change he would make would be to select custom bullet symbols, perhaps ♣ or ☽. Lastly, Chip would remove Vi Krieg's name from the Slide Master and replace it with his favorite quote, "Do what you love and the money will follow!" All of these changes would take some time, but he knew the payoff would be worth the effort.

Once finished, Chip proceeded through a dry run of his presentation using the Slide Show view. Happy with the results, he saved the presentation as "School Presentation 1" to the Data Files location.

3. Chip arrived at the high school 30 minutes early for his presentation. He was just opening the front door to the school when he was greeted by a well-dressed woman in her mid-thirties. "Mr. Yee, I presume?" Chip smiled and extended his hand to the teacher. "Yes, I hope I'm not too early for your class, Ms. Deviq?" "Oh, no, no . . . but we've experienced a small technical problem this morning with our A.V. system. I'm afraid we won't be able to connect your laptop computer to an LCD projection panel. I was hoping that you could print out your presentation onto black-and-white overheads using my laser printer. I'm sorry to make you deliver your presentation the old-fashioned way, but I'm sure my students would enjoy it all the same."

    Chip immediately began rehearsing the procedure in his mind. He would have to change his template from an on-screen presentation to a black and white overhead presentation. He would display the presentation in black and white and then review it on-screen to see how the objects looked. Realizing that he had been staring at Paula and saying nothing for the past ten seconds, Chip apologized and assured her that it was not a problem to convert his presentation to overheads. He then asked to be shown to her office to begin the process.

    Save this presentation as "School Presentation 2" to your Data Files location.

4. Back at his office, Chip received an official "Invitation to Quote" from the federal government. The government is nearing completion on a million-dollar expansion of their administration wing and requires landscaping services to be completed for their opening next month. Each vendor is being asked to prepare a 15-minute presentation on their company's strengths and present it to the selection committee this coming Monday.

    Using the storyboards shown below, Chip completed the handwritten version of the presentation. Unfortunately, he had to fly to Denver on family business and could not finish converting the presentation to PowerPoint. As his office assistant, you must now take Chip's storyboards and create a presentation appropriate for the federal government's selection committee, complete with introduction and closing slides. Chip also mentioned that you should choose templates, color schemes, typefaces, clip art, and AutoShapes for the presentation. Good luck!

Introduction #1	Company Background #2
(Remember to put the title of the presentation, my name, and the company's name on this slide!)	Started in 1992 by Mr. Chip Yee, H2U has become an innovator in the business of underground sprinkler systems.
Why We Are the Best #3	Partial Client List #4
The Most-Talented Designers The Most-Dedicated Staff The Most-Current Technology The Most-Satisfied Clients!	Mount Rushmore Society New Jersey Turnpike Assoc. Yasgusa's Farm, Inc. Willy's Motor Inn, Route 66
Summary #5	Closing Slide #6
(Remember to put a summary of the presentation here.)	(Remember to thank them for attending the presentation and provide time for questions.)

Save the presentation as "Federal Government" to your Data Files location.

Microsoft PowerPoint 97 for Windows

Adding Visual Effects

INTRODUCTION

PowerPoint provides you with powerful graphic and visual support, which makes it relatively easy to add professional touches to your presentations. In this session, we show you how to work with many kinds of visual objects including clip art images, graphs, and organizational charts. In addition, we lead you through adding special effects to your electronic presentations.

CASE STUDY   **IMMACULATE PERCEPTIONS, INC.**

"Creating a memorable corporate identity for all of our clients!" screamed the black letters on a bright yellow sign. This sign did not appear on a billboard, or even on a bus stop bench; it was placed dead center over the reception desk for Immaculate Perceptions, Inc. (IPI), a young and striving advertising agency in Brandon, Oregon. Started in 1991 as a partnership between Connie Appleton and Bobbie Brukowski, IPI now specializes in providing customers with marketing and advertising materials for trade shows and point-of-purchase (POP) displays.

Last week, Bobbie introduced the company's creative staff to Microsoft PowerPoint as a vehicle for communicating their clients' images and as a possible source of revenue. "It's great!" exclaimed Bobbie, pacing around the boardroom table. "You can add pictures and clip art, create graphs of financial and statistical information, and even match the presentation to their corporate colors. And the best part is that you can create a self-running slide show for use at a trade show booth—they don't even have to be present!" The staff was very receptive to Bobbie's pitch. Connie, who had listened to every word but had not spoken until this point, summarized the meeting with "Let's find out as much as we can about PowerPoint's visual tools and then meet again on Monday to discuss its uses for the upcoming Computer and Communications Show at the Shoreline Center. Remember, learn as much as you can about PowerPoint in the next week!"

WORKING WITH OBJECTS

Microsoft provides several Office tools, or **mini-apps,** that can be used by Power-Point. These mini-apps enable you to create objects that may be embedded into a presentation. To find out which mini-apps are available to you, choose the Insert, Object command from the menu and then browse through the list of objects that appears in the dialog box. You may also see the names of other software applications such as CorelDRAW!, depending on which applications you have installed on your computer. The Insert Object dialog box lists all the programs on your computer for which you may insert output, such as a drawing object from CorelDRAW!, into your PowerPoint presentation.

Although not all of these may be installed on your computer, Microsoft's mini-apps include the following:

Clip Gallery   Enables you to select and insert clip art from a library of cataloged images. For example:

Equation Editor   Enables you to create complex equations using special math symbols and typesetting standards. For example:

$$\sigma^2 = \frac{\sum_{i=1}^{N}(X_i - \mu)^2}{N}$$

Graph   Enables you to easily insert a graph into your document without having to launch Excel. For example:

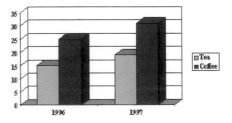

Organization Chart   Enables you to design, build, and insert an organization chart into your document. For example:

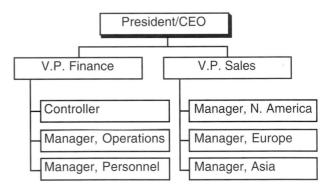

WordArt   Allows you to apply special effects to textual information in your document. (*Note:* This mini-app has been integrated into Microsoft Office so it doesn't appear in the list in the Insert Object dialog box.)

For further information on inserting and manipulating objects, refer to the In Addition boxes that appear throughout this guide and to the *Integrating Microsoft Office 97* Student Learning Guide in the Advantage Series for Computer Education.

INSERTING CLIP ART

A picture is worth a thousand words! Although this phrase is overused, its truth is undeniable. Graphics add personality to your presentation and convey information more efficiently than text alone. Unfortunately, many new computer users struggle with the tendency to place too many graphics on a single screen. To assist your planning of how and when to use graphics, apply these basic principles: strive for simplicity, use emphasis sparingly, and ensure a visual balance between graphics and text. Fortunately, PowerPoint's AutoLayouts already encourage a balanced and visually appealing use of graphics.

The Microsoft Clip Gallery provides a one-stop shopping mall for all your clip art images. You worked with clip art in Session 2 when you chose the "Text & Clip Art" AutoLayout. PowerPoint provides the following additional methods for inserting a clip art image on a slide:

- CLICK: Insert Clip Art button (🖼️) on the Standard toolbar
- CHOOSE: Insert, Picture, Clip Art from the menu
- CHOOSE: Insert, Object from the menu and select Microsoft Clip Gallery from the dialog box

In the following sections, you use the Insert Clip Art button (🖼️) on the Standard toolbar and then format and edit the image using the Picture toolbar.

INSERTING A CLIP ART IMAGE

Now you will insert an image from the Clip Gallery.

Perform the following steps . . .

1. Open "Software" from the Advantage Files location and then review the contents of the presentation in Slide Show view.

2. Ensure that slide 1 of the "Software" presentation appears in Slide view.

3. Let's use the Insert Clip Art button (🖼️) to insert a clip art image on this slide.
CLICK: Insert Clip Art button (🖼️)
The Clip Gallery dialog box appears.

4. SELECT: Shapes from the list of categories on the left
SELECT: the image shown in Figure 4.1 from the area on the right
CLICK: Insert button
Your screen should now appear similar to Figure 4.1. The image currently covers up the text on the slide. Notice that the Picture toolbar appears. Whenever a clip art image or picture is selected, the Picture toolbar appears so that you can edit the image, if necessary.

FIGURE 4.1

SLIDE 1 OF THE
"SOFTWARE"
PRESENTATION

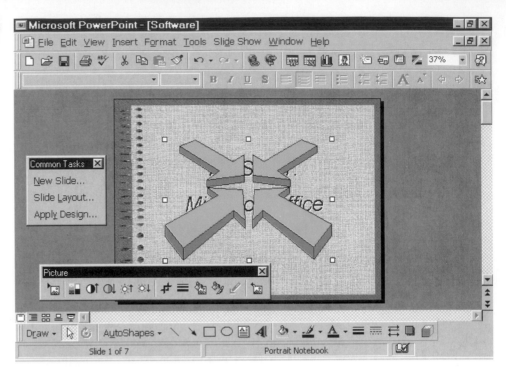

5. Let's experiment with moving the clip art image to behind the text on this slide. To do this, the image must be selected. While pointing to the clip art image on the slide:
RIGHT-CLICK: to display the shortcut menu
CHOOSE: Order

6. Since the clip art image is the currently selected object, the command you choose now will affect the clip art image.
CHOOSE: Send to Back
The clip art image now appears behind the slide's text (Figure 4.2).

FIGURE 4.2

THE IMAGE WAS
MOVED TO BEHIND
THE TEXT

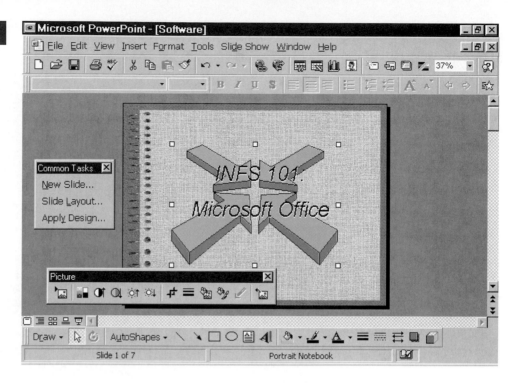

FIGURE 4.2

THE IMAGE WAS
MOVED TO BEHIND
THE TEXT

7. At this point, the text is somewhat difficult to read. If we increase the brightness of the image, the dark letters in the title may stand out more. To do this, you will use More Brightness button (⊡) on the Picture toolbar. Before continuing, ensure that the clip art image is still selected.
CLICK: More Brightness button (⊡) about ten times

8. The text should be easier to see, but let's now add the bold attribute to the title text. First you must select the Title placeholder.
CLICK: any letter in the title
The Title placeholder should now be selected.

9. To change the formatting of the title:
CHOOSE: Edit, Select All
CLICK: Bold button (**B**)

10. CLICK: outside the Title placeholder
Your screen should now appear similar to Figure 4.3.

FIGURE 4.3

THE TITLE TEXT IS
EASIER TO READ

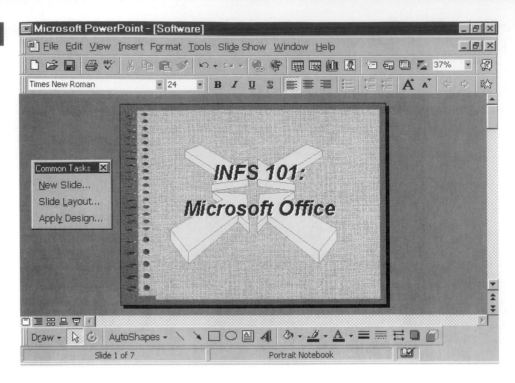

FIGURE 4.3

THE TITLE TEXT IS
EASIER TO READ

11. Save the presentation as "INFS 101" to your Data Files location.

QUICK REFERENCE	**1.**	**SELECT: the object you want to move**
Changing the Order of	**2.**	**RIGHT-CLICK: to display the shortcut menu**
Slide Objects	**3.**	**CHOOSE: Order**
		CHOOSE: an option from the menu

QUICK REFERENCE	**1.**	**SELECT: the object you want to edit**
Changing the Brightness	**2.**	**On the Picture toolbar:**
Level of an Image		**CLICK: More Brightness button (⬚), or**
		CLICK: Less Brightness button (⬚)

IN ADDITION INSERTING MOVIES AND SOUNDS

 You can insert movies and audio tracks for playback from within your presentation using the Insert, Movies and Sounds command. To play back the video clip or sound, display the presentation in Slide Show view and then click on the object.

IN ADDITION INTERNET LOCATIONS FOR CLIP ART, MOVIES, MUSIC, AND SOUNDS

- If you have access to the Internet, choose Tools, PowerPoint Central and then follow the on-screen instructions for finding what you want.

- From the Clip Gallery dialog box: CLICK: Connect to Web for additional clips button

IN ADDITION DOWNLOADING ADDITIONAL TEMPLATES AND WIZARDS FROM THE WEB

If you have access to the World Wide Web, you can download additional templates and wizards from Microsoft's Web site. To do this:

1. CHOOSE: Help, Microsoft on the Web

2. CHOOSE: Free Stuff

Then follow the instructions on the Web page to download the files you want.

INSERTING PICTURES

In addition to clip art images, you can insert graphic files into your presentation. A computer **graphic file** is usually created by an artist, designer, or desktop publisher. However, you can easily create your own graphic files if you have access to a **scanner.** A scanner is a hardware device that converts photographs and other paper-based material into computer images. Just as a photocopier makes a representation from paper to paper, a scanner makes a copy from paper to computer. You can insert an image directly from your scanner using the Insert, Picture, From Scanner command. Or, if you save the image to disk, you can insert the image file into your presentation using the Insert, Picture, From File command.

QUICK REFERENCE
Inserting Graphics

1. **Position the insertion point where you want to insert the object.**
2. **CHOOSE: Insert, Picture, From Scanner, or**
   CHOOSE: Insert, Picture, From File

CREATING GRAPHS

Most people recognize the benefit of using graphics to improve their effectiveness in communicating information. Clearly, a chart or graph is easier to decipher than rows and columns of tiny numbers. Fortunately, PowerPoint makes it relatively easy for you to include graphs in your presentations. It comes with a powerful supplementary program called **Microsoft Graph.** The Microsoft Graph 97 mini-app helps you produce great-looking charts and graphs—right from within PowerPoint! Graph does not replace a full-featured spreadsheet application like Microsoft Excel, but it does provide a more convenient tool for embedding simple charts into presentations.

There are a variety of methods for adding a graph to a slide (concentrate on using the first two).

- CLICK: Insert Chart button (📊) on the Standard toolbar
- DOUBLE-CLICK: graph placeholder on an AutoLayout slide
- CHOOSE: Insert, Chart from the Menu bar
- CHOOSE: Insert, Object from the Menu bar and select Microsoft Graph from the dialog box

In this section, you add a graph to a slide.

Perform the following steps . . .

1. Ensure that the "INFS 101" presentation appears in the presentation window and that the Common Tasks toolbar appears.

2. Display the last slide in the presentation (slide 7) by dragging the elevator scroll box to the bottom of the vertical scroll bar.

3. To insert a new slide:
CHOOSE: New Slide from the Common Tasks toolbar

4. In the Slide Layout dialog box:
SELECT: Chart layout

5. To display the slide:
PRESS: (ENTER) or CLICK: OK
Your screen should now appear similar to Figure 4.4.

FIGURE 4.4

SLIDE 7 WITH THE PLACEHOLDERS VISIBLE

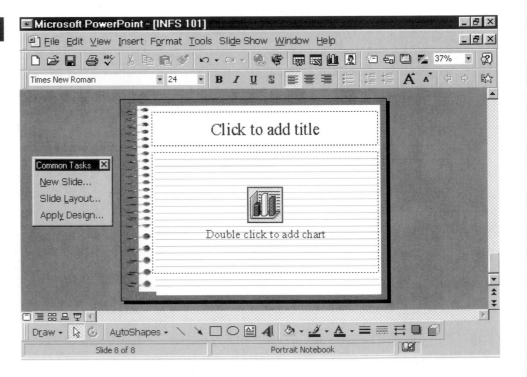

6. CLICK: Title placeholder
TYPE: **HOW YOU'RE GRADED**

7. To insert a graph:
DOUBLE-CLICK: the graph placeholder
The Graph datasheet appears in a separate window with sample information. Similarly to using an electronic spreadsheet, you add and edit data in the datasheet that you want to plot on a graph. Figure 4.5 shows the datasheet as it first appears and how it will look after you edit it.

FIGURE 4.5

EDITING THE DATASHEET

Before

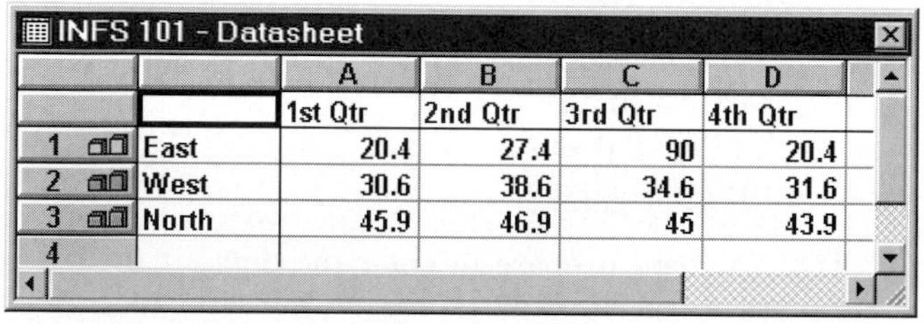

		A	B	C	D
		1st Qtr	2nd Qtr	3rd Qtr	4th Qtr
1	East	20.4	27.4	90	20.4
2	West	30.6	38.6	34.6	31.6
3	North	45.9	46.9	45	43.9
4					

INFS 101 - Datasheet

After

		A	B	C	D
1	Word	25			
2	Excel	25			
3	Access	20			
4	PowerPoint	15			
5	Integrating	15			

INFS 101 - Datasheet

8. In this step, you delete all the data that currently appears in the datasheet. To do this, you first select the entire datasheet by clicking the upper-left corner of the datasheet, directly below the Title bar. You then press the (DELETE) key.
CLICK: the upper-left corner of the datasheet (refer to Figure 4.6)
PRESS: (DELETE)

FIGURE 4.6

DELETING THE CONTENTS OF THE DATASHEET

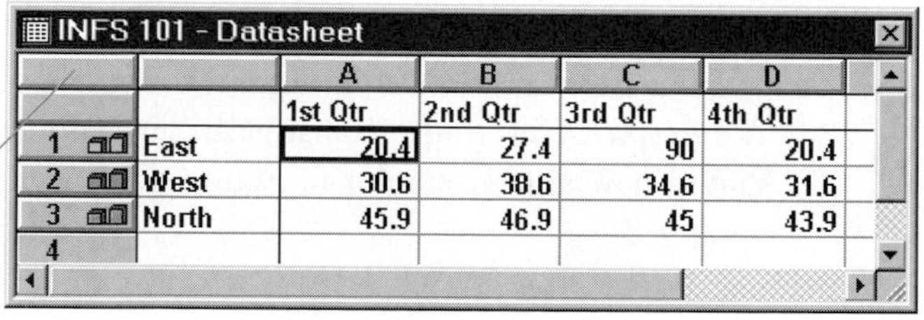

Click here to select all the cells in the datasheet

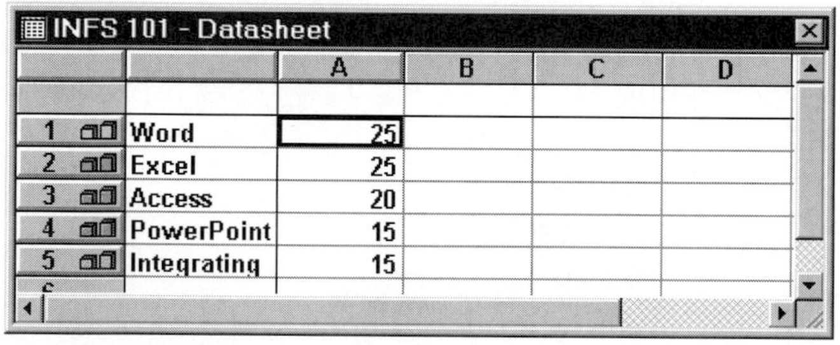

INFS 101 - Datasheet

		A	B	C	D
		1st Qtr	2nd Qtr	3rd Qtr	4th Qtr
1	East	20.4	27.4	90	20.4
2	West	30.6	38.6	34.6	31.6
3	North	45.9	46.9	45	43.9
4					

9. To enter data into the datasheet, you click the cross hair mouse pointer on the appropriate *cell* (the intersection of a row and a column) in the datasheet. In this step, you enter the titles.
CLICK: in the cell to the right of the number 1
TYPE: **Word**
PRESS: `ENTER`
The cursor automatically moves to the cell below.
TYPE: **Excel**
PRESS: `ENTER`
TYPE: **Access**
PRESS: `ENTER`
TYPE: **PowerPoint**
PRESS: `ENTER`
TYPE: **Integrating**
PRESS: `ENTER`

10. Now you prepare to enter the data.
PRESS: `CTRL` + `HOME`
The cursor automatically moves to where you will type in the first value (25).

11. To enter the data:
TYPE: **25**
PRESS: `ENTER`
TYPE: **25**
PRESS: `ENTER`
TYPE: **20**
PRESS: `ENTER`
TYPE: **15**
PRESS: `ENTER`
TYPE: **15**
PRESS: `ENTER`
If you drag the bottom border of the datasheet downward and then press `CTRL` + `HOME`, the datasheet should appear similar to the completed datasheet in Figure 4.5. (*Note:* Some of the headings may be obscured in your datasheet.)

12. Let's now display the graph on the slide:
CLICK: anywhere in the background of the presentation window
The graph is inserted automatically into your presentation. Your screen should now appear similar to Figure 4.7.

FIGURE 4.7

THE GRAPH IS
INSERTED ON THE SLIDE

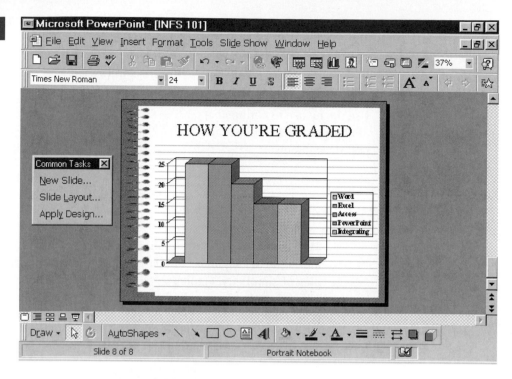

---

13. Save the presentation as "INFS 101" to your Data Files location.

Once you've inserted a graph on a slide, you can edit it at any time by double-clicking the image on the slide to load Microsoft Graph. While displaying a presentation in Slide view, you use the same techniques for sizing and moving a graph as you use for manipulating other types of objects.

QUICK REFERENCE
Inserting a Graph

- **CLICK: Insert Chart button (📊) on the Standard toolbar**
- **DOUBLE-CLICK: graph placeholder on an AutoLayout slide**
- **CHOOSE: Insert, Chart from the menu**
- **CHOOSE: Insert, Object and then select Microsoft Graph**

IN ADDITION INSERTING AN EXCEL WORKSHEET

1. CLICK: Insert Microsoft Excel Worksheet button (📗) on the Standard toolbar

2. Use the mouse to outline the dimensions of the worksheet in the pull-down menu.

3. Edit the worksheet object using Excel's commands and procedures.

4. Resize and move the object as necessary.

IN ADDITION INSERTING A WORD TABLE

1. CLICK: Insert Microsoft Word Table button (▦) on the Standard toolbar

2. Use the mouse to outline the dimensions of the table in the pull-down menu.

3. Edit the table object using Word's commands and procedures.

4. Resize and move the object as necessary.

CREATING ORGANIZATIONAL CHARTS

Microsoft Organization Chart allows you to create organization charts and other hierarchical diagrams. Similarly to working with graphics, you apply the principles of simplicity, emphasis, and balance to creating **organization charts.** In the following steps, you will insert a simple organizational chart into the "INFS 101" presentation.

There are a few methods for inserting an organization chart on a slide.

- DOUBLE-CLICK: organization chart placeholder on an AutoLayout slide
- CHOOSE: Insert, Picture, Organization Chart from the Menu bar

In this section, you add an organization chart to a slide.

Perform the following steps . . .

1. Ensure that slide 8 of the "INFS 101" presentation appears in the presentation window.

2. To insert a new slide:
   CHOOSE: New Slide from the Common Tasks toolbar

3. To select the Organization Chart AutoLayout slide:
   SELECT: Organization Chart layout
   PRESS: [ENTER] or CLICK: OK
   Your screen should now appear similar to Figure 4.8.

FIGURE 4.8

ORGANIZATION CHART
PLACEHOLDER ON A
NEW SLIDE

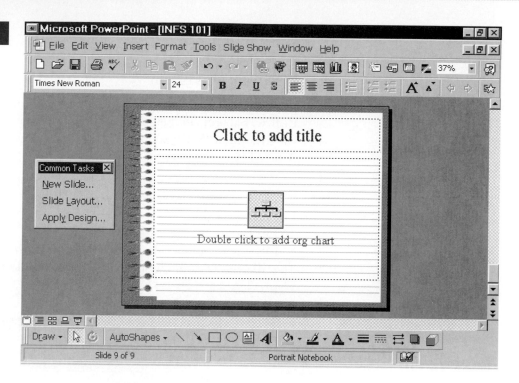

4. CLICK: Title placeholder
TYPE: **NEED HELP?**

5. To insert an organization chart:
DOUBLE-CLICK: the organization chart placeholder
You should see four boxes on the screen; the topmost box should already be selected.

6. To edit the content of the organization chart boxes:
TYPE: **Maria D. Perez**
PRESS: (**ENTER**)
TYPE: **Lead Instructor**

7. CLICK: the far left box, located in the second row of the chart
TYPE: **Feliberto Reyes**
PRESS: (**ENTER**)
TYPE: **Assistant Instructor**

8. CLICK: the box in the center of the second row
TYPE: **Frank Rogers**
PRESS: (**ENTER**)
TYPE: **Lab Assistant**

9. CLICK: the box on the right of the second row
TYPE: **Maritza James**
PRESS: (ENTER)
TYPE: **Lab Assistant**

10. To add a new box to the chart:
CLICK: Subordinate button (Subordinate: 凸) in the toolbar
CLICK: Maria D. Perez' box
A new box appears on the second level.

11. Because the new box is already selected, do the following:
TYPE: **Roxanna Adams**
PRESS: (ENTER)
TYPE: **Network Manager**
CLICK: anywhere outside of the chart to remove the active selection
The Microsoft Organization Chart window should now appear similar to
Figure 4.9.

FIGURE 4.9

THE COMPLETED
ORGANIZATION CHART

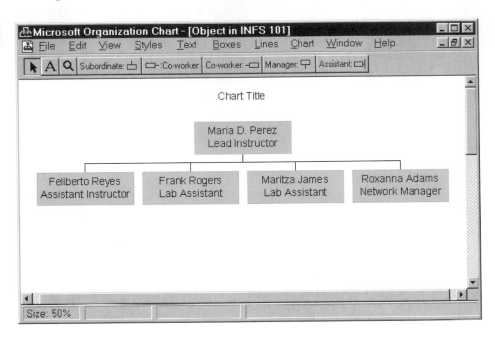

12. To return to PowerPoint and update the slide:
CHOOSE: File, Exit and Return to INFS 101
(*CAUTION:* Choose the command from the Microsoft Organization Chart
Menu bar and not the PowerPoint Menu bar.)

13. CLICK: Yes command button to update the presentation
The organization chart should now appear on the slide.

14. On your own, you may want to select the organization chart object and
enlarge it by dragging its top border upward. The chart's text may be easier
to read.

15. Save the "INFS 101" presentation to your Data Files location.

Once you've inserted an organization chart on a slide, you can edit it at any time by double-clicking the image on the slide to load Microsoft Organization Chart. You may, for example, decide to change the box colors, border color, border style, and so on. While displaying a presentation in Slide view, you use the same techniques for sizing and moving an organization chart image as you used for manipulating other types of objects.

QUICK REFERENCE
Inserting an
Organization Chart

- **DOUBLE-CLICK: organization chart placeholder on an AutoLayout slide**
- **CHOOSE: Insert, Picture, Organization Chart from the Menu bar**

IN ADDITION COPYING AND MOVING BETWEEN MICROSOFT OFFICE APPLICATIONS

1. Select the text, data, or other object that you want to copy. Then click the Cut button (✂) or the Copy button (📋).

2. Switch to the application you want to move or copy into and then position the cursor.

3. Click the Paste button (📋) to insert the contents of the Clipboard at the cursor location. (*Note:* If you choose Edit, Paste Special from the Menu bar and then choose the Paste Link option, the pasted information will be linked to its source application. Any changes you make to the data in the source application will show up in the linked application.)

DESIGNING AN ELECTRONIC SLIDE SHOW

So far in this learning guide, you've viewed a slide show using PowerPoint's default settings. No transitions between slides or timed pauses have been added to Slide Show view. In the following sections, you learn how to take control of your electronic presentations by setting timings, adding transitions, creating build slides, and adding animation. You also learn how to customize a slide show for a specific audience.

SETTING TIMINGS

Timing refers to the amount of time a slide stays on the screen during Slide Show view. Timing is especially useful for those occasions when you want to let a presentation run unattended in a continuous loop. You specify timings for your presentation by choosing the Slide Show, Rehearse Timings command or by clicking the Rehearse New Timings button (🖼) in Slide Sorter view.

In this section, you add timings to the "INFS 101" presentation.

Perform the following steps . . .

1. Ensure that slide 1 of the "INFS 101" presentation appears in the presentation window.

2. To build timings into the slide show:
   CHOOSE: Slide Show, Rehearse Timings from the Menu bar

3. To set timings:
   CLICK: [▷] after the clock reaches 5 seconds
   CLICK: [▷] every 5 seconds, for each remaining slide

4. When the slide show is finished, PowerPoint displays a dialog box showing the total number of seconds that have elapsed. To record the timings:
   CLICK: Yes command button

5. To review the timings in Slide Sorter view:
   CLICK: Yes command button

6. To view the presentation with the new timings:
   CLICK: Slide Show view button (▣)
   Now, sit back and watch the show! (*Hint:* You can also choose Slide Show, Set Up Show from the Menu bar and then select the *Loop continuously until 'Esc'* check box for self-running displays at trade shows and other presentations.)

7. Save the "INFS 101" presentation to your Data Files location.

QUICK REFERENCE
Setting Timings

1. **CHOOSE: Slide Show, Rehearse Timings**

2. **CLICK: the mouse button after the desired seconds on each slide**

3. **After viewing the entire presentation:**
   CLICK: Yes command button to record the slide timings
   CLICK: Yes command button to review the timings

IN ADDITION PLAYING MULTIPLE PRESENTATIONS CONSECUTIVELY

With PowerPoint, you can run multiple presentations consecutively, even unattended. When the first presentation is finished, the second presentation automatically begins. To do this, you assemble a *play list*.

For more information on this topic, choose Help, Contents and Index and then click the *Index* tab. Type **play lists** and then click the Display button to display a list of related topics.

ADDING TRANSITIONS

In this section, you learn to incorporate transitions between slides. Transitions are the special effects you see when you go from one slide to the next. Previously only available in higher-end multimedia authoring programs, transitions can now be easily inserted into any of your PowerPoint presentations.

Now you will add transitions to the "INFS 101" presentation.

Perform the following steps . . .

1. Display "INFS 101" presentation in Slide Sorter view. (*Note:* Ensure that slides 1–6 appear.)

2. To add a transition to slide 1:
SELECT: slide 1
CLICK: Transition button ([□]) on the Slide Sorter toolbar
(*Note:* You can also choose the Slide Show, Slide Transition command from the menu.) Your screen should now appear similar to Figure 4.10.

FIGURE 4.10

TRANSITION DIALOG BOX

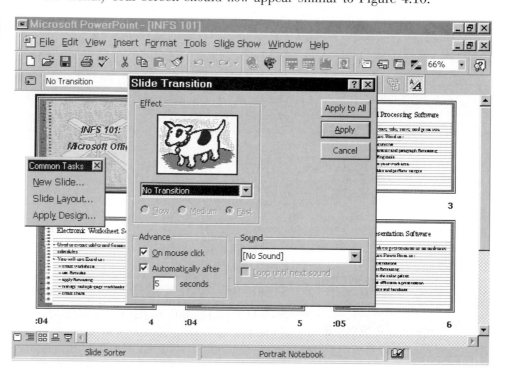

3. CLICK: down arrow beside the *Effect* drop-down list box
(*Note:* You can also display the same options by selecting the *Transition Effects* drop-down list box in the Slide Sorter toolbar.)

4. CLICK: several transition effects
Notice that they appear in the preview area of the dialog box.

5. SELECT: Checkerboard Across

6. PRESS: (ENTER) or CLICK: Apply
When you run the slide show, slide 1 will display with the Checkerboard Across transition.

7. SELECT: slide 2
SELECT: Blinds Vertical from the *Slide Transition Effects* drop-down list box in the Slide Sorter toolbar

8. For each of the remaining slides:
SELECT: a different transition effect from the *Slide Transition Effects* drop-down list

9. To view the slide show:
CLICK: Slide Show view button (🖥️)
CLICK: the left mouse button until you've seen the entire show

10. When the presentation is finished, the presentation will again display in Slide Sorter view. (*Note:* In this view mode, you can see how a particular slide will transition by clicking the transition icon that is located on the bottom-left of each slide. Also, if timing is present, it appears below its image.)

QUICK REFERENCE
Applying Transitions

1. **CLICK: Slide Sorter view button (**🔲**)**
2. **SELECT: any slide in the presentation**
3. **CLICK: Transition button (**🔳**) on the Slide Sorter toolbar**
4. **SELECT: a transition effect**
5. **PRESS:** ⌈ENTER⌉ **or CLICK: OK**

CREATING A BUILD SLIDE

Build slides let you reveal one bullet at a time in Slide Show view. You can also specify how the bullet appears (e.g., enters from the right), and whether you want to dim previously displayed items when you display a new bulleted item.

Next you create a build slide.

Perform the following steps . . .

1. Ensure that the "INFS 101" presentation appears in Slide Sorter view.

2. To add a build slide to the presentation:
SELECT: slide 4 in Slide Sorter view
(*Note:* This slide contains bulleted items describing electronic worksheet software.)

3. To create a build slide:
CLICK: down arrow beside the *Text Preset Animation* drop-down list box on the Slide Sorter toolbar
(*Note:* You can also choose the Slide Show, Preset Animation command from the menu.)

4. SELECT: Fly From Top

5. To display slide 4 in Slide Show view:
CLICK: Slide Show view button (🖥️)
The bullets appear one by one on the slide. If no timings were built into this presentation, you would need to click to display each bullet.

6. On your own, experiment with adding build effects to the remaining slides in the presentation.

7. Save the "INFS 101" presentation to your Data Files location.

QUICK REFERENCE
Creating a Build Slide

1. **CLICK: Slide Sorter view button ( )**
2. **SELECT: any slide in the presentation**
3. **CLICK: down arrow beside the *Text Preset Animation* drop-down list box on the Slide Sorter toolbar**
4. **SELECT: a build effect**

ADDING ANIMATION

Does your computer have a sound card and speakers? If so, you can play sound effects and add animation to your presentations. For example, you can listen to screeching brakes as text rolls in from the left side of the screen; how about hearing a laser sound as each letter drops into place or a whoosh sound as text races in from the left. These animated effects combine sound and motion and are only a few of the effects accessible from the Animation Effects toolbar. By adding a bit of drama to your presentation, these effects will not only keep your audience interested but also entertained. The Animation Effects toolbar appears below.

In this section, you use the Animation Effects toolbar to animate a slide in the "INFS 101" presentation.

Perform the following steps . . .

1. Ensure that slide 4 of the "INFS 101" presentation appears in Slide view.
2. To display the Animation Effects toolbar:
   CLICK: Animation Effects button ( ) on the Standard toolbar
3. If the Animation Effects toolbar is covering part of your slide, drag it to one of the edges of the presentation window.
4. Notice that many of the buttons on the Animation Effects toolbar aren't available. This is because you must first select the object you want to animate. To select the Text placeholder:
   CLICK: in the Text placeholder (containing the bulleted items)
   Your screen should now appear similar to Figure 4.11.

FIGURE 4.11

THE ANIMATION
EFFECTS TOOLBAR

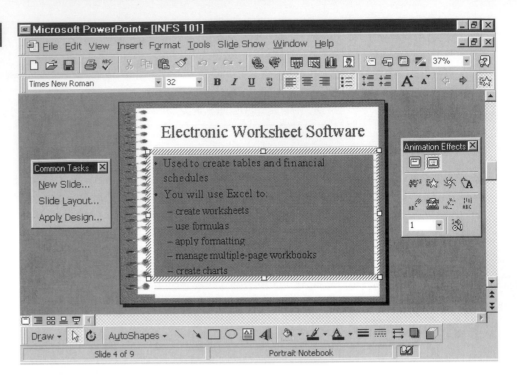

5. In this step, you are going to add the Laser Text Effect (⬛) to the bulleted text on slide 4.
CLICK: Laser Text Effect button (⬛)

6. To see the effect of the animation:
CLICK: Slide Show view button (⬛)
The bulleted text should be "flying" into place.

7. PRESS: `ESC` to display the presentation in Slide view

8. On your own, try out other animation effects.

9. Before proceeding, remove the Animation Effects toolbar from view.
CLICK: Animation Effects button (⬛) on the Standard toolbar

10. Save "INFS 101" to your Data Files location.

QUICK REFERENCE
Adding Animation Effects

1. **CLICK: Animation Effects button (⬛) on the Standard toolbar**
2. **CLICK: the area of the slide you want to animate**
3. **CLICK: the desired effect on the Animation Effects toolbar**

CREATING A CUSTOM SLIDE SHOW

With PowerPoint, you can customize a slide show to meet your specific needs. For example, in its current form, the "INFS 101" presentation is suited to an audience of students that is already enrolled in the INFS 101 course. It contains very specific information about the course. But what if you want to show the same slide show to an audience of prospective students? You would probably want to reduce the level of detail, eliminating slides that get too specific.

Using the Slide Show, Custom Show command, you can easily customize a slide show to your needs. You simply select the slides you want to include in the custom show and decide how you want them ordered. The major advantage of this feature is that you don't need to store multiple copies of the same presentation on disk.

Now you practice creating a custom show from the "INFS 101" presentation.

Perform the following steps . . .

1. Display the "INFS 101" presentation in Slide view.

2. CHOOSE: Slide Show, Custom Show from the Menu bar
The Custom Show dialog box appears.

3. To create a new custom show:
CLICK: New command button
The dialog box in Figure 4.12 appears.

FIGURE 4.12

CREATING A CUSTOM
SHOW

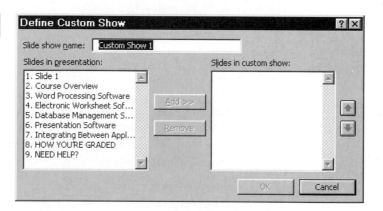

4. Let's type in a name for the custom show. The default name is *Custom Show #*.
TYPE: **Prospective Students**

5. You will now add slides 1–7 in the custom show, excluding slides 8–9 because they contain information that is too specific for the intended audience.
CLICK: the first slide in the *Slides in presentation* list box
CLICK: Add command button
Slide 1 was added to the *Slides in custom show* list box.

6. To add a group of slides, you hold down CTRL and click the slides in the *Slides in presentation* box that you want to select.
PRESS: CTRL and hold it down
CLICK: slides 2–7 in the *Slides in presentation* list box

7. Release the CTRL key.

8. To add the selected slides to the custom show:
   CLICK: Add command button
   The Define Custom Show dialog box should now appear similar to
   Figure 4.13.

FIGURE 4.13

DEFINING THE
CUSTOM SHOW

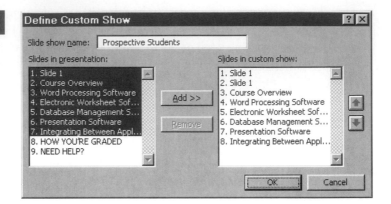

9. To proceed:
   PRESS: ENTER or CLICK: OK
   The Custom Show dialog box appears.

10. To view the show, click the Show button.
    CLICK: Show command button
    The slide show will run in a continuous loop.

11. To exit Slide Show view:
    PRESS: ESC
    In the future, when you want to view the custom show, you choose Slide
    Show, Custom Show and select the custom show you want to view. Then
    click the Show command button.

12. To remove the Custom Shows dialog box:
    CLICK: Close

13. Save "INFS 101" to your Data Files location.

14. Exit Microsoft PowerPoint.

QUICK REFERENCE
Creating a Custom
Slide Show

1. **CHOOSE: Slide Show, Custom Shows**
2. **CLICK: New button to create a new custom show**
3. **SELECT: the slides in the *Slides in presentation* list box**
4. **CLICK: Add command button**
5. **PRESS: ENTER or CLICK: OK**

IN ADDITION LINKING YOUR PRESENTATION TO THE INTERNET AND OTHER MICROSOFT OFFICE DOCUMENTS

You can create links in your presentation to Internet addresses or to other Microsoft Office documents on your hard drive or network drive. When you click the link, you move to the desired location. These links are called *hyperlinks*. To include hyperlinks in your presentation, you click the Insert Hyperlink button ( ) on the

Standard toolbar and then answer the questions in the Insert Hyperlink dialog box.

For more information, choose Help, Contents and Index. Click the *Contents* tab and select the "Working with Presentations on Intranets and the Internet" topic. Then explore the "Working with Hyperlinks" topic.

SUMMARY

This session focused on adding visual objects and effects to your presentations. You learned about editing clip art using the Picture toolbar. You also learned to insert a graph and an organization chart on a slide using Microsoft Graph and Microsoft Organization Chart. Next you added some special effects to an electronic presentation. Specifically, you added timing and transitions, created build slides, and added animated effects. The session concluded by showing you how to create a custom slide show.

COMMAND SUMMARY

Many of the commands and procedures appearing in this session are provided in Table 4.1 below.

TABLE 4.1	*Task Description*	*Menu Command*	*Alternative Method*
Command Summary	Insert a clip art image	Insert, Picture, Clip Art	
	Insert a graph	Insert, Chart	
	Insert an organization chart	Insert, Picture, Organization Chart	
	Build timings into a slide show	Slide Show, Rehearse Timings	
	Add transitions to a slide show (from Slide Sorter view)	Slide Show, Slide Transition	
	Create build slides (from Slide Sorter view)	Slide Show, Preset Animation	
	Add animated effects		

KEY TERMS

graphic file

A computer graphic, created by an artist or scanned from an existing picture or photograph, that you can insert into your document using the Insert, Picture command.

Microsoft Graph

A supplementary program or *mini-app* that lets you create graphs and insert them onto a PowerPoint slide.

Microsoft Organization Chart

A supplementary program or *mini-app* that lets you create organization charts and insert them onto a PowerPoint slide.

mini-apps

Small application programs that are bundled with Microsoft Windows products to enhance the primary applications; most mini-apps are accessed using the Insert, Object command.

organization charts

A diagram showing the internal management reporting structure of a company, organization, institution, or other such group; also used for flowchart diagrams.

scanner

A hardware device that converts an existing picture or photograph into a computer image that is stored digitally on the disk.

EXERCISES

SHORT ANSWER

1. How would you brighten a clip art image?

2. What is a custom show? Provide an example of when you might want to create a custom show.

3. What is the difference between inserting a clip art image using the Clip Art button on the Standard toolbar and using a Clip Art autolayout?

4. Describe some of the effects accessible using the Animation Effects toolbar.

5. What is the procedure for editing a graph object once it has been inserted on a slide?

6. Why would you want to build timing into a presentation?

7. Describe two methods for inserting an organization chart object on a slide.

8. In an electronic slide show, what is a transition? Give some examples.

9. Describe the process of creating and inserting a graph on a slide.

10. What is a build slide? Give some examples of build effects.

HANDS-ON

(*Note:* Ensure that you know the location of your Advantage Files and where to store your Data Files. If necessary, ask your instructor or lab assistant for additional information.)

1. Open the "Melon" presentation that is stored in the Advantage Files location. Perform the following modifications to the presentation:

   a. Make slides 2–4 build slides.

   b. Specify timings and transitions between all the slides in the presentation.

   c. Create a custom show called "December Trade Show" that includes slides 1 and 2.

   d. Save the presentation as "R.C. Melon" to your Data Files location.

2. Create a presentation that includes the five slides pictured in Figure 4.14. Create build slides, and add transitions and timings. Then, save the presentation as "PC Hardware Components" to your Data Files location.

FIGURE 4.14

SLIDE 1

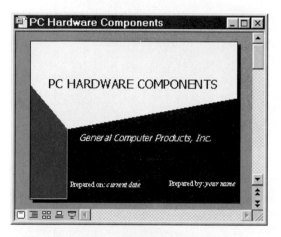

SLIDE 2

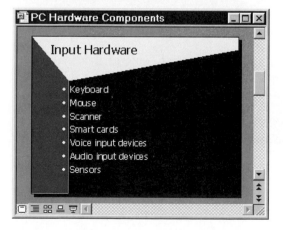

SLIDE 3

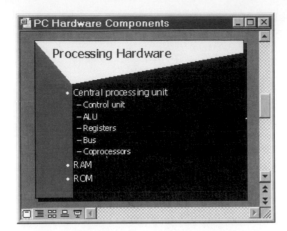

SLIDE 4

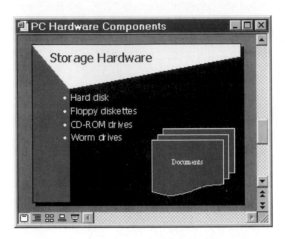

SLIDE 5

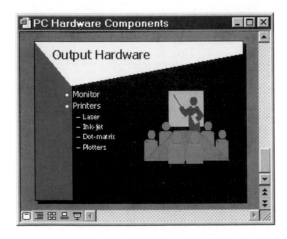

3. On your own, create a slide show describing a fictitious company, such as *Wally's Widgets.* The presentation should include six slides that contain the information listed below. When you're finished, save the presentation as "On Your Own-5" to your Data Files location.

   a. Company name, address, and phone information (include a clip art image)

   b. Description of the product (features and benefits)

   c. Pricing information

   d. Projected sales (include a graph)

   e. Personnel (include an organization chart)

   f. Summary slide

4. On your own, create an electronic presentation using PowerPoint's "Generic (Standard)" presentation template. You access this template in the *Presentations* tab of the New Presentation dialog box. Adapt this presentation to a topic you're interested in. When finished, save the presentation as "On Your Own-6" to your Data Files location. The presentation should contain at least five slides and include the following:

   a. A clip art image

   b. An autoshape image

   c. Text that you've inserted with the Text tool

   d. Customized bullets

   e. Build slides

   f. Timings and transitions between slides

   g. Animated effects

CASE PROBLEMS   **IMMACULATE PERCEPTIONS, INC. (IPI)**

(*Note:* In the following case problems, assume the role of the primary character or characters and perform the same steps that they identify.)

1. It was late Friday afternoon and most of the staff had already left the IPI offices for the long weekend. Roy MacGregor, on the other hand, was just arriving at IPI for the first time that day. Roy is the marketing manager for IPI and had taken an early commuter flight to Portland that morning to spend the day with a new client. Both Connie and Bobbie went to their office doors to greet him, but Roy got the first words out. "You're never going to believe this! I just spent an entire day with Gloria Gallego at Windermere's Windshield Wiper Warehouse. We had a $400,000 contract tied up by lunch and then she asked me some ridiculous questions about

presentation software." Connie and Bobbie stole a quick glance at each other as Roy proceeded with his story. "Four hundred big ones down the drain because we can't deliver some sort of electronic slide show for their trade show exhibit. I've never even heard of the thing before—something like PowerPress or Point-to-Power, I don't know!"

Connie and Bobbie led Roy to the boardroom and explained the meeting they had held with the creative staff that morning. Connie added, "We can do this presentation for them, Roy. I want you to call Gloria immediately and tell her that we'll send a sample presentation by Tuesday afternoon. Did you take any notes of what they wanted in an electronic slide show?" After shuffling some papers back and forth, Roy handed Connie one page of notes and left for his office to call Gloria.

Upon Roy's return, Connie had summarized what the presentation should look like and what information it should contain. Using the following notes, you must now create a presentation for Windermere's Windshield Wiper Warehouse.

PowerPoint Presentation for Windermere's Windshield Wiper Warehouse

The presentation must include the following features:

- *Be continuously self-running for display in trade show booths*
- *Use their corporate colors of White, Black, and Red*
- *Use transitions that wipe left and right like windshield wipers*
- *Contain transportation-related clip art, like the image of a car*
- *Contain 8 slides with the following content*

#1: An introduction slide with the company's name and the clip art image of a car	#2: Why W4 Wipers Work Best • Lifetime rubber compound • Durable steel construction • Tested and guaranteed
#3: Lifetime Rubber Compound • Lasts forever and a day • New coating stops streaking • Good from −30 to over 100 degrees in temperature	#4: Durable Steel Construction • Lasts forever and a day • Maintenance-free parts • Carried by hundreds of mechanics on the West Coast
#5: Tested and Guaranteed • Used on many makes and models of automobiles • Certified by the Windshield Manufacturer's Association	#6: Company name again • Friendly, courteous staff • Toll-free phone number • Terms of credit available (make this a build slide)
#7: A summary slide of the major points. Make it the same as slide #2 to save time.	#8: A conclusion slide with the company name and a message that the presentation will begin again in 15 seconds.

After viewing the presentation in Slide Show view, save the file as "Windermere" to your Data Files location.

2. Connie and Bobbie have been asked to present a company overview to the board of directors of IPI. This is a very formal presentation to their lawyers, accountants, bankers, and major investors. Create a PowerPoint presentation with an introduction and conclusion slide, and include the following components. Save the presentation as "IPI Board" to your Data Files location.

Company Products

- *Image consulting*
- *Trade show materials*
- *Point-of-purchase displays*
- *PowerPoint presentations*

Growth History (1991 to 1996)

- *Staff: 2 to 14*
- *Clients: 8 to 26*
- *Sales: $65,000 to $1.6 million*

Staff

- *Two directors*
- *Two managers*
- *Six creative staff*
- *Four administrative personnel*

Organization Chart

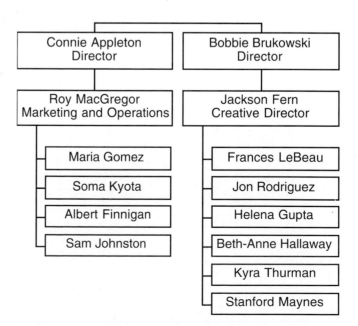

3. Add the following financial projections to the "IPI Board" presentation, complete with a table of figures on one slide and a graph on another. Also, incorporate slide transition effects and use build slides in the presentation. Save the presentation back to your Data Files location.

(in 000s)	1995	1996
Sales Revenue	$1,450	$1,620
Cost of Sales	580	700
Gross Profit	870	920
Fixed Costs	450	480
Net Profit	$420	$440

Microsoft PowerPoint 97 for Windows

Notes, Handouts, and Printing

SESSION OUTLINE

Public Speaking Tips
Speaker's Notes
Audience Handouts
Print Options for Slides
Packaging Your Presentation
Summary
Key Terms
Exercises

INTRODUCTION

In this session, you learn to create and print speakers notes and audience handouts, two useful components of any presentation. Like slides, notes and handouts have associated masters called the Notes Master and the Handout Master, respectively. You also learn to print the different elements of your presentation, including how to set up a 35 mm slide format for output.

SPRINGS COLLEGE, COLORADO

Situated on a hillside of fir trees with a breathtaking view of the valley, the Springs College campus provides a beautiful and convenient retreat for residents of Denver and Colorado Springs. In addition to its surroundings, the school is well known in the state for its progressive business and computer programs. Bradley Neumann was very fortunate to land his first-ever teaching position with Springs College, especially considering his alternative offer from Wolf Bay University in Canada's Northwest Territories!

After two months, Bradley felt comfortable with the marketing courses that he had recently assumed from Gayle Fanning, who was taking a year's sabbatical to conduct marketing research for a large computer manufacturer. He wasn't expecting to hear from Gayle for another ten months when he received an e-mail over the Internet: *Hi Bradley, I trust that you're into the full swing of things now that it's been a couple of months. I've been collecting some very interesting research that I think you should include in your Marketing Research 201 curriculum. I've received authorization from the company I'm working with to send you reports every two weeks with my findings and conclusions. I think this information will greatly benefit your students. I'll be in touch soon, Gayle.*

In this session, you and Bradley will learn to create speaker's notes pages and audience handouts. These two elements of a presentation are extremely valuable when you are presenting someone else's ideas and need the supporting documentation close at hand. You also learn to create 35 mm slides for taking your presentations on the road.

PUBLIC SPEAKING TIPS

One of the greatest skills that you can possess is a talent for public speaking. Whatever career choice you've made or will make, the time will come when you must present an opinion, train a co-worker, or give an impromptu speech at your son's or daughter's kindergarten class. In the real world, however, some people would rather streak across the field during the Super Bowl than say a few words in front of their peers.

Here are some techniques to help you combat your platform jitters and pull off a winning presentation:

- Prepare your presentation materials thoroughly.
- Practice your delivery in front of the mirror or using a tape recorder.
- Polish your delivery (e.g., remember to make eye contact).
- Psyche yourself up and project positive thoughts.
- Visualize yourself doing an excellent job!

When preparing to give a presentation, allot yourself approximately two minutes to present each slide. Therefore, a 30-minute presentation will have about 15 slides. You may feel that you need more content than this to "save you" for half an hour, but the actual time that it takes to present a slide to an audience is rarely less than two minutes. You do not want to put all your information into your slide presentation anyway. Otherwise, you might as well just distribute handouts to the audience and send them on their way. Remember, the audience is there to listen to what you will say and how you will say it! Every successful speaker communicates his or her interest and enthusiasm in a topic and remains courteous to the audience at all times.

SPEAKER'S NOTES

In preparing for a presentation, you should consider creating cheat sheets or crib notes. These notes help you avoid a common pitfall among novice presenters—putting too much text on the slides. Keep your slides brief and to the point. Use the notes pages in PowerPoint (as a replacement or complement to your recipe cards) to store reminders to yourself, relevant facts, and anecdotes. These notes pages also come in handy for question periods at the end of presentations.

In PowerPoint, a typical **notes page** provides a smaller, printed version of a slide at the top of the page with an area for text and graphics appearing below. Using the Notes Master, you can add designs and logos to all of your notes pages, or you can edit individual pages. To select the Notes Page view, click the Notes Page view button (🖳) or choose View, Notes Page from the menu.

CREATING AND PRINTING SPEAKER'S NOTES

In this section, you create a notes page for the "Training" presentation that is stored in your Advantage Files location.

Perform the following steps . . .

1. Open the "Training" presentation from the Advantage Files location.

2. The first slide of the "Training" presentation should appear in the presentation window.

3. CLICK: Notes Page view button (🖳)
   SELECT: 50% from the *Zoom* drop-down list box
   Your screen should now appear similar to Figure 5.1.

FIGURE 5.1

A NOTES PAGE FROM
THE "TRAINING"
PRESENTATION

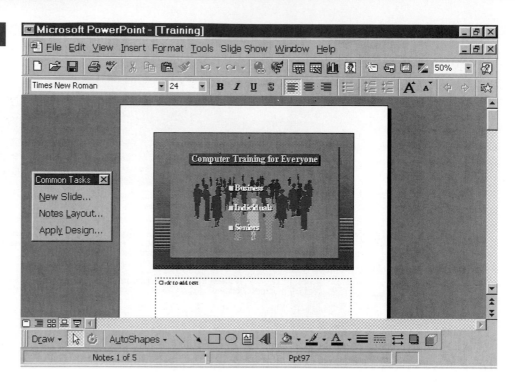

4. To add notes:
CLICK: anywhere in the notes box to position the insertion point

5. To enlarge your view of the notes box so it's easier to see:
SELECT: 75% from the *Zoom* drop-down list box
(*Hint:* As needed, you can also resize the page space taken up by the image or notes area by selecting the area's border and dragging its handles.)

6. Ensure that the insertion point or cursor is blinking inside the notes box. Do the following:
TYPE: `Welcome to MPC College.`
PRESS: ENTER twice
TYPE: `And welcome to our first computer training orientation meeting. We are anxious to share with you the elements of our training program and to take you on a tour of MPC's training facilities.`
PRESS: ENTER twice
TYPE: `Please feel free to ask questions at any point during the presentation.`

Your screen should now appear similar to Figure 5.2.

FIGURE 5.2

ENTERING TEXT INTO
A NOTES PAGE

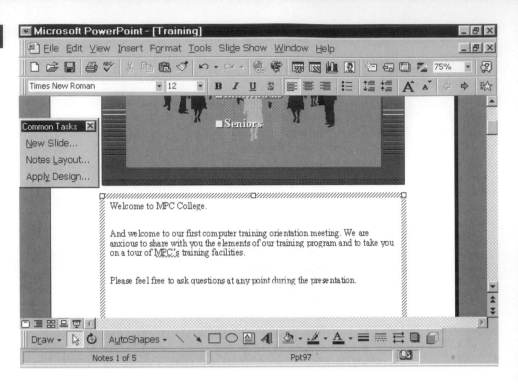

7. To print the notes page:
CHOOSE: File, Print
CLICK: down arrow beside the *Print what* drop-down list box
SELECT: Notes Pages

8. To print just the current slide:
SELECT: Current Slide option button in the *Print range* area
PRESS: [ENTER] or CLICK: OK

QUICK REFERENCE

Creating a Notes Page

1. **Make the desired slide active in the presentation window.**
2. **CHOOSE: View, Notes Page, or**
   CLICK: Notes Page view button (🖳)
3. **CLICK: anywhere in the Notes placeholder box**
4. **TYPE:** *desired notes*

MODIFYING THE NOTES MASTER

Let's place your name in the footer of the Notes Master. A *footer* is a word processing term for the area that appears at the bottom of every page. A *header* is a word processing term for the area that appears at the top of every page. This page currently has a footer with the page number and current slide number. You can also insert clip art images and other graphic pictures in the header and footer of a page.

Perform the following steps . . .

1. To create a footer that appears on every page, you need to modify the Notes Master. Let's display this master page:
   CHOOSE: View, Master, Notes Master
   (*Note:* You can also press **SHIFT** and then click the Notes Page view button (🖳) to display the Notes Master.)

2. DRAG: the elevator scroll box to the bottom of the vertical scroll bar so that you can see the bottom of the page

3. Click the mouse button in the bottom left-hand corner of the page in the Footer Area text box. The text box is selected.

4. To change the point size of the text:
   CLICK: down arrow beside the *Font Size* drop-down list box
   SELECT: 12

5. TYPE: **Presented by** *your name*
   Enter your name where specified in the above instruction. Your screen should now appear similar to Figure 5.3. (*Note:* The <footer> placeholder is non-printing and will not appear in your printout.)

FIGURE 5.3

THE MODIFIED NOTES MASTER

![Microsoft PowerPoint - [Computer Training] window showing the modified Notes Master with Common Tasks panel, Notes Body Area, Footer Area containing "<footer>Presented by your name", Page <#> in the center, and Number Area. Status bar shows "Notes Master" and "Ppt97".]

6. To return to the Notes Pages view:
   CLICK: Notes Page view button (🖳)
   Notice that the text you entered above now appears in the footer of the active page. Also, the current page number appears centered and the current slide number appears in the bottom-right corner.

7. Save your work as "Computer Training" to your Data Files location.

IN ADDITION INSERTING COMMENTS

When a presentation is produced as part of a collaborative effort, a handy feature is to be able to insert comments directly into the presentation. To do this in PowerPoint:

1. Display the Reviewing toolbar.

2. Display the appropriate slide.

3. CLICK: Insert Comment button (⬚) on the Reviewing toolbar

4. TYPE: a comment into the text box

If you don't want comments to appear in the presentation, click the Show/Hide Comments button (⬚) on the Reviewing toolbar.

Audience Handouts

Preparing handouts for your audience is a courtesy. However, you do not want to provide too much information in audience handouts; otherwise, there is no incentive to sit through your presentation. Many presenters create audience handouts in which important information is missing from the slide representations on the page. As the speaker proceeds through each slide, important information is provided so that the audience can fill in the blanks in their notes. Not only does the audience have to pay attention in order to compile a complete set of notes, they may also remember the important concepts better by having to write them down.

In PowerPoint, a handout is essentially a printout of the slides in your presentation. As with the notes pages, you can add text and art—such as your company logo—to all of the handout pages. You also choose whether to include two, three, or six slides on a handout page. Another option to consider is leaving space on the handout so that your audience can take notes during the presentation. In the following sections, you create a handout for the "Computer Training" presentation that is stored in your Data Files location.

MODIFYING THE HANDOUT MASTER

You add text and graphics to a handout by modifying the Handout Master. Unlike notes pages, handouts cannot be edited individually. In fact, you see them only after they are printed.

Perform the following steps . . .

1. Ensure that the first slide of the "Computer Training" presentation appears in the presentation window.

2. CHOOSE: View, Master, Handout Master
Your screen should now look similar to Figure 5.4.

FIGURE 5.4

HANDOUT MASTER
WITH OUTLINES
SHOWING WHERE TWO,
THREE, AND SIX SLIDES
WILL PRINT

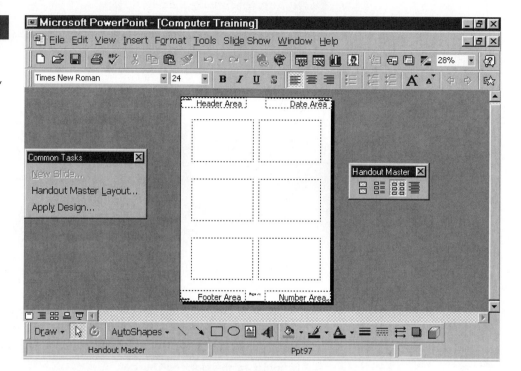

3. To enlarge your view of the handout page:
CLICK: down arrow beside the *Zoom* drop-down list
SELECT: 75%

4. DRAG: the elevator scroll box to the top of the vertical scroll bar

5. In this step, you insert a title in the header. Do the following:
CLICK: the mouse pointer in the upper left-hand corner of the page (in the Header Area text box)

6. To change the point size of the text:
CLICK: down arrow beside the *Font Size* drop-down list box
SELECT: 18

7. TYPE: **MPC College:**
PRESS: (ENTER)
TYPE: **Computer Training Center**
Your screen should now appear similar to Figure 5.5.

FIGURE 5.5

TEXT INSERTED IN THE
HEADER OF THE
HANDOUT MASTER

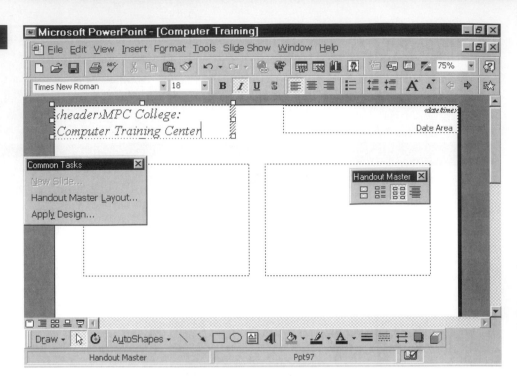

8. Display the presentation in Slide view.

QUICK REFERENCE
Modifying the
Handout Master

1. **CHOOSE: View, Master, Handout Master**
2. **Modify the formatting specifications of the Text placeholder or add text and graphics to the Handout Master.**

PRINTING AUDIENCE HANDOUTS

To print audience handouts for the "Computer Training" presentation, perform the following steps.

Perform the following steps . . .

1. CHOOSE: File, Print
   CLICK: down arrow beside the *Print what* drop-down list box
   SELECT: Handouts (6 slides per page)

2. To print the entire presentation:
   SELECT: All option button in the *Print range* area
   PRESS: (ENTER) or CLICK: OK

3. To prepare for the next section:
   CLICK: Slide view button
   CHOOSE: Fit from the *Zoom* drop-down list box

PRINT OPTIONS FOR SLIDES

As you've seen throughout this learning guide, the process of printing involves first opening the presentation you want to print, identifying what you want to print (slides, outline, notes pages, audience handouts) and then specifying the range of slides to print.

In the following sections, we describe some additional options that you should be familiar with when printing your presentations.

SETTING UP THE SLIDE FORMAT

The size of your printed slides is determined by the settings in the Page Setup box (Figure 5.6). If you don't want to use the default settings, you should choose File, Page Setup to establish the settings *before* you begin creating slides. Review the options in Table 5.1 for more information. **Landscape orientation** means that what you print will print across the length of the paper. In **portrait orientation**, a slide image would appear taller than in landscape orientation.

	Slide Output	Width	Height	Orientation
TABLE 5.1				
Slide Dimensions	On-Screen Show	10 inches	7.5 inches	Landscape
	Letter Paper (8.5 × 11 inches)	10 inches	7.5 inches	Landscape
	A4 Paper (210 mm × 297 mm)	10.83 inches	7.5 inches	Landscape
	35 mm slide	11.25 inches	7.5 inches	Landscape
	Overhead	10 inches	7.5 inches	Landscape
	Custom (your own settings)			

Perform the following steps . . .

1. Ensure that the first slide of the "Computer Training" presentation appears in the presentation window.

2. To display the Slide Setup dialog box:
   CHOOSE: File, Page Setup
   The Page Setup dialog box appears (Figure 5.6).

FIGURE 5.6

PAGE SETUP DIALOG
BOX

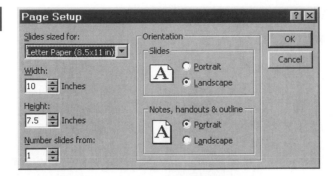

3. CLICK: down arrow beside the *Slides Sized for* drop-down list box

4. Review the options in the drop-down list box and do the following:
   SELECT: Cancel command button to leave the dialog box

5. Save the "Computer Training" presentation to your Data Files location.

6. Close the presentation and exit Microsoft PowerPoint.

35 MM SLIDES

If you will be creating 35 mm slides of your presentation, make sure to first select 35 mm slides in the Page Setup dialog box (described in the previous section). Then you choose File, Print to display the Print dialog box. Select the *Scale to Fit Paper* check box to have PowerPoint scale your slides so that they will fit. Select the *Print to File* check box in order to create a file that can be turned over to an outside service bureau for the creation of 35 mm slides. (*Note:* After you press **ENTER**, PowerPoint prompts you for the name of the slide file.)

For more convenience, if you are in North America and have a modem in your computer, you can send your presentation directly from PowerPoint to Genigraphics, a company that specializes in the output of color 35 mm slides and other types of color output. Choose the File, Send to Genigraphics command from the Menu bar and then follow the instructions presented by the Genigraphics wizard. (*Note:* If the "Send to Genigraphics" option doesn't appear in the File menu, then this option wasn't installed on your computer.)

QUICK REFERENCE Creating 35 mm Slides	**1.** **CHOOSE:** File, Page Setup **SELECT:** 35 mm slides in the *Slides Sized for* drop-down list box **PRESS:** ENTER or **CLICK: OK** **2.** **CHOOSE:** File, Print **SELECT:** Slides in the *Print what* drop-down list box **SELECT:** *Print to File* check box **SELECT:** *Scale to Fit Paper* check box **PRESS:** ENTER or **CLICK: OK** **3.** **PowerPoint will prompt you for the name of the output file.**

PACKAGING YOUR PRESENTATION

If you typically present PowerPoint presentations on different computers, you need to know about the Pack And Go Wizard. This helpful wizard packages your entire presentation, including the PowerPoint Viewer program (if desired), into a single file. In fact, you can even package multiple presentations together on the same diskette or across several diskettes. For an added sense of security and to ensure that the presentation looks the same on another computer, the Pack And Go Wizard lets you include linked files and embed TrueType fonts. Lastly, the wizard compresses the presentation so that it takes a lesser number of diskettes to take your show on the road! For more information on this topic, refer to the PowerPoint online Help facility or run the command by choosing File, Pack And Go.

IN ADDITION EXPORTING YOUR SLIDES AND NOTES PAGES TO A WORD DOCUMENT

1. CHOOSE: File, Send To

2. CHOOSE: Microsoft Word

3. SELECT: *Notes next to slides* or *Notes below slides* option button

4. PRESS: ENTER or CLICK: OK

SUMMARY

In this session, you learned how to create and print notes pages and audience handouts. You used the Notes Master and the Handout Master to include text or other objects in the headers and footers of every notes or handout page. The session concluded by showing you how to use the Page Setup dialog box and how to print 35 mm slides.

COMMAND SUMMARY

Many of the commands and procedures appearing in this session are provided in Table 5.2 below.

TABLE 5.2

Command Summary

Task Description	Menu Command
Display the Notes Master	View, Master, Notes Master
Display the Handout Master	View, Master, Handout Master
Display the Page Setup dialog box	File, Page Setup
Print 35 mm slides	File, Print
Package a presentation for delivery on another computer	File, Pack And Go

KEY TERMS

landscape orientation
In this mode, your slides print across the length of the page.

notes page
A notes page, used by the presenter, that includes a smaller printed version of a slide on the top of the page and an area for notes below.

portrait orientation
In this mode, your slides print across the width of the page.

EXERCISES

SHORT ANSWER

1. When might you need to use the Page Setup dialog box?
2. When might you want to modify the Notes Master?
3. What are the dotted lines that appear on the Handout Master?
4. What is the *Zoom* drop-down list box used for?
5. How do you change the orientation of the slides you print?
6. What does the Pack And Go Wizard do?
7. If you want all your notes pages to print with a larger notes area and a smaller screen image, what should you do?
8. How do you create 35 mm slides?
9. What does a notes page look like? What does a handout look like?
10. How do you include text on an audience handout?

HANDS-ON

(*Note:* Ensure that you know the location of your Advantage Files and where to store your Data Files. If necessary, ask your instructor or lab assistant for additional information.)

1. Open the "Travel" presentation that is stored in the Advantage Files location. This presentation contains a few slides from a more in-depth presentation. Perform the following steps.

    a. Display slide 1 in Notes Page view.

    b. Type in a few sentences of notes that would be helpful when presenting this slide.

    c. Create notes for slides 2 and 3 also.

    d. Print the notes pages.

    e. Display the Handout Master.

    f. Type the current date in the upper right-hand corner of each page and your name in the bottom-left corner of each page.

    g. Print the handouts.

    h. Save the presentation as "Travel Today" to your Data Files location.

    i. Close the presentation.

2. Open "Palette," a two-slide presentation, from the Advantage Files location. This presentation is intended to run in a continuous loop at a Home Improvements trade show. Embellish the presentation with the features we list below. Then save the presentation to your Data Files location as "The Master Palette."

    a. Apply a design to the presentation.

    b. Insert an autoshape on slide 1 that captures the viewer's attention.

    c. Add a clip art image to slide 2.

    d. Make slide 2 a build slide and add transition effects to both slides.

    e. In order to be prepared in case you're asked questions, create a Notes Page for each page for both slides, containing data you can refer to.

    f. Print the notes pages for your reference during the trade show.

3. On your own, use what you've learned in this learning guide to create an informative presentation about a topic of your choice or one given to you by your instructor. Your presentation should be organized with a clear objective and should contain at least 5 slides. Try to make your presentation as visually captivating as possible. When you're finished, save the presentation as "On Your Own-7" to your Data Files location.

CASE PROBLEMS **SPRINGS COLLEGE, COLORADO**

(*Note:* In the following case problems, assume the role of the primary character or characters and perform the same steps that they identify.)

1. Ten days pass before Bradley receives an e-mail from Gayle (shown below). After perusing the information, he determines that the content fits nicely with an upcoming lecture he is giving on the general steps involved in conducting market research. After printing the message, Bradley highlights the points that he wants to include on the slides. The remaining information will have to go into his speaker's notes. He proceeds to create a presentation consisting of seven slides: five content slides, an introduction slide, and a summary slide. After adding some clip art images, transitions, and build slides to the presentation, he saves his work as "Marketing" to his Data Files location. As the final step, Bradley prints the slides, speaker's notes pages, and audience handouts.

Date: Nov. 15, 1996
To: Bradley Neumann
From: Gayle Fanning
Subject: Steps in Marketing Research
cc:

A marketing research project involves the following steps:

1. ***Specify Your Objectives***
   *As a marketing researcher, you must know the **reasons for conducting the research**. Also, you must **properly define the process** to ensure that you will gather information on which you can base decisions. Don't let managers request unnecessary research based on their own excitement.*

2. ***Determine the Data Sources***
   *You must determine whether the information can and should be gathered from **internal sources** or from **external sources**. Internal sources are a company's financial statements and management information system reports. External sources include newspapers, trade journals, and government or industry reports.*

3. ***Define the Sample***
   *To provide information of any use, you must find a representative population sample. Issues that you must take into consideration include the **size of the sample** and the **data collection methods** you will use.*

4. ***Collect, Process, and Analyze the Data***
   *Data collection consumes a large portion of the research budget. The processing of data involves **reviewing the data for accuracy and completeness** and then **tabulating or coding the results**. Most data analysis is conducted using computers.*

5. ***Present the Results***
   At the end of the research process, you communicate your results to management through an **oral presentation** *and/or a* **written report.** *Ensure that you keep the presentation simple—your audience is there to be informed, not won over by your technical prowess.*

2. Bradley has been asked to deliver his "Marketing" presentation to the local chapter of the AASP (Association of Advertising and Sales Professionals), and Gayle and her client have agreed. The association has rented the lecture theater on the Springs College campus for an expected attendance of 200 members. They've also asked Bradley to produce a copy of his presentation on 35 mm slides so they can send it to their head office in Atlanta. Bradley decides to change the presentation's template for use as a 35 mm slide and add a copyright notice to the bottom of the audience handouts. The notice reads, "Copyright © 1997 by Gayle Fanning and Bradley Neumann." He outputs the presentation for 35 mm slides to a print file called "Marketing-35mm" on the Advantage Diskette.

3. Wally Fong had to dodge several people and trays to make it safely to where Bradley was sitting in the cafeteria. He politely asked to join Bradley and quickly took the seat across from him at the small round table. "I understand that you're the new guy who is taking over for Gayle. I'm Wally Fong, an instructor in computer sciences. I was communicating with Gayle over the Net and she mentioned that you had done some outstanding work in PowerPoint." Bradley smiled shyly and went back to his half-eaten salad. "I'd like to get your help on developing a PowerPoint presentation that reviews some of the newest operating system software." After further clarification and two espressos, Bradley agreed to help Wally with his project.

   Given that Bradley's time was limited, he encouraged Wally to develop the content for the presentation using the AutoContent Wizard. He would then take Wally's work and add clip art images, slide timings, transitions, and build slides. To get Wally started, the two men developed an outline for the presentation together, as provided below:

General	Operating System Software Review • Prepared by Wally Fong, Computer Sciences, and Bradley Neumann, Business Admin.
Introduction	This presentation reviews the strengths and weaknesses of operating system software currently available for the personal computer.
Topics of Discussion	The main ideas to be discussed include looking at three operating system software solutions: Windows, OS/2 Warp, and System 7.5.

Topic One	Windows • Graphical user interface (GUI) • 32-bit, preemptive multitasking • Plug and Play technology • Access to the Internet and the Microsoft Online Network
Topic Two	OS/2 Warp • Graphical user interface (GUI) based on System Object Model (SOM) • 32-bit, preemptive multitasking • Runs DOS, Windows, and OS/2 applications software in separate sessions
Topic Three	System 7.5 • Most mature and developed of all graphical user interfaces (GUI) • 32-bit preemptive multitasking • Excellent for graphics and multimedia • Runs on new PowerPC platform
Real Life	The User's Perspective • Will it run the applications I need to use? • Will it provide a more stable environment? • What are the real costs of switching from my current operating system software?
What This Means	Learn to review the features of an operating system software with respect to your computing needs. Do not get consumed by the advertisements pervading every trade journal that promise the world for only $99. The real costs are much greater than this!
Next Steps	1. Build a checklist of the features you require in operating system software. 2. Review each operating system based on this checklist. 3. Consider all the costs associated with switching or upgrading your system software.

As Wally, create a presentation using the AutoContent Wizard. Next, assume the role of Bradley and apply an on-screen template and special visual effects to the presentation. Save your work as "Operating Systems" to your Data Files location.

Appendix

Microsoft PowerPoint 97 Toolbar Summary

STANDARD

FORMATTING

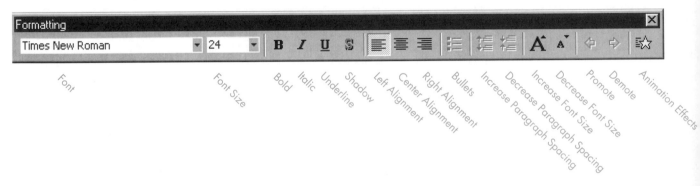

DRAWING

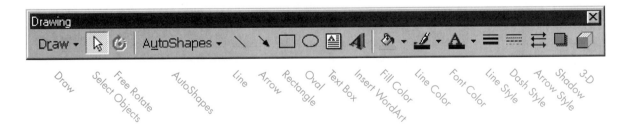

PICTURE

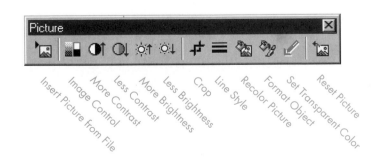

ANIMATE

OUTLINE

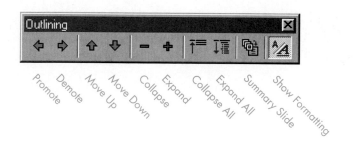

Index

The page numbers in boldface indicate Quick Reference procedures.

Integrating Microsoft® Office 97 Professional for Windows®

Sarah E. Hutchinson

Glen J. Coulthard

THE IRWIN/MCGRAW-HILL ADVANTAGE SERIES FOR COMPUTER EDUCATION

Boston, Massachusetts Burr Ridge, Illinois Dubuque, Iowa
Madison, Wisconsin New York, New York San Francisco, California St. Louis, Missouri

Irwin/McGraw-Hill

A Division of The **McGraw·Hill** Companies

INTEGRATING MICROSOFT® OFFICE 97 PROFESSIONAL for WINDOWS®

This book is printed on acid-free paper.

3 4 5 6 7 8 9 0 WC/WC 9 0 9 8 7

ISBN 0-256-26003-6

Publisher: *Tom Casson*
Sponsoring editor: *Garrett Glanz*
Developmental editor: *Kristin Hepburn*
GTS production coordinator: *Cathy Stotts*
Marketing manager: *James Rogers*
Senior project supervisor: *Denise Santor-Mitzit*
Production supervisor: *Pat Frederickson*
Art director: *Keith McPherson*
Prepress buyer: *Heather D. Burbridge*
Compositor: *GTS Graphics, Inc.*
Typeface: *11/13 Bodoni Book*
Printer: *Webcrafters, Inc.*

http://www.mhcollege.com

WELCOME TO THE IRWIN ADVANTAGE SERIES

The Irwin Advantage Series has evolved over the years to become one of the most respected resources for software training in the world—to date, over 200,000 students have used one or more of our learning guides. Our instructional methodologies are proven to optimize the student's ability to learn, yet we continually seek ways to improve on our products and approach. To this end, all of our learning guides are classroom tested and critically reviewed by dozens of learners, teachers, and software training experts. We're glad you have chosen the Irwin Advantage Series!

KEY FEATURES

The following features are incorporated into the new Microsoft Office 97 student learning guides to ensure that your learning experience is as productive and enjoyable as possible:

CASE STUDIES

Each session begins with a real-world **case study** that introduces you to a fictitious person or company and describes their immediate problem or opportunity. Throughout the session, you obtain the knowledge and skills necessary to meet these challenges. At the end of the session, you are given an opportunity to solve **case problems** directly related to the case scenario.

CONCEPTS, SKILLS AND PROCEDURES

Each learning guide organizes and presents its content in logically structured session topics. Commands and procedures are introduced using **hands-on examples in a step-by-step format,** and students are encouraged to perform the steps along with the guide. These examples are clearly identified by the text design.

PERFORM THE FOLLOWING STEPS

Using this new design feature, the step progression for all hands-on examples and exercises are clearly identified. Students will find it surprisingly easy to follow the logical sequence of keystrokes and mouse clicks. No longer do you have to worry about missing a step!

END OF SESSION EXERCISES

Each session concludes with **short answer questions** and **hands-on exercises.** These comprehensive and meaningful exercises are integrated with the session's objectives; they were not added as an afterthought. They serve to provide students with opportunities to practice the session material. For maximum benefit, students should complete all the exercises at the end of each session.

IN ADDITION BOXES

These content boxes are placed strategically throughout the guide and provide information on related topics that are beyond the scope of the current discussion. For example, there are three typical categories that are visually identified by the following icons:

Integration

The key to productive and efficient use of Office 97 is in the integration features for sharing data among the applications. With a few mouse clicks, for example, you can create a PowerPoint presentation from a Word document, copy an Access database into an Excel workbook, and incorporate professional Office Art into your annual report. Under this heading, you will find methods for sharing information among the Microsoft Office 97 applications.

Advanced

In a 200+-page learning guide, there are bound to be features that are important but beyond the scope of the text. Therefore, we call attention to these features and offer suggestions on how to apply techniques or to search for more information.

Internet

The Internet is fast becoming a standard tool for gathering and exchanging information. Office 97 provides a high level of Internet connectivity, allowing the user to draw upon its vast resources and even publish documents directly on the World Wide Web. Although not every student will have a persistent Internet connection, you can review the content under this heading to learn about Office's Internet features.

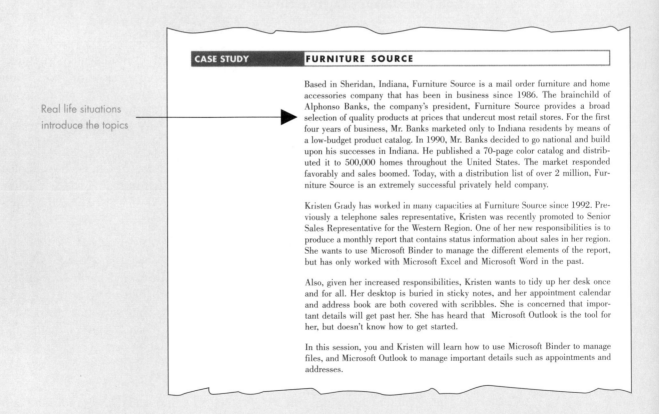

Real life situations introduce the topics

CASE STUDY   **FURNITURE SOURCE**

Based in Sheridan, Indiana, Furniture Source is a mail order furniture and home accessories company that has been in business since 1986. The brainchild of Alphonso Banks, the company's president, Furniture Source provides a broad selection of quality products at prices that undercut most retail stores. For the first four years of business, Mr. Banks marketed only to Indiana residents by means of a low-budget product catalog. In 1990, Mr. Banks decided to go national and build upon his successes in Indiana. He published a 70-page color catalog and distributed it to 500,000 homes throughout the United States. The market responded favorably and sales boomed. Today, with a distribution list of over 2 million, Furniture Source is an extremely successful privately held company.

Kristen Grady has worked in many capacities at Furniture Source since 1992. Previously a telephone sales representative, Kristen was recently promoted to Senior Sales Representative for the Western Region. One of her new responsibilities is to produce a monthly report that contains status information about sales in her region. She wants to use Microsoft Binder to manage the different elements of the report, but has only worked with Microsoft Excel and Microsoft Word in the past.

Also, given her increased responsibilities, Kristen wants to tidy up her desk once and for all. Her desktop is buried in sticky notes, and her appointment calendar and address book are both covered with scribbles. She is concerned that important details will get past her. She has heard that Microsoft Outlook is the tool for her, but doesn't know how to get started.

In this session, you and Kristen will learn how to use Microsoft Binder to manage files, and Microsoft Outlook to manage important details such as appointments and addresses.

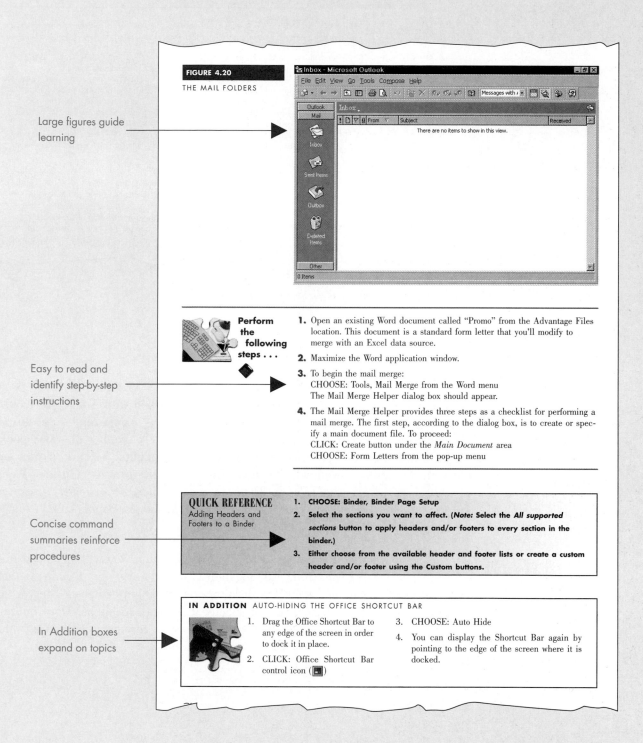

Large figures guide learning

FIGURE 4.20

THE MAIL FOLDERS

Easy to read and identify step-by-step instructions

Perform the following steps . . .

1. Open an existing Word document called "Promo" from the Advantage Files location. This document is a standard form letter that you'll modify to merge with an Excel data source.

2. Maximize the Word application window.

3. To begin the mail merge:
   CHOOSE: Tools, Mail Merge from the Word menu
   The Mail Merge Helper dialog box should appear.

4. The Mail Merge Helper provides three steps as a checklist for performing a mail merge. The first step, according to the dialog box, is to create or specify a main document file. To proceed:
   CLICK: Create button under the *Main Document* area
   CHOOSE: Form Letters from the pop-up menu

Concise command summaries reinforce procedures

QUICK REFERENCE
Adding Headers and
Footers to a Binder

1. CHOOSE: Binder, Binder Page Setup
2. Select the sections you want to affect. (*Note:* Select the *All supported sections* button to apply headers and/or footers to every section in the binder.)
3. Either choose from the available header and footer lists or create a custom header and/or footer using the Custom buttons.

In Addition boxes expand on topics

IN ADDITION AUTO-HIDING THE OFFICE SHORTCUT BAR

1. Drag the Office Shortcut Bar to any edge of the screen in order to dock it in place.
2. CLICK: Office Shortcut Bar control icon (▣)
3. CHOOSE: Auto Hide
4. You can display the Shortcut Bar again by pointing to the edge of the screen where it is docked.

Students practice with
real life projects

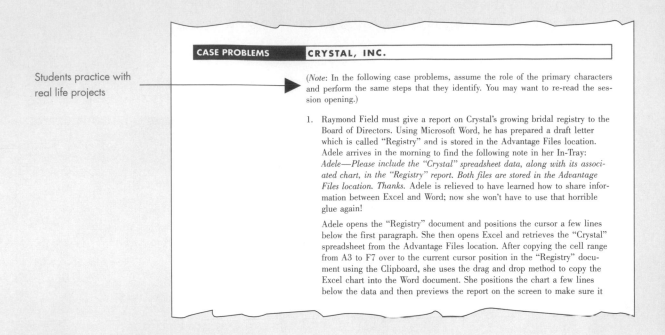

CASE PROBLEMS   **CRYSTAL, INC.**

(*Note*: In the following case problems, assume the role of the primary characters and perform the same steps that they identify. You may want to re-read the session opening.)

1. Raymond Field must give a report on Crystal's growing bridal registry to the Board of Directors. Using Microsoft Word, he has prepared a draft letter which is called "Registry" and is stored in the Advantage Files location. Adele arrives in the morning to find the following note in her In-Tray: *Adele—Please include the "Crystal" spreadsheet data, along with its associated chart, in the "Registry" report. Both files are stored in the Advantage Files location. Thanks.* Adele is relieved to have learned how to share information between Excel and Word; now she won't have to use that horrible glue again!

   Adele opens the "Registry" document and positions the cursor a few lines below the first paragraph. She then opens Excel and retrieves the "Crystal" spreadsheet from the Advantage Files location. After copying the cell range from A3 to F7 over to the current cursor position in the "Registry" document using the Clipboard, she uses the drag and drop method to copy the Excel chart into the Word document. She positions the chart a few lines below the data and then previews the report on the screen to make sure it

TEXT SUPPLEMENTS

ADVANTAGE FILES

Certain hands-on examples and exercises are marked with a disk ◆ icon, indicating the need to retrieve a document file from the **Advantage Files location.** These document files may be provided to you in a number of ways: packaged on a diskette accompanying this text, or on the computer network at your school. You may also download the files from the ***Advantage Online*** Web site (http://www.irwin.com/cit/adv). *These documents files are extremely important to your success.* Check with your instructor or lab advisor for details on how to acquire the Advantage Files.

In addition to identifying the Advantage Files location, you will also need to specify a **Data Files location.** This location is used to save the documents that you create and may either be a blank diskette or a folder on the network server. Again, your instructor or lab advisor will specify the proper locations. More information on the file locations and the proper techniques for retrieving and saving information is provided inside the back cover of this book.

CD-ROM INTERACTIVE TUTORIALS

In addition to using this book, you may have access to our *Advantage Interactive* software. These interactive multimedia tutorials are fully integrated with the material from each session and make effective use of video clips, screen demonstrations, hands-on exercises, and quizzes. You will enjoy the opportunity to explore these tutorials and learn the software at your own pace. For ordering information, please refer to the coupon inside the front cover.

INSTRUCTOR'S RESOURCE KIT

For instructors and software trainers, each learning guide is accompanied by an **Instructor's Resource Kit (IRK).** This kit provides suggested answers to the short-answer questions, hands-on exercises, and case problems appearing at the end of each session. Furthermore, the IRK includes a comprehensive test bank of additional short-answer, multiple-choice, and fill-in-the-blank questions, plus hands-on exercises. You will also find a diskette copy of the Advantage Files which may be duplicated or placed on your network for student use.

SUPPORT THROUGH THE WWW

The Internet, and more specifically the World Wide Web, is an important component in our approach to software instruction for the Office 97 application series. The *Advantage Online* site at http://www.irwin.com/cit/adv is a tremendous resource for all users, providing information on the latest software and learning guide releases, download options for the Advantage Files, and supplemental files for the Instructor Resource Kits. We also introduce new methods for you to communicate with the authors, publisher, and other users of the series. As a dynamic venture, *Advantage Online* will evolve and improve over time. Please visit us to see the latest developments and contribute your valuable feedback.

NETWORK TESTING

Evaluation and assessment are important components of any instructional series. We are committed to providing quality alternatives to traditional testing instruments. With our Irwin Network Test Interactive software, instructors can select questions, create and administer tests, and then calculate grades—all on-line! Visit the *Advantage Online* site for more information on how we are progressing in this exciting area.

Before you begin

As with any software instruction guide, there are standard conventions that we use to indicate menu options, keystroke combinations, and command instructions.

MENU INSTRUCTIONS

In Office 97, all Menu bar options and pull-down menu commands have an underlined or highlighted letter in each option. When you need to execute a command from the Menu bar—the row of menu choices across the top of the screen—the tutorial's instruction line separates the Menu bar option from the command with a comma. Notice also that the word "CHOOSE" is always used for menu commands. For example, the command for quitting Windows is shown as:

CHOOSE: File, Exit

This instruction tells you to choose the File option on the Menu bar and then to choose the Exit command from the File pull-down menu. The actual steps for choosing a menu command are discussed later in this guide.

KEYSTROKES AND KEYSTROKE COMBINATIONS

When two keys must be pressed together, the tutorial's instruction line shows the keys joined with a plus (+) sign. For example, you can execute a Copy command in Windows by holding down CTRL and then pressing the letter **c**.

The instruction for this type of keystroke combination follows:

PRESS: CTRL+c

COMMAND INSTRUCTIONS

This guide indicates with a special typeface and color the data that you are required to type in yourself. For example:

TYPE: **Income Statement**

When you are required to enter unique information, such as the current date or your name, the instruction appears in italic. The following instruction directs you to type your name in place of the actual words: "your name."

TYPE: *your name*

ACKNOWLEDGMENTS

This series of learning guides is the direct result of the teamwork and heart of many people. We sincerely thank the reviewers, instructors, and students who have shared their comments and suggestions with us over the past few years. We do read them! With this valuable feedback, our guides have evolved into the product you see before you. We also appreciate the efforts of the instructors and students at Okanagan University College who classroom tested our guides to ensure accuracy, relevancy, and completeness.

We also give many thanks to Garrett Glanz, Kristin Hepburn and Tom Casson from Irwin for their skillful management of this text. In fact, special recognition goes to all of the individuals mentioned in the credits at the beginning of this guide. And finally, to the many others who weren't directly involved in this project but who have stood by us the whole way, we appreciate your encouragement and support.

WRITE TO US

We welcome your response to this book, for we are trying to make it as useful a learning tool as possible. Write to us in care of Garrett Glanz, Richard D. Irwin, 1333 Burr Ridge Parkway, Burr Ridge, IL 60521. Thank you.

Sarah E. Hutchinson
sclifford@mindspring.com

Glen J. Coulthard
current@junction.net

Contents

SESSION 1
Fundamentals

SESSION 2
Sharing Information

SESSION 3
Working with Objects

SESSION 4
Managing Your Desktop

SESSION 5
Step-by-Step with OLE

SESSION 6
Comprehensive Case Study

Integrating Microsoft Office 97 for Windows

Fundamentals

SESSION OUTLINE

Introducing Microsoft Office 97
The Office 97 Applications
Working with Multiple Applications
Summary
Key Terms
Exercises

INTRODUCTION

For the price of a single software program only a few years ago, you can now purchase a complete assortment of the hottest new programs available. Microsoft Office 97 for Windows provides the most powerful suite of Windows applications ever assembled into one box. In this session, you are introduced to Windows and each of the component applications that make up Office 97. You learn how to work efficiently with multiple application programs, use the Windows taskbar, and access the Microsoft Office Help facility.

CASE STUDY   **MOUNTAIN WEAR**

Antonio is a sales representative for Mountain Wear, Inc. of Austin, Texas, a manufacturer of rugged footwear. He shares a small office with two other sales representatives and the district manager, Rita Bingham. Only Rita has her own private office. Antonio and the two other representatives share an open space separated by shallow cubicle walls. In other words, nobody, except for Rita, has any privacy. As a result, Antonio ensures that he looks the part of the diligent employee and keeps his desk area extremely tidy. This is Antonio's preferred working environment; he even wants the information showing on his computer screen to be neatly organized!

Being relatively new to the job, Antonio wants to do everything he can to prove his competence to his peers, which includes making full use of his desktop computer. Microsoft Office 97 for Windows came installed on his computer, but Antonio has only used Microsoft Word and Microsoft Excel in the past. He wants to learn about all the applications that are part of Microsoft Office, because just maybe a powerful software tool that would save him some time is sitting right under his nose. He would also like to learn more about sharing information among programs and about the general workings of Office so that he can improve his own productivity.

By the end of this session, you and Antonio will be familiar with the primary applications in Microsoft Office, how to switch between them, and how to organize them on the desktop.

INTRODUCING MICROSOFT OFFICE 97

Microsoft Office 97 for Windows combines the most popular and exciting software programs available into a single suite of applications. In the Professional edition, Office 97 includes Microsoft Word, Microsoft Excel, Microsoft PowerPoint, Microsoft Access, and the all-new Microsoft Outlook, an integrated desktop information tool that manages your e-mail, calendar, contacts, to do lists, journal, and Office documents. Office 97 also provides shared applications (sometimes called "server applications") that let you create and insert clip art, organizational charts, and mathematical equations into your word processing documents, electronic spreadsheets, and presentations.

All software products are born with specific design goals. For Office 97, Microsoft concentrated on maintaining consistency across the primary applications and supporting the easy sharing of data between applications. Of particular interest is how Microsoft incorporated support for the Internet into the primary applications. We describe these features in more detail below.

CONSISTENCY ACROSS APPLICATIONS

One of the major design objectives of Office 97 was to maintain consistency among the primary applications. The result of keeping the interface consistent is an extraordinary boost in your productivity by lessening the time required to learn how to use a product. To promote consistency within the Office family, all applications share common menus, dialog boxes, toolbar buttons, keyboard shortcuts, and miniapps. Figure 1.1 illustrates how the top-level menus in Word, Excel, Access, and PowerPoint are almost identical except for some application-specific menu commands. After working with these applications, you will also notice that each program has two general toolbars, named *Standard* and *Formatting*. Many of the buttons or icons on these toolbars are available across all of the Office applications.

FIGURE 1.1

TOP-LEVEL MENU BARS IN MICROSOFT OFFICE'S PRIMARY APPLICATIONS

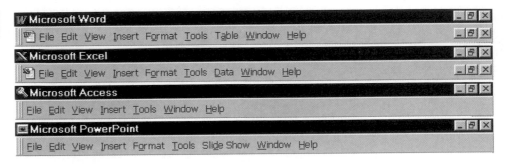

Another Office feature that improves consistency is the use of keyboard shortcuts, sometimes called **accelerator keys.** For example, you can press `CTRL`+**s** in any Office application to save the current document and `CTRL`+**p** to send it to the printer. After learning to perform these keyboard shortcuts in Word, you already know how to save and print a worksheet in Excel.

All of Office's primary applications use Intellisense technology, helping users focus on their work and not on their software. Examples of Intellisense are automatic spell and grammar checking, wizards that lead you through performing basic and complex tasks, and the *Auto Web Link*, which automatically converts a World Wide Web address into a hyperlink. (*Note*: We define *hyperlinks* shortly, in the Internet Features section.) Office 97 offers additional help system features, including an animated and customizable character called the Office Assistant who provides helpful information as you work.

INTEGRATION FEATURES

Many would say that the essence of Office 97 is its ability to share data among the suite of applications. For example, you can place an Excel chart in a report that you write using Word, a Word document in a PowerPoint presentation, an Access database in an Excel worksheet, and so on. You can also create and insert objects using shared applications—such as Microsoft Office Art and Microsoft Organization Chart—without ever leaving the current application. Using Microsoft Binder, you can assemble Word, Excel, and PowerPoint documents into a single file for distribution. Binder also allows you to print a collection of documents with consistent headers and footers and with consecutive page numbering.

INTERNET FEATURES

One of the most exciting innovations in Office 97 is its ability to take advantage of the World Wide Web and the Internet. For those of you new to the online world, the **Internet** is a vast collection of computer networks that spans the entire planet, connected by standard telephone lines. The term **Intranet** is used to refer to a local or wide area network that uses Internet technologies to share information within an organization. To access the Internet, you need a network or modem connection that links your computer to an account on the university's network or to an independent Internet Service Provider (ISP).

Once connected, you use web browser software, such as Microsoft Internet Explorer or Netscape Navigator, to access the **World Wide Web (WWW)**. The WWW provides a visual interface for the Internet and lets you search for information by simply clicking on highlighted words and images, known as **hyperlinks**. When you click a link, you are telling your web browser to retrieve and then display a page from a web site. Each web page has a unique location or address specified by its **Uniform Resource Locator** or **URL**. One example of a URL is: http://www.microsoft.com. For more information on the Internet and World Wide Web, visit your local bookstore, campus computing center, or computer users group.

Microsoft Office 97 provides a consistent set of tools for publishing documents, spreadsheets, presentations, and databases to the web and for accessing help directly from Microsoft's web site. Specifically, each Office application includes a Web toolbar that lets you quickly open, search, and browse documents on your local computer, Intranet, and the Internet. Furthermore, you can create your own hyperlinks and share your document with the entire world after publishing it to a web server.

INSTALLING MICROSOFT OFFICE

The Microsoft Office installation program copies the desired applications, along with several smaller applications called **mini-apps**, to your hard disk. A typical installation of Microsoft Office Professional creates folders for the Office applications in the "Microsoft Office" folder, which is located in the "Program Files" folder. Folders are also created for the mini-apps within the "\Windows" folder. Because you can specify the desired directories for each application during the installation process, the directory structure on your computer may be different.

THE OFFICE 97 APPLICATIONS

Without further ado, let's take a closer look at the applications available in Microsoft Office 97.

 ## MICROSOFT WORD

Microsoft Word 97 for Windows is a word processing software program that lets you create, edit, format, print, and permanently store documents such as letters, memos, and reports. In addition to the standard word processing capabilities, Word 97 enables you to do the following:

- view your documents in a number of different formats including normal, page layout, and outline view modes
- use wizards and templates for creating tables, performing mail merges, and writing standard documents such as agendas and resumes
- show and edit multiple pages on-screen at the same time using the multi-page print preview feature

MICROSOFT EXCEL

Microsoft Excel 97 for Windows is an electronic spreadsheet for organizing, analyzing, and charting statistical, financial, and mathematical data. Some of Excel's key capabilities include:

- create a workbook that contains worksheets, chart sheets, macro sheets, and Visual Basic programming modules
- enhance your worksheets with fonts, borders, colors, and patterns
- use wizards for entering functions, importing text files, creating tables, and charting worksheet data

MICROSOFT POWERPOINT

Microsoft PowerPoint 97 for Windows is a presentation graphics program that enables you to create on-screen presentations, overhead transparencies, speaker's notes, audience handouts, and 35mm slides. In addition to hundreds of predefined templates for slide backgrounds, PowerPoint enables you to do the following:

- use text, clip art, graphics, charts, and other media in your slides
- apply special transitional effects and time-coding options
- use wizards and templates for creating slides, recommending content, and picking styles and colors for presentations

MICROSOFT ACCESS

Available in Office Professional Edition, Microsoft Access 97 for Windows is a relational database management system for microcomputers. Access enables you to store and manipulate large amounts of data. For example, you can use Access to maintain inventory records, sort personnel lists, and summarize accounting data. Some key capabilities include the following:

- store millions of records in databases up to 1GB in size
- specify which records to view using the new Filter-By-Selection and Filter-By-Form tools, and then save these as queries for later use
- use graphical query-by-example (QBE) for performing complex search and retrieval operations

- use wizards for creating standard business and home database applications, importing information, designing forms and reports, and producing mailing labels

MICROSOFT OUTLOOK

Microsoft Outlook is a desktop information tool that provides a central location for keeping track of messages, appointments, addresses, to-do lists, and other activities. The following is a sampling of the tasks you can perform with Outlook:

- schedule and view appointments on a daily, weekly, or monthly basis
- set tasks and reminders in a task list, and then view their status using a variety of retrieval methods
- track and maintain a list of business and personal contacts
- track annual events, such as birthdays, anniversaries, and holidays
- organize e-mail and fax messages

MICROSOFT MINI-APPS

Rather than building similar features into each application, Microsoft makes several mini-apps accessible to all applications. Some of these mini-apps include the following:

Clip Gallery

Enables you to select and insert clip art, pictures, sound, and video into your documents. The following is a sample clip art image from the Clip Gallery:

Equation Editor

Enables you to create complex equations using special math symbols and typesetting standards. For example:

$$\sigma^2 = \frac{\sum_{i=1}^{N}(X_i - \mu)^2}{N}$$

Graph   Enables you to easily insert a graph into your document, without having to launch Excel. For example:

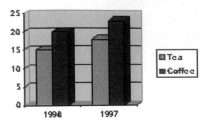

Organization Chart   Enables you to design, build, and insert an organizational chart into your document. For example:

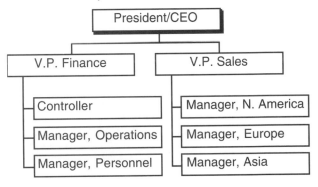

WordArt   Allows you to apply special effects to textual information in your document.

In Session 2, you will use several of these mini-apps in preparing documents, worksheets, and slides.

WORKING WITH MULTIPLE APPLICATIONS

With the multitasking capabilities of Windows, you can load and work with multiple application programs concurrently. Multitasking distributes the computer's processing time among running applications, ensuring that each program gets its fair, or required, share. The Windows feature that you will use frequently in multitasking is called the **taskbar.** By default, the taskbar borders the bottom of your screen. The name of each application you use is represented by a button on the taskbar; to switch to a different application, you simply click its button. You can also organize application windows using the taskbar. This section describes how you use the taskbar to switch among programs and to better organize your desktop.

MULTITASKING

The taskbar acts as the control center for multitasking in Windows. It enables you to switch easily between applications, arrange application windows on the desktop, and close applications. And the best part—the taskbar can remain visible on your screen while you are working in an application program.

In this section, you load Windows, followed by Word, Excel, and PowerPoint.

Perform the following steps . . .

1. Turn on the power switches to the computer and monitor. After a few seconds, the Windows desktop will appear (Figure 1.2.). (*Note:* The desktop interface on your computer may look different from Figure 1.2.)

FIGURE 1.2

THE WINDOWS DESKTOP

Desktop icons —

Start button —

Taskbar

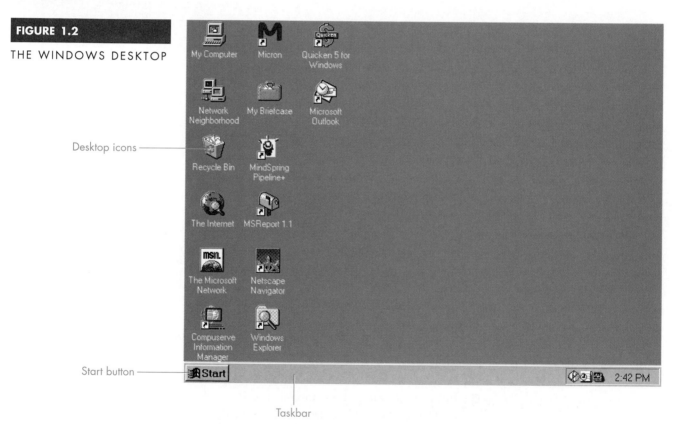

2. If a Welcome to Windows dialog box appears, do the following:
CLICK: Close button (☒) in the top right-hand corner of the window

3. Next you load Microsoft Word from the Start menu. Assuming Microsoft Office is installed on your computer, the New Office Document and the Open Office Document menu options appear in the Start menu. To load Word:
CHOOSE: New Office Document from the Start menu
The dialog box in Figure 1.3 should appear. From this dialog box, you

choose the type of document you want to create from the list of available wizards and templates. Office will then load the appropriate application.

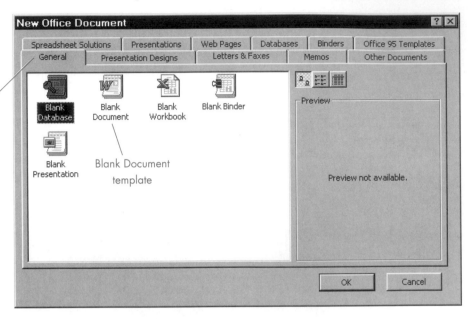

4. DOUBLE-CLICK: Blank Document (📄) template option
   A Word document appears on the screen. Notice that the taskbar is still visible.

5. Ensure that the Word application window is maximized. If the window is not maximized, click the Maximize button (🔲) in its Title bar.

6. To practice multitasking, let's load a new Microsoft Excel document.
   CHOOSE: New Office Document from the Start menu
   DOUBLE-CLICK: Blank Workbook (📊) template option
   You will now have two applications (Word and Excel) open and running in memory. You can always tell which applications are currently open by looking at the button names on the taskbar.

7. Currently, you are viewing Excel's application window. To switch to Word's application window:
   CLICK: Microsoft Word's button on the taskbar

8. Before continuing, let's open a new PowerPoint document.
   CHOOSE: New Office Document from the Start menu
   DOUBLE-CLICK: Blank Presentation (📄) template option
   (*Note*: You may notice that your computer is slowing down as you open new documents and launch additional programs. This often indicates that your computer is using the hard disk to simulate random access memory, or RAM. Adding more memory to your computer will alleviate this problem.)

9. If the New Slide dialog box appears:
   CLICK: Cancel command button

10. Ensure that the PowerPoint application window is maximized. You should now have three applications (Word, Excel, and PowerPoint) open and

running in memory. Review the buttons that now appear on the taskbar and then click them to practice switching among the open applications.

QUICK REFERENCE
Starting a New Document

1. **CHOOSE: New Office Document from the Start menu**
2. **DOUBLE-CLICK: a wizard or template option**

QUICK REFERENCE
Switching Between Applications

- **CLICK: application's button on the taskbar, or**
- **CLICK: application's Title bar on the desktop**

ORGANIZING YOUR DESKTOP

Working with multiple application windows open at the same time can be quite confusing. To better organize your desktop interface, you use the taskbar's context-sensitive shortcut menu and the Minimize ( ), Restore ( ), and Maximize ( ) buttons that appear in the application's Title bar. In this section, you practice minimizing, maximizing, cascading, tiling, and manipulating application windows.

Perform the following steps . . .

1. To minimize the PowerPoint window:
CLICK: Minimize icon ( ) for the PowerPoint application window
(*Note*: The application window's Minimize button is located in the Title bar, near the top right-hand corner of the application window. If you click the Minimize button for the presentation window by accident, the current presentation window will be minimized, but the application will remain maximized. Refer to the graphic below for clarification.)

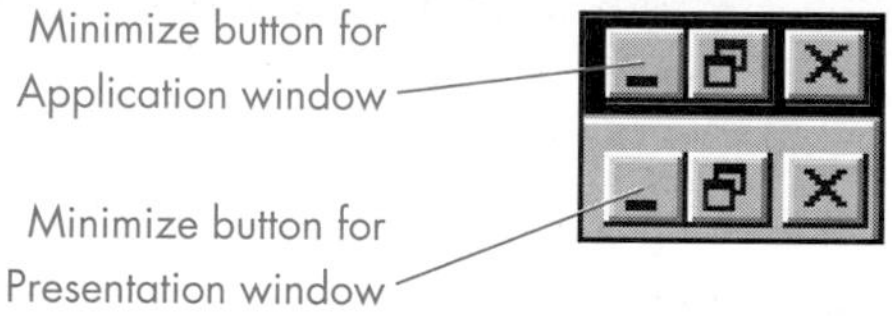

2. To tile the open application windows, you right-click an empty part of the taskbar and then make a selection from the shortcut menu that appears. Do the following:
RIGHT-CLICK: a blank area on the taskbar (to the left of the clock)
The following menu appears:

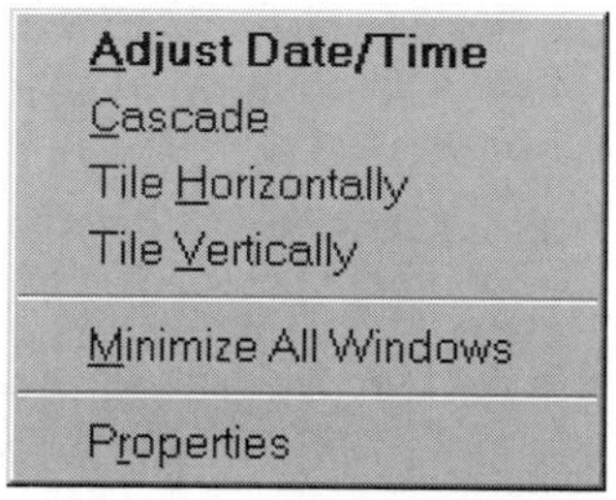

(*Note*: Depending where you positioned the pointer when right-clicking, the Adjust Date/Time option may or may not appear.)

3. CHOOSE: Tile Horizontally
Your screen should now appear similar to Figure 1.4. Notice that the Power-Point window was not tiled with the other applications; only windows that are open are arranged on the desktop. Notice that neither window is selected as the active window, as typically displayed by a different color and type style in the active Title bar.

FIGURE 1.4

TILING APPLICATION WINDOWS ON THE DESKTOP

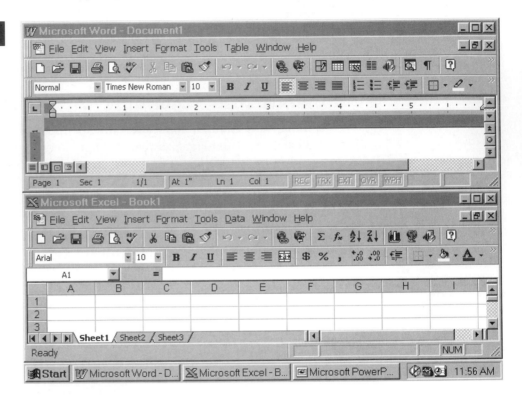

4. To make the Word application window the active window:
CLICK: the Word title bar

5. To maximize the Word application window:
CLICK: Maximize button (◻) in Word's Title bar

6. To switch to the Excel application:
CLICK: Excel button on the taskbar
Notice that the Excel window still conforms to the tiled view and, therefore, only covers half of the desktop area.

7. To close the Excel window, you can either click the application window's Close button (✕) or do the following:
RIGHT-CLICK: Excel button on the taskbar
CHOOSE: Close

8. At this point, the PowerPoint window should appear minimized. Let's display the PowerPoint window and then arrange the windows as you would fan out a hand of playing cards. Do the following:

CLICK: Microsoft PowerPoint on the taskbar
RIGHT-CLICK: an empty part of the taskbar
CHOOSE: Cascade

9. To make the PowerPoint application window the active window:
CLICK: an edge of the PowerPoint window (the Word window covers most of the PowerPoint window)
Your screen should now appear similar to Figure 1.5.

FIGURE 1.5

CASCADING
APPLICATION WINDOWS
ON THE DESKTOP

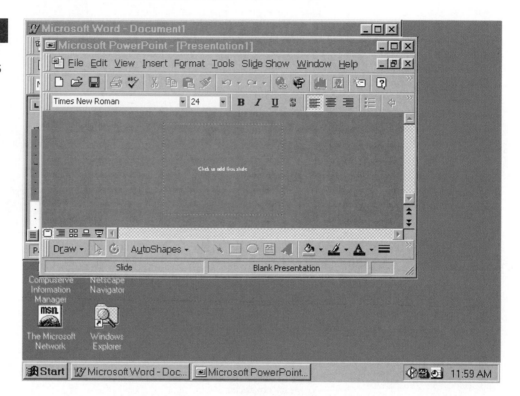

10. Now arrange the two windows to appear similar to Figure 1.6. (*Hint*: To change the size or shape of a window, you drag its borders or the sizing corner, as shown below. To move a window, you drag its Title bar.)

Sizing Corner

FIGURE 1.6

ARRANGING WINDOWS
ON THE DESKTOP

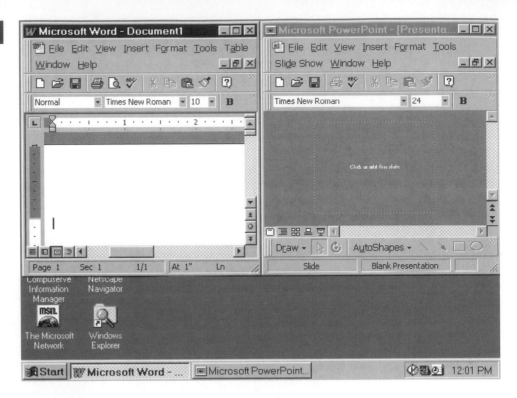

11. Close PowerPoint and Word using either the taskbar or the application's Title bar.

QUICK REFERENCE
Tiling and Cascading
Application Windows

1. **RIGHT-CLICK:** a blank area on the taskbar

2. **CHOOSE: Cascade, Tile Horizontally,** or **Tile Vertically** from the shortcut menu that appears

THE OFFICE SHORTCUT BAR

The Office Shortcut Bar provides another means of launching applications from the Windows desktop or from the primary Office applications. We label the Office Shortcut Bar, in a sample formation, below:

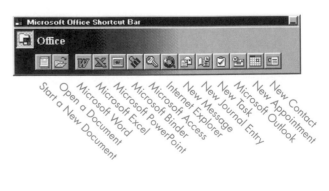

You can customize the Office Shortcut Bar to meet your needs. If the Office Shortcut Bar is installed on your computer, it may load automatically when you load Windows, depending on how Office is set up on your computer. (*Note*: The Office Shortcut Bar is installed on your computer if "Msoffice" appears in the Windows Programs menu.) When you load an Office application, such as Word, the Office Shortcut Bar remains visible, usually in the application's Title bar. Because the Office Shortcut Bar isn't installed on your computer during a typical installation of Office, we don't lead you through using it now.

IN ADDITION AUTO-HIDING THE OFFICE SHORTCUT BAR

1. Drag the Office Shortcut Bar to any edge of the screen in order to dock it in place.

2. CLICK: Office Shortcut Bar control icon (▦)

3. CHOOSE: Auto Hide

4. You can display the Shortcut Bar again by pointing to the edge of the screen where it is docked.

SUMMARY

Microsoft Office is an application suite of the most popular applications for Windows, including Microsoft Word 97, Microsoft Excel 97, Microsoft PowerPoint 97, Microsoft Outlook 97, and Microsoft Access 97 (Professional Edition only.) This session described the individual components that comprise Microsoft Office. You also practiced using the taskbar to switch between applications and to manipulate application windows on the desktop.

KEY TERMS

accelerator keys

Speed keys or keyboard shortcuts that allow you to perform a menu command by pressing a quick key combination.

Clip Gallery

A mini-app provided with Microsoft Office that lets you manage clip art images, pictures, sounds, and video clips and insert them into other applications.

Equation Editor

A mini-app provided with Microsoft Office that lets you create and insert complex mathematical and scientific equations into other applications.

Graph

A mini-app provided with Microsoft Office that lets you create a graph and insert it into other applications.

hyperlinks

Highlighted words or phrases that appear when viewing information on the World Wide Web. You click the hyperlink to view a different document.

Internet

A collection of computer networks that spans the globe.

Intranet

A local or wide area network that uses Internet technologies to share information.

mini-apps

Small application programs bundled with Microsoft Office applications. Rather than being stand-alone applications, they act as servers that provide data to the primary applications.

Organization Chart

A mini-app provided with Microsoft Office that lets you create and insert organizational charts into other applications.

taskbar

A Windows feature that lets you switch among running applications, organize running applications on the desktop, and close running applications.

URL

Standing for *Uniform Resource Locator*, a name given to an address or location on the Internet.

WordArt

A mini-app provided with Microsoft Office that lets you manipulate and apply special effects to text and then insert the text into other applications.

World Wide Web (WWW)

A visual interface for the Internet.

EXERCISES

SHORT ANSWER

1. What applications are included in the Office 97 Professional Edition?

2. Name the mini-apps that were introduced this session.

3. What kind of Internet functionality has Microsoft built into Office 97?

4. How does Microsoft Office provide *consistency* among applications?

5. How does Microsoft Office provide *integration* among applications?

6. What is meant by the term *Intellisense*?

7. Describe two methods to switch between applications.

8. What is the purpose of the Windows taskbar?

9. How do you arrange application windows in a fan-like formation using the Windows taskbar?

10. What is the purpose of the Office Shortcut Bar?

HANDS-ON

1. In the following exercise, you will practice organizing applications on the desktop.

    a. Turn on your computer and load Microsoft Windows.

    b. Start a new document in Microsoft Word using the Start menu.

    c. Maximize Word's application window.

    d. Start a new workbook in Microsoft Excel using the Start menu.

    e. Maximize Excel's application window.

    f. Switch to Word using the taskbar.

    g. Switch to Excel using the taskbar.

    h. Using the taskbar, cascade the application windows.

    i. Using the taskbar, tile the application windows.

    j. Using the mouse, position the application windows to match the screen in Figure 1.7.

    k. On the taskbar, right-click the Word button and choose the Close command.

    l. Using the taskbar again, close the Excel application window.

FIGURE 1.7

ARRANGING
APPLICATION WINDOWS
ON THE DESKTOP

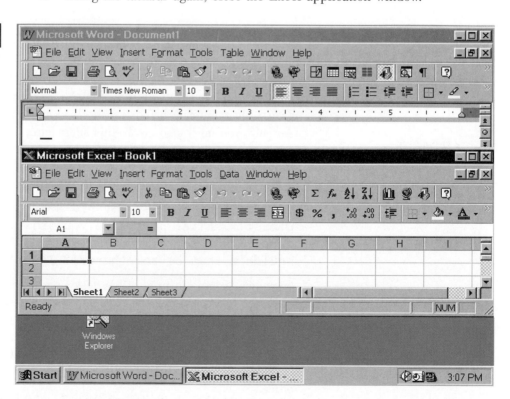

2. If the Office Shortcut Bar is installed on your computer, do the following:

    a. Load the Office Shortcut Bar.

    b. Using the Start a New Document button (▣), open a blank PowerPoint presentation and a blank Excel worksheet. (Notice that the Office Shortcut Bar remains visible in the Title bar.)

    c. Do the following to display help for the Office Shortcut Bar:
        RIGHT-CLICK: Shortcut Bar control icon (▣) on the left side of the toolbar
        CHOOSE: Contents and Index

    d. Using the *Contents* tab, review some of the tasks you can perform using the Office Shortcut Bar.

    e. Exit the Help Topics window.

    f. Close PowerPoint and Excel.

    g. Exit the Office Shortcut Bar by right-clicking the Shortcut Bar control icon (▣) and then choosing Exit.

CASE PROBLEMS   **MOUNTAIN WEAR**

(In the following case problems, assume the role of the primary characters and perform the same steps that they identify. You may want to re-read the session opening.)

1. At the end of a long day, Rita makes her way to Antonio's cubicle to congratulate him on a recent report he delivered. Antonio is relieved. Although he had spent a whole day preparing the report, he wasn't sure if she would appreciate his suggestions. Now that it's quitting time, Antonio decides to draft a short letter to his sister who lives in Memphis, Tennessee. (*Hint*: As Antonio, you must also create this short letter.) He starts a new Word document and then types the following text:

    Dear Rita,

    You won't believe it, my new boss's name is...(drumroll, please)...Rita! Just like you, sis. I'll have to be careful not to call her by your nickname, Ree-Ree. Ha! Wouldn't that be something?!? I was wondering if...

    Somehow arriving in front of his desk unnoticed, Rita startles Antonio with a question. Before looking up or responding, he minimizes Word to hide the letter from view. "Antonio, how do you arrange multiple applications on the desktop? You seem to be the computer expert around here." Pleased to be referred to as the "computer expert," Antonio describes how to tile and cascade open windows. Rita thanks Antonio for his help and heads back to her office.

Alone again, Antonio uses the taskbar to switch back to Microsoft Word. Instead of finishing his letter, he deletes the text that he has already written and replaces it with a summary of his lesson with Rita. Specifically, he describes the procedure for arranging document windows on the desktop. Antonio prints and then saves the document as "Arranging Windows" to the Data Files location.

2. The next morning Antonio enters the office at 7:22 AM, one hour before most of the remaining staff will make an appearance. To get prepared for the day's work, he starts a new PowerPoint presentation and then opens a new document in Microsoft Word. He then sizes the two application windows on the screen so they are both visible. Because he wants to know what new features are available in Microsoft PowerPoint 97, Antonio chooses Contents and Index from the Help menu. He then selects the Contents tab and double-clicks the "Key Information" topic. While reviewing the list of new features, one of his co-workers arrives at work. Not wanting his co-workers to think that he's slacking off, Antonio clicks the Cancel button in the Help Topics window. He then maximizes the Microsoft Word window.

Just at this point, Rita enters and informs everyone present that she wants an office meeting in ten minutes. Antonio quickly exits Word and Power-Point. On paper or using the computer, describe the steps taken by Antonio to perform the tasks outlined above.

Integrating Microsoft Office 97 for Windows

Sharing Information

SESSION

HTTP://WWW

2

IRWIN

COMPUTER & INFORMATION TECHNOLOGY

INTRODUCTION

Ever since we were old enough to understand, most of us have been told that sharing is a good thing. Microsoft now adds a new dimension to sharing, making it, in fact, a "great thing." With Office, you can share databases with tables, tables with reports, reports with presentations, and the list goes on. In this section, you learn how to perform some common integration tasks using Word, Excel, PowerPoint, and Access.

CASE STUDY	CRYSTAL, INC.

In 1935, Mr. Roger P. Field opened Crystal, Inc., in Boulder, Colorado. At first, the store carried and sold only the finest crystal. "Business was good for the first ten years, but it wasn't what I had hoped for when we first opened the store," said Mr. Field, who is now in his late 80s. Nonetheless, Mr. Field's store slowly became known as one of Boulder's finest institutions.

In 1955, Mr. Field listened to his most respected advisors, his children, and decided to expand Crystal's product line to include fine silver and china, linens, European pottery, cutlery, and even some paintings. Business immediately picked up and his store became financially successful, as well as a popular tourist stop. The store was always full of excitement and, as Mr. Field likes to remind people, "the cash registers were always busy."

Mr. Field's youngest son, Raymond, took control of the store over 15 years ago. Adele Suderman has been his assistant for the past five years. Situated on the fourth and top floor of the store, Adele's office is small but inviting, with a spectacular view of the neighboring mountains. She likes her job, which entails writing letters to customers and generating reports for Raymond. Sometimes she creates and prints charts using Microsoft Excel and then manually pastes those charts into reports. She also uses Microsoft Access to manage Crystal's growing customer database.

Adele realizes that she could perform some aspects of her job more efficiently. Specifically, she's heard that Microsoft Windows and Microsoft Office let users share data between applications. She definitely wants to know more, but has never had the time to learn. For example, she would like to send a standard announcement letter to selected customers in her Access database. Rather than manually cutting and pasting charts, she wants to copy data from her Excel worksheets directly into Microsoft Word. Being experienced at using the applications separately, Adele now wants to learn to work with multiple programs and to share data among them.

In this session, you and Adele learn how to copy and move information between Microsoft Office applications, insert and edit objects, and perform mail merges.

COPYING AND MOVING INFORMATION

Windows enables you to easily exchange information among different applications. The three primary methods for sharing information are **pasting, linking,** and **embedding.** Regardless of the method, the process is very similar to a regular cut or copy and paste procedure. For instance, to copy a cell's contents from a worksheet into a word processing document, select the cell and then issue the Edit, Copy command to place it on the Clipboard. After moving to the word processing application, issue the Edit, Paste command to place a copy of the Clipboard data into the document.

USING THE CLIPBOARD

When you cut or copy information from a document, Windows places the information in a temporary storage area called the Clipboard. You can paste the contents of the Clipboard into another location in the same application or into another application. When you paste information, you are not supplying a link between applications or document files; you are simply placing a snapshot of information into the destination document. To update the pasted data in the destination document, you must repeat the process of copying from the source document. Pasting is used when you need to perform a one-time exchange of information.

The general process for copying and moving information using the Clipboard is summarized in the following steps:

a. Select the text, graphic, or object that you want to copy or move.

b. Cut or copy the selection to the Clipboard.

c. Move the insertion point to where you want to place the information.

d. Paste the information from the Clipboard into the document.

e. Repeat Steps c and d, as desired.

Information resides on the Clipboard until it is cleared or until another piece of information is cut or copied. The Clipboard tools for cutting, copying, and pasting, common across all Microsoft Office applications, appear in Table 2.1.

TABLE 2.1 Copying and Moving Information Using the Clipboard	*Description*	*Menu Command*	*Toolbar Button*	*Keyboard Shortcut*
	Moves the selected object from the document to the Clipboard	Edit, Cut	✂	CTRL + x
	Copies the selected object to the Clipboard	Edit, Copy	📄	CTRL + c
	Inserts the contents of the Clipboard at the insertion point	Edit, Paste	📋	CTRL + v

---

QUICK REFERENCE

Copying and Moving Moving Information Using the Clipboard

- To move information using the Clipboard:
  CLICK: Cut button (✂)
- To copy information using the Clipboard:
  CLICK: Copy button (📄)
- To paste information using the Clipboard:
  CLICK: Paste button (📋)

USING DRAG AND DROP

The drag and drop method is the easiest and most intuitive way to copy and move information short distances. The Clipboard is not used during a drag and drop operation; therefore, you can only copy or move a selection from one location to another. In other words, you are not able to perform multiple "pastes" of the selection. This method works well for simple "from-here-to-there" copy and move operations.

In addition to using drag and drop within an application, OLE 2.0 technology now lets you use drag and drop to copy and move objects between applications. To perform drag and drop copying, select an object (for example, an Excel chart), drag it to its destination in another application window (perhaps a Word document), and then release the mouse button to drop it into place.

WHAT IS OLE, ANYWAY?

OLE is an acronym for Object Linking and Embedding, a technology that facilitates sharing and transferring data among Windows-based applications. OLE enables you to move from application-centric computing, where you perform a specific task in a specific application, to document-centric computing, where you perform a specific task using whichever applications are necessary. Before proceeding, you should be familiar with the following terms:

- The document in which the data was first composed, before being transferred to a compound document, is called a **source document.**

- The application that you use to create the source document is called the **server application.**

- A document that receives data from another application is called a **compound document** or a destination document.

- The application that accepts data into its compound document is called the **client application.**

In the following diagram (Figure 2.1), the two server applications (Microsoft Excel and Microsoft Word) are providing the data from their source documents to the compound document in the client application (Microsoft PowerPoint). For more detailed definitions on linking and embedding terminology, refer to Table 2.2.

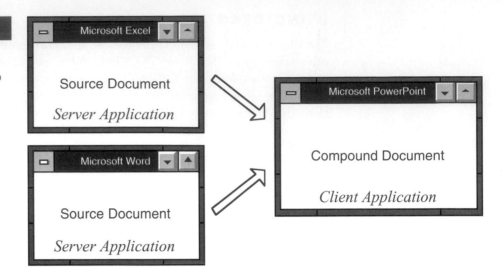

FIGURE 2.1

DIAGRAM SHOWING
SOURCE DOCUMENTS
SERVING A COMPOUND
DOCUMENT

TABLE 2.2

Definitions:
Object Linking
and Embedding
Technology

Term	*Definition*
Object	Any type of data, such as a document, table, chart, database, slide, sound file, or video clip, that has been linked or embedded into a document. An OLE object can be an entire file or a part of a file.
Linking	The process of inserting an object into a compound document. With linking, only the location of the object's source document is actually stored in the compound document.
Embedding	The process of inserting an object into a compound document. With embedding, the object's data is stored in the compound document along with the name of the server application.
Server Application	The application that provides objects for linking or embedding into compound documents. For example, Excel is the server application for worksheet tables and charts presented and stored in a Microsoft Word compound document. (*Note:* An application can be both a client and a server.)
Client Application	The application used to create a compound document. A client application accepts linked or embedded objects from server applications. For example, Microsoft Word is commonly a client for Excel tables and charts.
Compound Document	A single document that contains data in several different formats; for example, a Word document may contain a bit-mapped graphic, an Excel table, a sound file, and a video clip.

LINKING

Rather than using the Clipboard's static method for pasting information, you can use the Edit, Paste Special command to establish a link between a source and a compound document. When you make changes in the source document (using the server application), the information in the linked compound document (in the client application) is automatically updated.

You link files when the information you need from a source document is also used by other compound documents. For example, you may have a monthly sales forecast that needs to be included in several related reports. In this case, linking the compound report documents to the one source document is the most efficient method for automatically updating the reports when the forecast changes. As you may expect, linking is also very useful for sharing information with workgroups over a network.

EMBEDDING

Embedding information involves inserting an object into a **compound document (client application)** from a **source document (server application).** Unlike a linked object, an embedded object does not retain a connection to the source document; everything is contained in the compound document. Therefore, an embedded object is not automatically updated when information in its source document changes.

LINKING VERSUS EMBEDDING

To the person reading or using a compound document, linked and embedded objects appear identical. The primary difference between a linked object and an embedded object is where the data is stored. With a linked object, the data remains in the original source document file and the client application stores only a reference to the file in the compound document. With an embedded object, the data is stored in the compound document file along with information about the server application.

To determine which method you should use for inserting objects, review the comments in Table 2.3 and then ask yourself these questions:

- "How am I going to use the information?"
- "Who else needs the information?"
- "Who is responsible for updating the information?"

TABLE 2.3 Linking Versus Embedding	*Link an Object When...*	*Embed an Object When...*
	The information is shared among multiple users on your network.	You are the only user of the information.
	The information must be updated dynamically (done in the source document and updated automatically in all compound documents).	You want to edit or format the data from within the compound document.
	Disk storage space is a concern; a compound document that uses linked objects is typically much smaller than one that uses embedded objects.	You plan on showing your presentation or giving your document to users not on your network. In other words, the source documents to which your compound document is linked are not available to them.

INSERTING AND EDITING OBJECTS

This section explains the "how to" of inserting objects. In the next section, you'll learn these same methods using a hands-on approach.

EMBEDDING AN OBJECT

To insert clip art, WordArt, and chart objects, you use the Insert, Picture command. To insert other types of objects such as an organization chart or an equation, you use the Insert, Object command. In Figure 2.2, we show the Object dialog box. Using this dialog box, you select an object type on the Create New tab and click OK to proceed. The selected object's server application is launched and you may begin creating the object that you want to insert into the current document.

FIGURE 2.2

ONE EXAMPLE OF THE OBJECT DIALOG BOX

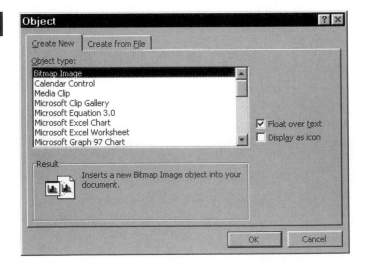

There are two methods for returning to the document after you've finished creating the object. If the server application supports Visual Editing, you simply click in the document outside of the object's frame. If, however, the server application launched itself in a separate window, choose the File, Exit and Return to Document command. When asked to update the object in the document, click the Yes command button or press (ENTER).

To insert an existing object, you can use one of the following methods:

- Choose the Edit, Copy command to place the object on the Clipboard and then choose Edit, Paste after positioning the insertion point in the destination document. The pasted information is automatically embedded.

- Choose the Edit, Copy command to place the object on the Clipboard and then choose Edit, Paste Special. From the dialog box, select the first option in the *As* list box (usually the object type).

- Choose the Insert, Picture command and then choose From File to specify the desired filename.

- Choose the Insert, Object command and select the *Create from File* tab to specify the desired filename.

- Drag the object from the server application's window to the compound document in the client application's window.

VISUAL EDITING

Visual Editing, a feature of OLE, makes it easy to update an embedded object in a compound document. To edit an embedded object, such as an Excel table, you simply double-click the object. Rather than being launched into the server application in order to perform the changes, you remain where you are and the current application's menus and toolbars are replaced with those of the server application. You can perform the same functions as in the original server application, and you don't have to leave the current document window!

LINKING AN OBJECT

The two methods for establishing a link between a source document and a compound document are as follows:

- Once an object is placed on the Clipboard, choose the Edit, Paste Special command to specify how it should be inserted into the document. To link the information, you select the *Paste Link* option in the dialog box that appears.

- Similarly to embedding an object, choose the Insert, Object command and then select the *Create from File* tab to specify a source document for linking. To establish the link, you select the *Link to File* check box before pressing (ENTER) or clicking on OK.

APPLICATIONS WORKING TOGETHER

Here's what you've been waiting for! In this section, you will learn how to integrate Microsoft Office's primary applications.

SHARING DATA BETWEEN WORD AND EXCEL

Microsoft Word and Microsoft Excel work very well together. Word even places an "Insert Microsoft Excel Worksheet" button (⊞) on its Standard toolbar, making it easy to insert a table of figures without leaving the comfort of Word. It is also surprisingly simple to drag and drop an object, such as a chart, between the two applications. In most scenarios, Word plays the part of the client application while Excel acts as its server.

In this section, you retrieve a worksheet file named "Cruises" from one of the following locations:

- *Advantage Files location* - This location may be on a diskette, in a folder on your local hard drive, or in a folder on a network server. The Advantage Files are the document files that have been created for you and that you will retrieve in the remaining exercises in this guide.

- *Data Files location* - This location may also be on a diskette, in a hard drive folder, or in a network folder. You will save the documents that you create or modify to the Data Files location. It may even be the same disk or folder where you keep the Advantage Files, however **if you are using diskettes we recommend you keep the Advantage Files and Data Files on separate diskettes.** Otherwise, you may run out of storage space.

> ***IMPORTANT:*** *Before continuing, ensure that you know the location of your Advantage Files and where to store your Data Files. If necessary, ask your instructor or lab assistant for additional information.*

Now we demonstrate the ease with which Word and Excel exchange data. Let's start with an example of drag and drop.

Perform the following steps . . .

1. Make sure that you have identified the location for retrieving your Advantage Files and for saving your Data Files. If you require a diskette, place it in the diskette drive now.

2. Start a new Word document and a new Excel worksheet using the method you're most comfortable with. Ensure that both document windows are maximized.

3. Close the Office Assistant window if it appears in either Word or Excel.

4. Since you won't be using the Standard or Formatting toolbars in the next few sections, let's remove them from view in order to free up more real

estate in the document windows. In Excel:
RIGHT-CLICK: the Menu bar to display the toolbar menu
CHOOSE: Standard
RIGHT-CLICK: the Menu bar again
CHOOSE: Formatting

5. Now switch to Word and remove the Standard and Formatting toolbars from view.
CLICK: Microsoft Word button in the taskbar
RIGHT-CLICK: the Menu bar to display the toolbar menu
CHOOSE: Standard
RIGHT-CLICK: the Menu bar again
CHOOSE: Formatting

6. Using the taskbar, tile the windows vertically to appear similar to Figure 2.3.

FIGURE 2.3

TILING APPLICATION
WINDOWS ON THE
DESKTOP

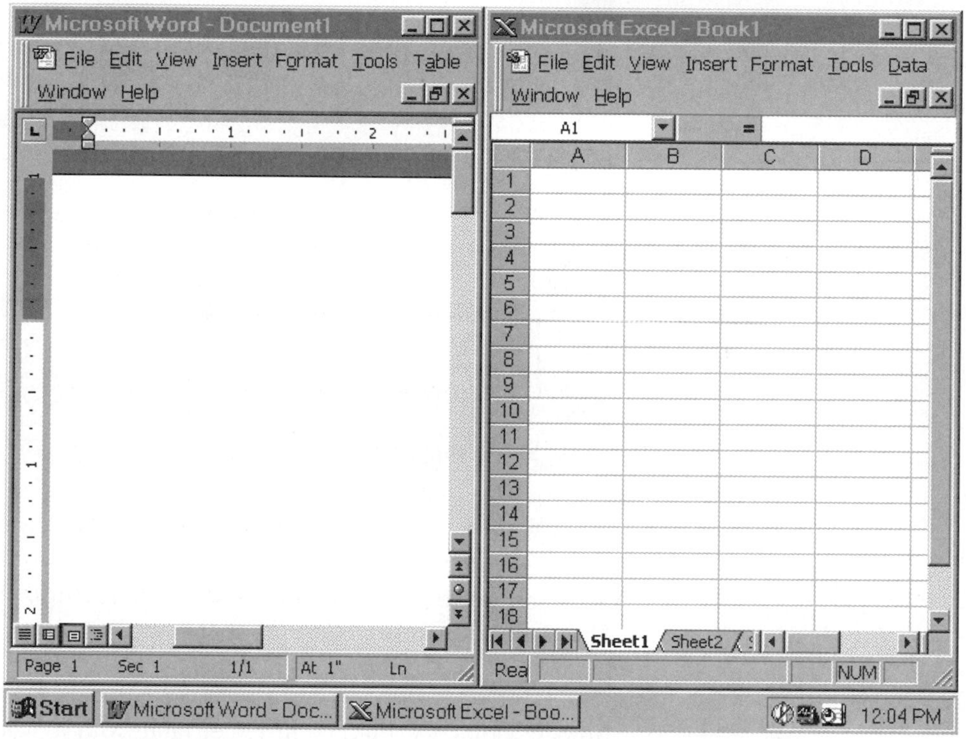

7. In Excel, load the "Cruises" worksheet from the Advantage Files location. This worksheet includes a small table of values and a chart.

8. To copy the chart between applications using drag and drop, position the mouse pointer over the chart and do the following:
PRESS: CTRL and hold it down
CLICK: the chart and hold down the left mouse button
DRAG: the chart from the Excel worksheet to the Word document, positioning it approximately ½ inch from the left margin and ½ inch from the top margin (refer to Figure 2.4)

Notice that the mouse pointer changes to a frame as you move it over the top of the Word document.

9. Now release the mouse button. The chart is immediately embedded into the Word document. (*Note*: You would perform the same steps to *move* a chart, except you do not hold down the [CTRL] key.) Your screen should now appear similar to Figure 2.4.

FIGURE 2.4

DRAG AND DROP
COPYING BETWEEN
APPLICATIONS

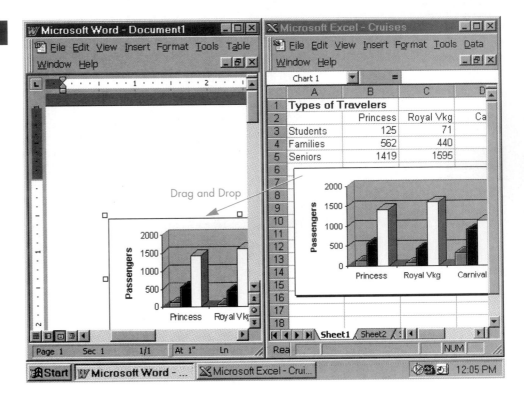

In addition to using drag and drop to copy or move objects between open application windows, you can drag and drop objects to an application's button on the taskbar. The target application will maximize so that you can position the object. This procedure will work even if the application window you're copying or moving data to is minimized.

Now let's practice linking an Excel table with a Word document.

Perform the following steps . . .

1. Make Excel the active application. (*Hint*: Click once on its Title bar.)

2. SELECT: the cell range from A1 to D5

3. To copy this information to the Clipboard:
CHOOSE: Edit, Copy from the Excel menu

4. Make Word the active application.

5. Position the insertion point above the chart object and then click. The cursor should now appear at the top of the document.

6. To set up the link between the Word object and the Excel worksheet:
CHOOSE: Edit, Paste Special from the Word menu
SELECT: *Paste Link* option button
SELECT: Formatted Text (RTF) in the *As* list box
The Paste Special dialog box should now appear similar to Figure 2.5.

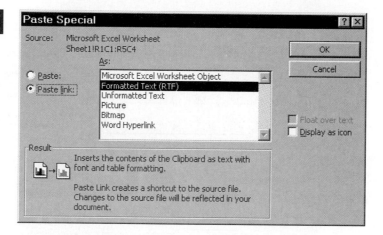

7. To complete the operation:
PRESS: (ENTER) or CLICK: OK

8. Let's prove that the Word object is linked to the Excel worksheet. First, ensure that you can see the Word document:
CHOOSE: View, Zoom
SELECT: *75%* option button
PRESS: (ENTER) or CLICK: OK

9. Now, make Excel the active application and enter a new value for the Student travelers on Princess lines:
SELECT: cell B3
TYPE: **1150**
PRESS: (ENTER)
You may have noticed two things when you modified the value in cell B3. First, the Word table object was immediately updated since it is linked. Second, the graph in Excel changed to reflect the new value but the embedded chart in Word did not change because it is *not* linked. Your screen should now appear similar to Figure 2.6.

FIGURE 2.6

LINKING AND
EMBEDDING OBJECTS
BETWEEN WORD AND
EXCEL

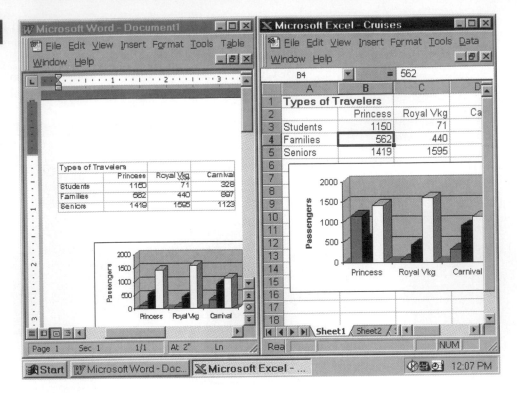

10. Practice changing some other numbers in the worksheet before continuing.

11. Remove the chart from the Word document by selecting the chart and then pressing the **DELETE** key.

12. Copy the new chart from the Excel worksheet to the Word document using the Clipboard. (*Note*: In Excel, make sure you select the entire chart object, including labels, and not just the graph itself.) In Word, paste the chart as a linked "Microsoft Excel Chart Object" using the Paste Special command.

13. Make Excel the active application window.

14. Manipulate the numbers in the worksheet. The table and chart in the Word document should be updated automatically upon each entry since they are both linked to the worksheet.

15. Before continuing, redisplay the Standard and Formatting toolbars in both Word and Excel.

16. Close Word and Excel without saving.

QUICK REFERENCE Pasting and Linking Information	1. Copy or cut the desired information to the Clipboard from the source document. 2. Move the insertion point to the compound or destination document. 3. CHOOSE: Edit, Paste Special 4. SELECT: *Paste Link* option button 5. PRESS: ENTER or CLICK: OK

SHARING DATA BETWEEN WORD AND POWERPOINT

There are several opportunities for sharing data between Microsoft Word and Microsoft PowerPoint. If you've already written an outline in Word, you can transform it into a PowerPoint slide presentation in less time than it would take to send it to the printer. If you've created a spiffy set of slides in PowerPoint, you can convert the presentation to a Word outline as the basis for a report. And these activities are additional to the normal copy and paste, drag and drop, and linking and embedding topics that we've been discussing up to this point.

Now you practice converting a Word outline into a PowerPoint slide presentation.

Perform the following steps . . .

1. In PowerPoint, start a new Blank presentation using the method of your choice. When the New Slide dialog box appears:
CLICK: Cancel command button

2. Maximize the PowerPoint application window.

3. There are two methods for converting a Word outline into a presentation. In PowerPoint, you can open an existing Word outline document and it will automatically convert it to a presentation. In Word, you can send an outline to PowerPoint by choosing File, Send To, Microsoft PowerPoint from the Menu bar. Since you are already working in PowerPoint, let's open the Word outline into PowerPoint. The name of the Word document file is "Hardware." Do the following:
CLICK: Open button (⬚)
SELECT: *your Advantage Files location*
SELECT: All Files from the *Files of type* drop-down list box
SELECT: "Hardware" from the *Name* list box
PRESS: ENTER or CLICK: Open command button
After a few moments, PowerPoint's outline view appears, as shown in Figure 2.7. The six main topics (formatted using the Heading 1 style in Word) have become the titles for six slides in a new PowerPoint presentation. All text formatted using the Heading 2 style in Word has been transformed into bullet points on the six slides.

FIGURE 2.7

CONVERTING A WORD
OUTLINE INTO A
POWERPOINT
PRESENTATION

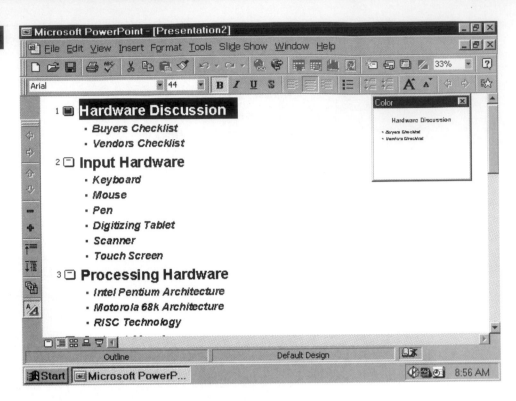

4. To apply a design to the presentation:
CLICK: Apply Design button (⬜) on the Standard toolbar
SELECT: Contemporary Portrait from the list box
PRESS: **ENTER** or CLICK: Apply

5. To display the slides as they will be seen by your audience:
SELECT: Slide Show button (⬜) at the left-hand side of the horizontal scroll bar
CLICK: with the mouse to proceed through the presentation

6. Save the new PowerPoint presentation as "Hardware" to the Data Files location.

QUICK REFERENCE
Creating a PowerPoint
Slide Presentation from
a Word Outline

Retrieve the desired Word outline document using PowerPoint's File, Open command. (*Note:* To list non-PowerPoint files, make sure to select All Files from the *Files of type* drop-down list box.)

PowerPoint allows you to copy entire slides, or individual objects from a slide, into a Word document or an Excel worksheet. This feature may become important to you if you've added special objects such as tables, charts, and graphics to your slides and need to use them elsewhere. Now you will practice copying an entire slide from a PowerPoint presentation into a Word document.

Perform the following steps . . .

1. Start a new Word document and ensure that the application window is maximized.

2. Switch to PowerPoint using the taskbar.

3. View the "Hardware" presentation in Slide view.

4. Using the vertical scroll bar, move to the slide titled "Output Hardware" (slide 4).

5. To copy the slide to the Clipboard:
CHOOSE: Edit, Select All
CLICK: Copy button ([icon])
(*Note:* The Edit, Select All command selects all of the objects on the slide. However, there is no way to select the background template.)

6. Switch to Word using the taskbar.

7. In Word, the cursor should be blinking at the top of the document.

8. To paste the slide into the Word document:
CHOOSE: Edit, Paste Special
CHOOSE: Picture
PRESS: (ENTER) or CLICK: OK
Notice that the entire contents of the slide were copied, except for the background template.

9. To size the slide:
CLICK: slide object to select it
DRAG: the sizing corner until the slide covers half its original size

10. Close Word and PowerPoint without saving any of the changes to the document or presentation.

QUICK REFERENCE
Displaying a PowerPoint
Slide in a Word Document

1. Open a PowerPoint presentation and move to the desired slide.
2. CHOOSE: Edit, Select All from the PowerPoint menu
3. CLICK: Copy button ([icon])
4. Position the insertion point in the Word document.
5. CLICK: Paste button ([icon]) to insert the slide into the document

PERFORMING MAIL MERGES

One of the most powerful features of word processing software is the ability to merge names and addresses into standard documents for printing. This process, called **mail merge,** allows you to create a single document and then print personalized copies for numerous recipients. Mail merge activities are not limited, however, to producing form letters. Merging can be used to print a batch of invoices, promotional letters, or legal contracts.

Merging requires two files: the **data source** and the **main document.** The data source contains the variable data, such as names and addresses, to be merged with the main document or form letter. In this section, you perform two separate mail merges. In the first scenario, you merge an existing Word document with a list of names stored in an Excel worksheet. In the second scenario, you merge the same Word document with selected records from an Access database. You will use Microsoft Word, Microsoft Excel, and Microsoft Access in this section.

MERGING WITH AN EXCEL DATA SOURCE

In this section, you merge a Word form letter with information stored in an Excel worksheet.

Perform the following steps . . .

1. Open an existing Word document called "Promo" from the Advantage Files location. This document is a standard form letter that you'll modify to merge with an Excel data source.

2. Maximize the Word application window.

3. To begin the mail merge:
   CHOOSE: Tools, Mail Merge from the Word menu
   The Mail Merge Helper dialog box should appear.

4. The Mail Merge Helper provides three steps as a checklist for performing a mail merge. The first step, according to the dialog box, is to create or specify a main document file. To proceed:
   CLICK: Create button under the *Main Document* area
   CHOOSE: Form Letters from the pop-up menu

CLICK: Active Window command button

Your Mail Merge Helper should appear similar to Figure 2.8. (*Note*: The path to the Advantage Files location may be different on your computer.)

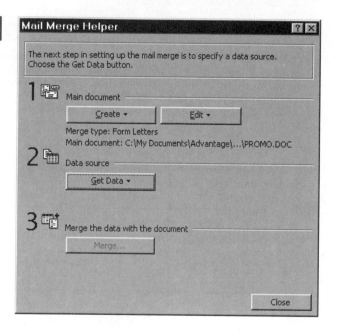

5. To complete the second step:
CLICK: Get Data button under the *Data Source* area
CHOOSE: Open Data Source

6. In the dialog box that appears:
SELECT: *your Advantage Files location*
SELECT: MS Excel Worksheets in the *Files of type* drop-down list
SELECT: "Clients" from the file list
PRESS: **ENTER** or CLICK: Open
Microsoft Excel is launched in the background and the worksheet is opened.

7. After a few moments, a new dialog box appears asking you to specify the range of worksheet cells that contain the database. Since the entire spreadsheet file is a database and the option is already highlighted:
PRESS: **ENTER** or CLICK: OK

8. The next dialog box to appear informs you that there are no merge fields in the main document:
CLICK: Edit Main Document button

9. Using the Insert Merge Field button appearing at the left-hand side of the Merge toolbar, create a merge document that matches Figure 2.9. (*Note*: You select a field by clicking the Insert Merge Field button and then selecting the appropriate field from the list. The field list corresponds to fields in the "Clients" worksheet.)

FIGURE 2.9

THE MAIN DOCUMENT
WITH MERGE FIELDS

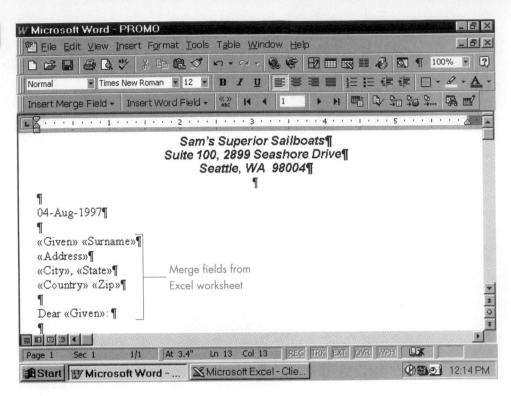

10. Now that the data source file and the main document have been created or specified, you are ready to perform the merge. The output of the merge is typically sent to a new document or to the printer. If there are only a few records in the data source file, you may prefer to merge to a new document, save the document for review, and then print the document at a later time. If there are several hundred records in the data source file, merging directly to the printer is probably your best option. To merge the names from the Excel worksheet into the form letter document:
CLICK: Merge to New Document button (🔳) in the Merge toolbar

11. After a few seconds, the new document appears with the first record merged onto Page 1 of the form letter. Scrolling down the document will reveal the remaining merged letters. Save this new document as "Excel Form Letter" to the Data Files location. Your screen should now appear similar to Figure 2.10.

FIGURE 2.10

THE COMPLETED
"EXCEL FORM LETTER"
MERGE DOCUMENT

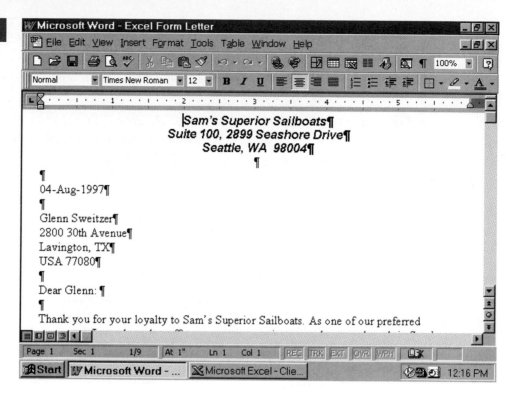

FIGURE 2.10

THE COMPLETED
"EXCEL FORM LETTER"
MERGE DOCUMENT

12. Close the "Excel Form Letter" document and the "Promo" document without saving the changes.

QUICK REFERENCE
Performing a Mail
Merge Using an
Excel Data Source

1. **CHOOSE: Tools, Mail Merge**
2. **Specify a main document file.**
3. **Specify an Excel worksheet file as the data source.**
4. **Specify the desired worksheet range (or the entire spreadsheet file) containing the data for merging.**
5. **Edit the main document, inserting merge fields as desired.**
6. **On the Merge toolbar, select either the Merge to New Document button ( ) or the Merge to Printer button ( ).**

MERGING WITH AN ACCESS DATA SOURCE

When you require more database power than Excel can provide, you can always turn to Access. Rather than merging all of the records stored in an Access database, you can even specify particular records using an Access query. In this section, you merge information from an Access table into a Word form letter.

Perform the following steps . . .

1. To save memory, ensure that Microsoft Excel is closed.

2. In Word, open the "Promo" document from the Advantage Files location. (*Note*: This is the original "Promo" document, without merge fields.)

3. You begin the mail merge as before:
   CHOOSE: Tools, Mail Merge
   The Mail Merge Helper dialog box appears again.

4. To specify the Word merge document:
   CLICK: Create button under the *Main Document* area
   CHOOSE: Form Letters
   CLICK: Active Window command button

5. To specify the Data Source:
   CLICK: Get Data button under the *Data Source* area
   CHOOSE: Open Data Source

6. SELECT: *your Advantage Files location*
   SELECT: MS Access Databases in the *Files of type* drop-down list
   SELECT: "Customer" from the file list
   PRESS: ⟨ENTER⟩ or CLICK: Open

7. Microsoft Access is loaded and a new dialog box appears (as shown in Figure 2.11). This dialog box lets you specify a particular table or query that is stored in the database file. To accept the Customer table as the desired data source, do the following:
   PRESS: ⟨ENTER⟩ or CLICK: OK

FIGURE 2.11

MICROSOFT ACCESS
DIALOG BOX

8. The next dialog box to appear informs you that there are no merge fields in the main document:
   CLICK: Edit Main Document button

9. Using Figure 2.9 as a guide, insert the merge codes using the Insert Merge Field button on the toolbar.

10. To merge the names from the Access database into the form letter:
CLICK: Merge to New Document button (🔳) in the Merge toolbar

11. After a few seconds, the new document appears with the first record merged onto Page 1 of the form letter. Save this new document as "Access Form Letter" to the Data Files location. Your screen should appear similar to Figure 2.12.

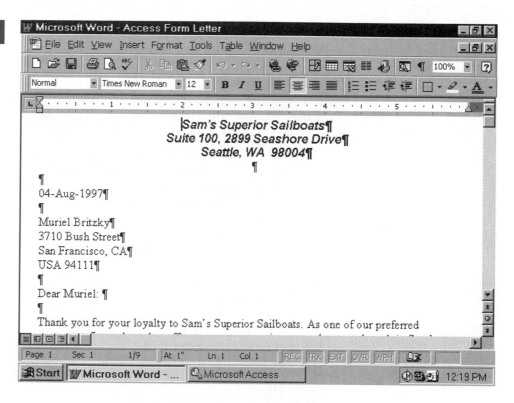

12. Close the "Access Form Letter" document and the "Promo" document without saving the changes.

13. Close all the applications.

QUICK REFERENCE
Performing a Mail Merge Using an Access Database

1. **CHOOSE: Tools, Mail Merge**
2. **Specify a main document file.**
3. **Specify an Access database file as the data source.**
4. **Specify the desired table or query that contains the data for merging.**
5. **Edit the main document, inserting merge fields as desired.**
6. **On the Merge toolbar, select either the Merge to New Document button (🔳) or the Merge to Printer button (🔳).**

IN ADDITION   PERFORMING A MAIL MERGE USING AN ACCESS DATA SOURCE

 You perform the same basic steps as when merging with other types of data sources. After clicking the Get Data button in the Mail Merge

Helper dialog box, choose Use Address Book and then Outlook Address Book.

SUMMARY

This session discussed the various methods for sharing information in the Windows environment. Topics included using the Clipboard, drag and drop, linking, and embedding. The latter half of the session provided an opportunity to illustrate the OLE concepts in hands-on exercises. You learned how to embed an Excel object into a Word document using drag and drop, link a table of values to an Excel worksheet, create a PowerPoint presentation from a Word outline, and merge information from an Excel worksheet and an Access database into a Word document.

Table 2.4 provides a list of the commands and procedures covered in this session.

TABLE 2.4 Command Summary	*Task Description*	*Menu Command*	*Toolbar Button*	*Keyboard Shortcut*
	Move the selected object from the document to the Clipboard	Edit, Cut	✂	CTRL + x
	Copy the selected object to the Clipboard	Edit, Copy	📋	CTRL + c
	Insert the contents of the Clipboard at the insertion point	Edit, Paste	📋	CTRL + v
	Insert the contents of the Clipboard at the insertion point, and specify whether to create a link with the original source document or whether to embed the object	Edit, Paste Special		
	Create an object or insert an existing object into your document	Insert, Picture or Insert, Object		

KEY TERMS

client application
An application that accepts data into a compound document.

compound document

A document that contains data from another application.

data source

A Word document file, Excel spreadsheet, or Access database that captures and stores variable information, such as a list of names and addresses, for the merge process.

embedding

A way of sharing and exchanging information; refers to the process of inserting an object into a compound document that is linked to the server application.

linking

A way of sharing and exchanging information; refers to the process of copying information from a source document into a compound document and establishing a dynamic link between the two.

mail merge

A procedure that typically involves combining data stored in a data file with a form letter created in a word processing software program.

main document

A type of form letter document used by Word in the merge process. The main document file contains codes to insert information from the data source file.

pasting

A way of sharing and exchanging information; refers to the process of copying static information from a source document into a destination document without linking the two documents.

server application

An application that you use to create a source document.

source document

The original document in which information is created for transfer to a compound document.

EXERCISES

SHORT ANSWER

1. What is the most common method of copying and moving information?

2. What is OLE?

3. What is an object?

4. When might you use a compound document?

5. How do you copy an object using drag and drop between applications?

6. How do you link an object that you've copied to the Clipboard?

7. What is meant by the term *Visual Editing*?

8. Name two methods for automatically creating a PowerPoint presentation from a Word outline.

9. Name two data source alternatives for performing a mail merge.

10. After creating a source document and specifying a data source, what are the two options for outputting merged information?

HANDS-ON

(*Note*: Ensure that you know the location of your Advantage Files and where to store your Data Files. If necessary, ask your instructor or lab assistant for additional information.)

1. In this session, you created a PowerPoint presentation from a Word outline. Using the File, Send To, Microsoft Word command, create a Word outline from the "Employee" presentation stored in the Advantage Files location. Save the Word document as "Employee Outline" to the Data Files location. Exit Word and PowerPoint.

2. Using the mailing list information from the Students table in the Access database called "Training," create a new document that personalizes a copy of the "G-Arches" document for each student. Both of these documents are stored in the Advantage Files location. Save this new document as "Golden Mail" to the Data Files location and then close all the applications. Do not save your changes to the "G-Arches" document.

CASE PROBLEMS	CRYSTAL, INC.

(*Note*: In the following case problems, assume the role of the primary characters and perform the same steps that they identify. You may want to re-read the session opening.)

1. Raymond Field must give a report on Crystal's growing bridal registry to the Board of Directors. Using Microsoft Word, he has prepared a draft letter which is called "Registry" and is stored in the Advantage Files location. Adele arrives in the morning to find the following note in her In-Tray: *Adele—Please include the "Crystal" spreadsheet data, along with its associated chart, in the "Registry" report. Both files are stored in the Advantage Files location. Thanks.* Adele is relieved to have learned how to share information between Excel and Word; now she won't have to use that horrible glue again!

   Adele opens the "Registry" document and positions the cursor a few lines below the first paragraph. She then opens Excel and retrieves the "Crystal" spreadsheet from the Advantage Files location. After copying the cell range from A3 to F7 over to the current cursor position in the "Registry" document using the Clipboard, she uses the drag and drop method to copy the Excel chart into the Word document. She positions the chart a few lines below the data and then previews the report on the screen to make sure it looks balanced. Perhaps she should insert a line above the table data or move the chart slightly to the left or right. After previewing the report, she decides to underline the table headings and then saves the letter as "Registry" to the Data Files location. While marveling at her own efficiency, she prints the report and hands it to Raymond as he walks through the door. "Finished already? Adele, this report looks great! Thanks!"

2. As part of her monthly tasks, Adele sends a brief announcement letter to each person in the "Customer" database about upcoming events. Having created many letters of this type in the past, Adele jots down the general format for the announcement on a piece of paper before accessing the computer:

[given] [surname], you are invited to a Coffee reception to meet the famous Italian painter,

Fabio Mortellini

WHEN: January 21

TIME: 10:00 AM–2:00 PM

P.S. Please accept a personally autographed sketch as your free gift!

Adele uses Microsoft Word to create the document and saves her work as "Fabio" to the Data Files location. She then merges the letter with the "Customer" database that was created using Microsoft Access. The "Customer" database is stored in the Advantage Files location and contains nine records. (*Hint*: After choosing Open Data Source, select "Customer" from the Advantage Files location, and then select the Customer table.) To complete the merge document, she then inserts the «Given» and «Surname» merge codes in place of "[given]" and "[surname]" in the "Fabio" document.

When finished, she performs the merge to a new document, saves the document as "Mortellini" to the Data Files location, and then prints the merged letters. Before leaving for lunch, she exits Word, saving the "Fabio" document to the Data Files location.

Integrating Microsoft Office 97 for Windows

Working with Objects

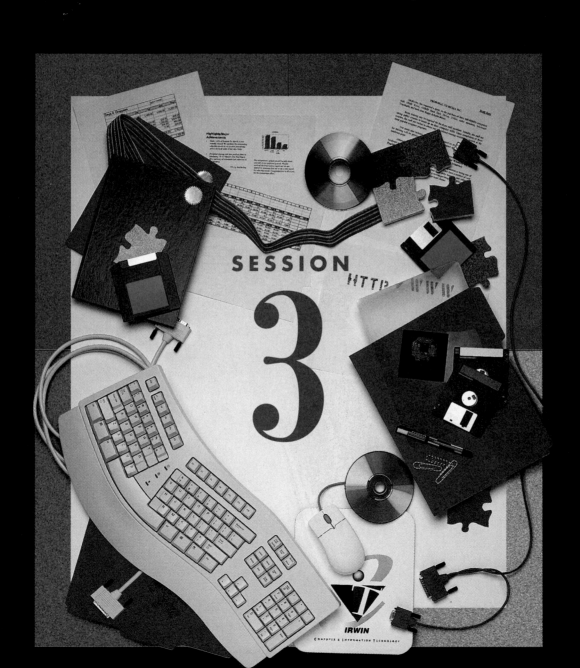

SESSION OUTLINE

About Mini-Apps
Using Microsoft Clip Gallery
Inserting Pictures
Using Microsoft Equation Editor
Using Microsoft Graph
Using Microsoft Organization Chart
Using Microsoft WordArt
Summary
Key Terms
Exercises

INTRODUCTION

If you performed a complete installation of Office on your computer, several Microsoft mini-applications were copied to your hard disk in addition to the primary applications. These applications stay relatively unknown to novice users until they are accidentally stumbled upon. However, they are not complex, nor are they difficult to learn. In this session, you use these mini-apps to practice embedding and editing objects.

CASE STUDY　　　　　**LAKELAND GYM**

Peter Iverrson, the manager of the Lakeland Gym in St. Paul, Minnesota, needs to put a monthly status report together for the president of the club. Peter's assistant, Josephine Keller, has looked through last month's report and suggested several ways to improve on it using Office's mini-applications. Because Peter wants to impress the president, he listened closely to Josephine's comments.

Peter considers himself competent using Word, Excel, and PowerPoint, but he has never worked with the mini-applications that Josephine has mentioned. For example, Josephine suggests that Peter use an organization chart to show the club's employees and their reporting relationships, rather than the existing textual list. Also, she feels that he could jazz up the report by inserting a few graphics. Peter agrees with Josephine's comments, but doesn't believe they can complete the report by tomorrow.

In this session, you and Peter will learn how easy it is to create objects using the following mini-applications: Clip Gallery, Microsoft Equation Editor, Microsoft Graph, Microsoft Organization Chart, and Microsoft WordArt.

ABOUT MINI-APPS

When most of us read the term "application software," we immediately visualize Word, Excel, PowerPoint, or Access. However, an important aspect of any software suite is the availability of mini-applications that add value to the primary applications. **Mini-apps** act as servers to the primary applications, as opposed to being stand-alone, independent programs. These mini-apps enable you to create objects that may be embedded into a document, worksheet, or presentation. In Office 97, Microsoft refers to mini-apps as **Office Tools.** Several Office Tools can be accessed using the Insert, Picture command while others are accessed using the Insert, Object command.

USING MICROSOFT CLIP GALLERY

The Clip Gallery mini-app provides a one-stop shopping mall for all your clip art images, pictures, sounds, and video clips. Figure 3.1 shows the Microsoft Clip Gallery dialog box. In a typical Office installation, a number of clip art images are copied into the Clip Gallery. A **clip art image** is a computer graphic or picture that you can insert into your documents, usually without having to pay royalties or licensing fees to the artist or designer.

FIGURE 3.1

THE CLIP GALLERY
DIALOG BOX

Select a category
to limit the number
of images that
appear

For the selected
category, images
appear in this area

Words that
describe the
selected image

You can also use the Gallery to add your own clips, delete existing clips, and move clips. In the next few sections, you practice working with the Clip Gallery.

INSERTING CLIP ART

A picture is worth a thousand words! Although this phrase is overused, its truth is undeniable. Graphics add personality to your documents and convey information more efficiently than text alone. Unfortunately, many new computer users struggle with the tendency to place too many graphics on a single page. To assist your planning of how and when to use graphics, apply these basic principles: strive for simplicity, use emphasis sparingly, and ensure a visual balance between graphics and text. In this section, you insert a clip art image in a Word document.

Perform the following steps . . .

1. Open Word and then open "Clover" from the Advantage Files location. This letter is a promotional piece for Clover's Car Center, which is offering an opportunity to loyal customers who want to purchase seed stock. Your task is to find a clip art image for the company logo and then insert it under the heading at the top of the page.

2. Position the insertion point immediately below the address line, centered on the screen.

3. To find a logo in the Clip Gallery:
   CHOOSE: Insert, Picture
   CHOOSE: Clip Art
   CLICK: *Clip Art* tab
   The Clip Gallery dialog box should appear similar to Figure 3.1.

4. Rather than trying to scan through all of the images, you can limit your search to a group of clip art images dealing with a specific category. To begin our search for a logo for Clover's Car Center:
SELECT: Transportation from the list of categories

5. SELECT: the red sports car
(*Note*: If this image isn't available on your computer, select a different image.)
PRESS: **ENTER** or CLICK: Insert command button
You are immediately returned to the document. The sports car is disproportionately large, as shown in Figure 3.2. You resize the image in the next step.

FIGURE 3.2

INSERTED CLIP ART
IMAGE

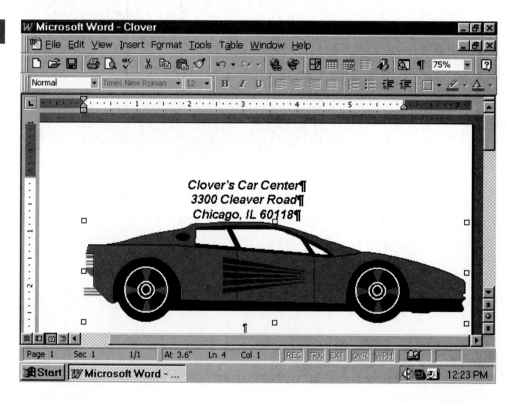

6. Notice that the image is already selected. To resize an object so that it is more proportional to the document, you drag its sizing handles. To move an object, you point at the selected object until a double-headed arrow appears, then drag the object to the new location.

On your own, by referring to Figure 3.3, resize and move the inserted clip art image. Your screen should now appear similar to Figure 3.3.

FIGURE 3.3

SIZING AND MOVING
A CLIP ART IMAGE

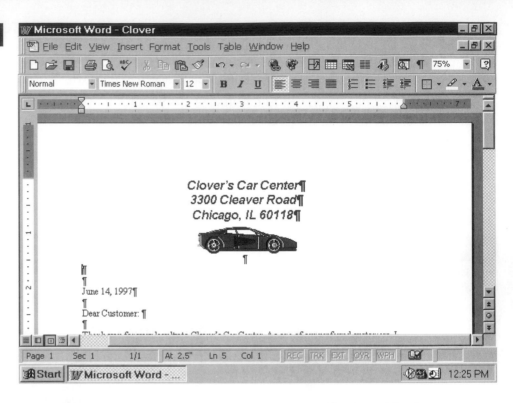

7. Save the document as "Clover's Car Center" to the Data Files location.

8. Close the document.

QUICK REFERENCE
Inserting Clip Art Images

1. **Position the insertion point where you want to insert the object.**

2. **CHOOSE: Insert, Picture, Clip Art**

3. **CLICK:** *Clip Art* **tab**

4. **SELECT: the category and then the desired graphic**

5. **PRESS:** (ENTER) **or CLICK: Insert**

6. **Move and resize the graphic, as necessary.**

INSERTING SOUND AND VIDEO CLIPS

"Sit down and listen to my document." Does the previous sentence sound strange to you? When we think of reviewing documents, we typically think of *reading* them. But now you can include sound clips, and even video clips, in your letters, spreadsheets, and presentations. You can create the sound and video files yourself using one of the many digital recording devices on the market today, or obtain the files from a third party. In these cases, you insert the files in your document by choosing Insert, Picture, From File, or by choosing Insert, Object and then clicking the *Create from File* tab. Or you can choose from the library of sound and video clips in the Clip Gallery. Once it is stored in your document, you experience a sound or video clip by double-clicking its associated object.

Perform the following steps . . .

1. To get a better idea of the types of sounds and video clips you can include in a document:
   CLICK: New button () on the Standard toolbar
   CHOOSE: Insert, Picture
   CHOOSE: Clip Art
   CLICK: *Sounds* tab

2. If a selection of sound clips is available, select a sound clip and then click the Play button. Repeat this procedure for a few more clips.

3. Now:
   CLICK: *Videos* tab

4. If a selection of video clips is available, select a video clip and then click the Play button. Repeat this procedure for a few more clips.

5. Close the Clip Gallery dialog box before continuing.

IN ADDITION DISPLAYING CLIPS STORED ON THE MICROSOFT OFFICE CD

Approximately 3,000 clip art images, 140 pictures, 20 sounds, and 20 video clips are available on the Office 97 installation CD. If this CD is in your CD-ROM drive when you access the Clip Gallery, these additional clips will automatically be accessible from the Clip Gallery dialog box. (*Note:* If you're using Office 97 on a network, you may already have access to these clips.)

IN ADDITION ACCESSING CLIPS STORED ON THE WEB

If your computer has an Internet connection and access to a Web browser, you can access additional clips stored on the Web. In the Clip Gallery dialog box, click the Connect To Web For Additional Clips button. This action connects you to Clip Gallery Live, a web location where you can find, preview, and download clips.

INSERTING PICTURES

You can easily insert photographs in an Office document by clicking the *Picture* tab of the Clip Gallery and then selecting from the library of available photos. (*Note*: Depending on how Office is set up on your computer, these picture files might not be available to you.) Or you can create your own picture files if you have access to a **scanner.** A scanner is a hardware device that converts photographs and other paper-based material into computer images. Just as a photocopier makes a representation from paper to paper, a scanner makes a copy from paper to computer. Once it is saved to the disk, you can insert a picture file into Word, Excel, or PowerPoint by using the Insert, Picture, From File command.

In this section, you use the Insert, Picture, From File command to insert a picture into the "Computer" document, stored in the Advantage Files location.

Perform the following steps . . .

1. Open the "Computer" document located in the Advantage Files location. This file contains a monthly article or flyer that is designed to be given away at local computer stores. Your task is to insert a scanned photograph at the end of the document.

2. Move to the bottom of the document.

3. Make sure that there is at least one blank line between the last paragraph and the end of the document. Position the insertion point on the last line.

4. To insert a photograph that has been stored in the Advantage Files location:
CHOOSE: Insert, Picture, From File
SELECT: *your Advantage Files location*
SELECT: "Lab" from the list box
CLICK: Preview button (⊞)
The dialog box should now appear similar to Figure 3.4.

FIGURE 3.4

THE INSERT PICTURE
DIALOG BOX

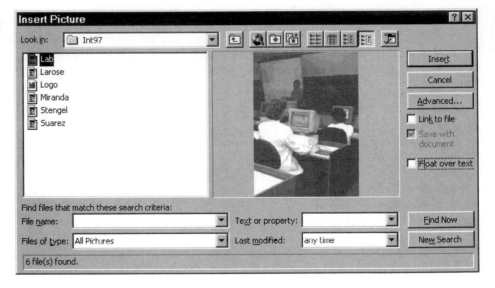

5. Before continuing, ensure that the *Float over text* check box isn't selected. Otherwise, the picture will cover up the document's text.

6. To proceed with inserting the graphic picture into the document:
PRESS: **ENTER** or CLICK: Insert
The graphic appears at the insertion point.

7. You size the image as you do any other object:
CLICK: once on the image
DRAG: the sizing handles to reduce its height and width

8. To add a caption to the graphic:
CHOOSE: Insert, Caption from the Menu bar
Notice that "Figure 1" is inserted automatically.

9. TYPE: : Computer Class at City College
Your dialog box should appear similar to the one shown in Figure 3.5.

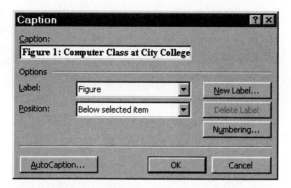

10. PRESS: (ENTER) or CLICK: OK

11. Print the document. (*Note*: You can skip this step if you don't have a printer connected to your computer.)

12. Save the document as "City College" to the Data Files location, replacing the existing version.

13. Close the document.

QUICK REFERENCE
Inserting Pictures

1. **Position the insertion point where you want to insert the picture.**
2. **CHOOSE: Insert, Picture, From File**
3. **SELECT: the desired disk drive and filename**
4. **CLICK: Preview button (▦) to preview the graphic**
5. **To prevent the picture from covering up the document's text, ensure that the *Float over text* check box isn't selected.**
6. **PRESS: (ENTER) or CLICK: OK**

IN ADDITION INSERTING A SCANNED PICTURE

1. Ensure that you've installed Microsoft Photo Editor on your computer and that your computer is connected to a scanner. (*Note:* Microsoft Photo Editor can be installed from the Microsoft Office installation disk.)

2. Position the cursor where you want to insert the scanned picture and then choose Insert, Picture, From Scanner from the Menu bar.

3. Scan the picture and then follow the instructions that your scanner displays on the screen.

4. Edit the image, if necessary, and then choose File, Exit and Return to *Application* from the Menu bar.

USING MICROSOFT EQUATION EDITOR

The Microsoft Equation Editor mini-app allows you to insert mathematical equations into your documents without leaving your current application. Whether you are writing a paper on quantum physics or working in the engineering lab of Motorola, the Equation Editor provides an invaluable tool for compiling complex mathematical elements, such as fractions, exponents, and integrals, into a legible equation.

To build an equation, you select mathematical elements from over 120 templates and 150 symbols. A **template** is an empty form or framework for an equation or expression, such as a fraction. You access templates using the bottom row of buttons on the Equation Editor's toolbar (shown in Figure 3.6). A **symbol** refers to a mathematical symbol. Since these symbols are not typically found in TrueType fonts, they are provided on the top row of the Equation Editor's toolbar. When you click a button on the toolbar, a **palette** of additional options is displayed for that template or symbol.

FIGURE 3.6

THE EQUATION EDITOR'S TOOLBAR

Symbols row
Template row

In this section, you insert an equation into a document.

Perform the following steps . . .

1. The Equation Editor isn't installed as part of a typical Office installation. Before continuing, let's check to see that it's installed on your computer
CLICK: New button (▢)
CHOOSE: Insert, Object
CLICK: *Create New* tab

2. Now scroll through the list of object types until you see Microsoft Equation Editor 3.0 (or 2.0). If you don't find this object type, click the Cancel button and then skip to the "Using Microsoft Graph" section.

3. CLICK: Cancel

4. Open the "Finance" document located in the Advantage Files location. This document provides an income statement for a fictitious company. Your task in this section is to document a simple ratio that measures the company's operating results.

5. Move to the bottom of the document. In the table provided for you, position the insertion point in the second row of the first column.

6. To create a ratio that measures the net profitability of each dollar of sales, do the following:
TYPE: **Profit Margin =**
(*Note*: You are only entering the ratio into the document. Unfortunately, the Equation Editor has no ability to actually perform the calculation.)

7. PRESS: Space Bar once to insert a space between the equal sign and the new equation

8. To create the equation using the Equation Editor:
CHOOSE: Insert, Object

9. In the Object dialog box:
CLICK: *Create New* tab
SELECT: Microsoft Equation 3.0 (or 2.0) from the *Object Type* list box

10. Ensure that the *Float over text* check box isn't selected.

11. PRESS: (ENTER) or CLICK: OK
The Equation Editor toolbar and menu appear in the Word document. (*Hint*: If inserted properly, the object will be surrounded by a hatched or shaded pattern.)

12. The first step in building an equation is to select the appropriate template. Since the Profit Margin ratio is a fraction and cannot be properly created using Word's formatting styles, do the following:
CLICK: Fraction Template button (▯) to display its palette

13. SELECT: Full-size vertical fraction (▯)
The Equation Editor inserts the selected template into your document.

14. With the insertion point in the numerator (above the line):
TYPE: **Net Income**
PRESS: (TAB) to move to the denominator (below the line)
TYPE: **Net Sales**
Notice that the Equation Editor doesn't let you put spaces within the variables' names; they will appear as NetIncome and NetSales.

15. To insert a space manually within the word NetIncome, position the insertion point between the "t" and the "I" and then do the following:
CLICK: Spaces & ellipses button (▯)
SELECT: Thick space (one third of an em) button (▯)
(*Note*: Look at the Status bar to see a description of the button you're pointing to.)

16. To insert a space manually within the word NetSales, position the insertion point between the "t" and the "S" and then do the following:
CLICK: Spaces & ellipses button (▯)
SELECT: Thick space (one third of an em) button (▯)

17. To finish using the Equation Editor and return to Microsoft Word:
CLICK: in the document, outside of the equation's frame
(*Note*: The Visual Editing feature of OLE technology allows you to click in the document to return control to the client application, Word.)

18. Using the steps that you learned above to create the ratio, enter the values (4,750,000.00 and 1,000,000.00) in a full-size vertical fraction in the Computation and Result column. (See Figure 3.7 for a sample.)

19. Position the insertion point immediately to the right of the equation object (in the document) and do the following:
PRESS: Space Bar
TYPE: = .21

20. Ensure that the object isn't selected. Your screen should now appear similar to Figure 3.7.

FIGURE 3.7

THE PROFIT MARGIN RATIO

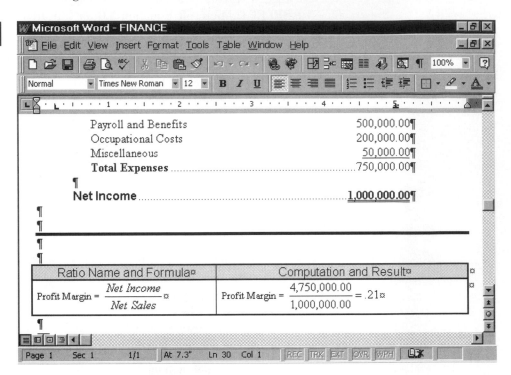

21. Save the document as "Ratios" to the Data Files location.

22. Close the document.

QUICK REFERENCE
Using Microsoft Equation Editor

1. **Position the insertion point where you want to insert the object.**

2. **CHOOSE: Insert, Object**

3. **SELECT: Microsoft Equation 3.0 (or 2.0) on the *Create New* tab**

4. **Check the status of the *Float over text* check box**

5. **PRESS: ENTER or CLICK: OK**

6. **SELECT: templates and symbols from the toolbar**

7. **TYPE: textual and numeric information, as required**

8. **CLICK: in the document to return to the client application**

USING MICROSOFT GRAPH

The Microsoft Graph mini-app is a full-featured charting application that helps you produce great-looking charts and graphs from within a Word document or Power-Point presentation. Graph does not replace Excel, but it does provide a more convenient tool for embedding simple charts into documents. For example, you would use Graph to plot the values already stored in a Word table. If you had a situation that required further analysis of the figures, you would want to use Excel to perform the analysis and chart the data. In this section, we demonstrate how easy it is to add professional graphics to your work using Microsoft Graph.

Perform the following steps . . .

1. Open the "Faxnote" document located in the Advantage Files location. This fax provides a brief note with a table of research values. Your task in this section is to plot the values in a chart that will appear immediately below the table.

2. Move to the bottom of the document and position the insertion point inside the table.

3. To plot the values from a Word table, you must first select the table:
   CHOOSE: Table, Select Table
   The table should appear highlighted before proceeding.

4. To load Microsoft Graph:
   CHOOSE: Insert, Picture
   CHOOSE: Chart
   (*Note*: You can also create a chart from scratch. To do so, position the insertion point where you want the chart to appear and then load Microsoft Graph. A datasheet window appears where you enter the values that you want to plot. You can then proceed as illustrated in this exercise.)

5. Microsoft Graph immediately goes to work and displays a 3-D column chart. (*Note*: You can easily change the chart type using the Chart Type button (◣▾) on the Standard toolbar.) To better view the chart, let's temporarily remove the Datasheet window.
   CLICK: View Datasheet button (▦) in the Standard toolbar
   Your screen should now appear similar to Figure 3.8. Next, you label the X axis.

FIGURE 3.8

THE GRAPH OBJECT

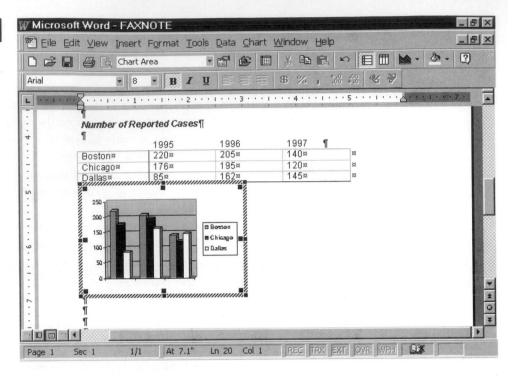

6. To redisplay the datasheet:
CLICK: View Datasheet button (▦)

7. To add labels to the X axis:
CHOOSE: Chart, Chart Options
CLICK: *Axes* tab
SELECT: *Category* option button in the *Category (X) axis* area
PRESS: **ENTER** or CLICK: OK
Now, what you type into the cells above the first row of data will appear along the X axis.

8. Now you need to type the X-axis labels into the first row of the datasheet, directly above the data.
CLICK: the cell above the number "220"
TYPE: **1995**
CLICK: the cell above the number "205"
TYPE: **1996**
CLICK: the cell above the number "140"
TYPE: **1997**
PRESS: **ENTER**

9. To view the graph:
CLICK: View Datasheet button (▦)
Labels should now appear along the X axis.
(*Note*: The process of formatting the chart in Microsoft Graph is identical to the way you would format a chart in Excel. To apply formatting, click the right mouse button on any item in the chart to display its shortcut menu. From this menu, choose the desired formatting command.)

10. Size the chart to the width of the table by dragging the sizing handle on the right border of the chart.

11. If you are still viewing Microsoft Graph's commands, to exit Microsoft Graph and return to the document:
CLICK: in the document, outside of the chart frame

12. In this step, you select the chart and then drag it downward about ½ inch so it isn't so close to the table above.
CLICK: the chart object
DRAG: the chart downward about ½ inch

13. Save the document as "Faxdone" to the Data Files location.

14. Zoom the display to 75%. Your screen should now appear similar to Figure 3.9.

FIGURE 3.9

THE COMPLETED CHART, CREATED USING MICROSOFT GRAPH

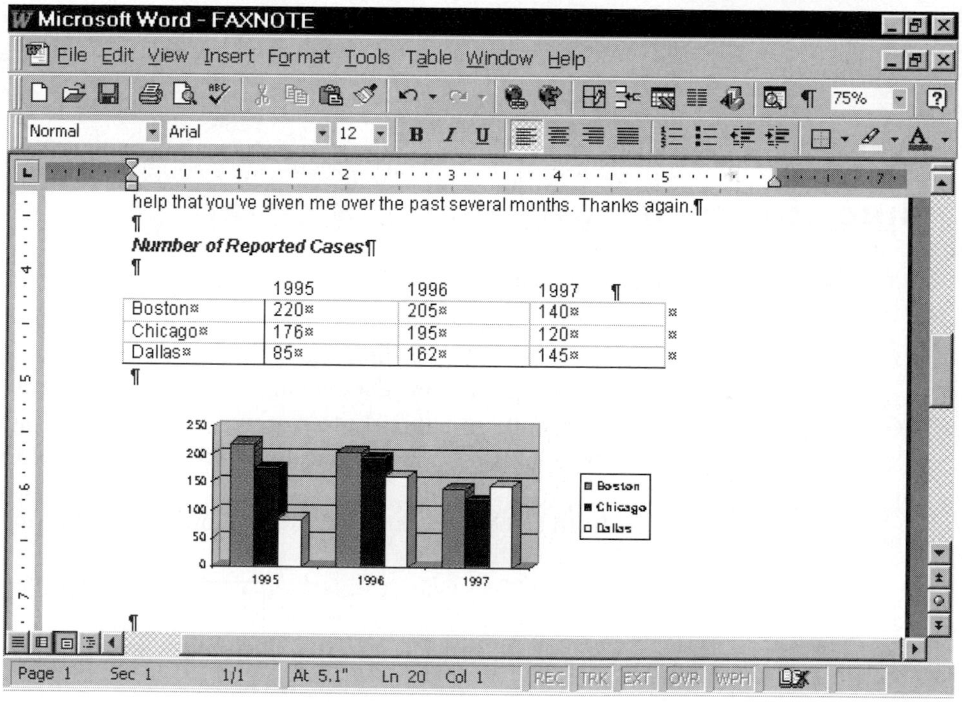

15. Let's assume that you made a mistake in entering Dallas' figures for 1995. The number in the Word table should read 185, not 85. Position the insertion point in the Word table and correct the value for Dallas.

16. Notice that the chart is not linked to the Word table. When you change a value in the table, there is no effect on the chart. To update the chart, you must enter the new value into the Datasheet window as well:
DOUBLE-CLICK: the chart object

17. In the datasheet:
SELECT: cell A3 (for Dallas in 1995)

18. TYPE: 185
PRESS: `ENTER`
The chart is refreshed to show the new value.

19. To complete the editing process:
CLICK: in the document, outside of the chart frame

20. Save the document as "Faxdone" to the Data Files location, replacing the existing version.

21. Close the document.

QUICK REFERENCE
Using Microsoft Graph

1. **SELECT: a Word table (or position the insertion point in the document)**
2. **CHOOSE: Insert, Picture from the Menu bar**
3. **CHOOSE: Chart**
4. **Edit the chart using Graph's commands and procedures.**
5. **CLICK: in the document to return to the client application**

USING MICROSOFT ORGANIZATION CHART

Microsoft's Organization Chart mini-app is a scaled-down version of Banner Blue Software's Org Plus for Windows that allows you to create organizational charts and other hierarchical diagrams. Most commonly, you create an organizational chart to include in a Word document, such as a report or internal memo, or a PowerPoint presentation. Similarly to working with graphics, apply the principles of simplicity, emphasis, and balance to creating **organizational charts.**

In this section, you create the following organizational chart:

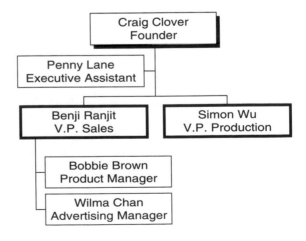

Perform the following steps . . .

1. Open the "Clover" document located in the Advantage Files location. This letter is a promotional piece for Clover's Car Center, which is offering an opportunity to loyal customers who want to purchase seed stock. Your task is to create and embed an organizational chart showing the Clover management team.

2. Move to the end of the first paragraph and insert two blank lines by pressing **ENTER** twice.

3. To create the organizational chart:
CHOOSE: Insert, Object

4. In the Object dialog box:
CLICK: *Create New* tab
SELECT: MS Organization Chart 2.0 from the *Object Type* list box
PRESS: **ENTER** or CLICK: OK
The Organization Chart window appears as shown in Figure 3.10. Notice that the chart begins with only two levels: one box at the top level and three boxes directly underneath on the next level. Levels are also called **groups** in Organization Chart.

FIGURE 3.10

THE ORGANIZATION
CHART WINDOW

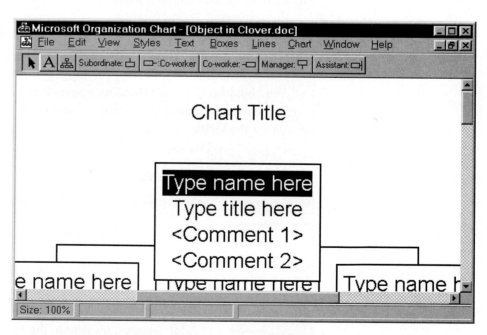

5. With the top box in the chart selected (as shown in Figure 3.10):
TYPE: **Craig Clover**
PRESS: **TAB**
TYPE: **Founder**
Notice that the information you type automatically replaces the selected text in the box.

6. SELECT: lower left-hand box by clicking it once
(*Note*: Only click once on the box you want to select. If you click twice by mistake, the insertion point is placed in the box and you must then drag the I-beam mouse pointer across the text you want to replace.)

7. Because we need only two branches under this organizational chart:
PRESS: DELETE
The selected box is removed from the chart and the other two boxes on the same level re-align themselves under Craig Clover's box.

8. SELECT: the left-hand box in the second level

9. TYPE: **Benji Ranjit**
PRESS: TAB
TYPE: **V.P. Sales**

10. SELECT: the right-hand box in the second level

11. TYPE: **Simon Wu**
PRESS: TAB
TYPE: **V.P. Production**

12. CLICK: on a blank area inside the Organization Chart window to remove the selection

13. To add a subordinate to Benji's team:
CLICK: Subordinate button (Subordinate: ⌐) in the toolbar
CLICK: Benji's box once
You should see a new subordinate branch attach itself to Benji's box. Table 3.1 summarizes the buttons that are available in the toolbar for adding people to the chart.

TABLE 3.1	*Button*	*Description*
The Organization Chart's Toolbar	Subordinate: ⌐	Adds a subordinate below the selected box.
	☐─:Co-worker	Adds a co-worker to the left of the selected box.
	Co-worker: ─☐	Adds a co-worker to the right of the selected box.
	Manager: ⌐	Adds a manager above the selected box.
	Assistant: ☐┤	Adds an assistant beside the selected box.

14. To add another subordinate to Benji's box:
CLICK: Subordinate button (Subordinate: ⌐) in the toolbar
CLICK: Benji's box once again

15. To return the mouse pointer to an arrow and remove the highlighting:
CLICK: Select button (↖) in the toolbar (if it is not already selected)
CLICK: on a blank area inside the Organization Chart window

16. To select an entire group or level of boxes:
CLICK: either subordinate box under Benji's box
CHOOSE: Edit, Select
CHOOSE: Group from the cascading menu
Notice that both boxes under Benji are now selected.

17. To change the style of a group of boxes:
CHOOSE: Styles from the menu
SELECT: the middle style on the first row (as shown at
the right)

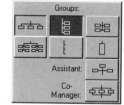

18. Enter the following two individuals into the boxes
appearing beneath Benji Ranjit: Bobbie Brown, Product
Manager and Wilma Chan, Advertising Manager.

19. Let's add an assistant for Craig Clover:
CLICK: Assistant button (Assistant ☐)
CLICK: Craig Clover's box
TYPE: **Penny Lane**
PRESS: TAB
TYPE: **Executive Assistant**

20. To make Craig Clover's box stand out from the rest:
CLICK: Craig Clover's box
CHOOSE: Boxes, Shadow
SELECT: any box shadow

21. To add a border to the two V.P.'s boxes:
CLICK: Benji Ranjit's box
PRESS: CTRL +**g** as a shortcut to selecting all the boxes at the same
level or group
CHOOSE: Boxes, Border Style from the Menu bar
SELECT: any box border
(*Hint*: You can also press CTRL +**b** to select an entire branch.)

22. To display more of the chart in the window:
CHOOSE: View, 50% of Actual

23. Let's return to the document:
CHOOSE: File, Exit and Return to Clover.doc

24. When asked to Update the Object in CLOVER.DOC:
PRESS: ENTER or CLICK: Yes
You are returned to the "Clover" document and the organizational chart
appears at the insertion point.

25. Select the organization chart if it isn't selected already.

26. DRAG: the sizing boxes to reduce the size of the chart
CLICK: outside the chart object
Your document should now appear similar to Figure 3.11.

FIGURE 3.11

THE COMPLETED
ORGANIZATIONAL CHART

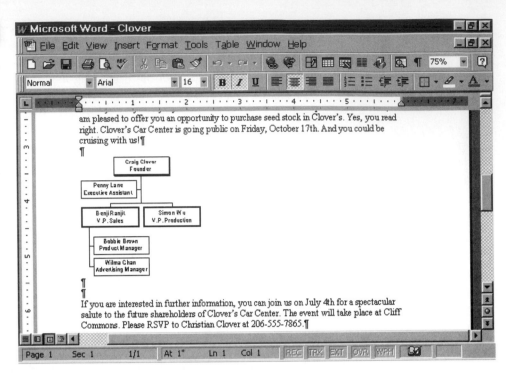

27. Save the document as "Organization Chart" to the Data Files location.

28. Close the document.

QUICK REFERENCE	1.	**Position the insertion point where you want to insert the object.**
Using Microsoft	2.	**CHOOSE: Insert, Object**
Organization Chart	3.	**SELECT: MS Organization Chart 2.0 on the *Create New* tab**
	4.	**PRESS: ENTER or CLICK: OK**
	5.	**Edit and format the chart boxes.**
	6.	**CHOOSE: File, Exit and Return to document**

USING MICROSOFT WORDART

The Microsoft WordArt mini-app is an excellent tool for jazzing up standard documents. If you need to create company logos, newsletter headlines, or promotional pieces, WordArt can make your job easier and much more fun. Some examples of WordArt appear below:

WordArt can definitely help you grab and keep the reader's attention. However, you should avoid inserting too many WordArt objects on the same page. Instead of enhancing your work, too many special effects can distract the reader.

In this section, you practice using WordArt.

Perform the following steps . . .

1. Open the "City College" document located in the Data Files location. You used this file previously to insert a graphic file and add a caption to a picture. Your task now is to insert a WordArt object in the heading of this flyer.

    Notice that the heading is arranged into a two-cell table. In the left-hand cell, the title "Computer Corner" appears. You will size and move the WordArt object to fit in the right-hand cell.

2. To create the heading using WordArt:
    CHOOSE: Insert, Picture
    CHOOSE: WordArt
    The WordArt Gallery dialog box appears, as shown in Figure 3.12.

FIGURE 3.12

WORDART GALLERY

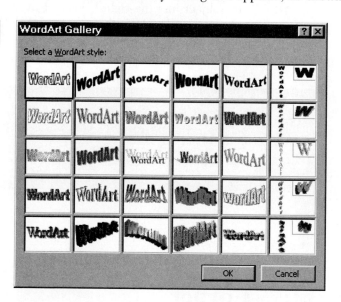

3. Now you select a style for your WordArt.
    SELECT: the style in the fourth column of the fourth row
    PRESS: (ENTER) or CLICK: OK

4. In the Edit WordArt Text box:
    TYPE: **June 97**

5. To see how the text will appear in your document:
    CLICK: OK
    The June 97 object appears selected and the WordArt toolbar appears. The WordArt toolbar is labeled in Figure 3.13.

FIGURE 3.13

WORDART'S TOOLBAR

Insert WordArt
Edit Text
WordArt Galley
Format WordArt
WordArt Shape
Free Rotate
WordArt Vertical Text
WordArt Same Letter Heights
WordArt Alignment
WordArt Character Spacing

6. If the toolbar currently appears in the document area, drag it to one of the borders of the application window. We suggest dragging it to the right-hand border. Now more of your document is visible.

Let's move and resize the WordArt object and then change the displayed font.

Perform the following steps . . .

1. The June 97 heading should already appear selected.
DRAG: the object into the right-hand cell in the heading area
DRAG: the sizing corners until the object fills the cell
CLICK: outside the WordArt object to deselect it
Your screen should now appear similar to Figure 3.14.

FIGURE 3.14

WORDART OBJECT AFTER
BEING MOVED AND
SIZED

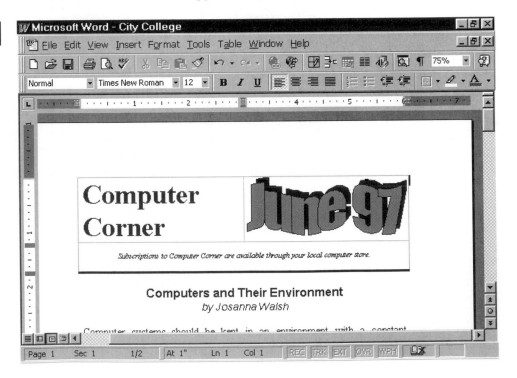

2. To select a different font for the WordArt object:
CLICK: the WordArt object
CLICK: Edit Text button
SELECT: Times New Roman from the Font drop-down list box
PRESS: (ENTER) or CLICK: OK

3. To return to the document:
CLICK: in the document, away from the object

4. Print the document.

5. Save the document as "City College," replacing the previous version.

6. Close the document.

QUICK REFERENCE Using Microsoft WordArt	**1.** Position the insertion point where you want to insert the object.
	2. CHOOSE: Insert, Picture
	3. CHOOSE: WordArt
	4. SELECT: a style from the WordArt Gallery dialog box PRESS: (ENTER) or CLICK: OK
	5. Type text into the Edit WordArt Text dialog box PRESS: (ENTER) or CLICK: OK
	6. Edit the WordArt image using the WordArt toolbar, as necessary.
	7. CLICK: away from the object to deselect the object

Summary

This session let you practice inserting and editing objects using Microsoft's set of Office Tools. You used the Clip Gallery to find a logo for a company, Equation Editor to create a profit margin ratio, Graph to plot the values from a Word table, Organization Chart to insert a management diagram into a document, and WordArt to spice up the heading of a flyer. Also in this session, you viewed an embedded video clip and learned how to insert a graphic image file as a picture object.

Table 3.2 provides a list of the commands and procedures covered in this session.

TABLE 3.2	*Task Description*	*Command*
Command Summary	Create an object or insert an existing object into your document	CHOOSE: Insert, Object
	Insert a clip art image	CHOOSE: Insert, Picture CHOOSE: Clip Art
	Insert a graphic image that is stored as a file on the disk	CHOOSE: Insert, Picture CHOOSE: From File
	Insert an equation	CHOOSE: Insert, Object SELECT: Microsoft Equation Editor 3.0 or SELECT: Microsoft Equation Editor 2.0
Graph	Insert a chart at the insertion point or create a chart from an existing table of values	CHOOSE: Insert, Picture CHOOSE: Chart
	Remove or display the Datasheet of values to plot in a chart	CLICK: View Datasheet button ( )
Organization Chart	Insert an organization chart	CHOOSE: Insert, Object SELECT: MS Organization Chart 2.0
	Add a shadow effect to a chart box	CHOOSE: Boxes, Shadow
	Add a border to a chart box	CHOOSE: Boxes, Border Style
	Leave Organization Chart and update your document	CHOOSE: File, Exit and Return
WordArt	Insert a WordArt object	CHOOSE: Insert, Picture CHOOSE: WordArt
	Select a font for the WordArt text object	CLICK: Edit Text button CLICK: Font drop-down menu
	Add special shape effects to text, such as the Wave applied to the article heading	CLICK: Edit Text button CLICK: WordArt Shape

KEY TERMS

clip art image
A computer graphic that you can insert into your document to make it more interesting or entertaining; the Microsoft Clip Gallery organizes clip art images for all Office applications.

group
In Organization Chart, an entire horizontal level of co-workers.

mini-apps

Small application programs that are bundled with Microsoft Office to enhance the primary applications; some mini-apps are accessed using the Insert, Picture command, while others are accessed using the Insert, Object command.

Office Tools

See *mini-apps*.

organizational chart

A diagram showing the internal management reporting structure of a company, organization, institution, or other such group; also used for flow-chart diagrams.

palette

In Equation Editor, a list of additional options accessed through the toolbar for templates and symbols.

scanner

A hardware device that converts an existing picture or photograph into a computer image that is stored digitally on the disk.

symbol

In Equation Editor, a mathematical symbol (usually Greek) that is not available in the typical TrueType fonts provided by Windows.

template

In Equation Editor, a form or framework for entering mathematical elements, such as a fraction or square root.

EXERCISES

SHORT ANSWER

1. Which Office Tool can you use to insert a video clip in a document?

2. How do mini-apps differ from the primary applications in Office?

3. What two commands are used to insert Office Tool objects?

4. What three principles should you keep in mind when inserting clip art?

5. Name the Office applications that can access the Clip Gallery.

6. The Equation Editor's toolbar is divided into two areas. Explain.

7. How do you insert a space between words using the Equation Editor?

8. When would you want to use Excel to create a chart instead of using Microsoft Graph?

9. How do you change the shape of an object? move an object?

10. How would you correct a misspelled word in a WordArt object?

HANDS-ON

(*Note*: Ensure that you know the location of your Advantage Files and where to store your Data Files. If necessary, ask your instructor or lab assistant for additional information.)

1. In the following exercise, you practice inserting objects using Microsoft's Office Tools.

    a. Close all open documents.

    b. Start a new PowerPoint presentation using the New Office Document option in the Start menu.

    c. From the New Slide dialog box:
        SELECT: Title Slide autoLayout option

    d. CLICK: "Click to add title" text on the new slide that appears

    e. TYPE: **Microsoft Clip Gallery**

    f. CLICK: "Click to add sub-title" text
        TYPE: **Choose from hundreds of pictures, sounds, and video clips!**

    g. Insert a clip art image of your choice anywhere on the slide using the Insert Clip Art button (▣).

    h. Move and resize the image as desired.

    i. CLICK: New Slide button (▣) on the Standard toolbar

    j. SELECT: Chart AutoLayout

    k. CLICK: "Click to add title" text

    l. TYPE: **Microsoft Graph**

    m. DOUBLE-CLICK: "Double click to add chart" text

    n. Create and format a new 3-D column chart based on the following values, using Microsoft Graph:

	Actual	Budget
Widgets	120	125
Grapples	24	35
Grommets	88	90

        (*Hint*: Type over the existing information.)

    o. So that columns C and D aren't included in the graph:
        RIGHT-CLICK: "D" in the border area for column D
        CHOOSE: Delete
        RIGHT-CLICK: "C" in the border area for column C
        CHOOSE: Delete

After removing the datasheet, your screen should appear similar to Figure 3.15.

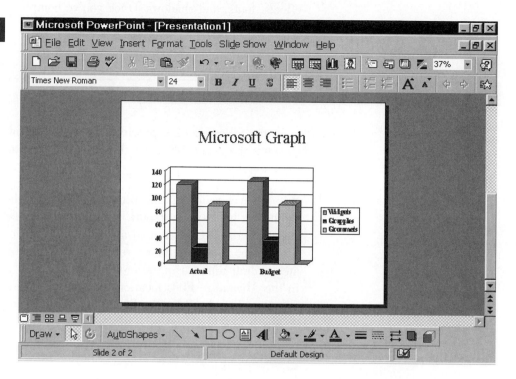

p. CLICK: New Slide button (🖫) on the Standard toolbar

q. SELECT: Organization Chart autoLayout option

r. CLICK: "Click to add title" text

s. TYPE: **Microsoft Organization Chart**

t. DOUBLE-CLICK: "Double click to add org chart" text

u. Insert the following organizational chart into the slide:

v. Save the presentation as "MiniApps" to the Data Files location.

w. Exit PowerPoint.

2. Create a new document in Microsoft Word that presents ten different versions of the same WordArt object. Use the text "WordArt" and apply shape effects, fonts, and shadows. Once you've completed creating the objects, print the document and save it as "Art Class" to the Data Files location. Exit Word.

CASE PROBLEMS   **LAKELAND GYM**

(*Note*: In the following case problems, assume the role of the primary characters and perform the same steps that they identify. You may want to re-read the session opening.)

1. With sleeves rolled up and fingers poised over the keyboard, Peter is ready to enliven his monthly report. He is now convinced, after learning more about Microsoft Office's mini-applications, that Josephine was right on target with her suggestions. Before receiving Josephine's feedback, Peter had created a draft report using Microsoft Word called "Lakeland," which is stored in the Advantage Files location. Peter now retrieves the draft report and creates a letterhead for the first page. He tries to make the letterhead look as much like the following example as possible.

President's Report   1920 Bush Street
                                                     St. Paul, MN 92111
                                                     Tel: 222-222-2222

When finished, Peter saves the document as "President's Report" to the Data Files location.

2. Peter's next task in preparing the monthly status report is to insert an organization chart into the "President's Report" document. (*Note*: You saved this file in the last exercise.) He creates the chart and includes it under the Employees section of the report. The chart shows the following reporting relationships:

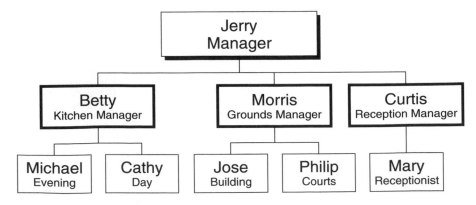

When finished, Peter saves "President's Report" to the Data Files location.

3. Rather than using a table of numbers, Peter creates and inserts a bar chart of the following sales data into the Food Services section of the "President's Report" document.

Sales ($)	Last Month	This Month
Restaurant	2100	3900
Bar	1950	4175

When finished, Peter saves "President's Report" to the Data Files location. He then prints the final report for submitting to the president.

Integrating Microsoft Office 97 for Windows

Managing Your Desktop

SESSION

4

IRWIN
COMPUTER & INFORMATION TECHNOLOGY

INTRODUCTION

What comes to mind when you think of a desktop? A stack of papers, an appointment calendar, an address book, a notepad with a scribbled list of to do items, a computer? Whatever your vision, Office 97 can help you tidy your desktop and keep it organized using two powerful applications: Microsoft Binder and Microsoft Outlook. Microsoft Binder helps you organize documents that pertain to the same topic or project and Microsoft Outlook provides folders for managing e-mail, appointments, business and personal contacts, tasks, and more. Let's now take a look at how we might use these two tools to manage our desktops.

CASE STUDY	**FURNITURE SOURCE**

Based in Sheridan, Indiana, Furniture Source is a mail order furniture and home accessories company that has been in business since 1986. The brainchild of Alphonso Banks, the company's president, Furniture Source provides a broad selection of quality products at prices that undercut most retail stores. For the first four years of business, Mr. Banks marketed only to Indiana residents by means of a low-budget product catalog. In 1990, Mr. Banks decided to go national and build upon his successes in Indiana. He published a 70-page color catalog and distributed it to 500,000 homes throughout the United States. The market responded favorably and sales boomed. Today, with a distribution list of over 2 million, Furniture Source is an extremely successful privately held company.

Kristen Grady has worked in many capacities at Furniture Source since 1992. Previously a telephone sales representative, Kristen was recently promoted to Senior Sales Representative for the Western Region. One of her new responsibilities is to produce a monthly report that contains status information about sales in her region. She wants to use Microsoft Binder to manage the different elements of the report, but has only worked with Microsoft Excel and Microsoft Word in the past.

Also, given her increased responsibilities, Kristen wants to tidy up her desk once and for all. Her desktop is buried in sticky notes, and her appointment calendar and address book are both covered with scribbles. She is concerned that important details will get past her. She has heard that Microsoft Outlook is the tool for her, but doesn't know how to get started.

In this session, you and Kristen will learn how to use Microsoft Binder to manage files, and Microsoft Outlook to manage important details such as appointments and addresses.

INTRODUCING MICROSOFT BINDER

When using a computer, people typically organize their documents using folders or directories. However, no matter how tidy you try to be, your disk can sometimes become cluttered and it can prove difficult to locate a group of files pertaining to a particular topic or project. Microsoft Binder can help you better organize your work. With Binder, you store related documents in a single file called a **binder,** similar to placing pages into a three-ring notebook. Binder provides a solid framework for compiling multiple documents for copying, reviewing electronically, and printing.

Let's look at an example. Pretend that you manage the advertising for a paint company named The Master Palette and that you are in the process of gearing up for an advertising campaign. You've begun working on the following documents: (1) a company description in Word, (2) a product listing in Word, (3) an advertising budget in Excel, and (4) a presentation file in PowerPoint. If you store these documents in a single binder, you only have to look in one place to find all the files relating to your ad campaign. As well, you can easily print all of the documents in the binder, called **sections,** in a single command.

Specifically, you can perform the following types of tasks in Binder:

- Add, remove, and reorganize sections in a binder

- Edit and apply a consistent formatting style to binder sections

- Spell-check binder sections

- Print the sections in a binder as a single document, with consecutive page numbering, headers, and footers

- Preview the binder

- Send the entire binder via e-mail to coworkers for review and editing

- Save the binder as a template so that you can use it again for a future project

- Use a Binder template to help you get started quickly on new projects

When editing an individual section in a binder, Binder activates the source application and displays its Menu bar, Standard toolbar, and Formatting toolbar. For example, while editing a document you created in Microsoft Excel, Excel's Menu bar and toolbars appear in the Binder application window. This provides a document-centric framework for working with related files; you simply focus on the documents at hand while Binder takes care of the rest for you, such as loading the application you need.

STARTING BINDER

You load Binder the same way you load any other Office application. If you use the Programs menu to load Binder, a blank binder will appear. To start Binder and load a binder template, choose the New Office Document command in the Start menu and then select the *Binders* tab in the New dialog box. Then double-click the template you want to open. To open an existing binder file, use the same procedure you use to open other types of document files. Now let's load Binder.

Perform the following steps . . .

1. Use the Programs menu to start Binder. A blank binder will appear.

2. Make sure the Binder application window is maximized. Your screen should now appear similar to Figure 4.1. The Binder application window is composed of the Title bar, Menu bar, left pane, and right pane.

FIGURE 4.1

AN EMPTY BINDER

Title bar

Menu bar

Left pane

Right pane

Binder Status bar

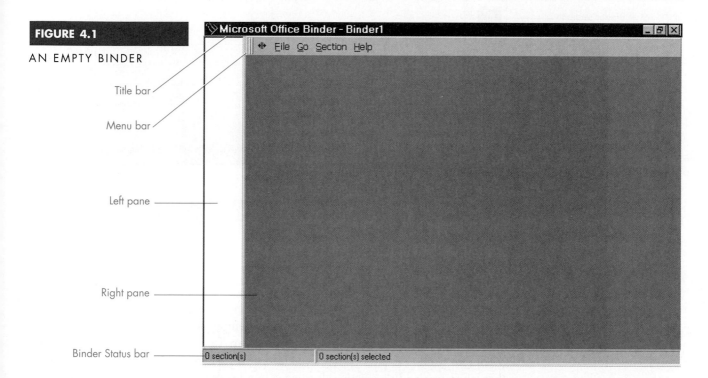

Figure 4.2 shows the Binder application window after sections relating to your advertising campaign have been added. When managing binder sections, you will use the Show/Hide Left Pane button (■) located to the left of the File menu to hide or display the left pane. To edit an individual section, simply click its icon once. The document will appear in the right pane along with the Menu bar and toolbars of its source application.

FIGURE 4.2

A BINDER WITH
ADDED SECTIONS

Show/Hide
Left Pane button

Binder section

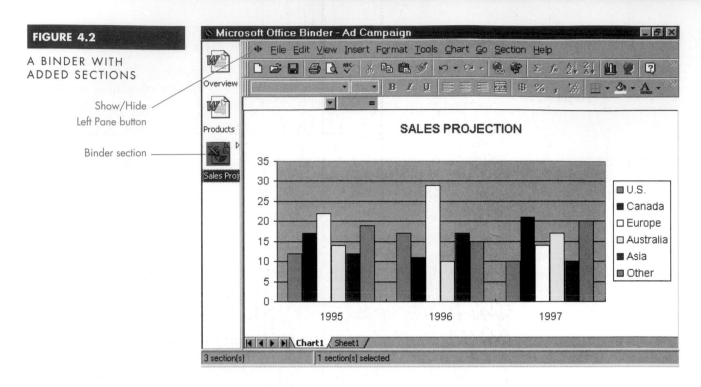

CREATING A BINDER

To create a binder, you can either add an empty section to a binder or copy an existing document into the binder. To add an empty section to a binder, you choose the Section, Add command from the Menu bar. To add an existing document to a binder, you choose the Section, Add from File command. It is important to note that when you add an existing document to a binder you are *copying* the document to the binder; that is, the original document remains unchanged on the disk. To conserve disk space, you may consider deleting the original document from the disk. If you later decide that you no longer want a section to be part of the binder, you can always save a section back to the disk as a document.

ADDING DOCUMENTS TO A BINDER

In this section, you add two documents relating to your advertising campaign to a binder. The files "Overview" and "Products" are stored in the Advantage Files location.

Perform the following steps . . .

1. Ensure that an empty binder appears in the Binder window and that the Binder window is maximized.

2. To add the "Overview" document to the binder:
   CHOOSE: Section, Add from File

3. To specify the Word document "Overview" as the new section:
   SELECT: *your Advantage Files location*
   SELECT: "Overview" from the list box
   PRESS: (ENTER) or CLICK: Add
   The "Overview" document is copied into the binder. Because "Overview" is a Word document and is the currently selected section, Microsoft Word is activated in the right pane. Notice that the Section menu now appears next to the Help command in Word's Menu bar. Your screen should now appear similar to Figure 4.3.

FIGURE 4.3

ADDING THE WORD DOCUMENT NAMED "OVERVIEW" TO THE BINDER

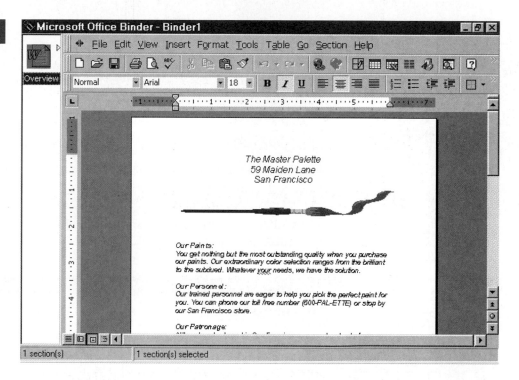

4. To add the Word document named "Products" to the binder:
   CHOOSE: Section, Add from File from the Menu bar
   SELECT: *your Advantage Files location*
   SELECT: "Products" from the list
   PRESS: (ENTER) or CLICK: Add
   The "Products" document is copied into the binder. Notice that the Overview section is still selected.

5. CLICK: Products icon in the left pane
   The Products document appears. (*Note*: Make sure to click the section's icon, otherwise Binder simply selects the name of the section.)

6. To hide the left pane and display more of the current section in the right pane, do the following:
CLICK: Show/Hide Left Pane button (⏮)
Your screen should now appear similar to Figure 4.4.

FIGURE 4.4

THE LEFT PANE IS
HIDDEN FROM VIEW

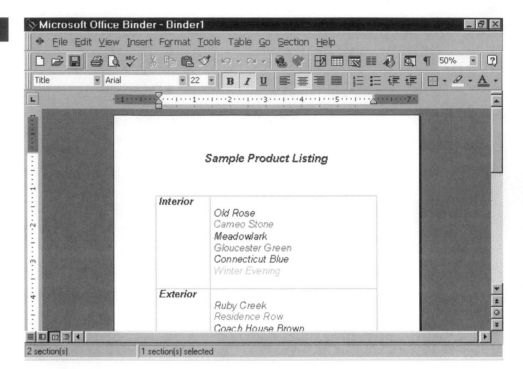

7. To redisplay the left pane:
CLICK: Show/Hide Left Pane button (⏮)

QUICK REFERENCE
Add a Section to a Binder

- **CHOOSE: Section, Add to add a new section to the binder**
- **CHOOSE: Section, Add from File to add an existing document to the binder**

QUICK REFERENCE
Hide/Display the Left Pane

CLICK: Show/Hide Left Pane button (⏮)

IN ADDITION ADDING ACCESS DATA TO A BINDER

Although you can't add an Access file directly to a binder, you can output an Access table to a Word or Excel document, and then include the document in the binder.

SAVING A BINDER

If you make changes to the binder as a whole or to an individual section in the binder, you should save it to the disk using the File, Save Binder command. If you've edited a section that was added from a document on the disk, the original document remains unchanged when you save the binder. You use the same procedure to save a binder as you would to save a document.

In this section, you save the binder to the Data Files location.

Perform the following steps . . .

1. CLICK: Save button () in the Standard toolbar
    Notice that the Save As Binder dialog box appears instead of Word's Save As dialog box.

2. To save the file as "Ad Campaign":
    TYPE: **Ad Campaign** in the File name text box
    SELECT: *your Data Files location*
    PRESS: (**ENTER**) or CLICK: Save command button

QUICK REFERENCE
Save a Binder

1. **CHOOSE: File, Save Binder**
2. **TYPE: a name into the *File name* text box**
3. **SELECT: a drive in the *Save in* drop-down list box**
4. **PRESS: (ENTER) or CLICK: Save command button**

CREATING A NEW SECTION IN A BINDER

When you choose the Section, Add command to insert a new section, the section is positioned immediately after the selected section in the Binder pane. Next you add a Microsoft Excel chart to the "Ad Campaign" binder.

Perform the following steps . . .

1. CHOOSE: Section, Add
    The Add Section dialog box appears, as shown in Figure 4.5.

FIGURE 4.5

ADD SECTION DIALOG
BOX

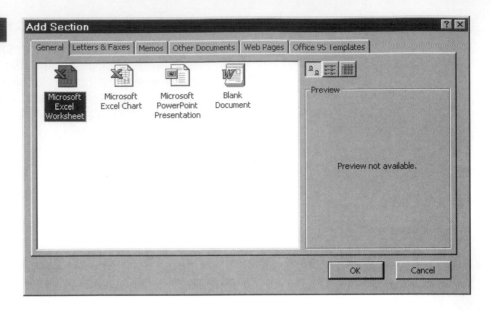

2. SELECT: Microsoft Excel Chart
    PRESS: **ENTER** or CLICK: OK
    Your screen should now appear similar to Figure 4.6. Notice that Excel's
    Menu bar and toolbars appear.

FIGURE 4.6

ADDING A MICROSOFT
EXCEL CHART TO THE
BINDER

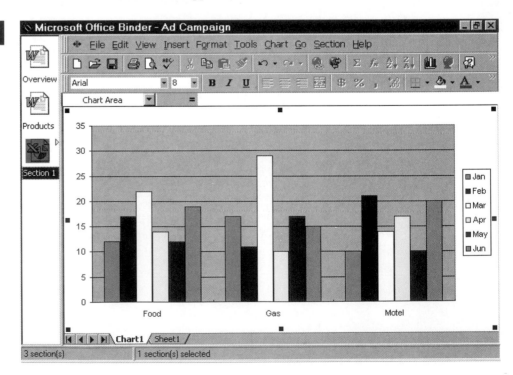

3. The newly inserted section is highlighted and an Excel chart with sample
    data appears in the right pane. To rename the section to "Sales Projection":
    CHOOSE: Section, Rename
    TYPE: **Sales Projection**

4. Now let's display the Excel datasheet and edit the data.
   CLICK: *Sheet1* tab on the bottom of the document window

5. Edit the datasheet to look like Figure 4.7. (*Hint*: Only the data in column A and row 1 needs to be retyped. The rest of the data remains the same.)

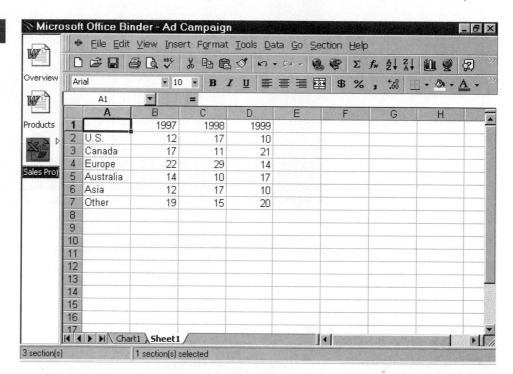

6. To preview the Sales Projection section, you use the Print Preview button (⬚) on the Standard toolbar. (*Note*: You can preview the entire binder using the File, Binder Print Preview command.)
   CLICK: *Chart1* tab
   CLICK: Print Preview button (⬚)
   Your screen should now appear similar to Figure 4.8.

FIGURE 4.8

PREVIEWING THE SALES
PROJECTION SECTION

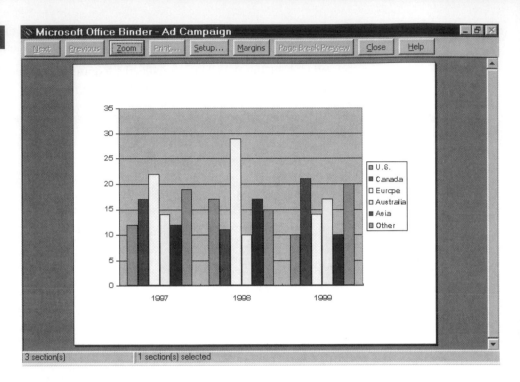

FIGURE 4.8

PREVIEWING THE SALES
PROJECTION SECTION

7. CLICK: Close command button in the toolbar

QUICK REFERENCE Rename a Section	**1.**	**SELECT: the desired section in the Binder pane**
	2.	**CHOOSE: Section, Rename**
	3.	**TYPE:** *new name*

EDITING A BINDER

When editing, formatting, and proofing binder sections, you must often work with each section individually. For example, to spell check a binder that contains five sections, you must run the spelling checker five times, once for each section. Likewise, to apply consistent formatting to the contents of a binder, you must apply the formatting to each section in the binder. Only the File menu provides commands that affect the entire binder at once. For example, you can add headers and footers to the entire binder using the File, Binder Page Setup command or preview the entire binder using the File, Binder Print Preview command.

In the next few sections, you add a footer to the "Ad Campaign" binder, move a binder document, and copy between binder documents.

EDITING BINDER SECTIONS

In this section, you prepare to print a few sections in the "Ad Campaign" binder. Your immediate objective is to add a footer to the Overview and Products sections. You will print these sections later for inclusion in an advertising brochure.

Perform the following steps . . .

1. CHOOSE: File, Binder Page Setup
The dialog box in Figure 4.9 should appear.

2. SELECT: Overview in the *Only sections selected below* area
SELECT: Products in the *Only sections selected below* area

FIGURE 4.9

BINDER PAGE SETUP
DIALOG BOX

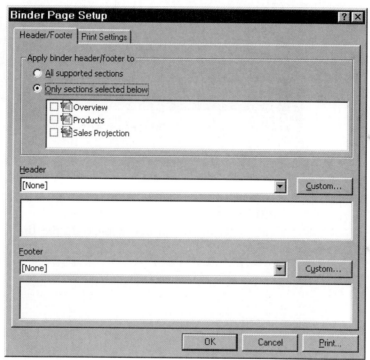

3. Let's look at some of the sample footers that Binder has collected for you:
CLICK: down arrow to the right of the *Footer* display box
A selection of footers appears. Since we're going to define a custom footer:
CLICK: down arrow again to remove the list

4. CLICK: Custom button in the *Footer* area
The Custom Footer dialog box should appear.

5. The cursor should be blinking in the *Left section* text box.
TYPE: **your name**

6. Let's include the page number in the center section.
CLICK: *Center section* text box
TYPE: **Page**
PRESS: Space Bar
CLICK: Insert Page Number button (⊞)
PRESS: Space Bar
TYPE: **of 2**

7. Let's include the current date in the right section.
CLICK: *Right section* text box
CLICK: Insert Date button (⊞)
The Custom Footer dialog box should now appear similar to Figure 4.10.

FIGURE 4.10

DEFINING A CUSTOM
FOOTER

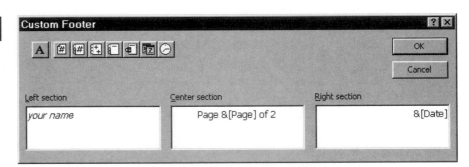

8. To complete the operation:
PRESS: (**ENTER**) or CLICK: OK
The footer definition now appears in the Binder Page Setup dialog box (Figure 4.11).

FIGURE 4.11

THE COMPLETED FOOTER
DEFINITION

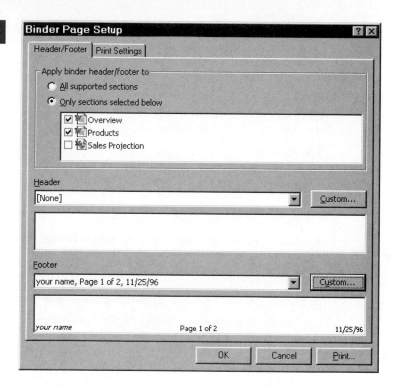

9. To further define how you want to print your binder:
CLICK: *Print Settings* tab
The Print Settings tab appears in Figure 4.12.

FIGURE 4.12

CHOOSING SECTIONS
TO PRINT

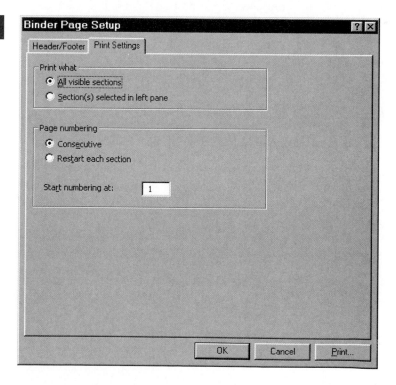

10. Before continuing, ensure that the settings on your computer match those in Figure 4.12.

11. PRESS: ⌐ENTER⌐ or CLICK: OK

12. To see the inserted footer, select the Overview or Products section and then drag the vertical scroll bar downward. Later in this session you will get a better view of the footer when you preview the binder sections.

13. Save the "Ad Campaign" binder to the Data Files location.

QUICK REFERENCE Adding Headers and Footers to a Binder	1. **CHOOSE: Binder, Binder Page Setup** 2. **Select the sections you want to affect. (*Note:* Select the *All supported sections* button to apply headers and/or footers to every section in the binder.)** 3. **Either choose from the available header and footer lists or create a custom header and/or footer using the Custom buttons.**

MOVING BINDER SECTIONS

Once you've added sections to a binder, it's quite easy to change their order in the left pane. You simply select the section you want to move and then drag it up or down. A miniature page icon shows you where the section you're dragging will be positioned.

Let's try moving the Sales Projection section to the top of the left pane.

 **Perform the following steps . . .**

1. CLICK: Sales Projection section in the left pane
The Sales Projection section is now the selected section.

2. By pointing to the Sales Projection document icon, drag the section to the top of the left pane. The Sales Projection section should now appear first in the list.

3. On your own, drag the Sales Projection document downward so it appears in its original position, after the Products section.

QUICK REFERENCE Move a Section	1. **SELECT: the desired section in the left pane** 2. **DRAG: the section up or down in the left pane**

COPYING AND MOVING BETWEEN SECTIONS

Copying and moving between binder sections is the same as copying and moving between applications. Select the text you want to move or copy and then click the Cut button (✂) or Copy button (📋) on the Standard toolbar. Switch to the target section and then click the Paste button (📋) or choose Paste Special from the Menu bar.

Let's practice copying the clip art image from the Overview document to the Products document.

Perform the following steps . . .

1. SELECT: Overview document
   SELECT: the clip art image
   The clip art image should be surrounded with selection handles.

2. CLICK: Copy button (📋) on the Standard toolbar
   The clip art image was copied to the clipboard.

3. Now let's select the Products document.
   SELECT: Products document

4. Position the cursor one line below the heading, in the center position.

5. CLICK: Paste button (📋)
   Your screen should now appear similar to Figure 4.13.

FIGURE 4.13

THE CLIP ART IMAGE WAS COPIED INTO THE "PRODUCTS" DOCUMENT

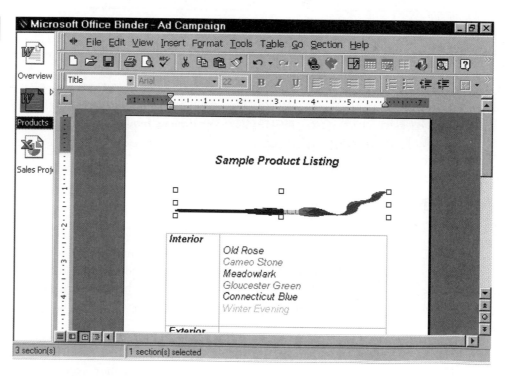

6. Save the "Ad Campaign" binder to the Data Files location.

UNBINDING A BINDER

You may decide at some point that you no longer want a particular document to be part of a binder. Or you may decide to unbind every document in the binder so that each section becomes a separate document on the disk. To save a single section as a document on the disk, select the section and then choose the Section, Save as File command. Then proceed as if you were saving any Office document. The binder file will remain unchanged. You can delete a section permanently from a binder by selecting the section and then choosing the Section, Delete command.

To unbind an entire binder at once, right-click the binder name in "My Computer," Windows Explorer, or on the Windows desktop. Choose Unbind from the shortcut menu that appears. The sections in the binder will be saved as individual files in the same folder that holds the binder file. Again, the binder file will remain unchanged.

PRINTING A BINDER

To print a binder section, select the section and then click the Print button (🖨) on the Standard toolbar. To print multiple sections or the entire binder, use the File, Print Binder command. The Print Binder dialog box (Figure 4.14) is slightly different from the Print dialog box used in other Office applications. Below we describe a few options that may be unfamiliar to you:

• Choose a *Print What* option to print all sections in the binder at once or just the selected section(s). If you select *All visible sections*, Binder prints the sections in the order that they appear in the binder.

- Choose a *Numbering* option to determine whether sections are numbered consecutively from section to section or whether each section is numbered individually. Set a starting page number using the *Start numbering at* text box.

FIGURE 4.14

PRINT BINDER DIALOG BOX

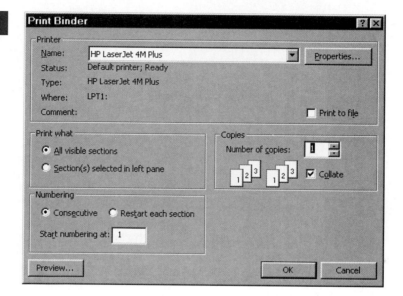

You may want to preview the binder before you print it. To preview an individual section, select it and then click the Print Preview button () on the Standard toolbar. To preview multiple sections in the binder, select them in the left pane and then choose File, Binder Print Preview. If only one section is selected in the left pane, choosing File, Binder Print Preview will preview the entire binder.

In this section, you preview and print a few sections in the "Ad Campaign" binder.

Perform the following steps . . .

1. Let's preview the Overview and Products sections. First you must select them.
   SELECT: Overview section
   To select an additional section, you hold down Ctrl while clicking the additional section.
   PRESS: CTRL and hold it down
   CLICK: Products section
   Both sections should appear selected in the left pane.

2. To preview these sections:
   CHOOSE: File, Binder Print Preview
   Your screen should now appear similar to Figure 4.15. Other than the addition of the Binder Print Preview toolbar, this dialog box looks the same as when using other Office applications.

FIGURE 4.15

PREVIEWING THE BINDER

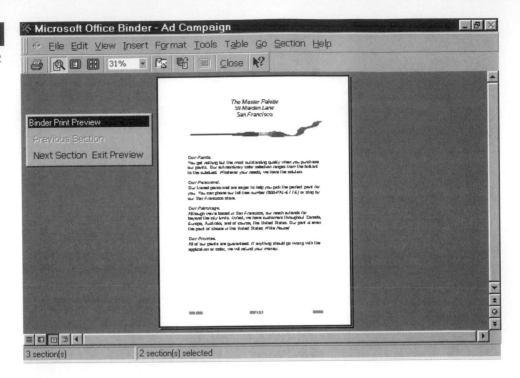

3. To view the next section:
    CHOOSE: Next section in the Binder Print Preview toolbar

4. To view the previous section:
    CHOOSE: Previous section in the Binder Print Preview toolbar

5. To return to the binder:
    CHOOSE: Exit Preview in the Binder Print Preview toolbar

6. To print the selected sections:
    CHOOSE: File, Print Binder
    SELECT: *Section(s) selected in left pane* option button

7. PRESS: ENTER or CLICK: OK
    The selected sections, complete with footers, are sent to the printer.

QUICK REFERENCE
Printing a Binder

1. **CHOOSE: File, Print Binder**

2. **Make a selection in the *Print What* area.**

3. **Review the *Numbering* options.**

4. **PRESS: ENTER or CLICK: OK**

INTRODUCING MICROSOFT OUTLOOK

Now that you know how to manage files that pertain to a common topic, let's look at how you might use Microsoft Outlook to manage other types of information. **Microsoft Outlook** is a desktop management tool that enables you to manage the information you typically deal with when working at your desk, such as dates, addresses, reminder notes, and fax and e-mail messages. Microsoft Outlook features are integrated throughout the primary applications in Office 97.

Outlook uses folders to keep track of your desktop information. When you type in a note, Outlook stores it in your Notes folder. When you add an address to your address book, Outlook stores the new address in your Contacts folder. When you enter a date in your calendar, Outlook stores the new information in your Calendar folder, and so on. Outlook uses the following folders to help you keep your desktop organized:

- *Inbox folder.* Here you store any e-mail or fax messages that you receive. Before you can send and receive e-mail and faxes, you must choose an *information service*, such as Microsoft Exchange Server or Microsoft Fax. An **information service** defines the rules for sending and receiving e-mail, faxes, and files on your computer. To add an information service, choose Tools, Services and then click the *Services* tab.

- *Calendar folder.* Here you keep track of your schedule. This folder provides the functionality of your paper calendar or schedule book, but with more flexibility since you can easily change how information is viewed.

- *Contacts folder.* Similar to a rolodex card file, you store personal and business contact information in this folder, such as name, address, phone, fax, and e-mail information. Later, you can create a letter to a contact with Word 97 or use the contacts as a mail merge data source.

- *Tasks folder.* Here you list your To Do tasks and when you want them completed. You can add tasks to the Tasks folder from Word, Excel, and Power-Point using the Reviewer toolbar.

- *Journal folder.* This folder keeps track of your Word, Excel, Access, Power-Point, and Binder files by storing a shortcut to the file in a dated timeline. This folder is useful when you want to work with a particular file, but can't remember its filename. If you remember the approximate month or day that you last worked on the file, you can open the Journal folder, go to the appropriate date, and then open the file.

- *Notes folder.* This folder provides a location for storing notes, similarly to how you might use sticky notes. In Outlook, simply choose File, New, Note to add a note to the Notes folder.

STARTING OUTLOOK

There are a couple of ways to load Outlook. You can use the Programs menu to load Outlook or double-click the Microsoft Outlook shortcut on the Windows desktop, if it is available.

Perform the following steps . . .

1. Load Outlook using the Programs menu.

2. If the Office Assistant appears, click OK in the tip window to remove the Office Assistant from view.

3. Make sure the Outlook application window is maximized. Your screen should now appear similar to Figure 4.16, although the messages (if any) on your computer will be different. By default, the Inbox is open when you first load Outlook. The Outlook application window is composed of the Title bar, Menu bar, toolbar, Outlook Bar, and Information viewer.

FIGURE 4.16

THE OUTLOOK INBOX

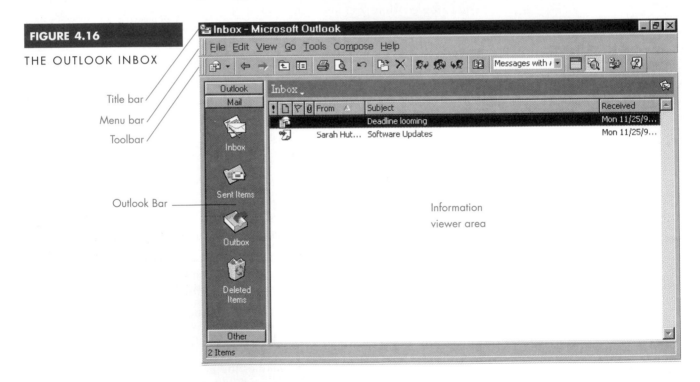

Now let's put Outlook to work.

ADDING DATA

In this section, you will again assume the role of the advertising manager for The Master Palette, an esteemed paint company based in San Francisco. Specifically, you will add a contact to your contact list and an appointment to your calendar. You will also "jot" down some notes about upcoming events. (*Note*: Because Outlook is so easily customizable to meet your needs, the Figures in this section might not match your screen exactly.)

As an ad campaign manager, you're not without an extensive contact list. You just learned of someone who creates colorful brochures at reasonable rates. Let's add this contact to the Contacts folder.

Perform the following steps . . .

1. CHOOSE: File, New
   CHOOSE: Contact
   The Contact window appears.

2. Ensure the Contact window is maximized. Your screen should now appear similar to Figure 4.17.

FIGURE 4.17

THE CONTACT WINDOW

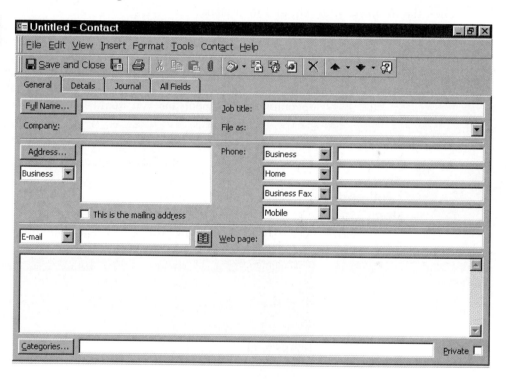

3. As you can see, Outlook provides a form into which you can type very detailed information about your contact.
   TYPE: **Peter Renshaw** into the *Full Name* text box
   TYPE: **Pete's Printing** into the *Company* text box

4. Type the following into the *Address* text box:
   14 Ownby Circle
   San Francisco, CA 94111

5. Type the following into the message area at the bottom of the window:
   Remind Pete of the 25% discount he promised me.

6. To save the contact information:
   CLICK: Save and Close button in the toolbar
   You'll review your entry in the Contact folder shortly. First, let's enter a date in the Calendar.

IN ADDITION CREATE A LETTER IN WORD 97 TO AN OUTLOOK CONTACT

1. In Outlook, select the Contacts folder.

2. CHOOSE: Contacts, New Letter to Contact
Microsoft Word will open and the Letter Wizard will prompt you for some information.

3. To choose a contact from the Contacts folder, click the *Recipient Info* tab, and then click the Address Book button.

4. In the *Show Names from the:* drop-down list box, select Contacts and select a contact from the list. Then press **ENTER** to continue.

5. Click the Finish button after you've reviewed the remaining tabs in the Letter Wizard dialog box.

6. Edit the letter, as necessary.

In your current role, you have to maintain strict control of your calendar. Any missed deadlines ultimately rest on your shoulders! Let's say that you have an upcoming appointment that you would like to schedule.

Perform the following steps ...

1. To add a new date to the calendar:
CHOOSE: File, New
CHOOSE: Appointment
Your screen should now appear similar to Figure 4.18, with a different date. A form appears into which you type appointment information.

FIGURE 4.18

THE APPOINTMENT
WINDOW

2. Let's pick a date that is one month from the current date. To do this:
CLICK: the down arrow next to the *Start Time* text box
A drop-down calendar appears.

3. The name of the current month borders the top of the drop-down calendar. You click the left arrow (←) to display the previous month and the right arrow (→) to display the next month. To advance the calendar to the next month:
CLICK: right arrow (→)

4. Now select the day that is one month from the current date.

5. TYPE: **Open House** into the *Subject* text box
TYPE: **The Master Palette** into the *Location* text box

6. Type the following into the text area at the bottom of the window:
TYPE: **Don't forget to hand out our latest color brochures.**
PRESS: [ENTER]
TYPE: **Remember to honor the 15% discount coupons that ran in the Examiner.**

7. Let's now format the text with bullets.
SELECT: the two lines of text you entered in the previous step
CHOOSE: Format, Paragraph
SELECT: *Bullets* check box
PRESS: [ENTER] or CLICK: OK

8. Because you'll be busy with this appointment the entire day:
SELECT: *All day event* check box
Your screen should now appear similar to Figure 4.19. Notice that the *Reminder* check box is checked and 15 minutes appears in the list box to the right. On the date of the Open House, if your computer is equipped with speakers, you will hear a reminder alarm every 15 minutes until you deselect the *Reminder* check box.

FIGURE 4.19

THE APPOINTMENT
WINDOW WITH ADDED
INFORMATION

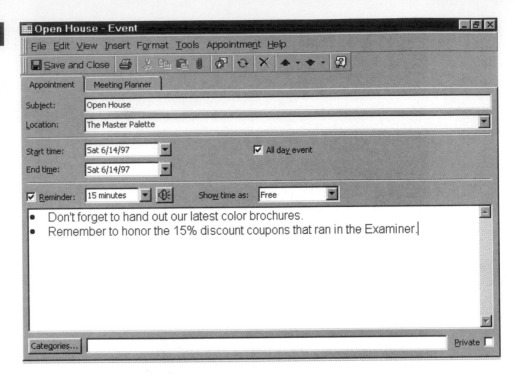

9. To save the appointment information:
    CLICK: Save and Close button in the toolbar
    In the next section, we'll review your entry in the Calendar folder.

OPENING CATEGORIES AND FOLDERS

Outlook provides three folder categories: Outlook, Mail, and Other. The buttons
that enable you to switch between categories appear in the Outlook Bar. To display a different category you click its button in the Outlook Bar. To open a folder,
such as Calendar or Contacts, you click its icon in the Outlook Bar.

**Perform
the
following
steps . . .**

1. CLICK: Outlook button in the Outlook Bar
    The list of Outlook folders appears in the Outlook Bar. The Inbox is the
    currently selected folder. Notice that the label "Inbox" appears above the
    Information viewer area.

2. Let's look at the Mail folders.
    CLICK: Mail button in the Outlook Bar
    Your screen should now appear similar to Figure 4.20.

FIGURE 4.20

THE MAIL FOLDERS

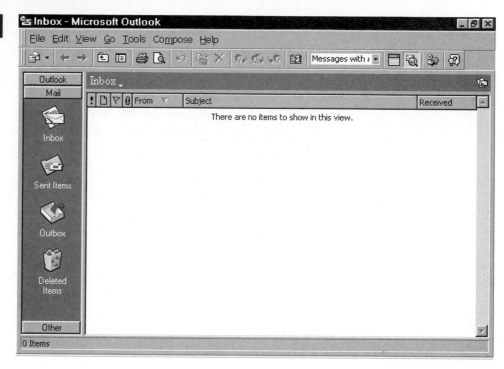

3. Let's now look at the Other folders.
CLICK: Other button in the Outlook Bar
As you can see, with the Other folders you can easily access all the files on your computer or network.

4. To open a folder, you click its icon. To illustrate, let's open the Calendar folder.
CLICK: Outlook button in the Outlook Bar
CLICK: Calendar icon

5. On your own, practice switching between the categories and folders available in the Outlook Bar.

Now let's look at the date you entered in the previous section.

Perform the following steps . . .

1. Ensure that you are viewing the Calendar folder, and that the Day/Week/Month view is selected in the Current View pull-down menu (Day/Week/Mon).

2. To further ensure that our screens look the same, let's click the Day button (1) in the toolbar.
CLICK: Day button (1)
In this view mode you can enter hourly appointments into your calendar.

3. Let's view a month at a time.
CLICK: Month button (31)

4. Now click the down arrow at the bottom of the vertical scroll bar until you can view the dates for next month. Notice that the "Open House" appointment that you entered earlier appears in the calendar.

5. Guess what? The date of the Open House was changed to the following week. To change the date:
DRAG: the appointment to the next week
To view the detail behind an appointment, you simply double-click it.

6. Earlier, you added a contact to the Contacts folder. On your own, view the contents of the Contacts folder.

7. On your own, practice navigating around the Outlook folders. To find out more about using the Outlook folders, choose Help, Contents and Index and then click the *Contents* tab. Then double-click a topic you're interested in.

8. Now close Microsoft Outlook.

IN ADDITION ADD A REMINDER TO THE TASKS FOLDER FROM WORD, EXCEL, OR POWERPOINT

From Word, Excel, or PowerPoint, you can create a reminder that relates to the current document. For example, you may want to remind yourself to include next month's budget data, when it becomes available, in your Word document. To create a reminder:

1. Open the document that needs a reminder.

2. In Word, Excel, or PowerPoint, click the Create Microsoft Outlook Task button on the Reviewing toolbar.

3. In Outlook, type reminder information that relates to the task.

4. In Outlook, click the Save and Close button to return to your application.

SUMMARY

Microsoft Binder is useful for organizing documents that belong together, such as all the files that relate to a particular project. You learned how to add existing documents to a binder, add a new section to a binder, and save a binder. Next you added footers to the binder, moved a binder section, and learned how to copy between binder sections. You also learned how to preview and print a binder.

In the latter portion of the session, you learned the fundamentals of using Microsoft Outlook, a software tool that is helpful in organizing the types of information you typically deal with at your desk. Specifically, you added an address to the Contacts folder and an appointment in the Calendar folder. You also learned more about opening the different folders in Outlook.

Table 4.1 provides a list of the commands and procedures covered in this session.

TABLE 4.1	*Task Description*	*Command*
Command Summary	Add an empty section to a binder	CHOOSE: Section, Add
	Add an existing document to a binder	CHOOSE: Section, Add from File
	Hide/display the left pane	CLICK: Show/Hide Left Pane button ()
	Save a binder	CHOOSE: File, Save Binder, or CLICK: Save button (⊞)
	Rename a section	CHOOSE: Section, Rename
	Delete a section	CHOOSE: Section, Delete
	Move a section	DRAG: the section up or down in the left pane
	Add headers and footers to a binder	CHOOSE: File, Binder Page Setup
	Print a binder	CHOOSE: File, Print Binder
	Unbind a binder section	CHOOSE: Section, Save as File
	Unbind an entire binder	RIGHT-CLICK: the binder name CHOOSE: Unbind
	Add a contact to Microsoft Outlook	CHOOSE: File, New CHOOSE: Contact
	Add an appointment to Microsoft Outlook	CHOOSE: File, New CHOOSE: Appointment

KEY TERMS

binder

In Microsoft Binder, the file used to organize documents that relate to a common subject.

information service

An information service is software instructions that make it possible for you to send and receive e-mail, faxes, and files on your computer.

Microsoft Outlook

Microsoft Outlook provides a framework for keeping track of many of the tasks you perform at your desk such as maintaining your calendar, accessing addresses, and sending and receiving e-mail and faxes.

section

In Binder, the name given to a document, worksheet, or presentation.

EXERCISES

SHORT ANSWER

1. What are some advantages of using the Outlook Calendar folder to manage appointments rather than a paper-based calendar?

2. What types of tasks can you perform using Microsoft Binder?

3. When would it be useful to use the Journal folder in Microsoft Outlook?

4. What is the procedure for moving sections in a binder?

5. In Microsoft Outlook, what do you need to do before you can send and receive e-mail messages?

6. What is the procedure for copying text from one binder section to another?

7. How do you print the entire contents of a binder?

8. What does it mean to *unbind* a binder?

9. How do you rename a binder section?

10. How would you approach spellchecking a multi-document binder?

HANDS-ON

(*Note*: Ensure that you know the location of your Advantage Files and where to store your Data Files. If necessary, ask your instructor or lab assistant for additional information.)

1. In the following exercise, you practice adding documents to a binder and then editing the binder.

   a. Start a new blank Binder document by choosing New Office Document from the Start menu.

   b. Add the "Guests" workbook and the "Invite" Word document. Both documents are stored in the Advantage Files location.

   c. Move the Guests section so that it displays after the Invite section.

   d. Select the heading "Drake's Tennis and Swim Club" in the Invite section.

   e. Copy the selected section to cell A2 in the Guests section.

   f. Save the binder as "Celebration" to the Data Files location.

2. In the following exercise, you insert a footer in the "Celebration" binder and then preview and print the binder.

   a. Ensure that the "Celebration" binder appears open in Microsoft Binder. (*Note*: You saved this binder in exercise 1.)

   b. Insert your name and the current date in the page footer of each binder section.

        c. Preview both sections in the binder.

        d. Print the entire binder.

        e. Save the binder as "Celebration" to the Data Files location.

        f. Exit Binder.

3. On your own, create a report using the Report binder template. You access this template in the *Binders* tab of the New Office Document dialog box. Create a report about a class you're currently taking, your job, your hobby, or something else that interests you. Modify, add, or delete sections as needed to support your topic. When you're finished, save the binder as "My Report" to the Data Files location.

CASE PROBLEMS	**FURNITURE SOURCE**

(*Note*: In the following case problems, assume the role of the primary characters and perform the same steps that they identify. You may want to re-read the session opening.)

1. Having just finished a course on Microsoft Binder, Kristen is ready to tackle the summary report and create the sections for the report in Microsoft Binder. In future months, she can edit the sections to reflect new data. Kristen wants to include the following sections in the report: (a) Word cover sheet, (b) Word regional summary document, and (c) Excel top-ten products list.

    Kristen starts by creating a new Word section and naming it Cover Page. She includes the following information and formatting on the appropriate lines. When finished, she centers the information between the top and bottom margins:

Line	*Text*	*Formatting*
1	Sales Report for the Western Region	Arial, 22 point size, centered, boldface, underlined
4	April, 1996	Arial, 18 point size, centered
20	Prepared by: Kristen Grady	Arial, 14 point size, centered

Before continuing, Kristen saves the binder as "April Summary Report" to the Data Files location.

Now Kristen is ready to create the second section of the binder. She creates a new Word section and names it Sales Summary. She then includes the following information. (*Note*: Unless otherwise specified, use the Arial font in a 12 point size. If Arial isn't available on your computer, select a different font.)

Line	Text	Formatting
1	April Sales Summary	Arial, 18 point size, centered, boldface, underlined
3	1. Overall sales were strong, up an average of 25% from March. Home accessory sales were up 30% and furniture sales were up 20%. 2. Over 70% of the orders came from California, followed by Nevada at 15%, Oregon at 13%, and Washington at 2%. 3. More requests than we could handle came in for the damask couch slipcover, the iron fireplace screen, and the treasure chest. Customer satisfaction in the western region gets a high rating.	

"Only one more section and then I'm finished!" thinks Kristen. She creates a new Excel section and names it Top-Ten. She then includes the following information. (*Note*: Widen columns as necessary and use a 10 point size unless otherwise specified.)

Cell:Data	Formatting
A1: Top-Ten List: April	22 point size, boldface
A3: Item Name	boldface, underlined
B3: Units Sold	boldface, underlined
A5: Damask Couch Slipcover	
A6: Wrought Iron Fireplace Screen	
A7: Treasure Chest	
A8: Country Bench	
A9: Wrought Iron Candlesticks	
A10: Wrought Iron Chandelier	
A11: Rattan Bedside Table	
A12: Leather Picture Frame	
A13: Flannel Sheets	
A14: Wrought Iron Wine Rack	
B5: 2000	Currency format
B6: 2000	Currency format
B7: 2000	Currency format
B8: 1787	Currency format
B9: 1700	Currency format

Cell:Data	Formatting
B10: **1656**	Currency format
B11: **1500**	Currency format
B12: **1451**	Currency format
B13: **1420**	Currency format
B14: **1398**	Currency format

When Kristen is finished building the worksheet, she again saves the binder as "April Summary Report" to the Data Files location.

2. "Wow, that was easy!" Kristen thinks. She is pleased that she created her first binder without a hitch. She decides now to venture into lesser-known territory. First, she adds the following footer to the Sales Summary and Top-Ten sections: **Furniture Source, Western Region: Page # of 3**. She centers the footer in both sections and uses a 10-point font. Next, she spell-checks each section in the entire binder. Finally, Kristen saves "April Summary Report" again to the Data Files location.

3. Before printing the binder, Kristen decides to preview the entire binder and then print the entire binder. Kristen then faxes a copy of the binder to her boss. Kristen is pleased to think that May's report will take much less time to create than this month's. All she needs to do is retrieve the "April Summary Report" binder, edit it to include May's information and a new footer, and then save it as "May Summary Report."

4. After returning from her lunch break, Kristen listened to her voice mail messages. She had a message from Alphonso Banks, the company president! He had the following message for her: *Please arrange a breakfast meeting in Sacramento, California, for two months from today. I'll be there on business and want to meet the other representatives. If you need to reach me while I'm in California, I'll be at 2101 25th Avenue. My phone number will be 916-111-1111.*

   Using Outlook, she enters the date of the breakfast meeting in her Calendar folder. She also enters a note in the Notes folder reminding her to tell the representatives in her region to hold the date. (*Hint:* Choose File, New, Note.) Finally, she enters Alphonso Banks' contact information into her Contacts folder.

   Latté time! Make it a double!

Integrating Microsoft Office 97 for Windows

Step-by-Step with OLE

SESSION OUTLINE

Your Mission
Working with Text
Applying Special Effects to Text
Working with Graphics
Adding an Organizational Chart
Summary
Exercises

INTRODUCTION

Practice, practice, practice! Sound like an old gym coach you used to know? Well, we're probably emphasizing the same principles—essentially, practice makes perfect. In this session, you leave the "how to" of integrating Microsoft Office and work through a real-world example one object at a time. You'll experience the power of OLE firsthand in creating a newsletter using Microsoft Word. Okay, people, time to get out on the field!

CASE STUDY MINESTRONE SOUP COMPANY

You are the communications manager for the Minestrone Soup Company. One of your duties at Minestrone is to create and disseminate a monthly employee newsletter. Your objective in this session is to finish next month's issue. Fortunately, the body of the newsletter has already been completed and only the front page requires some extra work. Having just completed a course on using Microsoft Office, you're ready to tackle the newsletter's cover page. Your personal objective is to add some flash and appeal to the cover.

In this session, you create a compound document using Microsoft Word. You also use Microsoft WordArt to apply special effects to text, Microsoft Clip Gallery to insert an image, Microsoft Organization Chart to create an organizational diagram, and the Insert Picture command to paste a scanned photograph into the document. The tasks in this session focus on embedding objects from the Microsoft Office mini-apps.

YOUR MISSION

Your mission is to create the following newsletter cover page for the Minestrone Soup Company. All of the necessary items are either included in the Advantage Files location or must be created using the Office mini-apps. You should refer back to this page to clarify, or perhaps visualize, each section's objective.

WORKING WITH TEXT

In this section, you retrieve the newsletter's cover page that was initially prepared by your assistants. Although they entered the body text for all the articles, you must create the headings and captions. To speed up the process, your thoughtful assistants have placed text boxes where the headings should be entered. This section provides an example of using text boxes and tables as placeholders in a Word document.

Perform the following steps . . .

1. Load Microsoft Word.

2. Open an existing document called "Soupnews" that is located in the Advantage Files location. This document automatically loads in Page Layout View. Your screen should appear similar to Figure 5.1.

FIGURE 5.1

THE "SOUPNEWS" DOCUMENT FILE

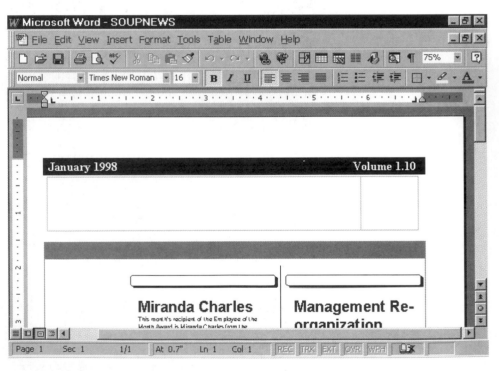

3. Position the mouse pointer over the text box that appears immediately above the article heading "Miranda Charles."

4. To position the insertion point in the text box, ensure that the mouse pointer is an I-beam and then do the following:
   CLICK: left mouse button once
   You should now see a flashing I-beam in the text box. (*Hint*: You can increase the display size of the document by choosing a zoom percentage from the *Zoom* drop-down menu in the toolbar.)

5. TYPE: **employee of the month**
(*Note:* Thanks to your assistants and their use of formatting styles, the text is automatically centered and formatted in uppercase as you type.)

6. Position the mouse pointer over the text box that appears immediately above the article heading "Management Reorganization" and click once to position the insertion point.

7. TYPE: **head office report**
Again, the text is centered and formatted in uppercase.

8. Scroll down the page using the mouse and scroll bars until you see a text box to the left of P. Minestrone's quotation for Miranda Charles. Position the mouse pointer over the text box and click once to position the insertion point.

9. TYPE: **Miranda Charles**

10. Scroll down further on the page until you see a table with the title "INSIDE." This table provides a quick glance at the topics contained in the newsletter. To enter the first topic in the table, position the insertion point in the second column of the first row. (*Hint:* You can always refer back to the sample cover page provided at the beginning of this session to clarify instructions.)

11. TYPE: **New Daycare Provider**
PRESS: ⬇ once

12. TYPE: **Safety Committee Report**
PRESS: ⬇ once

13. TYPE: **Christmas Report**
PRESS: ⬇ once

14. TYPE: **Travel Specials**
PRESS: ⬇ once

15. TYPE: **Message from Paulo**

16. Save the document as "Soup News-Revised" to the Data Files location.

Great! You now have headings for the articles, a caption for the graphic of Miranda Charles, and a table of contents for this issue of the newsletter. Let's proceed to the next section where you will use Microsoft WordArt to draw and retain the reader's attention to your newsletter.

APPLYING SPECIAL EFFECTS TO TEXT

In this section, you create a WordArt object for the heading of the newsletter, SOUPER NEWS. Once the heading is inserted, you will then edit it to practice working with embedded objects.

Perform the following steps . . .

1. To begin, scroll the document window to view the top of the page.

2. To create the heading using WordArt:
   CHOOSE: Insert, Picture
   CHOOSE: WordArt
   The WordArt Gallery dialog box appears.

3. SELECT: the style in the fourth column, fourth row of the dialog box
   PRESS: `ENTER` or CLICK: OK

4. In the Edit WordArt Text dialog box:
   TYPE: **SOUPER NEWS**

5. To insert the object in the document:
   PRESS: `ENTER` or CLICK: OK
   Your screen should now appear similar to Figure 5.2.

FIGURE 5.2

INSERTING A
NEWSLETTER BANNER
USING WORDART

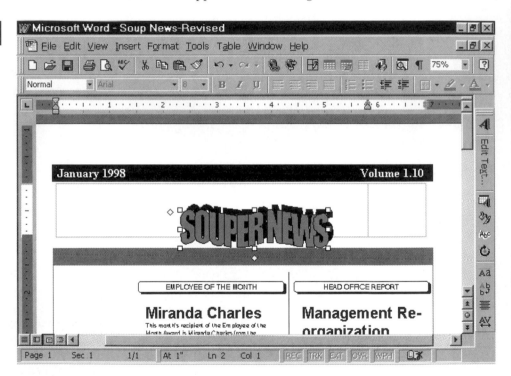

6. The heading, SOUPER NEWS, now appears as a selected object. On your own, move and resize the object to fill the left-hand cell in the table heading. Your document should now appear similar to Figure 5.3.

FIGURE 5.3

MOVING AND RESIZING
THE WORDART OBJECT

7. Save the document as "Soup News-Revised" to the Data Files location, replacing the existing version.

WORKING WITH GRAPHICS

Newsletters seem to gain personality with the inclusion of graphics, especially real-life photographs. In this session, you insert images from the Microsoft Clip Gallery and from a photograph stored as a bitmap file in the Advantage Files location.

Back to the scenario: Several people in the company have told you that they missed the last issue because it was "just another piece of paper in my in-box." You now realize the importance of getting and keeping their attention. To this end, you decide to peruse the ClipArt Gallery for a catchy logo to use in addition to the SOUPER NEWS WordArt heading. You've also learned that Human Resources has photos of each employee. After some in-house searching and bartering, you were able to borrow Marketing's image scanner and save a picture of Miranda Charles to the Advantage Files location. You will place Miranda's photo on the cover of next month's newsletter. Let's get to work.

Now you add a logo to the SOUPER NEWS heading.

Perform the following steps . . .

1. To begin, scroll the document window to view the top of the page.

2. Immediately below the date line, position the insertion point in the second column of the table, to the right of the WordArt object "SOUPER NEWS."

3. To find a logo in the Clip Gallery:
    CHOOSE: Insert, Picture
    CHOOSE: Clip Art
    The Clip Gallery dialog box appears.

4. To limit the clip art images to those dealing with Entertainment topics:
    SELECT: Screen Beans from the list box

5. SELECT: the graphic pictured in Figure 5.4
    PRESS: (ENTER) or CLICK: Insert command button
    The Clip Gallery is closed and you are immediately returned to Word and your newsletter.

6. The graphic is currently larger than the table. On your own, position and resize the graphic to fit into the table.

7. Save the document as "Soup News-Revised" to the Data Files location, replacing the existing version. Your screen should appear similar to Figure 5.4. (*Note*: Get into the habit of saving your work after each major addition or revision.)

FIGURE 5.4

INSERTING CLIP ART
INTO A TABLE

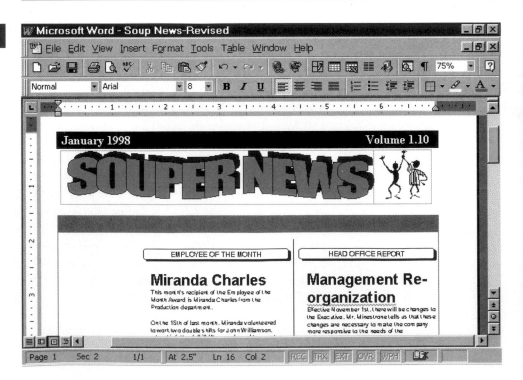

Now you add a clip art image beside the Contents table.

Perform the following steps . . .

1. To begin, scroll the document window to view the bottom of the page.

2. Fortunately, your assistants created a frame in Word to contain the graphic. To position the insertion point in the frame:
CLICK: to the left of the Contents table, in the blank area
You should see a hatched or shaded border appear around the area designated for the graphic.

3. To insert a clip art image:
CHOOSE: Insert, Picture
CHOOSE: Clip Art

4. SELECT: the magnifying glass graphic from the Academic category
PRESS: (ENTER) or CLICK: Insert

5. The image is inserted into the document, spanning a fairly large area at the bottom of the page. Resize and position the graphic to fit neatly in the area left of the Contents table. Refer to Figure 5.5 for proper positioning and sizing of the graphic.

6. Save the document as "Soup News-Revised" to the Data Files location, replacing the existing version.

FIGURE 5.5

INSERTING CLIP ART
INTO A FRAME

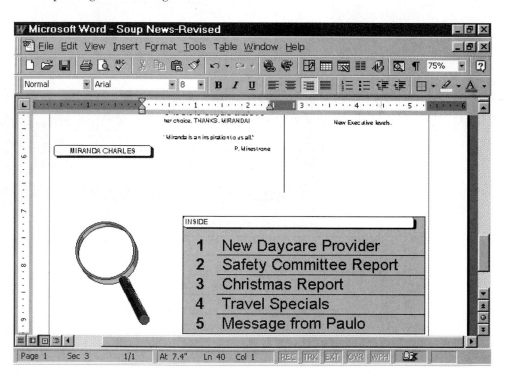

In this step, you add a photograph to the newsletter.

Perform the following steps . . .

1. To begin, scroll the document window to view the area above the caption for Miranda Charles and to the left of the article text.

2. Your assistants have placed another frame in the newsletter to hold the photograph. To position the insertion point in the frame:
CLICK: above the "Miranda Charles" caption, in the blank area
You should see a hatched border appear around the outline of the frame.

   (*CAUTION:* Make sure that you are clicking above the caption and not above the article heading.)

3. To insert a graphic file into the frame:
CHOOSE: Insert, Picture
CHOOSE: From File
SELECT: *your Advantage Files location*
SELECT: "Miranda" from the list box

4. To preview the picture:
CLICK: Preview button ([icon])
The Insert Picture dialog box should appear similar to Figure 5.6.

FIGURE 5.6

PREVIEWING A GRAPHIC FILE IN THE INSERT PICTURE DIALOG BOX

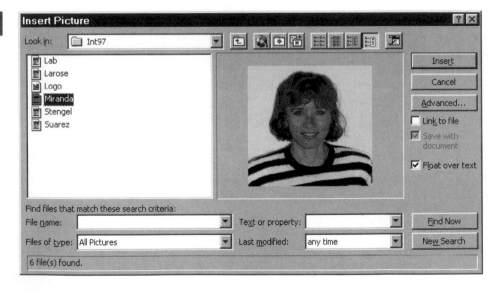

5. To insert the photograph into the newsletter:
PRESS: (ENTER) or CLICK: Insert

6. If the photograph requires sizing in your document, drag the sizing handles to position the graphic as shown in Figure 5.7.

   (*CAUTION*: You should only drag the corner handles of photographs to ensure proportional sizing. Otherwise, your photographs will look like reflections in a circus mirror.)

FIGURE 5.7

INSERTING A
PHOTOGRAPH

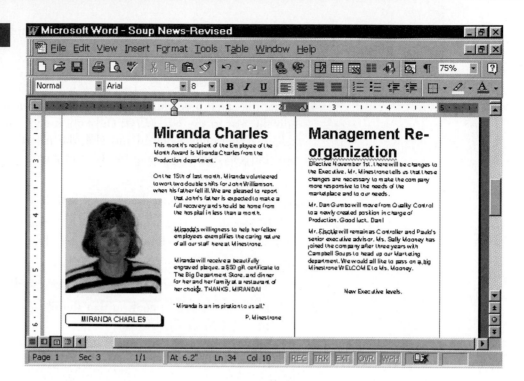

7. Save the document as "Soup News-Revised" to the Data Files location, replacing the existing version.

ADDING AN ORGANIZATIONAL CHART

The president of Minestrone Soups, Paulo Minestrone himself, has asked that you emphasize the new executive personnel in your newsletter. In addition to running the front-page article entitled "Management Reorganization," you decide to insert an organizational chart depicting the new executive level. You ask your assistants to create a caption for the chart near the end of the article, and you then proceed with the following steps.

Perform the following steps . . .

1. Let's insert the organizational chart with the cursor at the top of the document. (Your helpful assistants know that it will be easier to move the organizational chart into position from this location!)
PRESS: CTRL + HOME

2. To create the organizational chart:
CHOOSE: Insert, Object
SELECT: *Create New* tab
SELECT: MS Organization Chart 2.0 from the *Object Type* list box
PRESS: ENTER or CLICK: OK
The Microsoft Organization Chart mini-app is launched and you are presented with a blank organizational chart.

3. To edit the default text in the boxes of the sample chart:
   TYPE: **Paulo Minestrone**
   PRESS: TAB
   TYPE: **President**

4. Using the same procedure as above, click on each box to select it and then edit the text in the box. (*Hint*: Only click once on the box you want to select. If you click twice by mistake, the insertion point is placed in the box and you must then drag the I-beam mouse pointer across the text you want to replace.)

Left Box	*Center Box*	*Right Box*
Sally Mooney	Dan Gumbo	John Fisckle
Marketing	Production	Controller

5. When you are finished editing the chart:
   CHOOSE: File, Exit and Return to Soup News-Revised.doc

6. When you are asked to confirm that the object needs to be updated:
   PRESS: ENTER or CLICK: Yes
   At this point the organizational chart appears selected at the top of the document.

7. Drag the organizational chart into position below the article on Management Reorganization. Ensure that the caption appears below the chart. Refer to Figure 5.8.

FIGURE 5.8

INSERTING AN
ORGANIZATIONAL CHART

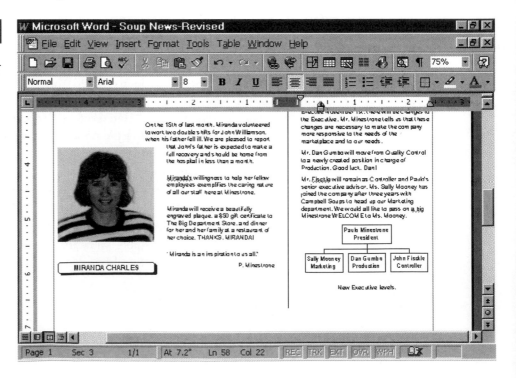

8. Now that you've finished creating the initial chart, let's go back and edit Mr. Minestrone's box to make it more distinctive. To begin:
DOUBLE-CLICK: the organizational chart object
After a few seconds, the chart appears in the Microsoft Organization Chart window.

9. To enhance Mr. Minestrone's entry with a shadowed box:
CHOOSE: Boxes, Shadow
SELECT: any box shadow option

10. To return to the newsletter:
CHOOSE: File, Exit and Return to Soup News-Revised.doc

11. When you are asked to confirm that the object needs to be updated:
PRESS: `ENTER` or CLICK: Yes
The new organizational chart sports a fancy shadowed box for Paulo Minestrone and plain boxes for the rest of the executives.

12. Save the document as "Soup News-Revised" to the Data Files location, replacing the existing version.

13. Congratulations, you've completed the newsletter! Print it out to review your masterpiece:
CHOOSE: File, Print
PRESS: `ENTER` or CLICK: OK

14. Compare the output from your printer with the sample page provided at the beginning of this session.

15. Close the document and exit Word.

Summary

This session led you step-by-step in creating a newsletter using Microsoft Word. Building a true compound document, you inserted a WordArt object, a clip art image, a photograph stored as a bitmap file, and an organizational chart. In addition, you used the Visual Editing feature of OLE to edit the objects once they were embedded into the document. (By the way, the president was so impressed that he personally authorized the purchase of a new computer for you to make the next issue even better!)

EXERCISES

HANDS-ON

(*Note*: In the following case problems, assume the role of the primary characters and perform the same steps that they identify. You may want to re-read the session opening.)

1. In this exercise, you select a new image from the Microsoft ClipArt Gallery to appear next to the Contents table.

   a. Open the "Soup News-Revised" document, stored in the Data Files location.

   b. To begin, scroll the document window to view the clip art image appearing to the left of the Contents table.

   c. Position the mouse pointer over the object and click the right mouse button to display its context-sensitive shortcut menu.

   d. CHOOSE: Clip Object
      CHOOSE: Replace

   e. Select a different clip art image and insert it in the document.

   f. Size and position the new clip art image to the left of the Contents table.

   g. Save the document as "Soup News-Edited" to the Data Files location.

   h. Print the revised newsletter.

2. Using WordArt, change the heading from SOUPER NEWS to THE MONTHLY SOUP. Apply various special effects to the text. Print the revised newsletter.

3. Using Microsoft Organization Chart 2.0, add Miranda Charles as an Administrative Assistant to Dan Gumbo in Production. Print the revised newsletter. Save the document as "Soup News-Edited" to the Data Files location, replacing the existing version. When finished, close the document and exit Word.

Integrating Microsoft Office 97 for Windows

Comprehensive Case Study

SESSION OUTLINE

INTRODUCTION

Although presenting a complicated subject like OLE in a two-dimensional book is difficult, it doesn't compare to the challenges you face in assimilating and applying the material. Now we let the truly inspired students demonstrate their creativity and perseverance. You will not find step-by-step instructions in this session. In fact, the only instructions that you will receive are provided in the objective statement at the beginning of each section. Although there are no new concepts presented, you will be surprised how much learning actually takes place!

CASE STUDY MINESTRONE SOUP COMPANY

As the technology manager for the Human Resources division, your mission is to create an Online Employee Manual for the Minestrone Soup Company. For years now, the company has been disseminating its policy manuals in three-ring binders. To reduce its paper flow, Minestrone has decided to merge onto the information superhighway. Each individual in the company has an electronic mail account, and the president has asked you to prepare an Employee Manual that staff can access directly from their computer workstations.

You will now create a living document that includes an audio greeting from the company president, the company logo, photos and sound bites from several key executives in the Human Resources division, and the company's safety record presented as a table and a chart. Now's the time to apply what you've learned!

YOUR FIRST STEP

Rather than starting from scratch, you've decided to edit the existing Employee Manual (written in Microsoft Word) and add some new features. Some of the new items must be created using the Microsoft Office mini-apps. Other items have been created by staff members and are provided in the Advantage Files location. Table 6.1 provides a summary of the items you've received from other departments for inclusion in the manual.

TABLE 6.1	Filename	Description
Items to be Added to the Online Employee Manual	MANUAL.DOC	The existing Employee Manual, written using Microsoft Word
	LOGO.WMF	A graphic of the company logo in a Windows Metafile format, provided by Sally in Marketing
	MESSAGE.WAV	A sound clip from Paulo Minestrone, the president, welcoming the employee to the new online manual
	STENGEL.WAV	A sound clip about Margaret Stengel, the director of Human Resources
	LAROSE.WAV	A sound clip about Robert LaRose, the manager responsible for Employee Assessments
	SUAREZ.WAV	A sound clip about Maria Suarez, the manager responsible for Payroll and Benefits
	STENGEL.BMP	A scanned photograph of Margaret Stengel
	LAROSE.BMP	A scanned photograph of Robert LaRose

TABLE 6.1
Continued

Filename	Description
SUAREZ.BMP	A scanned photograph of Maria Suarez
SAFETY.XLS	An Excel worksheet detailing the company's safety record, supplied by Bob in Human Resources

Your objective for this section is to load the existing Employee Manual document into Microsoft Word. The document is stored as "Manual" in the Advantage Files location. Figure 6.1 provides a thumbnail view of the four pages contained in the document. Review the pages and note the items contained in the curly braces {}. You will replace these items with the object specified in the braces.

FIGURE 6.1

DISPLAYING PAGES
FROM THE "MANUAL"
DOCUMENT USING
A THUMBNAIL VIEW

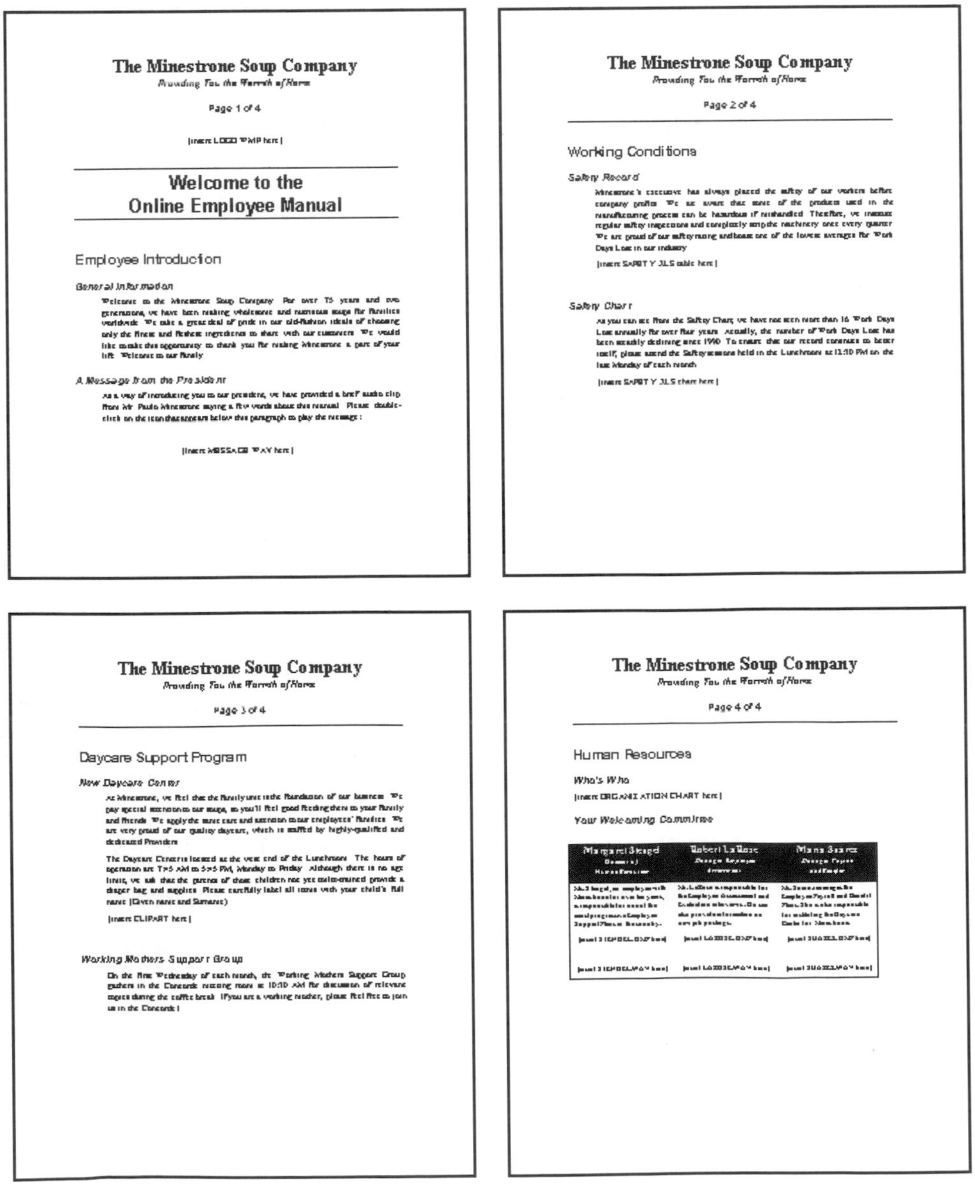

INSERTING GRAPHICS

In this section, you embed graphics from the Microsoft Clip Gallery and from graphic files stored in the Advantage Files location. You will have to size the graphics once they've been inserted into the document. Make sure that you delete the text in the curly braces when you insert the graphics.

Perform the following steps . . .

1. Move to the top of Page 1.

2. Delete the text "{insert LOGO.WMF here}."

3. Insert the LOGO.WMF file, that is stored in the Advantage Files location, as shown in Figure 6.2. Size and position the logo so that Page 1 does not run onto Page 2. (*Note*: Do not link the picture with the file on the disk.)

FIGURE 6.2

INSERTING THE "LOGO" GRAPHIC FILE

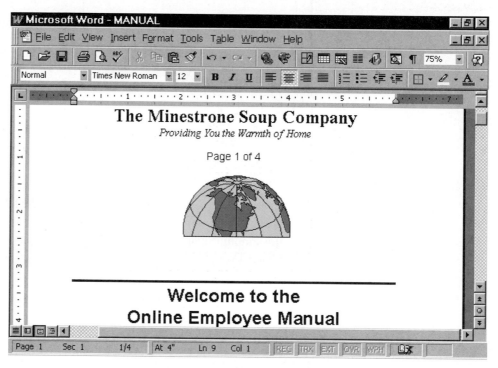

4. Save the document as "Manual-Revised" to your Data Files location.

5. Move to Page 3.

6. Replace the text "{insert CLIPART here}" with the clip art image that appears in Figure 6.3. Resize the image to prevent an extra page break from occurring.

FIGURE 6.3

INSERTING AN IMAGE
FROM THE CLIPART
GALLERY

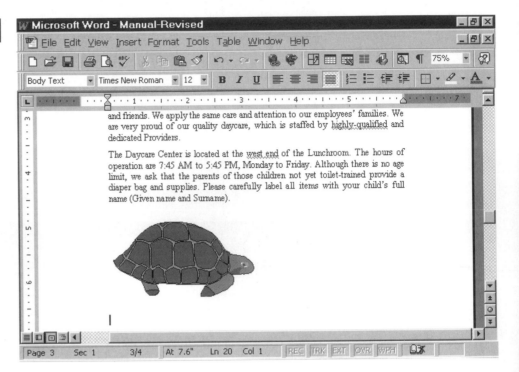

7. Move to Page 4.

8. In the table, replace the text "{insert *NAME*.BMP here}" with the correct graphic images stored in the Advantage Files location. After sizing each of the graphic images, your screen should appear similar to Figure 6.4. (*Note*: Do not link the pictures to the files on the disk.)

FIGURE 6.4

INSERTING SCANNED
PHOTOGRAPHS

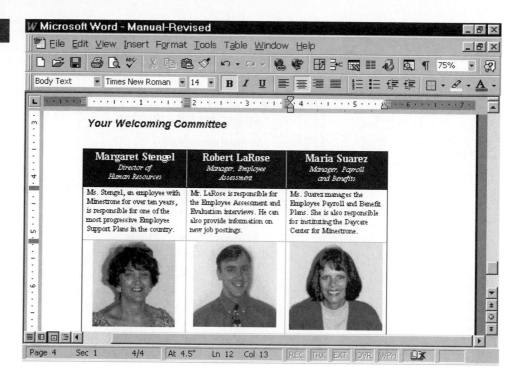

9. Save your work as "Manual-Revised" to the Data Files location.

INSERTING SOUND FILES

You can insert sound objects into a document using the same steps that you have learned for inserting graphic files. However, only computers that meet the MPC (Multimedia PC) hardware specification will be able to play the audio clips stored in the Advantage Files location. If you experience problems inserting or playing these sound files, skip to the Inserting an Excel Table and Chart section.

Perform the following steps . . .

1. Move to the bottom of Page 1.

2. Delete the text "{insert MESSAGE.WAV here}."

3. Create an object in the document that links to the MESSAGE.WAV file stored in the Advantage Files location. (*Hint:* You create an object from an existing file and then display the object as an icon in your document.) Before proceeding, ensure that Page 1 does not run onto Page 2. When you have finished inserting the audio clip, position it so that your screen appears similar to Figure 6.5.

FIGURE 6.5

LINKING TO A GREETING
MESSAGE FROM THE
PRESIDENT

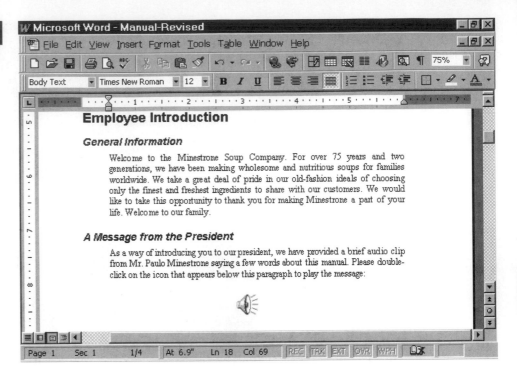

4. Save your work as "Manual-Revised" to the Data Files location.

5. To play the WAV audio clip:
    DOUBLE-CLICK: message.wav icon ()
    If your computer can play WAV files, the clip begins to play.

Now, you need to insert the audio clips for each person in the Human Resources division.

Perform the following steps . . .

1. Move to the table on Page 4.

2. Replace the text "{insert *NAME*.WAV here}" with the correct sound files stored in the Advantage Files location. (*Hint:* Ensure that the *Link to file* and *Float over text* check boxes aren't selected in the Object dialog box.) Your screen should appear similar but not identical to Figure 6.6.

FIGURE 6.6

INSERTING WAV AUDIO
FILES

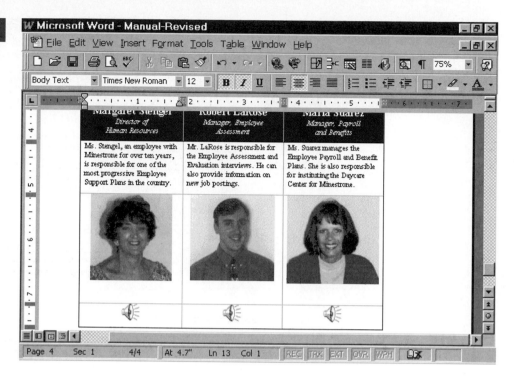

3. Play each of these audio clips.

4. Save your work as "Manual-Revised" to the Data Files location.

INSERTING AN EXCEL TABLE AND CHART

Now we'll add some hard figures to the Employee Manual document. In this section, you embed the SAFETY.XLS worksheet information into the Employee Manual document. The worksheet file is stored in the Advantage Files location.

Perform the following steps . . .

1. Move to Page 2.

2. Delete the text "{insert SAFETY.XLS table here}."

3. With the insertion point on the same line where you deleted the text, insert the table from the SAFETY.XLS file. (*Hint*: Remember to use the Create from File tab, but do not select the *Link to file*, *Float over text*, or *Display as icon* check boxes.) Your screen should now appear similar to Figure 6.7.

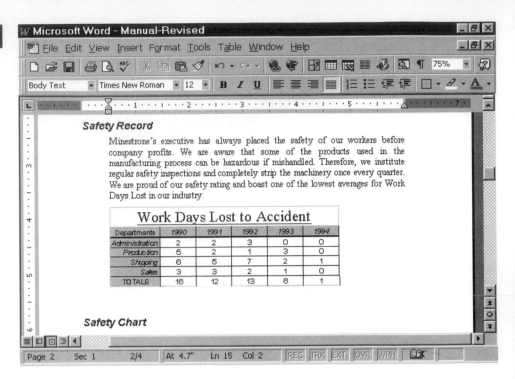

4. Delete the text "{insert SAFETY.XLS chart here}" near the bottom of the page.

5. Open the SAFETY.XLS worksheet into Microsoft Excel, and then arrange the Word and Excel application windows so that they are both visible on the screen.

6. In Excel, move to the second worksheet page named "Graph" and drag and drop the chart from this worksheet into the "Manual-Revised" document.

7. Exit Excel and then maximize the Word application window.

8. You may have to size the chart and remove some blank lines to ensure that all the information fits onto a single page. Your screen should appear similar to Figure 6.8 when you are finished.

9. Save your work as "Manual-Revised" to the Data Files location.

FIGURE 6.8

EMBEDDING AN EXCEL CHART

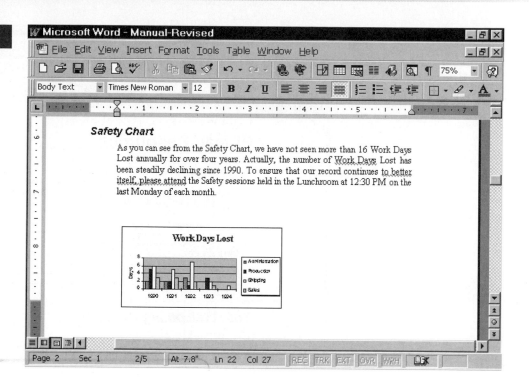

ADDING AN ORGANIZATIONAL CHART

To provide a visual representation of the management structure in the Human Resources division, you've decided to add an organizational chart of the three top-level managers. Use the following sample as a guide for creating your own chart:

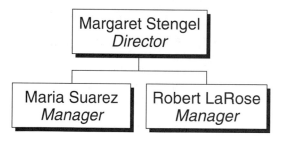

Perform the following steps ...

1. Move to the top of Page 4.

2. Delete the text "{insert ORGANIZATION CHART here}."

3. With the insertion point on the same line where you deleted the text, add a new organizational chart like the one that appears above. Your screen should appear similar to Figure 6.9. Again, you must be careful not to make the chart too big since you want the information to be displayed on a single page.

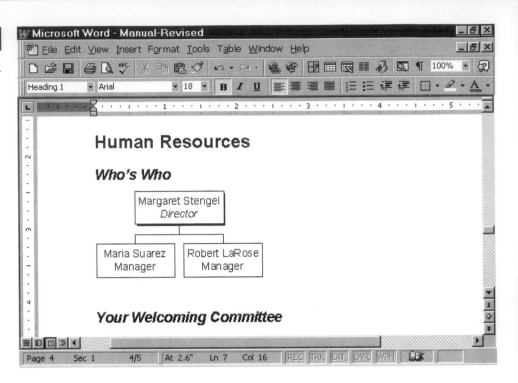

4. Save your work as "Manual-Revised" to the Data Files location.

5. Print the document and then compare it to the thumbnail view in Figure 6.10. (*Note:* Some printers may not be able to reproduce the graphics to match their display quality on your computer's monitor.)

6. Close the "Manual-Revised" document.

FIGURE 6.10

THE FINISHED PRODUCT!

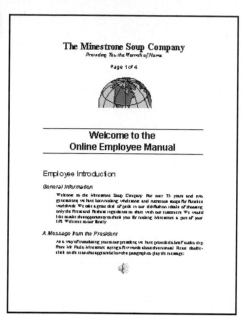

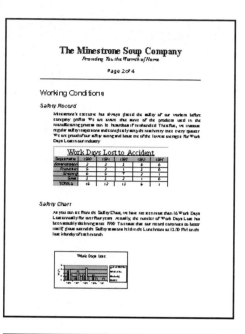

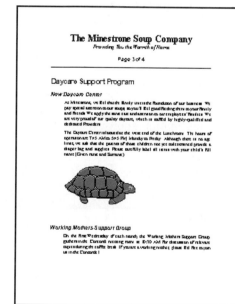

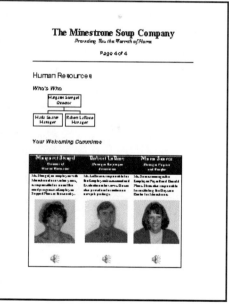

Summary

This session provided you with an opportunity to test your knowledge in using and integrating Microsoft Office. Starting with a basic Microsoft Word document, you inserted and manipulated clip art images, scanned photographs, sound bites, an Excel table and chart, and an organizational chart.

Congratulations on completing this guide. We hope that you can begin applying this knowledge in your work or school projects immediately. Good luck with Microsoft Office!

EXERCISES

HANDS-ON

(*Note*: In the following problems, assume the role of the primary characters and perform the same steps that they identify. You may want to re-read the session opening.)

1. In the following exercise, you select a new clip art image for the company logo.

    a. Move to the top of Page 1.

    b. Delete the LOGO.WMF object that you inserted into the document at the beginning of this session.

    c. Using the Clip Gallery, select a new object for the company logo and then size it accordingly.

    d. Move to Page 3.

    e. Replace the "Turtle" clip art image with a new image from the Clip Gallery.

    f. Save the document as "Manual-Edited" to your Data Files location.

2. You've just received a call from Bob in the Human Resources division. It seems that the SAFETY.XLS workbook file that he had given you contained some incorrect information. Edit and update the table and chart on Page 2 using the new information shown below:

Work Days Lost to Accident

Departments	1990	1991	1992	1993	1994
Administration	4	1	1	0	1
Production	5	2	3	3	0
Shipping	6	5	7	2	1
Sales	3	3	2	1	0
TOTALS	18	11	13	6	2

Index

The page numbers in boldface indicate Quick Reference procedures.

Index